SPYING IN SOUTH ASIA

In this first comprehensive history of India's secret Cold War, Paul M. McGarr tells the story of Indian politicians, human rights activists, and journalists as they fought against or collaborated with members of the British and US intelligence services. The interventions of these agents have had a significant and enduring impact on the political and social fabric of South Asia. The spectre of a 'foreign hand', or external intelligence activity, real and imagined, has occupied a prominent place in India's political discourse, journalism, and cultural production. *Spying in South Asia* probes the nexus between intelligence and statecraft in South Asia and the relationships between agencies and governments forged to promote democracy. McGarr asks why, in contrast to Western assumptions about surveillance, South Asians associate intelligence with covert action, grand conspiracy, and justifications for repression? In doing so, he uncovers a fifty-year battle for hearts and minds in the Indian subcontinent.

PAUL M. MCGARR is Lecturer in Intelligence Studies at King's College London and author of *The Cold War in South Asia, 1945–1965*.

SPYING IN SOUTH ASIA

Britain, the United States, and India's Secret Cold War

PAUL M. MCGARR
King's College London

Shaftesbury Road, Cambridge CB2 8EA, United Kingdom

One Liberty Plaza, 20th Floor, New York, NY 10006, USA

477 Williamstown Road, Port Melbourne, VIC 3207, Australia

314–321, 3rd Floor, Plot 3, Splendor Forum, Jasola District Centre, New Delhi – 110025, India

103 Penang Road, #05–06/07, Visioncrest Commercial, Singapore 238467

Cambridge University Press is part of Cambridge University Press & Assessment, a department of the University of Cambridge.

We share the University's mission to contribute to society through the pursuit of education, learning and research at the highest international levels of excellence.

www.cambridge.org
Information on this title: www.cambridge.org/9781108843676

DOI: 10.1017/9781108919630

© Paul M. McGarr 2024

This publication is in copyright. Subject to statutory exception and to the provisions of relevant collective licensing agreements, no reproduction of any part may take place without the written permission of Cambridge University Press & Assessment.

When citing this work, please include a reference to the DOI 10.1017/9781108919630

First published 2024

Printed in the United Kingdom by CPI Group Ltd, Croydon CR0 4YY

A catalogue record for this publication is available from the British Library.

A Cataloging-in-Publication data record for this book is available from the Library of Congress

ISBN 978-1-108-84367-6 Hardback

Cambridge University Press & Assessment has no responsibility for the persistence or accuracy of URLs for external or third-party internet websites referred to in this publication and does not guarantee that any content on such websites is, or will remain, accurate or appropriate.

CONTENTS

List of Figures   *page* vii
Acknowledgements   viii
A Note on Place Names   x
List of Abbreviations   xi

Introduction   1

1 Transfer of Power: British Intelligence and the End of Empire in South Asia   14

2 Silent Partners: Britain, India, and Early Cold War Intelligence Liaison   32

3 India's Rasputin: V. K. Krishna Menon and the Spectre of Indian Communism   52

4 Quiet Americans: The CIA and the Onset of the Cold War in South Asia   76

5 Confronting China: The Sino-Indian War and Collaborative Covert Action   100

6 Peddling Propaganda: The Information Research Department and India   124

7 From Russia with Love: Dissidents and Defectors in Cold War India   153

8 The Foreign Hand: Indira Gandhi and the Politics of Intelligence   181

9 Battle of the Books: Daniel Patrick Moynihan, Seymour Hersh, and India's CIA 'Agents'   209

10	Indian Intelligence and the End of the Cold War	233
	Conclusion	257

Notes 267
Bibliography 316
Index 335

FIGURES

I.1 Communist Party of India rally, New Delhi, c. 1960. *page* 5

I.2 Allen Welsh Dulles, Director of Central Intelligence (1953–1961). 11

1.1 Sir Percy Sillitoe, Director General of MI5 (1946–1953). 29

2.1 America's ambassador to India, Chester Bowles, attacks a proliferation of communist propaganda in the subcontinent, *The American Reporter*, 26 April 1967. 48

3.1 V. K. Krishna Menon (left) with Indian prime minister, Jawaharlal Nehru, London, 18 April 1949. 54

4.1 Members of the Jan Sangh Party demonstrate outside the Communist Chinese Embassy in New Delhi over China's occupation of Tibet, 1 January 1960. 94

5.1 Tibetan refugees after being evacuated from the Sino-Indian border by the United States Air Force, Pathankot, India, 1962. 112

6.1 The CIA's pervasiveness in Indian politics represented in *Thought* magazine, 26 April 1967. 144

7.1 'The most sensational defector the United States has ever attracted': Svetlana Alliluyeva, daughter of Josef Stalin, smiles for photographers at a press conference in New York, 26 April 1967. 169

8.1a–d Indian satirist, Laxman, lampooning the nation's obsession with the CIA in a selection of cartoons carried by the *Times of India*. 191

8.2 President Richard Nixon and India's Prime Minister Indira Gandhi talk at the White House, 4 November 1971. 193

8.3 *New Age*, the newspaper of the Communist Party of India, lambasts the CIA for its latest, purported, act of subversion in the subcontinent, 22 October 1972. 202

9.1 Morarji Desai, Indian prime minister (1977–1979). 211

10.1 All India Trade Union Congress members demonstrating against 'American Imperialism' in front of the US Embassy, New Delhi, 18 December 1971. 254

ACKNOWLEDGEMENTS

This book is the product of an intellectual and emotional interest in India and its people that stretches back over several decades. Its genesis lies in the AHRC research project, *Landscapes of Secrecy: The Central Intelligence Agency and the Contested Record of US Foreign Policy, 1947–2001*, with which I was fortunate to be associated. I have accumulated many debts in striving to better understand and explain the interventions of British and American intelligence services in Cold War India. The research underpinning this book is based on primary resources in archives on three continents and would not have been possible without the generous support of numerous colleagues and institutions. Funding has come from the British Arts and Humanities Research Council; the British Academy; the Department of American Studies at the University of Nottingham; and the Rothermere American Institute at the University of Oxford. Librarians and archivists in the United Kingdom, the United States, and India have extended invaluable help with the identification of research materials.

Without the encouragement of Professor Matthew Jones of the London School of Economics and Political Science, and Professor Richard J. Aldrich of the University of Warwick, this project would not have reached fruition. A number of other scholars have played important parts in bringing this book to press. In particular, I thank and acknowledge the contributions of Christopher Andrew, Sarah Ansari, Pauline Blistène, Rudra Chaudhuri, Christopher Clary, the late Patrick French, Amit Das Gupta, Sunil Khilnani, Genevieve Lester, Lorenz Lüthi, Tom Maguire, Chris Moran, Eric Pullin, Sergey Radchenko, Rob Rakove, Jairam Ramesh, Daniela Richterova, Jayita Sarkar, Ian Talbot, Damien Van Puyvelde, and Simon Willmetts, all of whom have contributed to making this a better book. The University of Nottingham is a wonderful place in which to work on the shared histories of Britain, the United States, and South Asia. At Nottingham, I have been privileged to know and to learn from Katherine Adeney, Rory Cormac, Tony Hutchison, Chun-Yi Lee, Stephanie Lewthwaite, Spencer Mawby, Ruth Maxey, Anna Meier, Joe Merton, Catherine Rottenberg, Maria Ryan, Bevan Sewell, Francesca Silvestri, Carole Spary, Jeremy Taylor, and Graham Thompson. The late Hugh Tinker, an acute observer of modern Asia, cautioned fellow authors that, 'Anyone who has the temerity to write about cultures other than his own (however long he may have tried to get to know them) must expect to be told that he has got something wrong.'[1] I acknowledge sole responsibility for any errors and omissions that follow.

My family have accepted, mostly cheerfully, the distractions and absences associated with researching and writing international history. My sons, Robert, William, and Oliver, continue to endure, if not entirely understand, their father's preoccupation with the Indian subcontinent. Minnie, my research assistant, offered abundant vocal encouragement and companionship as this book took shape. My wife, Louise was responsible, quite literally, for keeping the project, and her husband, alive. It is to Louise, with love, that this book is dedicated.

A NOTE ON PLACE NAMES

The renaming of States and cities in India started in 1947 after end of British imperial rule. Changes frequently stirred controversy and not all the alterations proposed were adopted. Many changes came into effect only after periods of considerable delay. Each change necessitated approval from the federal Government of the Indian Union. Many of the States, cities, towns, and streets referenced in the pages that follow retained their British colonial nomenclatures throughout the Cold War, and often for a considerable period beyond. Mumbai officially replaced Bombay in 1995; Chennai superseded Madras in 1996; and Kolkata was adopted in place of Calcutta in 2001. For practical purposes, and to avoid frequent modifications to verbatim quotations, the chronology associated with official changes to place names in India has been retained. In consequence, readers will encounter Bombay, Madras, and Calcutta more often than Mumbai, Chennai, and Kolkata.

ABBREVIATIONS

AID	Agency for International Development
BDOHP	British Diplomatic Oral History Programme
BIS	British Information Service
BJP	Bharatiya Janata Party
CAB	Cabinet Papers
CCF	Congress for Cultural Freedom
CCP	Chinese Communist Party
CDS	Chief of Defence Staff
CENTO	Central Treaty Organisation
CIA	Central Intelligence Agency
CPGB	Communist Party of Great Britain
CPI	Communist Party of India
CRO	Commonwealth Relations Office
DIB	Delhi Intelligence Bureau also Director Intelligence Bureau
DO	Dominions Office
FBI	Federal Bureau of Investigation
FO	Foreign Office
FRUS	Foreign Relations of the United States
GRU	Soviet Foreign Military Intelligence
HVA	Hauptverwaltung Aufklärung (Foreign Intelligence Service of East German Ministry of State Security – Stasi)
HMG	Her Majesty's Government
IAF	Indian Air Force
IB	Delhi Intelligence Bureau
ICA	International Cooperation Administration
INC	Indian National Congress
IPS	Indian Police Service
IPI	Indian Political Intelligence
IRD	Information Research Department
JCS	Joint Chiefs of Staff
JIC	British Joint Intelligence Committee
JFKL	John F. Kennedy Library

LIST OF ABBREVIATIONS

KGB	Committee for State Security
LBJL	Lyndon B. Johnson Library
MAP	Military Assistance Programme
MEA	Ministry of External Affairs
MI5	British Security Service
MiG	Mikoyan i Gurevich (Soviet fighter aircraft)
MOD	Ministry of Defence
NAFEN	Near and Far East News
NAI	National Archives of India
NEFA	North East Frontier Agency
NMML	Nehru Museum and Memorial library
NSC	National Security Council
OSS	Office of Strategic Services
PDB	President's Daily Brief
PIB	Press Information Bureau
PLA	People's Liberation Army
PREM	Prime Minister's Office files
PRC	People's Republic of China
R&AW	Research and Analysis Wing
RSS	Rashtriya Swayamsevak Sangh
SFF	Special Frontier Force
SIS	British Secret Intelligence Service or MI6
SLO	Security Liaison Officer
SOA	Office of South Asian Affairs, Department of State
SOE	Special Operations Executive
UKNA	United Kingdom National Archive
UNSC	United Nations Security Council
USNA	United States National Archives, College Park, Maryland
USIS	United States Information Service

Introduction

> Now, the problems of Asia . . . have to be solved, and great powers and others should necessarily, because they are great powers, have a great interest in solving them, but if the great powers think that the problems of Asia can be solved minus Asia in a sense, or minus the views of Asian countries, then it does seem to be rather odd . . .
>
> Jawaharlal Nehru (1954)[1]

> This conflict of ideologies, as it is being termed, by the people today – Russian way and American way – does not interest me much. Nor do I care to bother about it.
>
> Anand Niwas (1952)[2]

George Smiley, the eponymous Cold War intelligence officer, immortalised by the British novelist, John le Carré, first encounters his Soviet nemesis, Karla, in a stifling Indian prison cell, in the mid-1950s. 'The Indian authorities arrested him [Karla] at our request and carted him off to Delhi jail', Smiley reminisces to a colleague in the British Secret Intelligence Service (SIS), or MI6. 'As far as I remember we had promised the Indians a piece of the product. I *think* that was the deal.'[3] The early fiction of le Carré, a body of work that encompasses bestsellers such as *The Spy Who Came in from the Cold* and *Tinker, Tailor, Soldier, Spy*,[4] has been characterised as framing the Cold War in reductive terms that position the conflict exclusively as a struggle for global hegemony between a Socialist East and a Capitalist West.[5] In fact, and as George Smiley intimated, le Carré's writing reflected the importance of a proliferation in clandestine North-South interactions as European decolonisation coalesced with the collapse of the Soviet Union's alliance with Britain and the United States at the end of the Second World War.[6] The actual collaborative relationships that Western intelligence services forged with their nationalist counterparts in the Indian subcontinent were, intriguingly, more complex and involved than le Carré's readers can possibly have imagined.

Spying in South Asia provides the first scholarly examination of interventions made by the intelligence and security services of Britain and the United States in post-colonial India. It probes the nexus between intelligence and statecraft in South Asia, and questions relationships established between foreign intelligence agencies and South Asian governments for the promotion of democracy, which evolved into justifications for repression. It asks how Western societies came to think of intelligence in terms of surveillance and civil liberty, while today South Asians associate it with covert action and grand conspiracy. It challenges received wisdom on post-war intelligence by contending that Western clandestine agencies had a transformative political and socio-cultural impact not in Cold War Europe, but in the developing world. Paradoxically, between the early 1950s and the mid-1970s, as covert interventions by British and American intelligence services in the internal affairs of Iran, Guatemala, British Guiana, Indonesia, the Congo, and Chile, amongst others, were derided by Indian policymakers as unacceptable manifestations of neo-colonialism, New Delhi quietly consolidated intelligence links with the West. After 1947, India's leaders faced competing pressures to safeguard the national security of a diminished and debilitated post-colonial state while, at the same time, upholding popular conceptions of sovereignty that privileged autonomy and abjured foreign alliances. Part of the solution to this conundrum identified by India's leaders, was to work secretly with the intelligence and security services of Britain and the United States.

Decisions taken by the Indian government during the Cold War in the intelligence and security sphere produced outcomes that were often messy, contradictory, and counterproductive. The formation and implementation of policy was complicated by a national landscape in India within which competing groups of politicians, human rights activists, businesspeople, lawyers, and journalists both fought, and facilitated, interventions made by the intelligence services and covert propaganda agencies of Britain, the United States, and the Soviet Union. The significance of nonaligned states in the transnational story of Cold War secret intelligence has been obscured by a tendency on the part of historians, and producers of popular culture, to view clandestine activity in the context of a narrow East-West binary.[7] Attention given to espionage and covert action inside the developing world has concentrated on the personal narratives of prominent individuals, and marginalised or ignored the importance of Asian and African nations.[8] Recent studies have sought to correct the marginalisation of the global South in Cold War history. Important interventions by Paul Thomas Chamberlain and Lorenz Lüthi have gone some way to recover, and to account for, the extent to which post-colonial nations formed their own distinct visions of decolonisation, freedom, and sovereignty.[9] Nascent states across the global South responded to the Cold War in complex ways, collaborating with, co-opting, and resisting, superpower encroachment. The sophisticated manipulation of British, American, and Soviet anxieties enabled local actors to win support from powerful external forces, and to influence and disrupt their regional agendas. In India's case, the year 1947, as Ramachandra Guha has observed pointedly, did not, as a dearth of historical

INTRODUCTION

analysis on post-colonial South-Asia might suggest, signal the end of history.[10] Indian agency in South Asia's clandestine Cold War was considerable. *Spying in South Asia* breaks new ground by tilting the prevailing East-West axis of Cold War intelligence studies to examine the conflicts diplomatic and social impact from a North-South perspective.

An over-arching argument made in this book is that the Cold War interventions undertaken by British and American intelligence and security agencies in India proved to be misguided and largely self-defeating.[11] British and American policymakers mounted covert (and avowed) intelligence operations in the subcontinent on the basis of a series of questionable, and often conflicting assumptions: that covert action could steer Indian public opinion in a pro-Western and anti-communist direction; that popular perceptions of Western intelligence agencies could be insulated from deep-seated Indian attitudes to British colonialism and American neo-colonialism; that Western intelligence support provided to New Delhi would corrode India's relations with the Soviet Union; that global controversies surrounding American intelligence practice would not cut through with the Indian public; that the subcontinent's politicians would resist leveraging anti-Western sentiment and refrain from employing the Central Intelligence Agency (CIA) as a lightning rod for India's domestic travails; and, that secret intelligence activity could, ultimately, help to arrest a decline in British and American influence in the subcontinent. None of these assumptions proved correct. None of their associated objectives were realised.

In addition, *Spying in South Asia* re-periodises Cold War secret intelligence. To date, intelligence literature has focused predominantly on early Cold War intelligence events, such as the defections of Guy Burgess, Donald Maclean, and Kim Philby, members of the so-called of 'Cambridge Five' spy ring.[12] Much has also been made of espionage activity and covert action in the later Cold War period, when the process of détente faltered and East-West tensions intensified in the wake of the Soviet invasion of Afghanistan, in December 1979, and Ronald Reagan's elevation to the White House.[13] Yet, in the 1960s, the politics of intelligence in the global South entered a new temporal and geographic phase. At this time, the numbers of Soviet defections staged in Europe slowed as border controls between East and West Germany were tightened and, in 1961, the Berlin Wall went up. Meanwhile, defections at points of Cold War intersection outside Europe multiplied, and nowhere more so than in India. In 1967, Svetlana Alliluyeva, Joseph Stalin's daughter, fled to the West after evading her Soviet minders, stealing through the streets of India's capital, and walking into the US embassy in New Delhi. Before long, such shifts in the pattern of defections were reflected in popular culture. As noted, le Carré situated his account of Karla's would-be defection in *Tinker, Tailor, Soldier, Spy*, not in the well-worn literary borderlands between East and West Germany, but in India, a gateway between Europe and Asia.[14]

In India, as elsewhere, the process of decolonisation transcended a formal transfer of constitutional power from the coloniser to the formerly colonised.[15] Having shaken off almost two centuries of British hegemony, the post-colonial state that emerged in India desperately required financial aid to stimulate a moribund and under-developed economy. India's leaders also came under pressure to implement land reform; establish political institutions; frame a constitution; promote a common sense of national identity; consider health-care and educational provision; manage poverty; maintain law and order; and refashion the nation's armed services and bureaucracy. Maintaining close and constructive relations with Britain afforded one means of accessing external support.[16] The end of British rule in India did not eradicate informal levers of colonial control. Economically, socially, culturally, and politically, London continued to exercise a powerful influence within the subcontinent.

In national security terms, India remained dependent upon the United Kingdom to supply its armed services with senior leadership, training, and equipment. A British General, Sir Roy Bucher, served as head of the Indian army until 1949. Air Marshal Sir Thomas Elmhirst commanded the Indian Air Force until 1950. The Indian Navy was led by Royal Navy officers until April 1958. Shielded from public scrutiny, but no less important, was a decision taken by India's premier, Jawaharlal Nehru, and members of his inner cabinet, to sanction India's establishment of clandestine intelligence partnerships with Britain and the United States. Pressing strategic concerns superseded the personal misgivings and political complications that Indian officials faced when weighing the merits of working with London and Washington in the intelligence arena. As a state subject to formidable fissiparous pressures, India had much to gain from tapping into British experience and expertise in counter-subversion and internal security, a good deal of which was accumulated in the subcontinent prior to 1947. Ensuring that seditious movements were kept in check, whether of a religious or communal persuasion, or on the left or the right of the political spectrum, preoccupied Indian leaders. In the nominally secular Republic of India, with its significant Muslim minority, New Delhi was anxious to keep a lid on simmering Hindu nationalism.[17] Likewise, emerging Cold War threats, whether internal, in the guise of an active and well-supported Communist Party of India (CPI), or external, in the form of its powerful socialist neighbours, the People's Republic of China (PRC) and the Soviet Union, troubled prominent right-wing members of the ruling Congress Party, and notably the Home Minister, Vallabhbhai Patel.[18]

Nehru voiced concern that India's intelligence services were overly dependent on the British and had fallen into replicating British colonial methods. His intelligence chiefs, the Indian premier bemoaned, appeared content merely to repackage information supplied by London.[19] 'I do not think it necessary or appropriate', Nehru confided to one of his closest advisors, 'that our [India's] political intelligence should function as an annexure to theirs [Britain's]'.[20] Nehru had a point. A tendency was manifest on the part of India's fledgling intelligence establishment to valorise and to defer to British colleagues. In 1950, one Indian government report recorded that it was 'an undoubted fact' that the 'deadly effectiveness' of Britain's intelligence system had delivered victory in the First and the Second World Wars.[21] Recounting his arrival at New Delhi's Tihar jail to interrogate Karla, George Smiley underscored how everything, and yet seemingly nothing, had changed in India's intelligence relationship with Britain. Smiley, '... saw the iron gateway of the old prison engulf him, and the perfectly pressed British uniforms of the [Indian] warders as they waded knee-deep through the prisoners: "This way your honour, sir! Please be good enough to follow us, your excellency!"'[22] The imaginary representation conjured by le Carré of Indian obsequiousness in the presence of a British intelligence officer is exaggerated for literary effect. It was not, however, as Nehru and others bemoaned, entirely incongruous.

Constrained by a lack of alternative options, Indian governments endeavoured to resolve a conundrum of balancing security against sovereignty by secretly consolidating intelligence links with Britain and the United States in areas as diverse as training, information collection, analysis, and even covert action.[23] From Whitehall's perspective the cultivation of a strong intelligence relationship with India retained value as a means of preserving British interests

Figure I.1 Communist Party of India rally, New Delhi, c. 1960. United States Information Agency collection, US National Archives, College Park, Maryland.

in the subcontinent; keeping India ostensibly aligned with the West; acting as a barrier to communist penetration of the region; and, not least, demonstrating to the United States that Britain remained an international partner worth having.[24] The scope, scale, and significance of the intelligence partnership fashioned between India, the United Kingdom, and the United States passed largely unnoticed. In the late 1960s, when knowledge of New Delhi's intelligence partnerships with London and Washington filtered into the public domain, Indian politicians were exposed to uncomfortable scrutiny by an incredulous press and an uneasy public. Subsequently, a civil culture in the subcontinent riven with conspiracism and infused with paranoia, as mediated by politicians, journalists, social activists, and cultural producers, and exploited by forces of the left and the right, inside and outside South Asia, came to occupy an extensive, prominent, and pervasive role in popular Indian discourse.[25]

Constructing intelligence alliances with Britain and the United States also required Indian policymakers to set aside inequities of Western colonialism that, in the security and intelligence domain, had inflicted deep psychological scars. Indira Gandhi, Jawaharlal Nehru's daughter, and India's first, and to date only, female prime minister, attested to the emotional trauma that repression practiced by Britain's imperial security agencies inflicted on her family.[26] In December 1921, when her father was arrested by British authorities for distributing political leaflets on the streets of Allahabad, a four-year-old Gandhi had perched on her grandfather's knee to observe Nehru's appearance in court. Gandhi was present when a British magistrate sentenced Nehru and her grandfather to six months in prison and watched as they were hauled off to Lucknow jail in chains.[27] A decade later, having endured several periods in British custody, Nehru challenged Philip Kerr, the Marquess of Lothian, who had served as Under-Secretary of State for India, to deny that British rule in India was not despotic. The British hold on the subcontinent, Nehru charged, was 'based on an extreme form of widespread violence and the sanction is fear . . . . It surrounds itself with a vast army of spies and informers and agents provocateurs. Is this the atmosphere in which the more democratic institutions flourish?'[28] Bhola Nath (B. N.) Mullik, head of India's Intelligence Bureau (IB) in the 1950s, observed that Nehru's direct and sustained exposure to oppressive colonial security methods had left the Indian leader with a 'natural' and 'strong prejudice' against foreign intelligence services.[29] In other words, India's political class had ample reason not to co-operate with London and Washington in the intelligence field, and only did so by placing pragmatic security considerations before personal animosities.

More broadly, the political geography of the Cold War all but ensured that the subcontinent would become a locus of that conflict's clandestine struggle. Directly to India's north lay the communist colossuses of the Soviet Union and the People's Republic of China. In 1955, an exchange of state visits between

INTRODUCTION 7

Nehru and the Soviet leader, Nikita Khrushchev, invigorated Moscow's moribund relationship with New Delhi. Soviet economic and technical assistance flooded into India, while politically Moscow courted Nehru's goodwill by throwing its weight in the UN Security Council behind New Delhi's claim on the disputed state of Kashmir. In 1960, by the end of Dwight Eisenhower's second presidential term in the United States, Washington had become alarmed by the growth of Soviet influence in India and the strength of indigenous Indian communism. Eisenhower's efforts to bring India and the United States closer together, primarily through the provision of American economic assistance, were amplified by his successor, John F. Kennedy. Kennedy saw democratic India as a crucial strategic counterweight to the expansion of Chinese communist influence in Asia.[30] Cold War competition for non-aligned India's favour drew thousands of diplomats, non-governmental organisations, technicians, businesspeople, and journalists to the subcontinent from the Soviet Union, Eastern Europe, Britain, and the United States. In turn, this acted as a magnet for foreign intelligence agencies. By the end of the 1960s, India's Ministry of External Affairs worried that New Delhi's acquisition of an unwelcome reputation as a major Cold War clearing-house, or the 'Berlin of the East', threatened serious harm to the nation's international relations.[31] The former British SIS officer, and Soviet spy, George Blake, observed that alongside Berlin, India was seen as especially important in Western intelligence circles as it offered, 'the most favourable conditions ... for establishing contacts with Soviet citizens'. In New Delhi, Blake underlined, 'there was a wider intercourse than elsewhere between Soviet diplomatic personnel and local politicians and public and it would be easier therefore for our [SIS] agents to establish contact with them'.[32]

What applied to SIS, also held good for the CIA, and Soviet intelligence bodies, such as the Committee for State Security (KGB) and GRU, or foreign military intelligence. From humble beginnings, the American covert footprint in India expanded exponentially. As far back as 1827, Josiah Harlan, an American merchant who travelled to the subcontinent five years earlier in search of adventure, fortune, and fame, had initiated a campaign of covert action. Harlan, who the British writer and chronicler of empire, Rudyard Kipling, used as a model for his short story of intrigue on the North-West Frontier, *The Man Who Would Be King,* raised the Stars and Stripes in the city of Ludhiana, in the Punjab, in India's northwest, and enlisted a motley band of local fighters. Intent on fomenting rebellion against Afghanistan's ruler, Dost Mohammad Khan, Harlan's scheming came to nothing. He eventually returned to the United States, served in the Union army during the American Civil War, and died of tuberculosis in San Francisco, in 1871, a forgotten man.[33] Following India's independence, Harlan's compatriots in the CIA, having initially operated out of a single 'station', or office, in New Delhi, rapidly extended the geographical scope of the Agency's activities. The

8   SPYING IN SOUTH ASIA

CIA established a network of out-stations across the subcontinent, in Bombay, Calcutta, and Madras. One American diplomat, who served in New Delhi at the height of the Cold War, attested that the Agency's presence in India was, 'very large, and very invasive . . . the CIA was deeply involved in the Indian Government'.[34] From the late 1950s, when India's relations with the PRC came under strain, Nehru's governments elected to 'look the other way' as CIA aircraft violated Indian airspace in support of Agency sponsored resistance activities in Chinese controlled Tibet. In 1959, New Delhi infuriated Beijing by colluding in a CIA-sponsored operation to spirit the Dalai Lama out of Lhasa and into asylum in northern India.[35] Equally, in the early 1960s, a series of young and dynamic KGB chairmen, including Alexander Shelepin, Vladimir Semichastny, and the future Soviet leader, Yuri Andropov, came to see India as an important component in Moscow's policy of fermenting wars of national liberation as a means to undermine Western influence in the global South. Under Andropov's direction, Soviet foreign intelligence agencies concentrated a large proportion of their resources, outside of Europe and North America, on India.[36] Oleg Kalugin, then a rising star in the KGB's First Chief (Foreign Intelligence) Directorate, confirmed that, towards the end of the decade, the KGB 'had scores of sources throughout the Indian government – in intelligence, counterintelligence, the defense and foreign ministries, and the police. The entire country was seemingly for sale, and the KGB and the CIA had deeply penetrated the Indian government'.[37]

Participants in India's secret Cold War represented the latest in a long line of state and non-state actors who, in one form or another, established the Indian subcontinent as an historic centre in the development of spycraft. A tradition of using espionage to uphold state security in India can be traced back to the Vedic period in the late Bronze Age.[38] The *Arthashastra*, a treatise on diplomacy attributed to the scholar, Kautilya, and believed to date from the 3rd century BCE, features chapters on the 'Establishment of Clandestine Operations'; 'Surveillance of People with Secret Income'; and 'Investigation through Interrogation and Torture'. Rediscovered and translated into English in 1905, the *Arthashastra* is thought to have served as a blueprint for the expansion of the Mauryan dynasty, the subcontinent's first, and for many centuries, largest empire.[39] Somewhat later, between the sixteenth and seventeenth centuries, the extension of Mughal power into northern India was sustained by extensive intelligence networks responsible for monitoring civil and military functionaries, or *mansabdars,* and landowners, or *zamindars*, and ensuring their fidelity to the imperial state.[40] By the eighteenth century, the arrival of British power in India, in the form of the East India Company, saw the advent of sophisticated webs of local spies and propagandists. Fortune tellers, midwives, physicians, and entertainers were employed by the Company to report on signs of internal revolt and subversive activities of agents working for France and imperial Russia.[41] After 1857, the imposition of formal British

INTRODUCTION 9

rule in India brought with it the introduction of a more structured colonial system of political surveillance and military intelligence, underpinned by repressive force.[42] Reflecting on his experience serving in India at the height of the British *Raj*, one military officer recorded that, 'there can never be any secrets in India, it is rather like living in an illuminated greenhouse'.[43] India, the jewel in Britain's imperial crown, operated as an 'empire of intelligence', the preservation of which, hinged on the efficient collection and processing of information on the social and political lives of its subjects.[44]

The centrality of intelligence to the British imperial project in India caused unease amongst many colonial administrators. Officials, from British Viceroys to district officers, were reluctant to establish permanent secret services. In part, financial considerations came into play. British India was set up to run on the cheap and intelligence organisations were expensive. Indian public opinion was also sensitive to intelligence activity. Colonial rule relied on the acquiescence of India's masses and British bureaucrats were concerned that a heavy-handed approach to security would invite unrest. Moreover, British society evinced a wider cultural aversion to spies and intelligence work. Back at home, espionage was disparaged as ideologically distasteful and at odds with the British national character. It is notable that the United Kingdom operated without established foreign intelligence and counter-intelligence services of its own until 1909.[45] India did prove to be a useful place for would-be British intelligence officers to acquire operational experience. Both SIS and, more particularly, the British Security Service, MI5, recruited officers who had served in India. Sir David Petrie, a Scotsman from Perth, who joined the Indian Police Service (IPS) in 1900 after graduating from Aberdeen University, headed the Intelligence Bureau between the wars. In 1940, on his return to Britain, Petrie was appointed Director-General of MI5. Other prominent Indian alumni within MI5 included John 'Jack' Curry, who spent over two decades working for the IPS before joining the Security Service in 1934. Curry subsequently became a senior officer in MI5's B Branch, responsible for monitoring subversive communist and fascist activity. In the interwar period, several cryptologists working on Russian radio traffic for IB were brought back from India to work in MI5 and SIS. Two of them, Alistair Denniston and John Tiltman, became eminent codebreakers at the Government Code and Cypher School at Bletchley Park.[46] Before that, a requirement to expand metropolitan intelligence capacity occasioned by the First World War prompted large numbers of British policemen and intelligence officers to quit India and return to the United Kingdom to take up posts in MI5.[47] The movement of intelligence personnel between India and the UK ensured that MI5's relations with the DIB were close. So close, in fact, that the DIB's British arm, Indian Political Intelligence (IPI), was located inside the Security Service's London headquarters. Harmonious relations enabled MI5 to work effectively with the DIB to monitor communists travelling between Britain and the subcontinent. Broader cooperation between the two intelligence services, however, remained sporadic and was more limited. With less than a hundred staff on its books, of which only a quarter were active officers, MI5 was too small to provide wide-ranging direction and support to colleagues in India.[48]

In fact, the British colonial intelligence system in the subcontinent was never as extensive or as effective as its contemporary critics and adversaries claimed.[49] One scholar has gone as far as to suggest that the, 'confidence and self-assertion of the British in India was in truth illusory, and the vision of absolute control . . . as imagined in Kipling's *Kim* . . . was little more than wishful thinking'.[50] Popular culture, and the work of Kipling, most especially, helped to establish a 'myth' of British omnipotence in India. In 1901 Kipling published his novel *Kim*, which immortalised the intelligence war, or 'Great Game', fought on India's northern border between agents of the British and Russian governments.[51] The impression of a far-sighted and all-knowing colonial state that emerges from Kipling's account of Kimball O'Hara, a juvenile Eurasian spy who, along with Hurree Babu, a native informant, reports to British intelligence, left a deep imprint on generations of global readers. As late as the 1960s, Kipling's tale of espionage and covert action remained recommended reading for British diplomats posted to South Asia.[52] A decade earlier, uncomfortable Cold War echoes of Kipling had surfaced when the SIS officer, Harold 'Kim' Philby, a child of the *Raj*, who grew up in Ambala, in northern India, speaking Punjabi as his first language, came under suspicion as working for Soviet intelligence. Philby was given the nickname Kim by his father, St John, an officer in the Indian Civil Service, and Kipling devotee.[53] The influence of Kipling's South Asian spy fiction extended across the Atlantic to America's intelligence community. In his youth, Allen Dulles, the future Director of Central Intelligence, was captivated by *Kim* and devoured the novel on a long steamship journey to India. Five decades later, on his death, Dulles' tattered and treasured copy of the book was found lying at his bedside.[54] Kermit 'Kim' Roosevelt, a CIA officer best known for his involvement in the Agency-backed coup that removed Mohammad Mossadegh from power in Iran, in 1953, acquired his sobriquet in a similar manner to Philby. Fond of impressing his tutor with concocted tales of a childhood spent in the subcontinent, which he embellished with phrases in pidgin Hindustani, on discovering her son's deceit, his mother was reminded of Kipling's *Kim*, and the name stuck.[55] Roosevelt's vicarious relationship with India, mediated through Kipling's *Boy's Own* representation of British imperial adventurism, as one scholar of the CIA has noted, was influential in shaping the mentalities of the Agency towards the Middle East and South Asia in the period immediately after the Second World War.[56]

At the same time, a post-war extension of American power across the globe was interpreted by many Indians, Nehru included, as heralding the arrival of a new and pernicious form of imperialism. One of the first books to reference the CIA, and its purportedly nefarious designs on the developing world, L. Natarajan's, *American Shadow over India*, was published in Bombay in

Figure I.2 Allen Welsh Dulles, Director of Central Intelligence (1953–1961). Bettmann / Getty Images.

1952.[57] The CIA, as the 'covert' foreign policy tool of choice for US Presidents from Harry Truman onwards, quickly acquired an invidious reputation in South Asia as an anti-democratic socio-political malefactor. Much of the mistrust and fear that British colonial intelligence and security agencies had once engendered in the subcontinent was accordingly transferred to the Agency. Public opprobrium associated with the CIA in India eventually came to overshadow American diplomatic initiatives designed to win 'hearts and minds'. A report produced for the United States Information Service observed, presciently, that 'centuries of bitter experience have made the Hindu dread, above all things, the policeman, the foreigner, the official, the "420" [a term for British security officials derived from India's Penal Code] who rarely in history have done other than exploit them'.[58] The CIA's principal Cold War opposition in India, the KGB and GRU, worked tirelessly to amplify Indian conceptions of the Agency as an all-powerful miscreant. In the 1970s alone, the Soviets covertly bankrolled an Indian press agency, two daily and eight weekly Indian newspapers, and four popular magazines, in order to feed India's media with a stream of salacious CIA stories.[59]

The socio-political impact of British and American intelligence activity in India during the Cold War is not reflected in current literature. In the United Kingdom, the publication of authorised histories of MI5 and SIS have shed some light on the establishment and operation of intelligence liaison relationships between Britain and its former South Asian empire.[60] Path-breaking though they are, these state-sponsored works seldom stray far beyond the parochial field of intelligence operations and into the realm of transnational politics. Significantly, existing intelligence studies have, until very recently, neglected arguably the most significant clandestine operation mounted by Britain in post-colonial South Asia, that undertaken by the Foreign Office's Information Research Department (IRD).[61] The absence of a comprehensive account of the CIA's Cold War operations in India and, more precisely, that organisation's impact on the United States' wider relations with South Asia, represents a lacuna in the voluminous body of scholarship covering the American intelligence community.[62] Accounts of foreign intelligence agencies in India's domestic affairs, authentic and otherwise, have long occupied a prominent place in South Asian political discourse, journalism, and modes of cultural production. Indian scholarship has nevertheless largely eschewed serious engagement with the history of post-independence security and intelligence collaboration, and competition, with Britain and the United States. Indian intelligence literature remains dominated by the self-serving accounts of former intelligence officers, and sensationalist works in which unsubstantiated conspiracy theories, communal politics, and the spectre of a malevolent 'foreign hand', all loom large.[63] *Spying in South Asia* offers an archivally rich, transnational analysis of a clandestine Cold War that, as recently released official records in the UK, US, and India affirm, had a deep and enduring impact in the subcontinent.

Over the past seventy-five years India has confronted myriad threats to its national security. Indigenous communist movements, communal violence, a querulous Pakistani neighbour, and a regional rival in the form of the People's Republic of China, have all threatened the integrity of the Indian Union at various times. The nation's emergence in the twenty-first century as a nuclear-armed economic and strategic powerhouse has transformed its international strategic standing. India now matters locally, regionally, and globally. Scholarship scrutinising the history of India's association with secret intelligence, and the interaction of India's bureaucracy and people with external intelligence services, has been complicated by a post-colonial socio-political landscape preoccupied by intrigue, tinged with anti-Americanism, and obsessed with secrecy. India's uneven relationship with covert action, that has manifested periods of official suspicion and hostility, alongside phases of acceptance and active engagement, is currently in a state of flux. Restrictions imposed by previous Indian governments on covert operations undertaken by the Research and Analysis Wing (R&AW), Indian's foreign intelligence service, have been swept aside by a new bureaucracy under the leadership of Narendra Modi and the Hindu nationalist Bharatiya Janata Party (BJP). Under the direction of Modi's National Security Advisor, and former Director of the IB, Ajit Doval, India has

INTRODUCTION

embraced the potentialities of covert action. In 2015, allegations surfaced that the R&AW had intervened in Sri Lanka's presidential elections, successfully working to unite opposition to the pro-China incumbent, Mahinda Rajapaksa, and replace him with the India-friendly, Maithripala Sirisena.[64] The following year, Doval was rumoured to have authorised special forces to cross the line of control between India and Pakistan in Kashmir, and conduct 'surgical strikes' against *Jaish-e-Muhammad* (The Army of Muhammad), a Pakistan-based terrorist organisation that India held responsible for an assault on one of its military bases.[65] In addition, Doval has been credited with masterminding cross-border operations by Indian intelligence and special forces against Naga separatists operating from bases inside Myanmar.[66]

India's current leaders, it appears, have priced-in negative consequences of covert action on the nation's relations with its neighbours, and have calculated the associated diplomatic and reputational costs to be acceptable. Given that two of New Delhi's regional rivals are nuclear-armed states, the strategic risks associated with India's current covert action doctrine have never been greater. An absence of political and public support for intelligence reform has left the Indian government, and its intelligence services, dangerously exposed to calamitous missteps when it comes to covert action. In an observation that resonates with the crises faced by America's intelligence community in the mid-1970s, one national security commentator has noted that the R&AW would best serve India's interests, and help to promote stability and prosperity in Asia, by refocusing on intelligence gathering and analysis, and avoiding 'pulse-quickening operations built on . . . an anti-terrorism mindset'.[67] Absent a meaningful recalibration of existing and ineffective institutional mechanisms regulating Indian clandestine activity, Indian policymakers now faces a choice between sticking with the nation's twenty-two official languages, or adding 'a new language of killing'. India's emergence as an economic titan, renewed Sino-Indian tensions, continued regional backwash from a so-called 'War on Terror', and uncertainties surrounding New Delhi's security policy, have kept the subcontinent at the forefront of global news headlines. *Spying in South Asia* aims, above all, to foster debate on the evolution of South Asia's relationship with secret intelligence and to consider its wider global consequences. Recovering the hidden history of India's secret Cold War and critically assessing its impact on New Delhi's international relations has never been more important as we advance further into an 'Asian century'.

1

Transfer of Power: British Intelligence and the End of Empire in South Asia

In August 1947, Britain hauled down the Union Jack and departed from South Asia. At the Lucknow Residency, in Uttar Pradesh, a site revered by the *Raj* as a symbol of imperial resolve following the events of 1857, elaborate precautions were taken to ensure that the transfer of power passed off without incident. The Residency was the only building in the British Empire where the Union Flag was never lowered. In the run-up to independence some Indians called for the Union Jack to be replaced by India's tricolour. Instead, a day before India celebrated *swaraj*, or self-rule, the British flag was lowered under the strictest secrecy and its flagpole removed. Press photographers were banned from the ceremony, and in its aftermath a temporary police post was established to discourage public celebration.[1] The careful stage management of events at Lucknow underscored the value Britain placed on formal displays of imperial sovereignty to mediate the realities of local power. Projection of influence through the manipulation of images of authority had, by and large, served the British well in India.[2] However, by the end of the Second World War a resurgence in Indian nationalism exposed British overdependence on reputation and esteem as levers of statecraft. The previous December, the Viceroy, Archibald Wavell, confided to his diary that, 'the administration [in India] has declined, and the machine in the Centre is hardly working at all now ... while the British are still legally and morally responsible for what happens in India, we have lost nearly all power to control events; we are simply running on the momentum of our previous prestige.'[3]

In contrast to the progressive, if troubled, transfer of political power in the subcontinent, the handover of intelligence and security responsibilities was precipitate and problematic. The British left India without bequeathing the newly independent state an intelligence apparatus that was fit for purpose. India's leaders had assumed greater authority over internal policy once the post-war Labour administration of Clement Attlee had accepted that, in South Asia at least, Britain lacked the means to suppress the forces of nationalism. In the intelligence arena, the reassignment of authority from British to Indian hands occurred on a shorter timescale and a more limited basis. To a degree, this was unsurprising, given that the colonial intelligence effort in South Asia had largely been directed at manipulating nationalists prominent in India's pre-independence transitional governments.[4] It was not until March 1946, when a Cabinet Mission led by the British ministers Stafford Cripps, Lord Pethick-Lawrence, and A. V. Alexander arrived in the subcontinent, that Whitehall's secret agencies recognised that an Indian Home Minister with responsibility for intelligence could be appointed at any moment.[5] That summer, the Viceroy's secretary reminded British officials to screen their files for documents that an incoming nationalist administration might find useful, 'as material for anti-British propaganda'.[6] Residents of New Delhi were treated to the spectacle of thick black clouds swirling high into the sky for weeks on end as reams of records were torched in the courtyard of the IB's registry building in the *La Qila*, or Red Fort. A systematic destruction of decades of information saw much of the operational history of the Intelligence Bureau go up in smoke.[7]

Exposure to the power of the secret colonial state coloured the attitudes of Indian politicians towards intelligence agencies. Jawaharlal Nehru's aversion to intelligence was commonly attributed to the harassment and oppressive surveillance that Britain's imperial security apparatus had brought to bear on Nehru and his family.[8] Alex Kellar, MI5's resident expert on colonial matters, reasoned that, 'Nehru's critical views on "our [Britain's] intelligence organization" are doubtless due in considerable measure to his own personal experience as a political agitator . . . '[9] Once installed as India's prime minister, Nehru expressed reservations that, 'Indian Intelligence was still dependent on the British and was following old British methods taught to the Indian Officers in pre-independence days, and was also dishing out intelligence which the British continued to supply to it.'[10] Into the 1950s, Nehru complained to his friend, and India's last Viceroy, Lord Louis Mountbatten, about the product that he received from India's Intelligence Bureau. 'I always read our Intelligence reports very critically and I am not prepared to accept them as they are', Nehru confided. 'I have had a good deal of experience of the police and of Intelligence from the other side to be easily taken in by the reports we get.'[11]

That said, Nehru acknowledged India's need to develop an effective intelligence service of its own. In November 1947, reflecting on a series of pressing national security challenges, the Indian leader emphasised to his chief ministers:

> . . . the necessity for developing intelligence services. This is very important, both from the provincial and the central points of view. It is not easy to develop a good intelligence service suddenly as the men employed must be carefully chosen. Our old intelligence system has more or less broken down as it was bound to, because it was meant for other purposes, chiefly in tracking Congressmen and the like. The new intelligence service will have to be built differently.[12]

The intelligence vacuum that developed in India from 1946 was especially acute given the profusion of urgent problems confronted by Nehru and his ministers. India's political leaders were anxious to curtail communal tension

16   SPYING IN SOUTH ASIA

and to reassure the country's substantial Muslim minority that they could keep a lid on Hindu nationalism.[13] The wrenching effect of Partition, mass migration, the violent deaths of hundreds of thousands, if not millions of the subcontinent's citizens, and the enervating territorial disputes that ensued between India and Pakistan, not least over the former princely state of Kashmir, led policymakers to seek timely and accurate intelligence.[14] In addition, Indian officials were concerned to negate a subversive threat posed by a large and well-supported Communist Party of India (CPI). In the political tumult that accompanied Britain's retreat from South Asia, communist support threatened to gain traction beyond urban centres that accommodated the industrial working class and evolve into a broader peasant insurgency. A proliferation of red flags in Indian villages alarmed the British *and* their nationalist partners in the Congress Party.[15] Moreover, despite assurances provided to Attlee's Foreign Secretary, Ernest Bevin, by the Soviet leader, Joseph Stalin, that Moscow would not interfere in India's internal affairs, the British obtained evidence that financial aid was being directed by Moscow to the CPI.[16]

Once Attlee's government responded to dwindling British authority in India by bringing forward the timetable for independence from June 1948 to August 1947, the flow of intelligence reaching London from the subcontinent dried up. A month after Wavell's lament that Britain had lost its capacity to dictate events on the ground, the Joint Intelligence Committee in London noted that it was, 'no longer able to advise the Chiefs of Staff fully on the implications of future developments in that country [India]'.[17] Whitehall planned to retain independent India as a close international ally of the United Kingdom. The subcontinent's access to the Middle East's oilfields, its proximity to both the Soviet Union and China, its reserves of labour, and its untapped potential as an industrial base, made it imperative, in the minds of British military planners, 'that India should remain closely allied to the Commonwealth'.[18] With the end of British colonialism in India coalescing with the advent of the Cold War, London came to regard the maintenance of friendly relations with a nationalist government in New Delhi as *sine qua non* to the containment of Soviet power in Asia.

India did not figure as prominently on other nations' lists of global priorities. In the aftermath of Indian independence, while Britain's press gave blanket coverage to the political drama and social trauma unfolding in the subcontinent, reports in Soviet newspapers focused on crop yields in the Ukraine, an upcoming Latvian theatre season, and fawning eulogies of Stalin. The Soviet newspaper of record, *Izvestia*, made one brief reference, on its back page, to India's transition to independence.[19] Under Stalin's regime, the USSR's relationship with India was informed by the Soviet dictator's conviction that post-colonial states functioned as imperialist puppets. In 1950, one Indian official bemoaned that the state-controlled Soviet media was determined to represent India as, 'a stronghold of reaction, a persecutor of democratic forces, a hanger-on of the Anglo-American bloc, and the harbinger of a new Imperialism in the East'.[20] In the United States, American broadsheets reflected upon the termination of Britain's 200-year presence in South Asia only after discussing soaring domestic food prices, Soviet meddling in the Greek civil war, the Italian economy, and a heatwave sweeping the Atlantic seaboard.[21] President Harry Truman evidenced little interest in the momentous events taking place in India. At the time, Truman, and his Secretary of State, George Marshall, were pre-occupied by developments in Western Europe, where post-war economic and social tensions appeared set to sweep communist regimes to power in Italy, France, and across the Mediterranean littoral. Chester Bowles, who Truman appointed ambassador to India in 1951, chaffed at the disinterest senior US officials manifested towards South Asia. Washington's perceptions of the subcontinent, Bowles griped, were filtered through a distorted and 'Kiplingesque' prism. To Americans, the ambassador bemoaned, India appeared, 'an ancient land of cobras, maharajahs, monkeys, famines, [and] polo players, [that was] over-crowded with cows and babies'.[22]

Absent superpower interest in India, Whitehall was free to leverage its experience of managing intelligence systems in the subcontinent to influence the evolution of India's national security state. Another, and secret transfer of power, occurred in 1947. Its origins lay in plans hatched by MI5 and SIS to retain a British intelligence foothold in India. It came to encompass a protracted struggle for operational paramountcy between Britain's Security and Secret Intelligence Services. Bureaucratic turf wars inside Whitehall's secret world stirred debates at the highest levels of government over whether the United Kingdom should undertake covert action in India and, if so, how it should be conducted, and to what purpose? Decisions taken in London to employ Britain's intelligence services to uphold UK national interests in the subcontinent, and advance the West's wider anti-communist Cold War agenda, dovetailed with an Indian requirement for external support in the domestic security arena. A mutual dependency helped to forge and sustain close relations between the intelligence and security services of Britain and India during, and after, the transfer of power in South Asia. In the shadowy realm of secret intelligence, the transition of authority in India from the coloniser to the colonised was more complex and contested than has hitherto been acknowledged.

The Other Transfer of Power: The Indianisation of the Intelligence Bureau

In the autumn of 1946, the impending Indianisation of intelligence in South Asia unnerved MI5. As the nationalist push for independence gathered momentum, Guy Liddell, Deputy Director-General of the Security Service, ruminated on the prospect that, 'At any moment we might be faced with an Indian D.I.B. [Director Intelligence Bureau] and an Indian War Minister through whom any communications on Intelligence matters might pass.' 'What struck me', a concerned Liddell recorded, ' . . . was that we should anticipate the worst, namely, a completely chaotic situation over a period of months, if not years, when all communications [with India] would have broken down and the Government here would have very little idea about what was going on'.[23] Before the end of the year, MI5's anxiety that intelligence from India would dry up appeared all too real. In November, Liddell noted that the flow of material reaching the Joint Intelligence Committee from India had slowed to a trickle and Britain's Chiefs of Staff were no longer receiving meaningful reports on the security situation in South Asia.[24]

Apprehension in MI5 that its ability to monitor and react to events unfolding in India was rapidly diminishing was amplified by the uncertain fate of Indian Political Intelligence (IPI), or the Security Services 'Indian branch'. While IPI remained nominally under the control of the Secretary of State for India, from 1923 it had worked closely with MI5. At the direction of IPI's chief, Philip Vickery, MI5 officers kept leading Indian nationalists in the United Kingdom under surveillance and, on occasions, placed intercepts on their mail and telephone communications. In return, Vickery's organisation maintained intimate relations with the IB and acted as a *de facto* British clearing house for the collection, analysis, and dissemination of intelligence related to India from across the globe.[25] Once an interim Indian government took office in New Delhi, on 2 September 1946, IPI's days were numbered. Crucially, the Home Ministry, to whom the IB reported, passed from British control and into the hands of the nationalist leader, Vallabhbhai Patel. Patel wasted no time in stamping his authority on India's intelligence services. Norman Smith, the last British DIB, was summoned to see India's new Home Minister and told that the IB's operational mandate had changed. Surveillance operations against Congress Party officials were prohibited, although those targeting radical left-wing Indian politicians and suspected communists were allowed to continue. Significantly, Patel removed Smith's prerogative of direct access to the Viceroy. Moving forward, all IB reporting was channelled through the Home Ministry. At a stroke, the British government were cut out of the intelligence loop in their own colony. In Patel's mind, it was essential that the colonial security apparatus was placed in nationalist hands prior to a transfer of constitutional power. Once stripped of their eyes and ears in India, any last-minute change of heart on the part of the British would be rendered futile.[26]

The following spring, as Whitehall began to shut IPI down, British colonial intelligence officers packed up en masse and either departed for home or took up positions in alternative imperial outposts. Old Indian hands found that securing new jobs was problematic. Back in London, a young Enoch Powell, then working in the Conservative Party's central office, was approached by

TRANSFER OF POWER

anxious colonial officials for assistance. Gordon Thompson, commander of the British Indian army in Calcutta, asked Powell for help in securing employment with SIS. Powell effected an introduction, but Thompson was left disappointed by SIS's 'remarkably unenthusiastic' response. With the Ministry of Supply also turning him down, Thompson was reduced to soliciting work from the Tory Party.[27] Others proved more fortunate. By 1950, SIS had found room for three former British Indian officials on permanent, pensionable terms, and a further 12 on temporary or contract agreements.[28] Treasury objections that SIS's Indian recruits had been employed on more generous financial terms than existing officers, subsequently forced the Service's chief, Stewart Menzies, to discharge three of their number and commit to taking 'on no more new men from this [Indian] source'.[29] Such a regrettable step, SIS grumbled, represented 'a wicked waster of good potential'.[30] The Security Service found less trouble accommodating British colonial policemen and intelligence officers. Between the wars, MI5 absorbed several British officials who had served in the subcontinent. Institutional connections forged between MI5 and the IB that were rooted in imperial security drew colonial officials into the Security Service. In March 1947, Guy Liddell, Deputy Director-General of MI5, undertook a talent spotting mission in the subcontinent. With Norman Smith's assistance, Liddell interviewed promising British officers in the IB, some of whom were taken on by the Security Service.[31] By 1965, the process of British decolonisation saw almost two-thirds of MI5's officers with résumés that included a form of imperial service.[32]

Shortly after Liddell's visit to India, Smith was replaced by the first Indian Director of the IB, Tirupattur Gangadharam (T. G.) Sanjeevi Pillai. A forty-nine-year-old policeman from Madras, Sanjeevi had joined the Indian Police Service in September 1922 and made steady, if unspectacular, progress through its ranks as the nationalist campaign for *swaraj*, or independence, gained impetus. In 1946, following stints in the Madras Special Branch and CID, Sanjeevi was promoted to the post of Deputy Inspector General of Police. Within a year, he was posted to New Delhi and, in April 1947, was made chief of the IB. Writing to Omandur Ramasamy Reddy, premier of the Madras presidency, Vallabhbhai Patel apologized for ordering Sanjeevi north at a time, ' . . . that you can ill-afford to spare him, but it is of paramount necessity that we should have a first-class officer as Director'.[33] Sanjeevi's colleagues in the IB found their new boss to be a distant and difficult character. K. Sankaran Nair, who enjoyed a long and distinguished career in Indian intelligence, admired Sanjeevi for his intellect and the high professional standards that he demanded from IB officers. Nair was less impressed by Sanjeevi's prickly temperament and an abrasive self-confidence that bordered on hubris.[34] A propensity to lapse into fits of pique would, ultimately, lead Sanjeevi to fall foul of his political masters and bring his tenure as DIB to an abrupt and premature end. Guy Liddell questioned Patel's wisdom in appointing Sanjeevi, 'a Hindu

19

policeman from Madras without intelligence experience'. A highly competent Muslim intelligence officer of long standing, Liddell noted, had been passed over by Patel. 'This [Sanjeevi's appointment] and other incidents', Liddell mused, 'showed a tendency on the part of the [Intelligence] Bureau to degenerate into a Hindu Gestapo, whose principal target would be the Moslem League'. Such an unwelcome development, were it to materialise, Liddell reflected, was likely to restrict his Service's interaction with the IB, 'except on the subject of Communism, in which the Congress Party were showing particular interest'.[35]

The formidable set of challenges, and the inadequate resources, that Sanjeevi inherited when he assumed charge of the IB would have tested the capabilities of the most accomplished intelligence officer. In Sanjeevi's case, his relative inexperience was quickly and brutally exposed. The IB Director erred in alienating senior politicians by seeking broad executive powers for his organisation. Powerful figures in the governing Congress Party, Patel included, considered that Sanjeevi's grab for power threatened to place the IB beyond a level of legislative scrutiny appropriate in a democracy. Sanjeevi argued that his role managing, 'a very vast intelligence organization with centres flung far and wide in the country and outside it', demanded that he should be designated *primes inter pares* within India's intelligence community. In doing so, Sanjeevi exaggerated his own importance and overplayed his hand.[36] A suggestion by Sanjeevi that his title should be amended from 'Director, Intelligence Bureau', to, 'Director-General of Intelligence', met with a frosty response from Indian civil servants. Rejecting Sanjeevi's proposal, R. N. Banerjee, the administrative head of the Home Ministry, observed disapprovingly, 'I am rather surprised that such an unsound proposal should have been put up seriously by the Director, Intelligence Bureau.'[37] Sanjeevi's bid to secure control over all intelligence matters, civil and military, received an equally firm rebuff from India's armed forces. Thomas Elmhirst observed that Sanjeevi had courted 'a certain amount of trouble' by seeking to impose his authority over the country's Joint Intelligence Committee (JIC). Having proposed to his military colleagues that he should not only chair the JIC but, 'control all Intelligence–internal, external, military, naval and air', Sanjeevi was left in no doubt that such an idea was unthinkable, and that instead he should 'concern himself with internal security and with the running of a certain number of agents into adjacent territory'.[38]

The struggle for power in India's intelligence establishment was mirrored by a concurrent post-war battle between MI5 and SIS over their respective roles and responsibilities. At the beginning of 1947, representatives of SIS, MI5, and IPI held a series of discussions on how to 'maintain the future flow of intelligence relating to India'. The outcome was distilled into a single joint report, in which the three secret organisations put forward several recommendations. As an interim measure, it was suggested that IPI should be incorporated into the Security Service. A temporary dispensation was also proposed that allowed for

IPI to continue running covert operations in foreign territories. The latter ran counter to a directive that Clement Attlee had issued in April 1946, which prohibited the Security Service from engaging in such activity. Authorising MI5/IPI to mount covert operations abroad was justified as a necessary short-term expedient, given the exceptional nature of the security situation unfolding in India. Whitehall endorsed the recommendations and, on 1 August 1947, IPI was officially incorporated into MI5. To assuage concern in SIS that the Security Service's charter risked becoming unduly expansive, it was agreed that IPI activity conducted on foreign soil would only be undertaken in partnership with SIS.[39]

In addition, the joint report called for SIS to be granted an operational remit in India. Attlee's directive of April 1946 had included a clause prohibiting SIS activity in British territory overseas, including India. Or, in other words, Attlee instructed the Security Service to keep out of foreign countries, unless invited in by a host government, and SIS to stay away from the British Empire. The three secret services rationalised extending SIS's mandate to incorporate India on the basis that, 'India may be a foreign country before long [and] it seems justified as an experimental measure.' Even were a new independent Indian government willing to exchange security and intelligence information, the joint report argued, it seemed unlikely that, for reasons of inefficiency or policy, such an arrangement could furnish all the material required by customers in Whitehall. In a memorandum sent by Menzies to William Hayter, who oversaw intelligence matters at the Foreign Office, the SIS chief made plain that whatever the nature of the future relationship between the United Kingdom and India, his organisation could only pick up the slack left by the Indianisation of the IB by placing its officers on the ground in South Asia. For SIS to supply Whitehall with intelligence on Indian and foreign nationals in the subcontinent; to keep abreast of Indian links to individuals and organisations of interest further afield; and to advise on intelligence matters in countries adjacent to India; the Service needed an active office or station in the subcontinent.[40] An Indian nationalist government, one FO official underlined, was certain to be 'wholly unreliable' when it came to intelligence sharing, and could, 'never be in quite the same category as Canada or Australia'.[41] As an addendum, the joint report recommended the dispatch of a resident MI5 officer to the British High Commission in New Delhi. Patel had previously indicated that he would be receptive to an exchange of security liaison officers following the transfer of power, and Whitehall embraced the opportunity this presented to maintain strong links with the IB.[42]

The spirit of collective goodwill displayed by Britain's secret world in respect of India proved to be short-lived. By early February 1947, senior figures in the Foreign Office began pressing for a revision of the terms set out in the joint report, and for SIS to assume primacy in the subcontinent. Writing to MI5's Director General, Sir Percy Sillitoe, on 7 February, Sir Orme Sargent,

Permanent Under-Secretary for Foreign Affairs, declared, ' . . . we feel very strongly that it is undesirable to have two organisations [SIS and MI5] engaged in covert activities in a foreign country.' The activities of MI5, Sargent insisted, 'can in the nature of things never be fully overt'. Allowing two British intelligence services to run side-by-side in India, the FO mandarin insisted, risked duplication, confusion, and the unwelcome exposure of clandestine activity. One solution, Sargent ventured, would be to offer SIS officers posted to India training in MI5 work, and enable them to take on counterintelligence and security responsibilities.[43] At the same time, Sargent approached Sir Terence Shone, the British High Commissioner in New Delhi, to canvass support for the establishment of a local SIS station. Given the fluidity and uncertainty of the political situation in India, Shone was advised that, from an intelligence standpoint, the Foreign Office 'thought it best to take two bites at the cherry'. This, Shone was told, involved planning both to implement an interim intelligence structure in India, along the lines of that envisaged by the MI5-SIS-IPI joint report, and, concurrently, preparing the ground for a more permanent arrangement under which SIS would exercise exclusive jurisdiction in the subcontinent. Acknowledging that SIS had been excluded by Attlee from operating in Commonwealth territory, Sargent brushed the restriction aside and expressed confidence that India would soon come to represent foreign intelligence terrain, making SIS 'the natural collectors of covert intelligence'. Accordingly, Shone was asked by Sargent to accommodate an SIS officer in the British High Commission and to extend the intelligence officer diplomatic cover.[44] Weeks later, in March 1947, Attlee approved the relaxation of restrictions on covert action undertaken by MI5 and SIS that had been set out in the joint report on intelligence in India.[45] The scene was now set for a bureaucratic tussle between MI5 and SIS that, over the coming months, would see the subcontinent turned into a test case for the post-war delineation of Britain's global intelligence responsibilities.

Staying On: British Intelligence and Post-Independent India

Within MI5, Guy Liddell enthusiastically embraced the opportunity to establish an MI5 liaison office in New Delhi. Liddell's intention was to broker a reciprocal arrangement with the Indian government. This envisaged that MI5 would station one of its officers in Shone's High Commission and, in return, Sanjeevi and the IB would attach one of their men to the Indian High Commission in London.[46] During his visit to India, in March 1947, a delighted Liddell obtained Patel's agreement to exchange security liaison officers. The Deputy Director of MI5 was less pleased when Norman Smith suggested to Patel that, to avoid undue suspicion about the nature of the proposed security liaison arrangement, MI5's man in India should have no prior connection to the IB, Indian Police, or colonial civil service. Appointing an outsider with limited knowledge of India's security landscape, Liddell fumed, would be a mistake and needed to be overturned.[47]

The individual MI5 selected as its first Security Liaison Officer (SLO) in India was Lieutenant Kenneth Bourne. A former Chief of Shanghai Police, Bourne served in India with the Intelligence Corps during the war. Under the codename BRISTOL, he had run a counter-intelligence unit that functioned as a Chinese section of the Intelligence Bureau. Bourne's operation was bankrolled by the Special Operations Executive, but he reported to the IB, and his remit encompassed domestic Indian security duties that included monitoring local Chinese agents and watching over the political and criminal activities of Calcutta's large Chinese community.[48] Bourne's background contravened Smith's recommendation that MI5's SLO should have no prior association with the IB. Liddell pressed ahead with the appointment regardless, and Patel acquiesced. Bourne left London on 29 July 1947 to take up his new post in India.[49] Bourne operated from an office in Eastern House, a building occupied by British information and publicity staff and detached from the main High Commission. He remained in New Delhi for just six months before being replaced by Bill U'ren, another former British Indian police officer who had clocked up twenty years of service in the subcontinent. The experiment posting of an MI5 SLO to India proved successful and it was soon replicated in neighbouring Pakistan and, as the Cold War expanded, across the Empire and Commonwealth.[50] Over time, the SLO innovation came to play an important part in the history of British decolonisation. In more parochial terms, it also ensured that for decades to come relations between MI5 and the IB were more intimate and interdependent than those between any other departments of the British and Indian governments.[51]

Over at SIS, Stewart Menzies followed the Security Service's lead and recruited an ex-Indian policeman of his own to look after the Service's interests in the subcontinent. Vernon Thomas Bayley was born in October 1908 in Ferozepore, Bengalc, to a family steeped in the history of the British *Raj*. As far back as the sixteenth century, his relatives had acted as directors of the East India Company, worked for the Bengal civil service, sat on the subcontinent's judiciary, and served as commissioned officers in the British Indian Army. Bayley's grandfather, Sir Steuart Bayley, worked closely with British intelligence while acting as Secretary of the Political and Secret Department at the India Office. After joining the Indian Police in 1928, Bayley was posted to the North-West Frontier. In 1937, he relocated to New Delhi and took up a position with the IB. Bayley was recruited into SIS in 1946. He was married to the author Viola Powles. Powles enjoyed a successful career writing children's adventure stories under her married name, the locations of which frequently corresponded with Bayley's SIS postings. As a junior IB officer, the often cash-strapped Bayley made ends meet by cultivating his own public audience and moonlighting as a newsreader on Delhi Radio.[52]

On 17 September 1947, Bayley arrived in India in the company of two SIS secretaries. A second SIS officer, and Bayley's assistant, John Peter May, followed in mid-December.[53] May was captured by the Japanese following the fall of Singapore in 1942, and languished for the remainder of the war in a prison camp in Malaya. Patel and the Intelligence Bureau were not informed of Whitehall's decision to reactivate a covert British intelligence presence in India and the small SIS station operated on an undeclared basis. A requirement to build-up obsolete agent networks from scratch required Bayley to travel widely throughout the subcontinent. Accordingly, Menzies asked Shone to provide his SIS officer with a roving cover role within the UK high commission and suggested that a nominal designation of Information Officer or Trade Commissioner would be appropriate.[54] Bayley was eventually given the more amorphous title of 'Secretary', primarily out of concern that his ignorance of economics and public relations might be exposed and attract unwanted attention. The SIS station was housed in a large, single room in the High Commission, directly beneath Shone's private office.[55] The High Commissioner wanted to keep a close eye on his guests.

Shone had opposed an SIS presence in India. In particular, the High Commissioner expressed reservations that Bayley's links with the subcontinent were too conspicuous, and that the SIS officer would be viewed with misgiving by locals. William Hayter agreed, and cautioned Menzies that Bayley's employment seemed, '... an unnecessary risk for you to take'.[56] Menzies thought otherwise. Bayley, the Chief of SIS insisted, 'himself is convinced of his ability to work in India without detection'. While acknowledging that 'naturally some suspicion may attach to him when he first arrives', Menzies maintained, 'this suspicion will die down when Bayley carefully lives his cover'. Moreover, Menzies vouched that Bayley would, 'confine his activities, when they start, entirely to handling first-class, trustworthy British head agents'. It was essential, Menzies submitted, that he was able to utilise an officer in India with extensive experience of the subcontinent. '[N]o-one who has not had experience of handling Indian agents could possibly direct the British head agents in such a difficult task', Menzies informed the Foreign Office. 'Unpleasant repercussions are far more likely if we put in an inexperienced officer for this job.' Whitehall officials remained sceptical that Menzies insistence on appointing Bayley was entirely sound. 'In short', one mandarin summarised, 'the proposal is to "bluff it out"'.[57] In an effort to placate Shone, the High Commissioner was made aware that Bayley would not be permitted to run Indian agents directly. In addition, the local SIS station was instructed to recruit no more than five European cut-outs, or intermediaries, who would, 'collect ... information from "unconscious" Indians'. Such 'unconscious' Indian contacts were not to know, or were supposed not to know, that they were 'being pumped' for 'information about Soviet-inspired or Communist activities in the Dominion'.[58] Bayley's function, Shone was reassured, 'would be that of an organiser, the contact with the agents being made by others under his general direction and guidance'.[59] With Menzies refusing to give further ground, SIS was allowed to have its way and Bayley's Indian posting was confirmed.[60] In response, a disgruntled Shone fired off a brusque one-line note to the Foreign Office that stated simply, 'I am still not happy about this.'[61]

Shone's concern over Bayley's appointment was amplified after the SIS officer approached High Commission staff about the availability of modern air conditioning units; solicited advice on purchasing a car, preferably an American Chevrolet or Ford; and asked to be accommodated in the Cecil Hotel, in the heart of Old Delhi. The requests were met with dismay and deemed entirely contrary to the anonymity which Shone had been assured Bayley would cultivate. It was pointed out to Bayley that air conditioning units were in notably short supply in the Indian capital; that an imported British vehicle might provide a less ostentatious form of transport; and that it would seem odd for the SIS officer and his staff to lodge in Old Delhi, when other High Commission officials resided in the city's diplomatic quarter.[62] Worse still, Bayley blotted his copybook with Shone by corresponding with High Commission staff in his own name rather than a work name or pseudonym. 'This was noted by a locally recruited [Indian] member of staff who is the wife of one of the European Deputy Directors of the Intelligence Bureau', Shone complained to the Foreign Office. 'She promptly asked if the letter was from [Bayley] who her husband had heard (and told her) was coming out soon to join the staff of the Trade Commissioner.' 'Although this is a large country, people in the higher strata know one another (and what they are doing) from one end to the other', Shone made clear to Whitehall. 'We feel that whatever cover we might provide Bayley it will be virtually impossible to remove suspicion from the minds of the large number of intelligent Indians (who are bound to know his background).' Pressing the Foreign Office to reconsider a change of tack before it was too late, Shone implored bluntly that, 'they [SIS] may wish to reconsider the question of Bayley's appointment'.[63] The High Commissioner was overruled. Before landing in India, Bayley had quipped to British diplomats that, 'The next year or two should certainly not be dull.'[64] The SIS officer's words were to prove prescient, but for reasons other than he intended.

Covert Cold War

In part, the urgency surrounding SIS's efforts to get a station up and running in India was informed by the perception that post-war Soviet subversive activity was shifting focus from Europe to Asia. Fragile post-colonial governments, beset by pressing social and economic problems, it seemed, had been identified by Moscow as highly susceptible to the lure of communism. In 1948, SIS watched intently as Calcutta, long a hot bed of radical politics in the subcontinent, played host to a conference of the progressive Youth of Asia and the Congress of the Communist Party of India.[65] In the wake of the Calcutta meetings, the tactics of communist groups across Asia switched from support for a united front approach and collaboration with non-communist nationalists, to a more militant and often violent opposition to state power. Jawaharlal Nehru's interim government was itself embroiled in suppressing an armed communist insurgency centred on the Telangana region of southern India. In this context, Lenin's dictum that the decisive battle for world revolution would be fought and won on the banks of the river Ganges, appeared troublingly prophetic to SIS officers pondering the inception of the Cold War back at the Service's Broadway headquarters.[66]

Under pressure from customers in Whitehall to demonstrate its utility in blunting communism's appeal, SIS implemented a wide range of covert action. Most of the clandestine activity undertaken by the Service, espionage aside, centred on black propaganda operations that were combined, when needed, with the liberal use of bribery or blackmail.[67] Black propaganda was designed to give the impression that it originated with the target it was intended to discredit. Such propaganda was unattributable and did not identify its source. The working assumption of Menzies' organisation was that, in conjunction with a new Foreign Office propaganda unit, the Information Research Department (IRD), it would spearhead 'a comprehensive worldwide political warfare plan'.[68] This envisaged SIS exerting control over news agencies; covertly controlling newspapers and periodicals, 'by general subsidy and/or by bribery of owners and editors'; secretly running broadcast stations; and facilitating, 'the dissemination of rumours, distorted or untrue reports, etc. either through selected news channels or by pamphlets, posters, etc. or orally'.[69]

India was amongst the first countries that SIS targeted in its 'clandestine propaganda effort'. One estimate, for the years 1948 and 1949, calculated that SIS expended £350,000 on covert propaganda in India and the Middle East. The bulk of this money was spent on printing and publishing propaganda material; bankrolling 'whispering campaigns' that aimed to expose local politicians as being 'directed' by the Soviet Union; and operations designed to sow dissension within local communist parties by planting real or manufactured evidence pointing to the duplicity or dishonesty of their leaders. More exuberant, but much less common, were operations that sought to effect the 'framing' of foreign diplomats 'in order to effect their removal and possible liquidation'; the penetration of factories and trade unions; acts of minor sabotage and intimidation (including the use of stink bombs and microphone interference to disrupt meetings); the kidnapping of communist leaders or Russian nationals to give the appearance of defection; and assassination.[70] In March 1948, when pressed by the Chiefs of Staff to ramp up information warfare activities, the Foreign Office defended the effectiveness of its black propaganda operations by pointing to an assertion made by Menzies that, 'He [Menzies] had evidence of the usefulness of his machinery in India.'[71]

Precisely what covert action Vernon Bayley and the SIS station in India had undertaken remains unclear. However, in October 1947, Kenneth Bourne warned MI5 headquarters back in London that Indian colleagues in the IB had become concerned by the actions of his 'friends' in SIS.[72] The following March, with gossip swirling around New Delhi about Bayley's background and the nature of his mission in India, SIS deemed it prudent to order his recall to London. Such a drastic step, it was acknowledged, raised 'the distinct possibility of his [Bayley] not returning' to India and the local SIS station being closed.[73] As an interim measure, Orme Sargent recommended that SIS cease all activity in India and 'remain entirely inactive'.[74] The appointment of Archibald Nye to replace Terence Shone as High Commissioner later that year, increased the pressure on SIS to reconsider the merits of retaining an operational presence in India. On 15 October, Menzies briefed a meeting of the Joint Intelligence Committee that Nye, in common with his predecessor, 'had taken exception to even an embryo organisation of S.I.S. being set up in India and had so informed the Prime Minister'.[75]

From Menzies perspective, Nye's conviction that an SIS station was neither needed nor desirable in India was especially unfortunate. Lieutenant-General Sir Archibald Nye was stationed in the subcontinent as a young regimental officer and had risen to serve as Vice-Chief of the Imperial General Staff under Sir Alan Brooke during the war. A favourite of Winston Churchill, and a loyal and efficient deputy to Alanbrooke, Nye was lauded by the latter for having, 'a first-class brain, great character, courage in his own convictions, [and being a] quick worker with great vision'.[76] In 1946, on retiring from the Army, Nye returned to India to become Governor of Madras. In the autumn of 1948, when Nye's term in Madras came to an end, he received plaudits from Indian officials for his adroit handling of the transfer of power in southern India, and his success in quelling labour unrest and a communist-backed peasant uprising. Significantly, Nye enjoyed the respect and friendship of Jawaharlal Nehru. 'It may interest you to know what your premier [of Madras] told me about you', Nehru wrote to Nye, in August 1948. 'He was loud in praise of you and when I asked him if he had any suggestions about your successor, he said "send us someone like Nye." That is praise enough. Unfortunately, we cannot find Nyes easily.'[77] In Archibald Nye, Menzies was confronted with a powerful and well-connected adversary.

Nye's objection to SIS activity in India did not reflect a conviction on the High Commissioner's part that the subcontinent was peripheral to Britain's strategic Cold War interests, or that South Asia was in any way impervious to communist subversion. Far from it. 'The importance of a stable India from the point of resisting Communist infiltration in all that part of the world [Asia] could not be over-emphasised', Nye assured Whitehall.[78] Rather, Nye concluded that SIS operations in India were likely to yield little useful intelligence and would run an unwarranted risk of aggravating delicate Indo-British relations. The Security Service's declared SLO, Nye judged, could meet Britain's substantive intelligence requirements in India, and could do so without alienating Nehru's government.[79] Importantly, Nye's position was supported by British officials in India who had been galvanised by Shone's opposition to SIS operations in the subcontinent. Senior members of MI5, such as Alex Kellar, also lined up to question whether undertaking espionage and launching covert operations in colonial or Commonwealth countries was altogether wise or, indeed, morally, and ethically sound.[80]

Menzies and the Foreign Office were not prepared to sanction SIS's permanent retreat from India without putting up a fight. Shutting SIS out of the subcontinent even temporarily, FO officials speculated, would make it difficult to, 'start [intelligence operations] again and we might lose a lot of valuable information about Communism in the meantime'.[81] William Hayter queried whether, 'the Chiefs of Staff would feel strongly about a total shut down of intelligence activities in India'. 'There is almost no country', Hayter suggested implausibly, 'of which we know so little'.[82] It rankled with the Foreign Office that Nye had used a private meeting with Attlee to convince the prime minister that SIS could serve no useful purpose in South Asia. 'Evidently the Prime Minister has forgotten', one FO official recorded testily, 'that he [Attlee] approved Sir E. Bridges' minutes of 7th March and 21st July 1947 [authorising SIS activity in India]'. When it came to convincing Attlee that the Security Service could uphold British interests in the subcontinent absent SIS, Nye was pushing against an open door. Attlee had overcome an initial suspicion of the Security Service and grew to hold Percy Sillitoe and MI5 in high regard.[83] With Shone, Nye, MI5, and Nehru's government having all expressed unease about SIS's in-country presence, Attlee had ample reason to order Menzies organisation to quit India.

In late October, a dispirited Sargent informed Menzies that, 'The Prime Minister is . . . determined on the closing down of covert activities in India and there is, I am afraid, nothing more that we can do for the time being'. The Chief of SIS was duly ordered to close his station in New Delhi and confirm his organisation's withdrawal from India.[84] Attlee's intervention, set out in the so-called 'Attlee Directive', appears to have taken the form of an oral instruction and was not put in writing at that time. It may well, in any case, have been moot in respect of Bayley and SIS's India station. Sometime after the events of 1948, as MI5 worked to strengthen its relations with the IB, Alex Kellar noted that subsequent to the transfer of power the Intelligence Bureau had been, 'particularly irritated . . . by the activities of M.I.6. [SIS] personnel in India: two were in fact asked to leave'.[85] Whether SIS was forced out of India by Attlee or was pushed from the subcontinent by Patel and the Indian government, made little practical difference. Henceforth, the Security Service, through its overt liaison relationship with the IB, would exercise exclusivity in managing British intelligence interests in India.

The political decision communicated through the 'Attlee Directive' to exclude SIS from India had broader consequences. Sillitoe and MI5 proved successful in extending the Directives scope beyond India to cover the entirety of the British Empire and Commonwealth. Menzies organisation was not merely shut out of India but was also largely precluded from conducting clandestine operations in swathes of Asia and Africa.[86] The imposition of the Directive made little difference to SIS in respect of the 'old' Commonwealth, where Canada and Australia were in the process of setting up their own foreign intelligence organisations. Menzies was, however, troubled that, by setting a precedent that prohibited his organisation from operating in former British colonies, Whitehall had made it harder for SIS to respond to a global threat posed by communism.[87] The empire and Commonwealth remained under the sway of the Security Service until well into the 1960s and, thus, was largely shielded from SIS's 'cloak and dagger' operations.[88] In the subcontinent, it was not until 1964 when, in the wake of the Sino-Indian border war the Indian government reassessed the utility of covert action, that SIS reopened a station in New Delhi under the direction of Ellis Morgan, a protégé of the future head of the service, Maurice Oldfield.

Figure 1.1 Sir Percy Sillitoe, Director General of MI5 (1946–1953). Central Press / Stringer / Hulton Archive / Getty Images.

Security, Sovereignty and Secret Intelligence

By the close of 1948, and after a little local difficulty, a common purpose was established in London and New Delhi that would define the future intelligence and security dimensions of Britain's relationship with India. India's political leadership looked to Britain, primarily, to help rebuild an intelligence infrastructure in the subcontinent that had been created by the former colonial administration to function as a domestic security service rather than a foreign intelligence agency. From its inauguration, the Intelligence Bureau's focus was on disrupting nationalist conspiracies and preserving the stability and authority of imperial governance. The IB was infused with an insular mentality, fearful of sedition, ever watchful for rebellion akin to the events of 1857 and, latterly, preoccupied by the threat posed by communist subversion following the Russian revolution of 1917. The transfer of power in India in 1947, as commentators on contemporary Indian intelligence practice have noted, reinforced as much as reinvented a colonial intelligence culture shaped by fear and anxiety.[89] In the 1970s, Parmeshwar Narayan (P. N.) Haksar, principal secretary to India's premier, Indira Gandhi, and a leading architect of India's external intelligence service, the Research and Analysis Wing (R&AW), lamented that, in many respects, independence had come to represent a missed opportunity. 'Transfer of power meant continuation of elite domination', Haksar bemoaned, 'without any commitment to dismantle the colonial heritage and restructure the socio-economic relations on equalitarian and truly democratic lines'.[90] Haksar could just as well have been describing the evolution of India's intelligence community.

Nehru's interim Indian government approached secret intelligence in much the same way as their British colonial antecedents. The IB was conceived by a new generation of Indian leaders as a safety valve to help relieve internal pressures, to mitigate the influence of communism and communalism, and to serve the parochial interests of a domestic political elite. The intelligence organs of the state were not geared to meeting external threats from India's neighbours. It was entirely unsurprising that, given a congruence in attitude and approach towards intelligence between the former coloniser and the recently decolonised, Patel and India's Home Ministry identified merit in working closely with the British Security Service. In contrast, SIS, with its expertise in foreign intelligence, espionage, and covert action, as Shone, Nye, and other British officials cautioned Whitehall, was always likely to be regarded with suspicion bordering on hostility by a nascent post-colonial state sensitive to preserving hard-won national sovereignty. Menzies initial enthusiasm for establishing an SIS presence in India aside, policymakers in Whitehall were aware that assisting India in building up a foreign intelligence capability, not least in light of New Delhi's fractious relationship with Pakistan, a fellow Commonwealth state, would prove more problematic than aid offered by MI5 in the security field.[91] Tellingly, unburdened by the complication of having to sustain an appearance of impartiality between India and Pakistan, it was the United States, and the Central Intelligence Agency, more specifically, who would support India in the covert action arena in the aftermath of independence.

It was not until the early 1960s that SIS returned to India. By then, MI5, through a succession of resident SLOs in New Delhi, had been able to embed itself firmly into India's intelligence bureaucracy. Reflecting on the reintroduction of SIS to the subcontinent, one future Director-General of MI5, Stella Rimington, who began her career in the Security Service in India, recalled that the two services offices were located adjacent to each other in the British High Commission behind security doors, 'which had a combination lock that habitually stuck in the oppressive Indian climate and whose numbers had to be given a sharp hit with a shoe to get then to move into place'. Her SIS colleague, Rimington remembered, was 'a genial, rather low-profile character, with some sort of job in the political section, but notable mainly for his performances in character parts in the plays put on by the British High Commission Amateur Dramatic Society'.[92] A talent for acting, one assumes, proved useful in the context of the SIS officer's day job. Senior SIS officers, including a coming Chief, Maurice Oldfield, went on to establish a productive relationship with their Indian counterparts. One Indian intelligence officer, who briefly rose to lead the R&AW, has recounted spending time getting to know Oldfield during recreational trips to Jaipur and Jaisalmer, in Rajasthan, in Western India.[93] Renowned as an engaging storyteller with a playful sense of humour, Oldfield's highly developed sense of scepticism when it came to the utility of covert action was doubtless significant in securing Indian goodwill for SIS. In the period between the transfer of power in 1947, and the onset of the Sino-Indian War of 1962, it was not SIS, however, but its British partners and erstwhile rivals in the Security Service that, thanks to Clement Attlee, determined the course of Britain's intelligence relationship with India.

2

Silent Partners: Britain, India, and Early Cold War Intelligence Liaison

On 9 September 1965, the RMS *Caledonia* left Liverpool and headed into the Irish Sea. The British liner entered service just prior to the end of the Raj, in March 1947. It was launched by the Marchioness of Linlithgow, whose husband, Victor Hope, exasperated Indian nationalists during his period as Viceroy, between 1936 and 1943. Plying a colonial route that took in Gibraltar, Port Said, Aden, and Karachi before terminating at Bombay, the *Caledonia's* voyage to India was conducted in an atmosphere of opulence that belied Britain's diminishing global power. One passenger likened travel on the ship to, 'sailing slowly in a sort of time capsule to the Orient'.[1] Full of characters from a fading imperial landscape, the *Caledonia's* patrons numbered tea-planters, missionaries, boxwallahs, or European businessmen, and British diplomats destined for postings abroad. The latter included John Rimington, a young official bound for New Delhi and the position of first secretary at the British High Commission. During his tour, Rimington's wife, Stella, a future head of the Security Service, was inducted into the secret world.

Whitehall's approach to the transfer of power in the subcontinent was shaped by a desire to remain on friendly terms with India's nationalist government. 'It is a truism that the unique position of the United Kingdom in this country places a special responsibility on His Majesty's Government in handling western relations with India', Sir Archibald Nye, Britain's High Commissioner in New Delhi, underlined, in May 1951. 'By virtue of our old ties and friendships . . . we have opportunities for exerting influence over India far superior to those of the United States.' '[I]t remains a major interest of British policy to ensure that India does not drift . . . into the grip of Communism', Nye maintained. '[I]t is essential to deny India to Russia. The only way to secure this object is to work patiently for the closest Indian relationship with the West.'[2] By the time Stella Rimington arrived in the subcontinent change was in the air and Nye's emphasis on the importance of cultivating intimate British relations with India had lost much of its currency. During her stay in New Delhi, which lasted from September 1965 to February 1969, Stella Rimington reflected that, 'India crossed a water-shed in the modern development of that country.' Historic ties to the United Kingdom had worn thin and, as the Cold War gathered momentum in South Asia,

Indians looked to the American and Soviet superpowers for support. A decline in the UK's standing in India was hastened when Britain's premier, Harold Wilson, infuriated Indians by blaming New Delhi for an outbreak of Indo-Pakistan hostilities over Kashmir. In the wake of Wilson's injudicious public remarks, the Anglophile former Indian High Commissioner in London, Vijaya Lakshmi Pandit, informed UK ministers that, 'It would be difficult to exaggerate Britain's unpopularity in India.'[3]

In another sense, the 1960s also marked an inflection point in relations between India and Rimington's service, MI5. Britain's Security Service established close and convivial relations with India's Intelligence Bureau. In 1957, B. N. Mullik, India's then DIB, assured Roger Hollis, the Director-General of MI5, that, 'In my talks and discussions [with MI5], I never felt that I was dealing with any organisation which was not my own.'[4] The MI5 Security Liaison Officer who recruited Rimington as a clerical assistant, in the summer of 1967, certainly felt at home in India. A larger-than-life individual who appeared to have stepped from the pages of an Ian Fleming novel, the SLO was a baronet, and a bachelor, and resided in a spacious house in one of the more salubrious suburbs of India's capital. He was well-known for hosting lavish curry lunches that extended late into the night and cruised around town at the wheel of large Jaguar car.[5] A blurring of lines between intelligence fact and fiction extended to Rimington herself. An accomplished actress and stalwart of the British High Commission's amateur dramatic society, the coming leader of MI5 entertained Indian guests and the diplomatic community with star performances in sell-out stage productions. 'Stella was an extremely good actress', one of her contemporaries in India recalled, 'which must have come in very handy'.[6]

At the point Rimington packed up and headed home from India, the Security Service's halcyon days in the subcontinent were over. The reintroduction of SIS to India in 1964, coupled with swinging cuts to MI5's international footprint demanded by an impecunious Whitehall, diluted the Security Service's relationship with the Intelligence Bureau. Expertise in internal security that had underpinned MI5's association with the IB, although still valued, was relegated to a position of peripheral significance by Indian policymakers. The last MI5 SLO left India not long after Rimington and, in the process, severed a connection between the Security Service and the IB that stretched back to the 1920s. Perhaps fittingly, Rimington was unable to return to United Kingdom on the RMS *Caledonia*. No longer economically viable in an age of intercontinental air travel, the British ship was taken out of service before the end of 1965 and sent to Amsterdam, where it functioned as a floating hostel for students. Signposts of British retreat from the subcontinent, MI5's included, were hard to miss.

The subcontinent's intelligence landscape had looked very different in the 1940s. With India denuded of an effective intelligence service following independence, MI5's sway in South Asia was considerable. In May 1948, Guy Liddell crowed that, 'There is no doubt that Nehru, [Vallabhbhai] Patel, and the Minister of Defence are anxious to maintain [a] British connection. Their difficulty is to put their former policy of "driving the British out of India" into reverse without losing face.'[7] By fostering contacts with Indian counterparts, Whitehall was able to sustain a level of influence in Indian governing circles beyond that justified by Britain's waning authority. '[O]ne must face an inevitable running down [of British influence in India]', the CRO conceded, ' ... [but] this could be in a measure arrested if we had greater resources to apply in India to the maintenance of our links'. The Security Service could not have agreed more. The success of MI5's investment in its SLO programme in India underpinned wider relations between London and New Delhi. When the last MI5 SLO left the subcontinent, not at India's behest, but due to economies forced on the Security Service by the Treasury, Whitehall sundered a valued connection between the British and Indian intelligence communities. The DIB at the time, S. P. Verma, voiced incredulity that MI5 had abandoned, 'the longstanding contact at a personal level which has proved invaluable to us'.[8] In beating a retreat from India, MI5 terminated a partnership with the IB that, between the 1940s and the 1960s, represented arguably its most important foreign liaison relationship outside of Europe and North America.

Our Man in Delhi: MI5's SLO Programme in India

The Security Service's SLO concept predated the transfer of power in India. During the Second World War, MI5 had stationed SLOs and, in the case of overseas military bases, Defence Security Officers (DSOs), throughout the British Empire. The SLO's role was to provide advice and support to local security agencies and to act as a conduit for the exchange of information between London and Britain's imperial outposts. It was not to engage in acts of subterfuge or espionage. For SLOs to remain effective, the Security Service felt they needed to retain the trust of their host governments.[9] The success of post-war SLOs in India led to the expansion of the programme across Britain's colonies and Commonwealth.[10] In October 1949, MI5 documented the functions of SLOs. Their responsibilities were divided into primary and secondary categories. Within the former, MI5 emphasised the importance of cultivating a liaison channel between SLO's and host governments. It was imperative, the Security Service stipulated, for SLOs, 'to ensure ... that all security intelligence and counter-espionage information flowing into Security Service channels and bearing in the particular security problems ... [of the] territory to which he [an SLO] is accredited, is made available to all appropriate Civil and Service Authorities in that territory'. An SLO was expected, 'to volunteer and supply on request' assistance to local security services in areas such as preventive security, vetting, and travel control. Alongside these primary tasks, SLOs were encouraged to win the confidence of intelligence and security colleagues abroad with a view to obtaining information that might not otherwise be available. As the Chairman of the Joint Intelligence Committee, Sir Patrick Dean noted, Whitehall's belief was that, 'one of the functions of the Security Service; [is] to obtain secret intelligence by its own means'.[11]

It was also an SLO's responsibility, in Guy Liddell's words, 'to keep ... [a host country] aware of the wider implications of subversive movements ...'[12] Or, in India's case, to ensure that Jawaharlal Nehru's Congress governments remained attuned to the threat posed by communism. The first conference of the Communist Party of India (CPI) was convened in the industrial city of Kanpur, in the United Provinces of northern India, in December 1925. Indian nationalists had been attracted by the Bolshevik Revolution in Russia, and prominent political radicals, such as Manabendra Nath (M. N.) Roy, benefited from support offered by Lenin and the Comintern. In 1920, Roy inaugurated an émigré Indian communist organisation at a gathering convened in the Soviet central Asian city of Tashkent. Between the wars, the British Indian government prosecuted several high-profile conspiracy cases that targeted individuals, Roy included, who were alleged to have engaged in communist-inspired sedition. One of MI5's first significant imperial interventions occurred in 1929, when Sir Eric Holt-Wilson, MI5's deputy director, was sent to India to assist the Intelligence Bureau in the Meerut Conspiracy trial.[13] British concern at India's vulnerability to communism, however, proved largely misplaced. During the struggle waged by nationalists for independence, and in its immediate aftermath, Marxism-Leninism, as one senior British official conceded, did 'not make much ground in India'.[14]

Active, but relatively small, the CPI concentrated winning support amongst an amalgam of university students, industrial organisations, and the subcontinent's peasantry, with mixed results. In practical terms, disorder stoked by communists in areas such as Kerala, Telangana, and West Bengal, met with a robust response from the Indian authorities. In November 1951, reflecting on India's reaction to communist agitation, Archibald Nye reassured London that, 'The Central and all the Provincial Governments have come out wholeheartedly against communism.' 'They have', Nye added, 'dealt with the communists with a firmness, indeed one might say with a ruthlessness and brutality, which we ourselves never at our most difficult times showed in this country'. British officials were less impressed by what they considered to be an unwarranted sense of complacency on the part of Indian officials in suppressing cheap CPI propaganda. Indian ministers, Nye bemoaned, 'are inclined to think that the Hindu way of life is so contrary to the concept of communism that no one need worry about the result of communist penetration'.[15] After meeting one Indian journalist, William Haley, editor of *The Times*, felt equally uneasy at the indifference with which colleagues in the subcontinent's press approached communism. Haley was unpersuaded when his Indian associate pronounced

36 SPYING IN SOUTH ASIA

that communism in South Asia was essentially constitutional in outlook, and more benign and less threatening than 'anyone else's Communism'. 'One might almost say that this belief', a startled Haley recorded in his diary, 'is the Communists' secret weapon'.[16]

In September 1946, on forming an interim government, Nehru took to the airwaves to spell out his commitment to a non-aligned foreign policy. 'We propose as far as possible to keep away from the power politics of groups, aligned against one another', India's premier stated.[17] When it came to the Soviet Union, Nehru acknowledged the admiration many Indians felt for a country that had transformed itself from a backward peasant economy into a global superpower. Moreover, as a neighbour of India's, Nehru reasoned that his government, 'cannot afford to antagonise Russia merely because we think that this may irritate someone else'.[18] Likewise, as one Indian official noted, Soviet calls for, 'the end of colonialism and racial discrimination and for redistribution of world wealth, are by no means disagreeable to India'.[19] Under Stalin, India was largely ignored by the Soviet Union. In 1953, the dictator's death changed the dynamic of Moscow's relations with the subcontinent. Andrey Vishinsky, the USSR's foreign minister, began to attend receptions at the Indian Embassy in Moscow. In New Delhi, the Soviet ambassador displayed a 'sudden affability' towards his Indian hosts. Much of the 'tendentious propaganda' that the Soviet Union had directed against India ceased.[20] Most significantly, as the Soviets adopted a new foreign policy of courting friends inside the developing world, in the United Nations, Moscow extended India its support in the dispute with Pakistan over the state of Kashmir.

Accordingly, Security Service SLOs posted to India were confronted by a seemingly paradoxical Indian approach to communism. At home, the activities of the CPI were closely monitored by the IB and, whenever they threatened to disrupt social order or promote violent political dissent, were ruthlessly suppressed. Abroad, Nehru's governments sought close relations with their Soviet neighbours and, in the process, tolerated support funnelled to communists in the subcontinent from Moscow. Squaring the circle of assisting the IB in containing indigenous communism, while simultaneously pushing Indian colleagues to adopt a less benign appreciation of international communism, was never easy for SLOs. The Security Service's decision to post officers to India who were both affable and well-disposed towards the country did, to some extent, mitigate the impact of policy differences between London and New Delhi. A short but successful SLO tour undertaken by Kenneth Bourne in 1947, was followed by a series of equally productive secondments to India completed by Bill U'ren, Eric Kitchen, Walter Bell, and John Allen. The SLO programme nurtured a sense of familiarity and interdependence between MI5 and the IB. British SLOs became regular visitors to the IB's headquarters in New Delhi and toured the Intelligence Bureau's outstations to get to know regional Indian security and intelligence colleagues. In turn,

Mullik valued the opportunity that MI5 provided to consult with senior intelligence officers from Australia, Canada, New Zealand, and South Africa at Commonwealth Security conferences held in London. At a lower level, a steady stream of IB staff made the journey from India to the UK to attend MI5 tradecraft courses. In practical terms, the Security Service proved useful to the IB by, amongst other things, tracing covert financial subsidies passing from Moscow to the CPI.[21]

Although close and convivial, MI5's relationship with the IB did encounter problems. Mullik expressed dissatisfaction that, on occasion, the Security Service was inclined to short-change his organisation. The DIB objected when IB officers sent to Singapore to attend British courses in counter-espionage and observation techniques received only the most basic instruction. In protest, Mullik suspended the Intelligence Bureau's participation in the programme. The DIB was equally put out when MI5 questioned his request to send IB officers to London for three-months' coaching in long-term penetration. The Security Service agreed to provide general training for Mullik's officers but insisted that devoting such prolonged attention to a single facet of security work was impractical. Mullik reacted by making clear that he would no longer send IB officers to London unless they received appropriate direction in agent running. 'Something has obviously got into Mullik's hair', Guy Liddell responded disparagingly, '. . . it may well be heat or that he is getting very mistaken information about our capabilities'. India's intelligence chief, Liddell reflected, seemed blissfully unaware that, 'most of what we [MI5] achieve is through hard work and a certain amount of luck'.[22] While not always harmonious, the intimacy that MI5 enjoyed with the IB was sufficiently strong to overcome occasional tensions and periodic diplomatic squalls. In the mid-1950s, when political relations between India and the UK were strained by the Suez Crisis, Mullik reassured MI5's SLO, John Allen, that it was important to insulate their two services bilateral intelligence association from broader disagreements between London and New Delhi. Taking care to mask the full extent of collaboration between the IB and MI5 was one means of doing so. India's Ministry of External Affairs (MEA), Mullik assured Allen, would welcome the opportunity to lobby Nehru for the termination of MI5's presence in New Delhi. The Indian premier's aversion to the work of intelligence services, Mullik claimed, left Nehru susceptible to entreaties from the MEA that MI5 should be sent packing from the subcontinent.[23] Mullik's exhortations aside, the Security Service had reasons of its own to obscure its connections to the IB. Aside from anything else, Whitehall was conscious that their security and intelligence liaison relationships with foreign governments were vulnerable to penetration and suspectable to exploitation by Soviet propagandists looking for ways to undermine British diplomacy.[24]

Nehru's unease that the Intelligence Bureau risked becoming too close to MI5 was made abundantly clear when the Indian premier acquiesced, reluctantly, and with strict conditions, to a request from his intelligence service to station its officers in India's High Commission in London. Nehru was initially unpersuaded that a permanent Indian intelligence presence was needed in the UK, and asked the resident High Commissioner, Balasaheb Gangadhar (B. G). Kher, for 'much greater justification than has been given to me so far for the establishment of a Security Unit in London'. Subsequent interventions by the IB and India's Home Ministry, which was responsible for intelligence oversight, persuaded Nehru to change his mind. Under an arrangement that mirrored MI5's SLO programme, the Intelligence Bureau was authorised to place officers in London under diplomatic cover and to declare their presence to the British authorities. Nehru was determined, however, to ensure that a geographical expansion in the IB's operations did not compromise India's diplomacy, weaken political supervision of intelligence agencies, or lead to excessive and inappropriate monitoring of Indians abroad. The IB could establish a Security Liaison Unit (SLU) in London, the prime minister stipulated, only on the understanding that its officers had, 'absolutely nothing to do with the staff of ... India House'; the SLU was answerable to India's High Commissioner; and, that IB officers abstained from routine surveillance of India's student population and wider diaspora in the UK. On the latter point, Nehru made plain that if the IB felt compelled to operate outside Indian territory, not least to reduce India's reliance on information furnished by friendly foreign intelligence services advancing their own parochial agendas, it should do so in the most transparent manner possible. Here, the Indian premier drew a distinction between MI5's SLO arrangement in India, 'that is not secret so far as we are concerned, and we were told about it', and the activities of other, undeclared, foreign intelligence agencies in the subcontinent. '[T]the US has a very widespread Intelligence net', Nehru noted pointedly. 'But they [Washington] have not told us officially anything about it.' As SIS had discovered to its cost, while India's premier acknowledged that, 'many so-called Attaches in every foreign embassy are really intelligence agents', his tolerance of covert intelligence activity on India soil had limits.[25]

Nehru was persuaded to push ahead with the establishment of an Indian SLU in London, and in a limited number of other locations abroad, chiefly on the basis that it would promote useful dialogue between the IB and its foreign counterparts on areas of common concern. London, especially, the Indian premier rationalised, constituted 'a clearinghouse of communications ... between the Cominform and the Far-Eastern countries, including India'. The CPI, Nehru noted, was 'largely guided through London', as were communists front organisations such as the Word Federation of Trade Unions, Women's International Democratic Federation, and World Federation of Democratic Youth. Drawing on MI5's knowledge of transnational communist networks was clearly in India's interest. Moreover, Nehru recognised that Indian deficiencies in the 'technical side of Intelligence' could best be remedied by leveraging the superior resources and know-how of the Security Service. Nevertheless, Nehru remained adamant that the IB 'remain apart' from their colleagues in MI5 and avoid a blurring of operational boundaries and responsibilities. 'We do not want any tie-up between our Intelligence and any other foreign Intelligence, including UK Intelligence', India's prime minister decreed. '[A] certain association is often helpful, provided we keep wide awake ... [but] we [India] have to be careful so as not to get entangled with British Intelligence and be exploited by it.'[26] The relationship between the IB and British intelligence was a source of perennial anxiety for Nehru. Writing to India's cabinet secretary in October 1956, he expressed incredulity that IB officers were being sent to London to learn Russian rather than being tutored in Moscow. 'It seems to me that our intelligence people cannot get out of the habit of thinking of two or three countries in the Commonwealth, especially the UK ... ', an exasperated Nehru complained, 'for any kind of training'.[27]

Winning Friends and Influencing People: MI5 and India's Intelligence Chiefs

Britain's Security Service invested considerable time and energy fostering personal connections with India's intelligence chiefs. In the case of the IB's first Indian director, T. G. Sanjeevi, senior MI5 officers encountered little difficulty in promoting the idea that the UK and India had much to gain from working together. Having tried, and failed, to wrest additional power and authority from the Indian government's bureaucracy, Sanjeevi also had ample reason to look abroad to bolster his own fortunes and those of the IB. In November 1948, Sanjeevi welcomed an invitation from MI5's Director-General, Sir Percy Sillitoe, to visit the UK for discussions on 'matters of mutual interest'.[28] Arriving in London on 4 December, the DIB's talks with MI5 extended over two weeks. To colleagues in India's Home Ministry, Sanjeevi represented his encounter with MI5 as, 'extremely important and urgent'. Its purpose, the DIB disclosed, was 'primarily to establish contacts with his opposite numbers' in Britain's Security Service, and 'to co-ordinate intelligence work'.[29] On meeting Sanjeevi, Guy Liddell observed that the DIB was, 'obviously appalled by the size of his task. He [Sanjeevi] told me pathetically that the Indian Government expected him to know everything well in advance.' Having listened to Sanjeevi's complaints that political jealousies within the ruling Congress Party threatened to cripple the effectiveness of IB as a national intelligence agency, Liddell reflected with surprise that his counterpart appeared to be seeking 'almost dictatorial powers'. Political pressure to deliver results beyond the capabilities of IB, Liddell mused, appeared to have induced Sanjeevi to contemplate the creation of 'an enormous Gestapo, which will cost the country a great deal of money and may well be corrupt and inefficient'.[30]

Sanjeevi arrived in London with a reputation as a sensitive and capricious individual who was prone to fits of impetuosity. His wife, who was equally high-handed, travelled with Sanjeevi to the UK. Sanjeevi was devoted to his spouse. Having met and become enamoured with his partner when she was married to another man, Sanjeevi remained a bachelor for many years and, when his wife's first husband passed away, married her, and assumed responsibility for a stepson and an extended family.[31] A strict Hindu and a vegetarian, MI5 officers discovered that Mrs Sanjeevi appeared to 'live largely on eggs'. With London burdened by post-war rationing, eggs were troublingly hard to come by. To avert a culinary crisis, the Security Service's staff were mobilised in a covert operation to source black market produce. Having failed to secure a sufficient supply of metropolitan eggs, disaster was narrowly averted when an enterprising young officer cajoled a relative with a smallholding to send a fresh batch up from the country. This was just as well, Guy Liddell recorded wryly in his diary, as, 'Unless all these things are provided for her, Sanjeevi won't come to the office!'[32] Dietary dramas aside, Sanjeevi's visit proved a success in cementing relations between MI5 and the IB. Liddell ensured that the DIB went away satisfied that he had been taken into the confidence of the Security Service on a range of issues, from the operation of Joint Intelligence structures to more mundane matters such as the control of foreign aliens. During a farewell lunch in Sanjeevi's honour, hosted by Sillitoe at the Savoy, Liddell took satisfaction that the DIB seemed, 'very pleased with his visit and is going back [to India] full of ideas'. 'How far he will be able to put them into practice', Liddell questioned, 'is another mater!'[33]

From the Security Service's perspective, Sanjeevi lacked the qualities and experience necessary to transform the IB into an effective intelligence service. Scepticism in London that Sanjeevi was up to his job, did not stop the DIB from acting as an advocate for close ties between his service and MI5. In his interactions with the Security Service, MI5 officers noted that the DIB wasted, 'no opportunity of stressing the value which he places on maintaining our relationship on a professional and personal basis'.[34] Contacts between MI5 and the IB on Sanjeevi's watch became so amiable that the Security Service approached India for help in collecting intelligence behind the Iron Curtain. In July 1949, SIS had come under criticism for its lack of sources inside the Soviet Union. With a view to improving British intelligence coverage of the USSR, MI5 approached Sanjeevi to enquire whether the IB would be willing to run Indian citizens travelling to the Soviet Union as joint-informants.[35] Equally, back in October 1948, when the Soviet ambassador in New Delhi lodged a request with the Indian government to operate a wireless transmitting and receiving set in his embassy, it was to MI5 that Sanjeevi turned for advice. Disinclined to sanction the presence of a Soviet transmitter that could be used to coordinate interference in India's internal affairs, Sanjeevi was also aware that a straight refusal would displease Moscow. Rather than rebuff the Soviets, the DIB took the Security Service's advice to string the Russians along. '[W]ith a view to delaying matters [surrounding the transmitter]', MI5 counselled Sanjeevi, 'the Government of India might ask [the Soviets] for details of the proposed installation, frequency, wave lengths to be used etc'.[36]

Collaboration between MI5 and the IB on matters related to Chinese communism was just as familiar. In June 1949, with the advent of the PRC a few months away, Sanjeevi disclosed to British officials that, within India's national security establishment, 'there is some anxiety that the Chinese Communists may turn their attention to Burma and India rather sooner than was anticipated'. Reports reaching the IB that thousands of Chinese Communists had infiltrated northern India through Burma and East Pakistan, perturbed the DIB.[37] In an effort to assuage Sanjeevi's concerns, MI5 harnessed the SLO system to, 'do our best to keep D.I.B. informed regarding the main trends of CCP [Chinese Communist Party] policy'. Communist documents seized during raids on the South China Bureau of the CCP, which the British judged to be 'extremely revealing', were passed on to Indian colleagues.[38] As greater volumes of Chinese communist propaganda appeared in bookstores and newsstands across India, MI5 also assisted the IB in identifying the networks through which Beijing filtered publicity material into, and across, the subcontinent.[39] By the beginning of 1950, interaction between MI5 and the IB had become so engrained that Liddell was prompted to crow, 'India is relying more and more on us [MI5] and they could not do without our S.L.O. there at all. This is satisfactory.'[40]

Less pleasing to the British was a reluctance on the part of Sanjeevi to fully comprehend the magnitude of the communist threat facing India. British diplomats complained that the DIB had difficulty understanding the danger communist expansion posed to Asia. To British alarm, Sanjeevi professed that manifestations of communism in India represented little more, 'than a radical and possibly violent Indian political movement, aimed against the present Congress Government'.[41] Having met with Sanjeevi at the beginning of 1948 to review CPI activity, MI5's SLO, Kenneth Bourne, was surprised to learn that, in the DIB's estimation, 'Communist influence over the whole of India vis-a-vis other political parties was about 15%.' While Sanjeevi conceded that communist authority was increasing in some areas, notably East and West of Madras, and in Bombay city, Bourne was advised that, 'in most other parts of India its [communist] influence was . . . at a standstill and was possibly decreasing . . .'. 'The Party [CPI] could not be regarded as a threat', Sanjeevi maintained, 'either to the Government or to Congress for at least a decade'. Although accepting that communists had 'a very strong hold' over most of India's trade unions, Bourne was reassured by the DIB that the Army and the civil service were relatively free of communist sympathisers. In the latter case, it was not communism, but a 'strong affiliation' within sections of the government bureaucracy to the Rashtriya Swayamsevak Sangh (RSS), a right-wing Hindu nationalist organisation, that most concerned the IB. On this point, India's intelligence services were fully in step with Nehru. For India's premier, the forces of communalism represented more of a threat to the nation's freedoms than communism. In May 1948, writing to his sister in Moscow, Nehru opined that although communist violence remained a clear and present danger to the Indian state, 'the fact remains that we are looking in the wrong direction'. 'Of course, our major problem continues to be some form of communalism and the narrow communal outlook that has affected large numbers of Hindus', India's prime minister observed. 'We have by no means killed the spirit of the Hindu Mahasabha or the RSS.'[42]

Sanjeevi was equally untroubled by the volume of 'Russian money' filtering into India and funding communist agitation. This, the DIB informed Bourne, was 'very small ... [and] of little consequence'. More cash, Sanjeevi claimed, was diverted to the CPI by the British Communist Party via Indian students travelling back and forth between the UK and the subcontinent.[43] The British saw Sanjeevi's assessment of Indian communism as misguided and overly sanguine. An uptick in communist support in the subcontinent, in Whitehall's view, was 'exert[ing] a considerable indirect political influence by swaying Indian outlook towards the left'. Commenting on this difference in viewpoint, Alexander Symon, Britain's Deputy High Commissioner in India, concluded that, '... [Sanjeevi's] opinions serve the ... purpose of showing us how very far the Director of the Intelligence Bureau has yet to go in his Communist education'. 'He [Sanjeevi] seems to regard the movement as a purely internal nuisance to be classed with any other political body in India', Symon grumbled, 'and he shows no signs of regarding Communism as an international conspiracy aimed at the Sovietization of Asia and the World. His views seem to me to be somewhat superficial.' More specifically, the DIB's claim that covert Soviet funding of communist bodies in the subcontinent was minimal was not seen as credible. 'I cannot see how he [Sanjeevi] can really say this unless he were in possession of a great deal more inside knowledge, than he appears to have, of the party's [CPI's] financial and organisational secrets', Symon fulminated. 'From our [British] information we can say the party is well organised and well financed ... whenever there is a strike or other agitation led by the Communists, they manage by one means or another to finance the movement to some considerable tune.'[44]

British misgivings that Sanjeevi was too lax when it came to addressing communist subversion were overtaken by events in New Delhi. In July 1950, Sanjeevi was sacked as DIB and sent back to the police service in Madras. Nehru had expressed frustration with the quality of reports produced by the Intelligence Bureau and wasted few opportunities to make his dissatisfaction known.[45] In October 1948, when responding to an intelligence summary on communist activity in Hyderabad, the Indian premier noted acerbically that he had received, 'a very vague report which does not help very much ... [it] is not the kind of report which normally intelligence men should send'. Disparaging a paper that was absent 'any actual or factual information', Nehru skewered, 'a bad report ... [that] is apt to mislead and create a wrong impression'. 'I have found a tendency to be vague and to judge of events without finding out if they actually took place', India's disgruntled leader complained. 'The Intelligence Department should be asked to present facts and not opinions.'[46] Three years into his tenure at India's intelligence chief, Sanjeevi's abrasive manner, appetite for power, and reluctance to overstate the communist threat to India, had also exhausted the goodwill of his boss at the Home Ministry, Vallabhbhai Patel, and fatally depleted his standing within the Home Ministry.[47] In Sanjeevi's place, Patel appointed Mullik as India's second DIB. Mullik had served as Deputy Director of the IB since September 1948. Inside India's intelligence community, Mullik was regarded as an exceptionally hard-working and industrious individual, someone imbued with firm opinions, and a leader that evidenced genuine concern for the welfare of subordinates.[48] Articulate and politically astute, Mullik's rise to the top of Indian intelligence did not pass without comment or criticism. Yezdezard Dinshaw (Y. D.) Gundevia, India's Foreign Secretary, took a dim view of the new DIB, characterising him as a sycophant incapable or unwilling to speak truth to power.[49] Further afield, Liddell found Mullik to be a less agreeable personality than his opposite number in Pakistan, Kazim Raza. In Liddell's judgement, Mullik was also 'rather shifty' and less 'balanced and intelligent' than his deputy at the IB, Madan Hooja.[50] While he considered Mullik's personality as 'not a very pleasant one', Liddell attributed the DIB's asperity, in part, to 'the fact that as a rather young man he has been put into a very big job and is a little conscious of his position'.[51] Liddell may not have warmed to Mullik, but a significant point of continuity between India's first and second DIBs lay in the field of foreign intelligence liaison. Mullik continued, and amplified, Sanjeevi's emphasis on the IB working in close partnership with MI5.

Under Mullik's direction, the IB strengthened its position within the Indian government. One contemporary observer of post-Independent India attributed the political power accumulated by Mullik to the personal relationship that the DIB forged with Nehru. 'Access to, and the confidence of the Prime Minister, were the prerequisite of influence in the Government in those days', it was noted, 'and Mullik enjoyed them to the full'.[52] Politically to the right of Nehru, the Indian prime minister came to value his spy chief as, 'able, conscientious and thoroughly straightforward'.[53] Mullik's control of security dossiers on many of Nehru's colleagues and political adversaries, coupled with the increasingly important role played by intelligence in domestic Indian politics, ensured that Nehru had good reason to keep the DIB inside his inner circle. Much as Sanjeevi had before him, Mullik's accumulation of bureaucratic authority provoked concern in the senior ranks of India's armed forces. A suspicion festered in military circles that the DIB was not above feeding disinformation to Nehru on purported military plots against the civil government and, in the process, bolster the IB's standing at the expense of the Army.[54] Equally, Mullik held a less benign attitude to communism than his predecessor, and sought to place the IB, rather than the Army, at the forefront of Indian anti-communist counter-insurgency activity.[55] In March 1951, less than a year after becoming DIB, Mullik authored a report on communist subversion in the north-eastern state of Tripura. The report cast the CPI as an existential threat to Indian democracy. Emphasising a 'phenomenal' growth of communist support in Tripura, that was driven by strong party discipline and a willingness to embrace political violence, Mullik argued that agitation in the state represented, 'a serious danger, which therefore threatens the security of the Indian Union ... ' Pushing for the adoption of an aggressive counter-insurgency policy that mirrored tactics employed by the British against communist irregulars in Malaya, the DIB sought to establish twenty-one armed police camps in Tripura and to fortify villages that had 'not yet gone over to the Communists'. Calling for swift central government action before it was too late, Mullik declared, 'There has been enough wastage of time already giving the Communists sufficient opportunity to build up their strength. ... The problem of Tripura should be considered to be an all-India problem.'[56]

At times, the extent of Mullik's anti-communist zeal exasperated his political masters. In September 1951, Nehru's reacted with dismay to an IB a proposal to counter subversive communist activity in the nation's schools. Students and their wards, Mullik suggested, should be forced to sign a written undertaking not to participate in political activities. Some of Nehru's Chief Ministers were appalled by what they considered to be an IB charter to spy on parents and their children. A student activist and political radical in his youth, Nehru professed himself amazed by 'the complete lack of intelligence shown [by the IB] in issuing such a circular'. 'For our Intelligence service to issue circulars about guardians of students being asked ... not to take part in political activities', Nehru fumed, 'appears to me so extraordinary as to be almost past belief'.[57] Complaints lodged by Russian nationals in India regarding excessive IB surveillance elicited a similar reaction from the Indian leader. Nehru noted that he had repeatedly received intelligence reports on supposedly suspect individuals with whom he was personally familiar. 'The conclusions arrived at in such reports were often, to my knowledge, manifestly wrong', the Indian premier asserted. Nehru attributed the difficulty that IB officers encountered in making rational assessments on political issues to the colonial training in the Indian Police Service that many had undergone before switching to an intelligence role. 'It does not often happen that an Intelligence Officer, however good for his work', Nehru reasoned, 'has political flair or an understanding of basic events'.[58] Nehru questioned why the IB kept every Russian in India under watch. 'I do not think', he argued, 'that we need be afraid of these Soviet citizens doing much propaganda here or indulging in undesirable activities'. Intelligence Bureau officers were poor watchers in any case, Nehru reflected, and 'patent to everybody' as 'their face and manners proclaim them'. 'I doubt', he concluded, 'if [IB surveillance] ... can do anything particularly useful'. The IB was instructed by the prime minister to stop shadowing groups of Russian tourists.[59]

While Nehru was uncomfortable with Mullik's uncompromising aversion to communism, the British Security Service considered the DIB to be an exceptionally useful ally and well-positioned inside the Indian government to drive home the pernicious threat posed by the CPI and its external sponsors. Eric Kitchen, who succeeded Bill U'ren as MI5's SLO in New Delhi, in June 1950, noted that Mullik met with India's prime minister at least twice every week and, 'reinforced by information from ourselves, had ... succeeded in making Nehru more aware of the dangers of Communism'.[60] The idea that Mullik could serve a useful purpose by exposing India's premier to anti-communism sentiment retained currency amongst British officials until Nehru's death, in 1964. In August 1960, Morrice James, Britain's Deputy High Commissioner in India, pondered whether, 'we here [in New Delhi] can or should do more vis-a-vis Nehru himself, or perhaps more promisingly through such senior Indian officials as Mullik (the D.I.B.) who have access to Mr. Nehru, to put the Soviet treatment of their nationalities in a somewhat less rosy perspective'. On reflection, James concluded that having, 'looked into this ... [I] am satisfied we have in fact been making good use vis-a-vis Indian officials, including Mullik, of the material on this subject [Soviet communism] which has reached us from various sources'.[61] Back in May 1958, when Roger Hollis visited India, he recorded that the DIB's appraisal of the danger posed by communism in the subcontinent was much closer to the British Security Service's position than that of the Indian government.[62] Mullik's politics did not go unnoticed by some of his more progressive Indian colleagues. In June 1972, looking back on Mullik's long and influential career in intelligence, P. N. Haksar, a committed socialist, reminded his boss, and India's premier, Indira Gandhi, that, 'the first head of the Intelligence Bureau [sic], Shri B. N. Mullik, has great passion for studying what was then fashionable "international communism". He took a great deal of personal interest in it.' 'Now', Haksar added witheringly, 'every intelligent person knows that all these studies of so-called international communism are not worth the paper on which they are written'.[63]

Managing Moscow: MI5, the IB, and Soviet Intelligence

Nehru's scrutiny of the IB's efforts to contain communist activity in India frequently frustrated MI5's counter-subversion officers. The Security Service became 'depressed' as the 1950s progressed and their Indian colleagues in the IB struggled to respond to an increase in Soviet intelligence activity in the subcontinent. One MI5 officer grumbled that, when it came to India, 'in effect they [the Soviets] are having an almost free run for their money both in the espionage and subversive fields'.[64] In turn, Mullik expressed his irritation to MI5 over the quality and quantity of information that he received from its SLO's on the Soviets regional intentions and capabilities. While sympathetic with the DIB's desire for more and better intelligence on Moscow's thinking, senior MI5 officers reflected sardonically that they felt much the same. 'If Mullik only knew the extent to which we chrystal-gaze[sic] at the J. I. C. on this subject', Guy Liddell ruminated, 'he might not be so insistent in his demands!' On one occasion, having pressed Bill U'ren for specific details on Soviet economic policy, Mullik was taken aback when the SLO replied that such matters were outside his sphere of expertise. 'But you are an officer of M.I.5', the DIB responded incredulously, 'surely you know these things?' Liddell found Mullik's faith in the Security Service's omnipotence perplexing and indicative of the IB's limited appreciation of the wider intelligence Cold War. 'Mullik is obviously reluctant to believe that we have not got agents in the Kremlin', the Deputy Director of MI5 observed disdainfully.[65]

Tensions between MI5 and the IB simmered as Moscow's efforts to penetrate the political, economic, and social fabric of India gathered pace. By 1955, mounting concern at the extent of Soviet covert interference in India's internal affairs prompted Nehru to use the opportunity afforded by the presence in South Asia of the Soviet leaders, Nikita Khrushchev, and Nikolai Bulganin, to broach the issue of Moscow's financial support for the CPI. During talks held in New Delhi, Nehru warned his guests that Indians would react badly were it to become apparent that 'the Soviet Union was directly encouraging the local Communist Party'. 'It was commonly believed in India', Nehru noted, 'that large sums of money came to the Communist Party from outside in various ways'. Brushing aside his hosts insinuation that Moscow was meddling in India's affairs, Khrushchev, implausibly, denied any knowledge of the CPI's sources of funding. 'Mr Khrushchev said on his word of honor', the official Indian text of his exchange with Nehru recorded, 'they (the Communist Party of the Soviet Union) had no connection with the Indian Communist Party'.[66] Nehru was less concerned with Khrushchev's passing acquaintance with the truth when it came to Soviet funding of the CPI, and more concerned about the potential for Moscow's clandestine interference in the subcontinent to compromise Indo-Soviet relations were it to become public. The Indian premier confided to a colleague that he, 'was not worried about their [the CPI's] behaviour very much as we could easily deal with them. They were neither strong nor very intelligent.' Rather, Nehru was troubled that, by continuing to bankroll 'objectionable' communist behaviour in India, Moscow would reveal its hidden hand, and his governments relations with the Soviet Union would wither. 'I think my talk produced some effect on them [Khrushchev and Bulganin]', the Indian premier concluded optimistically. 'Though what they will continue to do about it I cannot say.'[67]

Western diplomats and intelligence officers were less convinced that the Soviets would turn over a new leaf in India. Khrushchev's claim that Moscow had nothing to do with the subcontinent's communists flew in the face of evidence that suggested the opposite. As early as 1948, America's ambassador in India, Henry Grady, had remarked wryly that, 'The Soviet ambassador in Delhi was more preoccupied with opening secret channels to India's communists than contacting responsible officials of the Ministry of External Affairs.'[68] American intelligence reports validated Grady's point and concluded that the exceptionally well-funded CPI was able to operate paid agents at all levels in India's state governments, from low-salaried clerks, engaged in routine espionage, to officials working with senior police offers who were privy to national security policy. The proliferation of cheap Soviet propaganda in India's cities, and a willingness among sections of the Indian press to follow a pro-Moscow line, and benefit from advertising revenue derived from Eastern European sources, pointed to 'a marked increase in [covert] Soviet activity regarding India'. 'Soviet representatives in India were careful to avoid any impression of aiding or directing Communist activity in India', one US intelligence assessment underlined, 'but they assisted several front organizations in direct and indirect ways to spread their anti-American propaganda'.[69] Chester Bowles, one of Gray's successors, confirmed that a surge in communist publicity in the subcontinent had coincided with Russian officials, including the then ambassador, Kirill Novikov, playing a more prominent role in India's social and political milieu. The same could not be said for his Chinese colleagues, Bowles noted. China's Army, Air, and Naval attachés in New Delhi lived next door to Bowles, but conspicuously avoided acknowledging their American neighbour. 'My daughter Sally has been able to wangle smile from some of the younger Chinese children', Bowles informed Washington, 'but she reports no (repeat no) progress above age of ten'.[70] Moscow's increasingly convivial relations with New Delhi allowed Soviet intelligence agencies to channel an increasing proportion of their resources into India under the guise of trade and cultural missions.[71] By the 1960s, the KGB boasted that it had assets in place at every strata and in every division of the Indian government.[72] At the same time, an officer from E branch, responsible for MI5's overseas liaison, was sent to India to brief the IB on developments in counter-espionage. The officer reported back that while the Intelligence Bureau had recorded some successes in disrupting clandestine communist activity, 'the overall impression of the Bureau's work against the huge Soviet Embassy staff is depressing indeed'.[73]

Stella Rimington was similarly taken aback by the number of Soviet 'advisers', or undeclared KGB and GRU officers, that she encountered in India. 'The country was overrun with . . . military advisers, agricultural advisers, industrial advisers, economic advisers and every other kind of adviser you can imagine', Rimington remembered. 'As we toured the country, we kept falling over them.'[74] One aspect of the MI5 SLOs work in New Delhi was to identify

Figure 2.1 America's ambassador to India, Chester Bowles, attacks a proliferation of communist propaganda in the subcontinent, *The American Reporter*, 26 April 1967.

foreign intelligence officers, and to monitor efforts they made to attach themselves to British High Commission staff. To Rimington's amusement, she was targeted in a recruitment operation mounted by Soviet intelligence. Rimington and her husband had made the acquaintance of a young lecturer at Delhi University. Having been entertained by the man and his wife on a few occasions, one evening the future head of MI5 found that two new guests had been added to their usual dinner party, a Soviet KGB officer, under diplomatic cover, and his partner. Rimington immediately broke off contact with her Indian 'friends'. On a separate occasion, Rimington suspected that she had been subjected to a crude *kompromat* operation by the KGB. Some other Indian 'friends' approached Rimington and requested that she carry medicines through customs in the High Commission's diplomatic bag. The drugs were unobtainable in India and purportedly needed for a sick child. Doing so would have breached diplomatic regulations and contravened Indian law. It would also have left Rimington vulnerable to future coercion from Indian or Soviet 'friends' seeking 'favours'.[75] Everything that MI5 was hearing, seeing, and experiencing on the ground in India, it seemed, pointed to a worrying intensification in Soviet covert intelligence activity.

Beating A Retreat: Ending MI5's Indian Experiment

As the Soviet intelligence footprint in India expanded from the late 1950s, MI5 fought a rear-guard action to stave off swinging cuts to its budget demanded by a Whitehall bureaucracy searching for overseas economies. The sacrifice of MI5's entire SLO programme, it seemed, might be necessary to satisfy Treasury demands for deep cuts in the secret vote. In 1964, the reestablishment of an SIS station in India added to the pressure on MI5 to justify a continuance of its in-country presence. Having reluctantly accepted Downing Street's adoption of the Attlee Directive, the Foreign Office did its best to ensure that the 'ban' on SIS activity in India remained provisional and was subject to challenge.[76] As the Cold War expanded and intensified, covert action, the preserve of SIS, became more appealing to British governments as a cost-effective means of achieving foreign policy goals.[77] At the same time, the British Chiefs of Staff presented an apocalyptic picture of the global threat confronting UK policymakers. 'The free world continues to be menaced everywhere by the threat of communist subversion and expansion', military planners declared, 'which has world dominion as its ultimate aim'. In placing an emphasis on 'techniques of subversion', backed by the clandestine supply of arms and finance to its allies, Moscow and Beijing appeared to have seized control of the post-colonial world. More effective use of Britain's 'covert agencies', the Chiefs of Staff argued, was needed to 'wrest the covert initiative from the enemy'.[78]

Within the CRO, while it remained understood that, 'the policy . . . has been that there should be no Secret Service activity in the Commonwealth', it was also accepted that SIS had on a 'few occasions', and with appropriate authority, conducted operations in India.[79] Moreover, by late 1959, Dick White, Chief of SIS, with the full support of the Cabinet Secretary, Norman Brook, was pushing hard for the ban on intelligence collection operations by his service within the commonwealth to be overturned. '"C" [White] was not now suggesting that "carte blanche" should be given for such activities', a record of one Cabinet Office meeting noted, 'he was asking that the general doctrine should not preclude us from mounting Intelligence operations in the case of a particular country if this was justified on merits'. Over at MI5, Roger Hollis took exception to an initiative that threatened to destroy the goodwill that the Security Service had established with foreign counterparts and on which the SLO system depended. 'It was desirable that we should be able to deal openly with the security organisation in emergent territories', Hollis insisted, 'and so far, we had been able to do so because the United Kingdom had not carried out clandestine activities in them'. In search of a way forward, Brook suggested that it appeared 'preferable' not to seek a wholesale revision to the Attlee Directive, but instead to 'justify specific [SIS] projects [within the Commonwealth] on their individual merits'.[80]

Alexander Clutterbuck, who had been born in India to a family of the *Raj*, and was then Permanent Under-Secretary at the CRO, reminded Brook that, 'it [the Attlee Directive] was a principle by which we set considerable store, since we considered it was fundamental to our relationship with other Commonwealth countries'. Nevertheless, Clutterbuck agreed that, in special circumstances, where the national interest demanded that SIS undertake covert operations within Commonwealth territory, 'we [the CRO] would certainly be prepared to consider the making of an exception and, indeed, some exceptions had already been made'. As Clutterbuck intimated, and was no doubt fully aware, SIS had been busy contravening the Attlee Directive in India for some time.[81] In due course, Harold Macmillan formally endorsed qualifying his predecessor's blanket prohibition on covert action inside the Commonwealth. In a meeting of Cabinet principles, held in December 1959, the British premier confirmed that, '... while there was no question of reversing the "Attlee Directive" altogether, there might be occasions when the intelligence to be gained by operations carried out for a specific purpose might outweigh the general objections and the dangers'. The Indian subcontinent was referenced explicitly at the meeting as a region where such a 'specific purpose' could manifest and would offset 'objections and dangers'.[82]

Pressure from the Cabinet Office to revise the Attlee Directive and facilitate SIS operations in the subcontinent diluted a core rationale underpinning the local MI5 SLO programme, namely the collection of intelligence that Britain could not otherwise expect to receive from the Indian government. It was not the return of SIS in 1964 in the wake of Sino-Indian hostilities, however, that prompted MI5 to quit India. Rather, the Security Service found it increasingly difficult to resist demands from the Treasury to trim its costs. In 1965, MI5 was required to implement annual cost savings of £100,000 on the Secret Vote for 1966/67. In response, the Service's post-war SLO programme, the genesis of which lay in India, was effectively wound up. Security Liaison Officers were recalled from Tanzania, Ghana, Ceylon, and Gibraltar, and preparations made to shut down MI5 stations in Australia and Malta. Roger Hollis enlisted the support of John Freeman, Britain's High Commissioner, in a bid to preserve his Service's presence in India. Freeman informed Whitehall that removing MI5's SLO would, 'risk destroying a liaison [with India] which it might be very difficult if ever to re-establish'. The exercise in diplomatic special pleading left Brook's successor at the Cabinet Office, Sir Burke Trend, unmoved. For want of annual savings totalling £8,038, MI5's twenty-year presence in India was ended.[83] It fell to Hollis' replacement as MI5's Director-General, Martin Furnival Jones, to inform his opposite number at the IB, S. P. Verma, that the current SLO in New Delhi would not be replaced on completion of his tour. Reflecting on the wider benefits which had accrued to both sides from their association, Verma expressed deep regret that by withdrawing from India MI5 would sever, 'the longstanding contact at a personal level which has proved invaluable to us'. Concluding a sombre and plaintive exchange with Furnivall-Jones, the DIB confessed that he, 'did not know how he [Verma] would manage [to run the Intelligence Bureau] without it [MI5]'.[84]

3

India's Rasputin: V. K. Krishna Menon and the Spectre of Indian Communism

On 21 October 1954, Sir Alexander Clutterbuck, Britain's high commissioner in India, sat down at his desk in Albuquerque Road, New Delhi, to compose a private and confidential letter. Clutterbuck's note was addressed to Joe Garner, deputy under-secretary of state at the Commonwealth Relations Office in London. The subject was V. K. Krishna Menon, a native of the southern Indian state of Kerala who, during the first two decades and more of India's post-colonial history, established a reputation as one the most controversial and divisive figures in international politics. 'While it is true that Krishna has helped us [the United Kingdom] on occasion ... ', Clutterbuck cautioned Garner, 'I nevertheless rate him for my own part as a thoroughly dangerous man, indeed as Nehru's evil genius – a born conspirator and intriguer, making mischief wherever he goes, utterly unscrupulous, determined to mark his mark in the world, and now gradually undermining, whether deliberately or not ... the whole conduct of India's foreign relations.'[1]

Menon's political education had begun back in the early 1920s when he enrolled as a student at Madras Law College. The British theosophist and political activist, Annie Besant, took Menon under her wing and introduced him to the Indian Home Rule movement. By the end of the decade, with the benefit of Besant's financial support, Menon's commitment to Indian nationalism had been sharpened by a period of study at the London School of Economics, under the tutelage of the political scientist, and prominent socialist, Harold Laski. It was in London, in 1935, that Menon first met Jawaharlal Nehru. Menon went on to form a close personal and political bond with the future Indian leader, earning plaudits from Nehru for his service as secretary of the India League, the principal organisation promoting Indian nationalism in pre-war Britain.[2] Under Nehru's patronage, Menon experienced a meteoric rise to political power. In 1947, he was appointed to the prestigious post of Indian High Commissioner to the United Kingdom. Menon's abrasive personality and readiness to listen to and, on occasions, publicly endorse Soviet and Communist Chinese positions on a range of international questions, ruffled feathers in London and Washington. In the United States, government officials shared Clutterbuck's unflattering assessment of the Indian diplomat. Menon was described by State Department officials as 'venomous', 'violently

52

anti-American', 'an unpleasant mischief-maker', and 'a tough, poisonous bastard'.[3]

During the 1930s, British governments faced increasing pressure to grant India greater political autonomy. Indian nationalist organisations in the United Kingdom; Labour politicians such as Stafford Cripps, Aneurin Bevan, and Michael Foot; and intellectuals, including Bertrand Russell and Harold Laski, all pressed the case for Indian self-government in some form.[4] Menon, above all others, transformed the British-based campaign for Indian independence from an uncoordinated and ineffectual movement, into a cohesive and dynamic political force. Between 1932 and 1947, as Secretary of the India League, he set the Indian nationalist agenda in Britain. In the process, Menon's strident anti-imperial rhetoric and links to the Communist Party of Great Britain (CPGB) brought him to the attention of MI5, and its sister organisation, Indian Political Intelligence. Marked out as 'one of the most important Indian extremists in the country',[5] Menon's political activities were seen as a direct threat to Britain's colonial rule in South Asia. Following the transfer of power in 1947, the Attlee government, and its immediate successors in Whitehall, became convinced that India, and more particularly, Krishna Menon, constituted a weak link in the Commonwealth security chain.

With the onset of the Cold War, MI5 became fixated with the Indian government's vulnerability to communist subversion. Given his connections to British communism, the Security Service opposed New Delhi's decision to appoint Menon to the post of Indian High Commissioner in London.[6] The nature of Menon's links to British communists convinced senior MI5 officers that, if not a dyed in the wool Marxist, Menon was nevertheless politically suspect.[7] Moreover, the Indian High Commissioner's mercurial character and eccentric behaviour encouraged British and Indian officials alike to question his emotional stability, reinforcing the perception that Menon was unsound. 'As long as Menon and his associates remained in the High Commissioner's office', MI5's Deputy Director-General, Guy Liddell, observed in 1949, 'there could be no reasonable guarantee of [Commonwealth] security as far as India is concerned'.[8] At the same time, London sought, in part, to retain Britain's status as a global power by preserving strong political, economic, and as far as possible, intelligence and security links, with India.[9] The Attlee government was conscious that as an intimate of India's premier, Menon's position as High Commissioner carried important implications not only for Dominion security, but also for Indo-British relations. Post-war British administrations found themselves attempting to foster close ties with India while simultaneously containing a threat that New Delhi, and most especially, Krishna Menon, were deemed to pose to Commonwealth defence.

British disquiet at Menon's appointment as India's High Commissioner to the United Kingdom, and a subsequent alarm surrounding India House's susceptibility to communist subversion, led Whitehall to adopt a covert counter-subversion strategy that encompassed plans to engineer Krishna Menon's removal from office. Over subsequent decades, the persistence of a shared conviction amongst senior British and American officials that Menon was, at best, a communist fellow-traveller and, at worst, a fully paid-up agent of the Kremlin, saw Washington and Whitehall revisit various clandestine schemes to discredit the Indian statesman. Notably, following India's humiliation at the hands of China in a brief but bloody border war in late 1962, Western intelligence agencies, with encouragement from their political masters, dusted off secret plots to smear Menon by initiating and amplifying newspaper reports, inside and outside India, that blamed the then Defence Minister for his nation's misfortune.[10] As late as August 1972, two years prior to Menon's death, British officials in India continued to warn London that the ageing and, by now, former Indian politician remained, 'one

Figure 3.1 V. K. Krishna Menon (left) with Indian prime minister, Jawaharlal Nehru, London, 18 April 1949. Keystone-France /Gama-Keystone / Getty Images.

of the main instruments through which the Russians have worked in India'. Menon, Whitehall was cautioned, retained 'very considerable influence' with the Indian premier, Indira Gandhi, and 'through Krishna Menon ... Mrs Gandhi has been so imbued with ideas which closely fit Soviet requirements that no very great effort is needed now to induce her to adopt policies and attitudes which suit them well enough'.[11] Such exaggerated characterisations of Menon's power on the part of Western diplomats were commonplace, and misinterpreted the nature and extent of his authority over Indian government policy. This miscalculation, as much as Menon's own bellicose public rhetoric and acerbic persona, complicated and constrained British and American relations with India for much of the early cold war period.

'Near Communist': Krishna Menon, Congress, and the CPGB

In 1928, Krishna Menon was elected general secretary of the Commonwealth Group of India. He quickly set about re-organising and rebranding the organisation into the more militant and activist India League. Under Menon's leadership, the League's 'vicious' anti-colonial propaganda became a thorn in the British government's side.[12] By 1932, the League's call for immediate Dominion status for India was generating sufficient concern within IPI, for the Home Office to approve the interception of Menon's personal mail and telephone calls, alongside those of India League's London offices at 146 Strand.[13]

Within the Indian subcontinent, Menon's transformation of the India League was noted by leaders of the Indian National Congress (INC). From 1938, Nehru assumed the role of Menon's political mentor. Brushing aside complaints from Britain's Indian community that Menon's direction of the India League was high-handed and authoritarian, in August that year, Nehru made it clear that he, ' . . . would not consider any proposal that might tend to bring about a cleavage between either Congress or himself and the India League, and . . . was satisfied with the work done by the League on behalf of the Indian National Congress in this country'.[14] For his part, Menon worked assiduously to promote the impression within British left-wing circles that he was 'Nehru's right-hand man in London'. He took on the role of Nehru's literary agent, and acted as a chaperone to his daughter, Indira, while she studied at Somerville College, Oxford.[15] 'Menon is very jealous for his own prestige . . . ', the IPI noted, 'He has pointed out that he alone has any authority to speak for NEHRU and that he is invariably advised by the Congress Socialist Party on matters of importance'.[16]

The Security Service's interest in Menon was piqued once the India League established links to the CPGB. In October 1931, MI5 had assumed responsibility for investigating domestic communist activity. Up until 1936, however, there appeared, 'no evidence of any cooperation worth mentioning between the [India] League and the Communist Party of Great Britain'. The seeds of future CPGB-India League collaboration had been sown in the summer of 1935, when the Comintern's Seventh Congress directed Communists to enter the anti-imperialist struggle.[17] In response, the CPGB offered to work with the League against the passage of the Government of India Act, which despite granting India's provinces greater autonomy fell well short of nationalist demands for self-government. Concerned that Britain's Communists would seek to subvert his control of the League and having previously been subjected to their barbed criticisms, Menon initially rebuffed the CPGB.[18]

When the Government of India Act passed on the statute books, Menon changed tack and resolved to widen the India League's political base and raise its public profile. Reaching out to the CPGB, and its 15,000 members, appeared an obvious means of doing so. As a first step, Menon set about co-opting leading British communists onto the Indian League's Executive Committee, and struck up friendships with the CGPB's Secretary General, Harry Pollitt, and Rajani Palme Dutt, its principal theoretician.[19] Menon also began to draw on CPGB support to pack the India League's hitherto poorly attended meetings, and to supply speakers for its public events. Moreover, the CPGB's newspaper, *The Daily Worker*, with a daily circulation of nearly 40,000, became an important mouthpiece for the League's propaganda. By the end of 1936, collaboration between the India League and the CPGB was sufficiently close for IPI to suggest that Menon, 'took no important action of any kind in regard to the Indian situation without prior consultation with the higher Communist Party leaders'.[20] The following year, IPI went further, arguing at one stage that Menon's ultimate goal was the establishment of a 'soviet system for India'.[21] Although not a member of the CPGB himself, to Britain's security services Menon appeared well on the way to becoming so. Or, as one intelligence report put it, Krishna Menon appeared to be a 'near communist'.[22]

The Labour Party's leadership felt much the same way about Menon. From its inception, the India League had nurtured links with Labour's left-wing and, in 1934, Menon was elected as a Labour councillor for the north London borough of St Pancras. Senior Labour Party figures, however, became increasingly uncomfortable with Menon's association with British communists. In November 1939, Menon's standing in wider the Parliamentary Labour Party plummeted when, minded of the India League's reliance on communist support, he refused to condemn the Soviet Union's invasion of Finland.[23] In a bid to re-establish his Labour credentials, Menon stood as the prospective Labour candidate for parliament in Dundee, a city with strong links to India's jute industry. Given his association with the CPGB, MI5 found the Dundee Labour Party's endorsement of Menon, 'really rather remarkable'.[24] Labour's National Executive Committee agreed and, in November 1940, having concluded that Menon held a 'double loyalty', he was de-selected, and thrown out of the Party.[25]

In fact, Menon's relations with the CPGB were often strained. Rank and file communists questioned his flaky ideological credentials and disdain for Marxism.[26] To the CPGB's hierarchy, Menon's politics were largely immaterial. His value lay as a conduit between British communist leaders and the INC leadership, and more especially, Jawaharlal Nehru. In other words, Menon and the CPGB were drawn together by political necessity rather than a sense of shared dogma. In a letter Menon wrote to Minocher Rustom 'Minoo' Masani, a fellow LSE student and Lincoln's Inn barrister, who was also close to Nehru at that time, he confided that, 'while I am a left-wing socialist, a believer in the almost immediate establishment of a socialist equalitarian society I have little use for the C. P. [Communist Party] here [London] or in India. I have personal friends among them and some good ones, but my metaphysics and politics and economics lead me in a different direction.'[27]

In the absence of a common strategic purpose, the India League's relationship with the CPGB began to unravel under the pressure of international events.[28] At one time a 'frequent visitor' to its London headquarters at 16 King Street,[29] Menon's association with the CPGB soured following the Nazi invasion of the USSR in June 1941. Once the Soviets had joined Britain in the fight against fascism, to Menon's fury, the CPGB stopped attacking British colonialism and began emphasising the need for allied unity.[30] Simmering tensions between Menon and Britain's communists reached a head in December that year, as the Wehrmacht stood before the gates of Moscow. Tired of his posturing, in a succession of private exchanges with communist leaders Menon was taken to task for, 'behav[ing] as if it [the India League] existed in a vacuum, seeing everything only from the point of view of its own immediate advantage'.[31] The CPGB's disenchantment with Menon had little impact on the India League's propaganda activities. In early 1942, with Britain reeling from Axis advances in North Africa and the Far East, the League redoubled its information effort. Working around the clock, its presses churned out literature excoriating the British government for its double standard in professing to fight for the democracy while denying Indians their freedom. In May 1942, IPI expressed concern that the India League's activities were, 'quite definitely having a slowing-down effect on the war effort amongst Indians in this country'.[32] In response, Roger Hollis, then head of MI5's F1 section, responsible for communist surveillance, attempted to disrupt its work by drafting Menon for National Service. Approaching the Ministry of Labour in January 1942, Hollis enquired whether, as 'a leading light on the India League, an organisation with very close affiliations with the Communist Party', Menon could be conscripted in some capacity.[33] To Hollis' frustration, his efforts to register Menon for National Service came to nothing.[34]

In India, Menon's activities gave cause for even greater British concern. The *Raj* had come under severe pressure in 1942, as the Cripps Mission floundered, and the INC's 'Quit India' campaign of civil disobedience gathered momentum. Confronted by an explosive internal situation, India's Viceroy, the Marquess of Linlithgow, badgered the India Office to intern Menon. Writing to the Secretary of State for India, Leo Amery in November, Linlithgow suggested, ' ... we should take pains to break up Menon and break up the India League with him. I am certain that so long as he is there, he will be a focus of discontent and difficulty ... '.[35]

Amery rejected Linlithgow's appeal, explaining to a fellow conservative MP that Menon was, 'very clever and takes good care ... to keep sufficiently within the law ... but between ourselves we are watching him carefully'.[36] Unlike fellow Indian nationalists on the subcontinent, Menon managed to remain one step ahead of the British for the duration of the war.

'A Considerable Threat to Commonwealth Security': India's High Commissioner in London

In 1946, as Clement Attlee's Labour government began to rebuild a nation exhausted by six years of enervating conflict, Britain's control over its India Empire fractured.[37] Although committed to an early transfer of power, the Labour government's failure to advance a timetable for Indian self-government produced rumblings of discontent in the subcontinent. In February, with the illusion of British imperial power crumbling, the Royal Indian Navy mutinied in Bombay. The following month, with the internal situation in India threatening to spiral out of control, Attlee dispatched a Cabinet Mission to the subcontinent to negotiate terms for Britain's withdrawal.[38] By 2 September, a transitional Indian government was in place, with Jawaharlal Nehru acting as its premier and foreign minister.[39] Eager to initiate contacts between his interim administration and European governments, Nehru asked Krishna Menon to serve as his unofficial ambassador-at-large. Acting as Nehru's emissary, Menon called on foreign ministries in Paris, Copenhagen, Oslo, and Stockholm.[40] It was his meeting with the Soviet Foreign Minister, Vyacheslav Molotov, in Paris, in late September 1946, however, that provoked alarm in official British circles.

Menon's meeting with Molotov had ostensibly been arranged to negotiate the sale of Soviet grain surpluses to India. Frederick Pethick Lawrence, Amery's successor as Secretary of State for India, suspected Menon's real agenda was more sinister. As a fellow traveller, Pethick Lawrence argued, Menon had seized the first opportunity, 'to make contact with, express sympathy with, and generally indicate India's desire to line up in the international field with, Russia rather than the Western bloc'. The idea that Menon was pro-Soviet, had come to represent an article of faith within the India Office. Consequently, it was thrown into a panic late in 1946, when rumours surfaced on the subcontinent that Menon was manoeuvring to become India's High Commissioner to the United Kingdom. Writing to the Viceroy, Viscount

Wavell, on 1 November 1946, Pethick Lawrence stressed that Menon, 'would not be well received here ... and if the suggestion [that he become High Commissioner] were made to you by Nehru or one of his colleagues it might be as well to warn him'.[41] Taking the matter up with Attlee, later that month, Pethick Lawrence underlined Menon's 'disturbing' propensity to criticise British foreign policy. He would, Attlee was assured, 'influence Nehru against H. M. G. when he comes here'.[42]

The case against Menon set out by Pethick Lawrence was underpinned with intelligence furnished by MI5 and SIS. This indicated that Menon had used a meeting held with Nehru in New Delhi to lobby the interim Indian prime minister to adopt 'an entirely pro-Russian line in all international dealings'. In the Security Services judgment, Menon appeared to have succeeded, 'in some degree at any rate' in winning Nehru 'over to this point of view'.[43] At the same time, Kumara Padmanabha Sivasankara (K. P. S.) Menon, an Indian civil servant, and no relation to Krishna Menon, who would later serve as independent India's first Foreign Secretary and ambassador to Moscow, made Nehru aware of domestic concern surrounding his namesakes purportedly suspect political loyalties. In a letter sent to Nehru in December 1946, K. P. S. Menon argued forcefully that, 'if Krishna Menon had his way, he would have reduced India in the eyes of the world, to the position of a Soviet satellite ... His judgement is warped; he thinks that Russia is always on the side of the angels.'[44]

Menon's job prospects improved in early 1947, after Attlee announced his decision to install Lord Louis Mountbatten as India's last Viceroy. Mountbatten had befriended Menon in pre-war London when the British establishment treated Indian nationalists as social pariahs. In return, Menon never forgot Mountbatten's generosity of spirit.[45] As Attlee's confidence in Wavell drained away over the course of 1946, it was Menon who championed Mountbatten as a worthy successor in Congress Party circles.[46] When faced with the formidable challenge of steering India to independence on terms acceptable to his metropolitan masters, the Congress Party, and Muhammad Ali Jinnah's Muslim League, Mountbatten employed Menon as an informal back channel to Nehru, and other senior Congress Party figures. Menon's adroit performance as a political go-between over the spring of 1947 impressed Mountbatten and, in July, he supported Menon's bid to become High Commissioner in London.[47] Writing to Attlee on 10 July, Mountbatten played up the importance of Menon's connection to Nehru. As one of the few individuals outside Nehru's cabinet with a 'good idea of what is in the minds of present Congress leaders', Mountbatten argued, Menon's presence in London would prove invaluable in the years to come.[48] Nehru made much the same point the following day, when informing Attlee that, ' ... we have decided to appoint Krishna Menon to this post [high commissioner]. I feel sure that with his knowledge of both India and England and the intimate contacts he has in both countries, he will [be] of great help to us in the new conditions that we would have to face'.[49]

Attlee's decision not to challenge Menon's appointment drew howls of protest from the India Office.[50] Springing to Menon's defence, Mountbatten tartly informed a disgruntled Earl of Listowel, who had replaced Pethick Lawrence as Secretary of State in April 1947, that while *"persona non grata"* in many circles at home', as someone who enjoyed Nehru's 'complete confidence', Menon would be well placed to advance British interests in New Delhi.[51] MI5's Director-General, Sir Percy Sillitoe, took a different view. Having got wind of Menon's posting through a chance conversation with an India Office official, Sillitoe's first reaction was to send Nehru 'a friendly warning' regarding Menon's links to the CPGB. To Sillitoe's chagrin, however, his staff quickly established that Menon's appointment was a *fait accompli*, and he abandoned the idea. Instead, Sillitoe approved a suggestion made by Sir Philip Vickery, head of the soon to be defunct IPI, for the latter to send a personal letter to Tirupattur Gangadharam (T. G.) Pillai Sanjeevi, the director of India's Intelligence Bureau. By using Vickery to convey in the starkest possible terms, 'the full implications of this appointment and its effect upon our future [intelligence] liaison', Sillitoe hoped that India's spy chief would bring pressure to bear on Nehru to reconsider Menon's posting.[52]

Sanjeevi was eager for a declared Indian intelligence officer to be based in London to facilitate liaison between the IB and MI5. He was informed by the Security Service that, with Menon in post, doing so 'would be a waste of time because we [MI5] could not communicate information to a member of the High Commissioner's office'. Conceding MI5's point, Sanjeevi, who harboured doubts of his own in respect of Menon's political loyalties, dropped the idea of appointing a liaison officer for the time being.[53] Not content with the warning his Service had issued to the IB, an irritated Sillitoe also drafted a memorandum on Menon for presentation to the Joint Intelligence Committee (JIC). This emphasised MI5's disquiet that Britain had been saddled with an Indian High Commissioner who had, 'close contacts with the Communist Party leadership in this country', and, was 'a warm supporter of Russia's foreign policy while equally opposed to that of our own'. In practical terms, Sillitoe's paper suggested that the flow of classified British material to the Indian High Commission be restricted once Menon was in post. 'Cabinet Ministers and other government officials with whom he [Menon] is likely to come into contact with', the head of MI5 cautioned, 'will have to be warned about him'.[54]

Contrary to British expectations, once in London, Krishna Menon enjoyed a honeymoon period as India's High Commissioner.[55] Menon played a pivotal role in negotiations that made it possible for India to remain within the Commonwealth as a sovereign republic, under the terms of 'The London Declaration'.[56] 'It is curious', Sir Stafford Cripps, Britain's Chancellor of the

Exchequer, wrote to Nehru, in April 1949, ' . . . that Krishna the revolutionary, the anti-British Indian Leaguer, has become one of the chief architects of the new and invigorated Commonwealth of Nations!'[57] Indeed, after a difficult start, relations between the Attlee and Nehru government improved considerably during the course of 1949. By then, Anglo-Indian friction generated by the Indo-Pakistani conflict over Kashmir and the 'police action' that enforced Hyderabad's integration into the Indian Union, had eased somewhat.[58] India's decision to remain in the Commonwealth, and booming bilateral trade, it seemed, augured well for future British-Indian relations. Writing to Britain's High Commissioner to India, Sir Archibald Nye, on 15 March 1949, Philip Noel-Baker, Secretary of State for Commonwealth Relations, expressed satisfaction that, 'general relations between London and Delhi are improving'. The perennial dark cloud on an otherwise sunny horizon remained Krishna Menon. With Menon looking set to stay in London 'for a considerable time to come', British officials fretted over the diplomatic storm that would ensue were India to discover the full extent of its exclusion from Dominion intelligence sharing arrangements. As Noel-Baker noted, the British continued, 'not in the least [to] trust the security or the general working of his [Menon's] Office'. The long-term prospects for Anglo-Indian relations would 'undoubtedly' improve, the British minister mused, if Menon were replaced as India's High Commissioner with 'someone sensible'.[59]

British misgivings surrounding Menon festered amidst a troubling backdrop of escalating Cold War tension. In the spring of 1948, Czechoslovakia came under communist control, the Western allies clashed with the Soviets over German currency reform and economic liberalisation, and in June the Berlin Blockade began. The spectre of renewed hostilities in Europe, produced a groundswell of anti-communist sentiment in Britain. On the domestic front, the Labour Party prohibited cooperation with domestic communists and purged several of its more left-wing members. The following year, the Transport and General Workers Union expelled shop-stewards linked to the CPGB and barred communists from holding union posts.[60] Within Whitehall, Attlee established a secret cabinet committee, GEN 183, to investigate subversive activity. The introduction of 'negative vetting' followed, under which the names of government officials working in sensitive areas were cross referenced against MI5's files.[61] Although not comparable with the McCarthyite purges that occurred subsequently in the United States, British civil servants found to have communist connections were sacked, forced to resign, or transferred to non-sensitive posts.[62]

Back in 1948, when Sanjeevi had travelled to London for talks with the Security Service, Philip Vickery had taken the opportunity to remind his Indian colleague of the detrimental effect that Krishna Menon was having on Anglo-Indian intelligence liaison.[63] In due course, Sanjeevi ensured that back in New Delhi, the Home Ministry was made fully aware that Menon's claim to

62   SPYING IN SOUTH ASIA

enjoy, 'the trust and confidence of Mr. Attlee and his colleagues ... was not true'.[64] Sanjeevi's interactions with Menon during the DIB's visit to the UK proved to be less amicable. In one report of a stormy encounter with the High Commissioner which Sanjeevi sent to his boss, and India's Home minister, Vallabhbhai Patel, the DIB stated that Menon had derided the Indian government's decision to crackdown on communist insurgents, labelling the policy as 'barbarous and inhuman'. '[T]he Government of India could with greater advantage use the Intelligence Bureau for rounding up black-marketeers and agents of corruption', Sanjeevi quoted Menon as saying, 'instead [of] hounding and harassing the communists'. In the process of explaining the Intelligence Bureau's position on indigenous communism to Menon, Sanjeevi relayed, he had been interrupted repeatedly by an exercised Menon who alleged that the DIB was intercepting and opening his mail.[65] Responding to evidence offered by Sanjeevi of atrocities committed by Indian communists, Menon supposedly retorted, ' ... that it was I [Sanjeevi] who was murdering Communists'.[66] A furious Patel complained to Nehru that in challenging government policy, and maligning the Intelligence Bureau, Menon had grossly exceeded his authority.[67] Nehru agreed that Menon's behaviour had been 'totally inexcusable'. The high commissioner received a stiff reprimand from the prime minister for suggesting that the Indian government 'tolerate' a 'virulent and violent' campaign of murder and criminality waged by the country's communists.[68] Menon subsequently apologised to Patel for slandering the Intelligence Bureau and Home Ministry and the row blew over.[69]

The persistence of a strong mutual enmity between Menon and the IB was all too apparent, however, in a series of private and exculpatory letters that the high commissioner sent to Nehru. Pulling no punches, Menon accused Sanjeevi of being 'an agent provocateur' whose purported attempt to smear his name ought to be considered, 'not even fair game in Intelligence work, unless it is intelligence as applied to enemy nationals when at war'. Denying that he had any particular concern for the plight of India's communists, Menon added that, nevertheless, he was uneasy at 'the imprisonment of people [in India] on the basis of secret service information'. During his interview with Sanjeevi, Menon conceded, he had said, 'that police reports on political opinions made, as they must be, by policemen who knew little about these affairs, placed people at the mercy of the police and the State would become a police state ... '.[70] Menon remained bitter that he had, in his estimation, been the unwitting victim of a ploy orchestrated between MI5 and the Intelligence Bureau to blot his copybook with Nehru. Whether MI5 and Sanjeevi had colluded to undermine Menon remains uncertain. Any such operation certainly proved ineffectual. Writing to Menon, in March 1949, Nehru made clear where his principal loyalty lay. Characterising Patel as 'nervous' and unduly sensitive to criticism after the censure he had received following Mohandas Gandhi's assassination in January 1948, Nehru reassured Menon that, 'I think

I have a fairly full realization of the pinpricks and other difficulties you have to contend against. I know that there is a small group bent on maligning you and on pushing you out of India House. This is not only irritating to you, but at least as much to me.'[71]

Nehru's expressions of faith in Menon did not stop MI5 from exploring ways to cut the high commissioner's tenure in London short. In May 1949, having reviewed Menon's case file, Guy Liddell's conviction hardened that the time had come to act decisively against the Indian diplomat.[72] Since 1947, Menon had troubled MI5 by, amongst other things, surreptitiously supporting the India League's ongoing anti-colonial activities.[73] Of more concern to MI5, however, was Menon's long-term affair with Bridget Tunnard, an India League secretary connected to the CPGB. In Liddell's judgement, Menon's relationship with Tunnard guaranteed, 'that anything of interest that MENON hears about will reach the Communist Party through her'. With MI5 having categorised India's high commissioner as a serious security risk, Liddell questioned whether, 'if it were at all possible, it would be better to cut our losses and get rid of MENON'.[74] In taking such action, MI5 felt confident that they could rely on India's Intelligence Bureau to, 'try and get some ammunition for us to get MENON'.[75] Likewise, while senior MI5 officers, including Vickery and Dick White, ruled out the possibility of conducting a formally sanctioned joint operation with the IB against Menon, the Security Service did point their Indian colleagues towards a firm of private detectives who began searching for evidence of illegality and impropriety in Menon's private life.[76] Other MI5 officers saw the aggressive targeting of Menon as counterproductive . Pushing Menon out of India House, some in the Security Service contended, risked, 'driv[ing] him back into the Communist fold carrying with him Commonwealth Defence secrets which he must have acquired as Nehru's right-hand man at the Commonwealth Prime Ministers' Conferences'.[77] Sillitoe found Liddell's argument the more persuasive. While Menon may have distanced himself from British communists since becoming high commissioner, MI5's Director-General conceded, he remained 'at least' a fellow traveller, and as such, a considerable threat to Commonwealth security.[78] In July that year, when briefing a closed session of the JIC on security in the Dominions, Liddell confirmed to fellow members of the British intelligence community, 'that we [MI5] were doing what we could to get rid of Krishna MENON'.[79]

Pushing Regime Change

In March 1950, British security concerns surrounding Menon became public when the London *Daily Graphic* broke a story that communists were on the payroll of India House. 'M.I.5 are concerned', the *Graphic* trumpeted, 'at [the] possible leakage of Imperial defence secrets in London through Communist

64 SPYING IN SOUTH ASIA

penetration of the offices of the High Commissioner for India'.[80] Fearful of the political fallout, both at home and abroad, that would follow on from India House's exposure as a nest of communist subversion, Whitehall, nevertheless, dithered over how to respond. It was not until early 1951, with the whiff of the treachery of British diplomats Guy Burgess and Donald Maclean hanging in the air, and with the CRO under new leadership, that a decision was made to tackle the security problem at India House head-on.[81] On 17 April 1951, Patrick Gordon Walker, who had replaced Noel-Baker as Secretary of State for Commonwealth Relations, met with Sir Percy Sillitoe at the CRO. Sillitoe brought an MI5 dossier to the meeting that documented Krishna Menon's contacts with British communists stretching back to 1936. The dossier acknowledged that Menon had never been a member of the CPGB. It made much, nonetheless, of his friendships with leading British communists.[82] Furthermore, evidence which suggested that Menon had broken with the CPGB after becoming Indian high commissioner was downplayed by MI5. Gordon Walker displayed less interest in Menon's past, however, than in the fourteen 'communists and fellow-travellers' that Sillitoe listed as working for India House, one of whom, a certain P. N. Haksar, headed its external affairs department.[83] Haksar had been a communist in his youth. In common with many Indian, and British, inter-war, left-wing activists, he had turned away from communism during the Second World War. To MI5, the *bona fides* of Haksar's political evolution remained suspect and the Security Service laid a heavy emphasis on his former flirtation with Marxism.[84]

Of even more concern to MI5 than Haksar, was Patsy Pillay. Married to a South African Indian, Pillay and her husband had been members of the South African Communist Party. They joined the Brondsbury branch of the CPGB on their arrival in Britain, in January 1949. 'Much to the delight of King Street', one MI5 officer observed, Pillay had gone on to secure a job in Menon's private office.[85] There was 'no doubt', in MI5's opinion, that the CPGB would exploit Pillay's access to classified information passing through India House, 'when it suited them.' Sillitoe informed Gordon Walker that MI5 had cautioned India's Intelligence Bureau that a communist cell was operating inside India House on three separate occasions, in December 1948, July 1949, and December 1950. The Indian government had passed the warnings on to Menon and emphasised the security risks involved in retaining communists on his staff. It appeared, Sillitoe added, that Menon had felt unable, or was simply unwilling, to purge the Indian high commission of communists. 'Taking everything into account', Sillitoe advised Gordon Walker, 'Menon and the offices of the Indian High Commission represent a security risk.'[86] Sillitoe left the CRO 'entirely convinced' that Gordon Walker had accepted that the security case against Menon was compelling. The Secretary of State, MI5's Director-General noted, now regarded India's high commissioner 'as a serious menace to security' and wanted 'to get rid of MENON'.[87] Gordon Walker had clashed repeatedly with

Menon after taking charge at the CRO and their mutual antipathy undoubtedly encouraged the British minister to favour Menon's removal. At one stage, Menon's 'bitter tirades of personal abuse' and 'unprovoked attacks' on Gordon Walker prompted the CRO to complain to the Indian government at their high commissioner's conduct.[88] Common gossip related to Menon's combustible personality and lurid rumours surrounding his personal life that circulated amongst the corridors of Whitehall meant that he was neither liked nor trusted by British officials, and only marginally more popular back in New Delhi.[89] As Sillitoe was well aware, many people in India shared MI5's assessment that Menon was 'a first class intriguer' with 'a bad moral record' and, as such, would be content to see the back of him.[90]

On 1 May, Sillitoe and Gordon Walker met again to discuss the practicalities of extricating Menon from India House. The option most favoured was to make a direct appeal to Nehru for Menon's removal. Three days later, Sillitoe called at 10 Downing Street to update Attlee on the Menon situation, and to lay the groundwork for an approach to India's prime minister. Attlee had clashed with Menon as far back as 1928, when the future British premier had sat on the Simon Commission. In 1940, Attlee had been instrumental in Menon's expulsion from the Labour Party.[91] In contrast, having previously been suspicious of the Security Service, Attlee had grown to hold both Sillitoe, and MI5, in high regard.[92] Menon's bulky MI5 file impressed Attlee. 'The Prime Minister was very interested in what I had to say', Sillitoe recorded after their meeting, 'especially with regard to the Communists and Fellow Travellers on Menon's staff'.[93] In the past, Menon's 'intimate' relationship with Nehru had dissuaded the British from airing their concerns over India House in New Delhi.[94] Denouncing a senior Indian official, it was felt, and more so, Menon, might be interpreted by Nehru as 'a direct criticism of his own judgement', and, 'have the effect of irritating him and inviting him to take an entrenched position'.[95] Moreover, MI5 was conscious that as a consequence of Nehru's personal experience as a political agitator who had been branded a communist by the colonial state, the Indian leader held a 'critical view' of intelligence professionals in general, and British intelligence officers, in particular.[96] Tellingly, when it came to Menon, although perturbed by the Indian high commissioner's communist connections, Sanjeevi's successor, B. N. Mullik, was happy for MI5 to tackle a thorny security question that threatened to prove politically toxic.[97]

Before deciding whether to recommend a British approach to Nehru, Gordon Walker took the precaution of consulting Sir Archibald Nye in New Delhi.[98] To bring Nye up to speed on Menon, Sillitoe arranged for him to receive a briefing from Eric Kitchen, who had taken over from Bill U'ren as MI5's Indian SLO, in June 1950.[99] Nye's advice, which Gordon Walker accepted, was not to approach Nehru on such a sensitive matter, and instead, to raise the issue of India House's vulnerability to communist subversion with

India's Minister for Home Affairs, Rajaji Rajagopalachari.[100] On 12 June, Nye secured an interview Rajagopalachari. Having informed the Indian minister that several of Menon's staff had connections to the CPGB, Nye suggested that, henceforth, the British government would prefer to channel sensitive information to New Delhi directly through the British high commission, and bypass India House. To Nye's disappointment, Rajagopalachari sidestepped his proposal, and merely asked that MI5 forward the names of communists working for Menon to Mullik.[101] News of Nye's encounter with Rajagopalachari soon reached Menon. Writing angrily to Nehru, Menon rubbished the charge that India House was susceptible to communist subversion. The Attlee government's scurrilous accusation, Menon raged, merely reflected its petty frustration that since 1947 India had proved willing and able to exercise autonomy in the conduct of its international affairs.[102]

Discounting Menon's bluster, MI5 took heart from signs that the timing of Nye's intervention had coincided with a groundswell of Indian dissatisfaction over Menon's performance in London. A decision that Menon took to bypass formal channels and purchase jeeps for India's army from European suppliers backfired spectacularly. When delivered, the vehicles were declared unusable. India's press accused Menon of wasting £3 million, while pocketing a sizable commission on the jeep deal for himself.[103] In July 1951, with Menon fighting for his political life, Alex Kellar, of MI5's Overseas (E) branch, reflected sanguinely that, 'Something may come of this [Nye's] approach. Nehru, although so unpredictable, may in any event feel, and for other reasons, that a change in High commissioner in London is desirable ... '.[104] Kellar's optimism appeared well founded. Cabling London on 8 November, Nye confirmed that a well-placed source, 'under an oath of secrecy', had confided in him that Menon's tenure as high commissioner might be about to end.[105] Nye's source was Mountbatten, who had become close to Nehru during his stint as India's last Viceroy. No doubt in collusion with Whitehall, and having obtained Rajagopalachari's prior consent, Mountbatten had written privately to Nehru, on 21 September, and urged him to sack Menon. Skirting around the security issue, Mountbatten instead used the pretext of Menon's failing health to press for his removal. Menon had a long history of physical and psychological infirmity. Following the death of his father in 1935, and the collapse of a long-term relationship, Menon had suffered a nervous breakdown and been hospitalised.[106] During the course of his rehabilitation, Menon became dependent on luminal, a barbiturate based sedative, the side-effects of which included confusion, loss of consciousness, and paranoia.[107] After he had appeared incoherent in public on several occasions in early 1951, stories began circulating that Menon had contracted tuberculosis, had a heart condition, was addicted to drugs, and had experienced a second nervous breakdown.[108] By, in Nye's words, 'not telling the truth, the whole truth and nothing but the truth', Mountbatten furnished Nehru with a plausible, and politically acceptable, excuse to terminate Menon's service as India's high commissioner.[109]

Facing pressure in India to recall Menon, in September 1951, Nehru dispatched his personal assistant, Mac Mathai, to London, to persuade Menon to take an extended leave of absence. On reaching India House, Mathai found Menon to be, 'terribly under the influence of drugs ... an ill man ... almost mad'.[110] Ignoring Mathai's plea to stand down on the grounds of ill health, Menon sent Nehru a raft of medical certificates attesting to his excellent physical and mental condition and, at one point, somewhat incongruously, threatened suicide were he to be forced from office.[111] Commenting on the unfolding drama, Nye observed to the CRO that, 'Krishna Menon seems to have dug his toes in and is fighting a strong rear-guard action to remain in his present job. I am told that Nehru is rather disgusted with Menon's attitude.'[112] Nehru was unwilling, nevertheless, to risk a public schism with Menon, particularly with India's first general election looming. Equally, with the Conservative Party having been returned to office that October, Nehru worried that sacking Menon would be interpreted as a sop to Churchill's government.[113] Consequently, the Indian premier resigned himself to a gradual transition of power at India House. With Menon's term as high commissioner due to expire early the following year, Nye was equally pragmatic. The prudent course, he suggested to London, was now to sit out Menon's final months in office, rather than risk unnecessarily ruffling Indian feathers.[114] The CRO was less eager to let the matter of Menon drop. In the form of Hastings Ismay, the CRO had a new Secretary of State who maintained that there was, 'no shadow of doubt that that K[rishna] M[enon]'s removal would be in the best interests of both England and India'.[115] Ultimately, with Nehru preoccupied by pressing domestic issues in the first half of 1952, time ran out on the CRO, and thoughts of a further approach to New Delhi in respect of Menon were shelved.

At the same time, the Security Service's began to fret that rather than return to New Delhi on leaving India House, or accepting another overseas posting, Menon might remain in London in a private capacity. Such an unwelcome development, MI5 worried, could see Menon, ' ... openly assume control of the India League and probably resume his King Street association and friendships'. Given his 'highly complex and unscrupulous character', MI5 officers speculated that, as a free agent, Menon would be tempted to, 'pass information acquired during his period in office to the Communists'.[116] British unease grew during the spring of 1952 after Menon rejected Nehru's offer of a seat in his cabinet, the Vice-Chancellorship of Delhi University, and the Indian Embassy in Moscow.[117] To MI5's chagrin, Menon seemed notably reluctant to leave Britain's shores. Menon's successor arrived in London in July. An efficient, if staid administrator, Bal Gangadhar Kher, was a former Governor of Bombay, who had not stepped foot in United Kingdom for forty years. Even so, and as

The Times pointedly observed, 'among officials in London his [Kher's] appointment is evidently regarded as most welcome'.[118] Substantiating MI5's suspicion that he would not 'sit quiet', Menon remained in London following Kher's arrival, and announced plans to reconstitute the India League.[119] By appearing uninvited at diplomatic receptions, and encouraging the impression that he continued to speak for Nehru, Menon acted as 'a constant thorn in the flesh of his successor'.[120] Almost as keen as the British to find him an alternative form of employment, Nehru finally cajoled Menon into joining the Indian delegation at the United Nations General Assembly in New York.[121] In the autumn of 1952, to MI5's considerable relief, Krishna Menon left Britain with a political whimper, rather than a diplomatic bang.

Éminence grise

On departing from the UK, Menon travelled directly to New York, where he assumed leadership of India's UN delegation. Acting as a self-appointed international mediator during the Korea, Indochina, Suez, and Taiwan Straits crises in the early 1950s, Menon achieved global renown as a diplomatic troubleshooter, or, as the then British foreign secretary, Harold Macmillan, put it, 'Nehru's Harry Hopkins'.[122] In February 1956, dismissing misgivings voiced by some his senior ministers, Nehru rewarded Menon's efforts by shoehorning him into the Indian cabinet as minister without portfolio. Elected to the *Lok Sabha*, the lower house of India's parliament, for the constituency of north Bombay the following year, in April 1957 Menon was promoted again, leapfrogging more established cabinet colleagues to become India's defence minister. Along the way, Menon's intellectual arrogance, duplicity, and cynical abuse of his relationship with Nehru, antagonised a sizable cross-section of Indian political opinion. Menon's militant socialism, fervent anti-colonialism, and willingness to engage with Soviet and Chinese Communists, induced a similar reaction amongst British and American policymakers and their political constituencies. One study of Indo-American relations undertaken in the United States at the time, underlined Menon's status as a pariah. A series of interviews conducted with prominent American academics, journalists, businessmen, and government officials, revealed the existence of a deep-seated and almost universal antipathy to Menon. Respondents labelled the Indian statesman variously as, 'a devil incarnate', 'a Machiavelli with a swelled head', and 'a pro-Communist anti-American blackmail agent'.[123]

Personality traits aside, Menon's relations with British and American officials continued to be coloured by a common perception that he leaned towards Moscow. Still, in the absence of a smoking gun implicating Menon in espionage activities, the CRO, and their colleagues at the British Foreign Office (FO), broadly discounted the possibility that Menon was an active Soviet agent.[124]

The same could not be said on the other side of Atlantic. The British may have concluded that Menon was not a communist stooge but, as Whitehall acknowledged, 'it was undoubtedly a fact, and a relevant one, that many high-ranking Americans did hold this view'.[125] President Eisenhower's Secretary of State, John Foster Dulles, counted as a prominent 'Menophobe'. As early as January 1947, when serving as a Republican Party advisor to America's UN delegation, Dulles caused a stir by publicly implying that Nehru's interim Indian government was under communist influence. Hauled into the State department to explain his indiscretion, a contrite Dulles insisted that he had not meant to suggest that India was a Soviet pawn. Rather, his analysis of Indian politics was based upon observations of India's UN delegation, and, more especially, Krishna Menon, whom Dulles described as a 'confirmed Marxian' and a disciple of Soviet foreign minister, Vyacheslav Molotov.[126]

The Truman administration had taken little interest in Menon.[127] In contrast, under the Eisenhower government, America's distaste for Menon intensified dramatically. Fed details of his links to British communists by MI5, and bitterly critical of his unsolicited intercessions into East-West disputes, Eisenhower's administration formed a bad impression of Menon.[128] In John Foster Dulles' moralistic vision of a binary Cold War world, where good battled evil, Menon was branded as, 'a pretty bad fellow' and a 'troublemaker'.[129] In turn, Menon bridled at Dulles' criticism of Indian non-alignment, promotion of a US-Pakistani alliance, and tolerance of Portuguese colonialism.[130] With a 'formidable incompatibility of temperament', adding spice to their political differences, Dulles and Menon clashed repeatedly in the 1950s.[131] In July 1955, in the aftermath of the first Taiwan straits crisis, one typically prickly exchange saw Dulles excoriate Menon for acting as a communist Chinese lackey. In response, Menon made it widely known that he regarded Dulles as the principal obstacle to peace and stability in Asia. Rather than engage meaningfully with the substantive international issues of the day, contemporary observes noted that 'a great part' of the diplomatic interplay between Dulles and Menon was invariably, 'taken up with the process of getting under each other's skins'.[132]

In April 1957, to Washington's alarm, the *New York Times* opined that Nehru's 'faintly satanic confidante' appeared set fair to exert a growing and malevolent influence over India's foreign policy.[133] Uncomfortably for the Eisenhower administration, Menon's rise to political prominence in the second half of the 1950s coincided with a realisation on the part of the United States that India's burgeoning population, untapped economic resources, latent military power, and democratic credentials represented a valuable Cold War prize. In January 1961, John F. Kennedy's arrival in the White House added additional impetus to the reorientation in American thinking towards India that had begun under Eisenhower.[134] The Kennedy administration, however, soon found its relationship with India, and Krishna Menon, under strain. Kennedy was disappointed to find Nehru listless and disengaged when they met in Washington, in November, and failed to establish a rapport with the ageing Indian premier.[135] Menon too, quickly found himself on the wrong side of the New Frontier after launching barbed attacks on Kennedy's handling of a range of foreign policy issues, from the Congo crisis to Kashmir. Although irked by Menon's personal invective, Kennedy's overriding concern was that it risked poisoning American public opinion and would erode congressional support for the appropriation of much-needed US economic aid to India.[136] In December 1961, Kennedy's broader concern proved prescient, although, on this occasion, Krishna Menon was, it appeared, unjustly blamed for undermining bilateral relations. Stung by criticism that his government had failed to prevent China annexing Indian territory on the nation's northern border, Nehru authorised the use of military force to end Portugal's 460-year presence in the enclaves of Goa, Daman, and Diu, on India's Western coast. The Indian press characterised the Goa 'police action' as 'Krishna Menon's War', and Anglo-American officials speculated whether India's defence minister had, in fact, orchestrated the military operation.[137] Britain's chief of defence staff, Lord Mountbatten, certainly felt so, observing bitterly that, 'I will never believe he [Nehru] cooked [it] up.'[138] With a large Goan community resident in his north Bombay parliamentary constituency, America's press were quick to point out that Krishna Menon had a strong political interest in giving the Portuguese a bloody nose.[139] Analysts inside the CIA concluded otherwise. While many in Washington were only too willing to point a finger of blame at Menon, Langley's judgement was that Nehru had pulled the strings over Goa and allowed his defence minister to be served up to the international community as a convenient 'whipping boy'.[140]

Within India, perceptions of the CIA's interest in Menon extended beyond political analysis and into the realms of covert action. While preparing to launch his campaign for parliament in 1957, Menon had been warned by Nehru that internal and external forces were determined to compromise his candidacy. The Indian premier claimed that both the Catholic Church in India, and the Democratic Research Service, an anti-communist propaganda organisation founded by Minoo Masani, who turned to the right politically in the 1940s, were plotting to 'work against' Menon's election. The Democratic Research Service, along with the Indian Congress for Cultural Freedom, where Masani was president, served as 'front groups' for clandestine American propaganda activities. Both received funding, if not direct political direction, from the CIA. By stating that 'foreign agencies will also be indirectly involved' in attempting to discredit Menon in Bombay, Nehru was alluding to Langley's active involvement in India's internal politics.[141] Communist presses in the subcontinent, with the benefit of generous financial support from Moscow, picked up and promoted a narrative that American intelligence agencies had ruthlessly targeted Menon in a protracted and pernicious campaign of disinformation. 'The CIA methodically went about from one election to another in preparing the ground to remove Menon from the political scene', an American official who defected to the Soviet Union later claimed. 'The interference of the United States in the elections in northern Bombay, where Krishna Menon was a candidate, were crude and brutal.'[142] According to one Indian communist publication, Robert Boies, the US consul in Bombay, made a habit of touring the city in his official car and handing out wads of cash to returning officers in a bid to inflate the votes of Menon's political opponents.[143]

Nehru was scornful of the 'devious methods' employed by supposedly unscrupulous political enemies of Menon. Shortly before the Goa crisis broke, the Executive Committee of the Bombay Pradesh Youth Congress passed a resolution opposing Menon's candidature in Bombay. The resolution stated that, 'in the case of Shri Krishna Menon, many of us feel that his behaviour on several questions about the Communist countries and specially the Chinese aggression and his association with Communists, ex-Communists and fellow travellers in India has made him suspect in the eyes of youth and other citizens of India'. 'If Shri Menon is not pro-Communist', another Menon critic challenged Nehru, 'one wonders why the Communists of India are pro-Menon ... It is well-known that the Communists of India do not support anyone unless their purpose is served in one way of the other.' Nehru responded to such *ad hominem* attacks by doubling down and declaring that he would support Menon, 'all the more'. 'It seems to me that most of the people who are opposing him [Menon]', the Indian prime minister informed one detractor, 'have either no understanding of our policy or deliberately do not like it'.[144]

Nehru's unwavering support for Menon unnerved British and American officials who feared that, either by default or design, a door was being left open for Krishna Menon to step into his mentor's shoes. Under the headline 'Who's Next', in the summer of 1962, *Time* magazine ran a rule over Nehru's likely successors as prime minister. Speculating that the Congress Party favoured a 'straw man' for the top job, *Time* installed India's 'bland' home minister, Lal Bahadur Shastri as the frontrunner to become India's next leader. Morarji Desai from the conservative wing of the Congress Party, and the Socialist leader, Jayaprakash Narayan, were also mentioned as potential prime ministers in waiting. According to *Time*, however, Nehru's preferred candidate was Krishna Menon.[145] Intriguingly, as the doyen of Congress' left-wing, Menon was also Moscow's choice to replace Nehru. In May 1962, in a singularly ineffective covert operation, the Soviet presidium, presumably without Menon's knowledge, authorised the KGB residency in New Delhi to bankroll a pro-Menon leadership drive.[146] Menon's appearance as a runner in the premiership unnerved the Kennedy administration. Robert Komer, who covered the India brief in the White House, cautioned his boss, and Kennedy's national security advisor, McGeorge Bundy: 'If there's even a one in five chance [of Menon seizing power], we ought to run plenty scared.'[147]

The possibility that Menon might seize power through unconstitutional means also entered the minds of Western officials.[148] Menon's political rivals in India had repeatedly assured the British that he retained the capacity to launch a coup d'état. In February 1962, Vijaya Lakshmi Pandit informed Sir David Eccles, Britain's minister of education, that, 'Krishna Menon had threatened the Prime Minister with a military coup if Mr. Nehru refused to give the order to invade [Goa].' Her brother, Pandit added, had refused to challenge Menon at the time, judging that his protégé's growing power over India's defence establishment made him, 'capable, in all senses of the word', of following through on his threat. Gore-Booth dismissed Pandit's allegation as overblown. Menon's political ambition was indeed palpable, the British high commissioner acknowledged, but 'he must be aware of his own unpopularity . . . with a considerable proportion of the Army, and in political circles, which must make him doubt whether a coup would be successful'. In sum, it appeared to the British that Menon was 'highly unlikely' to consider 'a naked seizure of power', not least because with the outcome so uncertain, 'Mr. Menon is too clever to run this kind of risk.'[149] Nonetheless, rumours that Menon was busy consolidating his grip over India's armed forces in preparation for 'a forcible bid for power', continued to circulate in New Delhi throughout the summer of 1962.[150]

In the autumn of that year, diplomatic gossip was overtaken by a dramatic and unexpected turn of events. On 20 October, the catalyst for Krishna Menon's political downfall appeared when a long simmering border dispute between India and the PRC erupted into open conflict. Within a week, Indian forces had been routed by the People's Liberation Army who occupied large swathes of northern India. With the nation facing an ignominious defeat, on 26 October, a shell-shocked Nehru qualified his commitment to non-alignment, and made an unprecedented appeal for international 'sympathy and support'.[151] Determined to leverage India's desperate need for military assistance to bring about a 'closer understanding' between India and the West, American officials were also inclined, 'to have decently in mind the pounding we have been taking from Krishna Menon'.[152] On 23 October, the US ambassador in New Delhi, John Kenneth Galbraith, candidly informed India's foreign secretary, M. J. Desai, that Krishna Menon's retention of the defence portfolio represented one of the 'more serious problems' standing in the way of US military aid to India.[153] Two days later, on 25 October, Galbraith sent a private backchannel message to Kennedy through his embassy's CIA station in which he reiterated the idea of linking the provision of American military support to Menon's, 'effective elimination from [the Indian] Defense-UN scene'.[154] The next morning, when Kennedy met with India's ambassador in Washington, B. K. Nehru, the President remarked pointedly that, 'We don't want to, in any way . . . to have Krishna enter into this . . . he is a disaster and makes the thing much more complicated. Your judgment is that he will continue, however, as defense minister?'[155] Although emphasising, 'the importance of avoiding the slightest appearance of U.S. initiative and responsibility in removing Menon', the White House made it known to Galbraith that in dealing with the Menon 'problem' it was, 'leaving [the] next steps up to you'.[156]

Galbraith responded by hatching a plan with Carl Kaysen, Kennedy's deputy national security advisor, to co-opt British support for a covert scheme designed to discredit Menon. Specifically, it was suggested to the British government that stories could be planted in European newspapers by intelligence and propaganda agencies that stressed Menon's culpability for India's humiliation at the hands of the Chinese. While agreeing that Menon was 'somewhat ill in mind', the British rejected the American approach.[157] Attacking Menon in the Western press, Britain's ambassador in Washington, David Ormsby Gore, advised Kaysen, was 'more likely to save Menon than send him under'.[158] Ultimately, Krishna Menon's fate was sealed not by clandestine intrigues hatched in Washington or London, but by Indian public opinion. Exposed to charges that his mismanagement of the defence portfolio had left India at the mercy of the perfidious Chinese, by the end of October 1962 Indians were clamouring for Menon's head.[159] His compatriots took to silencing Menon, the British noted, by sabotaging his microphone at open-air meetings.[160] After a last ditch bid by Nehru to save his friend's political career floundered, Menon resigned from the Indian cabinet on 7 November 1962.[161]

India's Rasputin?

British and American policymakers never reaped the political dividend of closer relations with India that they anticipated would follow once Krishna Menon's purportedly Machiavellian hold over Nehru had been severed. After a brief honeymoon period between late 1962 and early 1963, when Britain and the United States were lauded in New Delhi for furnishing India with diplomatic and military support against the Chinese, Western relations with Nehru's government came under renewed strain. By the middle of 1963, an embittered Nehru had grown to resent British and American attempts to extract a political *quid pro quo* from his government in return for continued military assistance. Determined to preserve the appearance, if not the substance, of Indian non-alignment, Nehru fought an acrimonious, and ultimately successful, rear-guard action against British and American efforts to negotiate an air defence pact with India.[162] Similarly, having long painted Menon as a major barrier to an improvement in Indo-Pakistani relations, Britain and the United States found it no easier to facilitate progress towards a Kashmir settlement in his absence, despite cajoling India and Pakistan to undertake six rounds of bilateral talks.[163] Indeed, by the end of 1963, frustrated at its inability to impose external solutions on complex regional problems, and with a new president in the White House whose focus was increasingly drawn to events elsewhere in Asia, India slipped down the list of Washington's global priorities. In the absence of American support, the British government found its voice on the Indian subcontinent increasingly marginalised.

All too often in the early Cold War period, officials in London and Washington attributed the tensions that bedevilled their interaction with India to Krishna Menon's malevolence. The inconvenient truth was that India, Britain, and the United States, held different, and often incompatible perspectives, on how to tackle the Cold War challenges that confronted the subcontinent. Invariably, each side preferred to demonise the baleful actions of individual 'foreign devils' rather than face up to an uncomfortable reality. Looking back on his tumultuous political career, Krishna Menon asserted that he had been neither, 'a buffoon nor a Rasputin'.[164] The historical record suggests that he had a point. Krishna Menon was, if anything, more Western folly, than communist instrument or evil Indian genius. Over the course of several decades, and in the guises of nationalist activist, Indian diplomat, international mediator and, latterly, Indian cabinet minister, Menon was cast as a communist fellow-traveller in hoc to Moscow and Beijing.[165] The British Security Service never wavered in its conviction that, 'the negative state of our information and the inference that Menon has dropped his communist contacts does not necessarily mean that the danger of his abusing his potential position . . . can on that account be ignored'.[166] Doubts planted by MI5 in the minds of British policymakers regarding Menon's political loyalties encouraged Whitehall to view India's habitual challenges to Western Cold War orthodoxy in terms of the nefarious influence of one man. In June 1962, the then Secretary of State for Commonwealth Relations, Duncan Sandys, was to be found carping that Indian diplomacy was hamstrung by 'Mr. Krishna Menon and the pro-Russian faction' in Nehru's cabinet.[167,168]

The absence of any evidence to substantiate charges that Menon colluded with Communist governments also failed to dent the conviction of America's policymakers and intelligence agencies that Menon was a security threat. Long after he had ceased to be an Indian minister, the CIA inserted references to the 'acid mouthed' Menon in the President's Daily Brief (PDB), the top-secret summary of intelligence delivered by the Agency each morning to the Oval Office. Menon, one PDB from March 1967 stated, remained 'one of the world's bitterest baiters of the US'.[169] In reality, following the expansion of Soviet intelligence operations in India in the early 1960s, KGB attempts to cultivate Menon met with a conspicuous lack of success. No proof has yet emerged that links Menon with Soviet intelligence services prior to the 1962. Subsequent active measures undertaken by the KGB in India did seek to promote Menon's political fortunes and, on one occasion, in 1967, encompassed the covert funding of his election expenses. However, the KGB were simultaneously attempting to advance the interests of seemingly every significant left-of-centre figure in India's ruling Congress Party including, amongst others, Gulzarilal Nanda, Lal Bahadur Shastri, and Indira Gandhi herself. If anything, the absence of material linking Menon to the KGB tends to confirm his long-standing ambivalence towards communism.[170]

Prior to 1947, Britain's intelligence services were overly influenced by Krishna Menon's willingness to collaborate with the CPGB in pursuit of Indian self-government. Following India's independence, British and American intelligence agencies proved unduly dismissive of signs that Menon had severed connections with former communist collaborators. In misinterpreting and exaggerating the security case against Menon, London and Washington ran excessive risks in their relationships with India. To Indian diplomats, their Western colleague's antipathy to Menon often appeared deeply irrational and akin to a 'neurosis requiring psychiatric treatment'.[171] Perhaps fittingly, neither Britain nor the United States was ultimately responsible for Krishna Menon's political Waterloo. Paradoxically, that distinction, after Menon was held culpable for India's ignominious defeat in the Sino-Indian war of 1962, fell to, of all people, Mao Zedong, and the Chinese Communist Party.

4

Quiet Americans: The CIA and the Onset of the Cold War in South Asia

Howard Imbrey's career as a CIA field officer began in India. After enlisting in the United States Army during the Second World War, Imbrey was posted to South Asia. Talent-spotted by the OSS, Imbrey ended the war running intelligence operations out of India, Ceylon, and Burma. In 1948, he was hired by the recently inaugurated CIA. Marked down for service in India on account of his language competencies and experience in the subcontinent, in December that year, Imbrey arrived in Bombay.[1] He was amongst the first CIA officers to embark upon a well-established path to advancement within the Agency's Directorate of Operations, or clandestine service. Some thirty years later, newly minted CIA officers assigned to the Agency's Near East Division continued to be dispatched to India 'on probation'. In the late 1970s, having been told that his first operational assignment would be in Madras, in southern India, one fledgling CIA officer remembered being informed by superiors that, 'I needed a tour in one of its [the Agency's] true shit holes to see if I could make it as a case officer.' At that time, the CIA rotated its Arabic-speaking recruits through Sana, in north Yemen. The remainder of the Near East Division's annual intake was sent to India, or what became known as 'the night soil circuit'. The Agency's decision to road test recruits in the subcontinent was driven by a belief that, 'India was better than most places to get your feet wet in operations.' As an early, and outspoken advocate of non-alignment, India hosted diplomatic and military missions from every corner of the world. From Langley's perspective, the presence in India of thousands of Eastern bloc officials, military officers, technicians, and journalists, presented an alluring intelligence target. Moreover, India's Intelligence Bureau was regarded as a worthy adversary against whom CIA officers could hone their tradecraft. The IB's ubiquitous counter-surveillance activity ensured that for American intelligence officers, 'short of Moscow or Peking, India was one of the toughest operating environments in the world'.[2]

Back in the 1940s, the resumption of Howard Imbrey's intelligence career, nominally as the US Vice Consul in Bombay, but, in actuality, as the head of the local CIA station, was occasioned by an unfortunate event. Imbrey's predecessor in Bombay was Lennox Fogg. The Fogg family were prominent in Boston society and were the benefactors of Harvard University's Fogg

QUIET AMERICANS 77

Museum. Lennox's career in intelligence was, however, complicated by his alcoholism. Following one particularly inebriate episode, Fogg became convinced that he had acquired the ability to fly and, having resolved to test his new powers from the second-floor window of his lodgings, was returned to reality with a bang. While Fogg survived, his career as a CIA officer in India did not. The State Department complained that Fogg's extracurricular exploits were attracting unwelcome attention from the Indian authorities, and he was recalled to the United States. With Fogg out of the picture, and with less interest in the potentialities of unpowered flight, Imbrey set about recruiting agents within India's military, police service, political parties, and labour unions. The CIA's priority was to acquire reliable information on the strength, disposition, and intentions of the Communist Party of India.[3] At that point, India's security and intelligence forces were battling to suppress a violent communist-led insurrection in Telangana, in the south of the country. With a global Cold War gathering momentum, American officials were hopeful that the threat posed by militant communism inside India would foster strategic cooperation between the two nations.

The CIA's early attempts to cultivate sources inside the Indian establishment met with mixed results. One senior Indian naval officer was targeted for recruitment after the Agency discovered that he had an interest in pornography. With the approval of Dick Klise, the CIA's principal officer, or station chief, in New Delhi, the Agency began supplying the Indian sailor with pornographic material. In return, Klise received copies of Indian military intelligence estimates that passed across the naval officer's desk. The arrangement functioned satisfactorily until Imbrey, on a visit to the Indian capital and accompanied by his wife, met with Klise, and his spouse, for dinner. On their way to a restaurant, the four Americans were accosted in the street by an Indian contact who, brandishing copies of several pornographic magazines, announced excitedly, 'Mr Klise, Mr Klise, I have some more for you.'[4] Unfortunate impromptu encounters aside, on Klise's watch the CIA in India built up a comprehensive network of local agents, or in the Agency's parlance, Controlled American Sources (CAS), across a wide spectrum of India's political, economic and security landscape. In doing so, the CIA benefited from the tacit support of numerous Indian legislators, policemen, labour leaders, journalists, and intellectuals, who saw varying levels of cooperation with the Agency as a useful insurance policy against the expansion of indigenous communism, outbreaks of communalism and, over time, the unwelcome attention of hostile neighbouring states.[5]

During the Second World War, the OSS was encouraged by the Roosevelt administration to keep a close watch on India. Mounting nationalist agitation, culminating in the Quit India campaign of 1942, led the OSS expand its footprint in the subcontinent with a view to safeguarding US interests in post-colonial South Asia.[6] In September 1942, in an effort to control OSS activity on

Indian soil, the British colonial authorities brokered an agreement with Washington. Under the terms of the agreement, American intelligence services were restricted to a liaison role, and prohibited from engaging in field operations.[7] Determined to override such constraints, the head of OSS, William Donovan, made it plain to his officers that, while the British may have tried to close the door on his organisation in India, he expected it to ignore an embargo on operations and to, 'come in through the transom'.[8] Donovan successfully sidestepped persistent British complaints that 'uncoordinated' OSS activity was 'detrimental' to the maintenance of colonial authority and had fostered a 'chaotic' intelligence environment in India.[9] Dismissive of 'increasing disquiet' voiced by British officials that the OSS was running agents and indulging in propaganda and psychological warfare in India, Donovan pressed ahead with building up his organisation's presence in the subcontinent. From its original office in New Delhi, the OSS eventually grew to encompass eleven Indian outstations.[10] By the end of 1943, the British had conceded defeat in their battle with Donovan, and effectively gave up trying to control OSS operations within their Indian empire.[11]

Once the war ended, and India secured independence, the CIA picked up where the OSS had left off. The Agency's assessment of the threat 'world communism' posed to India, and the urgency with which the United States should act to counter it, ran some way ahead of the State Department's own thinking. One CIA report, from September 1951, asserted that the Indian economy and bureaucracy were in such a parlous state that the country's communists might soon be able to 'seize control of the government'.[12] Having been supplied with transcripts by India's security services of interrogations conducted on local communist insurgents, the CIA concluded that external forces were fomenting unrest. 'Even the lowliest and most uneducated Communists', Agency analysts reasoned, 'display an intimate knowledge of Lenin, Stalin and Communist ideology. It is apparent that these . . . [insurgents] have not been led blindly by rabble-rousing Communists.'[13] Sherman Kent, Assistant Director of National Estimates at the CIA, subsequently recorded that the Operations Coordinating Board (OCB), which was established to oversee covert operations, became 'seriously disquieted, if not somewhat alarmed' by the deteriorating situation in India. The Board's anxiety was driven by a calculation that political and economic instability in India threatened to transform it from a 'friendly' into an 'unfriendly' state.[14] With the passing of Joseph Stalin in March 1953, and the emergence of a new Soviet leadership that identified value in cultivating India as a Cold War prize, American officials expressed apprehension that Moscow was now fishing in troubled India waters. 'The Kremlin today is using all the propaganda devices in its possession to make the Indians feel that we are their enemies; that we represent a new imperialism; that we intend to dominate their economy; that we are bent on involving the whole world, including India, in a new world war', a senior American diplomat observed the following year. 'We have ample reason to believe that domination of the Indian sub-continent is a part of the Soviets objective.'[15] The State Department came to share the CIA's anxiety at the threat that communism posed in India. Communist gains in Indian elections alarmed American diplomats, prompting one official to declare, 'There is no time to lose ... [conditions in India] are being successfully exploited by Communist agents ... [i]f South Asia is subverted it will be only a matter of time before all of the Asian land-mass and over a billion people will be under Communist domination, and our national security will face an unprecedented threat.'[16] The scene was set for the CIA to dramatically expand its role in India's intelligence Cold War.

Langley's New Best Friend: The CIA and Indian Intelligence

India's Intelligence Bureau saw considerable advantage in learning from and, on occasions, collaborating with, foreign intelligence services. Early in 1949, the DIB, Sanjeevi Pillai, accepted an invitation from Washington to visit the United States for talks with the Federal Bureau of Investigation (FBI) and the CIA. Prior to Sanjeevi's arrival in North America, Howard Donovan, Counsellor at the US Embassy in New Delhi, forwarded the State Department a biographical sketch of the Indian intelligence leader. Sanjeevi, Donovan noted, was 'a man of dignified appearance and bearing', spoke excellent English and, although a practising Hindu, was not a vegetarian. 'He never uses alcohol in any form ... and he does not smoke', the US official added. Sanjeevi's chief hobbies were gardening and astrology.[17] The latter pastime, one imagines, was more useful to Sanjeevi in his day job. In many ways, India's green-fingered spy chief was the antithesis of the stereotypical caricatures of rugged and swashbuckling Cold War intelligence officers that prevailed in the West. While Sanjeevi was certainly no James Bond or Jason Bourne, he did, in American eyes at least, have one important virtue. The DIB was, the US Embassy in Delhi reported, thought to be, 'very close to Prime Minister Jawaharlal Nehru'.[18] In fact, Sanjeevi was not nearly as intimate with the Indian premier as US officials believed. Revealingly, the DIB's visit to the United States saw him get on the wrong side of the Nehru family. India's ambassador in Washington, and Nehru's sister, Vijaya Lakshmi Pandit, took exception to the intelligence chief's failure to advise her of his presence in America, or to take Pandit fully into his confidence. On taking the matter up with her brother, an irritated Pandit was assured by Nehru that she had been 'perfectly justified' in protesting about Sanjeevi's behaviour. 'I was greatly annoyed myself', Nehru volunteered. 'As a matter of fact, I saw Sanjeevi before he went away and laid great stress on his contacting you and keeping in touch with you throughout his visit.'[19]

80 SPYING IN SOUTH ASIA

While in the United States, Sanjeevi had been instructed by India's Home Ministry to focus on studying the operations and methods of the Federal Bureau of Investigation.[20] Building external intelligence capacity was seen as a secondary concern next to developing India's internal security capabilities. Sanjeevi had formed a small overseas intelligence branch within the IB. Initially, two officers were detailed to work under diplomatic cover as First Secretaries in India's embassies in Paris and Bonn. Although not his main concern, the DIB hoped to glean useful information from the CIA on running foreign intelligence operations.[21] Ahead of Sanjeevi's arrival in Washington, Loy Henderson, America's ambassador in New Delhi, cautioned US intelligence officials that Sanjeevi's visit was likely to have 'wide ramifications in our over-all relations with India'.[22] American diplomats anticipated that the ongoing threat posed by militant communism in southern India would persuade Sanjeevi to solicit advice and support from experts in the United States. One of Henderson's deputies, J. Graham Parsons, confided to colleagues in the State Department that, 'We hope for a great deal as a result of his visit ... [Sanjeevi is] not only convinced of certain dangers which India faces but ... ha[s] a large measure of responsibility for meeting those dangers. In discharging that responsibility [he] may have increasingly to look beyond India's borders and seek to influence policy in regard to dangers from without.'[23] In Langley, the CIA made ready to school Sanjeevi on the insidious subversive threat posed by international communism.

Whatever the CIA plans, Sanjeevi's overriding objective was to draw upon the investigative expertise and counter-espionage experience of the FBI, and its enigmatic director, J. Edgar Hoover. The Indian intelligence leader confided to Henderson that he had 'been looking forward with particular enthusiasm to meeting and having a heart-to-heart with ... J. Edgar Hoover'. To Henderson's mortification, Sanjeevi subsequently confirmed that he had been left 'boiling with resentment' by the off-hand way that the imperious Hoover had treated him. Having been palmed off onto Hoover's deputies, and exposed to an FBI briefing that was 'hardly more enlightening than that given to a visiting high school class', the DIB griped that Hoover evidently felt he 'had little to gain by devoting any personal attention to me'. The 'deep-seated pique' that Hoover engendered in Sanjeevi was evident when the latter made it plain to a shocked Henderson that, 'if a liaison was contemplated [between US and Indian intelligence services] even remotely involving the F.B.I .... he [Sanjeevi] would not only advise against us making such a proposal but would personally oppose it if it were made'.[24] In contrast, the CIA went out of its way to court India's spy chief. Having been warmly welcomed, and lavishly entertained, by senior Agency figures, including Colonel Richard Stilwell, chief of the Agency's Far East division, Kermit "Kim" Roosevelt, shortly to achieve notoriety for his exploits in Iran, and Director of Central Intelligence, Roscoe Hillenkoetter, Sanjeevi came away from Washington with a notably positive impression of the Central Intelligence Agency.[25] Significantly, and to the CIA's satisfaction, the head of IB embraced the Agency's offer to explore 'the possibility of establishing an official liaison on Communist matters'.[26] Sanjeevi's experience in the United States was to cast a long shadow over Indo-US intelligence liaison and, more broadly, Washington's Cold War relationship with New Delhi. The DIB's visit to North America ensured that the CIA, and not, as Sanjeevi had originally intended, the FBI, became India's Cold War intelligence partner of choice.[27]

Winning Sanjeevi's confidence was seen as a significant coup by US officials. The DIB, it was noted, had come around to favour the easing of Indian restrictions on intelligence sharing arrangements with the United States and Great Britain that New Delhi had imposed as part its commitment to Cold War non-alignment. Specifically, Washington was optimistic that Sanjeevi would press to overturn a prohibition on Indian intelligence officers discussing indigenous communist activity with their British and American counterparts. Sanjeevi, American colleagues observed approvingly, was 'understood to have begun to insist that they [the IB] need the cooperation of other countries fighting Communism in making their own struggle more effective'.[28] In any case, Sanjeevi made it plain to Dick Klise that, 'regardless of the official attitude of his [India's] government, he would welcome the continuance of our unofficial contacts'. As a policeman, the DIB added, 'he frequently had to take independent action without the knowledge of his government, and ... he assumed that ... [CIA officers] also had a certain freedom of action. Klise was quick to confirm that this was indeed the case and, moreover, the Agency would be delighted to work closely with Sanjeevi, if necessary, without the approval of the Indian intelligence chief's superiors.[29]

Ugly Americans: Nehru and the CIA

Indian government officials did become aware of relationships forged between the Intelligence Bureau and its British and American counterparts. Nevertheless, Sanjeevi, and subsequently, B. N. Mullik, continued to work hard to downplay the significance of such links. Were Nehru to get wind of the scale of India's partnership with the CIA and MI5, B. N. Mullik once explained to a British intelligence officer, much of the liaison activity would have to be curtailed.[30] Mullik's caution was well founded. Nehru repeatedly counselled Indian officials to treat intelligence received from British and American sources with an abundance of caution, given the 'considerable interest in our internal politics' evident in London and Washington. 'I think our Intelligence ... should keep wide awake about these matters', the Indian premier advised his foreign secretary. 'We should avoid too close contacts with the Intelligence people of other Governments.'[31] Nehru reacted with irritation and exasperation whenever the extent of the Intelligence Bureau's dependency on Western training and support became apparent. In the mid-1950s, the Indian prime minister was stunned to learn that his intelligence officers were being sent to Australia for instruction. Noting caustically that, 'the general standard of efficiency of Australians ... has not been evident to me', Nehru wondered precisely how, in the intelligence sphere, 'the isolated position of Australia [was] conducive to this [transfer of] wider knowledge and efficiency'. To Nehru, the arrangement was symptomatic of muddled and hackneyed thinking. 'Our intelligence people', he fulminated, 'cannot get out of the habit of thinking of two or three countries in the Commonwealth, especially the UK, as well as the USA, for any kind of training'. Nehru was equally dumbfounded on discovering that Indian intelligence officers were not travelling to Moscow to learn the Russian language, but to London.[32]

The unease that Nehru manifested in relation to intelligence activity was compounded by the Indian premier's anxiety that CIA operations were being undertaken in the subcontinent without the knowledge of his government. In June 1955, in a speech he made to a gathering of Indian diplomats in Europe, Nehru observed that he regarded the CIA as an especially invidious threat to Indian democracy. 'The United States are carrying on their espionage and secret service activities [inside India]', Nehru assured his audience. 'They have also been buying up newspapers and spreading a network of publicity organisations ... We are more concerned with what the Americans are trying to do than the others.'[33] While the Intelligence Bureau had been tasked with keeping a 'watch [on] communist activity', the Indian premier added, there had been 'very little' external interference in India's affairs from communist states. When it came to indigenous communism, he continued, intelligence suggested that the CPI had been instructed by its sponsors 'not to embarrass our government'.[34] In a letter he wrote to the Indian academic and member of parliament, Shriman Narayan, shortly before travelling to Europe, Nehru voiced concern at unwelcome American intrusions into Indian politics. 'It might interest you to know', he informed Narayan, 'that some little time ago I received definite information that the United States were looking for agents in the Congress Party in India'.[35]

Evidence from Indian and American sources did suggest that the CIA was successful in recruiting 'assets' inside the Indian government. Notably, M. O. Mathai, who served as Nehru's special assistant between the mid-1940s and the late 1950s, is amongst those reputed to have worked for US intelligence. According to one authority, parliamentary unease surrounding Mathai's inability to account for the accumulation of considerable personal wealth, prompted an enquiry conducted by India's Cabinet Secretary. This concluded that Mathai had 'without doubt had received money from the C.I.A. as well as from businessmen in India'.[36] Nehru's most prominent biographer went as far as to state: 'It can ... be safely assumed that, from 1946 to 1959, the CIA had access to every paper passing through Nehru's

Secretariat.'[37] While charges levelled against Mathai remain contentious, former State Department officers have corroborated claims of collusion between Indian government officials and the CIA. One American diplomat who served in India in the early 1960s, recalled how the CIA station in New Delhi openly boasted that it could obtain a copy of any document produced by the Indian government. 'So, I put this to the test once', the US official claimed, 'and they [the CIA] provided it for me'.[38]

Any animus that Nehru harboured towards the CIA was complicated, in the minds of US diplomats, by an assumption in Washington that the Indian leader was intrinsically anti-American. Loy Henderson confided to a friend that Nehru's 'dislike' for America was, 'not caused by any specific action that had been taken by the United States Government'. Rather, Nehru embodied a 'Hindi aristocrat[s] . . . contempt for . . . the American people. He [Nehru] thought that they were a vulgar lot too deeply interested in making money.'[39] Characterising India's left-leaning premier as 'a non-communist rather than an anti-communist', Henderson concluded that Nehru's disdain for American political and social institutions suggested that, 'if he [Nehru] were compelled to choose between the Soviet and the American way of life he might well choose the former'.[40] The ambassador's characterisation of Nehru overstated the depth of the Indian premier's estrangement from the United States and misinterpreted its essential character. The Indian premier was frequently and sharply critical of American policy on issues ranging from colonialism and racial discrimination to free market capitalism and military containment. Nehru also repeatedly and publicly emphasised that a community of common values, centred upon commitments to liberal democracy and individual liberty, meant that India and the United States had much in common.[41] Nehru did baulk at the inability of US policymakers to face global realities, and to deal with the world as it was, not how America would like it to have been. The reluctance of Americans to acknowledge the existence of Communist China, to condemn the inequities of European imperialism, and get on the right side of history in a rapidly changing world, inevitably pitched Washington against New Delhi, and much of the Asian and African world besides.[42] As Nehru pointed out to Lord Mountbatten, who himself rarely missed opportunities to drive a wedge between India and the United States, many Indians felt, 'a little tired of the advice being given to us from time to time in minatory language from the U.S. . . . they seem to forget that we are not some little Central American Republic'.[43]

When it was published, in 1958, Nehru confessed that he had 'been much influenced' by reading the book, *The Ugly American*, by the US authors, William J. Lederer and Eugene Burdick. An excoriating critique of the gauche inadequacies of bludgeoning American diplomacy in a fictional South East Asian country, Nehru, while acknowledging that the work was 'a little exaggerated', nevertheless, praised the book as 'essentially correct, as most of us

84

know'.[44] Nehru's suspicion that the CIA was corrupting India's political landscape was tempered, to some degree, by an assessment that the intelligence agency, and the governments in Washington that it served, was prone to act in the maladroit and ham-fisted manner portrayed by Lederer and Burdick. In May 1960, in the aftermath of the U-2 affair, when Washington bungled in denying that a CIA spy plane had been shot-down over the Soviet Union, Nehru derided American handling of the intelligence debacle as 'exceedingly inept'.[45] Aware that the performance of India's own intelligence agencies left much to be desired, Nehru nonetheless bridled whenever his ministers implied that their British and American equivalents were superior. In one exchange with an official from India's Ministry of Education, the prime minister observed scathingly, 'You refer to the tremendous Intelligence set-ups of U.S.A. and U.K. Recent information and indeed some previous knowledge also has shown that the U.S.A. set-up is singularly inept. Both in the case of Laos and Cuba it has failed miserably.'[46]

The CIA remained on Nehru's mind throughout July 1961 when the workaholic Indian leader took a short break among the picturesque hills of Kashmir, his ancestral homeland. It was while on holiday in Kashmir that Nehru chanced upon an article published in *The Nation*. The progressive American political magazine carried a long essay on the CIA written by the investigative journalist, and Agency critic, Fred Cook.[47] Published in the aftermath of the Bay of Pigs episode, Cook's polemic took aim at the secretive yet 'lavishly financed CIA' for presiding over the latest in a long line of 'fiascos'. Recounting in detail how 'time and again, CIA has meddled actively in the internal affairs of foreign governments', the article called for the Agency to be stripped of its covert action role and to focus solely on intelligence gathering and analysis. '[T]oday we practice the "black" arts on such a far-flung, billion-dollar scale', Cook argued, 'we throw around them such a mantle of spurious patriotic secrecy, that neither the people nor their watchdogs in Congress have the faintest idea what is happening until it has happened – until it is too late'. The consequences of an Agency that was, to Cook's mind, unaccountable and out of control, were twofold. 'Abroad, the CIA destroys our prestige and undermines our influence. At home we do not even know what is happening.'[48] Having digested Cook's stinging attack on the CIA, Nehru fired off a note to his Foreign Secretary, M. J. Desai. Observing that the article was 'a very revealing one about the working of the CIA and, consequently, in regard to many aspects of US foreign policy', the Indian premier instructed Desai to bulk order 200 copies from its American publishers. These, Nehru ordered, should be distributed widely to India's missions abroad and shared around government departments at home.[49]

Nehru was still brooding over the hatchet-job undertaken on the CIA by the *Nation* six months later, when he considered reforming India's intelligence system. Writing to Badruddin Tyabji, Special Secretary at the MEA, in

QUIET AMERICANS

February 1962, the Indian premier suggested that Cook's article demonstrated 'what harm a wrongly directed intelligence service can do'. The CIA's missteps, Nehru confided, had made him 'anxious that we [India] should proceed cautiously in this matter [intelligence reform]'. Reluctant to sanction an Intelligence Bureau presence beyond countries directly adjoining India, the prime minister questioned the necessity of employing 'a large [intelligence] network'. 'Normally our foreign missions should be able to supply such information as may help us', India's leader opined.[50] Nehru's responses to the CIA were not predetermined by misgivings that the Indian premier evidenced towards Washington's foreign policymaking. Still, the challenge of operating in a political climate within the subcontinent in which intelligence agencies in general, and US intelligence agencies above all, were viewed with apprehension and suspicion did not make the CIA's job any easier.

Unleashing the CIA: Eisenhower and South Asia

From Washington's perspective, the 1950s had witnessed the troubling conjunction of a looming economic crisis in India, a resurgence in popular support for communist parties in the subcontinent, and burgeoning Soviet ties to Nehru's government. In response, the Eisenhower administration feted Nehru during the India premier's visit to the United States in December 1956. The following January, India's growing importance to America was confirmed by Eisenhower's approval of National Security Council report 5701. The NSC report acknowledged that a strong, non-communist India would challenge aspects of US foreign policy. By supporting New Delhi, however, Washington could promote a 'successful example of an alternative to communism in an Asian context and would permit the gradual development of the means to enforce ... security interests against Communist Chinese expansion into South and South east Asia'.[51] In endorsing NSC 5701, Eisenhower's Ambassador in India, Ellsworth Bunker, cautioned that, absent US support, an economic collapse in India presented 'a strong possibility of the accession to power of some kind of extremist government'. In such a scenario, Bunker underlined, communist elements were likely to profit the most, and the costs to US security would be 'even higher than the loss of China to the Free World'.[52] Eisenhower's enthusiasm for bringing India and the United States closer together, primarily through the provision of generous American economic aid, would also be embraced by his successor, John F. Kennedy, who saw India as a key counterweight to Communist Chinese influence in Asia.

Where the White House led, the CIA followed. The Agency quickly came to embrace Eisenhower's tilt towards India and ramped up its activities in the subcontinent. Pushing out from a main base of operations, or station, in New Delhi, CIA officers intensified work undertaken from smaller out-stations in Bombay, Calcutta, and Madras. The more active the CIA's presence in India

86 SPYING IN SOUTH ASIA

the more difficult it was for the Agency to preserve a pretence of anonymity. Abraham Michael 'Abe' Rosenthal, the *New York Times* correspondent in New Delhi for much of the 1950s, observed the transformation with interest. Writing to his editor back in the United States, Rosenthal reflected on the rising numbers of CIA staff working in India under the guise of Treasury experts, Air Force contractors, or members of specialised bodies, such as the Asia Foundation. Agency personnel, Rosenthal revealed, were easily identified by Indian government officials, and were commonly referred to as, 'the Halicrafter boys . . . because whatever their Embassy cover, they all had offices in the same part of the basement, and all had identical Halicrafter radios'. The CIA's focus, Rosenthal reported, appeared to be directed, 'more than anything else in getting inside the Congress Party for purposes of information or influence'.[53]

American embassy and consular staff in India soon became conscious of a new sense of activism amongst their CIA colleagues. One diplomatic officer working out of the Bombay consulate, later observed that 'my first wake-up experience with the Agency' followed on from the local CIA chief 'press[ing] hard' to co-opt his services in the recruitment of an Indian agent. The consular official had befriended a prominent Indian mathematician cum politician, who had held a research post at Princeton, the American's alma mater. The CIA became interested in the mathematician when he was appointed secretary to an Indian delegation that toured scientific institutions in the Soviet Union. Pushed by the Bombay CIA station to question the mathematician on the specifics of his visit behind the Iron Curtain, the consular officer was ruffled when his Indian friend snapped back, 'What is all this about? Who did you get this from? Did you get this from your CIA?' Fortunately for the Agency, the Indian target cooled down, experienced a change of heart, and decided it was preferable to work for the CIA rather than report his encounter to the Indian authorities.[54] Eugene Rosenfeld, who worked as a USIS officer in New Delhi around the same time, recounted his experience of a separate, but equally offbeat, intelligence recruitment incident. A disgruntled Indian journalist working at the CPI's headquarters had resolved to sell his services to the CIA. A walk-in, or individual that unexpectedly and voluntarily offers to act as an American agent, the journalist, on arriving at US embassy, was directed to Rosenfeld in the mistaken belief that he wanted to discuss a press-related issue. Having listened patiently to a lengthy list of the Indians gripes, which included the CPI's intimidation and physical mistreatment of his family, alongside minor complaints surrounding the inequitable allocation of air conditioning and pay at the communist party's offices, Rosenfeld realised the Indian's purpose, and turned the matter over to the CIA. The journalist proved to be 'a hell of a good walk-in' and, in return for financial compensation, 'provided inside information of communist party activities from the head-quarters for at least five years'.[55]

As the CIA's field operations in India developed, so did its reputation for intelligence gathering and astute analysis, at least in a narrow Cold War sense. Abe Rosenthal found the CIA station in New Delhi to be well supplied with political specialists and experts on Marxism, the Soviet Union, and Chinese affairs, many of whom, 'were extremely knowing in the field of Asian studies'. The *New York Times* correspondent was less enamoured with a propensity amongst the CIA officers to 'put an American screen over their eyes' when considering more parochial Indian matters. Whenever the subject of Nehru, or Kashmir, or Indo-Pakistan relations cropped up, Rosenthal noted, his CIA contacts found it difficult to conceive of them outside the 'reflection of American interests'. In strictly operational terms, Rosenthal was impressed by the 'wide range of high and medium level contacts' that the Agency managed to acquire in the subcontinent, and that ensured the CIA were 'quite up on the minutiae of Indian politics'. The success that came to be associated with the CIA's Indian operations was reflected in the close personal interest they attracted from the Agency's Director, Allen Dulles. It was on one of Dulles's inspection trips to India, that Rosenthal was provided with a personal highlight of his tour in the subcontinent. The journalist was invited to meet with Dulles at the US Embassy. On walking out of the temporary office allocated to the CIA Director, following two hours of discussions, Rosenthal was delighted to find, 'every spook in India lined up in the anteroom waiting and knowing they were looking at me and asking: "Is this one we don't know about?"'[56]

Allen Dulles's family had a long association with India. Dulles's great grandfather, John Welles Dulles, spent five years conducting missionary work in Madras for the Presbyterian church before ill health forced him to return to the United States. During his senior year at Princeton, Allen Dulles followed the family trail to the subcontinent and accepted an offer to teach English at Ewing Christian College, in Allahabad. Dulles landed in India on 20 July 1914, on the eve of the First World War. A far cry from Princeton, Ewing College was a small and austere institution with a compliment of a dozen or so staff. Nehru's hometown, Allahabad was a hub of incipient Indian nationalist activity. Displaying a sense of curiosity and activism that would later serve him well as an intelligence officer, Dulles immersed himself in local culture and politics, acquired a smattering of Hindi and, with his pupils vouching for his *bona fides* as a sympathetic observer, began attending clandestine meetings of nationalist groups coordinating resistance to British rule. Intriguingly, Dulles also struck up friendships within the Nehru family during his time in Allahabad. As a contemporary of Nehru, and his sister, Vijayalakshmi Pandit, the young Dulles cultivated what would prove to be enduring connections with these two future titans of the Indian nationalist movement.[57] Forty years later, in 1953, when Pandit was elected as the first

88   SPYING IN SOUTH ASIA

female president of the United Nations General Assembly, Dulles sent her a one-line note. It read, 'Allahabad 1914'.[58]

Dulles's exposure to India was cut short by his decision to return to Princeton and attend graduate school. The brief period that the future CIA Director spent in the subcontinent, however, left a strong impression. On the steamship that had carried him to India, Dulles poured over Rudyard Kipling's *Kim*, the classic tale of the great nineteenth-century espionage game waged between the British and Russian empires astride India's northern border. Dulles treasured his copy of *Kim*, and the well-thumbed tome was discovered lying on his bedside table following his death.[59] In September 1956, when Dulles stopped off in New Delhi for three days during a round-the-world tour of CIA stations, and provided Rosenthal with a memory to cherish, he dropped in on Nehru to talk shop and recall old times. One CIA officer accompanying Dulles on that trip marvelled that, 'when we arrived in India, Nehru was giving everyone trouble, but he stopped everything and had a long talk and kept calling Dulles "Mr. Allen" and there were these reminiscences about Allahabad so many years before'.[60]

India's communists extended a much less warm welcome to Dulles. A front-page headline in the left-wing newspaper, *Blitz*, asked its readership to ponder, 'What's Behind Allen Dulles' Mystery Mission to India?' Alongside a picture of the CIA Director, entitled, 'Allen Dulles . . . Cloak and Dagger', *Blitz* declared dramatically, 'Let Asia beware . . . [the] US intelligence agency!'[61] Unfortunately for Dulles, the timing of his stay in New Delhi coincided with the arrest of an MEA employee who had sold copies of Nehru's correspondence with Egypt's President Nasser on the Suez Canal crisis to a foreign agent. The IB quickly identified Pakistan as behind the espionage coup. Never a newspaper to let the truth get in the way of a good story, *Blitz's* take on the 'Delhi Spy Scandal' suggested that Pakistani agents had acted in collusion with American and British intelligence services. Dulles, the newspaper claimed, had been delighted to receive facsimiles of the stolen documents, 'from American sources in Delhi by way of a special gift from American intelligence in India'.[62] For the remainder of his tenure as CIA Director, and beyond, Dulles's association with India was targeted by communist propagandists in disinformation operations. In January 1961, Radio Moscow broadcast allegations that Dulles and his late brother, John Foster Dulles, had been implicated in a plot to assassinate Nehru by Indian defendants in a conspiracy trial.[63] Five years later, in January 1966, the then CIA Director, William Raborn, speaking before a Congressional CIA subcommittee, pointed to the persistence of slurs in the Soviet press that linked Dulles's office to purported plans to assassinate Nehru in the 1950s.[64]

Kerala, the CPI, and the Complexities of Clandestine Collaboration

In 1957, warnings of India's vulnerability to communist subversion that Ellsworth Bunker issued from New Delhi, were brought home to

Washington following the results of general elections held between February and March. Nationwide, India's electorate handed Nehru's Congress Party a clear mandate. Congress candidates secured 371 of the 492 parliamentary seats available. Regionally, Congress achieved a plurality in eleven of India's thirteen state assemblies. Global press coverage of the election, however, focused overwhelmingly on returns in the southern state of Kerala, where the Communist Party of India swept to power. 'This must be the first time in history', Malcolm MacDonald, the British High Commissioner in India, informed Whitehall, 'that a Communist administration with anything approaching the jurisdiction and powers of the Kerala Government has been put into office by wholly democratic means'.[65] MacDonald was largely right. As the Indian Embassy in Washington observed, the State Department had been surprised and dismayed that, 'with the insignificant exception of San Marino', India's communists had broken significant new ground by seizing power via the ballot box rather than the bullet.[66]

On touring Kerala shortly after the election, Henry Ramsey, America's consul-general in Madras, advised the State Department that, 'Communists are moving skilfully and non-dramatically within constitutional limitations to consolidate [their] position.' Ramsey did not share the sanguine assessment advanced by Congress Party leaders that the CPI 'beachhead' in Kerala would prove fleeting, and that support for the communists would wither once the hard economic realities of governing the state became apparent. The 'lack of realism' displayed by Congress Party officials in Kerala, whose mismanagement, graft, and complacency had been exploited by the CPI, alarmed Ramsey. '[N]either [the] Kerala Congress nor central [Congress Party] has evolved a clear strategic line either to displace or replace [the] Communists', he cabled to Washington, 'and in EMS [Namboodiripad, the CPI state leader] and his Cabinet, Congress is confronted with shrewd, young, zealous, closely-knit team'.[67] To an extent, Malcolm MacDonald shared his American colleague's anxieties. With Kerala being openly referred to in some circles as 'The Indian Yenan', the British diplomat felt that, if left unchallenged, the CPI's intention of exploiting the State as 'a shop window' to showcase the benefits of communism could foster a sense of political momentum which the Congress Party might find impossible to stop.[68] Following the CPI's success in Kerala, Washington ensured that US economic aid and development projects in the subcontinent were redirected, wherever possible, to, 'bear more directly on the situation in South India'.[69] In addition, Eisenhower authorised the CIA to initiate a covert operation to subvert the communist state government. Between 1957 and 1959, by secretly channelling funds to Congress Party officials and anti-communist labour leaders, including S. K. Patil, a Congress boss in the neighbouring state of Maharashtra, the Agency fomented industrial unrest and political turmoil in Kerala. In July 1959, amidst scenes of mounting violence and disorder, the CPI government was dismissed from office under an executive order issued by India's President. Ellsworth Bunker subsequently justified the CIA operation in Kerala on the basis that his embassy had been in possession of hard evidence that showed the Soviets were funding local communist groups. Rationalising the CIA's actions as reactive and defensive in character, the US ambassador confirmed that in India, 'as we [America] have done elsewhere in the world we've come to the assistance of our friends when we knew and had evidence [of] what the communists were doing, financially and in other ways'.[70]

In the run up to the 1957 elections, Nehru, who had long harboured misgivings over the extent of foreign funding reaching India's political parties, explicitly asked the Intelligence Bureau 'to be vigilant about this matter'. 'We have often suspected that the Communist Party in India manages to get some kind of financial assistance from outside', the Indian premier informed his Home Minister, in June 1956. 'They may not get it from any official sources abroad but there are many other ways of getting it.'[71] Although the decision to clandestinely fund the Congress Party and its non-communist allies was taken in Washington, as the man on the spot, Bunker was granted significant 'discretion as to how it might be done and in what amounts'. In feeding cash to S. K. Patil and others in the Congress Party, Bunker noted, the CIA had leveraged its 'very good and very close' relationship with India's intelligence agencies. Collaboration between the CIA and the IB was such, the American ambassador recorded, that it was possible to ascertain, with a reasonable degree of confidence, where US funds were being spent, in what sums, and to what effect.[72]

Given the suspicion and concern within Nehru's Congress Party that surrounded CIA activity, the Indian decision to work covertly with the Agency was reflective of a genuine anxiety that the CPI in Kerala was functioning as a Soviet puppet. In April 1957, Mullik presented Nehru with an intelligence report that indicated senior members of the CPI Politburo planned to visit Moscow to consult with the Soviets on how the communist government in Kerala should be run. Alarmed by the prospect of such blatant external interference in India's domestic politics, Nehru asked that the Soviet ambassador, Mikhail Menshikov, be summoned to the MEA. Menshikov, the Indian prime minister stipulated, should be left under no illusions that were Moscow to receive a secret delegation of senior CPI officials, New Delhi would be extremely displeased. 'Any such approach would be highly improper in our view', Nehru reiterated to the MEA, and Moscow should be reminded that, ' . . . we are sure that the Soviet Government will not in any way, directly or indirectly, interfere in our internal affairs'. During their visit to India the previous year, Khrushchev and Bulganin had been warned off providing the CPI with clandestine funding. The Soviet leaders had provided assurances to Nehru that, 'this kind of thing will not be encouraged in any way and they [the

Soviets] did not wish to interfere in the least with internal matters in India'. Khrushchev's word, the Indian premier discovered, could not be trusted.[73]

Had Nehru been fully aware of the extent of discussions taking place in Washington over how the United States might reorientate the political landscape in Kerala, he might well have instructed the MEA to summon Ellsworth Bunker for a similar dressing down. In electing to work with the CIA on occasions, as in Kerala, the Congress Party's senior leadership was conscious that it would not be taken entirely into the Agency's confidence. Nehru was uneasy about what he knew the CIA to be doing in southern India. The Indian premier was even more anxious, however, at what he did not know, and was not being told, in relation to Agency operations conducted on sovereign Indian territory. At the beginning of 1959, as the CPI government was buffeted by mounting protests and agitation on the ground, William Fulbright, Chairman of the Senate Committee on Foreign Relations, had his interest in southern Indian politics piqued by a letter that he received from Kerala. Purportedly written by a local Indian man, the letter asked for Fulbright's advice and guidance on how 'newly-independent countries create effective non-Communist political organizations'. In response, Fulbright turned to Allen Dulles. 'What [do] you think we could do in this area', Fulbright challenged the CIA Director, 'that we are not now doing?'[74] At a brief meeting held between the two men on 16 March, Dulles sought to put Fulbright's mind at ease. When it came to developing political organisations in the global South to meet threats posed by international communism, Fulbright was assured, the CIA had 'been devoting a great deal of attention over the past years ... to develop[ing] certain techniques which I should like to discuss with you [further] at your convenience'.[75]

Dulles had indeed been busy. Subsequent to the election of a non-communist government in Kerala, at the beginning of 1960, the CIA classified Kerala as a 'target of opportunity'. The OCB's Working Group on South Asia was tasked with exploring covert action that could be taken in the State to 'further U.S. interests and those of the free world in general'.[76] A special report submitted by the OCB on 17 February, entitled 'Exploitation of Kerala Elections', cautioned against any triumphalism now that the CPI government had been defeated at the polls. Rather, the OCB report advocated that 'discreet encouragement' be offered to Indian government probes into the CPI administration's corruption and mismanagement in Kerala, 'and their results worked into publicity for use inside as well as outside India'.[77] At the same time, the CIA continued to direct financial subsidies to influential Indians and Indian organisations willing to advance an anti-communist line. Such activity was not always successful. David Burgess served as a Labour Attaché at the US embassy in New Delhi between 1955 and 1960. He secured his posting to India on the recommendation of Walter Reuther, the progressive union leader, and President of the

United Automobile Workers. Burgess was approached by the CIA to act as a conduit to Indian trades unionists but rejected the Agency's overtures on ethical grounds. 'I refused to be the carrier of money to bribe labor leaders there [Kerala] during a parliamentary election', Burgess later recalled. 'The CIA chief at the Embassy was not overjoyed with my refusal.'[78]

Occasional setbacks aside, well into the 1960s, whenever the CPI appeared on the cusp of making electoral gains in Kerala, Washington invariably turned to the CIA in an effort to sabotage communist prospects. In March 1964, Robert Komer, then a National Security Council staffer, pressed the 303 Committee, the executive body under President Johnson responsible for co-ordinating and approving covert actions, to place Kerala back at the top of the CIA's agenda once again. 'Since the C[ommunist] P[arty] seems to be coming back in Kerala and may again capture the state in next election, I've suggested to [name redacted] another look at this matter', Komer advocated. 'My thought is of course that the agency [CIA] might want to put a proposition up to State and the [Special] Group [303 Committee].'[79] Agency officers stationed in southern India at that time have corroborated Washington's conviction that the CPI represented a clear danger to Indian democracy. Duane 'Dewey' Clarridge, who went on to head the CIA's Latin American division in the 1980s and was a prominent figure in the Iran-Contra affair, was stationed in southern India as a young intelligence officer. Clarridge noted that after the events of 1957, the CPI came to be viewed by 'Washington in general, not just the CIA ... as a serious threat to India's non-aligned status'. Accordingly, while Clarridge himself saw communist strength in India as overblown and exaggerated, the CIA continued to invest in 'an elaborate network' of Indian agents. The Agency's intelligence collection network, which extended beyond India's communist heartland in the south and east to cover much of the remainder of the country, 'monitored the activities of the splintered Communist Party factions' and enjoyed 'marvellous access to paper, the documents that all bureaucracies live by and suffer with'.[80]

British officials in India largely concurred with Clarridge's assessment that the potency of Indian communism was to some extent a chimera. Although relieved that the CPI had suffered a setback in Kerala, Malcolm MacDonald cautioned London that, 'the imminence of a really serious Communist menace in India should not be exaggerated'. In New Delhi, MacDonald was less exercised by the internal threat posed by the CPI in southern India, and more worried by, 'a new and very important element ... Communist China's recent tyrannical conduct in Tibet, and still more the aggressive incursions of Chinese troops across India's frontiers ...'. An existential threat to Indian democracy posed by communism, MacDonald suggested, was unlikely to manifest internally, and more plausibly would arrive via Himalayan passes in the form of Beijing's People's Liberation Army.[81]

China, Tibet, and India's Troubled Northern Border

In August 1947, the departing British left India with a contested northern border. In the eastern Himalayas, India and China claimed sovereignty over territory roughly approximating to the present Indian state of Arunachal Pradesh. In the northwest, another Sino-Indian territorial dispute centred on ownership of the Aksai Chin plateau, a strategically important area of arid desert nestled between the Indian region of Ladakh, Tibet, and the Chinese province of Xinjiang. Dormant until the late 1950s, the border dispute between India and China intensified as relations between the two countries, which had thrived briefly following the signing of the *Panch Sheel* accord, or 'Five Principles of Peaceful Co-existence', in 1954, turned rancorous.[82]

In 1957, New Delhi took exception to Beijing's construction of a highway between Xinjiang and Tibet that passed through the Aksai Chin plateau.[83] Two years later, bilateral relations deteriorated further after Nehru granted political asylum to Tibet's spiritual leader, the Dalai Lama, and thousands of his supporters, in the aftermath of an abortive Tibetan revolt against Chinese rule. Enraged that Nehru had furnished Tibetan exiles with a base to conduct anti-Chinese activity, Beijing resented what it saw as a provocative intrusion by India into China's domestic affairs.[84] A series of armed clashes between Indian and Chinese border patrols, prompted increasingly bitter exchanges on the boundary question between Nehru and Zhou Enlai. As India's relationship with the People's Republic of China deteriorated, the Intelligence Bureau turned to the CIA for support. As in Kerala, the willingness of Mullik's IB and, to a considerable extent, the Indian government, to collaborate with the CIA against a common Chinese enemy was fraught with political complications. Not least, Nehru's government remained wary that the CIA would utilise only part of its considerable resources in the subcontinent against China. The question of precisely how, and to what degree, the Agency would leverage Indian requests for assistance to mask interventions in the country's internal political affairs, unsettled Indian policymakers.

Indian intelligence collaboration with the United States in respect of Communist China had deep roots. In December 1949, a year before Beijing annexed Tibet, the CIA approached the British Joint Intelligence Committee with a request for political, economic, and topographical information on the Himalayan plateau. India's JIC had recently completed an in-depth study of Tibet, which it shared with the British. With New Delhi's blessing, the study was forwarded on to the CIA. Decades of intelligence cooperation between New Delhi and Washington, centred on safeguarding the security of India's northern border, followed.[85] For much of the 1950s, Nehru's government maintained a cautious and pragmatic policy on Tibet. Many Indians, as Nehru acknowledged, felt an affinity for, and harboured 'sympathy' towards, their Tibetan neighbours. Beijing's decision to assert control over Tibet by

Figure 4.1 Members of the Jan Sangh Party demonstrate outside the Communist Chinese Embassy in New Delhi over China's occupation of Tibet, 1 January 1960. Bettmann / Getty Images.

means of the People's Liberation Army provoked dismay in India. The Indian premier recognised, nonetheless, the limitations of New Delhi's capacity to influence events beyond its northern border. A 'policy of encouraging the Tibetans to oppose Chinese overlordship over Tibet', Nehru rationalised, 'would be raising false hopes in the Tibetans which we [India] cannot fulfill and is likely to react [sic] unfavourably on the Tibetans'. Furthermore, Nehru concluded that interfering in an issue that China insisted was an internal matter, would breach the terms of the *Panch Sheel* agreement and succeed in alienating Beijing to no obvious purpose. Unwilling to sanction Indian support for resistance activity inside Tibet, Nehru was more equivocal when it came to offering succour to Tibetan emigrés based in India. 'Whatever happens in Tibet proper is beyond our reach', the Indian premier stipulated, in June 1954.' We can neither help nor hinder it. The question is what we do in our own territory. Do we encourage this or not? It is clear we cannot encourage it. At best we can tolerate it, provided it is not too obvious or aggressive. A very delicate balance will have to be kept up.'[86]

In practice, the Indian government's policy of 'looking the other way' in respect of Tibet facilitated the transit of CIA aircraft through Indian airspace in support of Agency-sponsored resistance operations. It also enabled CIA operatives to spirit the Dalai Lama out of Lhasa, and into northern

India in 1959.[87] In turn, India's northern border towns, and notably, Kalimpong, in the far east of the country, developed into hubs of espionage. In June 1954, Nehru complained to the MEA that Kalimpong had become, 'a nest of intrigues and spies'. The picturesque hill-station, with its juxtaposition of colonial-era churches and Buddhist monasteries, the Indian premier grumbled, was overrun with a farrago of Tibetan emigrés, Chinese communists, Chinese nationalists, Americans, White Russians, Red Russians, Eastern Europeans, Western Europeans, and every other kind of intelligence agent and operative imaginable. 'It is a common joke in Kalimpong', Nehru wrote to Mountbatten, 'that there are more spies there than other folk'.[88] Nehru fretted that the Americans, in particular, were using Kalimpong as a base to encourage the irredentist ambitions of hot-headed Tibetans. Such machinations, the Indian leader scoffed, were 'childish and totally unrealistic'. By arming such a 'petty violent effort', Washington would do nothing for Tibet. Rather, Nehru suggested cynically, the CIA's operation, 'can only be thought of in terms of some aggressive Americans as a diversion from their larger world policy or in case a big war occurs'. Anxious that the situation in Kalimpong risked getting out of hand and embarrassing his government, Nehru reinforced to Mullik that the IB should ensure foreign intelligence activity on Indian's northern border was kept as 'unobtrusive' as possible. Beijing's patience could only be expected to stretch so far. 'We have to be very careful about our activities in Kalimpong', the Indian premier cautioned MEA officials, 'because of the espionage and counter-espionage that is continually going on there'.[89]

Nehru's call for circumspection failed to impress China. In meetings held between the Indian prime minister and Zhou Enlai in the spring of 1960, the Chinese premier excoriated New Delhi for allowing the Dalai Lama and his followers to freely criticise Beijing from the safety of their sanctuary in India. The anti-Chinese activity emanating from Kalimpong was singled out by Zhou as a particular irritant, and an impediment to harmonious Sino-Indian relations.[90] In addition, the Chinese took Nehru to task for failing to stop CIA overflights of the Sino-Indian border and enabling the Agency's support for American-trained guerrillas in eastern Tibet. To Nehru's discomfort, Zhou responded to Indian expressions of ignorance in respect of the CIA's Tibetan operations by providing a detailed account of the dates of the Agency's overflights, the airstrips that they had used, the routes they had taken, and the cargoes that they had carried. Having captured or killed several Tibetans trained by the Agency, China's security services were able to piece together a comprehensive picture of the CIA's activities in Tibet. Having done so, Zhou impressed upon Nehru just how much Beijing knew of the Agency's Tibetan operation and, by implication, the degree to which India's government was complicit in it.[91]

The New Frontier: Containing Covert Action?

In January 1961, the transition from the Eisenhower to the Kennedy administration in the United States ushered in a new and, it would transpire, seminal phase in the CIA's operational history in South Asia. Kennedy placed considerable importance on building India up into an economic and political counterweight to Communist China. It therefore came as little surprise when he nominated John Kenneth Galbraith as his ambassador to India. A Harvard economics professor, Galbraith came to public attention as the author of such left-of-centre polemics as, *The Affluent Society,* and *The Liberal Hour.*[92] He first encountered Kennedy in the 1930s, when the President attended Harvard as an undergraduate. Galbraith subsequently became a prominent figure in post-war liberal Democratic politics and was installed as Kennedy's chief economic advisor during the latter's bid for the White House.[93] Kennedy admired Galbraith's intelligence, energy, and acerbic wit.[94] Galbraith's many detractors decried his propensity for self-promotion, arrogance, and displays of pique. One member of the US embassy staff in New Delhi characterised the ambassador as a 'scold', who 'never did anything in his life to minimize his own importance'.[95]

Prior to his arrival in India, in April 1961, Galbraith fought a series of bruising bureaucratic battles with the State Department, the CIA, and the Pentagon. It fell to Richard M. Bissell Jr., the CIA's Deputy Director of Plans, to brief Galbraith on Agency activity in India. To Bissell's alarm, Galbraith took exception to the CIA's interference in the subcontinent's politics and made clear his intention to drastically curtail American covert action in India. In an account of the meeting recorded in his journal, Galbraith noted that he had been informed, 'by the CIA ... on various spooky activities, some of which I do not like. I shall stop them.'[96] Specifically, Galbraith recalled being 'appalled and depressed' to learn of the CIA's plans to spend a sum, 'well into the millions [of dollars]', to bankroll the election expenses of pro-Western Indian politicians and subsidise local anti-communist newspapers and magazines. Such activity, Galbraith judged, was unlikely to be decisive in influencing Indian opinion. It was, however, almost certain to leak into the public domain, damaging Indo-US relations, and compromising Galbraith's position in New Delhi. The ambassador-designate was 'especially disturbed' by the CIA's 'particularly insane enterprise' of overflying Indian airspace to ferry arms and supplies to Tibetan resistance fighters.[97] Galbraith proved only partially successful, at best, in restricting the Agency's activities. The ambassador's aversion to covert action did, nonetheless, lead senior American intelligence officers to dismiss him as, 'basically anti-CIA'.[98]

Once in post, Galbraith quickly became aware of the seemingly ubiquitous shadow that the Agency had cast over India's security establishment. Galbraith was surprised, and faintly amused, when on being introduced to a line of local dignitaries during a visit to southern India, a man stepped forward and exclaimed exuberantly, 'Mr. Ambassador, I am the superintendent of police here in Madras. I would like to tell you that I have the most satisfactory relationship with your spies.'[99] In a bid to assert his authority over the CIA station in New Delhi, Galbraith initiated a sweeping review of its operations. 'I was not troubled by an open mind', he later admitted. 'I was convinced that most of the [CIA] projects proposed would be useless for their own anti-Communist purposes and were capable, when known, of doing us [the US] great damage as well.'[100] Galbraith distilled the results of his review into a caustic memorandum that landed on the desks of senior officials in the Kennedy administration. The document laid out a case for terminating CIA covert programmes then underway in India. It also called for the CIA station to be limited to arms-length political reporting, and to cease providing 'subsidies to [political] parties, politicians or papers; [and engage in] no other unnecessary undercover activities'. On a trip back to Washington, in May 1961, Galbraith hammered home his call to scrap covert intelligence operations in India. In face-to-face meetings with President Kennedy, Robert Kennedy, the Attorney General, McGeorge Bundy, Kennedy's National Security Adviser, and both Bissell and Allen Dulles, the ambassador pulled few punches in presenting the CIA as part of the problem confronting the United States in India, rather than the solution.[101]

Kennedy was still smarting from withering criticism that he had received in the wake of the Bay of Pigs debacle, after which the CIA retained few friends the White House. At the same time, the State Department had expressed its concern that too many of the Agency's operations were being publicly compromised, to the embarrassment of America's diplomats abroad. Just prior to the ill-fated events in Cuba, Kennedy's Secretary of State, Dean Rusk, had cause to apologise to the premier of Singapore, Lew Kuan Yew, after a clumsy CIA operation undertaken in the city-state was exposed. Chester Bowles, a former ambassador to India, and no great fan of the CIA himself, subsequently leveraged his position as Under Secretary of State to coax Kennedy into clarifying the chain of command within 'country-teams', which included the chiefs of all agencies operating in a US post overseas. Under Eisenhower, a secret order had exempted the CIA from the direct supervision of ambassadors. Kennedy reversed that decision and made clear that ambassadors retained authority over all agencies operating within their embassies, the CIA included.[102]

Galbraith's proposal to clip the Agency's wings was, consequently, well-timed. In the ambassador's telling, on his watch, clandestine CIA operations in India, with the exception of Agency airdrops into Tibet, were promptly terminated. Even the airdrop programme, Galbraith claimed, was eventually subject to suspension. Between 1957 and 1961, some 500,000 pounds of arms, ammunition, radios, medical supplies, and other military equipment, was dropped by the CIA and its proprietary company, Civil Air Transport, to Tibetan resistance forces.[103] Mullik's Intelligence Bureau had been briefed by the local CIA station on the overflights of Indian territory. The US embassy in New Delhi was never entirely sure if the IB passed on details of the airdrops to Nehru and senior Indian government officials. On balance, the embassy judged that Mullik had likely kept such knowledge to himself, 'as private police information'. For Galbraith, the overflight programme, whether Nehru was fully aware of it or not, was foolhardy. Aside from one treasure-trove of classified Chinese documents, the results gleaned from the operation, the ambassador reasoned, had been 'negligible'. The political risks involved in its continuation, however, were considerable. 'There is always the chance of a ghastly accident which would expose the whole activity in the manner of the U-2 [spy plane downed over the USSR in May 1960]', Galbraith complained to the State Department. 'For the Communists here [India] and everywhere it would be a windfall.' A long-time critic of what he derided as the adventurism of US foreign policy, Vietnam included, Galbraith argued that the Tibetan air operation, 'shows a disturbing American willingness to fish in troubled waters however far from home'.[104] Harry Rositzke, the CIA station chief in India, subsequently qualified Galbraith's account of the extent to which Agency activity in India was pared back. Rositzke maintained that much of the support that the Agency provided to the Dalai Lama, Tibetan exiles in India, and guerrilla fighters inside Tibet, remained largely unchanged under the Kennedy administration.[105] During Galbraith's tenure in India, and that of his successor, Chester Bowles, the CIA in-country presence remained (in the eyes of many close observers) as pervasive and powerful as ever. Joseph Greene, Bowles's deputy chief of mission, observed ruefully that his boss's distaste for covert operations was exacerbated by the nagging sense that Kennedy's assertion of the primacy of ambassadors over CIA station chiefs was simply ignored by the Agency. 'CIA never really went along with that [Kennedy's directive]', Greene reflected, 'and were always keeping things from the front office'.[106]

American diplomats who worked in New Delhi at the time have corroborated Greene's misgivings. Mary Olmstead spent four and a half years working in the economic section of the US embassy in the 1960s. The CIA, she observed, 'was very, very active' in the country. State Department officials seconded to India were appalled at the extent of financial incentives offered by the Agency to attract local agents. Such largesse appeared morally questionable and, from a purely economic perspective, helped to sustain a national bureaucratic culture riven with corruption and graft. India, Olmstead lamented, came to represent 'another illustration of CIA having too much money, too many people'. By adopting a scattergun approach to intelligence collection in the subcontinent that sought to 'find out everything that's going on', important material was often obscured in a morass of incidental information.[107] Agency field officers who worked under Rositzke have suggested that the CIA station in India remained dynamic and aggressive, and anything but the passive and enervated enterprise depicted by Galbraith. 'He [Rositzke] wanted us roaming around the city, getting to know India, and meeting individuals with access to secret information whom we might recruit', one CIA officer recalled. Morning CIA staff meetings, he added, 'had a certain Dickensian quality, like a colloquy between Fagin and his young pickpockets'. Rositzke was known to push his team hard to be proactive, to recruit Indian and Eastern bloc agents, to counter communist propaganda with disinformation, and to constantly evidence 'development activity'.[108] It is possible that Galbraith overstated his capacity to bring the CIA to heal in India. Then again, as Bowles suspected, perhaps the Agency just kept him in the dark.

Opportunity Anew: The Descent to War

In the autumn of 1962, as the Agency adjusted to Galbraith's ambassadorship, the CIA's complex relationship with India's government took a new and unexpected turn. In October, the long-simmering border dispute between India and China erupted into armed conflict. In short order, a succession of rapid Chinese military advances led some commentators to question whether India would emerge from the border war as an independent sovereign state. Speaking to his fellow citizens on 22 October, Nehru characterised China's thrust into northern India as 'the greatest menace that has come to us since independence'.[109] With India's armed forces in full retreat, a national State of Emergency was enacted, parliament recalled, sandbags piled around public buildings, and military recruiting stations flooded with eager volunteers. On the streets of the nation's major cities, effigies of Mao Zedong were set alight.[110] A shocked Nehru conceded that his government had been found wanting and was guilty of drifting along 'in an artificial atmosphere of our own creation'.[111] India, the nation's premier announced publicly, was in dire need of international 'sympathy and support'.[112] From Washington, the Kennedy administration responded immediately with offers of political and material aid. Although obscured at the time, the CIA would play a pivotal role in assisting India during, and subsequent to, the Sino-Indian war of 1962. A new intelligence partnership between Washington and New Delhi, and one that would have profound consequences for Indo-US relations throughout the remainder of the Cold War and beyond, was cemented once waves of Chinese troops crossed the Himalayan watershed and planted their boots firmly on Indian soil.

5

Confronting China: The Sino-Indian War and Collaborative Covert Action

On 20 October 1962, as the first light of dawn crested the eastern Himalayas, two flares burst into the sky over the Thag La Ridge, a steep and thickly wooded ridge commanding the disputed border between India's North East Frontier Agency (NEFA) and the Tibet region of China. Taking a cue to advance, moments later units of the Chinese People's Liberation Army fell upon positions occupied by Indian forces in the valley below. Caught unawares, the Indians were quickly overwhelmed.[1] Within forty-eight hours, Chinese troops had decimated the crack 7th Infantry Brigade and advanced deep into Indian territory. At the same time, a thousand miles away in the western Himalayas, another Chinese border incursion, in Ladakh, met with similar success. In mid-November, following a brief lull in fighting, the PLA launched a second major offensive. Representing the most significant show of Chinese force since Beijing sent its armies across the Yalu River into Korea, in October 1950, Indian defences were swept away and the road to the nation's densely populated northern plains left open. In Assam, at Tezpur, the largest city on the northern bank of the Brahmaputra River, panic took hold. Any semblance of civil administration collapsed. Prison doors were thrown open and criminals set free. The district treasury burned Indian banknotes lest they fall into enemy hands. A local airfield was besieged by desperate civilians begging to be evacuated to safety. In a matter of hours, a once bustling metropolis of 50,000 inhabitants was reduced to a 'ghost city'.[2]

In New Delhi, journalists pressed India's shell-shocked Defence Minister, Krishna Menon, to confirm when the Chinese invasion would be checked. 'The way they [the Chinese] are going', a dejected Menon replied, 'there is not any limit to where they will go'.[3] Speaking to a stunned nation on All India Radio, Jawaharlal Nehru warned his fellow citizens to prepare themselves for a long and arduous struggle with China. The outbreak of Sino-Indian hostilities, a disconsolate Nehru cautioned, represented nothing less than the 'the greatest menace that has come to us [India] since independence'.[4] An atmosphere of jingoism gripped India. Citizens committees were convened to coordinate acts of patriotism that included donating blood and knitting for the *jawans*, or soldiers.[5] India's

100

premier was reluctant to accept that China's military onslaught might compel his government to abandon its cherished policy of non-alignment. In the lead up to the border war, the Indian premier had characterised other countries acceptance of foreign military aid as akin to, 'becoming somebody else's dependent'. This, Nehru asserted, India would not accept, 'even if disaster occurs on the frontier'.[6] In fact, the scale of the calamity confronting India forced Nehru to perform a screeching U-turn. Offers of political support and military aid from the United States and Britain were readily accepted by a grateful Indian government.[7] Shrouded in a cloak of secrecy at the time, American and British intelligence services played a vital part in strengthening Indian security during, and after, the conflict. India's China war was the catalyst for a profound, if short-lived, period of intelligence collaboration between Washington, London, and New Delhi that was to cast a long shadow over Western relations with India for the remainder of the Cold War.

India's Intelligence Bureau and Perceptions of 'Failure'

The origins of the Sino-Indian border conflict are complex and contested.[8] Equally contentious, is the extent to which India's intelligence system was later held culpable for failing to anticipate and respond to China's military onslaught. India's Intelligence Bureau had evolved under its second director, B. N. Mullik, into an essentially domestic security service with a limited capacity to run foreign intelligence operations. The meagre cross-border capabilities that the IB possessed were focused preponderantly on countering threats from Pakistan. Nevertheless, in the months leading up to the border conflict, the IB did monitor and report on Chinese military dispositions. In May 1962, an IB source discovered that the Chinese consulate in Calcutta had advised Indian communists that Beijing intended to occupy contested territory in Ladakh.[9] Evidence of Beijing's aggressive intent was passed on by Mullik to Nehru, Krishna Menon, and India's Home minister, Lal Bahadur Shastri.[10]

The Indian government's ineffectual response to warnings of looming Chinese aggression have been attributed by historians in the subcontinent less to a failure of intelligence collection, and more to undue influence wielded by the IB over intelligence analysis and policy formulation. In contravention with established intelligence practice, the IB was responsible for gathering information on Chinese political and military developments *and* evaluating likely Chinese intentions. In effect, India's intelligence agency was guilty of marking its own homework. Equally, through Mullik, who had ready access to Nehru and enjoyed the Indian premier's confidence, the IB was able to establish a position on the border dispute that few military or civilian officials were willing, or felt able, to challenge.[11] A leading proponent of the 'forward policy', which discounted the possibility that Chinese forces would forcibly eliminate Indian army outposts straddling the disputed border, Mullik, abetted by senior political figures close to Nehru, amplified the IB's influence over border policy and stifled dissenting voices.[12] In May 1961, in responding to anxiety expressed by one of his own ministers at the effectiveness of Indian intelligence, Nehru sprang to the IB's defence. 'I have no doubt that Intelligence set-up can be improved', the Indian premier conceded. 'But I think it is true to say that it is a fairly efficient organization even as it is. The Head of the intelligence Service has full access to me and reports to me frequently. There is a fair amount of coordination with External Affairs information and military information ... I do not think any Intelligence Service could have done much insofar as Chinese aggression was concerned.'[13]

In fairness to Mullik and the IB, they were not alone in misreading Chinese intentions when it came to India's northern border. British officials in northeast India responded to concerns raised by the expatriate UK community in Darjeeling with an assurance that, 'Indian intelligence sources were sufficiently good to rule out the possibility of China launching a surprise large scale attack on India (even if, which was not the case, we thought that she intended to do so).' 'The build-up on the Chinese side of the frontier which would be needed', nervous British residents were informed, 'could not possibly be concealed'. Having spoken to Indian administrators in Assam, British diplomats concluded that inhabitants of the border areas had, 'learned to live with the problem and to have convinced themselves that China will not launch a military attack on India'.[14]

The military debacle that took India by surprise in 1962, saw a narrative of intelligence failure become embedded in the subcontinent's political consciousness. In turn, this generated intelligence reforms that came to encompass the creation of a new and separate external intelligence agency, the Research and Analysis Wing (R&AW). A perception of intelligence inadequacy occasioned by the Sino-Indian war also created conditions in which New Delhi's reluctance to collaborate with Western intelligence agencies was cast aside.[15] From Nehru downwards, Indian government officials held a negative view of American intelligence agencies. In the spring of 1961, following the Bay of Pigs fiasco, the Indian embassy in Washington dispatched a scathing assessment of the US intelligence community to the Ministry of External Affairs. Observing that the CIA 'seems to have a lurid life of its own', Indian diplomats expressed satisfaction that having been dealt a 'severe blow' by its adventurism in the Caribbean, 'it seemed quite possible that the CIA may lose not only its political influence, but also some of the [covert action] functions which it had arrogated to itself'. Although welcoming such a development were it to transpire, the

CONFRONTING CHINA 103

Indian embassy cautioned that any reduction in the CIA's power and influence was likely to benefit its institutional rival, the Federal Bureau of Investigation. This, in turn, would prove problematic. 'The FBI ... to put it mildly', New Delhi was warned, 'is a nest of would-be fascists'.[16] The border war, and the existential threat that it presented to the Indian Republic, transformed the Nehru government's uneasy relationships with America in the intelligence sphere. China's military incursions into the subcontinent in 1962 ushered in a new, if transient, golden age of clandestine collaboration between India and the United States.

Covert Cold War Cartography

A secret Sino-Indian border war had been underway for some time prior to October 1962. One area in which this shadow struggle played out, centred on historic maps that both challenged and appeared to legitimise the respective territorial claims advanced by New Delhi and Beijing. Indian government officials took particular interest in securing access to British colonial maps that they believed would confirm India's interpretation of its contested border with China. In September 1959, under the supervision of Sarvepalli Gopal, director of the historical division of the MEA, Indian emissaries began to comb through dusty files in the India Office Library (IOL), at the Commonwealth Relations Office, in London.[17] The Indians' objective was to procure a facsimile of a British map of Ladakh, which dated from 1851. The chart, the Indian government believed, proved beyond doubt that its delineation of the Western Himalayan border with China was legitimate. Having located the map, Gopal received special permission from the CRO to remove the original from the IOL for the purpose of making a photostat copy. In an episode worthy of a John le Carré spy thriller, an Indian official, K. L. Madan, took possession of the sole copy of document and boarded a London bus to return to his office at India House. During the journey, Madan was approached by a fellow passenger, who he believed to be Chinese, and offered £100 in cash for the map, along with the promise that a further £100 would be made available to two of his work colleagues. Having rebuffed the offer, a flustered Madan jumped off the bus and took flight.[18]

Alarmed at what appeared to have been a crude operation mounted by Chinese intelligence agents, the Indian high commission alerted the CRO. Indian diplomats asked Alexander Clutterbuck, permanent under-secretary at the CRO, to impose restrictions on public access to maps and documents in Britain's possession that were relevant to the border dispute. Clutterbuck agreed to implement tougher access standards, the effect of which was to ensure that only British and Indian officials were able to consult politically sensitive material held by the India Office Library. The Indian high commission also tightened its own security procedures. Reasoning that Chinese intelligence operatives had learned of Indian plans to acquire the Ladakh map by tapping into the high commission's telephone lines, its staff were instructed not to discuss any important matters over the telephone.[19] Nehru took a personal interest in what he characterised as the 'incident of the map'. Writing to his sister, and India's high commissioner in the UK, Vijaya Lakshmi Pandit, the Indian premier observed that the suspected Chinese intelligence operation conducted in London had 'put us on our guard'.[20] When news of the 'incident of the map' was picked up by Indian journalists, Nehru amplified media interest in the episode by stating unequivocally during a press conference in New Delhi that 'Chinese spies' had sought to purloin important documents that validated India's position on the border dispute.[21] In October, when Gopal returned to Britain to undertake further research on the border question, he was afforded protection from the British police in an effort to forestall further 'dirty tricks' on the part of the Chinese.[22]

Some years earlier, Britain had collaborated indirectly with India in another intelligence gathering operation related to the border dispute. On this occasion, the drama played out on the ground in the far northwest of the subcontinent. The affair involved a British climber, Sydney Wignall, who was introduced to officials claiming to represent the Indian high commission in London by the Himalayan Club, a mountaineering organisation run by former members of the British Indian Army and civil administration. In fact, Indian military intelligence had become aware of Wignall's plans to scale several peaks in West Nepal, a sensitive area that overlooked PLA installations inside Tibet. An approach was made to the British climber, and he agreed to spy for India.[23] Shortly before Wignall became embroiled in clandestine exploits on the roof of the world, another British adventurer, James (later, Jan) Morris, the London *Times'* correspondent on the 1953 Everest expedition, had taken note of unusual Indian activity in the border region. Morris was determined that the *Times* would secure a famous global scoop by breaking the story of the first successful ascent of Everest. On route to Everest, Morris had been delighted to stumble across a wireless transmitter manned by an Indian police officer in the remote town of Namche Bazar, in the Khumbu area of northeastern Nepal. Perplexed 'that there should be a radio station so deep in the wilds, and in a region so secluded', Morris made use of it to ensure the *Times'* account of Norgay Tenzing and Edmund Hillary's triumph made headlines around the world and appeared in print on the morning of Queen Elizabeth II's coronation. The Indian radio post had been established to pass information on communist infiltration across the Nepalese border back to Indian Army headquarters in New Delhi. 'This was one of the ideological frontiers of the world. There were rumours that the communists were building airbases on the high Tibetan plateau over the mountains; and this little radio station was a side show of the cold war', Morris observed later.[24] Side show it may have been, but for a brief moment in early 1953, India's covert war in the high Himalayas played a crucial, and unintended part, in one of the greatest news stories of the twentieth century.

Two years later, when Sydney Wignall arrived in the subcontinent, he was greeted by Lieutenant Colonel B. N. 'Baij' Mehta of the Indian Army. Mehta would be killed in action, almost exactly seven years later, fighting in the Sino-Indian war. The Indian officer briefed Wignall on his responsibilities as an Indian agent and instructed him on the communication protocols he was to use to convey information to New Delhi on Chinese military activity in the border region. Wignall was led to believe that Nehru, and like-minded members of the Indian cabinet, had prohibited intelligence operations in the border area on the grounds that they were needlessly provocative. Senior Indian Army officers, including General Kodandera Subayya 'Timmy' Thimayya, a future Chief of the Army Staff, the British climber was assured, took a different view. Wignall was informed that he would be acting as one of 'Timmy's boys', or a select group of covert operatives sent into Nepal and Tibet by Indian military intelligence to spy on the PLA. On 25 October 1955, while moving through the border area, Wignall was apprehended by a Chinese patrol. For several weeks, Wignall, and his climbing partner, John Harrop, were held in 'a freezing cold, and rat-infested prison cell in south-west Tibet, accused of being an agent, not of India, but of the American CIA'.[25]

Prior to his capture, Wignall claimed to have acquired valuable intelligence on China's construction of the strategic highway between Xinjiang and Tibet. On his release, Wignall's India Army handlers suggested that his intelligence had been placed before Nehru and Krishna Menon. Indian's civilian leadership had, Wignall was told, judged the information he had obtained as suspect, and it was discounted. The British Foreign Office, and officers from SIS, who Wignall alleged debriefed him on his return to London, evidenced greater interest in a rare instance of eyewitness testimony from an inaccessible corner of the globe. With precision aerial surveillance of the Himalayas beyond the capabilities of Britain and India, and satellite imagery still some years away, utilising civilians for intelligence gathering operations on India's border offered the prospect of significant rewards, but also ran significant political risks. Intriguingly, Wignall's foray into a modern rendering of South Asia's 'Great Game' would later intersect with another multi-national intelligence enterprise in the Himalayas that also employed foreign mountaineers. While in Chinese captivity, Wignall fed his PLA interrogators disinformation. The CIA, the British climber informed his PLA guards, had placed listening devices on two Himalayan peaks to monitor military activity across Tibet and into China.[26] A decade later, India would engage in just such an exercise in partnership with the CIA.[27]

India's capacity to respond to Chinese threats developing beyond its immediate borders was more limited. Until 1949, only one desk within the IB was dedicated to foreign intelligence. Under Sanjeevi's direction, the IB did post officers to Indian diplomatic missions in Pakistan and a small number of European capitals. Plans to expand the Intelligence Bureau's international footprint, however, were compromised by Sanjeevi's removal as DIB, in July 1950.[28] Nehru was sceptical that India needed, and could afford, a geographically diffuse intelligence infrastructure. 'I do not think that we should go in a big way to expand our Intelligence services', the Indian remier maintained. 'That is beyond our capacity.'[29] Nehru had a point. The challenge of gathering reliable and timely information on an effectively closed society in China had defeated intelligence services that were far larger and better resourced than the IB. Efforts that were undertaken by the IB to enhance its coverage of China were hampered by structural and cultural obstacles, as much as financial considerations. The study of Chinese linguistics, culture, politics, and history were neglected in the Indian academic system until the middle of the 1950s. At the time, one study estimated that within the whole of India no more than half a dozen citizens of non-Chinese origin were capable of reading and writing Chinese.[30] British efforts to establish 'closer liaison' with Indian colleagues 'over information about Chinese [border] activities' also failed to gain much traction. British diplomats in Beijing were reluctant to broach such a sensitive matter with local Indian colleagues. In December 1954, when London authorised an approach to the Indian counsellor in Beijing, who had 'shown signs of wishing to exchange confidences', the initiative collapsed after the counsellor was posted away before any information sharing could occur. The local British mission tried and failed to identify an alternative Indian conduit 'suitable and willing' to share intelligence on China's domestic politics and foreign policy.[31]

In 1957, as Sino-Indian tensions increased, the IB persuaded Nehru to approve the posting of an intelligence officer to Beijing under diplomatic cover. In doing so, the Indian premier overrode objections from the MEA and India's ambassador in China, Ratan Kumar (R. K.) Nehru. It was agreed that the intelligence officer sent to Beijing should be a fluent Chinese speaker. India's prime minister also stipulated that the IB's man in China, 'should be a trained economist and should also have political training'. 'Mere intelligence training', Nehru reasoned, 'is very far from adequate for an appraisal of a [foreign] situation'. Having set the bar for Indian intelligence officers aspiring to serve in China so high, it was unsurprising when plans to station a second IB officer in Shanghai were later abandoned for a want of suitable personnel.[32] Two years later, in 1959, as Sino-Indian enmity grew, an Indian academic, and member of the Praja Socialist Party, expressed bemusement to Nehru that an Indian intelligence and propaganda organisation had yet to be established in wider Asia. Having recently toured the region, Dr Samar Guha informed Nehru that he had been struck by the fact that, 'our [India's] Embassies abroad ... might give greater publicity to our border issues and India's viewpoint. There was a great deal of interest in them, but our Embassies

were not utilizing this opportunity to publicize our case.' When it came to the matter of China, Guha observed pointedly, 'Hong Kong ... was an ideal place for [an] intelligence set-up to find out what was happening in China. But apparently, we [India] had no such set-up there.'[33]

Building Intelligence Bridges

When China launched its military offensive against India in the autumn of 1962, it was not only New Delhi that was caught off-guard. As Indians reeled from the trauma of being pitched unexpectedly into a battle with their northern neighbour, 4,000 miles away in London, John Kenneth Galbraith spent the evening of 20 October at a West End theatre. Galbraith had stopped off in Britain while travelling back from New Delhi to Washington. With the conclusion of one dramatic performance, the US ambassador stepped into the London night to be greeted by another, as newsstands proclaimed the outbreak of hostilities between India and China. Back at his hotel, Galbraith was handed an urgent message from President Kennedy that ordered him to return to India on the next available flight. Kennedy's message made no reference to Sino-Indian fighting. Galbraith was needed in New Delhi, the President explained, to brief Nehru on developments taking place in the Caribbean. The CIA had discovered that the Soviet Union was constructing intermediate range nuclear missile sites in Cuba, ninety miles off America's eastern seaboard.[34] With Washington's focus on events in Cuba, it was not until the end of October that the Kennedy administration began to devote sustained attention to India's plight.[35] Kennedy was awake to the wider significance of the clash between India and China. The President confided to aides that the border war might well prove as fateful for American global interests as the Cuban Missile Crisis. By forcing Moscow to side with either India or China; opening a window for rapprochement between India and Pakistan; and fostering closer military and intelligence relations between New Delhi and the West; the President speculated that Beijing's aggression could rebound to Washington's advantage.[36]

On 25 October, a humbled Nehru conceded that his government had been guilty of, 'getting out of touch with the modern world [and] ... living in an artificial atmosphere of our own creation'.[37] The next day, India's premier issued a call for international 'sympathy and support', as barely a week into the border fighting Indian forces stood on the brink of an ignominious defeat.[38] The Kennedy administration responded promptly with pledges of political and material assistance. Calling a press conference in New Delhi, Galbraith brushed aside opposition from Washington's Nationalist Chinese allies and announced the United States' formal recognition of India's border claims. Having received a direct request from Nehru for military aid, Galbraith began working closely with the Indian Ministry of Defence, the Pentagon, and his British counterparts, to expedite the delivery of automatic rifles, ammunition, and military spares to India.[39] On 19 November, a further Chinese offensive shattered India's defensive line in the north. Nehru reacted by confirming to a stunned nation that his government had approached the United States and Britain for 'massive' military support. 'We are not going to tolerate this kind of [Chinese] invasion of India', Nehru proclaimed, '... India is not going to lose this war, however long it lasts and whatever harm it may do us.'[40] Representing his nation's plight as 'desperate', the Indian leader informed an incredulous Kennedy that only direct American military intervention in the Sino-Indian conflict could avert, 'nothing short of a catastrophe for our country'. Twelve squadrons of American supersonic fighters, two squadrons of bombers, and a mobile radar network, were all needed by India, Nehru declared, to check the PLA's advance. Concluding that the India premier was 'clearly in a state of panic', Kennedy questioned whether the ageing Nehru's judgement had deserted him.[41] Having earlier rejected charges from the Indian Left that the Kennedy administration was plotting to coerce New Delhi into becoming a Western ally, Galbraith was dismayed to find Nehru's government, 'pleading for military association'.[42]

Alarmed by the political and strategic implications of Nehru's appeal for a *de facto* military alliance with the United States, Kennedy determined to cut through the fog of war by dispatching a high-level fact-finding delegation to the subcontinent. Modelled on the Taylor mission that had assessed the military situation in South Vietnam, in October 1961, the American taskforce was led by the veteran diplomatic envoy, Averell Harriman.[43] Simultaneously, the British government sent its own politico-military team to India, headed by Duncan Sandys, the Secretary of State for Commonwealth Relations.[44] Shortly before midnight on 20 November, with the Harriman and Sandys missions yet to arrive in New Delhi, the Chinese government stunned the world by announcing a unilateral ceasefire and the staged withdrawal of its forces from much of the territory that they had occupied over the previous month. In practice, by relinquishing China's hold on territory in the northeast and asserting its control of Aksai Chin in the west, Beijing imposed on Nehru's government a border settlement that it had previously tried, and failed, to secure diplomatically.[45] The timing of the ceasefire, as British officials noted, was significant, and left India 'somewhat more committed to the West than would have been the case had the Chinese acted two days earlier'.[46]

Once in India, the Harriman and Sandys missions wasted little time in bringing influence to bear on Nehru's government. The sizeable American and British delegations included political advisers, economists, military personnel, and intelligence officers. Prominent among the latter were Desmond Fitzgerald, chief of the CIA's Far Eastern division, James Critchfield, head of CIA Near East Operations, and John Knaus, who ran the Agency's Tibetan Task Force. The mission's discussions with Indian government officials spanned a wide range of issues, including the provision of military aid, funding

CONFRONTING CHINA

for economic development, and the intractable dispute between India and Pakistan over Kashmir, and were exhaustively covered by the subcontinent's newspapers. Little public comment was made of talks held between the British and American mission's intelligence officers and their Indian counterparts. Strenuous efforts undertaken by the United States and the United Kingdom in the wake of the Harriman and Sandys missions to bolster India's military capabilities, revitalise its moribund economy, and resolve the Kashmir dispute, came to little. Before the end of the 1960s, India had largely turned its back on the West and looked increasingly to the Soviet Union for fiscal support and military supplies. Kashmir remained a sore point in India's relations with Pakistan.

In contrast, the Harriman and Sandys missions had a more transformative and a less transient impact on Indian's intelligence relationship with Britain and the United States. Exchanges held between senior CIA officers and their British colleagues with India's intelligence leaders paved the way for the evolution of new and extensive joint covert action capabilities directed primarily at the People's Republic of China.[47] These came to encompass, amongst other things, the deployment of a clandestine warfare unit to monitor Chinese military supply routes into Tibet; the development of enhanced photographic signals and imagery intelligence capabilities; an operation to install nuclear-powered surveillance equipment on India's Himalayan peaks to monitor Chinese atomic tests; and offensive disinformation activity designed to erode international support for China and burnish India's global standing.[48] The border war also served as a catalyst for the expansion of British covert operations in India and the return of SIS to the subcontinent. If the origins of the 'Attlee Directive' lay in India in the late 1940s, its effective demise was sealed by events in the subcontinent in the early 1960s.

Before the United States moved to recalibrate its intelligence relationship with New Delhi, members of the Harriman mission presented Washington with a blunt assessment of the deficiencies within India's intelligence community. In a report sent to the Joint Chiefs of Staff by General Paul Adams, the senior military officer attached to the Harriman mission and head of US Strike Command, the history of Indian international relations was represented as 'basically one of passive resistance'. India had, Adams stated, focused too much attention on a threat posed by Pakistan, while overlooking China's aggressive intent. Prior to October 1962, Adams noted, 'India's intelligence system was erroneously considered reasonably efficient.' Poor intelligence collection, inadequate information processing, and faulty intelligence estimates had been exposed by China's incursion into northern India and had laid bare an 'inadequate national intelligence effort'.[49] Adams suggested that India's substandard intelligence performance was due to over reliance on organisational structures and procedures that were outmoded and not fit for purpose. British colonial practices that dated back to the early decades of the century retained currency inside the Intelligence Bureau, which wielded an 'extraordinary concentration of responsibility for police affairs, internal security, and foreign intelligence collection ... '. Improving the effectiveness of India's civil and military intelligence services and addressing weaknesses in intelligence coordination and control across the government of India, Washington was warned, would not be a quick or an easy fix.

American officials voiced additional concern that New Delhi had been reluctant in the past to exchange intelligence information with the United States and, while the border war had changed the intelligence liaison environment, 'the Indians continue to resist a freer exchange [of intelligence material]'. The fact that Mullik had worked closely with Britain and other Commonwealth countries on security matters was seen as reassuring, but it was deemed troubling that the DIB had cultivated 'no official liaison with other foreign intelligence services and *has* avoided official contact with foreign intelligence agencies'. In part, Mullik's parochial attitude was attributed to a sensitivity on the part of senior Indian intelligence officers to New Delhi's policy of non-alignment. Equally, members of the Harriman mission suspected that the Indians realised 'much of their intelligence product is of a low standard' and were disinclined to advertise that fact. Whatever the obstacles restricting intelligence exchange, America's spooks were eager to sweep them aside. Given Mullik's position as 'a close personal adviser' to Nehru, and his broad responsibilities for border intelligence and paramilitary activity, winning the trust of India's spy chief was seen as critical to the evolution of US-Indian intelligence relations. It would be of 'extreme benefit to US intelligence interests', Adams emphasised, to move rapidly in establishing 'joint intelligence collection projects [with India] designed to insure mutual exchange of information'.[50]

For some American diplomats, securing the cooperation of Mullik was no more important to the progression of US-Indian intelligence relations than ensuring that the CIA remained under tight bureaucratic control in the subcontinent. Galbraith was particularly concerned that the presence of Desmond Fitzgerald on Harriman's staff signalled the potential for trouble. Fitzgerald had established a reputation within the Agency's Directorate of Plans, or covert operations division, for sponsoring risky clandestine activity across Asia. He had been a driving force behind the CIA's Tibetan task force. Fitzgerald's involvement in the latter covert action, which Galbraith condemned as ill-judged and politically reckless, led the ambassador to characterise him as 'one of the most irresponsible' officers in Agency's history. Suspicious that Fitzgerald would attempt to lure Indians into undertaking insecure and inappropriate operations, Galbraith had the CIA officer trailed around Delhi by a trusted embassy official. 'A spy to watch a spy', as the ambassador later noted.[51] Meanwhile, the sober and steady figure of James Critchfield was encouraged by Galbraith to take the lead in Agency discussions with Mullik.[52] Galbraith need not have worried. The extensive programme of joint covert operations that the CIA went on to implement in partnership with India's Intelligence Bureau would escape public scrutiny for many years to come. Paradoxically, it was revelations surrounding illegal CIA involvement with educational and cultural bodies inside the United States that would eventually set-off a political firestorm in India. In the immediate aftermath of the border conflict, however, the focus of America's intelligence community in South Asia was directed towards reinvigorating the capabilities of a new Indian collaborator in Washington's decades long struggle with Red China.

India's Clandestine China War

The most significant agreement that James Critchfield reached with the Intelligence Bureau in November 1962 was to provide CIA support in training and logistics for a new paramilitary force that Mullik intended to deploy on India's northern border. The predominantly Tibetan-manned unit was designated as the Special Frontier Force (SFF). It was more commonly known as Establishment 22, a soubriquet acquired from its leader, Major General Sujan Singh Urban, who had commanded the Twenty-Second Indian Army Mountain regiment during the Second World War. Modelled on the Green Berets, or US Army Special Forces, the SSF, who wore distinctive red caps, eventually came to encompass 12,000 elite troops.[53] For CIA officers and their colleagues in the US Army, the attraction of supporting India's development of an unconventional warfare capability lay, primarily, in the impact it was expected to have relative to the costs involved. Referencing the use that the Soviets had made of partisan units employed behind German lines on the Eastern front two decades previously, American officials emphasised that 'the entire [Indian] border area is excellent terrain for guerrilla operations'. 'If advantage is taken of the opportunity that now exists to train defensive guerrilla forces for operations behind enemy lines as stay-behind forces in case of invasion', the Harriman mission reasoned, 'the defense of India can be greatly enhanced at small cost'.[54] Specifically, Washington was asked to commit the United States to assist India in building up a defensive guerrilla warfare capability in the border areas adjacent to Bhutan, Sikkim, and the NEFA. The Kennedy administration was also pressed to support the Intelligence Bureau's plans to expand Indian offensive unconventional warfare operations. This scheme envisaged the IB co-opting refugees from India's northern frontier and, following appropriate training, sending them back across the border into Tibet to disrupt Chinese communications and collect intelligence.[55]

On 28 November, before the Harriman mission departed from the subcontinent, Critchfield and his military colleagues attended a meeting with Mullik and senior Indian Army officers at the Ministry of Defence in New Delhi. The gathering agreed a series of specific actions to take forward the development of

Figure 5.1 Tibetan refugees after being evacuated from the Sino-Indian border by the United States Air Force, Pathankot, India, 1962. United States Information Agency collection, US National Archives, College Park, Maryland.

India's unconventional warfare capabilities. To facilitate the planning and coordination of 'a wide spectrum of possible operations', agreement was reached to establish a Joint Unconventional Warfare Task Force (JUWTF) headquarters in New Delhi, that would operate under the auspices of the American Joint Military Mission to India (AJMMI). In addition, it was decided to set up a Joint Unconventional Warfare Operations Base (JUWOB) at Hasimara, a town situated on the banks of the Torsha River in northern West Bengal, near India's border with Bhutan. The facility at Hasimara was earmarked to oversee the training and operational activity of Indian and refugee guerrilla forces and was to be managed locally by an American Special Forces team, a US Air Force commando detachment, and four US Army units. Eight 'sanitised' American and Indian aircraft, stripped of all markings and identification numbers, were allotted to operate out of Hasimara and provide the guerrilla forces with air mobility. The meeting between Indian and American intelligence officers ended on 'a note of enthusiasm'. Given the problematic political optics that surrounded India's clandestine joint venture with the United States, both parties to the arrangement were, nevertheless, at pains to stress 'a very definite desire that the entire operation be as covert as possible'.[56] Less is known about British involvement in India's unconventional warfare programme. It is clear, however, that small numbers of British military personnel and intelligence officers with experience in guerrilla tactics and stay-behind operations did contribute to the training of Indian personnel. Mark Scarse-Dickens, who served in Britain's special forces in the jungles of Borneo during the *Konfrontasi* with Indonesia and went on to enjoy a long and successful career in SIS, completed at least one 'shadowy' tour of India. Scarse-Dickens passed on skills in cross-border ambushes to Indian recruits in the Himalayas before he was invalided back home. Mercifully, the curtailment of Scarse-Dickens' Indian adventure was not brought about by Chinese action. He was laid low by a bout of jaundice acquired after eating with a remote group of mountain herders and drove several hundred miles in a service Land Rover back to a hospital in New Delhi, where he collapsed.[57]

In the days leading up to Critchfield's exchange with Mullik, Nehru had indicated his support for strengthening India's unconventional warfare capacity. On 25 November, writing to his newly installed Minister of Defence, Yashwantrao Balwantrao Chavan, the Indian premier applauded the decision to recruit 'our tribal people in the Northeast' for special operations. 'These border people are tough and fit', Nehru noted approvingly, 'and especially good at some kind of guerrilla warfare'.[58] The sense of personal shock and betrayal that tormented Nehru following the onset of Sino-Indian hostilities, prompted something akin to a damascene conversion when it came to unconventional warfare. During late 1963 and early 1964, Nehru toured the SFF's main training camp in the Himalayas. He also visited the secret Charbatia air base, code-named Oak Tree, an abandoned Second World War airstrip near Cuttack, in the state of Odisha, in eastern India, that had been converted for use by Indian and American clandestine forces.[59] For a leader who had long harboured misgivings about the activities undertaken by intelligence agencies in democratic societies, and those practised by American intelligence agencies in particular, Nehru's willingness to embrace covert action following China's incursion into northern India represented a remarkable *volte face*.

Back in Washington, senior officials on the National Security Council proved to be equally enthusiastic advocates of India's development of an unconventional warfare programme. Robert Komer, the resident NSC expert on South Asia, argued that offering 'greater [US] backing to India's U/W [unconventional warfare] effort makes a great deal of sense'. By 1965, the $13 million that India had received to fund its secret war against China, Komer reasoned, represented exceptionally good value for money. By bankrolling covert operations in India's northern border areas, he maintained, it was possible to reassure New Delhi that the United States was 'serious about

China'. Moreover, 'being helpful under the table' where India was concerned, was seen as useful in counteracting lingering suspicions amongst Indians that Americans were 'really Pak[istani]s at heart'.[60] The political dividend that Washington expected to garner from supporting Indian unconventional warfare operations, as opposed to the strictly military value of a programme that was likely to prove little more than an irritant to the Chinese, underpinned America's willingness to keep covert action dollars flowing into New Delhi. In April 1966, Walt Rostow, Lyndon Johnson's national security adviser, endorsed a new and larger tranche of funding for Indian clandestine operations on the basis that, 'it is a quiet way to build our links with India in the security field in ways which counter Soviet leverage.' Utilising Indo-US collaboration in covert operations to limit Moscow's penetration of India's national security establishment made good sense to Rostow. Concerns remained in the White House that American involvement in India's secret war, were it to become more widely known, would alienate Pakistan and, more seriously, 'engage us [the United States], against our will, in an India-China conflict'. Such risks, Rostow judged, while considerable, were worth taking to keep India closely aligned with the West, and China tied up in securing its borders. 'On balance', Rostow counselled Johnson, 'I support this [Indian unconventional warfare] venture.'[61] American's ambassador in New Delhi, Chester Bowles, added another voice to those promoting expanded US support for India's unconventional warfare capability. Writing to Rostow, in July 1966, Bowles urged the Johnson administration not to stint on the provision of financial aid. 'This [unconventional warfare] is a tangible operation which has significant possibilities from our point of view', Bowles urged, 'and at this critical point I would hate to have the Indians begin to feel that we are losing interest in them'.[62]

British defence officials, although little more than interested bystanders in the evolution of Indian clandestine warfare, harboured anxieties that the rapid expansion of the Special Frontier Force facilitated by American largesse left it vulnerable to communist penetration. In talks with General Jayanto Nath Chaudhuri, the Indian Army's Chief of Staff, Britain's Chief of Defence Staff (CDS), Lord Louis Mountbatten, expressed misgivings that Mullik's Intelligence Bureau had recruited large numbers of 'guerrillas' from India's northeastern border regions. Recommending that Mullik's recruits were screened or positively vetted by the Indian Army, Mountbatten emphasised that 'experience in the last war showed that it was mainly the people of Communist outlook or fellow travellers who volunteered to become guerrillas ... '.[63] During subsequent exchanges with Britain's high commissioner in India, John Freeman, Mountbatten reinforced his apprehension that Mullik and the IB were running undue risks by pressing ahead with the expansion of the SFF without first implementing a rigorous process of background checks on its recruits. Mountbatten informed Freeman that India's

President, Sarvepalli Radhakrishnan, had advised him in confidence that the Governor of West Bengal had 'written to him [Radhakrishnan] expressing fears about the reliability of the guerrillas being raised by Mullick [sic], which he feared contained a lot of Communists or at least fellow travellers'. The Indian president, Mountbatten added, had seen fit to raise concerns over the SFF's political reliability directly with Nehru's successor, Lal Bahadur Shastri.[64] The British intervention had no discernible effect on the pace with which Mullik continued to build-up India's paramilitary border force. Determined not to be caught out a second time by a surprise Chinese assault in the north, Mullik prioritised the deployment of SFF forces on the Sino-Indian border and ignored suspicions that some of his men might not be entirely trustworthy.

Mullik's conviction that clandestine warfare could help to offset deficiencies in conventional Indian military power before deliveries of foreign ordnance and new programmes of indigenous armaments production took effect, proved important in revitalising the CIA's covert programme in Tibet. Having lost impetus before the outbreak of Sino-Indian fighting in the face of criticism from the Kennedy administration that the programme ran significant political risks and yet delivered little in the way of results, the Agency's enthusiasm for revisiting unconventional warfare in Tibet was boosted by Indian support.[65] In partnership with New Delhi, the CIA launched a new Tibetan initiative that encompassed covert political action, propaganda, and paramilitary activity. Its purpose was to keep the concept of an autonomous Tibet alive, both inside Tibet and amongst sympathetic foreign states. In the longer term, the objective was to build a Tibetan resistance movement capable of exploiting favourable political developments within Communist China, should they occur. In 1963, the CIA flew 133 Tibetans to its training facility at Camp Hale in Colorado for instruction in political propaganda and paramilitary techniques. The Agency also sent some of the 2,000 or so Nepal-based Tibetans that had participated in its original resistance operations for retraining in Indian camps. By early 1964, the total cost of the broad-based Tibetan operation, including equipping, training, and transporting paramilitary forces, propaganda activity, and a subsidy of $180,000 paid to the Dalai Lama, had reached close to $2 million. 'This [Tibetan] program', Agency officers cautioned the Special Group, a high-level, inter-departmental body responsible for directing covert operations, 'will continue to require fairly large expenditures over a long period of time to keep the possibility of a non-Communist government alive to the Tibetan people'.[66]

Between 1964 and 1967, the CIA infiltrated over two dozen teams of irregular forces into Tibet. Mullik and the IB played a crucial part in the operation and helped to guide the insurgent teams safely across the line of control between India and Tibet. New Delhi had objected to plans to parachute the teams into Tibet on the grounds that, back in the 1950s, doing so had proved impossible to conceal, had infuriated Beijing, and would now invite punitive Chinese retaliation. Disappointingly for the CIA and the IB, the revived Tibetan operation proved no more effective than its earlier incarnation, elements of which dated back as far as 1956. Although one team sent into Tibet managed to survive for an extended period, the remainder were quickly compromised, and their members captured and killed. One CIA assessment conceded that, 'Chinese security has shown no signs of deterioration and their control over Tibet, both political and military, remains as pervasive as ever . . . a large number of underground [Agency] assets have been uncovered and neutralized.'[67] By the early 1970s, having registered a signal lack of success, and with the Nixon administration pursuing a rapprochement with Communist China, the paramilitary programme was disbanded.[68]

India's decision to collaborate with the United States in waging a covert war against China did incite occasional ripostes from Beijing. In March 1967, a large and vocal public demonstration outside the Chinese embassy in New Delhi saw protestors shout anti-Chinese slogans, plaster the embassy's outer walls with anti-Chinese literature, and, at one point, attempt to storm the buildings heavily fortified gates. In response, China's Charge d'affaires issued a statement lambasting the Indian government for failing to prevent an attack on Chinese sovereign territory, for sheltering the 'traitorous Dalai [Lama] clique', and 'fostering and training . . . Tibetan traitor bandits, who are living in exile in India, in the fond hope that someday they could fight back to Tibet and restore serfdom there'. Should New Delhi's anti-China policy persist, and its interference in China's internal affairs continue, Beijing warned, India would 'be held responsible for the serious consequences arising therefrom'.[69] Later that summer, China arrested two Indian diplomats in Beijing, Second Secretary, K. Raghunath, and the Third Secretary, P. Vijai, and charged them with spying. Declared *persona non grata*, the Indians were deported to Hong Kong and subject to sustained violence and humiliation on their journey between the Chinese capital and Britain's crown colony. At Beijing airport, before boarding a flight to Canton, Raghunath and Vijai were pummelled and kicked for nearly an hour by hundreds of protestors, one of whom was a member of the Protocol Department of the Chinese Ministry of Foreign Affairs. In Canton, Raghunath was paraded through the streets in the back of an open lorry, forced to wear large dunce's cap, and beaten with bamboo poles.

By way of retaliation, the Indian government expelled a Chinese diplomat from New Delhi, placed a police cordon around China's embassy, and imposed severe restrictions on the movements of its officials in India. On 16 June, the Indian police stood by as a riotous crowd burst into the Chinese embassy compound and assaulted several Chinese officials. The tit-for-tat cycle of reprisals shifted focus back to Beijing the next day, when Chinese authorities arranged for a mob to surround the Indian embassy and, over the course of a three-day siege, smash all its windows.[70] The message conveyed by China was unequivocal. Beijing's patience with what it perceived to be unwarranted

Indian meddling in China's internal affairs had been exhausted. If New Delhi persisted in fanning the flames of Sinophobia at home, and offering support to insurgent forces inside Tibet, China would hit back. Ultimately, India's effort to regulate a covert war against China, fought with American support, and avoid public scrutiny and diplomatic fallout, proved quixotic. A decade or so later, blowback from the IB's clandestine Himalayan partnership with the CIA would generate global headlines and almost spell domestic political disaster for an embattled Congress Party.

Eyes in the Sky

A more successful legacy of Indian intelligence cooperation with the United States in the wake of the border war manifested in the field of aerial reconnaissance. Prior to Sino-Indian hostilities, the Indian Air Force (IAF) had flown short-range photographic reconnaissance missions over south-central Tibet, the NEFA, and Burma using British-supplied Canberra aircraft. The IAF did not possess the capability to penetrate Chinese airspace regularly and in-depth.[71] In any case, the Indian government was wary of the political consequences of undertaking missions that risked IAF aircraft being lost over Chinese-controlled territory. In seeking to monitor security threats developing along its northern border without provoking a further round of fighting with Beijing, New Delhi turned to the United States for assistance. On 5 May 1963, at a meeting held between Nehru, Mullik, and Chavan, agreement was reached to allow American aircraft to use a network of Indian airfields for covert reconnaissance purposes. Given the sensitivity surrounding the use of sovereign Indian territory to launch clandestine air operations over China, Indian and American policymakers were anxious to obscure the nature of the operation. Care was taken to ensure that airstrips used by the Americans were not also used by the IAF, or any other Indian military units.[72] In June 1963, the Aviation Research Centre (ARC) was inaugurated by the Intelligence Bureau with American support. Initially, the ARC operated eight US-supplied C-46 aircraft and several smaller planes out of the secret Oak Tree air base at Charbatia. Operations quickly expanded to include ARC aircraft flying out of Sarsawa in Uttar Pradesh, Doom Dooma in Assam, and the military zone of Palam airport, in New Delhi. The ARC's purpose was to supply photographic and technical intelligence on PLA forces in Tibet and Xinjiang, in Western China. Over a period of two years, American intelligence officers and technicians worked closely with the IB to transform the ARC into an effective forward reconnaissance arm of Indian intelligence.[73]

Concurrently, Nehru's government approved a request from Washington to operate high altitude U-2 aircraft out of India. The U-2 had been developed by the CIA in the mid-1950s to overfly the Soviet Union at flight ceiling that made it near invulnerable to Russian air defences. On 11 November 1962, as

Sino-Indian hostilities were ongoing, Nehru brokered an agreement with Galbraith under which U-2's were permitted to refuel in mid-air within Indian airspace during missions to monitor Chinese military deployments on the battlefront. Given Nehru's previously rigid adherence to the principle of Cold War non-alignment and steadfast rejection of foreign military aid, the American ambassador quipped to colleagues that the 'most improbable conversation of the century was Galbraith negotiating with Nehru on U-2 overflights'.[74] Later that month, U-2s based in Ta Khli, in Thailand, began operating over the Sino-Indian border on a flight plan that took the aircraft over the Bay of Bengal and eastern India. By January 1963, U-2 flights infringing Chinese airspace were identified by Beijing as having transited through India, and a formal protest was lodged with New Delhi by the Chinese government. Nehru inadvertently exacerbated Beijing's ire when, having received confidential briefings from American intelligence on the photographic take from U-2 missions, he referenced specific details of Chinese troop movements in a statement to the Indian parliament. Journalists correctly surmised that information within Nehru's public statement had been based upon information obtained from U-2 overflights.[75] Although irritated by Nehru's indiscretion, the CIA were delighted by the Indian prime minister's fascination with the striking visual imagery produced by the U-2's. 'If this is to be Nehru's new secret vice', senior Agency officers messaged Galbraith, 'I think we can keep him provided with "feelthy peectures" from all around the world, so long as he latches on tight to this particular exercise.'[76]

Nehru's indiscretions aside, Washington pushed to expand and consolidate collaboration with India in the realm of covert aerial reconnaissance for two reasons. Faced with requests from New Delhi for the United States to underwrite a sweeping overhaul of India's defence establishment by means of a $1.6 billion five-year military assistance programme (MAP), the Pentagon wanted hard evidence to puncture what it regarded as inflated and unjustifiable Indian plans to guard against future Chinese aggression. Talk within Nehru's administration of establishing a twenty-five-division Indian army by 1965 was dismissed by US Secretary of Defense, Robert McNamara, as 'completely unrealistic on the grounds of finance, manpower and the demands which their requirements would make of the ... United States'.[77] Equally, America's intelligence community saw value in establishing a precedent for U-2 overflights in India. Such a development, some US officials anticipated, might lead to more permanent US basing rights in India that would facilitate missions against the Soviets anti-ballistic missile testing range at Sary Shagan, in Kazakhstan, and areas of western China that were difficult to reach from U-2 airfields outside the subcontinent. In April 1963, Galbraith and the local CIA Chief of Station, David Blee, met with Indian officials and formally requested the provision of base facilities for U-2 aircraft. Within a matter of weeks, President Kennedy added his weight to the U-2 issue by raising the matter

CONFRONTING CHINA

with his Indian counterpart, Sarvepalli Radhakrishnan. It was following Kennedy's intervention that the United States was offered use of the Charbatia airfield for U-2 operations.[78]

It was some time before dilapidated facilitates at Charbatia could be made serviceable and were brought into operation. In the interim, U-2 flights over Tibet and western China continued to be routed through Thailand. On 24 May 1964, the first U-2 mission was launched from Charbatia. Three days later, Nehru died suddenly from a heart attack. While a nation grieved, and a battle to succeed Nehru preoccupied the attention of Indian policymakers, the Indian U-2 programme was suspended and its American aircraft and support crews were flown out of the country. Operations resumed at Charbatia in December, when concern mounted that an increase in tensions between New Delhi and Beijing might see a resumption in Sino-Indian fighting. Three further U-2 missions were conducted from the Indian airstrip before the latest crisis in Sino-Indian relations abated. By that time, the Indian U-2 programme had helped to confirm that that a facility Beijing had constructed at Lop Nor, in south-eastern Xinjiang, was being developed as a nuclear test site. Operations at Charbatia were subsequently scaled back and the airstrip was employed primarily as a forward staging post for U-2 missions launched from Ta Khli. In July 1967, as relations between Washington and New Delhi cooled, the Indian phase of the CIA's U-2 programme at Charbatia was permanently shut down.[79]

The fact that Nehru's government was prepared to sanction U-2 flights from Indian territory, and accept the considerable political risks this involved, revealed much about the levels of national anxiety and vulnerability that Indians felt towards China after 1962. Back in May 1960, Pakistan had become embroiled in an embarrassing and incendiary Cold War incident when a U-2 aircraft flying out of Peshawar, in northern Pakistan, was downed by a Soviet air defence missile over the Urals. The 'May Day' affair sent US-Soviet relations into freefall, prompted the cancellation of a major Cold War summit meeting in Paris, and forced Pakistan to issue a grovelling apology to Moscow.[80] Pakistan's unfortunate experience of playing host to American spy planes must have weighted heavily on Nehru's mind as he weighed the merits of permitting U-2s to operate from Indian soil.

Operation Hat

Later in the decade, joint efforts by India and the United States to keep a watch on the PRC took in an ambitious scheme to position remotely operated and nuclear-powered monitoring devices near the highest points of the Nanda Devi range in the Himalayas. Codenamed Operation Hat, an allusion to the missions cover story, which linked it to the US Air Force's High Altitude Test (HAT) program and, at points, also referred to as Blue Mountain, the

120   SPYING IN SOUTH ASIA

collaborative endeavour between the CIA and the IB used a crack team of American and Indian mountaineers to haul the monitoring devices into place.[81] The surveillance equipment was designed to harvest technical data from Chinese nuclear test sites and missile ranges in Xinjiang, 500 miles to the north. On 16 October 1964, China successfully exploded its first nuclear bomb, a uranium-235 device, at its Lop Nor test site. With the PRC outstripping India in industrial capacity, literacy rates and domestic consumption, Western policymakers worried that a failure to contain a nuclear China would leave subsequent generations of their citizens facing an unenviable security dilemma. A year earlier, in August 1963, President Kennedy had publicly speculated that, left unchecked, the PRC, with 700 million people, nuclear weapons, a Stalinist internal regime and an expansionist outlook, would pose the gravest threat to global peace since the end of the Second World War.[82] Having been on the receiving end of a brutal demonstration of Chinese military power, the Indian government sought reassurance from Washington that in any future clash with Beijing they could count on Western support. Britain and the United States were concerned that China's accession to the atomic club would prompt India to develop its own nuclear capability, diverting precious resources from the country's economic development and risking a dangerous regional arms race. Britain's prime minister, Harold Wilson, had warned his cabinet that, 'the watershed of proliferation would be [broken] if India were compelled to make a nuclear weapon under threat from China'.[83]

India's premier, Lal Bahadur Shastri, was known to be against developing an Indian bomb. Other senior Indian ministers, including Chavan, and the Minister for Defence Production, Alunkal Mathai Thomas, made it clear to the British that 'a growing tide of opinion' in the Congress Party opposed the Indian premier's 'negative' policy. Indians were aware, Chavan observed, that they were, 'faced by an enemy [China] which believed in the inevitability of war, and of nuclear war at that'.[84] Washington reasoned that one means of ameliorating Indian apprehension regarding China's bomb, and strengthening the position of nuclear dissenters, such as Shastri, would be to work with New Delhi to obtain accurate intelligence on evolving Chinese nuclear capabilities. Three Indian premiers, Nehru, Shastri, and Indira Gandhi were briefed on Operation Hat at various points, and each gave the project their approval.[85] A decade or so later, Indian's then prime minister, Morarji Desai, dispelled notions that the CIA and Indian's intelligence services had exceeded their authority and acted independently when it came to executing the mission. 'They [the CIA and the IB] were just acting on orders from the highest political levels', Desai informed a stunned Indian public, in April 1978.[86]

Back in 1967, a group of Indian mountaineers, led by Manmohan Singh Kohli, a celebrated climber and naval officer seconded to the Indo-Tibetan Border Police, were sent from the subcontinent to Alaska to train with American colleagues and devise a plan for executing Operation Hat. One monitoring device was subsequently installed by a joint CIA/IB controlled climbing team near the summit of Nanda Kot, a 22,000-foot mountain, in the Pithoragarh district of the present-day Indian state of Uttarakhand. The monitor functioned satisfactorily for a year before it was removed. In 1965, the installation of an earlier device was compromised by a snowstorm near the summit of Nanda Devi, an adjacent 25,000-foot peak, and it was lost. Attempts made to locate and recover the monitor, and its plutonium 238 powerpack, failed. Extensive ground and aerial searches sponsored by the Indian government continued into late 1968 without success. Samples of the headwaters fed by the Nandi Devi range were analysed until 1970, and water quality remained under observation for some years afterwards, but no trace of contamination was ever detected. Indian officials eventually concluded that the lost device had most likely been buried by an avalanche or carried away into an inaccessible crevasse.[87] In 1969, a final collaborative mission was undertaken by the CIA and the IB in the Himalayas. This involved the insertion of two monitors, powered by a combination of gas generators and solar power, on peaks in Ladakh and Arunachal Pradesh, at opposite ends of the Himalayan range. Named Operation Gemini, the purpose was to intercept Chinese communications inside Tibet. In 1973, the mission yielded valuable information on Chinese ballistic missile tests. By then, however, the United States' satellite reconnaissance programme was beginning to come into its own, making ground-based sensors redundant.[88]

From Washington's perspective, the programme of joint measurement and signals intelligence operations undertaken with New Delhi were judged to have been a partial success. Joseph Greene stated later that the 'pretty sophisticated' joint operation with India directed against China had yielded useful data and 'when things went mechanically or scientifically wrong, they were able to get fixed, or at least concealed without public uproar'.[89] Indian governments later had good reason to question Greene's sanguine assessment. In May 1978, the investigative American magazine, *Outlook*, published an exposé on Operation Hat. Speculation that the nuclear-powered monitoring devices placed on Nanda Devi and Nanda Kot might have released radioactive material into India's sacred Ganges River generated an uproar in India. Under intense pressure to come clean and reveal what the Indian government knew about Operation Hat, India's prime minister Morarji Desai confirmed publicly, for the first time, that India had secretly conducted clandestine operations with the CIA during the 1960s. The admission sent shockwaves through the nation's political establishment.[90] Fallout from the Himalayan spying affair would endure in Indian politics for years to come, adding to the national sense of paranoia and suspicion surrounding the CIA, and, in the process, exacting a heavy personal and professional toll on Morarji Desai.

Implausible Deniability

The unease that Indian and American policymakers felt in relation to the CIA's expanded role in the subcontinent following the border war of 1962 was reflected in the Agency's resolve to conceal its operational presence in India. In 1965, shortly after being posted to New Delhi, the *New York Times* correspondent, Anthony Lukas, noted that in India the CIA did its best to operate, 'very much on the hush-hush'. In contrast to the more overt presence that it adopted in other parts of the developing world, such as the Congo, in India, Lukas found that the Agency went to, 'great efforts to pretend that it doesn't exist'. The Agency's challenge in disguising the ever-greater numbers of its officers seconded to the American embassy faintly amused Lukas, who found little difficulty in identifying US intelligence personnel. The CIA's determination to keep its presence in India out of the public spotlight was made abundantly clear to the American journalist after he published a 'light yarn' in his newspaper. Lukas's report referenced the emergence of a 'protest movement' amongst American diplomats, led by an unnamed CIA official, against plans to cull some ducks that had taken up residence in a pool within the US embassy compound. Within days of the story's publication, Lukas was summoned to the embassy by the resident press attaché, and tersely informed that he had been declared *persona non grata* by the local CIA station chief. 'I was told', Lukas advised his superiors back in New York, 'that I had gravely compromised the agency's security here'. 'What, I asked incredulously, had I done? The answer: I had informed the Indians that the C.I.A. was operating out of the Embassy.'[91]

The CIA's reaction to Lukas' article was influenced by the fact that India's broader relationship with the United States experienced increasing strain as the 1960s progressed. Once Lyndon Johnson entered the White House in November 1963, America's focus shifted from the Indian subcontinent towards Southeast Asia. Consequently, diplomatic tensions between Washington and New Delhi on issues ranging from the provision of military assistance, the supply of food aid, and the escalating conflict in Vietnam, were allowed to fester. Efforts made by Chester Bowles to maintain constructive diplomatic relations with New Delhi were not helped by a series of revelations that suggested the CIA had recruited assets, or informers, at the very top levels of the Indian government. Bowles was particularly uncomfortable, Joseph Greene noted, with the knowledge that the CIA were working hand-in-glove with Indian intelligence and, at the same time, running separate operations against Indian targets without the knowledge of their host government. An ambassador belonging 'to the school which didn't want to touch "dirty" things', Bowles left his deputy chief of mission to manage the local CIA station.[92] Before arriving in India, Bowles's well-known aversion to clandestine operations had seen him excluded from the Kennedy administration's planning for covert action.

Desmond FitzGerald quipped that giving Bowles authority over covert operations would be akin to, 'entrusting a ship to a captain who hated the sea'.[93] Paradoxically, for an individual deeply uneasy with the secret world, Bowles was fated to spend an inordinate amount of his time as ambassador in India damping down the diplomatic fires ignited by CIA activity in the subcontinent, important facets of which were a legacy of the Sino-Indian War.

6

Peddling Propaganda: The Information Research Department and India

In May 1962, a letter from India arrived at Leconfield House, the headquarters of MI5. The note was from MI5's resident Security Liaison Officer in New Delhi and warned of an awkward development in the close relationship that existed between the Security Service and India's Intelligence Bureau. The Intelligence Bureau had approached its local MI5 contact for advice on a suspicious document circulating in the subcontinent that purported to originate with the Secretariat of the Chinese People's Committee for World Peace. Surfacing at a point when sharp disagreements between Moscow and Beijing had arisen over the formers campaign of de-Stalinisation, the document suggested that the Chinese Committee was about to institute an International Stalin Peace Prize. Indian officials were aware that a similar letter, attributed to the Vienna-based International Institute of Peace had previously been denounced as a hoax. When shown a copy of the 'Chinese' document, MI5's SLO immediately recognised it to be a forgery produced by the Information Research Department, a shadowy clandestine propaganda arm of the British Foreign Office with close links to SIS.[1] Before being posted to India the SLO had visited the IRD, seen the document concerned, and been made aware that it was the work of the department's forgers. To mask its origin, the SLO was instructed by the Security Service to 'deny all knowledge' of the forged document and, in a remarkable display of bravado, to offer to examine it for the Intelligence Bureau and furnish an informed, and disingenuous, 'expert opinion' on its veracity.[2] In Whitehall, British officials worried about the diplomatic repercussions that would follow on from exposure of covert UK 'black' propaganda operations in India. Black propaganda involves influencing a target audience by means of deception or disinformation. Such a tactic is politically contentious, ethically questionable and, as the IRD were aware, risked 'blowback', or unintended and negative outcomes. In India, as elsewhere, the British employed black propaganda less often than more benign 'white' or 'grey' varieties of information management. All three forms of propaganda were utilised by the IRD as part of its anti-communist activity in the subcontinent during the Cold War. Between the outbreak of the Sino-Indian border war, in late 1962, and India's fourth general election, in early 1967, IRD operations in South Asia peaked. During this period, they were active and extensive. Most controversially, on occasions, they encompassed collaboration between the Information Research Department and the Indian government.

The catalyst for Indian collaboration with the United Kingdom in the field of covert propaganda arrived in October 1962, when India's long-simmering border conflict with China suddenly turned hot. An ill-prepared and under resourced Indian government welcomed British support in waging an information war against Communist China. Whitehall's propagandists supplied expert advice and material assistance to Indian colleagues. However, joint operations undertaken between London and New Delhi soon encountered difficulties. British information officers expressed concern that China's propagandists were outmanoeuvring their Indian counterparts, whose news management was seen as muddled and ineffective. At the same time, Britain's own information offensive in the subcontinent suffered from a lack of strategic coherence and cut across the grain of India's prohibition on anti-Soviet propaganda. Discord between Moscow and Beijing, which culminated in the Sino-Soviet split, provided New Delhi with a powerful rationale for courting the USSR. Consequently, the British Government's insistence that Soviet rather than Chinese propaganda posed a greater long-term threat to South Asia, left its Indian partner feeling unsupported. In this context, the British found it impossible to implement a consistent and integrated propaganda strategy in India. Ultimately, London's plans to leverage the Sino-Indian border war to discredit Chinese *and* Soviet communism in South Asia met strong local resistance and floundered.

Going Grey: The Hidden Hand of IRD

In the aftermath of India's independence, 'white' propaganda distributed by the British Information Service (BIS) and the British Council formed the mainstay of the United Kingdom's information effort in the subcontinent. Undertaken openly with State support apparent and declared, 'white' propaganda seldom incorporates material obtained from covert intelligence sources. The negative and manipulative associations attached to the term 'propaganda', however, meant that such activity was invariably represented by official British agencies as publicity work. In global terms, London classified South Asia as a priority for propaganda operations. When the Commonwealth Relations Office increased its information and publicity budget in the post-war period, additional spending was 'very largely concentrated' on the newly independent states of India, Pakistan, and Ceylon.'[3] Britain's high commissioner in India at the time, Sir Archibald Nye, characterised the BIS as 'quietly effective' at spreading anti-communist and pro-British literature. Nye was similarly impressed by the 'good work' conducted in an equally 'unobtrusive way' by the British Council.[4] Senior Indian government officials agreed with Nye's laudatory assessment of Britain's publicity machinery. Sir Girija Shankar Bajpai, secretary general of India's Ministry of External Affairs praised the British for their 'modest' and 'factual' publicity work. The understated British approach, Bajpai reflected, contrasted favourably with 'the extravagant propaganda' circulated by the United States' information agencies, which he deemed to be 'positively detrimental to the interests of the U.S.A. in India'.[5] Keeping India out of the communist bloc represented a 'cardinal point' of post-war British foreign policy. In pursuit of this objective, overt British information agencies in the subcontinent, as Nye underlined, came to represent 'the spearhead of our [Britain's] attack on Communism'.[6]

The IRD maintained close contacts with overt information departments, such as the BIS. In large part, this intimate relationship was driven by a realisation that to maximise its impact, the IRD's anti-communist material needed to be balanced with pro-Western publicity. In November 1951, the Cabinet Overseas Information Committee noted, ' . . . experience shows that negative propaganda fails largely of [sic] its effect unless it is accompanied by at least as great a volume of positive material, that is to say, material showing what is going on in the Western democracies and what hopes their example offers to the world'.[7] John Edmonds, who later supervised the International Section of the IRD, emphasised the importance of ensuring that unattributable propaganda the Department fed to 'opinion moulders' overseas remained in step with the diplomacy practiced by the Foreign Office and its public information bodies.[8] In India, directors of the BIS, beginning with W. F. King in the early 1950s, cultivated strong and effective liaison arrangements with IRD colleagues.[9] Equally, having worked hard to establish its reputation as an organisation 'remarkably free of the propaganda stigma which attaches to certain other foreign information agencies', and the United States Information Agency, in particular, the BIS was determined not to compromise its effectiveness by becoming associated with 'blatant, overt, or covert anti-Communist propaganda activity'. The BIS was prepared to make 'effective and discreet use' of the IRD's services. It was acutely aware, nonetheless, of the risks that working with the IRD entailed. 'One false move', British officials acknowledged, 'could undo the work of years'.[10]

Use of 'grey' propaganda, which constituted the mainstay of IRD activity in India, focuses on the dissemination of unattributable information and masks government involvement. The basis for such material was often derived from 'open sources', or publicly available information disseminated in newspapers, journals, books, and the broadcast media. Grey propaganda was largely factual, although carefully crafted by the IRD to promote a specific political agenda. It frequently manifested in government officials co-opting journalists and publishers to replay favourable content. One British grey propaganda operation of note in the subcontinent occurred towards the end of 1954. Two years previously, when India's relations with Stalin's Soviet Union were far from convivial, Moscow had published a Russian Encyclopaedia. The Encyclopaedia criticised the Indian nationalist icon, Mohandas Karamchand Gandhi, for supporting British imperialism by serving in a medical unit, in South Africa, during the Boer War. The IRD latched onto the Soviets censure of Gandhi and fed the story to media outlets inside and outside India.[11] The editor of the influential Madras newspaper, the *Hindu*, berated the Soviets for promoting a 'fantastically tendentious and perverted account of Gandhi'. In the Manchester *Guardian*, British journalists suggested that Moscow had 'made a grave blunder' by vilifying Gandhi and prompting a 'vigorous' adverse reaction from a nation that revered the *Mahatma*. Broadcasts on All-Indian Radio confirmed that Nehru's government had protested to the Soviet embassy in New Delhi about the Encyclopaedia. Peddling 'such a false' account of Gandhi's life, dismayed Soviet diplomats were informed by Indian officials, was 'completely contrary to the professed Soviet friendship and respect for India'. The Soviets quickly apologised and made clear that the offensive entry would be removed from future editions of the Encyclopaedia. By then, however, the damage had been done, and the IRD took satisfaction in exploiting a Soviet own goal to disrupt Moscow's relations with New Delhi.[12]

Black propaganda, as noted, was employed by the British in India, although it accounted for a relatively small proportion of the IRD's work in the subcontinent. Between the early 1950s and the mid-1970s, the IRD worked closely with SIS's Special Political Action (SPA) section and SPA (Prop) unit which oversaw operations encompassing bribery, forgery, and covert funding of political parties.[13] Producing effective black propaganda involved considerable time and effort. Forging a document required meticulous planning, and necessitated the acquisition of authentic stationary, signatures, and postmarks. Hans Welser, a Swiss immigrant who rose to prominence in the murky world of post-war British disinformation, observed that each forgery had to be laboriously crafted and required 'a skill which is not very common'.[14] In the summer of 1960, in preparation for a meeting intended to coordinate information operations with American colleagues, British officials discussed plans for black propaganda work, including the use of forgery. In suggesting that Britain 'take the lead' in this area, Whitehall revealed not only a willingness to engage in disinformation-by-forgery, but also fostered the perception that British covert propagandists were especially proficient in such matters and had a thing or two to teach the Americans. In reviewing forgery operations mounted against international trade union organisations with communist connections, including the World Federation of Trade Unions, British officials enthused that, 'we should not hesitate to draw a bow at a [forgery] venture', that offered, 'suitable targets'. 'Even if it [a forgery] achieves nothing else', the British concluded pragmatically, 'the [ensuing] investigation by the communists has its own disruptive effects'.[15]

In several respects, non-aligned India was an ideal environment in which to conduct black propaganda. An open democracy, with a large, free, and vibrant press, and a population broadly opposed to entering Cold War alliances of any ideological stripe, India offered ample, 'cover for covert political action operations directed towards the manipulation of groups not otherwise susceptible to ... manipulation'.[16] In part, the limited scale of black propaganda work carried out by the IRD in the subcontinent was reflective of the heavy investment in resources that such activity demanded. The IRD also encountered considerable resistance from the Commonwealth Relations Office whenever the subject of conducting covert action in Commonwealth countries reared its head. To the CRO, India's importance to the UK diplomatically, economically, and strategically, suggested that dividends derived from black propaganda would rarely, if ever, justify the political cost associated with their exposure. Black propaganda continued to be authorised at the most senior levels of the British government during the Cold War.[17] On occasions, forgeries produced by the IRD surfaced in the Indian press. In 1963, a year after MI5's SLO in New Delhi had been surprised by the appearance of a forged IRD document attributed to the Chinese Peace Committee, a second counterfeit circular, nominally from the same source, received prominent coverage in the *Hindustan Times*.[18] When it came to combatting a Communist threat to Indian democracy, as one IRD officer who served in New Delhi made clear, ' ... "black" propaganda techniques should not be excluded from our future planning'.[19] That said, it was less hazardous grey propaganda that the British generally employed as their disinformation weapon of choice in India.

India's Information War

The history of British covert propaganda operations in India predated the Information Research Department. During the Second World War, the Viceroy of India, the Marquess of Linlithgow, employed the Special Operations Executive (SOE), a clandestine warfare unit formed in 1940, to moderate Indian nationalist sentiment by placing unattributable articles supportive of Britain and the Allied war effort in vernacular newspapers. 'Had this been done a generation ago', one official crowed to the British premier, Winston Churchill, 'Gandhi would not have had it all his own way.' The British covert information programme in India, Churchill was assured, in a memorandum no doubt designed to appeal to the prime minister's well-developed sense of Anglo-Saxon superiority, demonstrated how effectively 'an "unacknowledgeable" organisation can by covert means further the policy of H.M.G. in presenting the British case to immature peoples, and in combatting subversive movements among them'.[20] In actuality, British propaganda operations in the subcontinent had little, if any, substantive effect in suppressing Indian nationalism in the lead-up to nation's independence. Once the British had departed from South Asia, officials in Whitehall expressed concern that in seeking to win 'hearts and minds' in India they were 'working under a heavy handicap'. In contrast to the Soviet Union and the People's Republic of China, both of whom made much of communism's anti-colonialism, the British fretted that Indians' 'deep-rooted antipathy' to imperialism, and its associations with racialism, had manifested in an instinctive mistrust of the West. The British High Commission in Madras, in southern India, observed ruefully that, 'anti-imperialism has got mixed up with racial sentiments; the white race versus the black, and this has not been helped by the apartheid policy in South Africa, the persecution of Negroes in the U.S.A., treatment of Blacks in the West Indies, to mention only a few example'.[21] It was against this background that, in February 1948, barely six months after India had secured self-rule, the Information Research Department was established.

The British Cabinet directive that inaugurated the IRD stressed that the threat communism posed to 'to the whole fabric of western civilisation' compelled Britain to respond with a new and robust information policy. It was envisaged that, from an initial European base, the IRD's work would quickly assume global proportions and 'require special application in the Middle East and Far Eastern countries'.[22] Drawing some of its funds from the Secret Vote, or intelligence and secret services budget, under the leadership of Ralph Murray, who had served in the Political Warfare Executive during the Second World War, the IRD rapidly built-up a broad international network of contacts, or clients, amongst politicians, government officials, journalists, and trade unionists. The new organisation's innocuous sounding name was intended to allay public suspicion that the Foreign Office was operating a 'lie Department'.[23] In 1951, the IRD formed an 'English Section' that concentrated on combatting communist subversion at home. The department's primary focus, however, was on countering communism abroad. In short order, the IRD's terms of reference expanded to cover threats posed by Arab nationalism, and to disrupt political regimes, such as President Sukarno's in Indonesia, that endangered British strategic interests.[24] In 1949, a regional information office, located in Singapore, began to harmonise British propaganda efforts across Asia. At its zenith, in the mid-1960s, the IRD's London headquarters employed over 350 staff in geographical sections covering Southeast Asia, China, Africa, the Middle East, Latin America, and the Soviet Union, and had separate units dealing with editorial issues and international organisations.[25]

When it came to India, Ralph Murray was highly critical of a local press that presented news stories 'in a Communist way'. The head of IRD attributed this unwelcome situation to a hangover from, 'the days when all Indian journalists could find popular approval by adopting an anti-Imperialist, anti-Colonial and anti-Capitalist line'.[26] The impact in post-colonial India of journalists promoting an anti-Western or pro-communist viewpoint, speaking with an indigenous voice, and being legitimised by mainstream newspapers, was not lost on the British. The British Information Service echoed Murray's concern at the effect on Indian public opinion of the 'persistent and most dangerous Communist propaganda' appearing in leading dailies with links to the ruling Congress party, such as *Amrita Bazar Patrika*, the *Hindustan Standard*, and the *National Herald*. Such journalism, the BIS judged, was as pernicious, if not more so, than Soviet literature distributed in the subcontinent, and as the Communist Party of India's newsletter, *New Age*.[27] After 1949, British officials were also troubled by an unwelcome upsurge in Chinese communist propaganda in India. Mao's fledgling People's Republic wasted little time in strengthening distribution channels for its press briefs, agency reports, radio broadcasts, and cheap political literature which began to reach the subcontinent in increasing quantity. Chinese propaganda was deemed 'particularly effective' by the British, as it tended to focus on communist successes in combating problems familiar to most Indians, and chiefly those surrounding agrarian reform and petty corruption. Moreover, analysis conducted by the BIS found that Chinese propaganda retained currency and was regarded as 'widely acceptable' in India, because it originated from a fellow Asian nation that was 'held up as the spearhead of Asian resurgence.' Beijing's propagandists were considered especially adept at 'deliberately exploiting' potent racial themes that touched upon raw nerves in India, and which cast Britain alongside the United States as exploitative agents of 'white imperialism'.[28]

Initially, Whitehall baulked at entering into a propaganda war with Communist China and held back from disseminating unattributable material that was overly critical of Beijing. An aggressive information offensive directed at the People's Republic of China was ruled out on the grounds that it would complicate the prospects of reaching a *modus vivendi* with Mao's regime and, in the process, endanger important British interests in Asia and, above all, those in the crown colony of Hong Kong. Towards the end of 1951, following the PRC's entry into the Korean War, rising concern at the volume and sophistication of Chinese propaganda circulating in the subcontinent prompted London to change tack. British missions overseas were subsequently informed that, 'the prohibition on criticism of the Chinese Government and the Chinese Communist Party need no longer remain in force'. Given India's standing as *the* preeminent post-colonial and non-communist power in Asia, the British identified New Delhi as of critical importance when it came to disrupting Chinese propaganda.[29] From the IRD's perspective, the easing of restrictions on the use of counterpropaganda aimed at China was well timed. India's efforts to cultivate good relations with its powerful communist neighbour had afforded ample opportunity for the Chinese to disseminate propaganda in South Asia. In March 1955, one BIS report grumbled that Indians appeared to be entirely unconcerned at the influx of communist propaganda entering the country across their northern border. 'There continues to be wide and enthusiastic reception for Chinese propaganda [in India] even at the highest levels', one exasperated BIS officer observed, 'and a great deal more at the lower'.[30]

It was the increasing inroads made by Soviet propaganda in India, however, that exercised Whitehall most. Indian nationalist leaders, and not least, Jawaharlal Nehru, had long appreciated the Soviets' skill in information management. In 1927, when attending the Brussels Congress against imperialism, Nehru noted not only the Russians strategic guile, but also their capacity to galvanise global communist support through the efficient and effective dissemination of propaganda.[31] Following Stalin's death in 1953, the blossoming of India's previously sclerotic relationship with the USSR saw bilateral economic relations invigorated, political cooperation strengthened and, in the cultural sphere, the initiation of a new era of educational and artistic exchange. Soviet film festivals became a regular feature of Indian life; troupes of travelling Russian entertainers criss-crossed the country; the TASS news agency set up shop in Delhi; and subsidised Soviet literature featured prominently on the shelves of Indian bookstores.[32] British diplomats began to voice alarm at the extent to which the average Indian appeared, 'impressed ... by the skilful propaganda put out by the Reds in the form of newspapers and pamphlets'.[33] Prominent Indians sympathetic to the West, such as the socialist turned conservative politician, Minocher Rustom 'Minoo' Masani, responded by openly chastising Britain and the United States for doing 'pathetically little' to counter a proliferation of 'fantastically cheap' Soviet publications being 'sold at every [Indian] street corner'. In a single year, the Soviet People's Publishing House, which operated out of an office in Bombay, in western India, sold 300,000 heavily discounted copies of the *Life of Joseph Stalin*. Prohibitively expensive British or American books on liberal political themes, such as Arthur Schlesinger's, *Vital Center*, struggled to generate any Indian sales. 'The Soviet Government', Masani warned an American audience in Detroit, 'is spending millions of rubles in India today to try and get the mind of the people on their side'.[34] The celebrated Trinidadian writer of Indian heritage, Vidiadhar Surajprasad (V. S.) Naipaul corroborated Masani's concern. While travelling through Kashmir, in northern India, Naipaul was struck by the 'armfuls' of Soviet publications that the proprietor of his guest house had accumulated from the local tourist office. An old writing-table in the sitting room of his accommodation, Naipaul marvelled, was 'stuffed with Russian propaganda'.[35]

India's Intelligence Bureau kept a close watch on Soviet-directed propaganda activity. The IB's analysts reasoned that in drawing primarily on practical examples of purported social and economic progress achieved under Marxism, Moscow's propagandists aimed to secure support from India's professional class of scientists, journalists, lawyers, and academics. In contrast, literature distributed by indigenous communists, led by the Moscow-backed CPI, tended to focus on common grievances held by broad swathes of Indian

132   SPYING IN SOUTH ASIA

opinion, and address issues ranging from unease over American neo-colonialism to calls for land reform and the abolition of feudalism.[36] Reasonably content with the effectiveness of the Indian government's ability to monitor communist propaganda, British officials were less enamoured by what they perceived as New Delhi's lassitude in taking concrete steps to neutralise an insidious pincer movement that was targeting the nation's social system from above and below. As early as 1948, Alec Symon, Britain's deputy high commissioner, lamented that the IB's first Indian director, Tirupattur Gangadharam Pillai Sanjeevi, had 'very far ... yet to go in his Communist education'. Sanjeevi, a concerned Symon reported back to London, 'seems to regard the [Communist] movement as purely internal nuisance to be classed with any other political body in India and he shows no signs of regarding Communism as an international conspiracy aimed at Sovietization of Asia and the World. His [Sanjeevi's] views seem to me to be somewhat superficial.'[37] A decade later, Whitehall continued to express anxiety that the Indian government's appreciation of Soviet intentions remained recklessly benign. The British conceded that Nehru's administrations had taken a firm line in cracking down on CPI activists suspected of inciting civil disorder, promoting political violence, or engaging in electoral malpractice. Externally directed communist subversion, however, seemed of less concern to India's leadership. It was the Pandora's box of religious strife, and the risk that this might fracture Indian national unity, that most preoccupied Nehru. 'The danger to India ... is not communism', the Indian premier was fond of reminding his civil servants. 'It is Hindu right-wing communalism.'[38]

India Calling: Recalibrating the IRD in South Asia

The IRD's involvement with India began inauspiciously. From 1947, as South Asian independence coalesced with the onset of the Cold War, Christopher Mayhew, Under Secretary of State at the Foreign Office in Attlee's first administration, wartime intelligence officer, and leading actor in the IRD's creation, became uneasy that colleagues in the Commonwealth Relations Office had marginalised the importance of propaganda in South Asia. In November 1948, Mayhew fired off a tart memo to his counterpart at the CRO, Patrick Gordon Walker, in which he claimed to be 'puzzled' by an apparent reluctance in Whitehall to utilise the IRD in South Asia. Over the preceding nine months, the CRO had requested just seven copies of IRD publications for distribution in India, Pakistan, and Ceylon. Moreover, the CRO had failed to pass on to IRD requests from BIS officers in the subcontinent for background information on communist propaganda operations.[39] Chastened by Mayhew's criticism, Gordon Walker convened a series of planning meetings that brought together senior officials from the Foreign Office, the IRD, and the CRO. These meetings energised the British counter-propaganda effort in South Asia and provided it with a new sense of purpose and direction. From early 1949, the CRO began forwarding increased quantities of IRD material to the British High Commission in New Delhi and, in return, furnished Murray's organisation with intelligence on communist publications circulating in India. In addition, Archibald Nye quietly arranged for IRD anti-communist literature to be passed directly to Haravu Venkatanarasimha Varadaraja Iengar, the Indian government's Home Secretary, and the senior civil servant responsible for internal security.[40] A former stalwart of the pre-independence British Indian administration, Iengar was deemed by Nye to be 'one of the ablest and most effective' operatives in Nehru's government and, more importantly, staunchly anti-communist.[41]

By the early 1950s, IRD literature proliferated in India and had begun to reach an ever-wider circle of 'friendly' contacts inside the Indian government; the ruling Congress party; the armed forces; the press; and academics working in prominent research institutions.[42] Not all IRD material sent to India hit the mark. IRD output received by the High Commission in New Delhi was often of a generic anti-communist type or based on examples of communist repression and tyranny drawn from Eastern Europe. Unsurprisingly, this proved of limited relevance to Indian 'customers'. The arrival of IRD articles decrying the persecution of the Roman Catholic Church in Bulgaria bemused British information staff in India. 'Even the ablest Information Officer', the CRO was informed, 'cannot succeed in making a vital issue [of Bulgarian Catholicism] amongst his Indian contacts'.[43] The propaganda offensive in the subcontinent, Whitehall was chided, would benefit were IRD to cast 'a rather more critical and selective eye' over the suitability of publications that it sent east of Suez.[44] The IRD took note and gradually developed its output from an initial offering of short, well-documented, and utilitarian briefing notes, or *Basic Papers*, to encompass the production and distribution of wide range of materials designed to pique the interest of opinion formers in different international markets. The *Interpreter*, a monthly publication, was devised to influence national elites. It was offered to senior IRD contacts on the pretext that it was a British Foreign Service document, and that recipients would be privy to inside information not usually distributed beyond Whitehall. Notable for its tight prose and methodical anti-communist analysis, the *Interpreter* featured an introduction not dissimilar to that of a broadsheet leader. An extension of the *Interpreter*, *Asian Analyst* focused specifically on developments inside China, on Soviet and Chinese foreign policy, and the insidious actions of communist parties across Asia. The *Digest* pulled together short, punchy anti-communist stories that were readily quotable, and appeared sufficiently topical to pass as news. Finally, a *Facts About* series of books complimented IRD's more easily digestible offerings and were designed to serve as reference tools on a variety of communist topics.[45] In keeping with its status as a covert organisation, none of IRD's output carried a publisher's imprint or was attributed to the British government.

134   SPYING IN SOUTH ASIA

Refinements in IRD output reaped immediate dividends for the British in India. In a significant coup, the high commission was able to add Indian's intelligence chief, B. N. Mullik, to its distribution list for IRD material. Mullik was regarded as a particularly important British asset on account of his close relationship with Nehru, and his willingness to provide critical assessments on the type of IRD material likely to resonate inside the Indian government. One British official noted that in seeking to refine counter-propaganda for Indian audiences, he had come to 'think of the D.I.B. [Mullik] being the perfect point d'appui'.[46] Unattributable research papers produced by the IRD, and the Foreign Office Research Department (FORD), were channelled through the IB to other Indian government departments. This process enhanced the credibility of the literature immeasurably and helped to camouflage its British origins. 'There is evidence', British officials crowed, 'that much of this [IRD product] is read by Mr Nehru himself. By Sir N. R. Pillai [Secretary General of the MEA and Cabinet Secretary] and by the Home Secretary (Mr Pai)'.[47] Mullik himself proved to be an avid consumer of the IRD's work. The Indian intelligence leader devoured copies of multiple IRD publications, including the *Interpreter, Asian Analyst, Digest, Trends in Communist Propaganda* and *Facts About.*[48]

The connection established between the IRD and India's intelligence service also proved instrumental in enabling Whitehall to place a steady flow of unattributable anti-communist material in mainstream Indian newspapers. In April 1956, the high commission heaped praise on the IB for ensuring that an IRD account of the 'Petrov affair' received widespread play in the Indian press. Vladimir Petrov, a colonel in the Soviet KGB, or Committee for State Security, had defected to the West while serving under cover in Australia. In a dramatic development, worthy of John le Carré, an attempt by armed Soviet officials to spirit Petrov's wife, Evodkia, out of the country, was thwarted on the tarmac of Darwin airport by officers of the Australian Security Intelligence Organisation. Newspaper articles that attacked communism or communist theory, the British had learned, went down badly with the Indian public. On the other hand, human interest stories, such as the 'Petrov Affair', that exposed limitations placed on human rights behind the Iron Curtain, were judged 'popular' and could 'create a desirable impression on the [Indian] reader'.[49] More broadly, as the 1950s came to an end, the British high commission advised London that it was, 'satisfied we have in fact been making good use vis-a-vis Indian officials, including Mullik, of the [IRD] material on this subject which has reached us . . . '. Whether such material was being digested by Nehru and his cabinet, and what effect, if any, it might have had on the Indian leadership's attitudes to the Soviet Union, and the dangers posed by communist subversion, was, British officials conceded, 'much harder to say'.[50] In fact, the answer was, it seemed, not a great deal. In a note Nehru sent to the Ministry of External Affairs special secretary, Badruddin Tyabji, the Indian premier confirmed that while he received regular reports from Mullik, these 'were sometimes useful but very often they do not convey to me any really pertinent information'. 'The gathering of Intelligence does not merely depend upon certain techniques employed', Nehru added, 'it depends also on an acute mind having knowledge of the issues at stake. Often, I have found that the information supplied [by the DIB], even though detailed, is not helpful.'[51]

In the late summer of 1960, a change of British leadership in India that saw Sir Paul Gore-Booth installed as high commissioner, had a transformative effect on IRD operations. Gore-Booth was struck by the ubiquity of Soviet propaganda in the subcontinent and became convinced that the IRD should be employed more aggressively to counteract it. In September, the new high commissioner asked the IRD to send an officer from its editorial division out to the subcontinent to review Britain's counter-propaganda operation. Between March and April 1961, Josephine O'Connor Howe, who had earned a formidable reputation within the IRD for efficiency and directness, completed a root and branch assessment of the Department's activity in India.[52] O'Connor Howe was tasked with addressing perennial concerns that too much of the IRD literature sent to New Delhi remained overly blunt and strident in its anti-communism, was too generalist, and took insufficient account of local socio-political grievances. Gore-Booth stressed that, from his standpoint, the counter-propaganda picture was by no means entirely negative. Substantial amounts of material requested from the IRD by his information officers, O'Connor Howe was reassured, remained 'valuable', and had 'registered some notable successes' in the Indian press. Nevertheless, Gore-Booth's overall impression was that the IRD 'could do better'.[53] Back in London, the IRD's management had arrived at the much the same conclusion, albeit for different reasons. Douglas Rivett-Carnac, head of the IRD's Far East and Southeast Asia section, accepted that greater progress ought to have been achieved in India in refining and strengthening Britain's counter-propaganda work. Rivett-Carnac hailed from a 'dolphin' family, a term coined by Rudyard Kipling to denote British households that served for generation after generation in colonial India, 'as dolphins follow in line across the open sea'.[54] Scores of Rivett-Carnac's had occupied positions in the subcontinent as civil servants, army officers, and policemen, with one rising to become governor of Bombay in the early nineteenth century. Local information officials, in Douglas Rivett-Carnac's view, were largely culpable for neglecting to put 'any real effort ... into IRD work'. Receptive to Gore-Booth's invitation to take a more prominent and active role in India, senior IRD officials embraced an opportunity to demonstrate the Department's effectiveness in pushing back against Soviet propaganda when afforded appropriate support.[55]

The pressure for change coming from inside and outside India ensured that O'Connor Howe's recommendations for reforming IRD operations met with general approval. Placing emphasis on improving cooperation between the

IRD and the BIS, O'Connor Howe underlined the need to balance and coordinate the dissemination of the IRD's anti-communist message with the 'positive' output celebrating liberal democracy and free enterprise that underpinned the BIS' work. In other words, taken together, the tone of Britain's overt and covert propaganda operations could still sound discordant rather than harmonious when filtered through an Indian ear. Marrying IRD and BIS output together more seamlessly, even on a modest scale, represented a formidable challenge and had occupied the attention of information officers from the late 1940s. In the circumstances, O'Connor-Howe argued for breaking with precedent and deploying an experienced IRD officer to serve in India alongside BIS colleagues.[56]

Gore-Booth employed O'Connor-Howe's report as ammunition to lobby for the appointment of a permanent IRD officer in New Delhi. The IRD had been exploring ways of sending 'field officers' overseas for some time. Following a period of relative amity between the United States and the Soviet Union in the late 1950s, the Cold War had again threatened to turn hot at the beginning of the 1960s. The downing of an American U-2 reconnaissance plane over southern Russia, the Kennedy administration's abortive operation to 'liberate' Cuba, and sabre-rattling between Moscow and Washington over the status of Berlin, all ratcheted up tensions between East and West. A renewal in superpower friction saw Whitehall place 'increasing importance' on the role of the IRD in combatting communist subversion. Funding for the IRD increased, its staff expanded, and for the first time the Department found itself in a position to station permanent representatives in British diplomatic missions abroad.[57] By the end of 1962, twenty-five IRD field officers had been dispatched to foreign posts, and an agreement reached with the Treasury to fund an additional nine field officers. Two years later, the IRD had more than fifty staff stationed across the globe. Field officers were instructed to spend much of their time, 'assessing local communist propaganda in all its forms, and carrying out unattributable counter-propaganda'. In practice this encompassed monitoring and reporting on local communist activity; procuring examples of communist propaganda; arranging for the local translation and distribution of IRD literature; and actively cultivating new contacts willing to receive and disseminate IRD material.[58]

India's standing as a British foreign policy priority ensured that the country was placed at the forefront of the IRD field officer initiative. In January 1962, the first IRD officer posted to India, Peter Joy, arrived in South Asia. Joy was an experienced propagandist, politically astute, and had excelled while seconded to the Central Treaty Organisation (CENTO) headquarters in Ankara. The Director of IRD, Donald Hopson, championed Joy's appointment. It was also enthusiastically endorsed by Hopson's predecessor, Ralph Murray, who agreed that Joy 'would be excellent [in India]', a posting that the former IRD head considered 'more important than CENTO'.[59] Operating covertly, and without the knowledge of the Indian government, ostensibly Joy's role was that of a publications officer in the BIS.[60] Initially, as incidents between Indian and Chinese forces along the contested Himalayan border increased in frequency, and New Delhi's relations with Beijing deteriorated, Joy struggled to expand IRD's network of local contacts. Reluctant to compromise its policy of Cold War non-alignment, and anxious to enlist Soviet support as a means of deterring Chinese aggression, Nehru's government shied away from any action that might be interpreted as overtly anti-communist or likely to antagonise Moscow. With the assistance of overstretched British information staff located in Bombay, Calcutta, and Madras, Joy undertook the 'slow and laborious' task of creating a central card index of Indians that had been recruited to disseminate unattributable IRD material on a confidential basis. Following months of hard work, Joy's index listed sixty local contacts, with each graded in terms of their influence and reliability.[61]

Cold War Propaganda Turns Hot

In October 1962, from the IRD's perspective, things took a decisive turn for the better in India after New Delhi and Beijing came to blows in the Himalayas. British officials were as disconcerted at the ease with which China managed to outgun India in propaganda terms, as they were with the performance of the Indian Army on the battlefield. The 'absolute consistency' with which Beijing presented itself to international audiences as a victim of Indian aggression, one Foreign Office diplomat observed, contrasted unfavourably with New Delhi's 'wavering and often self-contradictory' performance in the publicity sphere.[62] In India, the BIS voiced a grudging admiration for the way in which Radio Peking's English Service had shown itself to be 'highly skilled' in selectively quoting from the public statements of Indian leaders to portray its adversary as a belligerent warmonger. In a media operation that 'out-Goebbels Goebbels', Chinese state radio utilised the services of an Irishman 'slightly reminiscent of Lord Haw Haw', to hammer home the theme of Indian aggression, 'so repetitively that something must certainly stick in the minds of Asian/African listeners, if not of other peoples also'.[63] The British were especially concerned at the lack of sympathy and understanding that India garnered within the developing world. An apparent indifference to India's plight amongst the nations of Africa and Asia was attributed, in part, to the imperious way that Nehru's governments had conducted much of their diplomacy since 1947. Paul Gore-Booth suggested that the border war had demonstrated to Indians that, 'if you want goodwill from people in critical moments, you must not spend the rest of your time either ignoring them or loftily criticising the management of their affairs'. Gore-Booth was astonished to discover that although Sino-Indian relations had been deteriorating for some years, 'no proper briefing on the [border] dispute had . . . ever been sent to Indian missions abroad [and] no guidance was available to such Indian Government organs of publicity as existed at the moment when the crisis broke'. Meanwhile, 'the Chinese propaganda machine was working flat out on carefully prepared material and argument'.[64]

In London, Harold Macmillan's government came under considerable pressure to offer India assistance, not least, from the almost pathologically Sinophobe Kennedy administration in the United States. Washington insisted that Britain's Commonwealth connection with India obligated the UK to assume a leading role in the subcontinent's defence and, crucially, offered a mechanism by which this could be achieved without comprising Nehruvian non-alignment. Aware that offering India some degree of support was politically necessary, Macmillan's cabinet nevertheless bridled at overcommitting Britain's limited economic and military resources to a conflict in faraway South Asia. Worse still, London was alert to the calamitous prospect that rushing to India's side would pose a risk of Britain becoming enmeshed in a shooting war with China. Such a scenario threatened disaster for important British overseas interests and, above all, those in Hong Kong. Furnishing India with expertise and advice in the information realm, Whitehall determined, offered one means of proffering assistance with a minimum of risk. 'The propaganda field is one in which we could significantly help India', the Foreign Office emphasised in November 1962. 'The Indians themselves are doing little and are ill-equipped for the task.'[65] At a meeting held with Nehru, in New Delhi, later that month, Duncan Sandys, Macmillan's Secretary of State for Commonwealth Relations, underscored that the United Kingdom was, 'extremely anxious to help the Indians in every way in the presentation of their case [on the border war]'. Noting that the UK had 'a considerably developed network of Information Services', Sandys advised the Indian premier that Britain would 'be very glad' to work with his government in countering Chinese propaganda.[66]

Sandys was pushing against an open door in suggesting that Britain and India work together on counter-propaganda aimed at China. The Sino-Indian war found Indian government ministries, journalists, and national research centres, such as the Indian School of International Studies, clamouring for material on the inequities of Communist China, which Peter Joy and the IRD were only too happy to furnish. As a first step, a new Indian government committee for 'War Information and Counter-Propaganda', that included representation from the IB, Ministry of External Affairs, All India Radio, and the Press Information Bureau (PIB), sought assistance from the BIS, which continued to act as cover for the IRD's undeclared operations in India. Extra copies of the IRD's stock publications on Chinese communism, such as *China Topics* and *China Records*, were rushed out to the subcontinent to meet a welcome surge in demand. A special supplement of the *Asian Analyst* was also run up to address purported Chinese treachery in respect of the border conflict. To smooth the flow of British propaganda reaching India, a twice-weekly airmail service was established between the IRD's office in London and the high commission in New Delhi. This allowed IRD analysts to supply timely details of anti-Indian and pro-Chinese statements made by communist leaders and their governments. It was also used to ensure that the Nehru's administration received copies of disparaging quotations attacking the Indian premier and members of his cabinet. These were attributed to Beijing but had actually been fed by SIS to news agencies in the Far East that were covertly funded by London in a classic black propaganda operation. Not to be left out, the British Ministry of Defence also got in on the act, sending Peter Joy information for distribution to his Indian contacts on the mistreatment of British prisoners held by the Chinese during the Korean War.[67]

The information expertise that Britain made available to India left the IRD well positioned to exploit a wave of anti-Chinese feeling that swept across India. The Indian government was careful, however, to steer popular protest in an anti-Chinese rather than an anti-communist direction. Direct attacks on communism made by third parties inside India were proscribed under the so-called 'third country rule' and, more particularly, criticism of the Soviet Union by foreign missions was actively discouraged.[68] The External Publicity Division of the MEA had, the head of the BIS, Donald Kerr, reminded colleagues, given the green light for British information officers to support, 'the appropriate official [Indian] bodies – and indeed to non-official organisations if we wished'. The only limitation India placed upon what amounted to an unprecedented invitation to Britain to disseminate counter-propaganda material inside and outside government channels in the subcontinent, was that all such work remain confined, 'to China and Chinese activities in view of the continued official ban on propaganda against the Soviet Union or Communism as such'.[69] British hopes of exploiting the Sino-Indian war to turn Indians against communism more broadly, and New Delhi's Soviet friend, in particular, was not something the Indian government welcomed or was prepared to tolerate. To complicate matters further, the IRD's desire to dispel Indian distinctions between good Soviet and bad Chinese communism was complicated when the Moscow-backed CPI placed patriotism above ideological affinity and publicly denounced Beijing's aggression.[70]

In an attempt to resolve the IRD's dilemma, and under instruction from London, Peter Joy began running a twin-track propaganda operation in India. One strand, which was 'virtually requested by the Indian authorities', saw Joy support and develop the Indian government's counter-propaganda capability directed against China. In practical terms, this encompassed work that ranged from providing guidance and advice to Indian colleagues on the format and content of programming on AIR, to arranging for Indian information officers to attend propaganda and psychological warfare courses back in the UK. In December 1963, one Indian official from the PIB, P. M. M. Menon, and another from AIR, P. S. Bhatia, arrived in London for training in counter-subversion propaganda. 'Great care had to be taken not to offend them [Menon and Bhatia] by our attitude to Russia', IRD instructors noted, 'but we did tell them that it was our policy to combat Russian Communism as well as Chinese Communism'.[71] Links Joy managed to forge with the China Division of the MEA also began to bear fruit. The MEA asked for British input on semi-classified Indian government documents related to the border conflict and to the Sino-Soviet dispute. This development, Joy enthused, had enabled political officers within the British high commission, 'to encourage a dialogue [with Indian colleagues] on future Chinese and Communist bloc policy which may in time provide us with opportunities for influencing official thinking in this field'.[72]

A second, and unofficial strand of the IRD's India operation, continued to disseminate counter-propaganda aimed at the Soviet Union. It operated without the knowledge and approval of the Indian government. Although frustrated by the official embargo imposed by Nehru's government on counter-propaganda activity with an anti-Soviet tinge, the IRD had little option other than to acknowledge the boundaries imposed by political realities on the ground. 'Russia's position in India excludes our close liaison with the Government in countering Communist subversion', a senior IRD officer acknowledged, 'and our effort must be concerned primarily with alerting unofficial . . . opinion to the threat rather than with liaison in countering it'.[73] The 'unofficial' Soviet element of IRD activity in India was seen by the Department as 'much more important' in the long term than its 'official' Chinese programme. Consequently, the 'main effort' undertaken by Peter Joy was concentrated upon the 'infinitely more difficult tasks of weaning Indians away from the idea that the Soviet Union's dispute with China has transformed it into India's "guardian angel" in the Sino-Indian dispute, and that the aims and methods of Soviet Communism are, in some way, different in kind from those of the Chinese'.[74]

By prioritising counter-propaganda in India that targeted the Soviet Union, the IRD took on a momentous challenge. Back in February 1957, having concluded that the previous year's Hungarian crisis had shown its propaganda capabilities to be lagging behind those of the West, the Central Committee of the Soviet Presidium approved an expansion in the volume and reach of Soviet propaganda aimed at the developing world. The budget of the Soviet Ministry of Communications was boosted, and Radio Moscow was provided with new and more powerful transmitters directed at Asia, Latin America, and Africa. The quantity of Soviet literature despatched to the Indian subcontinent mushroomed. One Soviet publication alone, the fortnightly magazine, *Soviet Land*, was distributed in India in fourteen languages, and had a circulation of 300,000 by the early 1960s.[75] Moreover, the 'formidable Communist bloc effort in the Information field' in India, manifested in an ever-expanding cultural programme of Soviet films, exhibitions, and lectures. The India-Soviet Cultural Society (ISCUS) operated a national network of branches and affiliates that sponsored communist libraries and reading rooms. *Novosti*, the Soviets 'unofficial' press agency, had an active bureau in New Delhi. A second Soviet front organisation, *Inter-Ads*, subsidised communist newspapers by channelling spurious advertising revenue in their direction. Moreover, the aftermath of the border war witnessed an upsurge in indigenous communist propaganda carried by left-wing Indian newspapers, such as *Blitz*, *Patriot*, *Link* and *Mainstream*, and amongst workers organisations linked to the CPI, such as the All-India Trade Union Congress.[76]

The Indian government's appetite for coordinating counter-propaganda operations with Britain against China remained strong throughout the 1960s. Frustratingly for the IRD, however, periodic British hints that this arrangement might be extended to cover Soviet communism met with firm Indian rebuffs. In June 1963, Whitehall considered declaring to the Indian government that an IRD officer was operating out of the British high commission. The proposal met with opposition from Gore-Booth and Joy. Nehru's administration, London was reminded, had repeatedly made clear its objection to any form of broad anti-communist propaganda activity. Dispensing with Joy's cover, declaring him as an IRD officer, and explaining the role's primary function, was deemed likely to end in his expulsion from India, and the imposition of new and unwelcome restrictions on the work performed by the BIS.[77] The absence of Indian government support for the IRD's 'unofficial' counter-propaganda effort against the Soviet Union had, in any case, British officials in the subcontinent pointed out, not stopped Joy from expanding the scope and scale of IRD operations. Indeed, Joy was eventually able to build up a network of over 400 Indian contacts, or 'well placed and influential individuals', who received IRD material and assisted in its dissemination.[78]

In 1964, Joy successfully engineered a major breakthrough in IRD activity by co-opting the support of two Indian publishers, Gopal Mittal, owner of the National Academy Publishing House in New Delhi, and Ram Singh, a journalist on the *Hindustan Times*, editor of the right-wing magazine *Thought*, and manager of the Siddharta publishing group. Mittal and Singh would go on to become mainstays of Britain's counter-propaganda offensive against Soviet communism in India. Each covertly distributed IRD literature under payment of a financial subsidy. On occasions, Singh facilitated black operations. In one instance, he arranged for publication of a letter, purportedly written in 1924 from Kanpur prison by S. A. Dange, the chairman of the CPI. In the letter, which Dange denounced as a forgery, the CPI leader offered to work covertly for the British colonial government. One British official noted that the letter's publication, 'has done much to damage the pro-Russian faction of the CPI and has precipitated a split in the party'.[79] More generally, Mittal's company printed and distributed books with anti-communist themes in English, Hindi, Urdu, and Tamil editions, the texts of which were supplied by the IRD. Under the terms of a 'see-safe' agreement, the IRD paid Mittal a subsidy that covered a book's publication and distribution expenses and ensured that his business returned a healthy profit from its association with Britain's covert propagandists. The scheme, which by the spring of 1967 had seen 70,000 books gifted to key contacts, or sold at below market prices, cost the IRD £10,000 per annum.[80]

Joy later expanded IRD operations to encompass an article redistribution scheme. In collaboration with Mittal, whose publishing interests included ownership of a prominent Urdu magazine, *Tehreek*, Joy arranged for IRD copy to be translated into a range of vernacular languages and passed on to journalists working at Indian newspapers and magazines. In theory, the scheme enabled the IRD to react quickly to breaking news, and to reach Indian audiences with topical anti-communist material. On average, however, the scheme placed just two articles a month in Indian newspapers, and at an annual cost of £1,500. At the time, India's thousands of newspapers and periodicals had a combined circulation of 30 million readers.[81] The meagre output of the article redistribution scheme was defended by Joy on the basis that the news stories it produced invariably resulted in similar copy being carried by other news organisations and, as such, 'it seems to us good value for money.' The IRD's inability to quantify precisely how much replay its articles received in the Indian media suggested that the value for money argument was based less on hard facts, and more on professional wishful thinking. Other less structured arrangements were put in place to distribute IRD news items through alternative Indian publishers, such as Sagar Ahluwalia, editor of *Young Asia Publications,* and Professor A. B. Shah, of the Indian Committee for Cultural Freedom. The network of publishing contacts established in India by Joy, IRD officers enthused optimistically, enabled the Department, ' . . . to get the right article into the right paper at the right time'.[82]

The merits of paying financial subsidies to IRD contacts in India provoked 'prolonged and fairly heated . . . discussion' inside the British government. The BIS came out against money being passed to Indians through individuals associated with the high commission under any circumstances. Donald Kerr objected stridently to, 'the use of methods which might jeopardise the good name of BIS as an overt agency of HMG'. In Kerr's mind, the risks involved in authorising covert payments to Indians by the IRD were excessive, as there was 'no fool proof way of ensuring that they cannot be traced back to their origin'. Peter Joy disagreed. Joy maintained that the imposition of a 'blanket veto' on payments to local 'friends' would restrict his ability to 'increase the placing and plugging of articles, news items, cartoons etc.' in the Indian press. The Soviet 'opposition' in India, Joy stressed, had 'no inhibitions' whatsoever about using its financial muscle to ensure that communist propaganda material featured prominently in newspapers and magazines. A reliance on 'simple "good-will"' was insufficient to persuade hard-pressed Indian publishers, many of whom operated on a commercial shoestring, to disseminate IRD product.[83] A risk-averse British attitude taken to compensating

Indians collaborating with IRD, Joy griped, meant that 'We are fighting with one hand tied behind our back.'[84]

By way of a compromise, Joy suggested employing 'go-betweens', or cut outs, to pass funds to the IRD's contacts. These were trusted individuals, often within the British expatriate business community in India, who had no direct association with the high commission, and could act surreptitiously as the IRD's paymasters.[85] In August 1965, agreement was reached that small sums of under £50 could be passed by IRD officers to Indian contacts on the understanding that the total amount paid to any single individual would not exceed £300 per annum.[86] In order to secure the CRO's acquiescence, the IRD undertook that 'there would be no question of indiscriminate or "scattershot" funding; nor would funds be used in an attempt to "convert" or "bribe"'. Rather, the Department committed to employ financial incentives solely to expedite local action when significant counter-propaganda opportunities presented themselves. By way of reassurance, senior IRD officers suggested to their colleagues in the CRO that, 'All the major missions in New Delhi (including the British High Commission) were presumed by the Indians to carry out transactions of this kind, and . . . [doing so] was most unlikely to effect the "image of purity" which the High Commission was seeking to project overtly one way or the other.'[87] Fortunately for the IRD, John Freeman, who replaced Paul Gore-Booth as High Commissioner in India in earlier that year, made plain that he had 'no objection to cash payments being made locally'. At the same time, Freeman reminded his resident IRD officer of the principle that a 'diplomatic officer of this Mission should not get himself involved in a transaction which could be represented as a direct bribe'.[88] Having been given a green light by Freeman, the IRD moved immediately to 'take advantage' of their new financial freedom and in the process 'demonstrate to the sceptical the advantages which can be derived from direct funding'. Accordingly, IRD's 'most reliable contact', Ram Singh, and his weekly *Thought*, became the first recipient of an IRD financial subsidy in the form of a regular block purchase of advertising space.[89]

Concurrently, the IRD also increased the use of other incentives aimed at, 'consolidating existing [Indian] contacts or influencing potentially useful "waverers" in the right direction'. All expenses paid trips to Britain were considered an especially 'fruitful' means of securing Indian cooperation. An IRD-funded junket to the UK taken up by D. F. Karaka, editor of the anti-Communist Bombay weekly, *Current*, the Department recorded, 'produced not only greater immediate usage of our [IRD] material but a fund of good will on which we should be able to draw in the future'. At the other end of the political spectrum, H. S. Chhabra, the leftist editor of *Africa Diary*, was assisted to attend a conference in Birmingham organised by the African Studies Association. By 'leveraging' Indians that it had sponsored to visit Britain, IRD was able to develop relations with valuable new contacts, including

Figure 6.1 The CIA's pervasiveness in Indian politics represented in *Thought* magazine, 26 April 1967.

S. R. Mohan Das, labour correspondent of the *Economic Times*; A. G. Noorani, correspondent of the *Indian Express*; Professor P. C. Chakravarty, head of the department of International Affairs at Jadavpur University, Calcutta; and N. S. Jagganatahn, an assistant editor of the *Hindustan Times*, amongst others.[90]

The perception inside Whitehall that the IRD was making some headway against the Soviet information offensive in India enabled Joy to lobby successfully for the allocation of additional counter-propaganda resources. Joy had long complained that the IRD operation in India was over-stretched, under-resourced, and, in consequence, 'dependent on a pathetically small network of reliable contacts in New Delhi and the [regional British] posts'. In May 1964, protests at the difficulties in making and 'nursing' Indian contacts in a vast country subject to an increasing weight of Soviet propaganda were addressed, in part, when a second IRD officer was posted to Delhi. Catherine Allen arrived in India as a 'super PA' to offer Joy much needed administrative support. One of Allen's successors, and a future head of MI5, Stella Rimington, would be inducted into the 'secret world' having 'stuffed envelopes' for the IRD in India.[91] Raised in Kenya, Allen had been recruited by the Department while an undergraduate at Oxford University, and had previously served in the IRD's Africa section. Allen proved to be an exceptionally capable and enterprising officer. Even with additional assistance, however, Joy struggled with the logistical challenges of running a counter-propaganda programme within a subcontinent renowned for its social, political, ethnic, religious, and linguistic plurality.

Periodic fieldtrips that Joy undertook outside New Delhi underscored the enormity of the geographical and functional tasks faced by the Department. In Ranchi, in eastern India, Joy discovered that one IRD contact, Sen Gupta, the editor of the local English language daily, *New Republic*, was, 'busily engaged in playing both the Soviet bloc off against the West in his own parish'. A stock IRD contact, Gupta ran a small newspaper with insufficient staff or time to devote to sub-editing. As a consequence, Gupta had more use for small features on topical issues supplied to him by the information department of the Soviet Embassy in New Delhi, and rather less appetite for relatively long-winded and abstruse IRD copy. Short one-page Soviet bulletins, written in plain language, and focusing on basic themes calculated to attract the attention of rural readers, such as Soviet medical, scientific and agricultural breakthroughs, compared favourably with the 'far too sophisticated' fare offered up by the British propagandists.[92] Reliable and effective IRD contacts working in Indian journalism and publishing were highly prized and, as Joy rued, 'as scarce as gold dust!'[93] Such, contacts, as Gupta readily acknowledged, invariably felt an indifference to the ideological message contained within British and Soviet propaganda. Indians were more concerned with parochial issues of style, human interest and, ultimately, commercial appeal. Recruiting contacts was one thing, Joy found to his chagrin, having them do your bidding was quite another, much more difficult, proposition.

British anxiety that the Soviets were stealing a march on the IRD in the *mofussil*, or areas outside the subcontinent's major metropolitan centres, led to a regional dimension being added to the Department's Indian armoury. Jonathan Davidson, a young graduate recruited directly from Cambridge University, was despatched by the IRD to Calcutta to oversee and expand counter-propaganda operations in eastern and southern India, hotbeds of indigenous communist activity. As with Joy, Davidson was not declared to the Indian government as an IRD officer and worked undercover as third secretary in the political section of the British mission in Calcutta. Davidson's role was that of a mobile contact maker, identifying new outlets for unattributable IRD material amongst politicians, journalists, publishers, and academics.[94] His area of geographic responsibility was vast. Davidson's remit ran from Calcutta, in the north, to Madras, a thousand miles further south, and took in Bangalore, Hyderabad, and Kerala, hundreds of miles to the west. Davidson would go on to have a highly distinguished career in the Foreign Office's information service and, as an accomplished musician, play first flute in the Calcutta Symphony Orchestra.[95] On Davidson's watch, and that of his successor, Ian Knight Smith, who arrived in India in March 1967, the IRD added a new tranche of Indians to its burgeoning list of contacts. These grew to encompass members of the opposition Praja Socialist Party, faculty at Calcutta University, leaders of the tea workers union in Assam, and influential figures in the state politics of eastern and southern India, such as P. Thimma Reddy, president of Andhra Pradesh Congress Party committee. As in New Delhi, the IRD's regional work ran to subsidising local publishers, such as A. N. Nambiar and P. V. Thampy, who operated the news services, FABIANS, and Indian Press Features.[96]

The diversification of IRD operations to cover eastern and southern India was viewed with satisfaction by the Department. Senior managers nonetheless remained aware of a danger in spreading the IRD's limited resources too thinly across the subcontinent and, in so doing, sacrificing impact in search of greater reach. 'IRD should', one official had concluded by 1967, 'concentrate more than hitherto on the cultivation of influential Congress Ministers, M.P.'s and senior civil servants'. 'We have tended', another IRD officer added critically, 'to commit our armour in penny packets against peripheral targets of opportunity and at greater cost'.[97] Or, put another way, the Department was anxious that its Indian operation had fallen into the trap of recruiting contacts based on their availability, and had neglected more important but less pliant targets. Furthermore, IRD field officers began to express reservations that the Indian operation risked becoming too insular and excessively focused on indigenous communist influence in the regions. 'The local [communist] threat is very much less of a threat to British interests and, for that matter, to the Congress Party itself', one cautioned, 'than that posed by the Soviet Union in particular and the Soviet bloc in general'.[98] All of which, in Whitehall's view, suggested the need to rebalance IRD work in India, and to refocus on weakening Soviet influence at the centre of Indian politics.

Collaboration Curtailed

As the IRD prepared to realign its operation in India, broader political developments in the subcontinent conspired to throw a spanner in the

Department's works. To a considerable degree, the IRD had benefited from a reservoir of goodwill towards Britain that had accumulated in India in the wake of the Sino-Indian War. As early as 1963, however, London's relations with New Delhi had hit a bump in the road following an ill-fated and unwelcome British intervention in the Kashmir dispute between India and Pakistan. Worse still, the Labour government of Harold Wilson, which had come to power in October 1964, managed to infuriate Indians by charging New Delhi with unwarranted aggression during the Indo-Pakistan war of 1965. In a development that would have seemed unthinkable only a few years before, the peace talks that concluded the 1965 conflict were brokered not by Whitehall in London, but by Moscow, on Soviet soil, in the central Asian city of Tashkent. The Tashkent accord was widely interpreted as emblematic of waning British power and influence in South Asia. 'How strange and intolerable it would have seemed to [Lord] Curzon', *The Times* opined in January 1966, 'that the affairs of the sub-continent he ruled should be taken to Tashkent to be discussed under the patronage of a Russian'.[99]

Equally troubling for the IRD was the sudden and unexpected death during the Tashkent talks of India's prime minister, Lal Bahadur Shastri, who had come to power on Nehru's passing, in May 1964. Nehru's daughter, Indira Gandhi, who, unlike her father, had little time for, or interest in, the United Kingdom, was co-opted to replace Shastri. In New Delhi, officials in the High Commission soon began to refer to the 'Gandhi factor' in Indo-British relations. The new Indian premier was considered to carry a considerable 'chip on the shoulder' when it came to Britain. With Gandhi at the helm, India's diplomatic, economic, and military links with the Soviet Union went from strength to strength. John Freeman confided to the Labour cabinet minister, Tony Benn, that Moscow was actively exploiting its enhanced status to sow Indo-British discord and aggressively pursue a 'Russian interest ... to disengage the British from India'.[100] Back in London, IRD officials echoed Freeman's concern 'that [the] Russians are now stepping up disinformation activities'. Much of the Soviet covert propaganda output, the British rued, evidenced 'rather an I.R.D. character', and had taken to employing 'unconscious or semi-conscious "agents of influence"', encompassing both journalists and politicians, who worked within local laws and were frustratingly 'difficult to pin anything on'.[101] Against a backdrop of diminishing British authority in the subcontinent, a dispirited Freeman concluded that his mission had little option other than to, 'lie low for the time being and leave it to the Russians to make the running [in India], in the hope of gradually recovering our influence and eventually making a comeback later'.[102] Or, as John Gordon McMinnies, who, in January 1965, had taken over responsibility for the IRD operation in India from Peter Joy, put matters, 'It would be ... quite unrealistic in the present post-Tashkent era to expect the Congress Government as such to peddle any material critical of the Soviet Union.'[103]

148 SPYING IN SOUTH ASIA

In 1967, the political obstacles confronting the IRD in India increased further. In the states of Bengal in eastern India, and Kerala, in the west of the country, electorates returned communist governments to office. Overnight, IRD contacts in the Congress party that had been nurtured over many years were cast to the margins of Indian politics. At the same time, allegations surfaced in the Indian communist press that external interference had taken place in that year's national elections. The Indian media fed off reports first published in the American west-coast magazine, *Ramparts*, that exposed the CIA's long-standing financial relationships with a number of international educational institutions and cultural bodies, including the Indian Committee for Cultural Freedom.[104] With Indian suspicion of Western intelligence agencies running high, IRD's representative in New Delhi came under suspicion as an 'undeclared friend', or SIS officer.[105] In response, John Freeman ordered the IRD operation to proceed with 'particular caution', and to temporarily curtail its riskier activities. IRD officers were instructed to avoid seeking new Indian contacts; suspended meetings with existing 'assets'; and implement tighter security measures around the distribution of financial 'incentives'.[106] In rationalising the decision to 'pause' IRD activity, Freeman argued that the attention that had been focused upon the CIA in India threatened to, 'unearth the activities of other Western Missions and perhaps link these with the C.I.A. Here we [the British] should be an obvious target'. Furthermore, with the election of regional communist governments, Freeman was conscious that, 'the spread of communist influence is now likely to enter the field of Indian domestic politics, and . . . in the process, the ability of the State Governments to uncover – or fabricate – "foreign influences" is of course increased'.[107] Worryingly for the British, Indian officials began to display a heightened level of interest in the United Kingdom's intelligence services. At one diplomatic reception, Freeman was startled when, Triloki Nath Kaul, India's Secretary at the Ministry of External Affairs, directed 'a sharp question' in his direction, asking the High Commissioner pointedly, "What is the British equivalent of the C.I.A.?". The same question was repeated by a second Indian at a lunch hosted by Britain's Information Counsellor a few days later. 'We do not want to read too much into Kaul's behaviour', local British officials advised London, 'but it certainly shows the way in which his mind, for whatever practical objectives, tends to work'.[108]

Freeman's sense that Western intelligence services faced a rough ride in the subcontinent proved to be well founded. In an ironic twist, Freeman was himself subjected to a communist disinformation ploy. In February 1967, a copy of a forged telegram purportedly sent from the British High Commission was delivered anonymously to Frank Moraes, a journalist on the *Indian Express*. Framed as a secret diplomatic cable written by 'Sir John Freeman' the forgery outlined incidents of American interference in India's internal affairs. It named members of the US embassy staff in Delhi and suggested that they were involved in passing covert payments to pro-American Indian parliamentarians and right-wing political party's campaigning against the ruling Congress government in national elections. A former Labour politician and one-time editor of the *New Statesman*, Freeman held no truck with the honours system and had never accepted a knighthood. The forgery, which at first glance Freeman conceded looked 'plausible' and 'could certainly confuse and probably deceive those who are uninitiated in our professional ways', was, on closer inspection, full of clumsy errors. The CRO fulminated against, 'a contemptible and unskilful attempt to blacken the name of the United States and Britain in India'.[109] At first, the IRD suspected that the forger was an Indian communist. British officials were, 'reluctant to believe that a Soviet intelligence officer could have been so clumsy'.[110] Sir Saville Garner, Permanent Secretary at the CRO, found the forgery fascinating, but mused to colleagues why communists, Indian or Soviet, 'imagine that we [British diplomats] still write in the style of Gibbon?'[111] Intriguingly, American intelligence personnel in India concluded that the forgery was the work of Yuri Modin, a KGB officer then operating under cover in the Soviet embassy in New Delhi. In the immediate post-war period, Modin had acted as Soviet controller of the infamous 'Cambridge Five' spy ring, whose British members included Kim Philby, Donald Maclean, Guy Burgess, Anthony Blunt, and John Cairncross.[112] Eager to avoid placing themselves in the Indian media spotlight, British diplomats decided to deny the forgery the oxygen of publicity and ignore coverage it received in the left-leaning Bombay weekly, *Blitz*. 'A public denial', British officials judged, 'would merely widen the article's readership'.[113]

Freeman's American colleagues in India proved less willing to ignore what they perceived to be a crude Soviet attack on British and American interests. Some months after the 'Freeman telegram' story had broken in *Blitz*, an essay appeared in the news magazine, *Young India*, under the heading, 'Did KGB Man Forge Freeman Telegram?' The exposé noted that 'a mysterious white "sahib"', with short blonde hair, blue eyes, Slavic features, and a command of Hindi and heavily accented English, had attracted the attention of India's Intelligence Bureau. The description closely matched that of Yuri Modin. Modin had left India abruptly in April 1967, only nine months after arriving in the subcontinent. This abnormally short tour for a Soviet 'diplomat', *Young India* asserted, appeared 'proof, if any were needed, that Modin came to India only to interfere with the [national] elections'.[114] Having read the *Young India* exposé, David Lancashire, IRD's representative in the Indian capital, speculated that its focus on the KGB, and reference to Modin, had been orchestrated by the local CIA station. The magazine's editor, Sagar Ahluwalia, Lancashire reflected, was a shady character, and known to receive financial payments and titbits of political gossip from the Agency.[115] Whether British conjecture surrounding the CIA's robust response to Soviet active measures in India

150   SPYING IN SOUTH ASIA

was well-founded or not, the events of 1967 left John Freeman in little doubt that the relative anonymity British covert activity had enjoyed in the subcontinent up to that point, was now over.

Eyedroppers and Firehoses: IRD in Retreat

The 'pause' imposed by John Freeman on IRD work in India lasted only a matter of months. Further growth in Soviet influence in the subcontinent, however, exemplified by the signing of an Indo-Soviet treaty of friendship and cooperation, in 1971, ensured that British counter-propaganda efforts remained hamstrung. In the face of calls from Whitehall for economies in overseas spending, Freeman's successor as high commissioner, Terence Garvey, questioned the need for an IRD presence on his staff. Garvey informed Whitehall that if financial savings had to be made in India, he was prepared to make do without an IRD officer, and to transfer counter-propaganda responsibilities to a member of his chancery.[116] It seemed imprudent, the high commissioner argued, to pour money and manpower into contesting an, 'immense Russian information effort [that] consisted mainly of providing second-class material for mass publication in India'. Overt and semi-autonomous bodies, such as the BIS and the British Council, Garvey added, could protect British interests in the subcontinent just as well, if not better, than the IRD.[117] In London, IRD officials fought a rear-guard action to retain a foothold in India. It would be foolhardy, the Department argued, to denude India of a specialist counter-subversion presence at a time when, following the outbreak of another Indo-Pakistan war and the emergence of the new state of Bangladesh, 'the Soviet Union and China are more closely involved than ever before in the sub-continent'. Nevertheless, under new terms of reference, P. H. Roberts, the incumbent IRD representative, was compelled to undertake 'straight' information work alongside the Department's covert activities. The IRD's regional representation in India was phased out.[118]

More broadly, by 1972, a new and slimmed down version of IRD, or IRD Mark II, had come into being. This development reflected the consensus in London that, since its heyday in the 1960s, 'the [IRD] operation had tended to get out of hand; IRD became too big, too diffuse and had to be drastically reorganised'. The department's complement of staff was halved, and its headquarters in London was relocated from a tower block at Riverwalk House, Millbank, to smaller offices in Great George Street.[119] Reductions in IRD's presence in South Asia coincided with India's removal from Whitehall's list of information policy priorities. Moving forward, the high commission in New Delhi was warned by the Foreign Office that should further cuts be contemplated in the propaganda budget, 'India will be one of the first countries at which we shall have to look.'[120] Roberts was subsequently tasked with additional responsibility for IRD operations in Pakistan, Nepal, Bangladesh, and Sri Lanka. Enthusiasm for expanding the IRD's global role, that had been so evident in Whitehall in the early 1960s, waned as Europe became the primary centre of British concern. With neither the time nor the funds to sustain the IRD's network of South Asian contacts, Roberts found himself confined to New Delhi. There his administrative support was supplied by the wife of a British diplomat, whose remit ran to reading seven English-language Indian newspapers a day and, 'using her own judgment on matters of IRD interest'.[121]

In 1975, IRD imposed a second suspension, or 'partial embargo', on its operations in India. That June, the Allahabad High Court controversially found Indira Gandhi to be guilty of electoral malpractice. The legal ruling threatened to invalidate the Indian premier's status as a member of parliament and bring down her government. Scenting political blood, Gandhi's opponents took to India's streets and the prime minister responded by declaring a State of Emergency, suspended civil liberties, and jailed her political opponents. The IRD's Indian contacts ran for cover, fearful of being exposed or imprisoned by an increasingly authoritarian regime that appeared obsessed by threats to the nation's sovereignty, real and imagined. In turn, following discussions between the IRD and the Foreign Office's South Asia desk, it was agreed that the circulation of counter-propaganda material in India should be 'drastically reduced'. The supply of IRD anti-Soviet literature to 'unofficial recipients', or Indians outside government, stopped altogether. With Gandhi's administration intercepting and censoring communications, local mail was no longer used to deliver IRD copy, further restricting its circulation. Reference to Indian internal politics was stripped entirely from the Department's material. Roberts found himself reduced to servicing a shrinking group of trusted officials in minor Indian government departments.[122]

Prior to the IRD's demise, in 1977, on the initiative of Labour's foreign secretary, David Owen, the Department continued to justify its by now 'penny packet' activities in India on the basis that they retained impact. IRD official's argued, implausibly, that when it came to counter-propaganda activity in the subcontinent, the British 'eye-dropper can continue to be effective where Russian and American fire hoses may be too indiscriminating always to hit the target, and the solution this applies may sting more'.[123] Pressed for evidence of its continued utility, the Department was forced to concede that it was all but, 'impossible to quantify the effectiveness of information activities, whether covert or overt'.[124] Instead, the IRD asked for the value of its work in India to be taken as an article of faith. Drawing on an agricultural analogy, the Department drew a parallel between its labour and the effect of fertiliser. 'You cannot really tell how much it has affected a particular crop as opposed, say, to the weather. But like fertilizer you have to put it on.' Across Whitehall, where misunderstanding of the IRD and its responsibilities was commonplace, British mandarins drew a different, and less flattering interpretation, from a metaphor that associated the Department with the spreading of manure.[125]

Ultimately, the IRD proved incapable of making the political weather in New Delhi, Bombay, Calcutta, or Madras. Broader foreign policy decisions taken in London, Washington, Moscow, and Beijing dictated Indian responses to the Soviet Union, and not the actions of a handful of overstretched covert counter-propaganda officers on the ground in South Asia. British foreign policymaking and, by association, that of London's principal ally, the United States, undoubtedly handicapped the work of the IRD in India, as elsewhere in the developing world. Issues surrounding colonialism, racial discrimination, immigration, and economic exploitation, bedevilled Britain's propagandists across Africa, Asia, and the Middle East, and produced reactive and defensive responses.[126] Under such circumstances, selling anti-communism was difficult. Well before the department's dissolution the late 1970s, the IRD experiment in India had run its course.

7

From Russia with Love: Dissidents and Defectors in Cold War India

In January 1968, Suman Mulgaokar, editor of the *Hindustan Times*, published an editorial entitled, 'The Right of Asylum'. Mulgaokar's interest in political asylum was piqued by a series of high-profile incidents that saw nationals from behind the Iron Curtain seek to defect to the West through India. Noting the consternation that this unwelcome development had engendered in Indian government circles, Mulgaokar observed wryly that:

> To have three Russian defections occur in your country within three years is embarrassing enough. When one of the defectors is Stalin's daughter, the matter gets much worse. When the third of the defectors . . . goes about stating that . . . he had 'chosen' India to defect from because visas for India were relatively easy to obtain, the unusually high colour of Indian Home and External Affairs Ministry officials becomes easy to understand.[1]

Less easy to comprehend, in Mulgaokar's opinion, was an aide memoire that the Indian Government circulated to diplomatic missions in New Delhi on 30 December 1967. Originating in the Ministry of External Affairs, the note stated that it was, 'well established that the affording of asylum is not within the purposes of a Diplomatic Mission'. Should any foreign mission receive a request for asylum, the MEA directive added, it should be refused.[2] The instruction backed Indian officials into an awkward corner. Were the American or the Soviet embassies to take in a defector, Mulgaokar observed, the MEA faced, 'the choice of either doing nothing, which would make it look impotent, or of invading the Embassy premises which would be a violation of the conventions of courtesy between nations'. In respect of low-level and largely benign political refugees, the adoption of such a rigid policy appeared unnecessarily punitive and counterproductive. It made little sense in such cases, Mulgaokar opined, 'for India to get into a flap merely because its soil was used to stage the defection'.[3]

The Indian government's directive on political asylum was triggered by the defection of Aziz Saltimovitch Ulug-Zade, a teacher of Hindi at Moscow State University who had travelled to India as part of a Soviet youth delegation. On 19 December 1967, just hours before he was due to return to the Soviet Union, Ulug-Zade walked out of the Hotel Ranjit in New Delhi, hailed a taxi, and made for the British High Commission in the diplomatic enclave of Chanakyapuri.

153

Having been turned away by the British, Ulug-Zade tried his luck at the American embassy a few hundred yards further down the street. The Americans proved more welcoming. To the fury of the MEA and the Soviet embassy, the US ambassador, Chester Bowles, offered Ulug-Zade sanctuary and agreed to assist his defection to the West.[4] In the Indian press, Soviet officials charged their American counterparts with kidnapping the Russian teacher. Caught in the middle of a spat involving the United States, Britain, and the Soviet Union, the Indian government saw its relationships with all three countries, and its domestic credentials as a haven for victims of political persecution, come under pressure.[5]

Over the previous decade, New Delhi had been embroiled in a succession of diplomatic disputes involving defections from East to West. The Ulug-Zade case had been preceded a few months earlier by an incident that dominated global news headlines. In March 1967, Svetlana Iosigovna Alliluyeva, the only daughter of the former Soviet dictator, Joseph Stalin, defected through the US embassy in New Delhi. Further back, in 1962, concurrent with the Sino-Indian border war and the Cuban Missile Crisis, Vladislaw Stepanovich Tarasov, a twenty-five-year-old Soviet merchant seaman, jumped ship in Calcutta. After a protracted legal wrangle in the Indian courts, the Russian sailor was deported from the subcontinent and began a new life in the West. The Tarasov episode came at a point when India was reeling from a humiliating military defeat inflicted by China, and its national government was actively courting American *and* Soviet assistance to stave off what, at one point, appeared a threat to the India Republic's very survival.

The significance of non-aligned states and, more specifically, India, in the transnational story of Cold War asylum has been obscured by a tendency to frame questions surrounding defection in a narrow East–West context.[6] Attention given to such activity inside the developing world has privileged personal narratives and marginalised the agency of Asian and African nations.[7] Scant emphasis has been given to incidents of defection that occurred within the context of decolonisation. These placed considerable strain on the pursuit of Cold War non-alignment as practiced by states such as India.[8] They also acted as an irritant in relations between the Soviet Union, the United States, and Great Britain, when these countries were attempting to forge new and more productive ties in the wake of the Cuban Missile Crisis. The ten-year period between the Sino-Indian border war of 1962, and the Indo-Pakistan conflict of 1971, witnessed India distance itself from the West and become more reliant on Soviet support. It also saw the government of India scrambling to contain diplomatic fallout from defections staged in the subcontinent that threatened to derail its strategic tilt towards Moscow and undermine New Delhi's promotion of universal human rights.[9]

Spy Central

By the mid-1950s, a decade into the Cold War, the numbers of Soviet defections in Europe slowed as border controls between East and West Germany were tightened and, in 1961, the Berlin Wall went up. Meanwhile, defections staged at points of Cold War intersection outside Europe multiplied. Appeals for political asylum increased on the part of 'non-returnees' from state-sponsored Eastern bloc travel and trade groups visiting Asia, and from 'jumpers', or absconders, on Soviet ships docked in ports across the developing world.[10] The presence in non-aligned India of so many diplomats, non-governmental organisations, technicians, businesspeople, and journalists from the Soviet Union, Britain, and the United States provided ample scope for SIS, the CIA, and the KGB to encourage defections. Official rhetoric in India and the West that defectors were welcome and would be treated sympathetically as victims of political persecution, belied the fact that national governments often approached the issue of asylum as an unwanted problem. Paradoxically, as Western intelligence services hatched plans to stimulate defections, the politicians that they served recoiled from the diplomatic tensions such activity fostered.[11] A majority of the defectors moving from East to West were of limited value in strict intelligence terms.[12] Moreover, the propaganda bonanza associated with parading defectors before the world's media was frequently offset in the minds of politicians by the potential such events carried to upset broader foreign policy objectives.

The mere mention of defection induced neuralgic episodes in British premiers, such as Winston Churchill and Harold Macmillan.[13] In 1954, Churchill expressed alarm that the defection of a KGB officer, Nikolai Khokhlov, would undermine that year's Geneva summit, at which Britain, France, China, Russia, and the United States met to discuss the fate of Indochina, and the wider Cold War in Asia. Churchill's ultimately abortive plan to exploit the death of the hard-line Soviet dictator, Joseph Stalin, which had occurred the previous year, and engineer a thaw in Cold War relations between East and West, led the prime minister to veto a request from SIS to publicise Khokhlov's defection.[14] The same year, a dramatic escape to the West staged in Australia by Vladimir Petrov, a colonel in the KGB, and his wife Evdokia, an official in the Soviet Ministry of Internal Affairs, provoked a schism in Canberra's relations with Moscow. It was not until March 1959, that diplomatic contacts were re-established between Australia and the Soviet Union.[15] Although American governments were generally less squeamish about the pitfalls of embarrassing Moscow by exploiting defectors for propaganda purposes, US presidents did occasionally rue the politics of political asylum. In 1975, Gerald Ford became enmeshed in a damaging domestic controversy involving the Soviet dissident, and author of the acclaimed *Gulag Archipelago*, Alexander Solzhenitsyn. Wary of disrupting ongoing US–Soviet détente, Ford found himself excoriated by both the left and the right wings of American politics when he bowed to pressure from Moscow and declined to meet with Solzhenitsyn in the United States.[16] In a South Asian context, the appearance of Soviet Cold War defectors in the subcontinent invariably proved unwelcome in Moscow *and* Washington.

On their part, Indian leaders found challenges inherent in balancing the domestic and international dimensions of political asylum to be equally, if not more, exacting. At home, officials in New Delhi struggled to maintain a delicate balance between retaining sufficient American goodwill to sustain valuable economic and humanitarian assistance from the United States, while simultaneously managing a foreign and security policy that tilted increasingly towards the Soviet Union. In such circumstances, Cold War defections that threatened to upset the fragile equilibrium underpinning New Delhi's relations with Washington and Moscow troubled policymakers in India, the United States, and the Soviet Union. With a hardening of the Cold War's battlelines in Europe, and an embryonic East–West détente beginning to take shape, it was in Asia, in the 1960s, that the issue of political asylum coalesced with regional conflicts and local insurgencies to endanger an uneasy accommodation between the superpowers. The public scandals, uncomfortable parliamentary questions, and press scrutiny of security and intelligence activity that habitually accompanied defections staged in Europe in the 1950s would, a decade or so later, be replicated and amplified in the Indian subcontinent.

Czechs, Chinese, and Clandestine Conflict

While South Asia became a global locus for Cold War defection from the 1960s, the international politics of asylum had occupied the attention of policymakers in New Delhi from the very beginning of the Indian Republic. In October 1949, the advent of the People's Republic of China presented India with a refugee problem. Political and religious groups opposed to China's new communist regime began leaving the western Chinese province of Xinjiang and streaming into the northern Indian border towns of Srinagar and Leh. In February 1950, Chinese Muslim leaders, representing hundreds of refugees who had navigated a perilous journey to India from central Asia, petitioned New Delhi for asylum.[17] Nehru sympathised with the plight of the Chinese exiles. India's premier had formed a bond with the Chinese republican leader, Jiang Jieshi, a fellow Asian nationalist whose Kuomintang administration had championed Indian independence from British colonial rule. Once the Chinese Communist Party had defeated the Kuomintang and ended an enervating civil war, however, Nehru put sentiment to one side and swiftly recognised the legitimacy of the PRC. Rationalising his decision to America's ambassador in India, Loy Henderson, Nehru observed that India would 'firmly oppose' Chinese attempts to 'infiltrate India with Communist ideology or with Communist agents'. Nevertheless, his government, 'hoped [that] by maintaining friendly relations with Chinese nationalism to be of service to China and to assist in extricating that nationalism from the control of Communism'.[18] Nehru respected the way that the CCP, under Mao Zedong's direction, had unified and invigorated a nation that had been divided and exploited by foreign powers.[19] The Indian premier had no desire to see bilateral relations disrupted by the issue of asylum.

Nehru's stance on the question of asylum was complicated by an affinity many Indians felt towards political refugees given the nation's own and very recent anti-colonial struggle to win basic freedoms and secure fundamental human rights. That said, wider geo-political considerations and, not least, Nehru's policy of non-alignment, influenced the Indian government's approach to Cold War asylum. The inconvenient fact that political refugees arriving in India had overwhelmingly travelled from East to West, made the issue of defection and asylum awkward in the context of New Delhi's relationships with Moscow and Beijing. As Indian journalists noted, Chinese refugees flooding into India recognised that, 'it will be embarrassing for the authorities here [India] to be asked for help when they have recognized the Communist Government of China, but they hope they will nonetheless be able to give them refuge'.[20] Equally, contacts established inside India between Chinese refugee groups and US diplomatic and intelligence officials left Nehru exposed to charges that his administration was sheltering enemies of the Chinese state. Having been appraised by their American colleagues of plans hatched by Chinese dissidents to smuggle anti-communist literature from India back into Xinjiang, British diplomats noted with unease that, 'the request of these [Chinese] gentlemen for asylum may, quite apart from the activities which they propose to indulge in, give rise to considerable difficulties for the Government of India'.[21]

The Indian government's attempts to mitigate political tension generated by the influx of Chinese refugees into the subcontinent failed to impress Beijing. In October 1950, following the PRC's occupation of Tibet, the Chinese vice-minister for foreign affairs, Chang Han-Fu, berated Kavalam Madhava Panikkar, India's ambassador in Beijing, over the numbers of asylum seekers being allowed to cross into Indian-controlled Kashmir from Xinjiang. Panikkar was left in no doubt that the presence of Chinese political dissidents in India was seen by Mao's regime as 'a threat to national security'. Characterising the refugees as 'rebels', Han-Fu demanded that the Indian government take steps to prevent its territory from being exploited as a base for anti-Chinese activity. Chinese diplomatic barbs piled pressure on to an Indian state under severe logistical and financial strain. Asylum seekers added to the crushing burden faced by a country grappling with the socio-economic impact of the subcontinent's recent partition, and the accompanying crisis occasioned by one of the largest mass migrations in human history.[22] In 1954, the *Panch Sheel* accord, or five principles of peaceful co-existence, agreed

158 SPYING IN SOUTH ASIA

between New Delhi and Beijing, ushered in a brief period of *Hindee Chinee bhai-bhai*, or Indian Chinese brotherhood. Before the decade was out, however, bilateral tensions had resurfaced in relation to defection and political asylum. In 1957, Nehru's government locked horns with the PRC after Beijing announced the construction of a highway between Xinjiang and Tibet, part of which bisected territory claimed by India.[23] Two years later, Sino-Indian relations deteriorated further after India granted political asylum to Tibet's spiritual leader, the Dalai Lama, and thousands of his supporters, in the aftermath of an abortive revolt against Chinese rule. Incensed that India had offered a haven to Tibetan exiles and convinced that the Indian government was colluding with the CIA to foment unrest inside Tibet, Beijing took a dim view of what it interpreted as New Delhi's provocative and unwarranted intrusion into its affairs.[24]

In November 1959, a little over six months after the Dalai Lama had established a Tibetan government-in-exile in Dharamshala, a hillside city nestled in the cedar forests of the Kangra Valley in the shadow of northern India's Dhauladhar mountains, Beijing sent a pointed message to Nehru that China was prepared to go on the offensive when it came to political asylum. The warning to Nehru arrived in the form of a remarkable public charge levelled by China's consulate-general in Bombay, Chang Chi-ping, that his American counterpart had arranged to kidnap, intimidate, and extort information from a local Chinese official, Chang Chien-yu. In what many observers interpreted as a Chinese ploy designed to present the United States and India as co-conspirators in a 'serious political plot' involving 'underhand activities', Beijing alleged that Chien-yu had been abducted by American personnel after entering the US consulate on routine business. American diplomats insisted that Chien-yu had, in fact, requested political asylum. In a bizarre turn of events, Chien-yu subsequently engineered an 'escape' from American custody and, in the process, a US marine sergeant, Robert Armstrong, who had been assigned to chaperone the would-be defector, was himself briefly detained inside China's consulate building. A Chinese spokesman claimed that American consular staff had tried unsuccessfully to 'turn' or coerce their colleague into becoming a US 'agent and force him to furnish intelligence'. Municipal Indian authorities appeared bemused by the high drama that played out on the streets of Bombay. In New Delhi, Nehru was furious that Indian territory had been abused by China to enact a crude political stunt intended to embarrass his government. Beijing appeared much more satisfied with the outcome of the phantom 'defection'. In a subsequent address to Indian journalists, Chang Chi-ping made plain that every nation should remember that under international law no consulate of any country had the right to grant political asylum to a foreign citizen. It was not difficult to interpret the subtext that lay behind the Chinese official's words.[25]

The Indian government's problems with Cold War asylum were not limited to Communist China. In February 1948, following a Soviet-backed communist coup in Czechoslovakia, India found itself confronted by a European asylum issue. The death, in suspicious circumstances, of Czechoslovakia's pro-Western foreign minister, Jan Masaryk, unnerved Czech diplomats in the subcontinent. Having been summoned home at short notice, ostensibly to receive instructions on a new commercial agreement being contemplated with New Delhi, the Czech trade commissioner to India mysteriously disappeared. A second Czech diplomat, based in Bombay, was recalled to Prague on the understanding that he was being promoted and would be reassigned to different foreign post. The official's name later appeared on a list of individuals sent to work in Czechoslovakia's mines.[26] The Czech ambassador in India, Jaroslav Sejnoha, was a close associate of Masaryk. A month after the coup, Sejnoha approached local British and American officials and confirmed his intention to denounce the communist regime in Prague and declare himself a 'resistance representative' of Czechoslovakia.[27] The British were reluctant to associate themselves with Sejnoha and run the risk of alienating Nehru's government. 'We do not (repeat not)', Whitehall informed the British High Commission in Delhi, 'wish to embarrass Government of India by giving advice or asylum to representatives accredited to them'.[28]

While Sejnoha courted support from circumspect Western colleagues, his staff in India became increasingly alarmed as news filtered through to the subcontinent of political purges and restrictions on civil liberties back home in Czechoslovakia.[29] Attempting to barter a passage to the West, the counsellor at the Czech embassy, Dr Alfred Dutka, who had worked as an agent for the Office of Strategic Services, in Europe, during the Second World War, began passing confidential documents of 'considerable importance' to the CIA station in Delhi. Although anxious to appear a loyal servant of the Prague regime, at least until his close relatives could be spirited out of Eastern Europe, Dutka was playing a double game and, as he candidly informed his CIA handlers, 'had no intention whatever of returning to Czechoslovakia'.[30] To the Indian government's dismay, Sejnoha, and the Czech ambassador's successor in India, Dr Bohuslav Kratochvil, also defected to the West through New Delhi. In February 1949, Sejnoha fled from India after receiving an order from Prague to return home and was eventually welcomed into the UK. Two years later, and under similar circumstances, Kratochvil, with assistance from Britain's intelligence services, absconded from the Indian capital. Having burnt his private papers, Kratochvil walked out of the Czech embassy, took a train from Delhi to Bombay, and boarded a steamer bound for England, which, appropriately enough, was named *Jai Azad*, or 'Hail Freedom'.[31] Encouraged by 'friends' in British intelligence, on the long voyage from India to Europe, Kratochvil briefed journalists on the 'evils' of a Czech communist regime that he had served faithfully over the preceding three years.[32]

160 SPYING IN SOUTH ASIA

The Kratochvil affair proved embarrassing for New Delhi. To have one Eastern bloc ambassador defect to the West in India appeared unfortunate. Having his successor follow suit led to awkward questions being asked in the Indian press over the Nehru government's willingness to look the other way as British and American intelligence agencies courted communist diplomats.[33] The left-wing Indian weekly, *Crossroads*, claimed that Kratochvil had been recruited as a British agent in New Delhi, and pointedly enquired what measures Nehru would take to forestall such Cold War intrigues. In Bombay, the salacious newssheet, *Blitz*, alleged that 'Western imperialism' had inspired the Czech ambassador's defection, and demanded a robust response from the Indian state.[34] Nehru confided to his sister, Vijaya Lakshmi Pandit, that he had been 'greatly distressed' by the events in Czechoslovakia that had culminated in Masaryk's death. Still, concerned that the onset of the Cold War had destabilised global politics and threatened 'explosive possibilities', the Indian premier determined, as far as possible, to remain detached from superpower squabbles. 'We have', Nehru underlined to Pandit, 'to take step[s] carefully to avoid entanglements'.[35]

Indian press allegations of British collusion in Kratochvil's defection were well informed and strained Nehru's resolve to avoid Cold War 'entanglements'. British officials in Delhi coached the Czech envoy on how to maximise the political impact of his flight into exile, 'in India rather than in Czechoslovakia or Western Europe, where his name means little'.[36] Specifically, Kratochvil was instructed to ensure that his statements to journalists left Indians in no doubt about the 'communist menace to Asia'.[37] Lauding the 'effective service' that Kratochvil performed for the West, Sir Archibald Nye, Britain's high commissioner, recorded with satisfaction that the Czech national had, 'been able to tell the Prime Minister [Nehru] and others the real truth about conditions in his own country and behind the iron curtain generally, which they would be very reluctant to accept if it came from us or from the Americans or from any Western representatives'.[38] Kratochvil was among the first Eastern bloc defections through India that Britain, and its American ally, exploited for Cold War political purposes. It would not be the last.

Vladislav Tarasov and the 'Other' Crisis of Autumn 1962

On the evening of 25 November 1962, global tensions were high. The Cold War superpowers were observing an uneasy truce in the aftermath of the Cuban Missile Crisis. In India, a shell-shocked nation was licking its wounds following a humiliating military defeat at the hands of China. Amidst a febrile international atmosphere, the actions of a young Russian sailor in the subcontinent ignited a political storm, setting off a chain of events that placed India at the epicentre of worldwide debates on political asylum. Under cover of darkness, Vladislav Stepanovich Tarasov, a merchant seaman from the Ukraine, climbed out of a porthole on the *Tchernovtei*, a Soviet oil tanker anchored in Calcutta's King George's docks, and swam to a nearby American ship, the *SS Steel Surveyor*. Once aboard the American vessel, Tarasov, clad only in a pair of swimming trunks and carrying his identity papers, two Indian rupees, and a single Soviet banknote, announced that his life was in danger and asked the ship's captain for political asylum.[39]

The Soviet defector subsequently claimed to have become disenchanted with restrictions on personal freedoms behind the Iron Curtain. In a series of public statements crafted by America's Cold War propagandists, Tarasov asserted that after listening to Voice of America broadcasts and reading copies of *America*, a US magazine distributed in the Soviet Union under a cultural exchange agreement, he had decided to seek a new life in the United States.[40] In truth, the Russian sailor, who had a wife and young child back in the USSR, had been suffering from depression as a result of his spouse's infidelity. Tarasov also had a history of complaining about poor pay and working conditions in the Soviet merchant fleet and had fallen out with a political commissar assigned to the *Tchernovtei*. The discovery in Tarasov's possession of letters critical of the Soviet regime, and an accompanying threat made by the commissar that the papers would debar him from future voyages abroad, it seems, provided the catalyst for an impromptu decision to defect.[41] In an effort to thwart Tarasov's flight to the West, V. Londorev, the Soviet Consul in Calcutta, informed the Indian authorities that the sailor had stolen the small sum of 700 rupees from his ship before disembarking, was a common criminal, and should be arrested and extradited back to the USSR. Tarasov's case was the first of its kind in India. The Soviets had never previously made a request to the Indian authorities for the extradition of one of their nationals. On 28 November, after the Soviets had, somewhat improbably, provided twelve witnesses to Tarasov's 'crime', Indian policemen boarded the *SS Steel Surveyor* and removed the sailor to Calcutta's central prison.[42] Acting on instructions from Washington, local American officials made clear to the Indian administration in West Bengal that the United States regarded the Tarasov affair as a political matter, that Soviet allegations of criminality were demonstrably false, and that the defector should be permitted to seek asylum in the West.[43]

The Indian government was piqued at being caught in the middle of a Cold War dispute between the United States and the Soviet Union at a time when the nation's very survival appeared to hinge on retaining the support of both superpowers in its conflict with China. The *New York Times* reflected that New Delhi had been thrown into a panic by, 'a Soviet sailor ... put[ting] a new strain on India's embattled policy of non-alignment in the cold war by demanding asylum ... '.[44] On 29 November, the Calcutta daily, *Jugantar*, or 'New Era', noted that, ' ... the Government of India, now caught between the crossfire of two friendly governments, will not find it easy to take a decision on

162 SPYING IN SOUTH ASIA

the issue. One of them [an Indian government official] remarked, "now it appears that a Sobolev has appeared in Calcutta'".[45] The allusion to Arkady Sobolev, Soviet ambassador to the United Nations in the late 1950s, underlined the concern that Indian officials harboured in relation to the Tarasov case. Sobolev had been at the centre of a diplomatic furore in America after he was charged by the US State Department with coercing five Russian sailors who had defected to the West into returning to the Soviet Union.[46]

In London, the Information Research Department pressed Whitehall, 'to seek to prevent TARASOV's being handed over to the Soviets for return to the USSR for trial'. The Soviet national's return to Russia, the IRD rationalised, 'would, inter alia, discourage other defections'. The IRD also assumed that Tarasov would have 'useful information' to barter on Soviet economic and political developments that Western governments could exploit to their advantage. The Russian sailor had been active in Communist Party from a young age, having joined its youth division, the Komsomol, at sixteen. His father was also a senior kolkhoz, or collective farm manager, in the southern Ukraine. The best means of securing Tarasov's passage to the West, the IRD concluded, was to mobilise international publicity.[47] Shining a light on Tarasov's plight was easier said than done. IRD officers noted the absence of reporting on the case in Indian newspapers and in copy submitted by local Western journalists. This was attributed to the imposition of *de facto* press embargo by Nehru's government. One British diplomat reflected that in official Indian circles, 'there is a rather noticeable conspiracy of silence on the [Tarasov] subject'.[48] A local *Daily Express* stringer, Prakash Chandra, confirmed to the IRD that he and several other foreign correspondents have been trying to file a story on Tarasov, but had been frustrated by the Indian censor. Tom Brady, the *New York Times'* correspondent in India, did succeed in delivering a report on Tarasov to his editor, and was promptly threatened with deportation by the Indian authorities as a result.[49]

More encouragingly for the IRD, American colleagues made it clear to Indian officials that the United States would initiate a global media campaign critical of New Delhi were Tarasov returned to the Soviet Union against his will.[50] In the interim, the IRD arranged for Reuters and BBC correspondents in India to be briefed on Tarasov's situation and, in return, secured a commitment from the former to cover any extradition proceedings should the case make it to the Indian courts.[51] Indian journalists were also fed a stream of IRD material on Tarasov through nominally independent press agencies that were under British control, such as Near and Far East News (NAFEN). After weeks of concentrated effort, the Department was heartened when, in January 1963, news stories based on its material found their way into right-wing Indian newspapers, such as *Current* and *The Organiser*.[52] At the same time, the IRD worked closely with American propaganda and intelligence services to explore how best to 'add any gloss' to local media coverage of the

FROM RUSSIA WITH LOVE 163

Tarasov affair.[53] One means of spicing up press reporting surfaced after it became apparent that the cultural attaché of the Soviet embassy in New Delhi, Anton Fedoseev, who had become involved in the Tarasov saga, was an undeclared officer of the GRU. British and American covert propagandists agreed to blow Fedossev's cover and, in consultation with local CIA and MI5 representatives in India, debated the 'best way of using this information'.[54] The local IRD field office confirmed later that its 'Fedoseev' plan had encompassed tipping off Indian press contacts and spreading rumours on the diplomatic grapevine in New Delhi that Fedoseev was a Russian hood.[55]

As it was, the Indian justice system's reluctance to dispense with due process and bow to political pressure to expedite Tarasov's extradition ensured that the affair descended into a very public form of high farce. Having twice been refused bail by local Indian magistrates, Tarasov, with American assistance, took his case to the Indian High Court. On 5 January, as Nehru's government came under intense pressure from both the Soviet and American embassies to intervene in the case, Tarasov was freed on bail by an Indian judge and released into the custody of Hugh Haight, the US consulate-general in Calcutta.[56] Back in Washington, the State Department poured scorn on Soviet attempts to portray Tarasov as a common criminal and to deny that his actions were politically motivated. Referencing previous Soviet attempts to pin spurious criminal charges on defectors, a State Department spokesman, Lincoln White, defended Tarasov and reminded journalists pointedly that, 'we've heard of such charges [from Moscow] before'.[57] To Moscow's consternation, the Soviet legal case against Tarasov received a setback when Russian officials discovered that a criminal act committed inside Indian territorial waters did not constitute grounds for extradition. A new, and more expansive, Indian Extradition Act had passed through the country's parliament a few months previously but had yet to be ratified. In an exchange of diplomatic notes between Indian and Soviet officials in November and December, the MEA provided the Russians with a copy of the Extradition Act and, more significantly, indicated the precise evidence that an Indian magistrate might expect to see before approving an extradition request.[58] By coaching the Soviets in the intricacies of amendments to India's asylum laws, the MEA created the impression of having sacrificed its impartiality in the pursuit of national security. When news of the legal advice extended by the MEA to the Soviets became public, Indian jurists were highly critical and lambasted the action as tantamount to, 'providing the Russians with a ready-made machine for achieving their object'.[59]

On 10 January 1963, having finished taking initial evidence, a Calcutta court dismissed the Soviet extradition motion against Tarasov. Emerging from the court a free man, Tarasov, in full view of a large contingent of international reporters, was immediately rearrested by the Indian authorities on the basis of new information provided by the Soviets. Contrary to previous witness statements, and in line with the MEA's counsel, the fresh evidence alleged that theft committed by Tarasov had occurred on the high seas and not in Indian territorial waters.[60] The extradition case, which by now had assumed the appearance of a cause célèbre in the subcontinent's media, returned to India's courts. Two of the country's leading criminal lawyers, Jai Gopal Sethi and Diwan Chaman Lal, the latter a member of the Upper House of India's parliament, were engaged by the Soviet and the American embassies in a legal tussle that, as one Western newspaper noted, had 'all the nuances of a Cold War issue'.[61] In the background, Soviet and American officials continued to impress upon the MEA the imperative of concluding legal proceedings swiftly, before the global media circus surrounding the Tarasov case could do serious harm to New Delhi's relations with Moscow, or Washington, and possibly both superpowers. To the MEA's frustration, the ponderous wheels of Indian justice in West Bengal turned slowly. During January and February, a series of open court hearings saw Tarasov's defence counsel call a succession of Soviet officials as witnesses, and pillory each in turn for fabricating documents, withholding material evidence, and committing acts of perjury. To the amusement of the public gallery, one unfortunate Soviet diplomat was asked in court to explain how, precisely, Tarasov could have managed to steal money from his crewmates, when he had been fished out of Calcutta's harbour wearing nothing but a pair of flimsy swimming trunks.[62]

Following weeks of legal argument, New Delhi's patience eventually snapped. At the end of February, in a highly unusual move, a special magistrate, N. L. Bakkar, was appointed by the Indian government to rule on the Soviet case for extradition. Tarasov was put on a Viscount aircraft and flown to the Indian capital. The denouement to the Tarasov saga played out in a small, dingy court room close to the national Parliament. The large press corps of Indian, British, American, and Soviet journalists now covering the case endured further weeks of tedious legal debate. After a month of testimony, and four long months since Tarasov had jumped ship, Bakkar dismissed all charges against the defector, who was swiftly spirited out of the country by representatives of the American embassy. In a damning verdict, delivered in a detailed forty-page judgement, Bakkar undoubtedly went much further in condemning Soviet actions than his own government would have wished, given India's ongoing dependence on Moscow to provide a deterrent against renewed Chinese aggression. Soviet officials, the Indian magistrate concluded, had 'manufactured evidence' against Tarasov, had failed to produce credible witnesses, and had concocted a case that was 'wholly inadequate and rife with contradictions'.[63] Shocked by Bakkar's finding, the Soviets appealed the ruling. The appeal was heard on 7 March 1963, in the imposing marble chambers of the Punjab High Court building in Old Delhi. The judge presiding was Chief Justice Donald Falshaw, a former colonial official who had stayed on in the subcontinent after Indian independence and was the last British-era judge serving in India. What faith, if any, the Soviets retained in British administered

Indian justice remains uncertain. Falshaw dismissed the Soviet appeal in less than an hour and confirmed Tarasov's right of asylum in the United States.[64]

To New Delhi's discomfort, India's press and, more predictably, its counterparts in the West, represented the outcome of the Tarasov affair in stark, binary terms. On 30 March, Prem Bhatia, editor of the *Indian Express*, pronounced in the *Guardian* that 'a cold war ended today between the Russian and American Embassies over a Russian who wanted to live in the West. The Americans seem to have won.'[65] Two days later, Calcutta's *Statesman* roundly condemned 'Socialist legality' in an editorial entitled 'The Ways of Justice'. The Tarasov case had, the newspaper informed its readership, accentuated fundamental differences between India's appreciation of the rule of law and individual freedoms and the absence of rights and justice behind the Iron Curtain, 'a grim reality of which there have been many reminders in recent years'.[66] The *Times of India* went further, editorialising that the 'shocking features' of the Tarasov case suggested that 'even after Mr. Khrushchev's much publicised de-Stalinisation campaign . . . the Soviet authorities are still not able to distinguish between prosecution and persecution'. In taking aim at the MEA, the leading Indian daily suggested that satisfaction at Tarasov's acquittal, 'will be shared by all who believe that justice is not a matter than can be subordinated to political expediency'.[67]

Svetlana Stalin heads West

As the 1960s progressed, the challenges that incidents of Cold War asylum presented to the Indian government continued to multiply. Most notably, the defection of Svetlana Alliluyeva, in March 1967, sparked a diplomatic uproar that succeeded in further straining India's relations with both the United States and the Soviet Union. The Alliluyeva drama unfolded early on the evening of 6 March. Taking advantage of the distraction provided by two receptions inside the Russian embassy, one of which, appropriately enough, was celebrating Soviet 'Women's Day', a neatly dressed woman carrying a small suitcase slipped quietly into the streets of India's capital. Her destination was the United States' chancery building. On arrival, speaking in good but heavily accented English, she informed the marine guard on duty that she was a Russian citizen and wished to see an embassy officer. Having been shown to the office of the US deputy chief of mission, Svetlana Alliluyeva confirmed to stunned American officials that she was the daughter of the former Soviet dictator Joseph Stalin and his second wife, Nadezhda Alliluyeva.[68] As the London *Economist* observed, Alliluyeva was nothing less than 'the most sensational defector that the United States has ever attracted'. Reflecting on the political conundrum that Stalin's daughter had presented to the American, Soviet, and Indian governments, the *Economist* added presciently that

Alliluyeva constituted a surprise package that 'is plainly marked "Handle with care"'.[69]

Alliluyeva was the common law wife of an Indian communist, Brajesh Singh, who she met while working at the Foreign Languages Publishing House in Moscow. She had travelled to India following Singh's death to scatter his ashes into the Ganges. Claiming to have become disillusioned with communism, Alliluyeva applied to the Soviet ambassador, Ivan Benediktov, for leave to remain in India. Her request was refused and, under orders to return to home, Alliluyeva took an impulsive decision to defect. The American embassy in New Delhi were not aware that Alliluyeva was in India. Chester Bowles, the US ambassador, later reflected ruefully on a widespread belief within the subcontinent that America had, 'this great intelligence network . . . this idea that we knew what was going on; [it] was nonsense; we didn't even know she [Alliluyeva] was there [India]'. Other Americans had encountered Alliluyeva. Two Peace Corps volunteers came across her in an Indian village. The young Americans were struck by the incongruous sight of a 'very attractive European lady' in the heart of rural India but had no idea that she was Stalin's daughter and failed to report the incident to US officials.[70]

Having received a written request from Alliluyeva for political asylum, Bowles took a momentous step. Reasoning that it would be only a matter of hours before the Soviets discovered that Alliluyeva was missing, the ambassador sent a flash cable to Washington. The message stated that 'unless advised to the contrary' Bowles would attempt to place Alliluyeva on a commercial Qantas flight leaving Delhi for Rome that evening. Having served as Undersecretary of State, Bowles experience told him, correctly, as it transpired, that Washington was unlikely to react with sufficient speed to countermand his decision. Shortly after midnight, Alliluyeva was issued with an American B-2 tourist visa, bundled into an embassy car, and driven to Palam airport in the company of a Russian-speaking CIA officer, Robert Rayle. Following a moment of high tension when the Qantas flight was delayed for ninety minutes due to a mechanical fault, at 2.45 am, on 7 March, Svetlana Alliluyeva departed from India and into political exile. Significantly, Alliluyeva's visa did not permit immediate onward travel to the United States from Italy, and she was left to kick her heels in Europe.

Bowles decision to facilitate Alliluyeva's defection was motivated by several factors. Denying her assistance and directing Alliluyeva back to the Soviet embassy was ruled out by the ambassador as, 'completely contrary to our [US] national tradition'. If it became known that the American government had turned its back on, 'an appeal for assistance from the daughter of Joseph Stalin, the public outcry in the United States and elsewhere would . . . [be] overwhelming'. Offering Alliluyeva refuge in the US embassy would have seen the American diplomatic compound surrounded by Indian police and international journalists, transforming the defection into a public soap opera. As with

Tarasov, Alliluyeva could have taken her case to the Indian courts and was considered to have a good chance of securing asylum. This outcome, Bowles recognised, was likely to prove a pyrrhic victory in the sense that it, 'would upset the Russians even more against us, because it would be so well publicized . . . '. The option of secretly exfiltrating Alliluyeva from India was rejected on the grounds that such an operation would run, 'unacceptable and unnecessary risks'. It was preferable, Bowles concluded, to place Alliluyeva openly and legally on a commercial flight to the West.[71] The fact that Alliluyeva's Soviet and Indian documentation was in order, and that she could be demonstrated to have departed from India of her own volition, provided some protection against Soviet charges 'of another CIA plot and against the accusation of kidnapping her [Alliluyeva] against her will'.[72]

Initial optimism voiced by Bowles that his embassy had successfully pulled off a 'ticklish' operation by spiriting Alliluyeva out of India, proved premature.[73] On 8 March, India's foreign secretary, Chandra Shekhar (C. S.) Jha, informed the American ambassador that the Soviet Embassy was 'extremely upset' and had 'stated to Indian officials that American secret agents abducted her [Alliluyeva] from India by force'.[74] Coming in the wake of recent failures in the Soviet Soyuz space programme, Alliluyeva's defection threatened to tarnish Moscow's long-planned celebrations to mark the fiftieth anniversary of the Soviet Revolution. One Indian newspaper noted that thousands of books, stage plays, exhibitions, lectures, and press articles lauding the events of 1917 were already, 'being churned out in an unending stream by the official [Soviet] propaganda machine'.[75] The Soviets made plain their displeasure with Bowles by breaking off all social contact with American officials in India. One moment of light relief amid the diplomatic turmoil occurred a week after Alliluyeva's departure. At a function in the Indian capital, Bowles literally bumped into Benediktov. The scowling Soviet ambassador responded by asking Bowles if it was true that anyone calling at the US embassy could expect to be issued with a visa and a ticket to America? Quick as a shot, a smiling Bowles replied, 'For you, we will'. At which point, the tension was broken and Benediktov dissolved into fits of laughter.[76]

The Indian government was less amused by Alliluyeva's defection. On 9 March, the MEA issued the US embassy with a formal note of protest. The note complained that Bowles's decision to act, 'in such haste, without giving any inkling to the Ministry of such impending action, is a source of serious embarrassment to the Government of India in their relations with the Soviet Union and the United States'. The MEA expressed particular concern that the Alliluyeva affair could adversely impact the 'close and friendly relations with the Soviet Union' that the Indian government 'greatly value'. Ending with a flourish of indignation, the Indian government's admonition underlined that it could not but, 'regret this action of the US Embassy which may put in jeopardy relations between India and the Soviet Union and may have serious repercussions on Indo-US relations'.[77] Bowles was sufficiently disturbed by the MEA's strident tone to fire off a mollifying letter to Jha. Addressing his palliative to 'Dear C. S.', the ambassador disclosed that Alliluyeva had threatened to approach the international press and plead her case in the court of public opinion should he deny her appeal for asylum. In the circumstances, the ambassador suggested, he had been left with little option but, 'to give her a visa to the United States and help her on her way'. Bowles also hinted that India's role in the Alliluyeva story was more complicated than publicly acknowledged. Specifically, the ambassador stated that Alliluyeva, whose deceased husband's nephew, Dinesh Singh, was minister for state at the MEA, claimed to have requested asylum from the Indian government. Dinesh Singh and colleagues at the MEA, Alliluyeva told Bowles, had informed her that India would take no action on the matter of asylum that ran contrary to the wishes of the USSR. Far better given this state of affairs, Bowles volunteered, for the Indian government to have been presented with a *fait accompli* by the Americans.[78]

Back in Washington, the State Department worried that such a high-profile defection might dislocate wider US–Soviet relations. The importance of securing Soviet goodwill on matters ranging from Vietnam and the Middle East to arms control and consular conventions, ranked higher on the Johnson administration's list of priorities than Soviet apostates, no matter how prominent. Undersecretary of State Foy Kohler, who had served a term as America's ambassador to the USSR and was committed to engineering a thaw in US–Soviet relations, reacted with fury to the news of Alliluyeva's defection. 'Tell them [Bowles' staff] to throw that woman out of the embassy', Kohler had raged, 'Don't give her any help at all.'[79] One American official confided to a British colleague that the Johnson administration hoped to remove some of the political heat from the Alliluyeva affair by denying it the oxygen of publicity. The defection, the British were advised, was 'being handled very restrictively indeed within the [Johnson] Administration and that only three to four people in the State Department and White House are au courant'.[80] Signals coming out of the Soviet Union indicated that Moscow was equally keen to downplay the Alliluyeva incident. On 21 March, at a meeting with Indian diplomats, the Soviet deputy foreign minister, Nikolay Firyubin, adopted a 'relatively mild' attitude to Alliluyeva's defection, at one stage making light of the fact that, by neglecting to confiscate Alliluyeva's passport, Benediktov had unwittingly facilitated her defection. Indian officials subsequently indicated to American colleagues that differences between Benediktov's belligerent response to the Alliluyeva affair, and Firyubin's more relaxed reaction, might reflect the Soviet ambassador's embarrassment at not keeping a close watch on his VIP guest.[81] This benign assessment of the Soviets position gained traction when, in April, Benediktov was demoted and transferred to Yugoslavia. British officials in Moscow broadly concurred, and advised London that, 'It is of course assumed here [by the Soviets] that in deciding not to give Svetlana Alleyuyeva [sic] [immediate] asylum [in America] the U.S. Government was motivated by the wish not to damage Soviet-U.S. relations at this important juncture.'[82] The Soviets did indicate to the American embassy in Moscow that their forbearance would last only so long as the United States continued to display sensitivity to the embarrassing position in which the USSR had been placed by Alliluyeva's actions. Notably, a KGB officer warned American officials that were Alliluyeva afforded asylum in the US, as opposed to another Western country, the Soviet intelligence agency would conduct a disinformation campaign, complete with forged documents, detailing how the CIA had coerced her into defecting.[83]

Just as the diplomatic storm surrounding Alliluyeva appeared set to subside, the American west coast magazine, *Ramparts*, broke the story of the CIA's relationships with several international educational institutions and cultural bodies, some of which were based in India. On 20 March, with Indians exercised by reports from the United States that American intelligence agencies had been busy interfering in their internal affairs, C. S. Jha summoned Bowles to the MEA to answer an accusation that Benediktov had made of CIA foul play in the Alliluyeva case. The Soviets, Jha informed Bowles, claimed to have received, 'information from U.S. sources that there had been correspondence between U.S. and Indian officials and that

Figure 7.1 'The most sensational defector the United States has ever attracted': Svetlana Alliluyeva, daughter of Josef Stalin, smiles for photographers at a press conference in New York, 26 April 1967. Bettmann / Getty Images.

this had indicated there was some kind of Indo-American complicity [in Alliluyeva's defection]'. Bowles dismissed the Soviet charge as nonsense. Whether the US had, or had not, enticed Alliluyeva to defect, a dispirited Jha responded, was, in any case, now a moot point. The Soviet embassy, the American ambassador was instructed, 'simply cannot believe that Indian officials did not know that Svetlana was leaving when she did. They have therefore convinced themselves of Indian duplicity.'[84] On March 23, Chagla bowed to a mounting clamour for government action and confirmed that an official inquiry would be conducted into CIA activity in the subcontinent. Indian communist MPs immediately called for the expulsion of several US embassy officials, including Robert Rayle, who they named as Agency officers. From his desk in the State Department, Dean Rusk bemoaned that Chagla's statement had reignited waning public interest in the defection saga and placed the United States, 'under great pressure to amplify ... [the] U.S. role in the Svetlana case ... '.[85]

In Whitehall, Sir Paul Gore-Booth, permanent Undersecretary of State at the foreign office, was a good deal less worried about renewed Indian interest in the Alliluyeva episode. Gore-Booth praised American colleagues for having taken the 'very wise step of not giving the defection what might be called "routine exploitation"' and ruffling Soviet feathers. However, the veteran diplomat, and former British high commissioner in India, suggested that there were, 'ways in which, so to speak, the free countries should "exploit this non-exploitation"'. Arguing that the Alliluyeva defection 'was of quite a different order' from anything the West had seen in recent memory, Gore-Booth noted that it had been presented to the world as an essentially humanitarian matter rather than an action driven by ideology. By encouraging and amplifying press comment on criticisms that Alliluyeva had levelled at Soviet constraints on individual liberties, the British mandarin added, the inequities of the communist system could be highlighted without London or Washington being accused of crude political point scoring. 'This [universal human rights] may not be a new doctrine', Gore-Booth reasoned, 'but its relaunching by the daughter of Stalin, in the fiftieth year of the Communist Revolution in Russia, is immensely important'.[86]

The Foreign Office quickly set about putting Gore-Booth's idea to 'exploit' American 'non-exploitation' into action. Whitehall's strategy was to stimulate contacts in the press 'not to play this [Alliluyeva's defection] as a cold-war operation', but rather to stress the 'absence of personal and cultural freedom' in the Soviet Union that Stalin's daughter had referenced as fundamental to her decision to seek exile in the West. Alliluyeva had, the FO noted, lambasted Moscow's decisions to proscribe Boris Pasternak's novel, *Doctor Zhivago*, and to sentence the writers Andrei Sinyavsky and Yuli Daniel to hard labour for publishing satirical works critical of the Soviet regime.[87] In a wider context, by the mid-1960s it was clear in the Soviet Union that neo-Stalinists were in the ascendency. Brezhnev had consolidated his grip on power having ousted the reform-minded Khrushchev. Solzhenitsyn's work was banned. The poet Joseph Brodsky was in a labour camp. Yuri Andropov, who had been appointed Chairman of the KGB in May 1967, took to publicly praising the Soviet secret police for its 'implacable struggle against state enemies'. In response, an underground intellectual and cultural movement emerged, led by Soviet writers and artists, which in time coalesced into a broad-based campaign for human rights.[88] Exploiting a decision by the United Nations to declare 1968 as an International Human Rights year, the IRD arranged for Gopal Mittal, one of its Indian publishing contacts, to circulate condemnations of the Soviets 'new attack on fundamental rights'. In an article entitled, 'Unending Soviet War on intellectuals', Mittal attacked Moscow for its mendacity. 'With all the talk of Soviet authorities' keenness to present an image of tolerance and moderation abroad', the Indian writer observed, 'there appears to be no relaxation. Their main interest is their own political self-preservation.'[89]

Journalists from the *Sunday Times*, which planned to serialise an autobiographical manuscript Alliluyeva had persuaded T. N. Kaul to smuggle out of Moscow, were encouraged by British officials to keep alive a story that was in danger of becoming yesterday's news by playing up its human rights angle.[90] Commentators in the press openly speculated that the Kremlin would 'undoubtedly' be worried by the impact that an illicitly distributed book written by Alliluyeva would have inside the Soviet Union. The effect, one Indian journalist suggested, could be 'comparable to Khrushchev's "secret speech"', the publication of which by the US State Department in 1956 had helped to ferment unrest in Poland and Hungary, and contributed to 'other political troubles which beset the Soviet empire'.[91] At one point, the Information Research Department proposed having Shirley Williams, the minister of state for education and science, review Alliluyeva's memoir on the flagship BBC Radio 4 programme, *Women's Hour*. The proposal was rejected as too incendiary by senior foreign office officials, 'because of the extreme sensitivity of Soviet Government on this matter'.[92] Not to be deterred, the IRD tried a different tack. Alliluyeva's memoir, *Only One Year*, which American propaganda agents in South Asia had declined to circulate, was, IRD officers observed, 'practically unobtainable in India . . . as the Indians, at Soviet insistence . . . were holding up imports'.[93] The Department set about boosting Alliluyeva readership in the subcontinent by distributing copies of her book to sympathetic Indian politicians and journalists. The department also employed NAFEN to secure serialisation rights for several Indian national newspapers, including the New Delhi *Indian Express* and the Bombay *Sunday Standard*.[94]

The IRD also took steps to counteract, 'a R.I.S. [Russian Intelligence Service] campaign against Svetlana designed to discredit her as a person and to frighten her publishers . . . '.[95] As the British discovered, the KGB planned to use assets inside Fleet Street and the UK publishing industry to expose alleged correspondence between Alliluyeva and her Indian husband that cast her in a bad light. These letters included photographs showing Alliluyeva relaxing with Lavrentiy Beria, Stalin's murderous secret police chief; the text of speech critical of Sinyavsky that she had purportedly drafted; and pornographic material that was intended to blacken her moral character.[96] The IRD suspected that the Russians would attempt to have the incriminating material published in the *Sunday Telegraph, Sunday Times,* or *Observer*, 'who have the space and the right readership'.[97] Consideration was given to suppressing the documents by purchasing them from an intermediary the Soviets had employed to peddle them on the international media market. However, that option, as the IRD noted, remained outside their operational purview, and was deemed something that their colleagues in SIS might consider.[98]

Senior officers from the IRD, MI5, and SIS did agree to act collectively against Soviet agents associated with circulating the documents smearing Alliluyeva. Articles and news stories were distributed by the IRD that denigrated Alexander Flegon, a UK-based Rumanian exile and founder of the Flegon Press, which reprinted Soviet journals and books, and Victor Louis, otherwise known as Vitaly Yevgenysvich Lui. Louis, a Soviet citizen, was married to a British subject, and served as Moscow correspondent for the *London Evening News.* He was believed to work for the KGB's Department 'D', or Disinformation. Department D had been set up in 1959, and busied itself producing hundreds of pieces of disinformation each year that were designed to influence the actions or polices of an individual, group, or country in ways beneficial to the Soviet Union.[99] Louis had come to the attention of British intelligence in 1966, when he coordinated a KGB operation to coerce the writer, Valeri Tarsis, author of works critical of the Soviet regime, such as *Bluebottle* and *Ward Seven,* into slandering fellow dissident Soviet authors. The media contacts Louis had cultivated, which enabled him, in the IRD's view, 'to play an important part ... [in] newspaper smear campaign against Svetlana', placed him firmly in the Department's crosshairs.[100] More broadly, the British intelligence community sought to use the Alliluyeva episode to send a signal to the KGB that it was no pushover. '[I]t would do no harm to show the KGB that we were capable of making a strong riposte to [text redacted] operations against the U.K', a joint meeting of the intelligence and security services resolved, in August 1967. '[T]he discrediting of LOUIS and FLEGON would be a valuable check.'[101]

In the United States, the Johnson administration faced criticism from the American press for its passivity in respect of Alliluyeva. In an article entitled, 'Svetlana Lost or Found?', *The National Review* chided Lyndon Johnson for ignoring the fact that, ' ... Svetlana Alliluyeva is playing out a momentous role in history ... [while Washington had decreed that] Svetlana's defection must be neutralized, drained of its large historical meaning ... so that the image of an increasingly benign Communist Russia may be permitted to stand undisturbed'.[102] At the same time, the Soviet press lambasted 'ruling-circles' in Washington for indulging in 'provocations of the highest level' that were designed to derail Soviet-American détente.[103] A succession of press conferences, media interviews, and public appearances made by Alliluyeva when she eventually reached the United States, coupled with the revelation that a tell-all memoir would shortly be rolling off American presses, shattered Soviet complacency that an accommodation could be reached with the Johnson administration to minimise political fallout from the defection. The fact that George Kennan, a former US ambassador to the Soviet Union, whom Stalin had declared *persona non grata*, and the architect of the American policy of Cold War containment, was known to be assisting Alliluyeva with her book, did little to assuage Moscow's sense of American bad faith.[104] On 27 May, *Pravda* accused the CIA and United States Information Service of exploiting, 'the Svetlana affair ... [to orchestrate] a massive anti-Soviet propaganda campaign'. 'In short', the official newspaper of the Soviet communist party declared, 'Washington is stooping to ... anything ... [in] making use of Soviet citizen S. Allelueva [sic].'[105]

In an ironic twist, following two unhappy decades spent moving between the United States and the United Kingdom, Alliluyeva eventually returned to Russia. In late 1984, the year in which year George Orwell had set his dystopian vision of a future totalitarian state, Svetlana Stalin came home. Anticipating a dose of their own propaganda medicine, one Western commentator, who had known Alliluyeva well, observed ruefully that, 'Naturally, she'll be expected and indeed required [in the Soviet Union] to make violently abusive attacks on America and Britain.'[106] The game of Cold War asylum, it seemed, had turned full circle. The Soviet news agency, TASS, duly carried an interview with Alliluyeva in which she professed not to have been 'free there [the West] for a single day'. The Americans, Stalin's daughter insisted, had her coerced into acting as 'the CIA's performing dog'.[107] Back in the 1960s, the Svetlana Alliluyeva affair was to have a profound effect on the way the Indian government approached the defection of another Soviet citizen, Aziz Saltimovitch Ulug-Zade. With the political fallout from Alliluyeva's decision to use New Delhi as a staging-post for her flight to the West still reverberating through the corridors of India's ministry of external affairs, Indira Gandhi's government adopted a heavy-handed, legalistic, and ultimately ineffective response to the increasingly vexing issue of political asylum. In the process, it attracted censure from domestic critics, and further strained its relations with the United States, the United Kingdom, and the Soviet Union.

Ulug-Zade and the Containment of Cold War Asylum

On 21 December 1967, with newsprint barely dry on the acres of paper that India's press had devoted to Svetlana Alliluyeva's defection, New Delhi was greeted by a raft of unwelcome headlines in the wake of Aziz Ulug-Zade's disappearance. On the *Times of India*'s front page a headline announced dramatically, 'Soviet youth vanishes in Delhi and causes Diplomatic sensation'. The MEA, the Indian daily reported, had taken a 'very serious view of this incident, since it does not want India to be turned into a cold war arena by the Big Powers in their game of international espionage and psychological warfare'. Indian government officials were said to be concerned that, coming just eight months after the Alliluyeva episode, Ulug-Zade's defection would have further and 'wider political repercussions' for Indo-Soviet relations.[108]

The Soviet embassy's reaction to Ulug-Zade's flight reinforced Indian anxieties that Russian patience on the issue of political asylum had worn thin. Nikolai Pegov, the Soviet ambassador in New Delhi, stormed into the MEA and demanded that the youth leader be returned to his custody. Having first rescinded Ulug-Zade's passport, Soviet officials informed Indian, American, and British counterparts that Moscow would consider it an unfriendly act were another nation to facilitate his defection to the West. Under Soviet pressure, the MEA instructed Delhi's police to find Ulug-Zade and ensure that he remained in India until the facts surrounding his disappearance could be established. As Indian journalists were quick to point out, however, the extent to which their government could satisfy Soviet demands in respect of Ulug-Zade were limited. Under Indian law, and in accordance with international conventions on political asylum, New Delhi had no authority to compel the defector to return to the Soviet Union. Having entered the country legally on a visa issued by the Indian embassy in Moscow, and following the cancellation of his Soviet passport, Gandhi's government was empowered only to deport Ulug-Zade to a country of his choosing.[109]

Soviet indignation at the latest defection to take place in India was magnified by a familiar suspicion that the CIA was behind the Ulug-Zade affair. Eastern bloc diplomats in New Delhi confided to Indian officials that they suspected the US intelligence agency of plotting to get even following the recent defection of an American citizen, John Discoe Smith. Before seeking political asylum behind the Iron Curtain, Smith had served as a communications clerk in the US embassy in Delhi. The Soviets subsequently arranged for a communist publishing house in India to release a salacious account of purported CIA misdeeds in South Asia that appeared under Smith's name.[110] Allegations of CIA interference in India's internal affairs had featured prominently in the Indian national elections that spring and had been amplified by the Agency's association with Alliluyeva's defection. Consequently, fresh rumours of American intelligence involvement in the Ulug-Zade case were politically explosive and spread panic inside the Indian government.[111] From an Indian perspective, other worrying echoes of the Alliluyeva case also emerged. Specifically, the international press began to insinuate that Ulug-Zade had been motivated to leave the Soviet Union by a denial of freedom of expression, constraints imposed on fundamental human rights, and the '[mis]treatment of Soviet writers and intellectuals'. The Russian defector, one newspaper emphasised pointedly, was the son of a well-known Uzbek poet.[112]

The diplomatic frenzy sparked by the Ulug-Zade affair, in part, explains the decision taken by John Freeman, Britain's high commissioner in India, to turn the Soviet teacher away when he came calling on the evening of 19 December. London's relations with India remained tense following a spat between Harold Wilson's government and New Delhi during the Indo-Pakistan war of 1965. Consequently, Freeman baulked at taking in the Soviet defector and attracting the Gandhi administration's ire. Any thoughts that Freeman may have entertained about offering Ulug-Zade sanctuary were further complicated by the intervention of Nikolai Pegov. Having been alerted by companions of Ulug-Zade that he might seek sanctuary within the UK high commission, the Soviet ambassador contacted Freeman directly and made it abundantly clear that Moscow would react strongly were the British mission to harbour a Soviet citizen.[113] To add to Freeman's problems, his communication links back to London had been temporarily compromised. At the time, Stella Rimington was working as an assistant to the resident MI5 Security Liaison Officer in India. Rimington recalled how, with a defector standing on their doorstep, the SLO was unable to locate the duty cypher clerk and dispatch a request to London for instructions. It later transpired that, anticipating a quiet night at work, the cypher clerk had slipped off spend the night with a Sikh boyfriend, and ignored repeated telephone calls and frantic knocks on her door.[114]

Isolated and under pressure to act, Freeman turned to colleagues at the American embassy for advice. Although wary that the United States might be subject to a Soviet deception exercise designed to compromise Washington's relations with New Delhi, Chester Bowles agreed to take-in Ulug-Zade while enquires were made as to his *bona fides*. One senior US embassy official later recalled that, 'the British ducked and he [Ulug-Zade] wound up as a houseguest in the American Embassy residential compound . . . We wanted to be more forthcoming than the British so we granted him asylum while we debated [what to do].'[115] Alarmed that Chester Bowles might act precipitately, as in the case of Alliluyeva, the MEA sought an assurance from the US embassy that Ulug-Zade would 'not be whisked out of the country without its knowledge'. With residual political fallout from the Alliluyeva affair having barely subsided, the last thing that the Johnson administration wanted was a second defection crisis on its hands. Accordingly, Galen Stone, senior counsellor at the US embassy, was quick to reassure Indian government officials that Washington would ensure every 'effort was made to find a way out of this tangle without undue embarrassment to either side'.[116] Having previously spurned Ulug-Zade, it was the British who, unexpectedly, offered a solution to the defection standoff. Freeman informed Kaul that the British government had received, and accepted, an application for political asylum from Ulug-Zade.[117] It remains uncertain what prompted London's volte-face. Averting the media spectacle of a second Soviet defector transiting from the subcontinent to the United States within the same year, may well have seemed more palatable to Moscow and New Delhi. Ulug-Zade had initially expressed a preference for relocating to the United Kingdom and had made the British High Commission his first port of call after deciding to defect. The British reversal was, therefore, able to be couched in humanitarian terms. Whatever the reason, it seems likely that a form of deal was struck between Bowles, Freeman, Pegov, and Kaul to recast the Ulug-Zade issue as something other than a direct confrontation between the US and Soviet superpowers. The effect, as undoubtedly intended, was to remove much of the political heat from the defection.

As Christmas approached, it was left to Joseph Greene, Bowles' Deputy Chief of Mission, to arrange Ulug-Zade's handover to Indian authorities on the understanding that he would not be transferred into Soviet custody against his wishes. In a scene reminiscent of a Cold War film noir, Greene led the young Uzbek through an underground tunnel that connected the main American embassy building to an annex across the street that housed the US Agency for International Development. After what must have seemed the longest four-minute walk of his life, Ulug-Zade was met at the tunnel's exit by an Indian MEA officer and ushered towards a waiting car. Greene snatched a moment to shake the defector by the hand, say goodbye, and wish him well. Having to stand by and watch while Ulug-Zade was driven away into a still uncertain future, Greene recalled decades later, had been 'one the most painful Christmas eves I had ever spent'.[118]

The endgame of the latest Soviet defection in India did not pass off totally without incident. As frustrated officials inside the MEA worked to bring the Ulug-Zade case to a satisfactory conclusion, opponents of the Gandhi administration attempted to exploit the country's latest defection drama. On 22 December, during a three-hour foreign affairs debate in the *Lok Sabha*, Indira Gandhi was repeatedly thrown on the defensive. Minocher Rustom 'Minoo' Masani, a leading figure in the conservative Swatantra Party, baited the Indian premier over her government's failure to confirm that Ulug-Zade would be allowed full freedom to determine his own destiny. Linking the Ulug-Zade case to a recent agreement reached by the Indian government with the Soviet news agency, Novosti, which had links to Russian intelligence services, Masani lambasted Gandhi's tendency to 'lean over backwards to please the Soviet Government'. Masani subsequently coordinated the publication of an open letter of support for Ulug-Zade. Signed by Koka Subba Rao, a former Chief Justice of India, G. L. Mehta, a former Indian ambassador to the US, and several other prominent citizens, the letter appealed to India's prime minister, 'on the grounds of fundamental human rights embodied in our Constitution and in the Universal Declaration of Human Rights to which India is a signatory to allow Aziz [Ulug-Zade] to go to the United Kingdom without further delay and in accordance with his choice'. Asserting that it would be a 'disgrace' to India were the Soviet defector coerced into returning home, the letter suggested that any impression Gandhi's government had succumbed to pressure from Moscow over the case, 'would injure India's international prestige'.[119]

The Ulug-Zade affair touched an especially sensitive nerve inside the MEA. As one Indian newspaper noted, the country's diplomats resented 'allow[ing] Indian soil to be used for cold war propaganda and thereby embarrass itself in its relations with other friendly [Eastern bloc] countries'.[120] Some of Gandhi's own MPs, such as Arjun Arora, lamented that, 'India was becoming a Cold War arena'. The time had come, Arora stated bluntly, to put an end to foreign powers abusing India's goodwill and using the country to score cheap propaganda points at the expense of India's wider political and economic interests.[121] However, as Indian lawyers advising Ulug-Zade made perfectly clear, should New Delhi proceed with returning defectors to the Soviet Union, the MEA could expect legal challenges in Indian courts. Gandhi's government was reminded that the State had come off badly when the issue of defectors rights had last been placed before the country's judiciary in the Tarasov case.[122] Still, piqued by what it regarded as an abuse of freedoms prevailing in India by three Soviet defectors over the previous five-years, the MEA formally notified all diplomatic and consular missions in the country that it did not recognise their right to grant asylum. 'The Government of India do not recognize the right of ... Missions to give asylum to any person or persons within their premises', a directive drafted by the MEA's Legal and Nationality department stated bluntly. Insisting that it was, 'well established international practice', that, 'the affording of asylum is not within the purposes of a Diplomatic Mission', foreign diplomats were warned not to grant, 'any request for asylum, or temporary shelter, or refuge'.[123]

In a private discussion with Freeman, Kaul went further, and confirmed that New Delhi was seeking to amend existing legislation with a view to making the sheltering of defectors an offence under Indian law.[124] British and American officials in India concluded that the MEA's threat was unenforceable and agreed to ignore it. In London and Washington, policymakers concurred that, 'the main purpose of the Indian circular was to discourage other would-be defectors from using India as their take-off point'. The terms of the 1961 Vienna Convention on Diplomatic Relations, it was noted, enshrined asylum on humanitarian grounds. Accordingly, British diplomats in New Delhi were instructed, 'not in any way to concede to the Indian authorities that asylum may not be granted on this ground'. Although 'anxious to promote friendly relations' with India, and 'willing to accommodate the Indian Government as far as possible', the British stopped short of publicly qualifying their support for Cold War asylum.[125] Embarrassingly for Indira Gandhi, some months later during a debate in the Lok Sabha, the Indian premier was forced to admit that

178   SPYING IN SOUTH ASIA

the MEA had not received a single formal reply to its circular on asylum from any foreign mission in New Delhi.[126] The noise generated by the Indian government on political asylum resulted in the international diplomatic community turning a collective deaf ear.

The British, as with the Tarasov and Alliluyeva defections, proved more active in formulating a covert response to the Ulug-Zade episode. The question of how best to exploit Indian criticisms of the Gandhi government's position on Ulug-Zade occupied the attention of the IRD. The Department debated passing unattributable material to Indian contacts in the press that highlighted growing political dissent amongst Soviet youth, noted resistance to Moscow's rule within the Soviet Central Asian Republics, and revisited elements of the Tarasov and Svetlana defections. In some quarters of the British intelligence community, Ulug-Zade's intellectual credentials were seen to offer up an excellent opportunity for publicising the suffocating cultural constraints imposed by the Soviet regime on its citizens. A senior MI5 officer categorised Ulug-Zade as, 'a man of great intelligence – in fact the most intelligent defector with whom he had ever had contact'. It was Ulug-Zade's 'intellectual penetration', the Security Service concluded, 'which had made him no longer content to endure the various shame imposed on him in the Soviet Union and so led him to defect'.[127]

Within India, additional effort from the IRD to capitalise on the theme of Soviet persecution of writers and intellectuals was dismissed by local Department representatives as unwise on two grounds. Firstly, bringing additional pressure to bear on Indira Gandhi and her ministers, it was reasoned, risked damaging delicate bilateral relations, and making the Ulug-Zade imbroglio 'harder to solve' by 'provoking those inside and outside the [Indian] Government who stand to lose most by Ulug-Zade's unwavering preference for Britain'. Secondly, Indians appeared to be doing an excellent job by themselves of holding their government to account. '[T]he facts of the case have been sufficient', the resident IRD officer in New Delhi informed London, 'both to provide a condemnation of Communism and to place the Indian authorities in a position where they would risk compromising themselves and their democratic freedoms if they had refused to accede to Ulug-Zade's wish [to resettle in the UK]'.[128] In the circumstances, the IRD was content to bide its time and delay public exploitation of Ulug-Zade's defection until after the Soviet national had departed from the subcontinent. As the chairman of the British Joint Intelligence Committee reasoned, while 'it would be quite normal for Mr. Ulugzade [sic] to give modest publicity to his experience ... we would not want to mount an operation on his behalf. He is not our answer to [Kim] Philby ... & the K.G.B.'.[129] The British did not have long to wait. On 30 December, the Indian government announced that the Soviet defector was free to travel to the United Kingdom. Three days later, Ulug-Zade was met at London's Heathrow airport by British security officers. Following an intelligence debriefing that stretched over several weeks, the IRD arranged for Ulug-Zade to take up employment in the BBC's Russian section. From the BBC, he worked with Britain's intelligence services publicising the plight of dissidents behind the Iron Curtain.[130]

Ultimately, although sympathetic towards the Gandhi government's concern at the unwelcome diplomatic tensions that accompanied defections staged on Indian soil, Indians questioned the wisdom of New Delhi's attempts to constrain a fundamental human right. An editorial in the *Hindustan Times*, cautioned the government that the problem of defection could not simply 'be wished away', and would remain an inevitable and 'continuing, human offshoot of the cold war'. Given India's non-alignment and close relations with both Cold War blocs, the newspaper underlined, it would continue to be an attractive 'jumping off place for potential defectors'. While regrettable, such a state of affairs was not reason enough for the Indian government to compromise a long-established national commitment 'to honour individual rights and freedoms'. It was 'unnecessary', the *Hindustan Times* argued, for the MEA to have sought to overturn the principle that foreign missions could grant asylum. Governments elsewhere, the newspaper reflected, had defended that right 'in far more difficult circumstances'.[131] A letter written to *Times of India* by one of its readers reinforced a general impression that Gandhi's government had panicked and erred in its approach to the thorny question of defection. In seeking to proscribe the right to political asylum on Indian territory, the MEA had, one citizen opined, 'taken . . . [a] hasty and possibly ill-considered step to cover its embarrassment over the defection of three Soviet citizens in a short period of time'.[132]

Failing to Square the Asylum Circle

India assumed a prominent role in the high drama of defection as the Cold War spread from Europe into Asia. The Indian government's engagement with the diplomatic problem posed by political asylum exposed the existence of deep fault lines between Indian domestic sentiment, which broadly favoured a liberal and compassionate policy on defection, and New Delhi's conviction that the nation's wider interests were best served by an uncompromising and legalistic response to political refugees originating from the Eastern bloc. Indian officials invariably found themselves squeezed by seemingly contradictory demands to defend New Delhi's post-independence commitments to freedom of political expression, individual liberty, and universal human rights, while, simultaneously, pursuing national security interests that hinged on the maintenance of constructive relationships with the Cold War superpowers.

The use of India by Eastern bloc defectors as a convenient route to the West continued to inject tension into bilateral relations between India and the Soviet Union beyond the 1960s. In February 1970, a year prior to the conclusion of an

Indo-Soviet Treaty of Friendship and Cooperation, a fourth Soviet citizen, Youri Bezemenov, slipped quietly out of India and into political exile in the West. An official posted to the USSR's Information Centre, Bezemenov had, appropriately enough, spent his last evening in the subcontinent watching an American film in a Connaught Place cinema, before vanishing into the Indian night.[133] By 1972, the *Times of India* had become blasé in reporting the latest Soviet national to abscond on Indian soil. Informing its readership that Mr. A. V. Tereshkov, a Russian engineer working at the Bokaro steel plant, in the east of the country, had disappeared with his family, the newspaper reflected ruefully that a nationwide alert and stringent checks placed on airports and border posts had failed to turn up the Russians. 'It is believed', the newspaper added, 'that they [the Tereshkov family] had already left India with the help of a foreign mission'.[134]

Indian domestic politics ensured that the issue of political asylum persisted as a choleric component of North–South dialogue. In June 1975, having come under investigation for electoral malpractice, and with protestors having taken to India's streets in almost equal numbers both to support and denounce her government, Indira Gandhi declared a national State of Emergency, suspended civil liberties, censured the press, and jailed political opponents. The large-scale and arbitrary detention of opposition politicians and activists, including the former deputy prime minister, Morarji Desai, prompted Amnesty International to categorise the Indian government's action as, 'perhaps the most significant event of the year in terms of human rights in Asia'.[135] The British and American governments found themselves inundated with applications for political asylum from Indian critics of Gandhi's government who had managed to evade arrest. In turn, the sympathetic line taken in London and Washington to requests from Indian citizens for refuge garnered New Delhi's disapprobation.[136] If the Indian government's campaign to inhibit Cold War defections in the subcontinent failed to yield tangible results in the long 1960s, it nevertheless represented a significant international event. The MEA's actions at the time are suggestive of a democratic government reinterpreting international law to suit diplomatic exigencies; and, taken together with ubiquitous and active covert foreign intelligence operations in India, it reinforces the scale of the Cold War's impact on South Asia. Once enmeshed in the politics of Cold War asylum, New Delhi attempted to actively discourage and disrupt defections on Indian soil while simultaneously working to minimise any adverse impact on its relationship with Moscow. In the process, Indian officials floundered in the face of competing local demands, domestic political rivalries, and external pressure. The politics of Cold War asylum represented a problem to which India could find no satisfactory solution.

8

The Foreign Hand: Indira Gandhi
and the Politics of Intelligence

In spring 1967, senior officials from the Central Intelligence Agency were horrified when the American west coast magazine, *Ramparts*, exposed the US intelligence organisation's long-standing financial relationships with a number of international educational institutions and cultural bodies.[1] In a series of damning articles, which were reproduced in the *New York Times* and the *Washington Post*, *Ramparts* documented the CIA's provision of covert funding to, amongst others, the National Students Association, Asia Foundation, and Congress for Cultural Freedom (CCF).[2] In India, an outpouring of public indignation ensued when it became clear that the Indian Committee for Cultural Freedom, a local offshoot of the CCF, had accepted money from the CIA. Chester Bowles, the US ambassador in New Delhi, lamented that the fallout from the *Ramparts* furore was likely to prove particularly damaging to United States' standing in India, a nation with whom it had fostered close academic contacts. The global spotlight that America's press cast on some of the CIA's more questionable activities was to have a profound and enduring impact upon Indian perceptions of America and its intelligence services. In the wake of the *Ramparts* scandal, the CIA came to occupy a prominent place in mainstream Indo-US cultural and political discourse. Blanket exposure given by the world's press to CIA indiscretions, exemplified by the international media circus that developed around Congressional probes into the US intelligence community in the mid-1970s, made a deep psychological impression in India. Having publicly catalogued the CIA's involvement in a series of plots to assassinate national leaders and subvert foreign governments, the chairman of one influential investigative committee, Senator Frank Church, famously characterised the Agency's behaviour as akin to, 'a rogue elephant on a rampage'.[3]

Remarkably, some reference to the CIA and its purportedly nefarious activities in the subcontinent intruded into almost every significant exchange that occurred between Indian and American diplomats during the premierships of Indira Gandhi, between the mid-1960s and the mid-1980s. During the latter half of the Cold War, what some commentators have referenced as an Indian national 'paranoia' towards the CIA and its clandestine activities, came to represent a constant and frustrating impediment whenever US policymakers

182   SPYING IN SOUTH ASIA

sought to forge closer and more constructive relations with India.[4] In public and privately, Indian leaders complained that the malevolent hand of the CIA lay behind many of the country's problems, foreign and domestic. Explaining away India's national ills in terms of the machinations of a 'foreign hand' was electorally expedient for Indira Gandhi. The Indian prime minister's vilification of the CIA, however, exacted a heavy and enduring toll on New Delhi's relations with Washington.

1967: India's Year of Intelligence

The year 1967 started badly for the CIA in India. In January, *New Age*, the weekly newspaper of the Communist Party of India, ran a series of articles in which it purported to name the CIA station chief in New Delhi, reveal the location of the station premises at Nyaya Marg, a quiet street behind the main US embassy building in Chanakyapuri, and expose the Agency's subversion of Indian democracy.[5] Concurrently, foreign missions in the Indian capital were struck by 'the intensity of the Soviet press and radio propaganda concerning India' that manifested in the run up to a general election in February. The British High Commission noted with concern an unusually high volume of 'bitter' anti-American vitriol emanating from Soviet publications and local communist weeklies. In part, the British attributed this unsettling development to 'exaggerated fears in Russian minds about the extent of American influence in India'. The US embassy, while remaining 'commendably thick-skinned' in the face of communist slanders had, the British observed, started to lose patience with baseless allegations levelled at specific American officials, and repeated references to 'mythical' plots hatched in Washington.[6] Prominent among the latter, was the extensive Indian press coverage given to 'Project Brahmaputra', a supposed CIA conspiracy to stimulate discontent among tribal communities in northeastern India.[7]

Communist attacks on the CIA were complicated by the unwelcome and unexpected appearance of ghosts from the Agency's past. A public intervention by John Kenneth Galbraith was met with astonishment and feelings of cold anger inside the CIA's Langley headquarters. Writing in the *Washington Post* on 12 March, Galbraith derided the CIA, with no little irony, as, 'a secret agency . . . with an excellent instinct for headlines'. The former ambassador publicly laid bare his interactions with the CIA in South Asia, and claimed that the Agency's, 'activities were generally known to, and involved no conflict with, local [Indian government] authorities'.[8] Infuriated by Galbraith's indiscretion, CIA Director, Richard Helms, fumed that Galbraith had succeeded in, 'rais[ing] unshirted hell in India and [had] . . . provided the central point of an acrimonious debate in the *Lok Sabha*'.[9] At the same time, a pamphlet appeared in India allegedly authored by the American defector, and former code clerk at the US embassy in New Delhi, John Disco Smith. First serialised in Moscow's

THE FOREIGN HAND   183

Literaturnaya Gazeta, Smith's scurrilous tract, *I was a CIA Agent in India*, detailed apparent Agency plots to subvert the Indian government. Derided as a ludicrous fabrication by Western officials, Smith's book nevertheless amplified many Indians' misgivings surrounding US encroachment into the subcontinent's political affairs.[10]

Groups on the left of India's political spectrum represented the combination of Galbraith's indiscretion and Smith's allegations as confirmation that the CIA had been actively subverting democracy in South Asia. Fresh from the campaign hustings, India's parliamentarians fed off rumour and suspicion surrounding America's foreign intelligence service and competed eagerly with each other to exhibit the toughest and most populist anti-CIA line possible. The general election returned the Congress Party to power, but with a weakened mandate and, for the first time since 1947, India's dominant political machine was left vulnerable to opposition MPs determined to hold ministers to account.[11] Congress's foreign minister, M. C. Chagla, came under pressure in parliament from George Fernandes, an MP for the Samyukta Socialist Party, to reveal what the government knew of CIA operations in India, and to confirm which Indian organisations were known, or suspected, to have received Agency funding. In response, an evasive Chagla parried Fernandes's enquiries and sought to reassure MPs that government ministers were alert to the dangers posed by a 'foreign hand'. 'By their very nature, activities such as those now attributed to the CIA are carried out secretly and such activities are not normally capable of verification', the foreign minister emphasised. '[The] Government are, however, constantly vigilant to protect the national interest. Whenever possible they take action against subversive and intelligence activities.'[12]

In briefing ministers on how best to deflect a flood of parliamentary questions on the CIA that surfaced post-*Ramparts*, officials from the Americas Division of the Ministry of External Affairs recommended adopting a pragmatic line. 'The fact is that all Governments carry out intelligence activities; it is an unfortunate but inescapable fact of international life', Indian officials stressed. 'When a State finds that the activities of foreign intelligence agents are affecting its interests, it takes whatever action it can to stop these activities.' The CIA had acquired an especially invidious international reputation for indulging in covert action, as opposed to intelligence gathering. But Indian ministers were reminded, 'No such activities have come to light in respect of India . . . [although the] Government are naturally vigilant and will remain so.' In addition, Chagla and his colleagues were informed by the Intelligence Bureau that the source of suspected CIA funding accepted by Indian organisations, including the Asian Student Press Bureau, International Confederation of Free Trade Unions, and Congress for Cultural Freedom, had been hidden from the recipients, and utilised for largely benign purposes. Indian beneficiaries of Agency cash, the MEA emphasised, 'have an apparently

184   SPYING IN SOUTH ASIA

worthy purpose and no known links with the CIA; like other beneficiaries of funds originating with the CIA, but passed on through innocent looking conduits, the Indian organisations appear to have been ignorant of the CIA's role'.[13]

Indian officials drew some solace from Galbraith's *Washington Post* article, which New Delhi, rather generously, interpreted as confirming, 'not that G[overnment].O[f].I[ndia]. acquiesced in C.I.A. activities but that these activities were ineffectual'. Highlighting a prominent case in point, MEA officials observed that US press reports had identified M. J. Desai, India's former foreign secretary and *de facto* head of the MEA, as a recipient of CIA funding. After retiring from the Indian civil service in 1964, Desai had taken up a temporary teaching post at the University of Hawaii's East-West Centre. Between June and August 1965, he embarked on a speaking tour of the United States, that subsequently expanded to cover appearances in Australia, Japan, Malaysia, and Thailand. The tour was financed by a private charitable foundation, the Granary Fund, which it later transpired was bankrolled by the CIA. On being informed by the MEA of his inadvertent connection with American intelligence, Desai 'pointed out that the tour enabled him to put across Indian views on various problems and it is a strange irony that the C.I.A. should now appear to have contributed to his spreading good-will and understanding on behalf of India!'[14]

During a raucous parliamentary session on 23 March, communist and socialist MPs returned to the attack and rounded on the government for being complacent while, 'the CIA has penetrated into all walks of Indian life with sinister effects, especially on our elections, and undermining our sovereignty'. Rejecting charges that the government had proved passive and inactive in the face of external intelligence activity openly conducted on Indian soil, Ministers defended the IB's counter-intelligence record and alluded to recent successes in uncovering foreign espionage rings. The Intelligence Bureau, MPs were promised, had been, 'alert and active . . . [and] constantly vigilant'. It was a 'misrepresentation', Ministers insisted, to assert that individual Indians, or Indian organisations, that had unwittingly benefited from funding traced back to the CIA had knowingly or materially advanced the Agency's interests.[15] Still, unable to silence government critics, Chagla bowed to pressure for more robust action and announced that a 'thorough' official inquiry would be conducted by his colleagues in the Home Ministry to ascertain whether external agents had interfered in Indian politics. 'We cannot permit foreigners or foreign governments to dictate to us what sort of a government we should have or what sort of people should be elected', Chagla asserted. 'We will unearth any activity that is objectionable, that is against the national interests.'[16]

In June, an Indian news magazine pre-empted the government, and released a sensational story detailing foreign interference in the nation's electoral politics. *Young India* published allegations that covert financial support had been provided to Indian politicians by the Soviet KGB. India's Home Ministry, the magazine claimed, had been obfuscating and 'sitting on the biggest story of the decade'. According to *Young India*, Chavan, was in possession of the eagerly awaited report on foreign intelligence agencies and, 'if made public [it] would blow "friendly" Indo-Soviet Relations" sky high!' The scoop claimed that a 'staggering' number of Indian legislators had been bankrolled by the KGB during that year's general election. The scale of Soviet subversion, it added, had come to light by accident, 'during [the] Home Ministry's much highlighted and much publicized investigation of the nefarious activities of the KGB's arch-rival, the dreaded CIA!' In total, India's security services were said to have established 'firm cases' that linked KGB money to forty national and eighty-nine regional political candidates that stood for office in constituencies across India. The individuals were associated not only with India's communist parties, but also to Indira Gandhi's ruling Congress faction and the Hindu nationalist, Jan Sangh.[17] David Lancashire, Britain's IRD representative in New Delhi, speculated that the *Young India* exposé had been orchestrated by the CIA. The magazine's editor, Sagar Ahluwalia, Lancashire observed, was 'a man of few scruples' who had come to rely heavily on secret American financial subsidies and scraps of political gossip passed his way by the Agency.[18] Lancashire's suspicions were later confirmed by Ahluwalia. In conversation with a colleague of Lancashire's at reception hosted by the British High Commission, the editor, 'true to his reputation', confessed that, 'he and his co-editors had made up the whole article on KGB involvement'. 'What he [Ahluwalia] probably meant, but would not admit', Lancashire informed his superiors back in London, 'was that it had been concocted, as we thought originally, by the Americans'.[19]

The Home Ministry's official report on foreign interference in Indian politics eventually leaked to the *New York Times*. Its contents implicated the CIA, along with West German, Israeli, and Eastern bloc intelligence services, in the covert funding of Indian political parties. On the right of the political spectrum, the Jan Sangh, or People's Party, and the Swatantra Party, were judged to have been major recipients of CIA cash. Likewise, left-wing candidates from both the Congress Party and the Praja Socialist Party were also confirmed as having benefited from secret American financial support. However, and somewhat conveniently for the CIA, given the vehicle through which the leaked report was disseminated, it also concluded that the amounts of money channelled through Communist embassies in New Delhi to Indian politicians from both the Communist Party of India and the Congress Party, comfortably outstripped America's covert investment in the 1967 elections.[20] The *Times* story was the subject of a heated debate in the *Lok Sabha*. On 15 June, faced with a barrage of criticism, a flustered Chavan conceded that the government had received a report on political funding from the Central Bureau of Investigation. Somewhat incredulously, the minister added that he had not yet found the time to read it. Rebutting charges that the government was engaged in a cover up, Chavan insisted that the report's broad conclusions would be placed before parliament once ministers had fully digested its contents. Pressed by disgruntled MPs to confirm when that might be, Chavan declined to provide a timeline for publication and suggested that further enquiries would be necessary to establish the veracity of some of the report's findings. Angry calls from Minoo Masani, the Swatantra leader, for the establishment of a judicial enquiry, were met with stony silence on the government benches. To the delight of his colleagues, one Communist MP wrapped up the debate by pointing out to an uncomfortable Chavan that for years the CPI had been accused by Congress of being funded by a foreign government. 'Now the shoe had begun pinch', the MP added mischievously, 'and all parties realized that such charges should not be bandied about lightly'.[21]

It later became clear that the KGB had employed an extensive variety of 'active measures' to smear the CIA during the 1967 general election. Several of these utilised fabricated American documents drafted by Service A of the KGB's First Chief Directorate, which specialised in disinformation. In one instance, a Soviet agent inside the American Embassy in New Delhi was able to pass templates of official US documents and sample signatures to the KGB. These were then used by Service A to forge a letter nominally from the US consul-general in Bombay, in which it was suggested that the CIA had been channelling large sums of money to right-wing Congress politicians.[22] By passing a steady stream of counterfeit letters to the Indian press, the KGB was able to keep the CIA firmly in the public spotlight. The Soviet disinformation campaign in India was assisted by an estimated seventeen English language Indian broadsheets, and a far greater number of vernacular newspapers, that were regarded as, 'fundamentally in sympathy with the Communist line'.[23] One Soviet intelligence officer, who served in the KGB residency, or station, in New Delhi, confirmed that in seeking to blacken the CIA's reputation in the subcontinent, the KGB had made full use of, 'extensive contacts within political parties, among journalists and public organizations. All were enthusiastically brought into play.'[24] British officials in India fretted that the 'very heavy Soviet reliance on the Soviet clandestine service in the subcontinent', threatened to undermine the bedrock of Indian democracy.[25] Moscow's concern at the weight of evidence accumulated by India's security service relating to KGB interference in the 1967 election was such that the Soviet embassy pressured Gandhi's government to suppress publication of the Home Ministry's report.[26]

There was little expectation that India's 'year of intelligence' would lead to a reduction in the covert activities of foreign states in the subcontinent. In December, as a tumultuous phase in Indian politics ended, C. P. Ramachandran, the *Observer's* correspondent in New Delhi, penned an article entitled, 'Where "I spy" is a national industry.' Reflecting on a period that had seen foreign intelligence services in India subject to intense and unfamiliar public and political examination, Ramachandran observed that, in the end, not that much had changed. 'There is no doubt at all about extensive activity by the CIA among the English-educated *elite* who run the administration of the country, man the top posts in the defence services and have influence in politics', the writer noted. 'The affluence of some comparatively low-paid journalists is also attributable to some easy money gained by giving information to foreign missions.' India remained, the *Observer* columnist determined, very much a nexus of Cold War intelligence competition. 'If there is anything that functions efficiently in India', Ramachandran concluded, 'it is the intelligence organisations of foreign missions and India's own huge intelligence set-up that taps most telephones, opens letters, prepares dossiers and keeps a large if fuzzy eye on what is going on'.[27] Eight years later, in 1975, Ramachandran's musings on the extent to which Cold War espionage had penetrated the social fabric of India remained valid. To the consternation of British officials in the Indian capital, local politicians continued to look upon foreign intelligence services as a useful source of ready cash. One representative of the Socialist Party of India, on presenting himself at the doors of the British High Commission, enquired of an incredulous consular officer, 'whether I could let him have the name of a CIA agent at the American Embassy, since the Indian Socialists were short of money and wanted the aid of the CIA'.[28]

Charpoys and Neem Trees: Indira Gandhi and the CIA

The psychological writing had been on the wall for Indo-US relations from the moment that Indira Gandhi became India's prime minister, in January 1966. Having assumed leadership of the world's largest democracy in her late forties, as one contemporary biographical sketch of Gandhi noted, years spent acting as Jawaharlal Nehru's consort had afforded her, 'a wealth of theoretical knowledge ... [but] limited practical experience [for] the enormous task of coping with India's problems over the coming years'. Raised in a household 'bubbling with political ideas, agitation, and tension', the future prime minister endured a lonely adolescence and grew up quickly within an environment where, as Gandhi herself noted, 'childhood games were political ones'. India-watchers in the State Department characterised Gandhi as intensely patriotic and deeply committed to the well-being of the Indian people. She was also, America's diplomatic service judged, handicapped by a 'proud temper and impatience, as well as much of the aristocratic manner of her distinguished forebear'. Reserved and socially awkward, Gandhi lacked her father's emotional connection with India's masses. Of impeccable political pedigree, yet largely untested amongst the cut and thrust of public affairs, few commentators expected much from Indira Gandhi.[29] Gandhi proved her many detractors wrong. Nehru had frequently reminded his daughter that the year of her birth, 1917, was also the year of the Russian Revolution.[30] The historical correlation sat lightly with Gandhi. She would go on to become the most transformative and controversial leader in modern Indian history.

Chester Bowles, who first encountered Gandhi in the 1940s, counselled Washington that derisory newspaper profiles that characterised the new Indian premier as the 'woolly minded daughter of a famous father', were wide of the mark. Less accurate was the American ambassador's assessment that he would, 'be able to work closely with her [Gandhi] and generally exert a constructive influence'.[31] In relatively short order, disillusioned American officials found cause to lament that, 'left-of-centre Indian officials, including Mrs. Gandhi, have long held a conspiratorial view of U.S. activities in India which has been a smouldering source of resentment against the United States'.[32] Western diplomats took to disparaging Gandhi as 'vain', 'emotional', 'authoritarian', and prone to 'irrational' fits of pique when events turned against her.[33] Of particular concern were undertones of anti-Americanism evident in Gandhi's actions and utterances, a character trait that she was perceived to have inherited from Nehru.[34] In October 1970, following one bruising encounter with Gandhi, US Secretary of State, William Rogers, complained that although the Nixon administration had, 'been in office only 20 months', the Indian premier was, 'holding against us a paranoia going back to John Foster Dulles'.[35] An avid consumer of literature with a strong CIA theme, in 1974 alone, Gandhi devoured Victor Marchetti and John Marks', *The CIA and the Cult of Intelligence*, Antony Sampson's, *The Sovereign State: The Secret History of ITT*, and David Halberstam's, *The Best and the Brightest*. 'The picture she would have [drawn of the CIA] from this selection [of books]', the American Embassy in New Delhi bemoaned, ' . . . would hardly be objective'.[36] One American intelligence officer who served in the subcontinent later recalled that, 'CIA agents . . . were to be found according to Madame Gandhi, beneath every charpoy and behind every neem tree.'[37]

Equally, as one of Nixon's ambassadors to India, Daniel Patrick Moynihan, pointed out, Gandhi had few qualms about cooperating with foreign intelligence agencies, including those of the United States, when it suited her interests to do so. In his 1978 memoir, *A Dangerous Place*, Moynihan confirmed that to his knowledge the CIA had twice intervened in Indian politics. On both occasions the Agency had funnelled money to the ruling Congress Party in a bid to head off the election of communist governments in Kerala and West Bengal. In one instance, the ambassador charged, CIA money had been passed directly to Gandhi in her capacity as Congress Party President.[38] Having served as Nehru's political confidante and, after 1964, a cabinet minister in her own right, it is hard to conceive that Gandhi was unaware of, if not complicit in, joint initiatives with the CIA that were sanctioned by the Indian government. In 1975, Gandhi's links to the CIA would come back to haunt her

THE FOREIGN HAND   189

when, in the midst of a crusade against the Agency's subversive practices, the
Hindustan Times began to publish details of the history of the Indian government's relationship with American intelligence. In response, Indira Gandhi
affected an awkward, and none too convincing case of prime ministerial
amnesia.[39]

Back in 1969, Gandhi had fallen out with the Congress Party's elder statesman, known as the Syndicate, after shifting to the political left. In July that year,
Gandhi nationalised fourteen of India's commercial banks, and sacked her
conservative finance minister, and bitter political rival, Morarji Desai. The
Syndicate reacted by expelling Gandhi from the Congress Party. In response,
she formed a new breakaway group, Congress (R). In February 1971, India
held its fifth general election, and Gandhi's reconstituted party, which drew on
support from the Moscow-sponsored wing of the CPI, was returned to power
on the back of the slogan, *Garibi Hatao*, or abolish poverty. The CPI subsequently piled pressure on its Congress (R) partner to adopt a radical socialist
agenda, and organised demonstrations of civil disobedience, or 'mass *satya-
graha*', in support of land reform, full employment, and wealth redistribution.
In the autumn of 1972, when confronted with communist-orchestrated protests against rampant inflation, food shortages, and rising unemployment,
Gandhi and senior Congress officials elected not to admonish the CPI, but
instead to implicate the CIA and the Agency's Indian 'accomplices' with
fomenting unrest. The Congress president, Shankar Dayal Sharma, who was
handpicked by Gandhi for his loyalty rather than political aptitude, delivered
a string of public speeches in which he accused the CIA of scheming to 'throttle
the Indian economy'. Sharma's transformation from a previously mild-
mannered and largely anonymous Congress functionary, into a prominent
anti-American firebrand, puzzled many observers. Noted for his good nature
and jovial disposition, in the past Sharma had expressed admiration for the
United States, where he had spent time researching constitutional law as
a Brandeis fellow at Harvard. Having reinvented himself as a benevolent
Indian leader locked in a desperate battle with the CIA, Sharma faced ridicule
from India's press. The US Embassy in New Delhi regarded Sharma as
anything but a dolt. The Congress president, American journalists were
assured privately by diplomats, knew exactly what he was doing by utilising
the Agency as a lighting-rod to explain away India's social and economic
problems.[40]

Gandhi was not above adding her voice to the chorus of anti-CIA rhetoric.
On 9 October, on the eve of a national Congress convention in Gujarat, the
Indian premier asserted that, ' . . . elements in India, who had always been
voicing opposition to the Government's political economic and foreign policies, were receiving encouragement from foreign sources'.[41] British officials in
India, and much of the country's English language press, dismissed the allegations levelled by Gandhi at the CIA, as a 'barefaced political stunt'. The British

High Commission in New Delhi reasoned that the 'CPI have plainly been up to their necks in recent agitation', while, 'Indian security professionals do not put down [the] agitation to [a] CIA conspiracy'.[42] The right-wing Indian periodical, *Thought*, noted sardonically that Gandhi had chosen to deliver her anti-CIA polemic in the state where Mahatma Gandhi's autobiography, *Experiments with Truth*, had played out. In a scathing editorial, Calcutta's *Statesman*, added that Gandhi's implication that India's economic difficulties were 'due to CIA "machinations"', was simply 'too infantile to be considered seriously'.[43] Casting a satirical, if equally damning eye on the CIA rumpus, the *Indian Express* printed a cartoon on its front page that depicted Sharma advising Gandhi that, 'This week's CIA activities include four price-rise demonstrations, seven buses hijacked by students, plus one cyclone in Orissa.'[44] Gandhi's willingness to conflate political opportunism and the CIA was in evidence in June 1975, when the Allahabad High Court found the Indian premier guilty of electoral malpractice during the 1971 general election. Justice Jagmohanlal Sinha, who handed down the decision, had effigies of him burned by Gandhi's supporters and placards brandished proclaiming "Is Mr. Sinha a CIA Agent?"[45]

Later that month, with her political opponents scenting blood, Gandhi declared a State of Emergency. 'Indira Gandhi', one US government report noted at the time, 'has become the constitutional dictator of India'.[46] In an ironic twist, Indian film censors later banned the Alan Pakula Hollywood movie, *All the President's Men*, based on a 1974 book of the same name written by the investigative journalists Carl Bernstein and Bob Woodward about the Watergate affair. Indian cinema audiences, the censor feared, might link the films biting critique of Richard Nixon's assault on democracy with Indira Gandhi's actions.[47] Congress Party figures loyal to Gandhi suggested that unrest preceding the imposition of martial law had been directed by a 'foreign hand'.[48] Members of India's political opposition that avoided imprisonment during the Emergency mocked the idea that external forces had been plotting to subvert the government. One Indian MP took to wearing a badge that proclaimed, 'I am a CIA agent', and made a tidy profit by selling copies to his parliamentary colleagues.[49]

Actions undertaken in the name of the United States government by the CIA in the early 1970s did play some part in reinforcing the negative perception of America's foreign intelligence service held by Indians in general, and by Indira Gandhi in particular. Circumstantial evidence linking the United States with those responsible for the assassination of Bangladesh's premier, Sheikh Mujibur Rahman, in August 1975, and exposés in the *New York Times* claiming that the CIA had run an agent inside Gandhi's cabinet during the 1971 Indo-Pakistan War, unnerved the Indian premier.[50] Still, to many observers, Gandhi's apprehension that US-sponsored regime change in India might figure on Washington's agenda appeared fanciful. Shortly after the declaration

Figure 8.1a-d Indian satirist, Laxman, lampooning the nation's obsession with the CIA in a selection of cartoons carried by the *Times of India*. Reproduced with permission of *Times of India*.

of a State of Emergency, the State Department discounted the possibility that Gandhi could be removed in a putsch. 'A surprise overthrow without prior disorders or other warning indicators seems unlikely', US officials reasoned, 'the [Indian] intelligence services have extensive resources, and it is hard to see how a conspiracy on the necessary scale could remain undetected for very long'.[51] Nevertheless, well into the 1980s, Gandhi continued to suspect that elements within the CIA were actively plotting her demise. Maloy Krishna Dhar, who later rose to become joint director of India's Intelligence Bureau, vividly recalled the suffocating paranoia that permeated India's bureaucracy under Gandhi. 'Those were the days of the CIA ghosts lurking in every nook and corner of the psyche of the scared politicians', Dhar remembered. Much like his prime minister, the young Dhar and colleagues within the IB, had 'started believing that the CIA was only a few steps away from breaking the country into pieces'.[52]

The Nixon Administration and the Politics of Intelligence

On entering the White House in January 1969, Richard Nixon quickly concluded that peace and stability in South Asia could best be maintained by furnishing India's rival, Pakistan, with sufficient American economic and military assistance to counterbalance New Delhi's preponderant regional power. Nixon interpreted the politics of the Global South through a reductive framework of superpower competition. Early on in his presidency, he instructed senior officials not to fritter away time on the problems affecting the developing nations. '[W]hat happens in those parts of the world is not, in the final analysis', Nixon intoned, 'going to have any significant effect on the success of our foreign policy in the foreseeable future'.[53] With South Asia rated as less important to the United States than Western Europe or the Pacific, the State Department's ambitions for the subcontinent encompassed little more than averting 'regional destabilization', and its attendant economic and political disruption.[54] As India's embassy in Washington made plain to New Delhi, ' . . . in the list of countries and regions of interest to the President's [Nixon's] concept of foreign policy, India is well near the bottom'.[55]

During the 1950s, Nixon earned India's disfavour by enthusiastically endorsing the Eisenhower administration's decision to enter into an alliance with Pakistan. At the time, Vice-President Nixon had failed to warm to Nehru, whom he considered cold, aloof, and bent on consolidating India's dominant influence not only in South Asia, but across the Middle East and Africa. Nixon's National Security Advisor, and latterly Secretary of State, Henry Kissinger, reflected that the President always felt more comfortable dealing with the 'bluff, direct military chiefs of Pakistan . . . than the complex and apparently haughty Brahmin leaders of India'.[56] On a visit to New Delhi in 1961, while he languished in the political wilderness, Nixon was snubbed by

Figure 8.2 President Richard Nixon and India's Prime Minister Indira Gandhi talk at the White House, 4 November 1971. Walter McNamee / Corbis Historical / Getty Images.

India's leaders. At the sole official function held in his honour, hosted by the Indian finance minister, Morarji Desai, Nixon groused at being presented with an indifferent vegetarian meal and lectured on the shortcomings of a US partnership with Pakistan that he had helped to broker. A second visit to the Indian capital, in 1967, proved equally unfortunate. Nixon did manage to secure a meeting with Indira Gandhi, but the encounter was kept short, and conversation proved stilted and awkward. One observer recorded that Gandhi could 'scarcely conceal her boredom' and, following twenty minutes of 'desultory chat', she beckoned over the Indian Foreign Officer escorting Nixon and asked in Hindi how much longer the interview would last.[57] The Director of the American desk at India's Ministry of External Affairs, Katyayani Shankar Bajpai, noted with relief that Nixon's discussions with other Indian ministers, on topics including China, Kashmir, and Indo-Pakistan relations, were more productive. Nevertheless, while conceding that Nixon was 'obviously clever', Bajpai judged that, 'he [Nixon] looks so patently untrustworthy, that I am surprised that he has got as far as he has'.[58] Nixon's problematic relationship with India was not helped by the disdain that Kissinger evidenced towards its policymakers. In August 1971, in conversation with Richard Helms, Kissinger responded to the CIA Directors assertion that emotions frequently outran good judgement in the subcontinent, by commenting acidly, 'Passions don't have to run very far to do that in India.'[59]

In December 1971, to Gandhi's fury, Nixon 'tilted' decisively towards Pakistan following the outbreak of Indo-Pakistan hostilities. In turn, having frustrated his effort to prevent East Pakistan's transformation into the independent nation state of Bangladesh, Nixon returned Gandhi's animus with interest.[60] That month, during talks with the British premier, Edward Heath, in Bermuda, Nixon railed against supposed Indian ingratitude for American aid. 'The United States had received nothing from India except a kick in the teeth, in exchange for $3/4 billion last year', the President grumbled. 'Was the Indian attitude that ... the white nations had no choice but to come in and bail India out?' At one point during the bilateral discussions, British ministers became so alarmed at the strength of Nixon's anti-Indian invective that they felt compelled to reiterate the Western self-interest in supporting India. 'The Indians were admittedly intolerably high-minded in relation to other people's affairs, and rather smug', Sir Alec Douglas-Home, Britain's foreign secretary reassured Nixon. 'But there was an important common interest in preserving Indian independence from Soviet and Chinese domination.'[61] An atmosphere of deep mutual distrust pervaded Washington's interactions with New Delhi after 1971. Strained bilateral relations were aggravated by differences over India's ties to the Soviet Union; the ongoing war in Vietnam; an outstanding debt which India had accumulated purchasing US grain shipments in 1960s; and the Gandhi government's fledgling nuclear weapons programme. Within the confines of Nixon's Oval Office, Indians were characterised as 'bastards', and 'a slippery, treacherous people' who deserved to experience 'mass famine'. Gandhi was derided by the President as an 'old witch' and a 'bitch'.[62]

The CIA ran India close in the disapprobation that it attracted from Nixon. One prominent historian of the Agency has observed that, 'No government institution elicited Nixon's sullen suspicion more than the CIA.' In Nixon's view, America's intelligence community was overstaffed, under supervised, and too expensive. It was also, the President frequently protested, incapable of furnishing him with information that he hadn't read first on the wire services. Thousands of people, Nixon was fond of quipping, appeared busily employed in Langley reading the *New York Times* and *Washington Post*.[63] Personal acrimony also shaped Nixon's adverse attitude towards the Agency. He harboured a festering grudge against the CIA that was rooted in John F. Kennedy's triumph in the 1960 presidential election. Nixon blamed the CIA for Kennedy's narrow victory, claiming that the Agency had allowed the Democratic ticket to exploit a so-called 'missile gap', or disparity in American and Soviet ballistic rockets, by withholding evidence that the 'gap' was illusory. Once in the White House, events conspired to reinforce Nixon's conviction that the CIA was not to be trusted. In 1972, Richard Helms infuriated Richard Nixon by refusing to embroil the Agency in his administration's efforts to cover up the Watergate scandal.[64] Nixon later confided to his chief of staff, H. R. Haldeman, that the CIA was, ' ... primarily an Ivy League and Georgetown set, rather than the type of people we get in the services and the FBI. I want ... to [know] how many people in CIA could be removed by Presidential action.'[65]

India's prominence as a Cold War intelligence hub posed particular challenges for the Nixon administration given its uneasy relationships with both New Delhi and the CIA. The close collaborative links that had were forged between American and Indian intelligence services from the early 1960s, continued to be valued by US policymakers a decade later. In March 1970, in assessing the state of Washington's relationship with India, the State Department emphasised that, 'an important area of our security relationship with India arises through liaison in the intelligence field'.[66] Strong channels of communication that continued to function between the CIA and R&AW, despite the vituperation heaped on the Agency by Indian politicians and sections of the country's press, proved their worth during the Indo-Pakistan war of 1971. Richard Viets, then a junior US political officer in India, who would subsequently serve stints as US ambassador to Tanzania and Jordan, recalled that, ' . . . our CIA liaison with the Indians was of the highest order at that point [1971] . . . I think it played a critical role in ending the war . . . Our Station chief could . . . [go to] his intelligence opposite numbers at the top and they in turn could go to their political masters.'[67] Moreover, India's standing within the non-aligned movement, and increasingly close connections with the Soviet Union, ensured that the subcontinent remained important and contested ground for Cold War propagandists. When it came to India, as one US official noted, ' . . . our [bilateral] relationships are affected by a variety of overt and covert information programs designed to project a sympathetic understanding of American policies and a favourable image of cultural developments in the United States and to discredit our international adversaries'.[68] Or, as one officer serving in the US Embassy in New Delhi noted at that time, 'We had a huge intelligence representation in India . . . We spent an awful lot of time monitoring what the Soviets were doing, and they spent an awful lot of time monitoring what we were doing.'[69]

Given the Nixon administration's uneasy relations with India, it was no surprise when the president nominated Kenneth Keating as his ambassador in New Delhi. A former senator for New York and appeals court judge, Keating had served in the US Army in India during the Second World War. By the time he returned to the subcontinent a quarter of a century later, to some US officials Keating seemed out of touch and out of sympathy with his host nation. Howard Schaffer, who accumulated decades of experience as a foreign service officer specialising in South Asia, briefed Keating before he left for India. Schaffer surmised that Keating was less than thrilled with his posting and would have preferred Nixon to have sent him to Israel, where he eventually served as ambassador. Schaffer found Keating to be 'vain', with 'a very well-developed self-esteem and self-importance', and someone who, 'considered himself God's gift to women'. The ambassador's misapprehension that his 'masculine charms' would impress Indira Gandhi, alarmed Schaffer. The relationship between Gandhi and Keating would, as Schaffer feared, prove to be distant and difficult.[70]

In New Delhi, the director of the US Agency for International Development (AID), Leonard Saccio, mirrored Schaffer's concern at Nixon's pick for ambassador. Saccio concluded that Keating had 'no know-how or understanding of India'. The ambassador's predecessor, Chester Bowles, had sought to correct stereotypical Indian conceptions of brash and superior Americans. Bowles had come in for ridicule in some quarters for riding a bicycle around the capital and encouraging his family to wear traditional Indian clothing. Keating adopted a different approach. 'I want you people [US officials] to get dressed as Americans', the ambassador announced on his arrival at the Roosevelt House embassy compound, ' ... no sandals. And I don't like beards.'[71] Keating's old-school conservatism quickly came into conflict with the political realities of 1970s India. Shortly after his arrival, Keating blanched at a speech that Gandhi gave in southern India which intimated that various US aid agencies were employed by the CIA to conduct espionage. Uncomfortable with the secret world of intelligence, at a meeting for senior embassy staff, the disturbed ambassador asked an Agency officer, 'What do I say if they [Indians] say we have CIA?' An awkward silence ensued while the local CIA station chief pondered precisely how to respond to a question whose naivety stunned the American officials present. 'He [Keating] was adrift, you see', a witness to the encounter later reflected. 'Nobody had briefed him, and he didn't have sense enough to realize everybody knows that we have [CIA] agents all over the place. But in those days, you would cover here, cover there. It was a lot of nonsense. But any rate, he had a real rough time.'[72]

Keating soon discovered how difficult it would be to overcome a suspicion of the CIA that was deeply engrained in India's political culture. In February 1971, as the country prepared to go to the polls in India's fifth general election, well-known American Indophiles pitched up in the subcontinent, including former ambassadors John Sherman Cooper, John Kenneth Galbraith, and Chester Bowles. India's communist press, abetted by broadcasts beamed into South Asia by Radio Moscow, implied that the American dignitaries' appearance had a malign purpose. 'There are grounds to believe that the arrival of prominent American politicians is connected with new plans to interfere in India's internal affairs', one Radio Moscow transmission charged. 'Public organisations in India are alarmed at these visits and calling upon the public at large to be more vigilant.'[73] Writing to Galbraith ahead of his arrival, Keating cautioned his predecessor that he would undoubtedly join a long list of American visitors whom, according to sections of the Indian press, 'have been here seeking to overthrow Mrs. Gandhi and install in power Swatantra, Jana Sangh, and the Opposition Congress ... '. Joking that he could not guarantee to provide the towering Galbraith with a super-length bed, Keating added, 'I will try to do so through the CIA which, according to the Indian papers, is the most important arm of the United States Government in India.'[74]

THE FOREIGN HAND 197

Before the end of the year, Keating had become disenchanted with, 'misrepresentations and falsehoods published and republished in the Indian press [about the CIA]', and a 'build-up of anti-U.S. passions' that these stimulated. British officials in the Indian capital sympathised with Keating's frustration at the upsurge in anti-American sentiment that had overshadowed his time in India. It appeared that 'no charge was too absurd and no imputation too scandalous to be laid at the door of the United States', Britain's high commissioner, Terence Garvey, reflected. Keating and his embassy were forced to endure an ever more 'puerile' campaign waged by senior Congress party figures, abetted by Indira Gandhi, 'to hold the hated CIA responsible for all of India's ills'. India's leadership, it seemed, had determined that the United States, and the CIA, above all, were ideally suited to assume the role of '1972's whipping boy'.[75] When the opportunity arose to leave India and return to the United States to manage Nixon's re-election campaign, a dispirited Keating jumped at the chance.

On meeting his American colleague prior to his departure, Garvey found Keating to be depressed and downbeat. The United States' relationship with India had been 'pretty good' at the beginning of his tenure, Keating lamented, but had steadily deteriorated ever since. Back in 1969, Keating noted, polls conducted by the Indian Institute of Public Opinion had ranked America second, behind the Japanese, in terms of nationwide appeal. Recent surveys had seen the Soviets top the Indian popularity stakes, while the United States languished in last place. Keating had no doubt that the reversal in America's fortunes was attributable in large part to the 'strongly prejudiced' view of the United States held by Gandhi and her followers. 'She [Gandhi] was far too ready to entertain the fabricated and malevolent stories which the Russians and their spokesman put out about the United States', Keating fulminated. 'These people were always going on about the CIA.' The ambassador's exasperation was compounded by his certainty that the Soviet smear stories targeting the Agency, to which Gandhi lent credence, were baseless. Keating assured Garvey that, 'He had told his government that this kind of thing had to stop and he made it his business to know pretty well what the CIA were up to ... in connexion to India.'[76]

Keating's vexation at the parlous state of Indo-US relations failed to prepare him for the ire that Indira Gandhi directed towards the United States when he paid a farewell call on the Indian premier. Keating had expected that his valedictory interview with Gandhi would prove awkward. Over the course of a thirty-minute audience with the Indian leader, the ambassador was, nonetheless, left dumbfounded by his host's 'emotional and distorted' assault on the Nixon administration and the purportedly heinous operations of the CIA. 'Everything the U.S. does', a rattled Keating was informed by Gandhi, 'is against India'. Forces inside the American government, she assured the incredulous ambassador, were 'working against us in India'; 'cooperating with communist extremists' to destabilise her administration; and encouraging 'a lot of American professors ... to engage in improper activities injurious to India'. Keating's insistence that the $10 billion dollars of aid which the United States had allocated to her country in the past could hardly be considered 'anti-Indian', was dismissed by Gandhi in a 'manner [that] was arrogantly confident, ready to believe the worst about the U.S., closed to any explanation, and thoroughly obnoxious'. 'Incredible!' a stunned Keating cabled back to Washington, 'My successor has an even tougher task ahead than I anticipated.'[77]

'The Paranoia Out Here is Thicker than the Dust': Moynihan and South Asia

Richard Nixon's decision to send Daniel Patrick Moynihan to India as Kenneth Keating's replacement blindsided many Washington insiders. Moynihan's reputation had been forged in domestic policymaking, with a focus on urban affairs, inner city deprivation, and race relations. A history PhD, Moynihan kick-started his political career as Assistant Secretary of Labor in the Kennedy administration, before transitioning to serve in the Nixon White House as an advisor and counsellor to the President. He had no previous diplomatic experience or expertise in international relations. Admired for his intellectual range and inquisitive mind, Moynihan embraced difficult challenges with alacrity, and came to earn Nixon's confidence. Intriguingly, Moynihan had anticipated that Nixon would turn to him when, during the president's second term, the White House sought to normalise its relationship with India. In 1972, in conversation with his wife, Liz, and against the backdrop of George McGovern's nomination as the Democrat's presidential candidate, Moynihan predicted that, 'Nixon will win [re-election] and he'll ask me to go to India.'[78] Commentators applauded Nixon's move as an unconventional but inspired play. Writing in the *New York Times*, Tom Wicker observed mischievously that, ' ... sending this imaginative and energetic Irishman as ambassador to India may be the best idea president Nixon has had; Mrs. Gandhi had best look to her neutralism and her wine cellar.'[79] In contrast, Moynihan's friends and colleagues were unsure whether his appointment merited celebration or commiseration. In a letter sent to Moynihan in December 1972, Theodore Barreaux, deputy director of the Securities and Exchange Commission, noted simply, 'India? Well, congratulations anyway.'[80]

In the subcontinent, Moynihan's arrival was eagerly anticipated. The *Times of India* predicted that he would carry, 'the process of thawing Indo-American relations one step further'. 'As a leading liberal intellectual, first associated with the Kennedy administration', the Indian daily noted, 'he [Moynihan] should find no difficulty in making friends in New Delhi'.[81] Columnists in the *Indian Express* concurred. 'It would be a fair presumption that President Nixon would not have appointed Mr Moynihan', the *Express* concluded, 'if he was not desirous of restoring some of the old warmth in the relations between the two countries'.[82] Other Indians evidenced less enthusiasm for Moynihan. The left-leaning Indian daily, *Blitz*, pronounced scathingly that 'Tricky Dick' Nixon could, 'not have chosen a trickier person ... as US Ambassador to India'. Disparaging Moynihan's reputation as a liberal scholar in sympathy with India, the Indian newspaper labelled the ambassador designate as, 'a double-thinking, double-talking and double-crossing politician [who] has no place in socialist, non-aligned India ...'.[83]

Moynihan characterised the troubled twenty-three-month period that he spent as US ambassador in New Delhi as 'the plague years'. From the outset, he resolved to maintain a low public profile in India.[84] In part, Moynihan's determination to work in the political shadows reflected his conviction that an ambassador should implement policy rather than make it. Emphasising his willingness to faithfully follow Washington's line, whatever that might be, Moynihan assured Kissinger that, 'my fixed principle ... has been to convey what I have thought policy was, and not what I might have wished it were'.[85] By the time he had completed a year in post, Moynihan had delivered only one set speech and made a total of three public appearances. 'I have tried to keep my head down out of a conviction that we [the United States] have previously been far too much in evidence and are still thought, by Indians, to be omnipresent', the ambassador explained to a friend.[86] 'We are not here to tell them how to run India', Moynihan subsequently reflected, 'That is all over.'[87] Moynihan appreciated that the failure of the United States to cultivate harmonious and productive relations with India had, 'been a central feature of Asian politics for a quarter century, and that by 1972 things had got about as bad as they could get'.[88] In the circumstances, an approach based on quiet diplomacy appeared a more likely means of burying political hatchets and placing bilateral relations on a positive footing. Moynihan's circumspection drew plaudits in India. In April 1973, writing in the *Hindu*, the prominent Indian journalist, G. K. Reddy, expressed satisfaction that, 'for the first time in recent years, there is an American ambassador in New Delhi who knows his mind, the limitations of his brief ... and the pitfalls of attempting to do too much in too short a time'.[89]

Equally, Moynihan was conscious of the toxic psychological prism of suspicion, fear, and loathing through which many Indians had come to view the United States. The noisy and intrinsically insecure covert operations mounted by the CIA across the developing world after 1947, which from the 1960s garnered headlines in the international media, left their mark in India. On arrival, Moynihan echoed the sentiments articulated previously by Keating, informing Kissinger that, 'the paranoia out here is thicker than the dust'. 'Stop sending India poisoned wheat', Moynihan quipped to Nixon's national security adviser, 'the Prime Minister is on to you'.[90] After three months in New Delhi, Moynihan was happy enough to be 'getting on very well' with Indian officials. The ambassador's one concern was a 'tremendous campaign mounting on the subject of U.S. spies'. The local press, Moynihan complained, appeared set on 'fingering one man after another' as a CIA agent. Some Indian government officers, the ambassador observed, had 'gone along' with the espionage game, and 'informally' accused a member of the US consulate in Calcutta, Peter Burleigh, of stoking civil unrest. Bridling at charges levelled against an American who had 'done nothing', Moynihan informed Indian officials that they were free to call for the expulsion of the diplomat, 'but they should understand that I will be going home on the same plane'.[91]

Moynihan had no personal axe to grind with the CIA. The ambassador liked and respected the Agency's station chief in New Delhi, a Dryden scholar and fellow academic from Cornell. Yet, in practical terms, Moynihan found the CIA to be moribund. Specifically, the Agency's officers in India appeared intellectually hidebound and ineffective. '[I]n a year of trying to get them [CIA] to think about Indian Communism for me, they have not been able to do so', he griped. Furthermore, in a wider regional context, Moynihan lamented that the CIA's public profile and operational ineptitude had come to represent serious and growing impediments to US diplomacy. In January 1974, the ambassador observed that:

> They [CIA] have just mercilessly fouled up in Thailand: with a student government which had denounced the new American ambassador as a CIA agent before he even arrived last month, some clown dreams up a letter to the Prime Minister offering a cease fire from the Communist insurgents in the North ... Alas, the illiterate youth who was given the letter to mail registered it with the home address of the agent who had given it to him. Result, black wreaths hung on the Embassy gates, apologies, silences ....[92]

A few months later Moynihan was taken aback when Indian government officials made public demands for the expulsion of US embassy personnel on charges of espionage and, at the same time, privately requested closer Indo-U.S. intelligence liaison. The head of the Indian prime minister's secretariat, Prithvi Nath Dhar, and the chief of India's external intelligence service, Rameshwar Nath Kao, quietly approached Moynihan to inquire whether CIA director, William Colby, would consider visiting India. 'The two [intelligence] services had worked together so well, and on so many important matters', Kao assured Moynihan. 'The training Indians had received in the United States was of such quality. The Director of C.I.A. would be so welcome.' Following his encounter with Kao and Dhar, a bemused Moynihan was left pondering, 'What is one to do?' Having earlier pressed the State Department to pull the CIA out of India altogether to keep the Agency off the front pages of India's newspapers, following his meeting with Dhar and Kao, Moynihan rescinded his request. 'They [the Indian government] want us', the ambassador advised Lawrence Eagleburger, Executive Assistant to Kissinger. 'Possibly they want even more of us.'[93]

Moynihan later confirmed that American intelligence collaboration with India that focused on the People's Republic of China was unaffected by Indo-US tensions or Gandhi's opportunistic public attacks on the CIA. 'Suffice that while Mrs. Gandhi was off making speeches about the ever present danger of subversion, and her Foreign Secretary was assuring reporters that a hapless young foreign service officer in our Calcutta consulate was indeed a dangerous provocateur and spy', Moynihan reflected ruefully, 'I was meeting with the director of the Indian intelligence service, and our subject was China.' Having 'been hard' on the Agency during his time in India and, like Keating, having conducted his own enquiries into its activities in the subcontinent, Moynihan 'ended satisfied that they [CIA] had been up to very little, save those things they did <u>with</u> the Indians'.[94] Nevertheless, as Moynihan discovered, his efforts to neutralise the impact of the CIA on bilateral relations, and recalibrate affairs between two nations that, in the words of one contemporary observer, had become 'locked in a corrosive limbo', proved elusive.[95]

Delhi is not Chile: The CIA and Subversion in the Global South

In September 1973, 10,000 miles from New Delhi, a bloody rightwing coup in Chile toppled the socialist government of Salvador Allende. The CIA's complicity in Allende's death, and his administrations replacement by a repressive military junta, led by Augusto Pinochet, sent shockwaves through India's political establishment. At the United Nations, Swaran Singh, India's Minister for External Affairs, denounced the coup and the assault on democracy in Chile.[96] Horrified by the speed and brutality with which Allende was swept from power, Indira Gandhi was concerned that she would be the next left-wing leader targeted by Richard Nixon for regime change.[97] The Indian premier privately fretted that 'big external forces' would combine with 'internal vested interests' to topple her government.[98] The news from Chile reached Gandhi during a dinner she was hosting for the Cuban leader, Fidel Castro. Given the many and varied plots that the CIA had hatched to liquidate Castro, it was unsurprising that discussion between the two leaders included the subject of American-orchestrated extra-judicial killing. Following Gandhi's assassination, in October 1984, Castro contributed to a commemorative volume celebrating her life. 'At that dramatic moment [back in 1973]', Castro wrote, 'Indira Gandhi, in a proof of her intimacy and confidence, said to me: 'What they have done to Allende they want to do to me also. There are people here, connected with the same foreign forces that acted in Chile, who would like to eliminate me.''[99] Gandhi expressed similar concerns to the Soviets, instructing India's ambassador in Moscow to ensure that Leonid Brezhnev was made aware that the CIA was 'aiming at killing her'.[100] An encounter, in New Delhi, in April 1974, between Gandhi and Allende's widow, Hortensia Bussi, one imagines, did little to ameliorate the India's premier's sense of foreboding.[101]

Figure 8.3 *New Age*, the newspaper of the Communist Party of India, lambasts the CIA for its latest, purported, act of subversion in the subcontinent, 22 October 1972. FCO95/1388, United Kingdom National Archives (UKNA).

THE FOREIGN HAND   203

The Indian leaders concern for her personal safety was well-founded. In 1975 alone, Gandhi was subject to several failed assassination attempts. A week before the murder of Mujibur Rahman in neighbouring Bangladesh, a former Indian army captain, Dhaja Ram Sangwan, was apprehended with a telescopic rifle and was believed to have the Indian premier in his sights. On 2 October, another attempt on Gandhi's life was made at a prayer meeting held at Raj Ghat, Mahatma Gandhi's memorial, in New Delhi. In the midst of a commemoration ceremony, a knife-wielding assassin breached Gandhi's security perimeter and was almost upon the prime minister before being intercepted by Shafi Qureshi, India's minister of state for railways. Earlier, in March, an assassin, wielding a twelve-bore shotgun, was detained outside the Allahabad High Court where Gandhi was testifying. No evidence emerged to link the assassination plots to external actors, CIA or otherwise.[102] At the time, senior Congress party figures declared defiantly that events in South America would not be repeated in the subcontinent. At a meeting of the All-India Congress Committee, one British observer reported, 'speaker after speaker condemned the CIA for putting the Chilean Army up to dethroning Allende'.[103] Gandhi had only recently returned to India from the fourth Conference of Non-Aligned Countries in Algiers where, in an address to the meetings plenary session, she noted Allende's absence and exclaimed, 'We miss President Allende of Chile who is fighting a battle which is common to us ... Each of our countries has a surfeit of its own domestic problems ... To these are added the problems created by external forces.'[104] Bellicose Indian leaders subsequently made a habit of reassuring the nation's public that they, 'would not allow Delhi to be turned into Chile'.[105] Gandhi too, would frequently return in her public statements to the events of September 1973. In an interview reproduced in the Congress newssheet, *Socialist Weekly*, nearly two years after Allende's downfall, Gandhi asked pointedly, 'Have these several Western countries not given full moral and material support to the most authoritarian regimes of Africa and Asia? Have we so soon forgotten what happened to Chile?'[106]

Not all Indians were as convinced as Gandhi that her government was in the CIA's crosshairs. Writing in the *Times of India*, the journalist, Girilal Jain, dismissed the notion that Allende's ouster would have any bearing on the politics of the subcontinent. 'Whatever the nature of the evidence of CIA involvement in the Chilean coup, one would be naïve to believe that it had not taken a hand at all in toppling President Allende', Jain opined. 'But one must be even more naïve to believe that the CIA could have brought down the regime with the co-operation of the giant multi-national corporation like the ITT and the so-called Chilean vested interests ... '. The chaotic economic problems and civil disorder that had plagued Chile prior to the coup d'état, Jain pointed out, had sealed Allende's fate, and those conditions did not yet prevail in India. '[I]t serves no useful purpose to draw a parallel between Chile and India', the journalist concluded. 'There does not exist so fundamental a clash of interest between Washington and New Delhi as to warrant the conclusion that the CIA is hell bent on bringing down Mrs. Gandhi's government.'[107]

The circumspection called for by some Indian commentators was undermined by an ill-judged American effort to convince the Indian premier that the Nixon administration wished her no harm. During the course of an interview with Gandhi, the US deputy chief of mission in New Delhi stated categorically, 'that of course the US had not' meddled in Chilean domestic politics.[108] Gandhi later witnessed the CIA's director, William Colby, testify before a US congressional committee that, between 1970 and 1973, the Agency had, in fact, spent more than $8 million in an effort to destabilise the Allende government.[109] Following Colby's testimony, a disconsolate Moynihan complained that, by handling the Chile question in such an inept manner, Washington had done a first-rate job of shooting itself in the foot. On 10 September 1974, the ambassador grumbled to Kissinger that Gandhi was now certain:

> that we would be content to see her overthrown, as we have, to her mind, been content to see others like her overthrown. She knows full well that we have done our share and more of bloody and dishonourable deeds. This as such is not her concern. She knows all too much of such matters. It is precisely because she is not innocent, not squeamish, and not a moralizer that her concern about American intentions is real and immediate. And of course, the news from the United States, as printed in the Indian press, repeatedly confirms her worst suspicions and genuine fears.[110]

Moynihan's gloom deepened when the investigative journalist, Seymour Hersh, obtained a copy of his message to Kissinger, and splashed the ambassador's insights over the front page of the *New York Times*.[111] Unable to resist ribbing Moynihan, John Kenneth Galbraith sent him a note stating that, 'your observations on Chile were highly to the point. I hope the new diplomatic practice of releasing telegrams on receipt did not cause you undue hardship with the Prime Minister.'[112] It was not only Gandhi that Moynihan had to worry about. To Kissinger's discomfort, the US Senate Committee on Foreign Relations grilled the Secretary of State over the 'very widespread publicity' Moynihan's cable had generated, and 'the fact there was concern by the Prime Minister of India that the CIA might become involved in some covert activity in India'. In response, Kissinger quipped that Moynihan was, 'given to flights of eloquence ... I think his dispatches, which are frequent and extensive, are always a joy to read ... Most of the time I get them first.' More substantively, the Committee were assured by Kissinger that he had, 'told the Government of India ... that if they find any American official or any other American, over whom we have any control at all, engaging in political activities in India, they should let us have the name and he would be removed from India within

THE FOREIGN HAND   205

24 hours'. 'We are not', the Secretary of State emphasised pointedly, 'involved in the domestic politics of India in any manner . . . '.[113]

Moynihan's mood darkened further when Colby compounded Gandhi's anxiety that the CIA was out to get her by launching into a spirited public defence of American covert action. On 13 September 1974, Colby addressed the annual conference of the Fund for Peace, a Washington DC based non-profit institution concerned with security and development in the Global South. Speaking in the context of a post-Watergate political climate laden with conspiracy and suspicion, Colby surprised his audience by making a case for greater 'openness' and transparency on the part of the Central Intelligence Agency. Alluding to CIA-led interventions stretching back to the late 1940s, that had sought to effect regime change in Italy, Iran, Guatemala, Indonesia, the Congo, and Cuba, amongst others, Colby acknowledged the Agency's record in, 'assist[ing] America's friends against her adversaries in their contest for control of a foreign nation's political direction'. Remarkably, America's spymaster went on to openly endorse the utility of CIA interference in the internal affairs of independent sovereign states. 'I . . . would think it mistaken to deprive our nation of the possibility of some moderate covert action response to a foreign problem', Colby volunteered, 'and leave us with nothing between a diplomatic protest and sending in the Marines'.[114]

On 2 December, Colby underlined his views on covert action in an interview published by *US News & World Report*. After being replayed in the Indian press, the interview had the effect, in Moynihan's words, of whipping up a 'wholly predictable storm' in the subcontinent. 'No one [should] have any illusions as to how bad it has been', Moynihan cabled back to Washington, 'or that it [the CIA issue] will go away'. The bemused ambassador was left 'groping' for an answer as to why Colby had considered it wise to publicly debate the merits and morals of CIA clandestine operations. The KGB, Moynihan noted dolefully, felt no compulsion to air its dirty intelligence laundry in public. On 3 December, in a bitter cable to Kissinger, Moynihan asked candidly, 'It is out of the question that some thought might be given in Washington to the effect in India of statements such as the Director has made? It is that nobody knows? Or is it that nobody cares?'[115] In his private journal, Moynihan added that Colby had behaved 'incredibly' and 'criminally' in talking out of turn to journalists. 'What can he [Colby] think he is doing', Moynihan raged, 'Is there nothing to which bureaucracy will not lead a man.'[116]

Daniel Patrick Moynihan departed from India, in January 1975, in a state of despondency. Two years earlier, the ambassador had been attracted to the subcontinent by the formidable challenge of recalibrating the troubled relationship between America and India, a land in which, he declared, Asian 'liberty resides'. An essential element in Moynihan's plan to reinvigorate Indo-US relations was predicated on quiet diplomacy. The United States had, in his estimation, alienated opinion within the developing world through a combination of overbearing rhetoric and the pursuit of an unnecessarily interventionist foreign policy. 'I have not overburdened either the Indian or American pubic with commentary or advice', Moynihan stated proudly on the occasion of his last public appearance in India. 'I have spoken in public only four times in two years, and two of these occasions took place a fortnight ago. I have not until this moment given a press conference.' Moynihan was acutely aware, however, that his diplomatic taciturnity had been compromised by a toxic legacy of CIA misdemeanours, past and present. 'Both the United States and India have far closer and more cooperative relations with the totalitarian powers of the world, than we have with one another', a dispirited Moynihan reflected as he prepared to leave New Delhi. 'Indeed, it is from one another that we are increasingly isolated.'[117]

No Nearer Normalisation: The CIA Conundrum

Indira Gandhi's repeated assertion that the malevolent hand of the CIA lay behind most of India's problems, whether genuinely held or not, undermined Washington's efforts to normalise Indo-US relations for much of the latter Cold War period. Despite the assurances provided to Gandhi by Moynihan, and his successor, Bill Saxbe, that they would resign if evidence emerged of CIA interference in Indian domestic affairs, Indian politicians and sections of the country's media continued to accuse the CIA of acts of subversion throughout the 1970s, and beyond.[118] For his part, Saxbe, a former attorney general and Republican senator from Ohio, saw little reason to depart from the policy of quiet diplomacy practiced by Moynihan. Noted for his candour and 'off-beat' character, Saxbe introduced himself to his staff in New Delhi by taking to the stage during an embassy variety show wearing judicial robes, and singing an aria from *Fiorello*, a popular musical about New York City mayor, Fiorello LaGuardia. Fond of whiling away days at the Delhi Golf Club, Saxbe favoured meetings with Indian businessmen over journalists and politicians. If the Indian government wanted to improve relations with the United States, Saxbe was reported to have stated, 'They know where I am.' Having asserted what had become, by now, a standard and tired public refrain on the part of American ambassadors that, 'there is no agency of the U.S. government that is in any way interfering in India', Saxbe was content to sit back and wait for Indira Gandhi's government to, 'decide the nature of the relationship that they want with Washington'. On being asked by an Indian newspaper editor why Saxbe had not initiated contact with the subcontinent's media, the US embassy press office responded curtly that the ambassador, 'had little to say, on or off the record'.[119] On the rare occasions that Saxbe did feel inclined to comment on Indo-US affairs, he made it abundantly clear that an improvement in relations, 'just cannot take place while the Prime Minister and other high Indian leaders continue to poke away at the US'.[120]

THE FOREIGN HAND 207

Having disregarded numerous private warnings from the State Department to desist from publicly criticising the CIA's alleged activities in the subcontinent, the Ford administration eventually lost patience with Gandhi and decided to punish New Delhi. In Washington, India's ambassador, Triloki Nath Kaul, was frozen out by the White House and denied access to Ford and Kissinger. In January 1976, the State Department ratcheted up pressure on Gandhi by announcing the curtailment of a range of joint Indo-US scientific and educational programmes, and the postponement plans to resume developmental assistance to India, which had been halted back in 1971 during the Indo-Pakistan War. Given India's continuing financial problems, the latter measure was expected to hit Gandhi's government particularly hard. Between 1965 and 1971, India had received $4.2 billion in American economic aid, $1.5 billion of which had been appropriated during the early years of the Nixon administration. In rationalising the United States' punitive policy to India's Foreign Minister, Y. B. Chavan, Saxbe confirmed that the United States had simply run out of road when it came to Gandhi and her government. '[We have] reach[ed] a point', Saxbe informed Chavan, 'at which we don't feel can continue to cooperate if [these] attacks [on the CIA] continue. We have said repeatedly that if the G[overnment] O[f] I[ndia] has any evidence of US interference we will act to eliminate it. I would resign.'[121] Reaffirming the Ford Administration's resolve, Brazil Brown, India desk officer at the State Department, confirmed to British officials that a policy review conducted on US-Indian relations had concluded, 'that there was probably no prospect of sustaining smooth, friendly relations with India so long as the suspicious Mrs Gandhi remained in charge'.[122]

The State Department's analysis was prescient. For the remainder of her life, Indira Gandhi informed sceptical foreign interlocuters that the CIA was up to no good in India. On meeting Denis Greenhill, a former head of the British diplomatic service, in New Delhi, in September 1980, the seasoned official was taken aback by Gandhi's insistence that the CIA was passing tens of millions of dollars through Thailand to subvert Indian rule in Assam. When Greenhill enquired how her government could be so sure the CIA was behind unrest in northeastern India, Gandhi astonished the British mandarin by responding that the 'trouble makers' in Assam had 'a mastery of the English language which was certainly not justified by their own capabilities'.[123] Likewise, the persistence of insinuations made by Gandhi, in public and private, that the Agency was supporting a successionist movement in the western Indian state of Punjab, maddened senior officials within the Reagan administration, including the vice president and one time CIA director, George H. W. Bush.[124]

In truth, the scope and effectiveness of CIA covert operations in India had declined after the late 1960s. Symptomatically, in 1975, British diplomats in New Delhi got wind of a spat between consular officers in the US embassy and their CIA colleagues over the role played by Gandhi's son, Sanjay, in the State of Emergency that had been declared earlier that year. A relative, Kuldip Narang, was believed to have supplied Sanjay Gandhi with a blueprint for the censorship guidelines and administrative rules used during the State of Emergency, and which were based on martial laws enacted by the Marcos regime in the Philippines. Sanjay Gandhi admired Marcos's authoritarian regime and looked to it for inspiration. Not a noted a bibliophile, one of the few books that occupied Sanjay's bookshelf was *Democratic Revolution in the Philippines* by Ferdinand Marcos. Marcos had presented the book to Indira Gandhi as gift. A copy of the specific martial law ordnances used by Marcos was passed to Narang by contacts that he maintained in the US Embassy in New Delhi.[125] Agency officers subsequently employed a highly questionable source to discredit their own embassy's political reporting of the Emergency. 'It strikes me as quite astonishing that the CIA should make use of this sort of material', one British official observed. 'After all, their resources are legendary (if not mythological). To use the unattributed opinion of an unidentified diplomat, quoted at second-hand by a non-specialist journalist, to cast doubt on a US Embassy report, strikes me as remarkably shoddy work.'[126] It is salient, in this context, that the CIA failed to anticipate nuclear tests conducted by India in 1974 and 1998. Towards the end of the Cold War, the Agency had become anything but the all-seeing and all-powerful force in South Asia that its detractors claimed.[127]

Indira Gandhi's death, in November 1984, at the hands of her Sikh body-guards and not, as she had feared, due of the machinations of the CIA, failed to free her from the Agency's embrace. Disinclined to let a good disinformation opportunity pass them by, the Soviets ensured the world was made aware that, in Moscow's view, the CIA had been culpable for Gandhi's demise. The 'black army of the American knights of the cloak and dagger', or the Agency, in Soviet parlance, had after all, TASS trumpeted, been linked to a litany of political assassinations, from Patrice Lumumba in the Congo to Maurice Bishop in Grenada.[128] It is arguable whether Gandhi would have given credence to indignant denials issued by the State Department, and which lambasted the Soviets for indulging in 'disgusting' and demonstrably false assertions, 'that the US, and specifically the CIA, were involved in, or inspired, this action of political terrorism'.[129] Perhaps the fallen Indian premier would have taken some solace from the knowledge that, with the Agency's assistance, witting or otherwise, she remained capable of disrupting superpower relations.

9

Battle of the Books: Daniel Patrick Moynihan, Seymour Hersh, and India's CIA 'Agents'

In November 1978, Daniel Patrick Moynihan released a memoir, *A Dangerous Place*.[1] Controversially, the book included revelations about historic CIA activity in India. Six months previously, the investigate journalist, Howard Kohn, had published an exposé, in *Outside* magazine, that laid bare details of 'Operation Hat', the joint covert endeavour that the Agency had conducted with India's Intelligence Bureau, in the 1960s.[2] The following year, the Pulitzer Prize-winning author, Thomas Powers, brought out *The Man Who Kept the Secrets*, a biography of former CIA director, Richard Helms. Indian opinion was outraged by the assertion in Powers' book, first aired in the American press back in 1971, that the CIA had run an agent inside Indira Gandhi's cabinet during that years' war between India and Pakistan.[3] All three publications appeared at a time when Gandhi was out of office, having been defeated at the polls by a Janata coalition led by Morarji Desai, a former Congress Party stalwart. To the right of Gandhi politically, and notable for his pro-business outlook and friendly disposition towards the United States, Desai hoped to reset strained Indo-US relations. By lobbing literary hand grenades into what one Western official described as a 'cauldron of Indian politics [that] never ceases to seethe', Moynihan, Kohn, and Powers, invigorated Indian animus for the CIA and, in the process, complicated Desai's efforts to recalibrate New Delhi's relationship with Washington.[4] Moreover, the subsequent appearance of a vituperative assault on Henry Kissinger penned by the American investigative journalist, Seymour Hersh, raised additional uncomfortable questions about CIA operations in India. Hersh's book, *The Price of Power*, named Morarji Desai as the CIA asset in the Indian cabinet in 1971.[5] The incendiary accusation levelled by Hersh prompted Desai to sue the journalist for defamation in an American court. The legal case developed into a media *cause célèbre* as the pedestrian wheels of US civil justice ground slowly to a conclusion during the 1980s. The press in India and the United States ensured that the defamation case's more dramatic moments received blanket coverage. At one stage, journalists were treated to the spectacle of a notably reluctant Kissinger, accompanied by two bodyguards, taking the stand in a Chicago courtroom having been subpoenaed as a witness by Desai's legal team.[6] The Hersh–Desai libel case represented the apogee of a drawn out and destabilising drama in

Indo-US relations that, towards the end of the Cold War, saw the CIA's interventions in the subcontinent pilloried in a slew of memoirs, books, and articles. The corrosive impact of such publications on the Agency's reputation saw competing state and non-state actors, in India and the United States, embark upon opposing campaigns designed to amplify and to suppress unofficial accounts of CIA history. Paradoxically, as the Cold War limped to a denouement, and Agency operations in India were scaled back, Langley's public profile in South Asia mushroomed. Caught up in a media frenzy, the CIA found itself assailed by detractors determined to exploit and to magnify the Agency's malignant reputation in South Asia.

Blowback: Secret Missions and Perilous Publications

On 17 April 1978, India's prime minister, Morarji Desai rose to speak in the *Lok Sabha*. Desai began his address by conceding that Indians were 'quite understandably exercised' by press reports that, a decade earlier, the United States had conducted a clandestine operation to install a nuclear-powered device on the second-highest peak in the Indian Himalayas, Nanda Devi. To audible gasps from packed parliamentary benches, Desai confirmed that enquires made by the governments of India and the United States had determined that the Nanda Devi operation was sanctioned at the highest levels in Washington *and* New Delhi. The joint Indo-American mission, India's premier revealed, was launched to obtain information on China's long-range missile capabilities. Desai reminded fellow MPs of the 'critical situation' that India had faced following its humiliation in the Sino-Indian border war. In the national climate of 'concern, apprehension and anxiety' that had prevailed at that time, he added, India's leaders felt compelled to take 'precautionary' action to better 'identify the various threats' the country faced from its enemies. The genesis of the covert operation, Desai disclosed, stretched back to the early part of 1964, and it had come to involve three prime ministers, Jawaharlal Nehru, Lal Bahadur Shastri, and Indira Gandhi. Calling for understanding rather than condemnation, India's premier nevertheless took the opportunity to drive home the serious implications, both political and environmental, of Operation Hat. Unable to resist making a barbed moral point about his personal objection to nuclear arms, Desai noted, 'Why do I say that I have nothing to do with atomic weapons and nothing to do with making atomic weapons? It is because of these hazards.' More significantly, an intervention by the Janata government's minister for External Affairs, Atal Bihari Vajpayee, disregarded Desai's admonition to avoid apportioning blame. Referring to press interviews that he had given prior to the debate, Vajpayee reiterated that he regarded the Nanda Devi revelation as a nothing less than a 'bombshell, because Mrs. Gandhi, who has been accusing America and the CIA and accusing us [Janata] also of joining hands with America before and during

Figure 9.1 Morarji Desai, Indian prime minister (1977–1979). Jacob Sutton / Gammo-Rapho / Getty Images.

the Emergency, herself joined hands with America when the situation demanded'.[7]

Howard Kohn, the journalist behind the Nanda Devi story, came to national prominence in the United States in March 1975, when he published a story in *Rolling Stone* on the Karen Silkwood case. Silkwood was killed in an automobile accident while travelling to meet a reporter from the *New York Times*. She had planned to hand over documents that laid bare shoddy safety practices at a nuclear fuel fabrication site where she worked in Cimarron City, Oklahoma. Almost exactly three years later, in April 1978, Kohn's second scoop involving possible plutonium contamination, entitled, 'The Nanda Devi Caper', sent shock waves through the corridors of power in Washington and New Delhi. Kohn's article contained several factual inaccuracies. The Central Bureau of Investigation was highlighted as the Indian agency that oversaw the Nanda Devi operation, when it had been coordinated by the Intelligence Bureau. The piece in *Outside* also claimed that Gandhi had been deliberately kept in the dark by India's intelligence services at the behest of the CIA who, Kohn alleged, retained 'absolute authority over the project'.[8] Although impossible to disprove while the archives of Indian's intelligence services remained closed, the notion that the Intelligence Bureau would 'go rogue' and conduct a major domestic covert operation, in collaboration with the CIA, and absent political approval, appears fanciful. Such a scenario was directly and explicitly contradicted by Morarji Desai in his statement to the Indian parliament. The substance of Kohn's account, however, was correct. India had undertaken a highly secret joint mission with the CIA to place nuclear-powered monitoring devices in the Himalayas; one device had been lost on Nanda Devi; and it did pose an ongoing environmental threat.

In the United States, *Outside* had barely hit the newsstands when letters from concerned members of Congress landed on President Jimmy Carter's desk. Writing to Carter on 12 April, the liberal Democrat, John Dingell, Representative for Michigan's 16th congressional district, and Richard Ottinger, Representative for New York's 24th district, expressed alarm that Kohn's article, 'raises serious allegations about a CIA operation in India during the 1960s – apparently carried out without the knowledge of the Indian Government'. 'If the [Kohn] article is in fact accurate', Carter was urged by his fellow Democrats, 'we strongly urge that the Nation take whatever steps may be necessary to resolve this serious and embarrassing situation'.[9] At the same time, Dingell and Ottinger appealed to Nani Palkhivala, India's ambassador in Washington, to share any information with them that New Delhi possessed on the Nanda Devi episode.[10] With American national broadcasters, including NBC's iconic *Today Show*, having picked up the Nanda Devi story, and with it splashed prominently over the front pages of the international press, Carter was left in no doubt that Kohn's revelations had the potential to wreck his administration's relationship with India.[11]

At ten o'clock the following morning, Carter's ambassador to India, Robert Goheen, found himself sitting opposite Indian's foreign secretary, Jagat Singh Mehta, in the Ministry of External Affairs, in the central secretariat's South Block, atop Raisina Hill, in the heart of New Delhi. India's most senior diplomat had summoned Goheen in the hope that the American ambassador would be able to shed light on an article that had appeared in that morning's *Indian Express*. Under the headline, 'CIA planted device may pollute Ganga', the *Indian Express* story rehashed a condensed version of Kohn's copy. Getting straight to the point, Mehta informed Goheen, 'that the article was bound to cause very grave concern in the Indian Government, Parliament and elsewhere and that there could well be a furore in Parliament'. 'It was, therefore, necessary', the foreign secretary emphasised, 'to know what the truth was as early as possible'. Goheen confirmed that the State Department were aware that the story had appeared in a 'radical left magazine' in the United States and were investigating its accuracy as a matter of urgency. Should the story prove true, Mehta stressed, public opinion in India would demand to know if any leakage of radioactive material into the Ganges headwaters had occurred and, if not, what measures could be taken to ensure that the monitoring device remained secure and presented no risk of future contamination. Until such assurances were forthcoming, Goheen was advised, 'there was bound to be a great deal of alarm all over the country'. Responding flippantly that 'one can hardly believe everything that newspapers said', the ambassador left a perplexed Mehta and rushed back to his embassy in search of further instructions from Washington.[12]

Mehta's next meeting that day was with Shiv Narain Mathur, director of the Intelligence Bureau. The DIB was instructed by Mehta to look into the background of the Nanda Devi operation with all possible speed. 'In view of the extremely sensitive and indeed explosive nature of the allegations made in the article', Mehta underlined to Mathur, 'I would be grateful if you could ascertain whatever details are possible, including the alleged involvement of our own intelligence agencies in the affair.'[13] At the same time, Indian officials moved to head off rising public anger in the subcontinent by briefing the press that Goheen had met with Mehta and had been left in no doubt that the Nanda Dev issue was of, 'great concern to the Indian government, the Indian parliament and the Indian people'. It was regrettable, Vajpayee confirmed to one journalist that, if true, the revelations surrounding collaborative IB-CIA operations in the Himalayas would damage US-Indian relations, which had undergone something of a renaissance under Desai and Carter. In an unusually caustic editorial, the nation's newspaper of record, the *Times of India*, largely absolved the country's former leaders of any blame and directed its ire squarely at the CIA. 'If it [the Nanda Devi operation] is so, no words can be too strong to condemn the CIA', the *Times of India* opined. 'It [CIA] has been guilty of a most dastardly act which can play havoc with the lives of millions of people for no one knows how long.'[14] Approached for his view of the unfolding drama in India, CIA director, Stansfield Turner, responded with a curt, 'no comment'.[15]

Back in Washington, Carter was informed by national security aides that press stories covering the CIA's involvement in placing two nuclear-powered monitoring devices in the Indian Himalayas were 'correct in major respects'. In the 1960s, an American plutonium-powered device placed on Nanda Devi to eavesdrop on the Chinese had been lost in an avalanche while being hauled into position. A second unit, positioned on an adjacent peak, Nanda Kot, operated successfully for several years before it was removed. The Indian government, Carter was assured, had known of, and approved, the CIA operation. The fact that Desai's Janata government had been blindsided by the publication of Kohn's expose was deemed unfortunate. India's intelligence services and bureaucracy had, however, been complicit, the president was reminded by US officials, both in facilitating the operation and keeping it secret. Privately, the State Department sought to soothe Indian concerns by passing on to New Delhi the findings of a 1967 study conducted by the Atomic Energy Commission. This had concluded that there were no obvious environmental dangers associated with the loss of the Nanda Devi device, which contained two to three pounds of plutonium-238. Publicly, Foggy Bottom adopted its standard position of not commenting on intelligence related matters.[16] Desai subsequently announced the establishment of an Indian scientific committee to confirm whether radioactive contamination had occurred as a result of the Nanda Devi mishap. Water samples were subsequently taken from the surrounding area over a number of years and flown for analysis to India's Atomic Research Centre at Trombay, in Bombay's eastern suburbs. To the Indian government's intense relief, no evidence of contamination was uncovered.[17]

The decision taken by Desai to come clean with India's public in his address to parliament on 17 April was welcomed by Robert Goheen. Advising Washington that the reaction to Desai's exercise in candour had been broadly positive, the American ambassador applauded India's premier for having, 'effectively defused what was becoming an increasingly emotional issue here [India] and one that might have had long-lasting reverberations'. The State Department had urged the Indian government not to comment on the Nanda Devi story. In ignoring the Carter administration counsel, Goheen conceded that Desai had made the correct call. '[T]he manner in which he [Desai] presented the matter not only was judicious and sound in the context of internal Indian politics', the ambassador judged, 'but . . . it also projects and reinforces the attitudes of cooperativeness and credibility which he seeks to have characterize the relationship between his government and ours'. Crucially, from Washington's perspective, Desai refrained from employing the CIA as a convenient domestic scapegoat once an intelligence operation that had been sanctioned by several of his predecessors became known. Carter might, Goheen suggested, wish to personally congratulate Desai on 'the judicious and effective' way that the Indian premier had handled an awkward diplomatic problem. Desai's deft political footwork, Goheen emphasised, had 'made it [the Nanda Devi episode] work to build a stronger acceptance of close Indo-U.S. relations when it might have been instead a cause of festering distrust'.[18]

The Indian embassy in Washington concurred with Goheen's assessment, noting with satisfaction that coverage of Desai's statement in the American media had dwelt on the 'great care' that India's prime minister had taken to avoid offending the United States. Writing in the *Baltimore Sun*, Fran Sabarwal informed the newspapers readers how, 'Opposition members of [India's] parliament who were hoping to cash in on CIA involvement to embarrass the [Desai] government were dumbfounded as Mr. Desai told them of the collaboration [between India and the United States].'[19] Likewise, the *Chicago Tribune*, a publication noted for its long-standing hostility to Indian governments and their adherence to Cold War non-alignment, heaped praise on Desai for refusing to hang the CIA out to dry. In taking early and decisive action to address the Nanda Devi revelations in a direct, and, in respect of a sensitive covert intelligence operation, unusually candid manner, Desai extracted the political sting from an incident that had threatened to undercut his own administration and compromise Indo-US relations.

'A Serious Affair': *A Dangerous Place* and the Covert Funding of Indian Politics

Daniel Patrick Moynihan's life and work could hardly have been more eclectic. From humble origins in poverty-stricken Oklahoma, via Manhattan's pre-war Hell's Kitchen ghetto, Ivy League academia, service in four presidential administrations, from John F. Kennedy to Gerald Ford, and election as US Senator for New York, Moynihan acquired a reputation as a hard-driving polymath. In 1973, Richard Nixon's unexpected decision to appoint Moynihan as America's ambassador to India was, in a sense, entirely appropriate. It was while serving in India, that Moynihan acquired what would become a lifelong scepticism of the utility of intelligence agencies and the merits of state secrecy.[20] Following his elevation to the Senate, in 1977, Moynihan became known for his criticism of the CIA. In April 1984, he stood down as vice chairman of the Senate Intelligence Committee in protest at the CIA's failure to 'properly' consult Congress on the mining of Nicaraguan harbours.[21] Having received a personal apology from CIA Director, William 'Bill' Casey, Moynihan resumed his post on the Intelligence Committee. Relations between the Senator and the Agency, however, remained uneasy. Back in the 1970s, after returning from India, Moynihan had disparaged inflated CIA estimates of Soviet power, dismissing as nonsense dire warnings from Langley that the United States risked being left behind by Moscow's planned economy.[22] As 'the quintessential liberal anti-Communist', Moynihan continued to use his political authority to challenge the institutional guardians of America's secret world.[23] In May 1991, in an op-ed written for the *New York Times*, Moynihan announced his intention to legislate for the abolition of the CIA, and to transfer of the Agency's intelligence functions to the State Department.[24] Four year later, Moynihan renewed his call for the Agency to be scrapped. 'Secrecy is a disease', he proclaimed. 'It causes hardening of the arteries of the mind. It hinders true scholarship and hides mistakes . . . The State Department must function as the primary agency in formulating and conducting foreign policy.'[25] Such radical prescriptions for intelligence reform unnerved conservative legislators, and Moynihan's proposed reforms stalled.

Between January 1995 and December 1996, Moynihan chaired a bipartisan commission on reducing government secrecy. This undertook a wide-ranging review of the US intelligence community. The commission's findings, which appeared early in 1997, were brought to a wider public audience the following year with the publication of Moynihan's book, *Secrecy: The American Experience*. In *Secrecy*, Moynihan depicted the CIA as an information-gathering organisation that had lost its way and succumbed to the lure of audacious, but often disastrous, covert operations. *Secrecy* confirmed that the genesis of Moynihan's interest in the interplay between intelligence, secrecy, and diplomacy, were not distilled in the cool, marble chambers of Capitol Hill, but in the fierce political heat of India.[26] The two years he spent in New Delhi as US ambassador, between February 1973 and January 1975, proved crucial in shaping Moynihan's attitudes, actions, and utterances in respect of the CIA. He had become exasperated in India by the local CIA station chiefs' habit of rushing excitedly into his office with special folders containing supposedly top-secret intelligence gleaned from sources inside the Indian government. Invariably, these turned out to be inaccurate or misleading. In an Indian context, as one historian of the Agency has noted, 'it was clear to him [Moynihan] that the CIA was missing a great deal'.[27] Shortly after leaving India, the debilitating impact of seemingly endless CIA scandals in the sub-continent was evident in Moynihan's thinking. In March 1975, writing in *Commentary* magazine, he made the case for placing less reliance on the dubious merits of secret operations, and more emphasis on open and honest dialogue with the United States' global partners. Anticipating the furore that *A Dangerous Place* would generate in India, Moynihan argued that American representatives overseas, 'should come to be feared in international forums for the truths he might tell'.[28]

One truth that Moynihan felt compelled to share in *A Dangerous Place* was that, while ambassador in New Delhi, he had ordered an enquiry into the history of CIA operations in India. Having resolved to establish 'just what we [America] had been up to', Moynihan claimed that over a period stretching back three decades, the CIA had twice, but only twice, interfered directly in India's domestic affairs by covertly channelling money to political parties. On both occasions, Moynihan claimed, once in the western Indian state of Kerala, and once in the eastern province of West Bengal, CIA funds had been given to the ruling Congress Party. In one instance, he added, Agency funds had been accepted personally by Indira Gandhi. Moynihan went on to speculate that the CIA's record of covert political funding may have fuelled Gandhi's paranoiac attitude towards the Agency when, on his watch, 'we were no longer giving any money to her'. Stark discrepancies between the marginal electoral benefit attributed to covert interference in India's internal affairs, and the considerable political risks such interventions carried, Moynihan argued, suggested that this was 'not a practice to be encouraged'.[29] In a first, and unpublished draft, of *A Dangerous Place*, Moynihan went further and suggested that he had 'been hard on the C.I.A.' in demanding a candid appraisal of 'what they [CIA] had really been up to in India'. The response, which Moynihan accepted as accurate, was not that much. Aside from clandestine payments made to Gandhi's Congress Party, the Agency had collaborated with Indian intelligence agencies in joint operations against China. The latter were not mentioned in *A Dangerous Place* but would, Moynihan speculated presciently, 'no doubt one day . . . make a great scandal in the Indian press'.[30]

In India, the appearance of *A Dangerous Place* was met with furious rebuttals from Gandhi and her supporters. The former Indian premier denied ever receiving money from the US government, and decried Moynihan's accusations as 'baseless', 'mischievous', and 'part of a conspiracy to defame me'. When pressed for further comment, Gandhi snapped angrily at reporters, 'All lies. They [Washington] are against me.' Kamlapati Tripathi, leader of Gandhi's Congress (I) party in the *Rajya Sabha*, or upper house of India's parliament, characterised Moynihan's claims as 'shocking', 'absurd', and a 'blatant lie' intended to damage Gandhi. 'Even making allowances for the fact that Mr Moynihan is a known "rabid Zionist" and has a grievance against Pandit Jawaharlal Nehru, Mrs Indira Gandhi, and the Indian National Congress for their consistent support to the just Arab cause', Tripathi stated, 'one would have expected of him [Moynihan] not to stoop to falsehood'.[31] Tripathi's Congress (I) counterpart in the *Lok Sabha*, Chembakassery Mathai (C. M.) Stephen, held a press conference in which he denounced Moynihan's book as an 'outrageous interference' in India's affairs and 'part of a CIA conspiracy'. The former ambassador, Stephen asserted, was a 'CIA agent' and a Zionist who hated India for its pro-Arab policies. If the US Embassy in New Delhi did not immediately disassociate itself from Moynihan's smear, Stephen fulminated, 'it deserves to be closed'.[32]

Outside the capital, in Jaipur, in northwestern India, pictures of Jimmy Carter were publicly set on fire in protest at what Congress supporters characterised as the American government's complicity in an unwarranted attack on Gandhi's integrity. In the east, exercised members of South Calcutta's Congress youth organisation marched on the local US consulate and delivered a letter of protest addressed to Carter. Moynihan, the letter claimed, had indulged in an 'ugly' political attack on Gandhi that 'may ultimately create severe bitterness between the people of these two countries'. India's left-wing tabloid press, led by lurid publications such as *Wave* and *Blitz*, ran banner headlines proclaiming, 'Moynihan a Zionist, Racist Scorpion', and 'Liar Moynihan's Accusations are a Cover-Up for Real CIA Lobby'. One indignant Indian citizen, Mohinder Singh, saw fit to file a defamation case in the Indian courts against Moynihan on Gandhi's behalf.[33] The strength of the backlash against Moynihan from within the Congress Party was reflective, one leading Indian newspaper suggested, of the 'embarrassment' its members felt that, 'Mrs Gandhi had been making the same allegation – that the CIA financed all Opposition parties when she was the Prime Minister.'[34] Seizing on Gandhi's apparent hypocrisy, Madhukar Dattatraya (Balasaheb) Deoras, head of the RSS, noted that Gandhi had accused her opponents of being on the CIA's payroll and had challenged them to prove otherwise. 'Now that the US Senator and former Ambassador to India, Mr Daniel Moynihan, has disclosed that CIA money was given to her [Gandhi]', Deoras maintained, 'she should abide by her own views'.[35]

Indian commentators agreed that Moynihan's intervention had given Gandhi's opponents a potent line of attack at a point when the former premier was politically vulnerable. Gandhi was still reeling from a public backlash that accompanied her imposition of a twenty-one-month State of Emergency, between June 1975 and March 1977, and a subsequent electoral rout. 'Gandhi's stock is low', one prominent Indian daily observed, 'and Moynihan's charges have sent it lower'.[36] Uncomfortably for Gandhi, India's mainstream press proved less willing than the Congress Party faithful to discount Moynihan's claims. In an editorial entitled, 'A Serious Affair', the respected Calcutta newspaper, *The Statesman*, insisted that, ' . . . the allegation cannot be dismissed as a casual remark or a bit of political gossip . . . Unless Washington comes out with an official explanation, Indians will find it difficult to believe that the practice of [America] financing political parties has really ended.'[37] Figures from within the ruling Janata Party, including its general-secretary, Madhu Limaye, began to call for the disclosure of government records relating to foreign funding of the nation's political parties. Looking back to controversies surrounding external intervention in the Indian general election of 1967, Limaye urged that a Central Bureau of Investigation report completed at the time was made public. 'We should find out whether the then government of India was aware of the "financial hand out" to Mrs Indira Gandhi . . . by the U.S. government', Limaye declared.[38] One Congress (I) MP threatened to retaliate if attempts were made to 'unmask' his colleagues as CIA agents, and to use parliamentary privilege to name Janata members whose relationships with the Agency had been exposed in *Inside the Company: CIA Diary*, a work published by the former CIA officer, turned Agency critic, Philip Agee.[39] With MPs from both sides of the *Lok Sabha* seemingly compromised by links to the CIA, Limaye's appeal for transparency was met with an awkward official silence.

The British High Commission in India kept a close watch on the political drama surrounding *A Dangerous Place*. Its officials noted that Gandhi had 'not very convincingly' denied receiving covert funds from the United States while president of the Congress Party. In citing Washington's satisfaction at her electoral defeat in 1977 as evidence that she could not have benefited from CIA funds, the British observed that Gandhi was 'conveniently forgetting that things were rather different in the 1960s'. It seemed doubtful to UK diplomats that definitive evidence would emerge to condemn Gandhi or to establish her innocence. '[S]o often in India these scandal stories are surprisingly not followed through by parliament . . . ', the high commission reminded Whitehall. Moynihan's book was nevertheless significant, the British reasoned, in landing a powerful blow on Gandhi when her popularity was at a nadir. '[T]his is another turn in the present downward spiral of Mrs Gandhi's fortunes', British diplomats concluded. 'Her [Gandhi's] supporters are still trying to put a brave face on things . . . But they fail to convince. The [Congress] party seems to be in disarray in a number of states . . . '.[40]

At the end of April 1979, in a meeting with press correspondents in his Senate Office on Capitol Hill, Moynihan robustly defended *A Dangerous Place*. Volunteering that he had been asked to speak to the media by India's foreign minister, Atal Bihari Vajpayee, who was visiting the United States, Moynihan reiterated his claim that Gandhi and the Congress Party had received CIA funds on two occasions. Crucially, Moynihan also retracted his assertion that Gandhi had herself been given CIA cash. '[H]e did not mean to give the impression that the money was put in a bag on one occasion and personally given to Mrs Gandhi by an American official', Moynihan informed journalists. Rather, he confirmed sheepishly, 'what he meant was that "Mrs Gandhi knew this" as the president of the [Congress] party when the money as passed over'. More broadly, Moynihan insisted that, 'What we [the United States] did was perfectly legitimate according to the standards of the time.' 'Today I would say "don't do it". Looking back, obviously that [CIA activity in India] caused us trouble. There was constant and incessant insinuation of some massive activity on our part which never existed . . . .' In the final analysis, Moynihan emphasised, the CIA had not foisted money onto the subcontinent's politicians, but that 'A democratic [Congress Party] regime asked for it [CIA money].' For Gandhi to deny the facts, and to claim that the Agency had engaged in activity designed to subvert Indian democracy was, Moynihan contended, an exercise in 'false, self-serving fantasy'. Every member of the Agency's station in New Delhi was known to the Indian government, Moynihan added, and the CIA had long enjoyed a close and collaborative relationship with India's Intelligence Bureau.[41] Indian and American diplomats were unimpressed by Moynihan's attempt at hedging his accusation against Gandhi. One State Department official expressed unease to British colleagues that Moynihan now appeared, 'in a muddle and simply cannot remember who took delivery of the [CIA] payments [to the Congress Party]'. India's press counsellor in Washington, Gopalaswami Parthasarathy, went further, and suggested to Western counterparts that Moynihan had erred badly by 'making a complete ass of himself' and not being able to substantiate his specific allegation against the former Indian premier.[42]

In the wake of Moynihan's press conference, the Carter administration became concerned that should India's parliamentarians be whipped into a frenzy of indignation over references to CIA interference in the subcontinent, a formal request might be made by the Indian government for the release of US records related to Gandhi's contacts with the Agency. Any such request would be refused, the British were assured by American colleagues, and enemies of constructive relations between New Delhi and Washington would then be gifted an opportunity to sabotage Carter's agenda for repairing brittle Indo-US ties.[43] Ahead of a parliamentary question tabled in the *Lok Sabha* on the 'Moynihan affair', Warren Christopher, Carter's Deputy Secretary of State, briefed Nani Ardeshir Palkhivala, India's ambassador in

Washington, that the US government had found no evidence of any payment made by the CIA to Gandhi. Christopher was careful, British diplomats took note, not to discount payments that the Agency may have made to other officials in the Congress Party. If necessary, Palkhivala was advised, New Delhi was free to use the information passed on by Christopher should it encounter difficulties during what was expected to prove a fractious parliamentary debate between the Janata government and its Congress opposition.[44]

The climax of the *Dangerous Place* imbroglio played out on the evening of 7 May. During a stormy four-hour session in the *Lok Sabha*, Congress MPs heaped abuse on Moynihan, while critics of Gandhi pressed the Indian government to appoint a commission of inquiry. Observing events from inside the parliamentary chamber, American diplomats watched the Congress leader, C. M. Stephens, launch a series of 'histrionic, vitriolic attacks on Sen. Moynihan [and] the CIA ... [both of] which he claimed were part of an "RSS/Zionist conspiracy"'. Senior figures in the Janata government, including Vajpayee, were also singled out by Stephen, and accused of cultivating links with the CIA through the RSS. Communist MPs piled further pressure on the government by demanding details of the Agency's relationship with India's Intelligence Bureau. 'We suspect', American officials remarked ruefully, 'that the Soviet embassy may have inspired the ... MPs to pursue this line'. The debate concluded with India's embattled Home Minister refusing to sanction an official inquiry, but assuring agitated colleagues that the government would take action to address irregularities in the funding of political parties and, 'try to plug as many loopholes as possible to stop the influx of illegal foreign money'. To prevent the political fallout from Moynihan's book spiralling out of control, both the US embassy in New Delhi and the State Department back in Washington declined all invitations from Indian journalists to comment on Moynihan's disclosures. Meanwhile, in India's cities, mobs of Congress supporters seized copies of *A Dangerous Place* from bookshops and burned them in the streets alongside effigies of Moynihan.[45]

The tumult in India that surrounded the publication of *A Dangerous Place* had two important consequences. Firstly, it entrenched attitudes on the utility of intelligence agencies and state secrecy held by Moynihan which had first germinated during his ambassadorship in the subcontinent, earlier in the decade. The Agency's capacity to act as a disruptive socio-political force in South Asia left a deep impression on Moynihan. In January 1974, from his vantage point in India, he had observed privately that the, 'CIA is not dead, but dying, I should think ... Too much white shoe fun in an unfunny world.'[46] The paradox that, having scaled back its covert operations in India, the Agency could still, years later, have a toxic impact on Indian perceptions of the United States, and its intelligence services, was brought home to Moynihan by the uproar that accompanied the release of his book. Moynihan's subsequent assault on the CIA would lead him to lobby relentlessly for reform of

America's intelligence community and against pervasive official secrecy. Moynihan's evangelical fervour in championing a more open intelligence bureaucracy, which came to incorporate the drafting of a Congressional bill; the chairmanship of a bi-partisan commission on government secrecy; the publication of a book; and innumerable speeches and articles; had its genesis in the political turmoil of the 1970s when he was afforded ample opportunity to gauge the CIA's deleterious impact on American diplomacy. Secondly, the 'Moynihan affair' of 1979 underlined the difficulty that the Carter administration faced in reframing Washington's relationship with New Delhi. Moving on from a troubled and discordant era of bilateral relations under Richard Nixon and Gerald Ford would clearly not be easy. As Jimmy Carter discovered to his chagrin, the Central Intelligence Agency had an unfortunate and, for a secret intelligence service, incongruous habit, of becoming an unwelcome point of public contention between India and the United States.

The Man Who Spilled the Secrets

Barely a year elapsed between Morarji Desai's efforts to extinguish the *Dangerous Place* CIA scandal and the eruption of another Agency-related furore in the subcontinent. In November 1979, a further political rumpus involving the CIA gripped the attention of India's press and public. In this instance, the release of Thomas Powers' biography of Richard Helms, *The Man Who Kept the Secrets*, attracted Indian ire. Powers' book revisited claims, first aired in the *New York Times* back in August 1971, that as tensions between India and Pakistan rose following moves by East Pakistan to secede and establish the nation state of Bangladesh, a CIA agent inside Indira Gandhi's cabinet had fed Washington highly sensitive material on official Indian thinking. In December that year, after hostilities erupted between India and Pakistan, it was alleged that the CIA's asset warned Washington that Gandhi's government was planning to escalate the conflict by engaging Pakistan's forces in the West of the subcontinent, as well as in the East. Richard Nixon later cited the intelligence that the White House received from the inner sanctum of Gandhi's administration as one of the rare occasions that the CIA furnished him with useful information. Unfortunately for Nixon and the Agency, the existence of a CIA mole in Gandhi's cabinet leaked to the press and was widely publicised by the syndicated columnist, Jack Anderson. According to the CIA's then Deputy Director of Plans, or head of clandestine operations, Thomas Karamessines, the Indian mole reacted to their exposure by ending the association with the Agency, and 'told us [CIA] to go to hell'.[47]

After becoming India's prime minister in 1966, Gandhi's predisposition to employ the CIA as an expedient political distraction for her government's failings had strained, but not yet broken, the Agency's relationships with the

Intelligence Bureau and Research and Analysis Wing. One American diplomat, who served in New Delhi during the Indo-Pakistan war of 1971, recalled that liaison relations between local American intelligence officers and their Indian counterparts could hardly have been closer.[48] The revelation that the CIA had run an asset at the heart of Gandhi's government saw much of the cooperation between Indian and American intelligence services curtailed, at least temporarily. In Washington, officials at the British embassy counselled London that American colleagues were having a particularly hard time maintaining their policy of not commenting on intelligence-related matters because, 'Anderson's revelations sound authentic.' 'Our CIA contacts', the British noted, 'have been uninformative or embarrassed when asked about them'.[49]

Ahead of a meeting between Nixon and Edward Heath in Bermuda in late December 1971, the UK's ambassador in Washington, George Baring, the Earl of Cromer, questioned whether Henry Kissinger had purposefully misinterpreted intelligence on India passed to the White House by the CIA. Nixon's then National Security Adviser, Cromer observed bitingly to the British Foreign Secretary, Alec Douglas-Home, had 'personally been running the United States policy in this [the Indo-Pakistan conflict] as if he were a latter day Metternich'. Kissinger had been passed intelligence, Douglas-Home was advised, 'which has consistently supported his worst suspicions that the Indians in one way or another wished to see the total collapse of Pakistan, East and West'. 'What these sources of intelligence are I do not know', Cromer confided, 'but I have been shown extracts of them purporting to report discussions in the Indian Cabinet confirming Kissinger's fears'. From the UK Embassy's own contacts with the CIA, the ambassador added tellingly, 'we have reason to believe that the CIA assessments do not confirm these reports [of aggressive Indian intent]'.[50] In contrast, when Nixon met with Heath on the tiny speck of British Overseas Territory in the North Atlantic, Kissinger made a point of emphasising his unwavering confidence in the CIA's Indian mole. 'The President had accurate information that the Indian Government at the highest level, including Mrs. Gandhi', Kissinger assured Douglas-Home, 'had been planning, in addition to the separation of East Pakistan, the break-up of West Pakistan . . . '.[51]

Eight years later, when Powers' book appeared in print, India's press and political class, absent the distraction of a sizeable regional war, leapt on the apparent confirmation that the CIA had run an agent in Gandhi's cabinet.[52] Raj Narain, recently India's Minister for Health, and a long-term opponent of Gandhi, wasted little time in suggesting that Jagjivan Ram, who served as Gandhi's Minister of Defence in 1971, had been the CIA's man. An indignant Ram dismissed the notion that he had been a CIA agent as patent nonsense. Unable to provide convincing evidence to substantiate his claim against Ram, Narain's accusation was also rubbished by the president of Janata, Chandra

Shekhar, as, 'the type of irresponsible statement that only deserves contempt. Does it deserve any comment? Nobody takes Raj Narain seriously.'[53] In an editorial entitled, 'From Bad to Worse', the *Times of India* joined those castigating Narain. '[I]t speaks to the depth to which our politics has sunk', the *Times* lamented, 'that he [Narain] should name the leader of a major party [Ram] as having been a CIA agent in Mrs Gandhi's Cabinet'. Politicians from both sides of the Indian political spectrum, from the then caretaker Indian premier, Charan Singh, to Gandhi herself, the *Times* opined, deserved to be censured for seeking to gain advantage from the uproar in the subcontinent that accompanied the publication of Powers' book. Gandhi, in particular, was excoriated for 'yielding to the temptation of making use of what an American author has written out of context' to attack her opponents and, in the process, risk destabilising national politics. 'After all', the *Times* reminded its readership, 'she [Gandhi] herself has been a victim of this kind of writing by no less distinguished an American that Mr. Patrick Moynihan'.[54]

In the United States, with an Indian general election scheduled for January 1980, the American press observed how the commotion surrounding Powers' book represented merely the latest example of an intelligence scandal coming to dominate the subcontinent's electoral politics. 'Allegations of involvement by United States and Soviet secret services in Indian political life are part of the campaign ritual here', the *New York Times* noted, 'and cries of "foreign money!" and "foreign interest!" often have the same impact as repeated cries of wolf'. It had been Indira Gandhi herself who, during a campaign stop in Kanpur on 9 November, had first brought Powers' book to the attention of the Indian public. At that point, Indian publishers had yet to release *The Man Who Kept the Secrets*. In an exchange with journalists, Gandhi quoted excerpts from Powers' biography of Helms that she claimed had been mailed to her from abroad, and which corroborated information that Kissinger had previously divulged to her in private. Reporters were perplexed that Gandhi had chosen to spotlight a story of a spy in her cabinet which, on the face of things, reflected poorly on her leadership. Several foreign diplomats suggested that Gandhi might have calculated that with a number of her former cabinet colleagues now political adversaries, including Janata's deputy prime minister, Y. B. Chavan, and minister for education, Karan Singh, any fallout from the cabinet affair would reflect equally badly on those standing against her in the January poll.[55]

In London, the *Times* echoed its sister publication across the Atlantic by remarking, somewhat wearily, that although not yet officially underway, India's election had already acquired a seemingly obligatory CIA scandal. The British newspaper found it illuminating that Charan Singh, who Ram was expected to challenge for the premiership in January, had instigated a formal investigation into the claims made by Powers. It appeared convenient, some sceptics suggested, for Charan Singh to entangle one of his

224   SPYING IN SOUTH ASIA

principle political rivals in a high-profile enquiry charged with rooting out a CIA-sponsored traitor at the epicentre of India's political establishment. As the *Times* observed caustically, 'The reference to India and the alleged CIA agent in the Cabinet [in Powers' book] is only brief but is more than enough to lend Indian politicians the kind of emotional material they evidently prefer to presenting rival programmes to the electorate for tackling India's immense development problems.'[56] For much of the remainder of 1979, the pernicious legacy associated with espionage that the CIA may, or may not, have undertaken in India at the beginning of the decade, remained, according to one press report, 'the hottest political issue in India these days ... '. While the Agency had been 'used routinely as a whipping boy in Indian elections', American journalists familiar with the subcontinent expressed a wry disbelief that, on this occasion, 'the ammunition was handed to Gandhi on a silver platter in the form of a biography by Thomas Powers ... '.[57]

Intriguingly, contemporaneous Indian accounts of the events of 1971 lent credence to the British suspicion that Nixon's administration had exaggerated the credibility and significance of intelligence acquired by a CIA mole in Gandhi's cabinet. In early 1972, India's ambassador in Washington, Lakshmi Kant (L. K.) Jha, informed P. N. Haksar that a trusted American source had confided to him that, as fighting had raged between India and Pakistan the previous year, the CIA received conflicting reports on India's intentions regarding West Pakistan. A consolidated intelligence assessment presented to Nixon and Kissinger marginalised the likelihood of aggressive Indian action against West Pakistan. 'The reason why it [the idea of aggressive Indian intent] is being played up', Jha suggested to Haksar, 'is to find support and justification for the policy which the President has pursued. The [intelligence] report does not provide the rationale of the policy, though it is being used as a method of rationalizing the policy.' An indignant Gandhi instructed Haksar to make it abundantly clear to Jha that if a CIA agent been operating in her cabinet, the information they provided to Langley had been fabricated. In a handwritten note scrawled on Jha's cable, the Indian premier recorded, 'that at NO time have I ever made such a statement [on action against West Pakistan]. Besides such a discussion had not taken place at my Cab[inet] Meeting.' In Haksar's response to Jha, sent on 3 March 1972, he duly emphasised that, 'While it is interesting to learn about the vagaries of the C.I.A., I should like you to know that at no time [has the] Prime Minister ever made a statement even remotely resembling what the C.I.A. agents have reported.' Gandhi's cabinet had been given no opportunity to discuss taking the 1971 war to West Pakistan, Jha was assured. The Political Affairs Committee of Gandhi's Cabinet did meet on 16 December, and a full Cabinet meeting had followed later that day but, Haksar confirmed, at no point had consideration been given to extending or expanding hostilities with Pakistan. 'The C.I.A. having led President Kennedy up the garden path', Haksar informed Jha, 'has done it again'.[58] Whether the

BATTLE OF THE BOOKS 225

CIA misled Nixon and Kissinger, as Haksar intimated, or the President and his national security adviser saw fit to manipulate intelligence to better suit their political agenda in the subcontinent, as Jha and British officials suspected, remains unclear. More certain, is that in seeking to extract political advantage from activity associated with the CIA in South Asia the early 1970s, Indian and American leaders bequeathed to their successors a toxic diplomatic legacy that poisoned bilateral relations.

'A Sheer Mad Story': Morarji Desai, Seymour Hersh and the CIA on Trial

In June 1983, Morarji Desai, who had recently turned eighty-seven years of age, was enjoying political retirement in Bombay. After stepping down as India's prime minister, in July 1979, Desai campaigned for the Janata Party in the following year's general election but did not contest a seat in the *Lok Sabha*. With Indira Gandhi and the Congress Party back in power, Desai seemed set to while away his remaining years in public obscurity. A respected, if not universally popular elder statesman of Indian politics, Desai's solitude was interrupted by an unexpected telephone call from New Jersey, in the United States. To Desai's surprise, he discovered an American stringer from the United Press News Agency was on the other end of the line. Struggling to be heard over a muffled international connection, the reporter asked Desai for a reaction to allegations made by the journalist and author, Seymour Hersh, in his recently published book, *The Price of Power: Kissinger in the Nixon White House*. Hersh had claimed, an incredulous Desai was informed, that the former Indian premier worked for the CIA as a paid agent during the Johnson and Nixon administrations. In return for an annual retainer of $20,000, Hersh asserted, Desai passed on highly sensitive intelligence to the Agency from within Indira Gandhi's cabinets. It was Desai, Hersh declared sensationally, who had been the CIA's mole and supplied the Agency with the information that convinced Nixon and Kissinger that India was poised to attack West Pakistan in December 1971. Stunned by the charges levelled against him, Desai dismissed Hersh's smear as a 'sheer mad story'. 'Madness is the basis, what else?', Desai asked his American caller. 'Can I be bought? Has anyone tried to do so earlier? Do you believe the story?'[59]

In Seymour Hersh, Morarji Desai faced a formidable adversary. Then in his mid-forties, Hersh came to global prominence by reporting on the My Lai massacre in the Vietnam War, for which he received a Pulitzer Prize in 1970. During the seventies, Hersh worked on the Washington bureau of the *New York Times*, where he focused on exposing some of the more dubious activities carried out by the CIA. Known for his irascibility and profanity, Harrison Salisbury, a colleague at the *Times*, characterised Hersh as a 'Vesuvius of a reporter'. To Henry Kissinger he was simply an 'extortionist'. One of the most influential investigative reporters of the late Cold War,

Hersh's determination to secure scoops occasionally led him astray. He would later run into trouble for the use of hearsay, anonymous sources, and documents that turned out to be forgeries, when advancing several controversial claims in a book on John F. Kennedy, *The Dark Side of Camelot*.[60] The 700-page work that Hersh produced on Kissinger was, the author claimed, based on interviews conducted with 1,000 people over a four-year period. The prodigious research Hersh invested in his Kissinger book, however, failed to prevent him from making some basic errors and relying on unsubstantiated claims in constructing what many Indian commentators decried as a flimsy and unpersuasive case against Desai. On 4 June, under the front-page headline, 'Blatant holes in charges against Desai', the *Times of India* took Hersh to task for including 'obvious mistakes' in his book. Hersh asserted that Desai was 'undoubtedly' a paid CIA informer and 'could only have been' the source that tipped off Nixon and Kissinger about Gandhi's alleged plan to attack West Pakistan.[61] But Hersh had erred, the newspaper noted, in stating that Desai had remained in Gandhi's cabinet after being relieved of the finance portfolio, in July 1969. In fact, Desai had left Gandhi's cabinet and effectively remained in the political wilderness during the two years leading up to Indo-Pakistan hostilities. How then, the *Times* asked, could Desai have then been privy to the inner-most thoughts of India's premier and his one of his bitterest political rivals?[62] Hersh's admission that, after 1970, his supposedly impeccable sources on Desai, 'were no longer in a position to see his reports', was also deemed problematic.[63] '[I]f Mr. Hersh's sources dry up in respect of events beyond that year [1970], as he himself admits', the newspaper wondered, 'how does he write so much about what happened in 1971? On the basis of conjecture?'[64]

In the face of Indian criticism, Hersh doubled down on his charge that Desai was the Agency's mole inside Gandhi's administrations. '[H]e [Desai] has been an informant for [the CIA] many years', Hersh reiterated to Indian journalists in Washington. 'He was a long-time informant, even before [the] Johnson administration. He was the key man. There may have been others also. I only write about what I know. I talked to people about his role, and I saw documents ... It [Desai's] has been a long-standing relationship with the CIA.' Pressed that he had been mistaken in claiming that Desai served in Gandhi's cabinet in 1971, Hersh lambasted his Indian detractors for splitting hairs. 'Mr. Morarji Desai was not in the government [in 1971]', Hersh conceded. 'He was only a member of parliament. All the same, he was a man with immense contacts. He had contacts in the ministries. He was not a cabinet informant but a cabinet-level informant. He was the informant in 1971 as he had been before that. I was terribly careful about checking that.' When reminded that Desai was renowned for 'his moral stature in Indian life', and that accusations that he had spied for the CIA would 'shock the Indian nation', Hersh appeared 'visibly peeved'. Desai's aversion to communism and affinity for the United States, combined with the enticement that, if backed by

Washington, he could engineer a political comeback and displace Gandhi, might, Hersh reasoned, explain the decision to work for the CIA. 'I am not in the business of running him [Desai] down', Hersh declared. 'It is painful for me to have to write about him.'[65]

In New Delhi, members of the Janata Party called on Indira Gandhi to distance herself from the claim that Hersh had made against Desai. Speaking in the *Lok Sabha*, the economist and Janata MP, Subramaniam Swamy, declared, 'The allegation that a prime minister of India was in the pay of the C.I.A. is an insult to the nation and it is the duty of the government to protect the fair name of the country.'[66] A slew of prominent Americans with intimate knowledge of India's relations with the United States also lined up to dismiss the idea that Desai could have worked for the CIA. Moynihan proclaimed that 'the charge was simply untrue'. From his position as vice-chair of the Senate Intelligence Committee, the former ambassador to India assured reporters, he had ordered, 'the agency (CIA) to go through the records and tell me. The agency informs me that whatever Mr. Hersh says about Mr. Desai in his book is simply not true.' Kissinger added to the chorus of disbelief, and declared publicly that, 'To the best of my knowledge the allegation is not true. I had never heard of the allegation before till I heard it in Mr. Hersh's writings.' A former NSC staffer and assistant Secretary of State, Harold Saunders, who had specialised in South Asian affairs for over a decade between 1961 and 1974, also went on record to confirm that he had, 'no knowledge of any relationship between Mr. Desai and CIA. Having checked with former colleagues, I believe the allegation is not true.' Unusually, former Agency officers also sprang to Desai's defence. Russell Jack Smith, who served with the CIA in India in the early 1970s, insisted that Desai had not worked for the Agency. 'The allegation [by Hersh]', Smith volunteered, 'is not true'.[67]

Unwilling to see Hersh's assault on Desai's reputation go unchallenged, a Chicago-based organisation, Indians for Truth Abroad, lodged a case against the American author in the US District Court of Northern Illinois. Following some initial equivocation, Desai was persuaded to support the legal action. On 17 June 1983, Hersh and his publishers, Summit Books, were named in a civil suit for 'wrongfully, maliciously and with intent to defame and injure [Desai]' including 'untrue, defamatory, libellous, and accusatory statements' in *The Price of Power*. Desai's lawyers argued that Hersh had subjected the former Indian premier to 'public hatred, ridicule and contempt', by knowingly publishing false statements, 'with reckless regard for the truth'. The court was asked to award libel damages of $50 million against both Hersh and his publisher.[68] In a written submission of evidence, Desai declared, 'What greater damage can there be than being stamped as a traitor of a country by this false and baseless charge [of being a CIA agent]? It is a matter of common sense for anybody to see that these serious charges are very deniable.'[69] At the same time, Desai was granted a temporary injunction by the Bombay High Court to

228

SPYING IN SOUTH ASIA

prevent the import, distribution, marketing, and sale of Hersh's book in India, although this was later overturned on appeal.[70] Desai was, nevertheless, able to draw some satisfaction from the appeal court's decision that every copy of Hersh's book sold in the subcontinent should include a disclaimer stating that its distributers had no reason to believe that the claim Desai was a CIA agent was true.[71] In Washington, Hersh stood by his story and prepared to contest the case. The CIA's star agent in India, he insisted to American reporters, 'was not his uncle, brother, or cousin, it was Morarji Desai'.[72]

News that Desai's dispute with Hersh was going to trial reignited public interest in the United States and India in the CIA's clandestine activities. Subramaniam Swamy's plea that politicians resist the temptation to exploit the affair for narrow partisan purposes proved futile. Addressing Indian journalists, Vajpayee, who following the collapse of the Janata Party had become President of the new Bharatiya Janata Party (BJP) in 1980, mischievously questioned why neither the State Department nor India's government had exonerated Desai. Claiming to be 'intrigued' by the silence of Gandhi's administration, Vajpayee asked, 'Why is it silent? If the allegation is true, what was the Prime Minister doing when her deputy prime minister was on the payroll of the CIA? Was there no security arrangement? The country would like to be assured that there are no KGB or CIA agents in the present cabinet.' It seemed equally odd, the BJP leader claimed, that the State department had elected to keep its own counsel. 'After all the (U.S.) state department cannot take the formal position that it does not comment on intelligence-related matters', Vajpayee noted. 'This is a special case. Mr. Desai is no ordinary person. He is the former prime minister of a friendly country.'[73] Responding for Gandhi's government, C. M. Stephen pointed reporters to the close links that he claimed Vajpayee maintained with US officials. 'Mr Vajpayee seemed to revel', the Congress Party luminary bit back, 'in the company of people with CIA trappings'. Perhaps, Stephens added, Vajpayee should spend less time clamouring for the government to intervene in the Desai case, and expend more effort, 'remind[ing] Mr. Desai of the "vulgar jubilation" his men had indulged in when Mr. Moynihan "dished out the [CIA] story against Mrs. Indira Gandhi."'[74]

With political tensions running high in India, opposition MPs persuaded the Lok Sabha's speaker to grant time for a debate on the Desai affair.[75] On 26 August, in a 'tumultuous' atmosphere and amid 'prolonged noisy scenes', the minister for external affairs, Pamulaparthi Venkata (P. V.) Narasimha Rao, was repeatedly berated by opposition members for refusing to comment on the specific charge that Desai had been a CIA agent. It was impossible, Rao maintained, to confirm the government's position while the matter remained subject to litigation in the United States.[76] Ratansinh Rajda, a Janata Party MP for Bombay South, reminded Rao that Hersh's book had been greeted in India with, 'fulminating fury ... from the masses, from the press, and the people alike'. It was regrettable, Rajda continued, that Gandhi's administration had disregarded public sentiment. 'I would have wished very much if [sic] Government had risen up to the occasion.' It was incumbent on every Indian politician, it was suggested to Rao, to confront 'any outsider or foreign power' that 'charge[d] leaders of one party or the other as CIA agents'. Such an accusation, Rajda insisted, 'militates against our self-respect and national grain, and we must oppose it unitedly. Unfortunately, that is not being done ... '. More generally, fractious parliamentary exchanges over India's response to the Hersh–Desai affair stoked a perennial debate in Indian politics over the ubiquity of external subversion and an insidious foreign hand. 'May I know', an excised Rajda demanded of Rao, 'whether our Cabinet secrets are being leaked out even at present? May I know whether Government has taken any precaution to see that no CIA or any other foreign agency works to the detriment of the interests of this country? ... Will you make a fool proof system in the Cabinet so that either CIA or KGB or any other agency will not be able to pounce upon, or have access to our national secrets?'[77]

Uncomfortably for Gandhi's administration, in Chicago Hersh's attorneys set about constructing their defence against Desai's lawsuit by seeking to establish a pattern of close links between the CIA and India's post-independence governments. As it had in the subcontinent, the focus of attention in the Chicago court room shifted away from the specific accusation made against Desai, and on to a more expansive range of questions involving the nature of interactions between US and Indian intelligence services.[78] To many of his compatriots, Hersh appeared to have acted in the wider public interest by shining a light on American covert activities abroad. In late 1987, an offer Hersh made to bring closure to a libel action that was then entering its fourth year, and that would have compensated Desai to the tune of $600,000, and seen him receive an apology for the inconvenience caused by the allegations printed in *The Price of Power*, was rebuffed.[79] Desai's insistence that Hersh unconditionally retract the allegation that he had been a CIA agent, and excise any mention of it from future editions of his book, appeared to many Americans as maladroit and, given the difficulty in making libel suits stick in US civil courts, reckless.

Having alienated American public opinion, Desai's lawyers irritated Washington's national security establishment by compelling the CIA's deputy director of operations, Claire George, to seek an injunction from a Federal Court excusing former Agency officers from appearing as witnesses. Desai's legal team had sought permission to question Russell Jack Smith, who they believed had acted as the Agency's station chief in New Delhi in the early 1970s. Citing Section 6 of the Central Intelligence Act of 1949, George successfully argued that 'The CIA cannot be placed in a position of having to confirm or deny a relationship with Mr. Desai or discuss it in any manner ....' The Federal Court concurred that, 'Any disclosure of Mr. Smith's CIA

230   SPYING IN SOUTH ASIA

employment would necessarily reveal intelligence methods ... [and] in order to accomplish its mission, the CIA must be able to protect the identity of its intelligence sources.'[80] The judge presiding over the Desai case, Charles R. Norgle Sr., reinforced the Federal court ruling by determining that while Hersh must testify in general terms about the nature of his sources, he need not identify them. By compelling other high-profile individuals, and notably, Henry Kissinger, to take the stand in Chicago, Desai's attorneys guaranteed that the CIA would garner yet more unhelpful press headlines. Kissinger proved a decidedly reluctant witness who tried, and failed, to evade a subpoena to testify on the spurious grounds that he was too busy to travel to Chicago. Having swept into the windy city in the company of a phalanx of bodyguards, a team of personal attorneys, and attendant news crews, the former Secretary of State volunteered that to his knowledge Desai had not been an CIA asset. Under cross-examination from Hersh's lawyers, Kissinger begrudgingly conceded that, as he was never informed of the identities of intelligence sources in India or elsewhere, he could not definitively state that Desai had no connection with the CIA. 'I had nothing to do with getting the [intelligence] information', Kissinger confirmed. 'I had only to do with the end product.' Ultimately, during the course of testimony that stretched to over three-and-an-half hours, Kissinger generated more heat than light in respect of the CIA's activities in the subcontinent.[81]

Towards the end of 1989, as Desai's libel action limped towards a conclusion, the *New York Times* reflected that that the meandering and seemingly interminable proceedings had encompassed testimony that, 'ranged from American foreign policy during the India-Pakistan war of 1971 to the ideals of the Bhagavad Gita to the methodology of an investigative reporter to spy jargon like "cryptos" and "assets"'.[82] That October, a jury of eight, having deliberated for just six hours, concluded that the prosecution had not demonstrated that Hersh had knowingly libelled the former Indian premier, or had acted out of malice in asserting that Desai had been a CIA agent. The verdict had taken six-and-a-half years to arrive. 'What this court said today', a triumphant Hersh exclaimed following the ruling, 'is that a reporter like me can write a story based on confidential sources – even to the effect that a former Prime Minister of India had been a C.I.A. asset ... '.[83] In India, citizens in the subcontinent reacted with a mix of bewilderment and anger to the news from Chicago. While empathetic with Indians conviction that Desai had been wronged by the US justice system, one of the country's leading lawyers, the supreme court advocate, Anil Divan, suggested that the former premier had been poorly advised. Given the burden of proof that US courts demanded, Divan stressed, it was virtually impossible for a public figure to win a libel case.[84] In the final analysis, a combination of Desai's obstinacy in refusing to accept an olive branch extended by Hersh, and legal counsel that, at best, served the former Indian premier badly, saw him become embroiled in

BATTLE OF THE BOOKS

an enervating process of litigation in US courts that ended in bitter disappointment. More broadly, the Desai-Hersh saga ensured that, to Washington's vexation, the CIA remained a conspicuous and corrosive feature of the United States' relationship with India, and one that the subcontinent's politicians seemed unable to resist exploiting for partisan purposes.

The 'Truth' Will Out

Two decades after the conclusion of Morarji Desai's libel case against Seymour Hersh, the tangled politics behind the American journalist's accusation that Desai had been a CIA agent continued to occupy the attention of the subcontinent's press and public. On 8 November 2011, Indian national newspapers ran with headlines that Rao had misled parliament back in August 1983 when he stated that Hersh had not been in contact with any government official prior to publishing *The Price of Power*. Documents released by the National Archives of India revealed that Indian diplomats in Washington had met with Hersh and had offered him advice of aspects of his then unpublished manuscript. It was pointed out to Hersh at the time, that his claim that Desai was a member of Indira Gandhi's cabinet during the Indo-Pakistan war in 1971 was false. For reasons unknown, Hersh ignored the Indian embassy in Washington and neglected to correct the error before his book was released. Hersh was also revealed to have shared copies of classified US papers with Indian officials that contained references to Desai.[85] Desai's lawyers picked up on an assertion made by Hersh during the libel trial that he had run relevant sections of his book past the Indian embassy in Washington. A copy of the chapter featuring Desai, annotated with handwritten notes and comments was, it seems, passed back to Hersh by a member of the embassy's staff. Efforts by Desai's legal team to access the annotated manuscript proved unsuccessful. Approaches made to Indian officials that had worked in Washington at the time were similarly rebuffed. The Ministry of External Affairs, Desai's attorneys concluded, had no interest in establishing whether an Indian official had assisted Hersh in the production of his book and, if so, who that official might be.[86]

The connection between Hersh and Indian diplomats, it turned out, was facilitated by Jack Mitchell, who acted as Jack Anderson's managing editor. Gopalaswami Parthasarathy, the Indian embassy's press and information counsellor, had wanted to counter the impact of Kissinger's recently released memoir, *The White House Years*, that the Indian official considered to be 'pro-Pakistani' propaganda. Having learnt that Hersh was working on, 'an expose ... [that was] particularly critical of Kissinger's support for right-wing dictatorships', including that of Yahya Khan in Pakistan, Parthasarathy arranged to have lunch with the American author. During their meeting, Parthasarathy offered to help Hersh with his project. In addition to sharing Indian documents on the 1971 war, for which Hersh was 'particularly thankful', Parthasarathy obtained an assurance from his new American friend that he would, 'let me have a look at the chapter as soon as it is completed.' 'I am keeping in touch with him [Hersh]', Parthasarathy informed Jyotindra Nath (J. N.) Dixit, Joint secretary in the External Publicity division of the MEA, 'to give him any suitable published material of details he may ask for'.[87] In part, at least, the reluctance of the MEA to spring to Morarji Desai's defence after he was labelled a CIA asset was the result of an earlier decision taken by the Indian government to cooperate with Hersh in the production of his book. Amplifying the impact of Hersh's anti-Kissinger tome, New Delhi reasoned, offered a useful means of counteracting a tide of anti-Indian sentiment that Kissinger's memoir was expected to generate.

Whether Morarji Desai was a CIA agent is likely to remain a matter of contention. Shortly after the libel trial in Chicago concluded, a Bombay daily, the *Independent*, speculated that Hersh may have got his wires crossed in naming Desai as the CIA's mole. Sources in the US, Hersh had noted, informed him that the Agency's agent had served as Chief Minister of Maharashtra, Finance Minister of India, and, briefly, Deputy Prime Minister. Desai ticked all those boxes. But so did Yashwantrao Balwantrao Chavan. In the early 1960s, when Chavan was in charge in Maharashtra, he was believed to have had an intimate relationship with Jane Abel, an official in the American Consul in Bombay. In 1964, Chavan moved to New Delhi to become India's Defence Minister. At the same time, Abel was transferred to the US embassy in the Indian capital. Coincidentally, a private secretary working for Chavan was later arrested by the Intelligence Bureau for passing classified information to the CIA.[88] Others have suggested that Anand Kumar (A. K.) Verma, who became head of the R&AW, and who was stationed in Washington while Hersh was working on his book, may have had a malevolent reason to implicate Desai as the CIA's man. Verma was associated with repressive activity during India's Emergency and had been sidelined once Desai's Janata government came to power.[89] More certain, and paradoxical, is the powerful and pervasive influence that American literature exercised on Indian perceptions of the CIA, and its supposedly malevolent foreign hand, as the Cold War stuttered to a conclusion. Absent official history (Indian or American) covering the work of intelligence services, and in a period where actual covert CIA activity in India was at an historic low, memoir and biography addressing controversial episodes in Washington's relations with New Delhi excited political and public passions in the subcontinent. Such literature also ensured that the Agency remained firmly, as it had since the late 1960s, at the epicentre of Indo-US diplomatic discourse.

10

Indian Intelligence and the End of the Cold War

In April 1984, Rameshwar Nath Kao, former head of the R&AW, and Indira Gandhi's Director General of Security, sent a 'personal message' to George H. W. Bush, Ronald Reagan's vice president. Bush was due to visit India the following month for the first and, as it transpired, only time. Kao had got to know and like Bush when he served as the CIA's director, between January 1976 and January 1977. Having learnt from the CIA's station chief in New Delhi that R&AW officers had acquired the sobriquet 'Kaoboys', Bush presented Kao with a small bronze statue of a cowboy, during one of the Indian intelligence leaders visits to Langley. A keen amateur sculptor, Kao, having presumably swept the statue for bugs, afforded it pride of place on a table in his office. Kao later commissioned the noted Indian artist, Sadiq, to cast a large replica, and had it installed in the foyer of the R&AW's headquarters building.[1] Artistic sensitivities aside, the two men shared a reciprocal respect for the others professionalism and discretion and operated a long-standing and unofficial backchannel between Washington and New Delhi. Bush reminded Kao on one occasion just how mutually beneficial it had been to, 'have used our personal communications in the past to pass informal information between our two governments'.[2] Drawing on their association as former intelligence chiefs, Kao asked to meet privately with Bush during his brief stay in New Delhi. Acknowledging the 'problems and misunderstandings' that had plagued the United States' relationship with India for much of the previous decade, Kao worked hard to put a positive spin on the prospects for productive bilateral cooperation. 'We speak the same language ... We share a common political culture. We both have a federal structure', Kao emphasised. 'It should thus be easier for us to understand the political problems that arise not only internally but also externally. While we strive for maintenance and development of friendship, it should be possible for us to live with our differences.'[3] The 'differences' and 'difficulties' that Kao sought to raise directly with Bush, centred on threats to the Indian Union emanating from successionist movements in Kashmir and the Punjab. Elements within Gandhi's government suspected that the CIA were, if not actively abetting, then turning a blind eye to, actions by state and non-state actors that endangered Indian national security.[4]

234   SPYING IN SOUTH ASIA

Much of the four days in May that George Bush spent in India, was taken up by an abduction episode involving US nationals that had been staged to focus international publicity on the CIA's purportedly subversive activities in the subcontinent. Forty-eight hours before Bush landed in India, an American couple from Ohio, Stanley Bryson Allen, and his wife Mary, were seized in neighbouring Sri Lanka by a rebel group, the Eelam People's Revolutionary Liberation Front (EPRLF). The rebels accused Allen, who was working in Jaffna, in northern Sri Lanka, on a water resource project funded by the US Agency for International Development, of being an agent of the CIA. In exchange for the Americans return, the EPRLF demanded the release of twenty political prisoners held by the Sri Lankan government and a payment in gold of $50 million. The abduction had been planned, a spokesperson for the EPRLF claimed, to highlight the CIA's collaboration with Sri Lankan government forces in the repression of the island's minority Tamil community. As the senior US official on the spot, Bush coordinated Washington's response to the crisis. Working closely with Indira Gandhi and the R&AW, who had established links to the rebels through southern India's Tamil community, Bush helped to secure the Allen's release before leaving New Delhi.[5]

When not preoccupied with his side hustle as a hostage negotiator, Bush held a series of constructive meetings with Gandhi and Kao. 'I wanted to let you know', the vice president wrote to India's intelligence chief on his return to Washington, 'how valuable I thought our conversations were during my recent visit to New Delhi'.[6] It was all the more disappointing, Bush felt compelled to add, that Indian government officials had again seen fit to imply that his former employer in Langley was interfering in India's internal affairs. Specifically, the CIA had been linked by members of Gandhi's government to militant Sikh organisations that were waging a violent insurgency in the Punjab. Weeks after Bush returned from India, an ill-judged and bloody counter-terrorist operation conducted by Indian special forces to oust militants from the Golden Temple in Amritsar, one of Sikhism holiest sites, left hundreds dead and wounded, the temple complex heavily damaged, and India's domestic and diasporic Sikh communities enraged. Faced with intense international pressure to justify the botched operation, codenamed Blue Star, which had exacerbated rather than quelled the Punjab insurgency, some figures close to Gandhi found it impossible to resist suggesting that a familiar 'foreign hand' lay behind India's troubles. 'I must frankly express to you', a peeved Bush informed Kao, 'how taken aback I was to hear of recent Indian accusations concerning alleged CIA involvement in the Punjab. Media articles and statements by government officials linking CIA operations with occurrences in Amritsar are completely contrary to the fact and quite distressing.' Bush was particularly irritated that, having personally and publicly reassured Indians that the Reagan administration respected 'the unity and integrity of India', and after privately reinforcing the point in private talks with

INDIAN INTELLIGENCE AND THE END OF THE COLD WAR   235

Gandhi, the CIA had been employed by senior figures in the Congress Party as a political scapegoat. Ending his message to Kao with a characteristically understated, but no less withering, diplomatic rebuke, Bush asked his Indian colleague to 'express my concern with these accusations to the Prime Minister at your earliest opportunity'.[7]

Kao's reply to Bush was uncharacteristically defensive and impolitic. Falling back on a habit Indian officials exhibited to draw historical analogies that, intentionally or not, grated with American counterparts, Kao expressed confidence that 'painful' though the decision had been to send the Indian army into Amritsar, 'I am sure that our friends in U.S.A. would appreciate it if they recall the history of their own civil war to safeguard the unity and integrity of the country.' John F. Kennedy had bridled when Jawaharlal Nehru lectured the Catholic Irish-American President on the inequities of colonialism. ' . . . I can claim the company of most historians', Kennedy had snapped back at Nehru, 'in saying that the colonialism to which my immediate ancestors were subject was more sterile, oppressive, and even cruel than that of India. The legacy of Clive was on the whole more tolerable than that of Cromwell.'[8] Having presented Bush with a lesson in American history, Kao went on to assure the vice president that Indian intelligence was in possession of 'information' which confirmed, 'that this [the Punjab insurgency] was a deep-seated conspiracy for secession'. It was unfortunate, Kao continued, that allegations had been made in the subcontinent's media linking the CIA with Sikh militants. Sidestepping Gandhi's muzzling of newspapers during the Emergency, Bush was reminded, with no little sense of irony, that the Indian government was powerless to control the nation's free press. Back in 1975, the Bombay edition of the *Times of India* had felt otherwise. In creative show of resistance to Gandhi's imposition of press restrictions, the *Times* had listed on its obituary page, 'D'Ocracy – D.E.M, beloved husband of T. Ruth, loving father of L.I. Bertie, brother of Faith, Hope, Justice, expired 26th June'.[9] Still, Kao insisted to Bush that Gandhi's administration had refrained from suggesting that the CIA was behind trouble in the Punjab. The prime minister herself, Bush was reminded, had used a television interview, aired in the United Kingdom, on the BBC's *Panorama* programme, to deny that she had privately accused the Agency of continuing to meddle in India's internal affairs. 'We accept your Government's statement', Kao stressed to Bush, '[and] particularly yours, in this matter [CIA activity]'.[10]

Denials from within Gandhi's administration that it had reverted to using the CIA as a patsy for India's domestic woes made little impression on American legislators. One Congressional report noted that a process of Sino-American rapprochement, and a concurrent strengthening of Indo-Soviet collaboration, epitomised by Gandhi's reluctance to openly condemn Moscow's occupation of Afghanistan, had corroded the United States' relationship with India. Caustic public diplomacy emanating from the subcontinent and that targeted the CIA, 'provided grist for further congressional dissatisfaction with New Delhi'. 'Mrs. Gandhi's periodic swipes at the U.S. for interference in Indian internal affairs', the White House was cautioned, 'infuriate Congressmen and staffers alike'.[11] From an Indian viewpoint, one former R&AW officer, who served in senior intelligence positions throughout the 1980s, has asserted that Gandhi had good reason to question the Agency's *bona fides* when it came to covert activity. Gandhi herself, if the Indian intelligence officer is to be believed, was subject to a protracted psychological warfare operation that, up until her death in October 1984, co-opted pliant journalists into spreading disinformation designed to undermine popular support for the prime minister by characterising her as a Soviet stooge.[12] Whether Gandhi was, or was not, a victim of CIA dirty tricks, is uncertain. Beyond doubt, is the remarkable degree to which the CIA remained a fixture at the heart of Indian civil debate throughout the 1980s. To the very end of the Cold War, the political fortunes of Indira Gandhi, and her son, and successor, Rajiv Gandhi, were intertwined with a series of espionage scandals in which, almost inevitably, the CIA figured prominently.

A Pink-Tinted Country

Bill Casey, Ronald Reagan's Director of Central Intelligence, was a fan of visual analysis. Early in his tenure at the CIA, Casey asked the Agency's Office for Global Issues, in the Directorate of Intelligence, to run up a chart detailing Moscow's international footprint. A world map was produced that depicted countries in different shades of red to denote varying levels of Soviet influence. Eight countries considered to be under direct Soviet control were inked in dark red. Six Soviet proxies appeared in crimson, and a further eighteen nations deemed under strong Soviet sway were marked in maroon. Towards the end of the communist colour chart, were a selection of salmon pink states that had entered into treaties of friendship and cooperation with Moscow. In August 1971, with trouble brewing between India and Pakistan, and with the latter having found favour in Washington and Beijing, Indira Gandhi signed a twenty-year treaty of mutual strategic support with the Soviet Union. On Bill Casey's world atlas, India was a pink-tinted country.[13] In intelligence terms, Soviet clandestine services had played an increasingly important part in Moscow's interventions in the subcontinent after 1971. In May 1973, a British assessment of covert Soviet operations in South Asia estimated that of the 600 Soviet diplomats posted to the region, 131 had been identified as intelligence officers. Remarkably, in India, 100 per cent of the Soviets Defence attachés, military personnel, and press and information staff had backgrounds in intelligence. Overwhelmed by the sheer numbers of undeclared Soviet spooks roaming India, local British intelligence officers took comfort from the close relations they had cultivated with Indian colleagues, 'who were relatively efficient and passed us a great deal of useful information'. Nonetheless, faced with a glaring disparity in clandestine resources, British diplomats acknowledged that they could not hope to compete in a covert conflict with the Soviets, or for that matter, their American allies. 'Our best hope of success', one Foreign Office official observed meekly, 'was in working with these [Indian intelligence] organisations in order both to make them more efficient and derive better information from them'.[14]

The British high commissioner in New Delhi, Sir Terence Garvey, cautioned against exaggerating Soviet designs on India. Moscow's approach, Garvey argued, was 'not to establish any kind of socialist system but to extend their influence by small pushes at specific points'. Soviet economists were chary of being caught 'holding the Indian economic baby' and it was far from certain how far communism had gained traction in India's armed services. The Eastern bloc, however, continued to invest heavily in a propaganda offensive in the subcontinent and British officials worried that, 'the Congress Party had been infiltrated to a certain extent by Communists and left-wing ideas'. Large numbers of Communist Party members had defected to the Congress, some of whom had risen to high office. Nevertheless, in comparison to Maoist, Trotskyist, and other radical left-wing groups operating in the country, Garvey regarded the Communist Party of India as relatively benign and 'almost part of the establishment.' Given the extensive political, economic, military, and interpersonal connections between India and the United Kingdom, Garvey reminded Whitehall, 'If the Kremlin Research Department had a penchant for the conspiracy theory of history, they could certainly be able to make out a good case by using the figures for United Kingdom-India [interaction].'[15] Colleagues in the British Ministry of Defence (MOD) held a less sanguine view of the threat posed by growing Soviet influence in India. One MOD paper, prepared in 1977 for an interdepartmental working group on India, placed strong emphasis on the 'suspected penetration of Indian Government Departments and to a lesser extent the Armed Services by the Russian Intelligence Service'.[16]

Early in the Reagan administration, the State Department resolved to actively counter what officials perceived as an alarming and unacceptable expansion in Soviet subversive activities. In April 1981, Lawrence Eagleburger, Assistant Secretary of State for European Affairs, Ronald Spiers, director of the Bureau of Intelligence and Research, and Paul Wolfowitz, director of the Policy Planning Staff, composed a joint memorandum to Secretary of State, Alexander Haig. Calling for a more aggressive approach to counter rising Soviet Bloc subversion, the memorandum identified a need to 'better fix' the success Soviet intelligence had garnered from penetrating foreign intellectual movements, trade unions, and peace groups. Haig was asked to approve the production and distribution of materials highlighting, 'how the Soviets have worked over the years to achieve influence sufficient to manipulate the internal affairs of certain nations on key issues'. The CIA, Haig was informed, 'is doing some of this already, but they could use encouragement from us to do more'. India was referenced specifically as a country where examples of KGB and GRU operations could be usefully exposed. A carefully calibrated American effort to encourage governments, including that in New Delhi, to monitor Soviet intelligence activity more closely, place greater constraints on the movements of suspected intelligence officers, and trim back their numbers, where possible, was contemplated. This strategy looked to coordinate State Department, CIA, and International Communication Agency (ICA) resources in a mutually reinforcing diplomatic, intelligence, and public relations offensive to push back against Soviet covert action. Haig welcomed the initiative and gave a green light to its implementation.[17]

Within India, influential voices counselled Indira Gandhi not to expect much in the way of genuine cooperation or support from the Reagan administration. In July 1982, writing to the prime minister ahead of her first visit to the United States in over a decade, P. N. Haksar suggested that 'Reagan is beleaguered and besieged'.[18] Haksar had long considered India's relations with the Soviet Union to be of 'cardinal importance'. He had also questioned whether Washington could ever be, 'compelled to accept as part of their working hypothesis that they cannot affect India except on the basis of equality and co-operation'.[19] Even so, Haksar's disdain for the American president was striking. 'Of course, it is always possible to have conversations seeking to understand how Reagan's mind works', he suggested to Gandhi, 'assuming, of course, that Reagan has a mind. In America itself, respectable journalists are talking about his lack of I.Q.' It was disturbing, Haksar went on, that Reagan had intimated, 'he knew how to deal with Brezhnev because he had dealt with Hollywood Communists during the days of MaCarthy [sic]'. 'He [Reagan] is a prisoner of an ideology which is in desperate search for viable domestic and foreign policies', the Indian premier was advised. 'And since the neo-conservative ideology is based on frustration of American power, it can lead to serious miscalculations and fiascos.'[20] In conversations with American visitors, including the scholar and journalist, Selig Harrison, Gandhi revealed that she felt misunderstood and maligned by the current American administration. 'You think we are against you [the United States]', Gandhi complained to Harrison, 'whereas in fact we are closer to you than to the Soviet Union'. 'I can say anything I want to your Government or to President Reagan', the Indian leader clarified. 'But I can't do that with the Soviets. They have set patterns and can't understand anything outside. To Khrushchev, perhaps, I could say what I liked, and he also responded that way, but not with any of the others.' It was unfortunate, the Indian leader continued, that 'America (whether it was Reagan himself or [the] CIA or [the] Pentagon) seemed to think that Indira Gandhi should be countered, and India kept under pressure.' In a telling aside to Harrison, as his encounter with Gandhi concluded, the American was surprised to be asked for his impression of Harry G. Barnes, Reagan's ambassador to India. She had wondered, Gandhi confessed to a startled Harrison, 'whether he [Barnes] was in the C.I.A.'.[21]

Persona Non Grata

Gandhi's suspicions where the CIA was concerned was not entirely misplaced. In January 1981, less than a week before his inauguration, Reagan, Casey, and Bush met with the outgoing CIA Director, Stansfield Turner, in a private room in Blair House, just across Pennsylvania Avenue from the White House. Turner had requested the meeting to ensure that the new administration was up to speed on the Agency's clandestine operations. Turner began by appraising Reagan and his team of the CIA's ongoing support for resistance movements fighting the Soviets in Afghanistan, and the latest developments in the US hostage situation in Iran. He moved on to explain that 'the really dicey operations' being conducted by the Agency did not involve covert actions, but rather sensitive intelligence collection efforts. Prominent among the latter was the work of a senior official within the Indian government who had been recruited as a CIA asset. The Indian, Turner revealed, was providing the Agency with invaluable material on Soviet weapon systems supplied to New Delhi and, specifically, those concerned with air defence.[22] Awkward American attempts to cajole India's Intelligence Bureau into pooling information on the Soviets had proved unsuccessful and had served to irritate New Delhi. The IB did maintain an open channel of communication with the CIA. Senior IB officers visited the Agency's Langley headquarters regularly and received CIA assistance in areas such as VIP protection. Still, Indian intelligence officers experienced difficulty in building relationships with their American colleagues. In the early 1980s, Thangavelu (T. V.) Rajeswar, the IB's Director, found his interactions with Bill Casey to be more bemusing than beguiling. On one occasion, having been invited to lunch with Casey and a group of senior Agency officers, Rajeswar was mystified when he was asked to comment on the Soviets recourse to chemical warfare in countries ranging from Cambodia to Canada. On checking that Casey was referring to the so-called 'yellow rain' phenomenon, which independent observers had discounted as being linked to Soviet use of biological or chemical weapons, Rajeswar was taken aback when Casey insisted that there was no question that Moscow's use of chemical agents had precipitated 'yellow rain'. Rajeswar was equally troubled by requests from the CIA to furnish information on Soviet dignitaries visiting India, and suggestions that his service turn a blind eye to American technical surveillance of Eastern bloc embassies in New Delhi in return for access to the Agency's latest eavesdropping technology.[23] By seeking to inaugurate a new and more aggressive phase in the subcontinent's clandestine Cold War, Casey and the CIA won few friends in India.

240   SPYING IN SOUTH ASIA

It did not take long for simmering tensions between India and the United States in the intelligence field to burst out into the open. In September 1981, nine months into Reagan's presidency, in a move the State Department slammed as 'unprecedented', Gandhi's administration refused to accredit a senior American diplomat that Washington planned to send to New Delhi. As prospective political counsellor, George Griffin was earmarked to take up the third most senior post in the US Embassy. While questions were occasionally raised in government circles about the suitably of ambassadors selected for foreign posts, it was rare for a host nation to veto the appointment of lower-level diplomatic staff. In Griffin's case, the State Department was infuriated at what it interpreted as India's craven response to an obvious attempt by the Soviets to besmirch the American diplomat through the crude use of disinformation. Back in December 1980, *The Patriot*, a left-leaning Indian newspaper that Moscow had been secretly funding since the late 1950s, accused Griffin of meddling in the internal affairs of Afghanistan, where he was working in the US Embassy in Kabul. In a classic disinformation ploy, the Soviet news agency, TASS, picked up the story, which had likely been passed to the Indian newspaper by the KGB, and it was reported back into the subcontinent via Radio Moscow. The following May, a story carried by the pro-Soviet Bombay tabloid, *Blitz*, claimed that Griffin had orchestrated covert CIA operations against the Afghan government and, sensationally, had been party to an attempt to sabotage an Air India plane used by Indira Gandhi on a foreign visit. 'Now his bosses are sending him [Griffin] to a new sector of work', *Blitz* alleged, 'which will signify a broadening of diversionary and spy activities of the C.I.A. in India'.[24]

Washington responded by taking the usual step of denying that the experienced foreign service officer, who had completed tours in Sri Lanka and Pakistan, as well as Afghanistan and India, had ever worked for the CIA. In 1968, Griffin's name appeared in a bogus directory of American intelligence officers circulated by the Hauptverwaltung Aufklärung (HVA), the external arm of East Germany's Ministry of State Security, or Stasi. The US foreign service officer may have blotted his copy book with the KGB by attempting, and failing, to persuade a Soviet couple to defect to the West during his time in Sri Lanka. In late July 1981, just weeks before Griffin was due to take up his assignment in India, Gandhi's government reacted to the swirl of falsehoods and innuendo surrounding the diplomat and informed the State Department that he was *persona non grata*. The Reagan administration responded by declaring that an Indian diplomat of equal rank, T. Prabhakar Menon, who was due to take up a post in Washington, was no longer welcome in the United States.[25] The Griffin incident added to tensions between Reagan's and Gandhi's governments, which had bubbled to the surface following a decision by Washington to supply India's regional rival, Pakistan, with $3 billion dollars of cutting-edge weapons, including advanced F-16 fighter aircraft.

INDIAN INTELLIGENCE AND THE END OF THE COLD WAR   241

Implausibly, the Indian government defended its action as a sensible preventative measure that would avoid Indo-US ties becoming, 'further embittered'. Addressing the *Lok Sabha*, Narasimha Rao, Gandhi's minister for external affairs, claimed that the Indian government had acted to avoid a 'much more undesirable state of affairs coming into being'. 'We have exercised our judgment and felt it was not proper to have Mr Griffin here on account of the activities this person was likely to indulge in.' Contrary to media reports, Rao insisted, Soviet disinformation had played no part in the government's decision to object to Griffin's posting. '[W]e have not been influenced by books, by newspapers, by what any other country has stated', the minister emphasised. Rao's circumspection did not stop members of his own party from speculating on Griffin's supposedly dubious past. Somanahalli Mallaiah (S. M.) Krishna, a Congress MP from Karnataka, in southwest India, reminded his fellow parliamentarians, 'that India does not have anything like the CIA with its tentacles spread to almost every nook and corner of the world'. Evidence from American sources, Krishna continued, including Henry Kissinger's memoirs, and studies conducted by the American journalist, Lawrence Lifschultz, had exposed covert efforts made by US officials in 1971 to persuade representatives of Bangladesh's pro-independence Awami League to reach an accommodation with Pakistan.[26] At the time, Griffin was serving as a consular officer in Calcutta, in eastern India, where the Awami League had established a government in exile. 'He [Griffin] was very vitally connected with ... the CIA', Krishna charged, and had worked against the interests of India and Bangladesh to advance the Nixon administration's pro-Pakistan agenda.[27] By stirring up yet more CIA conspiracism, the *Guardian's* correspondent in New Delhi, Peter Niesewand, reasoned, Gandhi's government had incensed local American officials. ' ... Indo-American relations are now', the British journalist judged, 'as sour as they have ever been, and Mr Rao's parliamentary statement yesterday has done nothing to improve matters'.[28]

A positive encounter between Reagan and Gandhi at the North–South summit in Cancun, Mexico, later that year, and a productive visit that the India premier made to the United States in July, where notable agreements were reached on scientific exchange and India's civil nuclear programme, helped to reset Indo-US relations. Almost as soon as dialogue between Washington and New Delhi had taken a constructive turn, however, another spy scandal surfaced in India and dissipated much of the goodwill that the Reagan administration had banked with Gandhi. In December 1983, reports emerged in the press that three retired Indian military officers had been arrested, taken to New Delhi's Tihar jail, and charged with passing sensitive defence material to a foreign power in contravention of the Official Secrets Act. Rumours quickly spread in the Indian capital that the CIA was implicated in the subcontinent's latest espionage affair. Details of the alleged spy ring surfaced first in the *Indian Express*. The newspaper reported that Indian Air

Vice Marshal Ken Larkins, his elder brother, Major General Frank Larkins, Lieutenant Colonel Jasbir Singh, of the Indian Army, and a civilian, Jaspal Singh Gill, had been taken into custody. Two diplomats from the US embassy in New Delhi, the *Express* added, were under investigation on suspicion of receiving classified information related to Indian military equipment.[29] With the story out in the open, India's Defence Minister, Ramaswamy Venkataraman, rushed to parliament and made a brief statement confirming that four arrests had been made on national security grounds, and that these were linked to activities involving a foreign power. Within twenty-four hours, a first secretary at the US embassy, Harry Wetherbee, had been declared *persona non grata* and put on a plane back to Washington. Nominally responsible for policy planning, in reality, Wetherbee was an intelligence officer in the local CIA station. India's Intelligence Bureau, reports suggested, had stumbled upon the espionage operation after one of its members had erred in making a cold approach to a patriotic air force officer. Instead of passing on operating manuals for Soviet MiG fighters in exchange for cash, as intended, the officer went straight to the IB. Opposition politicians, including the Janata Party's, Madhu Dandavate, claimed that the spy ring had provided the CIA with key technical details of the $1.5 billion military assistance programme that the Soviet Union had in place with India. Other sources confirmed that the espionage activity had targeted Indian air force bases and obtained blueprints of Soviet aircraft and air defence systems operated by the IAF.[30]

British officials in New Delhi noted the 'predictably wide coverage' that the Larkins affair generated in the Indian press. 'There is no doubt that the Indians have been very embarrassed by the incident', the High Commission reported to London. 'The main tenor of . . . debate [in India] was concern that senior officers had been willing to betray their country for money.' That America's intelligence establishment was singled out for particular public criticism came as no surprise to British diplomats. A more troubling development was the extent to which the latest spy scandal to rock India had encouraged local commentators to question the activities of other external intelligence services in the subcontinent, including that of the United Kingdom. 'The wickedness of the CIA was naturally mentioned [by India's press and politicians]', Whitehall was advised, 'but some speakers also referred generally to the espionage activities of diplomatic missions, as well as of other agencies, including the KGB and the British Secret Service'. While the British acknowledged that 'Indo-US relations will clearly suffer most', they also fretted that, as a consequence of the Larkins affair, 'there may well be some effect on countries believed to be associated with the United States'. Whatever adverse consequences might accrue for British intelligence in India, it seemed certain, 'that the Indians will be generally more security conscious, particularly over defence'. Espionage operations targeting the Indian government were expected to become more challenging as well as politically risky. The British Defence

Adviser and his staff in the High Commission, it was recorded ruefully, were no longer permitted to meet singularly with Indian colleagues.[31]

Conjecture on what the Larkins affair might reveal about foreign intelligence activity in India persisted into 1985, as the Indian justice system conducted seemingly interminable closed-court hearings that were subject to a strict reporting embargo. In July 1985, more than eighteen months after their arrest, the suspects in the case were convicted of selling classified information related to Soviet military systems operated by India to representatives of the United States government. In ruling on the case, High Court Judge, K. B. Andley, sentenced the three former military officers, Frank Larkins, Ken Larkins, and Jasbir Singh, to 10 years each in prison. The civilian member of the spy ring, Jaspal Singh Gill, received a two-year prison sentence. Faced with a long period of incarceration, a shocked Frank Larkins declared that he felt 'a little weak in the knees'.[32] Much the same sensation would afflict Indian and American government officials as, over the course of the 1980s an unparalleled Soviet disinformation campaign centred on India, in conjunction with a succession of further espionage cases involving the United States, saw Washington's relations with New Delhi remain under severe strain.

Soviet Active Measures: From Assam to AIDS

In October 1981, the US State Department called a press conference in Washington. Its purpose was to brief journalists on the latest special report produced by the Bureau of Public Affairs. The report's subject was Soviet 'Active Measures', or *aktivnyye meropriyatiya*. Distinct from espionage or counterintelligence activity, the State Department defined Soviet active measures as encompassing written or spoken disinformation; efforts to control media in foreign countries; use of Communist parties; clandestine radio broadcasting; blackmail; and political influence operations. Active measures did not, American officials stressed to assembled journalists, include press releases, open public broadcasting, or information disseminated through cultural exchange programmes. 'Soviet active measures are frequently undertaken secretly', the State Department report noted, 'sometimes violate the laws of other nations, and often involve threats, blackmail, bribes, and exploitation of individuals and groups'. Moscow's engagement with active measures, it added, 'remain a major, if little understood, element of Soviet foreign policy'. In seeking to manipulate the press in foreign countries, the Soviets had, it was alleged, employed a broad spectrum of techniques from the forgery of documents to the exploitation of front organisations. Initiated at the highest levels of the Soviet state and sanctioned by the Politburo and Communist Party Central Committee, active measures were designed and executed by Service A of the KGB's First Chief Directorate, or in the parlance of some journalists, the 'KGB's dirty-tricks squad'. They drew on support from official and quasi-official Soviet representatives, including academics, students, and journalists. A tendency existed in Western and developing world countries, the State Department asserted, to 'ignore or downplay Soviet active measures until Soviet blunders lead to well-publicised expulsions of diplomats, journalists or others'. A reluctance to pre-empt Soviet interference in a nation's domestic politics, the report stressed, had helped to facilitate Moscow's efforts to disrupt relations between states, smear critics of the Soviet Union, and corrode trust in foreign leaders, institutions, and democratic values.[33]

India was represented as an epicentre of Soviet active measures in the State Department report. Dozens of Indian journalists, it was claimed, had been co-opted to plant stories favourable to the USSR in the subcontinent's press. The salacious weekly *Blitz*, in particular, was singled out as a willing Soviet vehicle for the reproduction of forged documents and spurious articles that falsely labelled American officials and citizens as CIA officers or agents. A marked proliferation of sophisticated political influence operations, many involving forgery, had troubled American diplomats. By the beginning of the 1980s, disinformation directed by Service A was believed to occupy the attention of fifty full-time personnel and consume an annual budget of $ 50 million dollars. In India, Moscow's insistence, back in May 1976, that India alter the exchange rate applied on the import of Soviet goods, from Rs 8.33 to the rouble to Rs. 10 to the rouble, was a boon to KGB's propagandists. The manipulation of India's currency had no direct impact on bilateral trade, as this was dominated in rupees. It did allow the Soviets to amass a considerable war chest of local Indian currency that the KGB *rezidentura* in New Delhi put to use expanding its campaign against Mrs Gandhi's 'enemies', and the CIA above all.[34] More generally, Moscow was estimated to be spending $ 3 billion on its global propaganda operations, overt and covert.[35] 'On the basis of the historical record', Washington warned, 'there is every reason to believe that the Soviet leadership will continue to make heavy investments of money and manpower in meddlesome and disruptive operations around the world'.[36]

Soviet policymakers did not disappoint. Prior to the seventh summit of the Non-Aligned Movement, held in New Delhi, in March 1983, left-wing news-papers in India published a forged document that was attributed to the US ambassador to the United Nations, Jeane Kirkpatrick. The bogus text outlined plans for a covert American operation designed to Balkanise India and sow division in the developing world. Surfacing first in January, in *The Patriot*, which drew substantial advertising revenue from the Soviet embassy's Information Department, the forgery was later picked up and replayed by other sympathetic Indian dailies and by tabloids outside the subcontinent. It alleged that having toured South Asia in August 1981, Kirkpatrick had circulated a top-secret report within the US government that focused on an upsurge in separatist movements in India. An opportunity existed, the counterfeit paper stated, to destabilise the Indian Union, destroy its influence in the Non-Aligned

INDIAN INTELLIGENCE AND THE END OF THE COLD WAR   245

Movement, and wreck Soviets efforts to use neutralist New Delhi as a wedge to weaken Western influence in the developing world. In a statement issued the day after the *Patriot* article appeared, Kirkpatrick lambasted the newspaper for peddling 'pure and malicious disinformation' based on a 'total fabrication'. 'I have never', the ambassador shot back indignantly, 'written a paper on "Balkanization" or any even remotely related subject'. Ignoring Kirkpatrick's denial, TASS duly reported the original *Patriot* piece as an established fact, and it was referenced by communist newspapers worldwide.[37]

The kernel of the *Patriot* story featured in a spate of newspaper reports in New Delhi, Calcutta, and Madras that had surfaced in the months preceding its appearance. Each of these were carried initially in Soviet publications. Most focused on fictious reports that the CIA had meddled in elections in Andhra Pradesh and Karnataka, in southern India; was aiding separatist movements in Assam, in the northeast, and the Punjab, in the northwest; that Washington was bent on fomenting chaos in the Global South; and that the Pentagon was secretly building up military forces in Pakistan, on India's doorstep. The Moscow daily, *Moskovskiy Komsomolets*, ran a series of stories on the so-called 'Brahmaputra Plan', a plot supposedly hatched by the CIA to exploit religious and economic tensions in northeast India and tie up New Delhi's resources in counter-insurgency operations.[38] Other Soviet tabloids, including the youth newspaper, *Komsomolskaya Pravda*, amplified the narrative of American intrigue in India by accusing the CIA of assisting secessionist activities of militants in the Punjab who were fighting for the establishment of an independent Sikh state of Khalistan. Soviet propagandists ensured that printed disinformation was afforded additional impact by broadcasting press stories, in Hindi, into the subcontinent via Radio Moscow.[39]

Later in 1983, a major Stasi operation reaffirmed India's status as a global hub of communist propaganda activity. At the time, Americans were concerned with the spread of a new retrovirus, HIV/AIDS. With infections and fatalities linked to HIV/AIDS increasing rapidly in the United States, and the virus's cause still unknown, officers from the Stasi's disinformation unit, Department X, observed that American national hysteria associated with the condition was proliferating faster than HIV/AIDS itself. In India, stories appeared in the press that linked the emergence of HIV/AIDS to scientific research carried out by the US government. On 16 July, the front-page of *The Patriot* proclaimed sensationally, 'AIDS may invade India: mystery disease caused by U.S. lab experiments'. The Indian newspaper reproduced a letter from an unnamed American scientist that, one academic authority on disinformation has estimated, comprised 20 per cent fiction and 80 per cent fact. The letter combined half-truths and outright falsehoods in a superficially authoritative and engaging manner that encouraged readers to draw their own conclusions on the consequences of Washington's irresponsible behaviour. 'AIDS, the deadly mysterious disease which has caused havoc in the

U.S.', *Patriot* trumpeted, 'is believed to be the result of the Pentagon's experiments to develop new and dangerous biological weapons'. It emphasised, accurately, the World Health Organisation's concern at an unexplained disease, which appeared highly transmissible, and was sweeping through elements of America's immigrant, gay, and narcotic consuming communities. Quoting selectively from official records that had been released years earlier by the CIA and the Department of Defence, Indian readers were informed that US government agencies had 'tested new types of biological weapons in the densely populated areas of the U.S. and Canada, such as New York, Philadelphia, San Francisco, and Winnipeg'. Medical trials conducted by the American military and the Agency, most notably the controversial MKULTRA investigations into mind-control, the *Patriot* added, had been proven to have exposed unwitting 'guinea pigs', including drug users and convicts, to psychotropic agents and communicable diseases.[40]

In this instance, the practitioners of disinformation in the Stasi and KGB blundered, and the attempt to harness Indian newspapers as a launchpad for the global dissemination of stories attributing the appearance of HIV/AIDS to Washington's reckless clinical experimentation, fell flat. Anxiety surrounding HIV/AIDS had yet to reach the subcontinent. Despite its exemplary use of propaganda techniques to craft a compelling and effective narrative, Indians largely ignored the *Patriot* exposé. Having failed to gain traction in the subcontinent, the report fizzled out and went unnoticed in North America and Europe.[41] British officials in India had previously observed that the subcontinent constituted something of an experimental laboratory in which Soviet covert propaganda techniques were trialled and honed before being deployed across the developing world. 'The Russians have, of course', one IRD officer mused, 'used their experiences in India in many ways as a model for penetration of other countries and indeed their connexions with India as a direct instrument'.[42] Over time, the KGB, and its Eastern European collaborators, discerned that the effectiveness of active measures, including forgery, hinged less on whether they resonated with reality, and more on their capacity to affect emotions, or the collective outlook of a target audience. Moscow learnt that disinformation likely to sharpen existing tensions and prejudices or, in the terminology employed by Cold War propagandists, which amplified prevailing contradictions, worked best.[43] Indians evidenced an ambivalence to concocted accounts of America's role in exposing the world to HIV/AIDS, however unconscionable Washington's actions were made to appear. Such considerations resonated little with the lived experience of most South Asians. It was a lesson that the KGB was quick to absorb. As the 1980s progressed, and a new, more belligerent phase of the Cold War developed, the Reagan administration became irritated and, ultimately, infuriated, by the Soviets return to a disinformation theme that animated Indians more than any other, that of the American foreign hand and its subversive agenda in the subcontinent.

Rajiv Gandhi and the Politics of Intelligence: Plus ça change, plus c'est la même chose?

Indira Gandhi's interactions with successive American administrations were complicated by the Indian premier's byzantine relationship with the Central Intelligence Agency. Following her assassination in October 1984, US officials hoped that her son, and successor, Rajiv Gandhi, would seek to improve relations with the United States. A technocrat, who studied engineering at Cambridge University and Imperial College, London, and later joined Indian Airlines as a pilot, Rajiv was seen as a pragmatist. It was believed that he favoured reducing India's dependence on Soviet financial and military support and increasing the role of private enterprise in the country's moribund economy. A relative political novice, Rajiv had rejected a legislative role in his youth, and it was only following the unexpected death of his younger and electorally ambitious brother, Sanjay, that the elder Gandhi sibling gravitated towards the family business. Recalibrating established Indian diplomacy represented a daunting challenge for the most adroit and experienced of politicians, and Rajiv Gandhi was neither. Still, as American observers noted, Gandhi had the good sense to recognise a need to move ahead cautiously with reforms. '[P]ro-Soviet elements within his Congress Party and the bureaucracy, aided by the Soviet propaganda machine', the US embassy in New Delhi reported to Washington, 'could conceivably seriously threaten his [Gandhi's] political position unless he institutes policy changes slowly'. 'This "institutionalized" Soviet influence within India', American diplomats added, 'could be decisive in blocking – through private, party or parliamentary pressure – government decisions which are perceived as diluting the special relationship or threatening other Soviet interests in India'.[44]

It was not only 'institutionalised' Soviet influence in India that sought to stymie improved relations between Washington and New Delhi. In Moscow, the KGB's disinformation officers set to work producing a series of forged documents, the release of which was intended to reinforce a well-worn narrative that a perfidious America could not be trusted. In August 1987, a notable forgery featured in two successive issues of *Blitz*. The document took the form of a letter, allegedly sent in December 1986, from Bill Casey to Edwin Feulner, director of the Heritage Foundation, a conservative Washington think-tank. In the text, Casey, who had passed away back in May 1987, thanked Feulner for overseeing a Heritage Foundation study that recommended ways of fuelling animosity within Indian opposition parties with a view to ousting Gandhi from office. 'So, we have it straight from William Casey, the late CIA Director', *Blitz* proclaimed, 'as to who masterminded the current "turmoil" in India designed to pull down the Rajiv government and cut India down to the status of pariah nation in the world'. 'The Heritage–CIA gang has been hatching one plot after another to destabilise and balkanise India since the eighties', the Indian newspaper exclaimed.[45] A week later, *Blitz* ran a second story on the forgery which, apparently without irony, quoted TASS as confirming the veracity of the Casey letter. 'So, ours was a "total and complete" forgery, was it Mr. Ugly America??!!' the tabloid crowed excitedly.[46] In reality, the 'Casey' letter did represent a crude and obvious fabrication. A State Department report on Soviet influence activity pointed out that the letter published in *Blitz* contained a blurred image of the CIA's logo, which was also off-centre, suggesting that the emblem had been cut-out from another document and transposed on to blank letterheaded using a photocopying technique. The language and style of the letter's text was also awry. Casey had known Feulner for over twenty years. The former's correspondence to Feulner always began with the salutation, 'Dear Ed' and not, as the published letter stated, 'Dear Edwin'. Even Casey's signature was inauthentic. The letter had not, as was Casey's unfailing habit, been signed using a felt tip pen.[47]

The Soviet disinformation campaign connecting the CIA with plots to undermine Gandhi and his government was abetted by left-wing Indian politicians who persisted in perpetuating the hackneyed notion that the American government was subverting democracy in the subcontinent. In October 1987, during a brief visit Rajiv Gandhi paid to Washington, the topic of CIA machinations in India dominated media coverage of the Indian premier's talks with Reagan administration officials. Pressed by journalists to clarify remarks he had made that alluded to CIA interference in India, a defensive Gandhi replied, 'That's not what I said. What I have said was not just Western nations, but most nations have [intelligence] operations functioning in most developing countries and it is our job to see that they remain within limits. It is not possible to totally get rid of such organizations.' Somewhat incongruously, Gandhi went on to volunteer that he had broached the specific question of CIA activity with Vice President George Bush. In an exchange that echoed the correspondence that R. N. Kao had conducted with Bush on behalf of Gandhi's mother, three years earlier, the Indian prime minister confirmed that, 'He's [Bush] assured me there is no such [CIA] action or intervention [in India], certainly not at the highest levels, and I take his word for it . . . I think what Vice President Bush told me about the CIA is accurate.'[48] During an appearance on NBC's *Today* programme the following morning, Gandhi felt compelled to revisit the CIA chimera. Brushing over substantive issues in Indo-US relations, the Indian premier reiterated the assurance that Bush had offered that the CIA was not engaged in subversive activity in the subcontinent. Dismissing the concept of a 'foreign hand' as an unhelpful 'newspaper term', Gandhi nonetheless spurned the opportunity to reassure Americans that his government rejected the politics of conspiracism favoured by his mother. '[To] say there is no involvement of foreign agencies in India', Gandhi asserted on US national television, 'would be absolutely wrong'.[49]

In domestic terms, Rajiv Gandhi's capacity to move on from enervating debates surrounding the actions of foreign intelligence services, and to expend greater political time and energy on pressing issues, such as economic reform, were constrained by events on the ground in India. In February 1985, with Gandhi having been in office barely three months, the Intelligence Bureau uncovered what commentators dubbed 'the biggest spy ring in Indian history'.[50] Senior officials in the personal secretariats of Gandhi and the President of India, as well as bureaucrats from the ministries of defence, commerce, and the planning commission, were found to have passed classified information to a group of Indian businessmen over a number of years. Chittur Venkat Narayan, who operated under the alias Coomer Narain, acted as the ringleader. Narain was found to have handed over sensitive strategy papers on defence, foreign, and economic policy, to three European embassies in exchange for cash. Nineteen individuals were implicated in what came to be known as the 'Photocopy Spy Case'. Secret documents, it transpired, had been smuggled out of government premises and photocopied in a local Xerox shop. Three of the officials accused worked in the prime minister's office, one of whom, T. N. Kher, was a personal assistant to Padinjarethalakal Cherian (P. C.) Alexander, Gandhi's principal secretary.[51] A chastened Gandhi was forced to make a statement to the Indian parliament confirming that government employees in 'sensitive positions' had engaged in 'activities detrimental to the national interest'. India's press compounded Gandhi's discomfort by affording blanket coverage to 'one of the most serious spy scandals since partition'. Gossip abounded in India's capital over the identity of the foreign states that Narain had served. Although the Indian government remained coy, the involvement of Pakistan, the KGB, and the CIA, was mooted. New Delhi's summary expulsion of a French deputy military attaché, Lt. Col. Alain Bolley, added to an air of mystery over which countries had been privy to some of India's most closely guarded secrets. Serge Boidevaix, the French ambassador, soon followed Bolley out of New Delhi and into diplomatic exile.[52]

Unofficially, sources inside the US government denied any association in the Narain affair. 'New Delhi has found no evidence of US involvement in the recent spy scandal', a CIA report observed, 'but is trying to find a US connection'.[53] For members of the Communist Party of India, who paraded outside the American Embassy adjacent to Shantipath in the capital's Chanakyapuri diplomatic quarter, American complicity was never in doubt. While waving placards declaring, 'Smash Reagan plans to dismember India', and, 'Stop CIA-French espionage', the communists kept up steady chants of 'End CIA activities in India', and, 'Down with the imperialist conspiracy against India'. Declining to take Washington at its word, the Press Trust of India, along with several national newspapers, alleged that Bolley and the French government had shared the secrets obtained from Narain with the CIA.[54] In contrast,

Western journalists quoted intelligence sources as sceptical that the French had cooperated with the Americans. Paris had harvested commercially valuable security information from the Indian espionage operation that was of benefit to its own arms industry. Few experts saw good reason why this would have been shared with Langley. 'For all of its traditional paranoia about the U.S. Central Intelligence Agency', one American writer noted, it was telling that 'the Indian government had yet to point a finger at Washington'. The CIA concluded that reports emerging of Polish, East German, and Soviet roles in the espionage scandal had likely tempered the KGB's enthusiasm for 'fan[ing] suspicions of the US within the Indian government'. 'If Moscow's involvement is publicized', analysts back in Langley surmised, 'Soviet efforts to stir up anti-American sentiments with the Indian public probably would be undercut as well.'[55] Gandhi was deeply affected by the Narain case. He spent long hours poring over incriminating material seized by the IB, which included highly sensitive papers on laser weaponry, nuclear research projects, counterintelligence, and cabinet minutes on India's troubled relations with Pakistan and Sri Lanka. Narain had even provided the French with copies of India's diplomatic ciphers. As a consequence of the unprecedented security lapse, Gandhi took a much closer interest in intelligence matters. In the final years of his premiership, Gandhi spent more time meeting with India's spy chiefs than any previous, or subsequent, Indian leader.[56]

Rajiv Gandhi's interest in intelligence and security issues ensured that he was kept busy. Within a year, another pseudo-espionage case surfaced in New Delhi that, on this occasion, did implicate Washington in snooping on the India state. In January 1986, reports emerged in the press that Rama Swarup, the Indian representative of a quasi-official Taiwan trade promotion body, had assisted government bureaucrats in passing secret documents to officials in the US embassy. The local CIA station, journalists reported, had paid Swarup for confidential material on Indian-operated Soviet arms and to stage protests in the Indian capital against the Soviet occupation of Afghanistan. Government papers lodged in an Indian court alleged that West German and Taiwanese diplomats collaborated with Swarup in an American-led operation to cultivate members of the Indian parliament as sources of information. Two senior Indian ministers and a state commission chairman named in the court papers resigned. Public interest in the case in India was fuelled by the release of a 200-page 'charge sheet' that listed the contacts Swarup had established with MPs, lawyers, journalists, and diplomats stretching back to the 1950s. 'At some later point Swarup is alleged to have become an agent for the Americans and the Germans', a British official reported back to London, 'cultivating on their behalf such people as the Supreme Court Lawyer Lekhi ... the Ministers and former Ministers Singh Deo, Chandrakar, Sanjeevi Rao and Arvind Netam, former Prime Minister Morarji Desai, leader of the Telugu Desam Party, P. Upendra and numerous others'.[57]

INDIAN INTELLIGENCE AND THE END OF THE COLD WAR   251

Seven American diplomats and one German colleague left India unexpectedly in the wake of the Swarup revelations. The foreign officials, speculation
suggested, had fed Swarup material on Indira Gandhi's assassination which
subsequently found its way into the national press. Swarup was also believed to
have played an important intermediary role in introducing Western contacts
to Indian MPs and bureaucrats and in passing information to his 'handlers' on
official Indian thinking in relation to foreign and domestic policy. The extent
to which Swarup's activities were illegal, or merely stretched the boundaries of
India's opaque laws governing interaction between foreign nationals and
policymakers, was unclear. No charges were brought against prominent
Indians identified as part of Swarup's network. Gandhi's government
remained uncomfortable, nevertheless, that the Swarup affair had reinforced
an impression that India's secrets were up for sale. 'The immediate fall-out
from the publicity [surrounding the Swarup case]', the British High
Commission informed Whitehall, 'is likely to be a [further] tightening of the
rules concerning contacts between MPs and officials and diplomats and
middlemen'.[58] Gandhi duly cautioned his MPs that in future they should
avoid private meetings with small groups of foreign representatives. 'It was
pointed out [by the prime minister to Congress members]', one Indian newspaper reported, 'that on such occasions, foreigners try to engage guests in
conversations and get information from them or try to put across their own
point of view'.[59] British diplomats in New Delhi subsequently complained of
'difficulty in getting appointments in various Ministries'.[60]

The diplomatic community in New Delhi was not alone in griping that
Gandhi's government had overreacted to the Swarup situation. In the *Lok
Sabha*, Brigadier Kamakhya Prasad Singh Deo, who stood down as Minister of
Food and Civil Supplies after being named as a contact of the Indian lobbyist,
used his resignation speech to assert that his conscience was clear and that he
had not compromised Indian national interests in any way. Taking a none too
subtle swipe at Gandhi for failing to support Congress figures linked to
Swarup, Singh Deo declared that '[P]ublic men should be saved from the
insinuations and slander of unscrupulous people who tried to implicate the
innocent.'[61] In an editorial entitled, 'Govt Must Explain', the *Times of India*
offered Singh Deo support that his own government had failed to extend. On
the face of things, the newspaper observed, India's intelligence agencies had
launched an investigation into an alleged espionage ring operated by Swarup
and compiled a charge sheet of suspects on which Singh Deo's name featured.
In consequence, the minister had felt compelled to resign. 'But things were not
so simple', the *Times* noted. 'Indian intelligence agencies are not known either
for their efficiency or integrity; on every critical occasion they have fallen in
[sic] their faces; it is common knowledge that they have manipulated evidence
to suit them or their political masters.' 'But the Rama Swarup case fell into
a category of its own', the newspaper opined. Specifically, intelligence officers

had not interviewed Singh Deo, or other prominent public individuals listed as suspects, 'before smearing them'. The Intelligence Bureau, it appeared, was 'so keen to publicise its "great achievement" [in wrapping up the Swarup network] that it had taken care to provide copies of the chargesheet to newspapers'. It appeared inconceivable to the *Times of India* that the IB had not shown the chargesheet featuring Deo Singh to Gandhi and, instead, had acted on its own initiative in a matter involving two government ministers. In which case, the newspaper fulminated, the prime minster had 'failed to do his duty'. 'This duty was to ensure that no one was maligned and made to suffer for crimes he had not committed', the editorial thundered. 'A democracy does not survive in an atmosphere of character assassination.'[62]

Much as Gandhi may have wished to distance his administration and party from politically debilitating intelligence imbroglios, espionage ghosts from the past continued to resurface and impinge upon the prime minister's policy agenda. In October 1986, another spy scandal returned to feed the seemingly insatiable preoccupation with subversion and sedition in the Indian media. Back in 1977, six officials from the US embassy in New Delhi, along with a Soviet diplomat stationed in the Indian capital, were declared *persona non grata* following an Intelligence Bureau enquiry into leaks of classified information relating to India's defence, foreign affairs, and petro-chemical interests, that stretched back over fifteen years. After a tortuous eight-year trial, Indian participants in the spy ring – which was directed by a businessman, P. E. Mehta, and included K. K. Screen, a director in the state planning Commission – were convicted of espionage and jailed. Confirmation that another tranche of Indian bureaucrats had been induced to sell the nation's secrets to the CIA and KGB strained New Delhi's relations with Washington and Moscow, and raised further questions over India's competency when it came to safeguarding national security. The release of court transcripts that detailed the actions of officials who had routinely passed highly classified documents to foreign intelligence officers in the public toilet of New Delhi's Oberoi Intercontinental Hotel in return for wads of cash, did little to inspire public confidence in the nation's security and intelligence establishment.[63]

Towards the end of the decade as the Berlin Wall fell and the Cold War's denouement began to play out, India's press continued to feature a slew of allegations that the CIA was conspiring to subvert Rajiv Gandhi's government and the Congress Party. In November 1989, on the eve of a general election in India in which Gandhi was expected to face a tough fight to secure a further term in office, the pro-government *Hindustan Times* claimed that a $1 million-dollar grant had been funnelled by the CIA to the prime minister's political rival, Vishwanath Pratap Singh. Accompanied by photostats of purportedly official documents originating from the US embassy in India, the State Department, and the CIA, the news report was dismissed by American officials as 'mischievous', based upon 'patent forgery', and 'designed to damage Indian-American relations

INDIAN INTELLIGENCE AND THE END OF THE COLD WAR   253

at a critical time'.[64] Daniel Patrick Moynihan attacked the Indian newspaper revelations as baseless, and informed by, 'a painful – dare I say, pathetic – forgery'.[65] Forgery or not, as the *New York Times* noted, 'In India's highly charged political atmosphere, accusations of involvement with American intelligence agencies can be extremely damaging, with or without evidence, because they are widely circulated.' Singh had previously charged Gandhi's Government with operating its own 'department of forgeries' that manufactured spurious allegations intended to destroy its political enemies. By way of evidence, Singh pointed to bogus stories offered to Indian and foreign newspapers by mysterious sources that, accompanied by counterfeit documentation, suggested Singh's son, Ajeya, operated bank accounts in the Caribbean nation of St Kitts and Nevis worth tens of millions of dollars.[66] In Washington, the latest forgeries implicating the CIA with subversive activity in the subcontinent were not thought to have originated with Gandhi's administration. Pressed for comment by US journalists, an anonymous Bush administration source observed that, 'The Soviets and the communist bloc are the only ones who systematically engage in this [forgery]. We have no knowledge that the Indian government has done it in the past.' The fact that *Blitz* had published a series of additional allegations linked to the original *Hindustan Times* scoop, the source added, all but confirmed Moscow as the originator of the Singh smear.[67]

In 1992, revelations in the Indian press suggested that Soviet support for Gandhi extended beyond the realm of disinformation. Quoting from *Izvestia*, the Soviet newspaper of record, Indian journalists reported that documents had been discovered in the KGB archives which detailed payments made by the Soviet intelligence service to fund Gandhi's political activities. According to Russian sources, letters sent by the former KGB chief, Viktor Chebrikov, to the central committee of the Communist Party of the Soviet Union, confirmed that Gandhi had expressed 'deep gratitude' for financial subsidies secretly channelled to members of his family over many years via commercial transactions between an Indian company and Soviet foreign trade organisations. In response, an indignant denial issued by the All-India Congress Committee (AICC) dismissed the revelation as 'preposterous'. 'In normal circumstances', the AICC statement declared, 'we would not have considered that it [Soviet claims of Gandhi's KGB links] merited a denial . . . but Mr. Rajiv Gandhi is dead, and the Congress party cannot allow his name to be sullied'.[68] Two years later, in 1994, a book written by the Russian investigative journalist, Yevgenia Albats, and American human rights activist, Catherine Fitzpatrick, entitled *The State Within a State: The KGB and Its Hold on Russia, Past and Present*, reproduced portions of the letter in which Chebrikov had outlined KGB support extended to Gandhi.[69] If Russian sources are to be believed, clandestine payments allegedly made to Gandhi's political opponents by Western intelligence agencies, were more than likely offset by covert financial subsidies, not to mention KGB disinformation operations, that Moscow used to support the Congress Party.

Figure 10.1 All India Trade Union Congress members demonstrating against 'American Imperialism' in front of the US Embassy, New Delhi, 18 December 1971. Keystone / Stringer / Hulton Archive / Getty Images.

New Wars and Familiar Narratives

In common with his mother, even in death Rajiv Gandhi found it impossible to evade the clutches of the Central Intelligence Agency. On 21 May 1991, Gandhi was on the campaign trail supporting Congress candidates in southern India. Towards the end of a long day, at a final public meeting held in the village of Sriperumbudur, a stone's throw from Madras, a lone women emerged from a throng of onlookers and headed towards Gandhi. In the process of bending down to touch the former Indian premier's feet, Thenmozhi Rajaratnam, a member of the Black Tiger suicide brigade of the Liberation Tigers of Tamil Eelam, detonated a belt laden with RDX explosives that was concealed beneath her sari. Gandhi was killed instantly, along with fourteen bystanders. Leading figures in India's political establishment wasted little time in airing suspicions, verbally and in print, that the CIA had been behind a plot to assassinate Gandhi. Western journalists in the subcontinent were struck by the strength of a knee-jerk reaction in India to Gandhi's murder that appeared both visceral and irrational. Writing in the *Washington Post*, the newspapers South Asia correspondent, Steve Coll, noted, 'The view that the CIA wanted Gandhi dead is pervasive even among those Indian politicians, bureaucrats,

INDIAN INTELLIGENCE AND THE END OF THE COLD WAR   255

academics and journalists who have lived or travelled in the West.' 'It is a difficult opinion to explain or refute', Coll added, 'since it seems to arise not from evidence or even coherent speculation, but from a deep-seated emotional conviction'. While acknowledging the Agency's murky past and the particular imprint made by Congressional hearings in the 1970s that had exposed CIA complicity in murder plots in the global South, the American journalist nevertheless observed that in the case of India, a widespread belief that Langley was somehow involved in Gandhi's demise was not rooted in 'tangible history' but rather 'a different kind of thinking'.[70]

The connection that many South Asians drew between conspiracy, subversion, and political assassination was epitomised by a 2,000-word article published by the communist commentator and politician, Sudheendra Kulkarni, in the *Sunday Observer*. Under the banner, 'Days of the Jackal', an allusion to the bestselling novel by the English author, Frederick Forsyth, that recounted a fictional attempt on the life of French president, Charles de Gaulle, Kulkarni detailed the history of political assassination in the subcontinent since the Second World War. A common thread linking all the extra-judicial killings, he asserted, was a determination on the part of the West, and more especially, the United States, to keep India, Pakistan, and Bangladesh in a state of poverty, instability, and dependency.[71] Such theories resonated with many well-educated Indians who interpreted Gandhi's violent death as confirmation that the CIA was not prepared to tolerate a strong leader with an agenda to transform India into a vibrant, modern, and technologically advanced nation capable of challenging American global hegemony. Throughout the Cold War, Eastern bloc propaganda had promoted a narrative of the CIA as a malevolent and destructive force operating beyond the control of elected politicians. India's left-wing intelligentsia, who generally baulked at reductive Western characterisations of the Soviet Union as an evil empire, harboured an intrinsic enmity towards the Agency that Moscow's disinformation operatives worked hard to amplify. Troublingly for Washington, in a post-Cold War landscape absent communist ideological adversaries, the CIA found it impossible to shake off an impression in the subcontinent that it had pivoted away from combatting communism and towards neutralising Third World threats to a new unipolar American world order.

In Gandhi's case, the Bush administration found allegations that the CIA had been behind the Indian premier's murder to be particularly puzzling. Some foreign policy disagreements aside, Washington had enthusiastically endorsed Gandhi's determination to bring radical, free-market reform to India's economy. Moreover, as a technocrat who shared Washington's emphasis on the promotion of regional stability in South Asia, Gandhi was seen as someone with whom the United States could do business. American officials had become resigned during the Cold War to the CIA being employed as a convenient scapegoat in India for the country's ills. Exaggerated accounts of the Agency's supposed omniscience, as well as periodic exposures of its more questionable covert operations, unnerved India's political and business elites and provided a rationale for a protectionist trade policy designed to exclude corporate America from the subcontinent. Gandhi's assassination had the unfortunate effect of rekindling and enlarging deep-seated fears of CIA machinations in the imaginations of Indians. One contemporary American observer ruminated that, in the wake of Gandhi's assassination, 'The agency is blamed for nothing less than robbing India of its future.' In a post-Cold War context where Hindu nationalism was resurgent, corruption rampant, and political violence endemic, national powerbrokers, it seemed, remained unable to resist urging Indians to 'look the other way' and ask whether the foreign hand of the CIA was not responsible for the country's plight?[72]

Conclusion

> ... despite the end of the Cold War, the importance of intelligence has not diminished.
>
> R. N. Kao (1998)[1]

> The thing is old boy – between ourselves, don't tell the trainees or you'll lose your pension – we didn't do much to alter the course of human history, did we?
>
> SIS officer in John le Carré, *Silverview* (2021)[2]

Secret intelligence loomed large in India's relationships with Britain and the United States at the turn of the millennium. The end of the Cold War, and the beginning of another global conflict following the terrorist strikes launched against the United States, on 11 September 2001, inaugurated a new and intense phase in the Indian subcontinent's perennial intelligence 'Great Game'. Less than a month after Washington and New York had come under attack, Britain's prime minister, Tony Blair, arrived in India for talks with his opposite number, Atal Bihari Vajpayee. Blair stopped off in Pakistan on his way to New Delhi. In Pakistan, Blair, whose entourage included Richard Dearlove, the chief of SIS, was focused on securing Islamabad's cooperation in a campaign against Al Qaeda and the organisation's base of operations in Taliban-controlled Afghanistan. Disconcertingly for the British, policymakers in Pakistan and India were more concerned with discussing the status of Kashmir than in providing unconditional backing for a Washington-led 'War on Terror'. On 1 October, shortly before Blair reached South Asia, a Pakistani-based terrorist group, Jaish-e-Mohammed, killed thirty-one people in a suicide attack on the Jammu and Kashmir State Legislature. With Vajpayee under domestic pressure to respond to the terrorist incident, British diplomats fretted that the proxy war nuclear-armed India and Pakistan had waged over Kashmir since the late 1940s, risked spiralling out of control with disastrous consequences. 'I think all of us [in the British delegation]', Alistair Campbell, the British premier's director of communications, confided to his diary, ' ... had been a bit taken aback at just how much Kashmir defined their relations and just how deep the mutual hatred and obsession was'.[3] Decades earlier, during the Cold War, Britain and the United States had been slow to comprehend, and to accommodate, ambivalence within the subcontinent towards an ideological conflict between East and West that had seemingly little to do with the economic, social, and security challenges confronting the region. The extension of another global conflagration into South Asia manifested familiar tensions between the roles and obligations that Western nations expected partners in India and Pakistan to assume, and the opportunities that those partners identified to leverage offers of assistance to further their own, often very different, local agendas.

In intelligence terms, Blair's visit to India confirmed that the Cold War pattern of competitive cooperation between the clandestine services of India, the United Kingdom, and the United States, remained essentially unchanged. On landing at Indira Gandhi International Airport just before midnight on 5 October, a weary Blair was shepherded from an ageing Royal Air Force VC-10 transport aircraft and whisked into the Indian capital at high speed. As Blair's motorcade headed north on national highway 48 towards the centre of New Delhi, the prime minister motioned silently to Britain's high commissioner to India, Rob Young. Was the limousine laid on by the Indians bugged, Blair signalled. Not likely, the diplomat responded. Blair's circumspection in the company of Britain's Indian friends proved well-advised. At the hotel set aside for the British visitors, Blair's travelling Security Service team swept his rooms for eavesdropping devices. Two bugs were identified in Blair's bedroom, neither of which could be removed without drilling through walls. To avoid embarrassing his hosts, the British prime minister said nothing and swapped rooms with a junior member of his staff.[4] For the remainder of Blair's stay in India, the purpose of over-attentive Indian 'valets' assigned to each of his senior advisers became a running joke. India's intelligence services it appeared, were keen to ensure that their British guests were never short of company. Alistair Campbell's valet, an indefatigable young man with the work-name, Sunil, drew the short straw and was tasked with shadowing the notoriously combative communications officer. Wherever Campbell went, Sunil followed. On being told by Campbell, in characteristically robust fashion, to disappear, Sunil would fade into the background, only to reappear minutes later by the exasperated official's side.[5]

The ubiquitous surveillance coverage that Blair and his party were subjected to by Indian intelligence provoked black humour amongst the prime minister's team. Campbell, and the politically adroit Dearlove, 'had a great laugh' about the name of India's external intelligence service, the Research and Analysis Wing (R&AW). Campbell joked about dividing Downing Street's research and information unit into 'RAW domestic' and 'RAW international'. The most sensitive material passing through Downing Street, Blair's advisor quipped, could be handled by a small and elite team of trusted personnel, known as 'RAW hide'.[6] The allusion Campbell drew between a popular American

CONCLUSION   259

television series from the early 1960s, that followed the exploits of upright cowboys battling bandits and murderers on a lawless and inhospitable frontier, and India's foreign intelligence service, was likely more apt than he intended. With the strategic landscape on the subcontinent having been turned upside down by the events of September 11, the Kaoboys of R&AW were poised to play an outsized role in the latest version of an enduring covert conflict on the contested borders of India, Pakistan, and Afghanistan. An equally familiar, and similarly timeless, aspect of Britain's relationship with South Asia also reared its head during Blair's whistle-stop trip. London had long entertained a conceit that it knew how the subcontinent worked and what was best for it. In the field of Cold War secret intelligence, as with most other aspects of Britain's relations with India, New Delhi was thought to have much still to learn from London. When appraised of the enervating impact of the Kashmir dispute and its intractable nature, Blair conformed to type in expressing confidence that his experience of brokering the Good Friday Agreement in Ireland left him well positioned to succeed where so many others had tried and failed in South Asia. The United Kingdom remained, the prime minister insisted to sceptical Indian audiences, a 'pivotal' player in the region.[7] The unfortunate history of British and American post-1947 interventions in the affairs of the subcontinent, intelligence and otherwise, one assumes, had been omitted from Blair's Foreign Office brief.

Other continuities between a covert Cold War that had been consigned to history and contemporary clandestine operations proved uncomfortable for the Indian government. During the Cold War, exposure of British and American intelligence activity in the Indian press had disrupted London's and Washington's diplomacy. The ham-fisted attempt by India's intelligence services to eavesdrop on Blair suggested that lessons remained unlearned when it came to striking a balance between the risks and rewards associated with inherently insecure and high-profile covert operations. Once details of the abortive bugging operation against Blair had filtered into the public domain, India's media excoriated Vajpayee and ridiculed the nation's intelligence services. Under the front-page headline, 'Delhi clumsily bugged Blair's room', the *Times of India* wondered how the country's spooks had managed to bungle so badly and fail to conceal 'dirty tricks' that exposed their political masters to 'embarrassing and deeply incriminating' charges of bad faith.[8] In response, both the Bharatiya Janata Party (BJP) and the Indian government scrambled to issue denials that the British had been targeted in a state-sponsored espionage operation. 'No such thing was done. It's a false accusation', a BJP spokesman insisted. 'These charges are baseless', added the former BJP finance minister, Yashwant Sinha. 'The charge has been made by a discredited officer.'[9] Quite what Alistair Campbell made of being labelled 'discredited' is unrecorded. With Blair having left Downing Street weeks earlier, and the transition to a new British Labour government under

Gordon Brown underway, it is reasonable to assume, nonetheless, that neither London nor New Delhi welcomed the timing of 'blowback' from an historic and ill-judged intelligence enterprise.

Clearly, interest within the subcontinent's press for reporting on the more salacious and sensational aspects of secret intelligence persisted beyond the Cold War. This was unsurprising and hardly novel. Scandal sells newspapers, after all. The preoccupation, verging on a national paranoia, evidenced by India's fourth estate and political class towards threats posed by foreign subversion was, nevertheless, marked. In the summer of 2006, Vir Sanghvi, a prominent Indian journalist, and broadcaster, conceded to readers of his popular column in the *Hindustan Times* that he was, 'utterly and completely fascinated by the extent to which foreign intelligence services have penetrated the Indian establishment'. Sanghvi was raised in a prosperous, middle-class, left-wing, Mumbai family. His father was a successful barrister and his mother worked as an industrial psychologist. The young Sanghvi was educated in Britain at Mill Hill School and Brasenose College, Oxford. In adolescence, he had 'learnt to laugh' and 'giggle' at Indira Gandhi's incessant invocations of a foreign hand. Yet, in adulthood, the effect of growing up in a 'progressive' family that reasoned 'anybody who supports American interests in the formulation of Indian foreign policy is necessarily a CIA agent', coupled with revelations surrounding Soviet and American interventions in the subcontinent contained in the Mitrokhin Archive, and books by former Agency officer, Robert Baer, altered Sanghvi's thinking.[10]

Sanghvi was too reasoned and discriminating to adhere to the absolutist position espoused by his parents, who discerned direct lines between Indians sympathetic to America and CIA agents. Sanghvi recognised, however, that he was a 'product of my background'. He came to believe that an Indian policy-maker, 'who supports US interests blindly when it comes to Indian foreign policy has been compromised in some way'. Indian civil servants, journalists, military officers, and politicians, Sanghvi concluded, should be considered, 'a CIA asset, if he follows policies that serve US interests over ours – unless he can prove otherwise'. In retrospect, ubiquitous rumours that Agency moles had penetrated the heart of India's government from the very beginning of the Republic, the journalist argued, appeared compelling and credible and could not simply be dismissed as 'anti-US hysteria'. India after all, he observed, was one of the world's most important countries. 'Why wouldn't the CIA want to suborn our government?'[11] Sanghvi's epiphany in respect of foreign intelligence agencies resonated with fellow Indians who had been exposed to decades of domestic media output that sensitised them to a looming menace posed by external actors. The journalist's observations reflected a tendency on the part of India's press to engage in confirmation bias, reinforcing rather than refuting an innate suspicion of foreign intelligence services in general, and the Central

CONCLUSION 261

Intelligence Agency, in particular. The subcontinent remained hostile terrain for post-Cold War British and American spooks.

A measure of the widespread suspicion and fear felt by Indians towards Britain and the United States was a legacy of London's and Washington's repeated involvement in covert regime change after 1945. In Iran in 1953, during the Suez crisis of 1956, when it came to Chile in 1973, and elsewhere across the global South, a hidden British or American hand had been complicit in coup d'états against nationalist leaders who, often as not, enjoyed a strong popular or electoral mandate. The Suez Crisis irrevocably tarnished Britain's reputation in the Middle East, not least because London insisted on maintaining the fiction in exchanges with regional allies that it had not colluded with the French and the Israelis against Nasser.[12] The United States made a near identical blunder two decades later when American diplomats assured Indira Gandhi, in several face-to-face meetings, that the CIA had played no role whatsoever in the murder of Salvador Allende, and the replacement of his socialist administration in Chile with a repressive military regime. As Daniel Patrick Moynihan emphasised to Henry Kissinger at the time, it was difficult to imagine a more effective means by which the Nixon administration could have alienated Gandhi and convinced her compatriots that India's premier, and the nation's democratic system, might be next on Washington's hit-list. India's intelligence counter-culture provided, and continues to provide, a considerable socio-political challenge to foreign intelligence agencies and governments invested in South Asia. Its strength and resilience were nourished by ill-judged Western intelligence interventions in the subcontinent, and farther afield, after 1947.

A domestic environment in the subcontinent that was predisposed to view intelligence services and their activities with unease, if not hostility, ensured that the clandestine Cold War relationships forged between Britain, the United States, and India were often fraught and proved difficult to manage. For the most part, British and American intelligence agencies worked discretely and effectively with Indian counterparts and senior political figures in the ruling Congress Party. That changed towards the end of the 1960s when revelations surrounding CIA transgressions, within India and abroad, saw the Agency swept up in a political maelstrom that, while varying in intensity, remained a constant irritant in Washington's relationship with New Delhi. In the 1980s, American diplomats continued to bristle at jibes from Indian leaders who, while willing to engage privately with the CIA, publicly accused the United States of undermining Indian democracy.[13] While by no means exempt from local scrutiny, British intelligence activity in India attracted far less criticism from local politicians and went largely unreported in the media. This reflected, no doubt, Britain's declining importance to India and London's waning global significance. While Washington's relations with India experienced increasing strain from the early 1970s onwards, Whitehall was content for the CIA to function as a lightning rod for populist anti-Western sentiment.

For their part, Indian politicians proved to be adept at co-opting potent and pernicious symbolism associated with the CIA and harnessing it as an instrument to consolidate state power and strengthen post-colonial nation-building. The success which Indian policymakers evidenced in manipulating British and American intelligence interlocuters challenges ideas that nations inside the developing world were hapless victims of asymmetric Western power. Local agency, in the Indian subcontinent, at least, was important in directing the course and the outcome of South Asia's intelligence Cold War. It was only once the Cold War had ended, the Soviet Union's relationship with India had faltered, and the stranglehold exercised by the Nehru/Gandhi family on Indian politics loosened, that the CIA became less of a defining element in India's relationship with the United States. The Agency's seemingly boundless capacity to complicate American diplomacy represented an enduring source of frustration to US government officials in the latter Cold War period. Indira Gandhi, in common with manifold other leaders in the Global South, was anything but a passive bystander buffeted by external ideological and material pressures. Rather, the Indian prime minister was an active agent of history, willing and able to manipulate superpowers to further India's own regional ambitions and local interests.[14]

Frequently, interventions by British and American intelligence agencies in India were misdirected, maladroit, and counterproductive. The operations underpinning such activity were formulated on the basis of misapprehensions in London and Washington that covert actions and clandestine propaganda could turn Indian opinion against communism; that the taint of repression associated with Western intelligence practice would not adversely colour Indian attitudes; that the provision of intelligence support would undercut New Delhi's relations with Moscow; that salacious Congressional interrogation of CIA misdeeds would not alienate Indians; and, above all, that their intelligence services could stem, if not reverse, an erosion in British and American influence in the subcontinent. Such expectations were unrealistic and were never realised.

At times, and most especially in the early Cold War period, Britain and India worked closely together in the intelligence field. Invariably, however, ideological differences and political tensions between London and New Delhi inhibited effective joint action. British and Indian spooks conspired against each other almost as much as they operated in unison. Reporting to London shortly after the Indo-Pakistan war of 1965, when British influence in the subcontinent was at 'a low ebb', one official from the UK High Commission regretted that it had been reduced to feeding Indian colleagues intelligence, 'without get[ting] much of value in return', simply to avoid being ignored.[15] Arguments elucidated elsewhere that Britain 'punched far above its weight' in global intelligence terms throughout the Cold War are not supported in a South Asian context.[16] In common with studies that have addressed the

CONCLUSION 263

consequences of British intelligence interventions in the Middle East after 1945, there is little evidence that MI5, SIS, or the IRD, played a material role in propping up British influence in post-independent India.[17] If anything, by ushering the intelligence Cold War into South Asia, Britain and the United States inadvertently encouraged and advanced a diminution of their power in the subcontinent by inviting a Soviet riposte, and by corroding Indian trust in the good faith of Western intelligence agencies and their political masters. Long after the Cold War had been consigned to the dustbin of history, a legacy of mistrust and paranoia engendered by intelligence activity in India remained. In May 2011, an Indian journalist was covering state elections in a remote corner of West Bengal, some hundred miles or so outside Kolkata. Stopping in a small village that had witnessed a clash between Indian security forces and Naxalite insurgents, the journalist was surprised to come across a lone British writer sitting in the shade of a Banyan tree. The 'unlikely' encounter in the midst of the Indian *mofussil* raised the Indian journalist's eyebrows and perplexed a group of his colleagues. Dismissing the British writer's claims that he was researching a book on Naxalites, the Indians concurred that their foreign 'friend' had been engaged in 'some kind of MI6 [SIS] intelligence-gathering operation'.[18]

Equally, ideological blind-spots in Britain's intelligence community, or an inability to appreciate and respond appropriately to myriad complexities and contradictions in India's byzantine political milieu, hampered its operational effectiveness. In 1968, Labour's Minister of Technology, Tony Benn, whose father had been a Secretary of State for India, was amused and confounded by MI5's antiquarian approach to the subcontinent's politics. Benn had arranged to meet with India's high commissioner in London, Apa Pant. A career diplomat who had spent much of his professional life in Africa, Pant was also educated at Brasenose College, Oxford, and had practised for a time as a barrister after studying for the bar at Lincoln's Inn. Prior to his interview with Pant, Benn received a note from the Security Service. In it, MI5 identified India's high commissioner as a 'suspect person', 'anti-British', and someone who should be treated with 'circumspection'. Following an entirely innocuous encounter, in which Pant expressed his commitment to religious education and lauded the value of India's public school system, Benn was left to ponder the basis on which MI5 judged an 'innocent ... ageing aristocratic Indian parlour pink' to be a security risk.[19] A predisposition on part of the Security Service to conflate left-wing nationalism with communism, and to draw a direct line between sources of covert funding channelled to politicians, publishers, and journalists, and their underlying loyalties, was replicated within the CIA. The case of Krishna Menon perhaps best illuminates the capacity within British and American intelligence services to fashion monsters of their own making. The excessive weight attached by MI5 and the CIA to security concerns surrounding Menon are difficult to explain in purely rationale terms and, in hindsight, they appear overblown. The damage that an engrained, visceral, and widespread antipathy towards Menon on the part of British and American officials inflicted upon New Delhi's relations with London and Washington was significant. It was damage that better, less partial, and more nuanced British and American intelligence assessments of Menon and his political objectives could, and should, have avoided.

It was only after the Cold War had ended that the United States was able to exercise a degree of hegemonic power in the Indian subcontinent. By then new threats were emerging, chiefly in the form of nuclear proliferation and Islamist terrorism. South Asia was on the way to becoming categorised, in the words of Bill Clinton and, later, Barack Obama, as 'the most dangerous place in the world'.[20] In May 1998, a decision taken by Atal Bihari Vajpayee and his BJP government to test nuclear weapons and, in the process, Washington's patience, placed the intelligence communities of India and the United States at loggerheads once again.[21] George Fernandes, India's Minister of Defence at the time, was kept in the dark about the decision to test and reassured American counterparts that India would not do so.[22] Concurrently, India's intelligence agencies were implementing a sophisticated deception plan that circumvented efforts by the United States to anticipate New Delhi's preparations to go nuclear.[23] The tests triggered a crisis in New Delhi's relations with Washington. They also weakened trust between politicians and their intelligence services in both countries. Fernandes, and other senior Indian ministers, were furious that they had been kept in the dark by Vajpayee and the nation's spooks. Clinton administration officials demanded to know why the CIA had let itself be out manoeuvred and embarrassed by the R&AW.[24] George Tenet, the director of central intelligence, subsequently offered an insightful assessment of how another intelligence-related incident had been allowed to disrupt the United States' relations with India. The problem, Tenet argued, lay not with deficiencies in America's intelligence collection capability. The issue, instead, was one of analysis, or the inability to adequately interpret and to understand what motivated India's political class and drove its policymaking process. 'We did not sufficiently expect', Tenet acknowledged, 'that Indian politicians might do what they had openly promised'.[25] Or, in other words, and much as Tony Benn had found with MI5 and Apa Pant, Americans had fallen into the trap of projecting their own political, cultural, and strategic perceptions and prejudices onto Indians. Salient lessons from secret India's Cold War, that illuminated the pitfalls of Western hubris and cultural myopia, had, Tenet's assessment implied, remained unlearnt.

The record of Western clandestine interventions in India between 1947 and the end of the Cold War in 1989, offers up important lessons for contemporary global policymakers as they confront a diverse range of threats, from state-sanctioned disinformation and influence operations to non-state transnational terrorism, all of which have an extended history in the subcontinent. Rarely effective, and often characterised by long-lasting and deleterious consequences, British and American intelligence operations in India illustrate how external actors stoking inflated fears of nebulous threats can have a profound psychological impact upon a nations sense of security. In an earlier age, the British Empire spent much of its time fretting about safeguarding India from an expansive and acquisitive Russian rival, whose designs on the subcontinent, whatever they might have been, remained largely confined to the imaginations of czarist officials in St Petersburg. In the wake of the Second World War, feverish anxiety over the inroads that the Soviet Union and People's Republic of China were making in the developing world, and the danger that this posed to Western interests, prompted Britain and the United States to undertake covert action in the subcontinent, both with and without the knowledge and support of Indian governments. As elsewhere in Asia, Africa, and the Middle East, the United States and its British ally discovered that nascent post-colonial states could prove unexpectedly resistant to external influence and foreign direction. Popular conceptions of power and potency attributed to American and, to a lesser extent, British security and intelligence agencies appeared hollow and wildly overstated when confronted by Indian nationalism. Having paid a high price to secure independence and assert national sovereignty, Indians were reluctant to barter away autonomy in return for protection from states, including the Soviet Union, and ideologies, such as communism, that they interpreted as largely benign and unthreatening. Indian manipulation of British, American, and Soviet anxieties often enabled local actors to pitch foreign states against each other, and to influence and disrupt their regional agendas. Indian agency in the intelligence Cold War was considerable and has been largely overlooked.

The overt policy objectives and interests of British and American governments in India were not materially advanced by the prosecution of a secret Cold War in the subcontinent. Instead, Western intelligence agencies succeeded in disturbing the region's political equilibrium; undermining British and American influence; amplifying a national culture of conspiracism and paranoia; retarding democracy; and, paradoxically, facilitating the very expansion of communist power that secret intelligence interventions were intended to arrest. Viewed from the perspective of recent events, London and Washington have absorbed few, if any, lessons from previous Western intelligence interventions in South Asia. In Afghanistan and Pakistan, where the United States and Britain have strived, and failed, to shape stable and pro-Western states, questions surrounding the hubris and the limitations of Western power remain as pertinent today as ever. In the summer of 2010, India's then premier, Manmohan Singh, committed to fostering constructive dialogue with neighbouring Pakistan. Stung by a series of bomb attacks against Indian targets in Afghanistan that were traced back to Pakistan, the R&AW advocated retaliating in kind against Islamabad. Reasoning that India's involvement in such action would be impossible to conceal and would perpetuate a retaliatory cycle of violence and public recrimination that could spiral out of control, Singh's national security adviser, Shivshankar Menon, instructed the R&AW to, 'Keep your hands in your pockets.'[26] Fatefully, such hard-headed pragmatism was absent in London and Washington a generation or more before as British and American spooks turned India's Secret Cold War hot.

NOTES

Acknowledgements

1. Hugh Tinker, *The Banyan Tree: Overseas Emigrants from India, Pakistan, and Bangladesh* (Oxford: Oxford University Press, 1977), p. x.

Introduction

1. Reply to debate on President's Address, 22 February 1954, Parliamentary Debates (House of the People), Official Report, 1954, vol. 1, part II, cols. 431–34 (New Delhi: Parliament Secretariat, 1954).
2. Anand Niwas, a resident of Bombay, expressed ambivalence to the Cold War in a letter sent to US Supreme Court Justice, William O. Douglas in 1952. Douglas was an inveterate traveller who visited the subcontinent several times and published best-selling accounts of his experiences. Niwas to Douglas, 31 January 1952, William O. Douglas Papers, Box 1714 Folder 7 Indian 1951–52 (1 of 2), Library of Congress, Manuscripts Division, Washington DC. See also, William O. Douglas, *Strange Lands and Friendly People* (New York: Harper & Brothers, 1951); *Beyond the High Himalayas* (New York: Doubleday, 1952); and *Exploring the Himalaya* (New York: Random House, 1958).
3. John le Carré, *Tinker, Tailor, Soldier, Spy* (London: Hodder & Stoughton, 1974), p. 232. For an analysis of India's centrality to le Carré's Cold War spy fiction, see, Paul M. McGarr, 'The Neo-Imperialism of Decolonisation: John le Carré and Cold War India', *Intelligence & National Security* (38, 2) (2023), pp. 271–84.
4. John le Carré, *Tinker, Tailor; The Spy Who Came in from the Cold* (London: Gollancz, 1963).
5. Toby Manning *John le Carré and the Cold War* (London: Bloomsbury Academic, 2018).
6. See, Daniela Richterova and Natalia Telepneva (eds.), 'The Secret Struggle for the Global South: Espionage, Military Assistance and State Security in the Cold War', *The International History Review* 43, no. 1, (2021), pp. 1–5.
7. Exceptions include, Philip Davies and Kristian Gustafson (eds.), *Intelligence Elsewhere: Spies and Espionage Outside the Anglosphere* (Washington, DC: Georgetown University Press, 2013); and, in an Indian context, Bruce Vaughn, 'The Use and Abuse of Intelligence Services in India', *Intelligence & National Security*, 8 (1) (January 1993), pp. 1–22; and, Ryan Shaffer, 'Indian Intelligence Revealed: An Examination of Operations, Failures and Transformations, *Intelligence and National Security*, 33:4, (2018), pp. 598–610.
8. Scholarship addressing India's Cold War has largely ignored secret intelligence. The otherwise authoritative account of US-Indian relations by former American

NOTES TO PAGES 2–6

diplomat, Denis Kux, avoids the issue entirely. See, Denis Kux, *India and the United States: Estranged Democracies, 1941–1991* (Washington, DC: National Defense University Press, 1993).

9. Paul Thomas Chamberlin, *The Cold War's Killing Fields: Rethinking the Long Peace* (New York: HarperCollins, 2018); Lorenz M. Lüthi. *Cold Wars: Asia, the Middle East, Europe* (Cambridge: Cambridge University Press, 2020).

10. Ramchandra Guha, *India after Gandhi: The History of the World's Largest Democracy* (New Delhi: HarperCollins, 2007), p. vi; Manu Bhagavan, *The Peacemakers: India and the Quest for One World* (New Delhi: Harper Collins, 2012), p. ix.

11. Other studies have corroborated the limitations of Western covert action undertaken in the developing world during the Cold War. See, for example, the analysis of British clandestine interventions in the Middle East in, Rory Cormac. *Disrupt and Deny: Spies, Special Forces, and the Secret Pursuit of British Foreign Policy* (Oxford: Oxford University Press, 2018).

12. Susan L. Carruthers, *Cold War Captives: Imprisonment, Escape and Brainwashing* (Berkeley: University of California Press, 2009).

13. For instance, Victor Cherkashin, *Spy Handler: Memoir of a KGB Officer – The True Story of the Man Who Recruited Robert Hanssen and Aldrich Ames* (London: Basic Books, 2005); Bob Woodward, *Veil: The Secret Wars of CIA 1981–1987* (New York: Simon and Schuster, 1987).

14. le Carré, *Tinker, Tailor*.

15. Simon Faulkner and Anandi Ramamurthy, eds., *Visual Culture and Decolonisation in Britain*, eds. (Aldershot: Ashgate Publishing, 2006), p. 1.

16. Pankaj Mishra, *From the Ruins of Empire: The Revolt Against the West and the Remaking of Asia* (London: Allen Lane, 2012), p. 304.

17. Y. D. Gundevia, *Outside the Archives* (New Delhi: Sangam Books, 1983), pp. 208–9.

18. 'Reds Hinder Nation's Advance, Says Nehru', *Hindustan Times*, 13 January 1960.

19. B. N. Mullik, *My Years with Nehru, 1948–1964* (New Delhi: Allied Publishers, 1972), p. 57.

20. Nehru to Krishna Menon, 2 December 1948, *Selected Works of Jawaharlal Nehru (SWJN)* 2nd Series, vol. 8, ed. S. Gopal, (New Delhi, OUP, 1989), f. 2, pp. 368–70.

21. 'Intelligence Reports, 1950', Private Papers of Sardar Patel, Indian National Archives, New Delhi (INA).

22. John le Carré, *Smiley's People* (London: Hodder and Stoughton, 2011) (First Published London, 1979), p. 1314.

23. B. Raman, *The Kaoboys of R&AW: Down Memory Lane* (New Delhi; Lancer, 2007), pp. 42–43.

24. Paul M. McGarr, *Cold War in South Asia: Britain, the United States and the Indian Subcontinent, 1945–1965* (Cambridge: Cambridge University Press), pp. 27–28.

25. See, 'Conspiracy Theories', *Hindustan Times*, 1 October 2005. On Indian literature and the 'foreign hand', see Pauly V. Parakal, *CIA Dagger against India* (New Delhi: D. P. Sinha for Communist Party of India, 1973); Kunhanandan Nair, *Devil and His Dart: How the CIA Is Plotting in the Third World* (New Delhi: Sterling Publishers, 1986); Satish Kumar, *CIA and the Third World: A Study in Crypto-Diplomacy* (London: Zed Press, 1981); and Rustem Galiullin, *The CIA in Asia: Covert Operations against India and Afghanistan* (Moscow: Progress, 1988). Insightful observations on civil conspiratorial mindsets, in an Iranian context, can be found in, Robert Jervis, *Why Intelligence Fails: Lessons from the Iranian Revolution and the Iraq War* (Ithaca, NY: Cornell University Press, 2010), p. 32; p. 49.

NOTES TO PAGES 6–10

26. Indira Gandhi, 'Women on the March', September 1963, in *India: The Speeches and Reminiscences of Indira Gandhi, Prime Minister of India* (London: Hodder and Stoughton, 1975), p. 17.

27. Alex Von Tunzelmann. *Indian Summer: The Secret History of the End of an Empire* (London: Simon & Schuster, 2007), p. 64.

28. Shashi Tharoor, *Inglorious Empire: What the British Did to India* (London: Hurst and Company, 2017), p. 89.

29. Mullik, *Years with Nehru*, p. 57. For an American perspective on this issue, see 'Nehru's Political Personality', 18 June 1956, RG59, Lot 59 D 75 folder 1956, United States National Archives, College Park, Maryland (USNA).

30. McGarr, *Cold War in South Asia*, pp. 85–88.

31. A. R. Wic, 'The Ulug-Zade affair', *Weekend Review* (2, 5), 6 January 1968, pp. 6–7.

32. George Blake, *No Other Choice: An Autobiography* (London: Jonathan Cape, 1990), p. 67.

33. Rudyard Kipling, 'The Man Who Would be King' in *The Phantom 'Rickshaw and Other Tales* (Allahabad: A. H. Wheeler & Co., 1888); See also, Josiah Harlan, *A Memoir of India and Afghanistan* (Philadelphia: J Dobson, 1842); and Ben Macintyre, *Josiah the Great: The True Story of the Man Who Would Be King* (London: Harper Press, 2004).

34. Mary Olmsted, 8 April 1992, Foreign Affairs Oral History Project (FAOHP), Library of Congress, Washington DC, http://memory.loc.gov/ammem/collec tions/diplomacy/

35. Kenneth Conboy and James Morrison, *The CIA's Secret War in Tibet* (Lawrence: University of Kansas Press, 2002).

36. Christopher Andrew and Vasili Mitrokhin, *The Mitrokhin Archive II: The KGB and the Wider World* (London: Aleen Lane, 2005), pp. 9–10 and pp. 312–14.

37. Oleg Kalugin, *Spymaster: My Thirty-Two Years in Intelligence and Espionage against the West* (New York, 2009), p. 141.

38. Manila Rohtagi, *Spy System in Ancient India from Vedic Period to Gupta Period* (Delhi: Kalpaz Publications, 2007), p. 274.

39. Sunil Khilnani. *Incarnations: A History of India in 50 Lives* (London: Allen Lane, 2016), pp. 24–30.

40. Richard J. Popplewell, *British Intelligence and the Defence of the Indian Empire, 1904–1924* (London: Routledge, 1995), p. 9.

41. C. A. Bayly, *Empire and Information: Intelligence Gathering and Social Communication in India, 1780–1870* (Cambridge: Cambridge University Press, 1996).

42. James Manor. *Politics and State-Society Relations in India* (London: Hurst & Company, 2017), pp. 29–30; See also, Patrick French, *Liberty or Death: India's Journey to Independence and Division* (London: HarperCollins, 1997).

43. Sir Adrian Carton de Wiart, *Happy Odyssey: The Memoirs of Lieutenant-General Sir Adrian Carton de Wiart* (London: Jonathan Cape, 1950), p. 131.

44. See, Martin Thomas, *Empires of Intelligence* (Berkeley: University of California Press, 2008).

45. Popplewell, *British Intelligence*, p. 33.

46. Ibid., p. 81; Calder Walton, *Empire of Secrets: British Intelligence, the Cold War and the Twilight of Empire* (London: Harper Press, 2013), pp. 26–27.

47. Popplewell, *British Intelligence,* p. 219.

48. Christopher Andrew. *The Defence of the Realm: The Authorized History of MI5* (London: Allen Lane, 2009), p. 137.

NOTES TO PAGES 10–12

49. Bayly, *Empire and Information*, p. 1; Jon Wilson, *India Conquered: Britain's Raj and the Chaos of Empire* (London: Simon & Schuster, 2016), pp. 293–94.
50. Kim A. Wagner, *Amritsar 1919: An Empire of Fear and the Making of a Massacre* (New Haven, CT: Yale University Press, 2019), p. 16.
51. Rudyard Kipling, *Kim* (London: Macmillan, 1901). India's lure as the backdrop to great power rivalry, sedition, and intrigue proved irresistible to subsequent British authors. See Somerset Maugham, *Ashenden: Or the Secret Agent* (London: Heinemann, 1928); and, John Buchan, *Greenmantle* (London: Hodder & Stoughton, 1916).
52. 'Notes for Newcomers to India', undated, c. 1960, DO 35/2644, UKNA; Paul Gore-Booth, *With Great Truth and Respect* (London: Constable, 1974), p. 264.
53. Ben Macintyre, *A Spy Among Friends: Kim Philby and the Great Betrayal* (London: Bloomsbury, 2014), p. 34.
54. Stephen Kinzer, *The Brothers: John Foster Dulles, Allen Dulles and Their Secret World War* (New York: St. Martin's Griffin, 2013), pp. 19–20.
55. Kermit Roosevelt, *A Sentimental Safari* (New York: Knopf, 1963), p. xiii.
56. Hugh Wilford. *America's Great Game: The CIA's Secret Arabists and the Shaping of the Modern Middle East* (New York: Basic Books, 2013), p. 17.
57. L. Natarajan, *American Shadow over India* (Bombay: People's Publishing House, 1952).
58. Goodfriend to Timberlake, 15 February 1951, FO 1110/418, UKNA.
59. Andrew and Mitrokhin, *KGB and the Wider World*, p. 324.
60. See, Christopher Andrew, *The Defence of the Realm: The Authorized History of MI5* (London: Allen Lane, 2009); Keith Jeffery, *MI6: The History of the Secret Intelligence Service, 1909–1949* (London: Bloomsbury, 2010). Also, Calder Walton, *Empire of Secrets: British Intelligence, the Cold War and the Twilight of Empire* (London: Harper Press, 2013).
61. See, Paul M. McGarr, 'The Information Research Department, British Covert Propaganda, and the Sino-Indian War of 1962: Combating Communism and Courting Failure?', *The International History Review*, (41:1), (2019), pp. 130–56.
62. Standard accounts of the Agency largely overlook CIA activity in India. See, for example, Victor Marchetti and John D. Marks, *The CIA and the Cult of Intelligence* (London: Jonathan Cape, 1974); John Ranelagh, *The Agency: The Rise and Decline of the CIA* (London: Weidenfeld & Nicolson, 1986); and, Timothy Weiner, *Legacy of Ashes: The History of the CIA* (London: Allen Lane, 2007). The memoirs of Agency directors, such as Richard Helms, *A Look Over My Shoulder: A Life in the Central Intelligence Agency* (New York: Random House, 2003); and, George Tenet, *At the Center of the Storm: My Years at the CIA* (London: Harper Press, 2007), mention India only sparingly. The former CIA officer, Duane R. Clarridge, provides some insights into the work undertaken by the Agency in Cold War India in, *A Spy for All Seasons: My Life in the CIA* (New York: Scribner, 1997). In addition, records of ambassadorial tours offer brief glimpses into CIA activity in the subcontinent. See, John Kenneth Galbraith, *A Life in Our Times: Memoirs* (London: Andre Deutsch, 1981); Chester Bowles, *Promises to Keep: My Years in Public Life, 1941–1969* (New York: Harper and Row, 1971); and Daniel P. Moynihan, *A Dangerous Place* (Boston: Little Brown, 1978). For the most recent survey of CIA interventions in India since 1947, see Paul M. McGarr, '"Quiet Americans in India": The Central Intelligence Agency and the Politics of Intelligence in Cold War South Asia'. *Diplomatic History*, 38 (5), (November 2014), pp. 1046–82.
63. Mullik, Years with Nehru; T. V. Rajeswar, *India: The Crucial Years*. (Noida: Harper Collins India, 2015); Raman, Kaoboys of R&AW; K. Sankaran Nair, *Inside IB and*

NOTES TO PAGES 13–16 271

RAW: The Rolling Stone that Gathered Moss (New Delhi: Manas Publications, 2007); and, Vikram Sood, *The Unending Game: A Former R&AW Chief's Insights into Espionage* (Gurgaon: Penguin Viking, 2018). Notable exceptions, which provide important insights into India's intelligence operations and culture are Vappala Balachandran, *National Security and Intelligence Management: A New Paradigm* (Mumbai: Indus Source Books, 2014); A. S. Dulat and Aditya Sinha. *Kashmir: The Vajpayee Years* (Noida: Harper Collins India, 2015); and A. S. Dulat, Aditya Sinha and Asad Durrani, *The Spy Chronicles: RAW, ISI and the Illusion of Peace* (Noida (India): HarperCollins India, 2018).

64. Nicolas Groffman, 'Indian and Chinese Espionage', *Defense & Security Analysis*, 32:2 (2016), p. 9.
65. 'Surgical strikes', *Indian Express*, 3 October 2016.
66. Sharma, Aman, 'Blow-by-blow account: How PM Modi, Ajit Doval & Army chief planned covert strike against militant', *Economic Times*, 11 July 2018.
67. Groffman, 'Indian and Chinese Espionage', p. 12.

1 Transfer of Power: British Intelligence and the End of Empire in South Asia

1. 'Union Jack at Lucknow Residency Hauled Down', *Statesman*, 29 August 1947.
2. Jon Wilson, *India Conquered: Britain's Raj and the Chaos of Empire* (London: Simon & Schuster, 2016), p. 471.
3. *Wavell: The Viceroy's Journal*, ed. Pendrel Moon (London: Oxford University Press, 1973), 31 December 1946, p. 402.
4. R. K. Yadav, *Mission R&AW* (New Delhi: Manas Publications, 2014), p. 24.
5. Patrick French, *Liberty or Death: India's Journey to Independence and Division* (London: HarperCollins, 1997), p. 235.
6. 'Disposal of old records in the External Affairs, Political, and Home Departments', File 1299/2/GG/43, IOR/R/3/1/149, July 1946–August 1947, India Office Records (IOR), British Library (BL).
7. Richard J. Aldrich, 'American Intelligence and the British Raj: The OSS, the SSU and India, 1942-1947', *Intelligence and National Security*, 13: 1 (Spring 1998), pp. 148–9.
8. B. N. Mullik, *My Years with Nehru, 1948-1964* (New Delhi: Allied Publishers, 1972), p. 57.
9. Kellar Minute, 2 July 1951, KV/2/2512/4, United Kingdom National Archives, Kew, London (UKNA).
10. Mullik, *Years with Nehru*, p. 57.
11. Nehru to Mountbatten, 18 September 1954, *Selected Writings of Jawaharlal Nehru (SWJN)*, vol. 26, eds. Ravinder Kumar and H. Y. Sharada Prasad (New Delhi: Oxford University Press, 2000), pp. 221–23.
12. Nehru to Chief Ministers, 2 November 1947, *Letters to Chief Ministers, 1947–1964, Volume 1, 1947–1949*, ed. G. Parthasarathi (New Delhi, Oxford University Press: 1985), pp. 10–11.
13. Nehru to Pandit, 5 May 1948, Vijaya Lakshmi Pandit Papers, Instalment, Subject File 54, Nehru Museum and Memorial Library (NMML).
14. Y. D. Gundevia, *Outside the Archives* (New Delhi: Sangam Books, 1984), pp. 208–9.
15. Wilson, *India Conquered*, p. 472.

NOTES TO PAGES 16–23

16. Pethick-Lawrence to Mountbatten, 12 April 1947, *The Transfer of Power, 1942–47*, vol. X, ed. Nicholas Mansergh (London: HMSO, 1970–83), p. 219; Attlee to George VI, 15 March 1947, PS/GVI/C 337/08, Royal Archives, Windsor.
17. JIC (47) 2 (0) (Final), 'India – Organisation for Intelligence', 4 January 1947, L/WS/1/1050, IOBL.
18. 'Strategic position of the British Commonwealth', 2 April 1946, CAB 131/2 DO (46) 47, UKNA.
19. David C. Engerman, *The Price of Aid: The Economic Cold War in India* (Cambridge, MA: Harvard University Press, 2018), p. 21.
20. 'India's Foreign Policy', 1950, Speeches & Writings File No. 35, K. P. S. Menon Collection, NMML.
21. *New York Times*, 15 August 1947, p. 1.
22. Chester Bowles, 'American and Russia', *Foreign Affairs*, 49 (July 1971), pp. 636–51.
23. 7 August 1946, Liddell Diaries, p. 284, KV/4/467, UKNA.
24. 11 December 1946, Liddell Diaries, p. 104, KV/4/468, UKNA.
25. French, *Liberty or Death*, pp. 97–101.
26. Ibid., pp 257–59.
27. Thompson to Powell, 21 May and 12 June 1947, POLL 3/1/5, Enoch Powell Papers, Churchill Archives Centre, Churchill College Cambridge.
28. Minute to Trend, 4 December 1950, CAB 301/112, UKNA.
29. Minute to Crombie, 3 November 1950, CAB 301/112, UKNA.
30. Minute from Hodges to Rampton and Harris, 13 November 1950, CAB 301/112, UKNA.
31. 28 February and 3 March 1947, Liddell Diaries, pp. 162–63, KV/4/468, UKNA.
32. Christopher Andrew, *The Defence of the Realm: The Authorized History of MI5* (London: Allen Lane, 2009), pp. 137, 333.
33. Bhashyam Kasturi, *Intelligence Services: Analysis, Organisation and Functions* (New Delhi: Lancer Publishers, 1995), p. 26.
34. K. Sankaran Nair, *Inside IB and RAW: The Rolling Stone that Gathered Moss* (New Delhi: Manas Publications, 2013), p. 90.
35. 'Liddell Visit to the Middle East', J.I.C./532/47, J.I.C (47) 33rd Meeting (C), 4 June 1947, CAB 159/1, UKNA.
36. DIB to Ministry of Home Affairs, 3 May 1948, File No. 16/50/48-Police, National Archives of India (NAI).
37. 'Proposals for the Reorganisation of the Delhi C.I.D.', Banerjee, 29 May 1948, File No. 16/50/48-Police, NAI.
38. 5 May 1948, Liddell Diaries, pp. 90-92, KV/4/470, UKNA.
39. 'Future of Indian Intelligence Liaison', 29 January 1947, FO 1093/359, UKNA.
40. 'C' (Menzies) to Hayter, 17 January 1947, FO 1093/359, UKNA.
41. Halford to Hayter, 22 January 1947, FO 1093/359, UKNA.
42. 'Future of Indian Intelligence Liaison', 29 January 1947, FO 1093/359, UKNA.
43. Sargent to Sillitoe, 7 February 1947, FO 1093/363, UKNA.
44. Sargent to Shone, 8 February 1947, FO 1093/359, UKNA.
45. Bridges to Monteath, 10 March 1947, FO 1093/439, UKNA.
46. 13 January 1947, Liddell Diaries, pp. 120–21, KV/4/468, UKNA.
47. 'Liddell Visit to the Middle East', J.I.C./532/47, J.I.C (47) 33rd Meeting (C), 4 June 1947, CAB 159/1, UKNA; 16 May 1947, Liddell Diaries, pp. 1-2, KV/4/469, UKNA.

NOTES TO PAGES 23–27 273

48. Bourne to Guild, 7 August 1945, HS8/888, UKNA. See also, Christopher J. Murphy, '"Constituting a Problem in Themselves": Countering Covert Chinese Activity in India: The Life and Death of the Chinese Intelligence Section, 1944–46', *Journal of Imperial and Commonwealth History*, 44:6 (2016), pp. 928–51.
49. 29 July 1947, Liddell Diaries, p. 41, KV/4/469, UKNA.
50. 'Security Service Representative in Pakistan', J.I.C. (47) 75th Meeting (O), 5 Nov. 1947, CAB 159/2, UKNA.
51. Andrew, *Defence of the Realm*, p. 442.
52. David Gilmour, *The British in India: Three Centuries of Ambition and Experience* (London: Allen Lane, 2018), p. 205; Viola Bayley, *Memoir of Life in India, 1933–46: One Woman's Raj* (Unpublished manuscript, 1975/76), Microfilm no.57, Viola Bayley Papers, Centre of South Asian Studies, University of Cambridge.
53. Garvey to Halford, 16 November 1947, FO 1093/359, UKNA.
54. C (Menzies) to Hayter, 15 March 1947, FO 1093/359, UKNA.
55. Shone to Halford, 16 April 1947, FO 1093/359, UKNA.
56. Hayter to C (Menzies), 29 April 1947, FO 1093/359, UKNA.
57. Menzies to Hayter and handwritten note from Halford, 2 May 1947, 'India', FO 1093/359, UKNA.
58. Street to Halford, 13 October 1948, FO 1093/439, UKNA.
59. Hayter to Shone, 9 May 1947, FO 1093/359; Hayter to Sargent, 16 October 1948, FO 1093/439, UKNA.
60. C (Menzies) to Halford, 23 April 1947, FO 1093/359, UKNA; Hayter to C, 29 April 1947, FO 1093/359, UKNA.
61. Shone to Hayter, 23 May 1947, FO 1093/359, UKNA.
62. SIS Officer to Symon, 7 April 1947, FO 1093/359, UKNA.
63. Shone to Halford, 16 April 1947, FO 1093/359, UKNA.
64. SIS Officer to Symon, 7 April 1947, FO 1093/359, UKNA.
65. Stephen Dorril, *MI6: Fifty Years of Special Operations* (London: Fourth Estate, 2000), p. 87.
66. Ibid., p. 87.
67. Sargent to Stapleton, 9 January 1948, FO 1093/375; Menzies 'The Capabilities of the Secret Service in Support of an Overall political Plan', 20 January 1948, FO 1093/375, UKNA.
68. 'Special Operations', J. P. (47) 118 (Final), 17 December 1947, FO 1093/375, UKNA.
69. 'Capabilities of S.S. in Peace in Support of an Overall Political Plan', 20 January 1948, FO 1093/375, UKNA.
70. Ibid.
71. 'Cold War Organisation', COS 36th Mtg, COS 409/8/3/8, 10 March 1948, FO 1093/375, UKNA.
72. 20 October 1947, Liddell Diaries, pp. 92–93, KV/4/469, UKNA.
73. Keith Jeffrey, *MI6: The History of the Secret Intelligence Service, 1909–1949* (London: Bloomsbury, 2010), p. 638.
74. Sargent Minute, 7 October 1948, FO 1093/439, UKNA.
75. 15 October 1948, Liddell Diaries, p. 176, KV/4/470, UKNA.
76. *War Diaries, 1939–1945: Field Marshal Lord Alanbrooke*, (eds.) Alex Danchev and Daniel Todman (London: Weidenfeld and Nicholson, 2001), 13 November 1941 and retrospective entry, pp. 198–200.

274   NOTES TO PAGES 27–34

77. Nehru to Nye, 4 August 1948, *SWJN* 2nd series, vol. 7, ed. S. Gopal, (New Delhi: Oxford University Press, 1988), p. 578.
78. 'Measures for the provision of economic aid to India', 20 July 1949, DO 35/2921, UKNA.
79. Jeffrey, *MI6*, p. 639.
80. Andrew, *Defence of the Realm*, p. 479.
81. Halford minute, 13 October 1948, FO 1093/439, UKNA.
82. Hayter to Sargent, 13 October 1948, FO 1093/439, UKNA.
83. Sir Percy Sillitoe, *Cloak without Dagger* (London: Cassell, 1955), p. 176; Andrew, *Defence of the Realm*, p. 333.
84. Sargent to 'C', 21 October 1948, FO 1093/439, UKNA.
85. Kellar Minute, 2 July 1951, KV/2/2512/4, UKNA.
86. Andrew, *Defence of the Realm*, p. 442. In 1952, an annexe to the Maxwell Fyfe Directive to the Director General of MI5 allowed for a more flexible interpretation of the Attlee Directive. Under this, SIS was, 'in certain circumstances', and on the understanding that MI5 would be kept informed, permitted to undertake operations in Commonwealth and Colonial territory. 'Report of Enquiry into the Security Service by Sir Findlater Stewart', PREM 8/1520, UKNA.
87. Jeffrey, *MI6*, p. 639.
88. Andrew, *Defence of the Realm*, p. 442.
89. Prem Mahadevan, 'The Failure of Indian Intelligence in the Sino- Indian Conflict', *Journal of Intelligence History*, 8:1 (2008).
90. Notes on India post-independence, Undated, P. N. Haksar Papers, III Instalment, Subject File Other Papers 7, NMML.
91. Richard J. Aldrich, '"The Value of Residual Empire": Anglo-American Intelligence Co-operation in Asia after 1945' in *Intelligence, Defence and Diplomacy: British Policy in the Post-war World*, eds. Richard J. Aldrich and Michael F. Hopkins (London: Frank Cass, 1994).
92. Stella Rimington, *Open Secret: The Autobiography of the Former Director-General of MI5* (London: Arrow Books, 2002), p. 69.
93. K. Sankaran Nair, *Inside IB and RAW: The Rolling Stone that Gathered Moss* (New Delhi: Manas Publications, 2013), p. 117.

2 Silent Partners: Britain, India, and Early Cold War Intelligence Liaison

1. Stella Rimington, *Open Secret: The Autobiography of the Former Director-General of MI5* (London: Arrow Books, 2002), p. 54.
2. Nye to CRO, 17 May & 20 November 1951, FO 371/92870, UKNA.
3. Freeman to Bottomley, 16 September 1965, PREM 13/394, UKNA; Foot/ Pandit talk, 26 November 1965, PREM 13/2160, UKNA.
4. Christopher Andrew, *The Defence of the Realm: The Authorized History of MI5* (London: Allen Lane, 2009), p. 445.
5. Andrew, *Defence of the Realm*, p. 67.
6. Peter Hall, BDOHP, www.chu.cam.ac.uk/archives/collections/BDOHP/Hall.pdf
7. 5 May 1948, Liddell Diaries, pp. 90–92, KV/4/470, UKNA.
8. Andrew, *Defence of the Realm*, p. 481.

NOTES TO PAGES 34–41

9. Philip Murphy, 'Creating a Commonwealth Intelligence Culture: The View from Central Africa, 1945–1965', *Intelligence and National Security* 17(3) (2002), pp.107–8; pp. 136–37.
10. 'Security Service Representative in Pakistan', J.I.C. (47) 75th Meeting (O), 5 November 1947, CAB 159/2, UKNA; Philip Murphy, 'Intelligence and Decolonization: The Life and Death of the Federal Intelligence and Security Bureau, 1954–63', *Journal of Imperial and Commonwealth History* 29(2) (2001), pp. 101–30.
11. Dean to Foreign Secretary, 16 December 1955, cited in Chikara Hashimoto, *Twilight of the British Empire: British Intelligence and Counter-Subversion in the Middle East, 1948–68* (Edinburgh: Edinburgh University Press, 2017), p. 26.
12. 23 January 1953, Liddell Diaries, p. 21, KV/4/475, UKNA.
13. Andrew, *Defence of the Realm*, p. 137.
14. Nye to CRO, 20 November 1951, FO 371/92870, UKNA.
15. Ibid.
16. 'Times' Diaries, 16 October 1958, GBR/0014/HALY/15/1, Churchill Archives Centre, Churchill College Cambridge.
17. *Hindustan Times*, 8 September 1946.
18. Nehru to Asaf Ali and K .P. S. Menon, 22 January 1947, *SWJN* 2nd series, vol. 1, ed. S. Gopal (New Delhi: Oxford University Press, 1984), pp. 575–76.
19. 'India's Foreign Policy', K. P. S. Menon Papers, Nehru Museum and Memorial Library, New Delhi (NMML).
20. P. N. Kaul, 'Trade Relations with U.S.S.R.' 1954, Ministry of External Affairs, D/3042/Europe, National Archives of India, New Delhi (NAI).
21. Andrew, *Defence of the Realm*, pp. 444–46.
22. 29 December 1952, Liddell Diaries, pp. 190–93, KV/4/474, UKNA.
23. Andrew, *Defence of the Realm*, pp. 444–46.
24. Strang Minute, 9 February 1950, FO 371/82314, UKNA.
25. Nehru to Kher, 9 September 1952, *SWJN* 2nd series, vol. 19, ed. S. Gopal, (New Delhi: Oxford University Press, 1996), pp. 632–34.
26. Ibid.
27. Nehru to Cabinet Secretary, 9 October 1956, *SWJN*, vol. 35, ed. Mushirul Hasan, H. Y. Sharad Prasad, A. K. Damodaran (New Delhi: Oxford University Press: 2005), p. 207.
28. Iengar to Menon, 19 November 1948, File No. 40/21/49, Police II, Home Ministry Records, NAI.
29. Gopal Minute, 27 November 1948, File No. 40/21/49, Police II, Home Ministry Records, NAI.
30. 7 December 1948, Liddell Diaries, p. 204, KV/4/470, UKNA.
31. T. V. Rajeswar, *India: The Crucial Years* (Noida, UP: Harper Collins India, 2015), p. 166.
32. 7 December 1948, Liddell Diaries, p. 204, KV/4/470, UKNA.
33. 21 December 1948, Liddell Diaries, p. 209, KV/4/470, UKNA.
34. Andrew, *Defence of the Realm*, p. 443.
35. 6 July 1949, Liddell Diaries, p. 141, KV/4/471, UKNA.
36. Shattock to Rumbold 29 October 1948, FO 371/69738B, UKNA.
37. 'Information received orally from Mr. Sanjevi [sic]', June 1949', DO 231/3, UKNA.
38. 'Infiltration of Chinese Communists into India', February 1949, DO 231/3, UKNA.
39. Condon to Harrison, 12 May 1950, DO 133/132, UKNA.

276   NOTES TO PAGES 41–47

40. 23 May 1950, Liddell Diaries, p. 91, KV/4/472, UKNA.
41. Masterman to Symon, 2 March 1948, FCO 37/521, UKNA.
42. Nehru to Pandit, 5 May 1948, Vijaya Lakshmi Pandit Papers, Instalment, Subject File 54, NMML.
43. 'Communist and Left-Wing Movements in India', 27 January 1948, DO 133/128, UKNA.
44. Symon to Patrick, 14 February 1948, DO 133/128, UKNA.
45. Bhashyam Kasturi, *Intelligence Services: Analysis, Organisation and Functions* (New Delhi: Lancer Publishers, 1995), p. 27.
46. Nehru to Reddiar, 2 October 1948, *SWJN* 2nd series, vol. 7, ed. S. Gopal, (New Delhi: Oxford University Press, 1988), p. 274.
47. K. Shankaran Nair, *Inside IB and RAW: The Rolling Stone that Gathered Moss* (New Delhi: Manas Publications, 2013), p. 90.
48. Ibid., p. 95.
49. Y. D. Gundevia, *Outside the Archives* (New Delhi: Sangam Books, 1984), pp. 211–12.
50. 11 May 1951 & 3 August 1951, Liddell Diaries, p. 60 & p. 135, KV/4/473, UKNA.
51. 17 May 1951, Liddell Diaries, p. 73, KV/4/473, UKNA.
52. Neville Maxwell, *India's China War* (London: Cape, 1970), p. 335.
53. Nehru to Krishnamachari, 2 November 1962, T. T. Krishnamachari Papers, NMML.
54. Nair, *Inside IB and RAW*, p. 98.
55. Ibid., p. 8.
56. Mullik, 'Report on Tripura', 14 March 1951, File No. 21 (32)-PA/ 51, Ministry of States, Political Branch, NAI.
57. Nehru to Rajagopalachari, 11 September 1951, New Delhi, *SWJN* 2nd series, vol. 16, part 2, ed. S. Gopal, (New Delhi: Oxford University Press, 1994), pp. 469–70.
58. Nehru to Home Minister, 1 June 1951, *SWJN* 2nd series, vol. 16, part 1, ed. S. Gopal, (New Delhi: Oxford University Press, 1994), p. 636.
59. Nehru to Foreign Secretary, 29 September 1956, *SWJN*, vol. 35, ed. Mushirul Hasan, H. Y Sharad Prasad, A. K. Damodaran (New Delhi: Oxford University Press: 2005), pp. 525–36.
60. 13 June 1952, Liddell Diaries, p. 97, KV/4/474, UKNA.
61. James to Belcher, 31 August 1960, FO 371/152546, UKNA.
62. Andrew, *Defence of the Realm*, pp. 445–46.
63. Haksar to Gandhi, 19 June 1972, cited in Jairam Ramesh, *Intertwined Lives: P. N. Haksar and Indira Gandhi* (New Delhi: Simon & Schuster India, 2018), pp. 123–24.
64. Quoted in Andrew, *Defence of the Realm*, p. 446.
65. 29 December 1952, Liddell Diaries, pp. 190–93, KV/4/474, UKNA.
66. Bulganin and Khrushchev talks, New Delhi, 12 December 1955, *SWJN*, vol. 31, ed. H. Y. Sharad Prasad and A. K. Damodaran (New Delhi: Oxford University Press: 2002), pp. 339–44.
67. Nehru to Sampurnanand, 12 February 1956, *SWJN*, vol. 32, ed. H. Y. Sharad Prasad and A. K. Damodaran (New Delhi: Oxford University Press, 2003), pp. 264–65.
68. Grady to Secretary of State, 18 March 1948, *FRUS* 1948 vol. 5, pt. 1, pp. 497–98.

NOTES TO PAGES 47–53

69. 'Communist Penetration in India', 8 March, 1951, Department of State Office of Intelligence Research, Office of Strategic Services (OSS)-State Department Intelligence and Research Reports, NARA.
70. Bowles to Secretary of State, No. 3310, 10 February 1953, CIA-RDP65-00756R000600030099-5, CIA FOIA Electronic Reading Room, www.foia.cia.gov.
71. Christopher Andrew and Vasili Mitrokhin, *The Mitrokhin Archive II: The KGB and the Wider World* (London: Aleen Lane, 2005), pp. 9–10 and pp. 312–14.
72. Oleg Kalugin, *Spymaster: My Thirty-Two Years in Intelligence and Espionage against the West* (New York: 2009), p. 141.
73. Quoted in Andrew, *Defence of the Realm*, p. 446.
74. Rimington, *Open Secret*, p. 71.
75. Ibid., p. 72; p. 75.
76. Name Redacted to Costley White, 17 November 1951, DO 231/40, UKNA.
77. Macmillan to Eden, 19 October 1955, PREM 11/1582, UKNA.
78. Memorandum by the Chiefs of Staff, C.O.S. (55) 262, 12 October 1955, CO 1035/16, UKNA.
79. Costley-White to Scott, 24 July 1958, DO 231/110, UKNA.
80. Note for Record, 30 September 1959, CAB 301/126, UKNA; 'Intelligence Activities Concerning Commonwealth Countries (Note by 'C')', October 1959, CAB 301/126, UKNA.
81. Walker to Costley-White, 10 November 1959, DO 231/40, UKNA.
82. 'Intelligence and intelligence Targets', December 1959, CAB 301/126, UKNA.
83. Hollis to Burke Trend, 13 November 1965, CO 1035/171, UKNA.
84. Andrew, *Defence of the Realm*, p. 481.

3   India's Rasputin: V. K. Krishna Menon and the Spectre of Indian Communism

1. Clutterbuck to Garner, 21 October 1954, KV 2/2514-3, United Kingdom National Archives, Kew, London (UKNA).
2. Sarvepalli Gopal, *Jawaharlal Nehru: A Biography, vol.1, 1889–1947*, (London: Jonathan Cape, 1975), p. 202.
3. Arthur W. Hummel, Jr. Oral History, 13 July 1989, Foreign Affairs Oral History Project, Library of Congress, Washington, DC.
4. See K. C. Arora, *Indian Nationalist Movement in Britain,1930–1949* (New Delhi: South Asia Books, 1993); and Nicholas Owen, *British Left and India: Metropolitan Anti-Imperialism, 1885–1947* (Oxford: Oxford University Press, 2008).
5. 'Krishna Menon', 15 May 1945, MEPO 38/107, UKNA.
6. The post of Indian High Commissioner in London was created in 1920. Menon is, however, commonly referred to as India's 'first' High Commissioner to the United Kingdom. Joe Garner, *The Commonwealth Office* (London: Heinemann, 1978), p. 306.
7. Sillitoe to Chief Constable, County Durham, 24 February 1950, KV/2/2512-18, UKNA.
8. Liddell note, 18 June 1949, KV 2/2512-1, UKNA.
9. Attlee, Sir Stafford Cripps, his Chancellor of the Exchequer, and India's Last Viceroy, Lord Mountbatten, amongst others, argued that the retention of strong politico-military ties with India would secure Britain's status as a global power. Anita

278   NOTES TO PAGES 54–57

Inder Singh, *The Limits of British Influence: South Asia and the Anglo-American Relationship, 1947–1956* (London: St Martin's press, 1993), p. 47; John Darwin, *Britain and Decolonisation: The Retreat from Empire in the Post-War World* (London: Macmillan, 1988), pp. 152–53, pp. 302–3.

10. New Delhi to Sandys, 14 November 1962, DO 196/172, UKNA.

11. Norris minute, 22 August 1972, FCO 37/1096, UKNA.

12. K. C. Arora, *V. K. Menon: A Biography* (New Delhi: Sanchar Publishing House, 1998), p. 27.

13. 'Vengalil Krishnan Krishna MENON', 23 September 1932, KV/2/2509-11; 'K. Menon', 20 November 1932, MEPO 38/107, UKNA.

14. Scotland Yard report No. 122, 10 August 1938, File 295/1926 Pt2, P&J (J) 295/26, Jawaharlal Nehru, Indian Political Intelligence Files, British Library (BL JN).

15. 'V. K. Krishna Menon', 18 July 1939, KV/2/2509-7, UKNA.

16. 'V. K. Menon's views on the Political Situation in India', 1 February 1937, P&J (S) 79, Krishna Menon, Indian Political Intelligence Files, British Library (BL KM).

17. Owen, *British Left and India*, p. 240.

18. Suhash Chakravarty, *Crusader Extraordinary: Krishna Menon and the India League, 1932–1936* (New Delhi: India Research Press, 2006), p. 646.

19. Menon to Pollitt, 14 November 1939, Harry Pollitt Papers, CP/IND/POL, Correspondence, Misc., Communist Party of Great Britain Archive, Labour History Archives and Study Centre, Manchester (CPA LHASC), 'V. K. Krishna Menon', 10 June 1940, P&J (S) 1363, BL KM.

20. 'V. K. Krishna Menon', 10 June 1940, P&J (S) 1363, BL KM.

21. 'V. K. Krishna Menon', 1 February 1937, P&J (S) 79 1937, BL KM.

22. 'V. K. Krishna Menon', 29 November 1938, MEPO 38/107; 'V. K. Krishna Menon', 1 November 1939, KV/2/2509-7; IPI note on Menon, 13 June 1940 P&J (S) 1363/40, f.126, BL KM.

23. 'Menon's plan to celebrate Indian Independence Day', 17 January 1940, P&J (S) 138, BL KM; Owen, *British Left and India*, p. 257.

24. DVW to Hollis, 16 December 1939, KV/2/2509-6, UNKA.

25. 'National Agent's Opinion on the Parliamentary Candidature of Mr. Krishna Menon', 27 November 1940, ID/IND/1/13, Labour Party Archive, Labour History Archives and Study Centre, Manchester (LPA LHASC). Arora, *Menon*, pp. 38-40.

26. 'V. K. Krishna Menon', 10 June 1940, P&J (S) 1363, BL KM.

27. Menon to Masani, 13 April 1934, cited in Jairam Ramesh, *A Chequered Brilliance: The Many Lives of V. K. Krishna Menon* (Gurgaon, India: Penguin Random House India, 2019), p. 89.

28. Owen, *British Left and India*, p. 258.

29. 'COMMUNIST ACTIVITY', 11 April 1941, KV/2/2509-3, UKNA.

30. John Curry, *The Security Service, 1908–1945: The Official History* (London: PRO, 1999), p. 349.

31. 'V. K. Krishna Menon's Activities', 5 August 1941; 'Reactions to the release of NEHRU, AZAD, and others of the Indian Political Prisoners', 9 December 1941, P&J (S) 49/25, BL KM.

32. IPI note to Fulford, 18 May 1942, KV/2/2510-5, UKNA.

33. Hollis to Ball, 2 January 1942, KV/2/2510-8, UKNA.

34. Ball to Fulford, 30 May 1942, KV/2/2510-5, UKNA.

NOTES TO PAGES 58–62

35. Linlithgow to Amery, 30 November 1942, in Nicholas Mansergh, *Transfer of Power 1942–1947 (TOP)*, vol. III (London: HMSO, 1971), p. 325.
36. Amery to Robertson, 12 November 1942, POL (S) 2409 1942, BL, KM.
37. Kenneth O. Morgan, *Labour in Power, 1945–1951* (Oxford: Clarendon Press, 1984), pp. 193–94; R. J. Moore, *Escape from Empire: The Attlee Government and the Indian Problem* (Oxford: Clarendon Press, 1983), p. 338.
38. Gopal, *Nehru, 1889–1947*, p. 311.
39. Michael Brecher, *Nehru: A Political Biography* (London: Oxford University Press, 1961), p. 122.
40. Arora, *Menon*, p. 71.
41. Pethick Lawrence to Wavell, 1 November 1946, *TOP*, vol. VIII, pp. 858-9.
42. Pethick Lawrence to Attlee, 30 November 1946, *TOP*, vol. IX, p. 233.
43. 1 October 1946, Liddell Diaries, pp. 7-8, KV/4/468; 24 October 1946, Liddell Diaries, p. 34, KV/4/468, UKNA.
44. K. P. S. Menon to Nehru, 9 December 1946, Nehru Papers, Second Instalment, File 185, Nehru Museum and Memorial Library, New Delhi (hereafter NMML). See also, K.P.S. Menon, *Many Worlds Revisited* (Bombay: Bharatiya Vidya Bhavan, 1965).
45. Mountbatten to Listowel, 25 July 1947, *TOP*, vol. XII, p. 331.
46. Philip Ziegler, *Mountbatten: The Official Biography* (London: Guild Publishing, 1985), p. 354.
47. 'Report on the Last Viceroyalty, Part F, 25 July–15 August 1947', DO 142/364, UKNA; 'Minutes of Viceroy's Thirty Ninth staff meeting', 6 June 1947, *TOP*, vol. XI; Alan Campbell-Johnson, *Mission with Mountbatten* (London: Hamish Hamilton, 1985), p. 88.
48. Mountbatten to Attlee, 10 July 1947, PREM 8/545, UKNA.
49. Nehru to Attlee, 11 July 1947, PREM 8/545, UKNA.
50. Attlee to Nehru, 17 July 1947, *TOP*, vol. XII, pp. 214–5.
51. Mountbatten to Listowel, 25 July 1947, *TOP*, vol. XII, p. 331.
52. 31 July 1947, Liddell Diaries, p. 42, KV/4/469, UKNA.
53. 12 May 1948, Liddell Diaries, pp. 97-8, KV/4/470, UKNA.
54. 'Statement to be made by D. G. at J. I. C. meeting', 1 August 1947, KV/2/2512-20, UKNA.
55. Sarvepalli Gopal, *Jawaharlal Nehru: A Biography, 1947–1956*, vol. 2 (London: Jonathan Cape, 1979), pp. 140–41.
56. 'India's Relations with the Commonwealth', 10 November 1948, CAB 129/30, UKNA.
57. Cripps to Nehru, 28 April 1949, CAB 127/43, UKNA.
58. Gopal, *Nehru: 1947–1956*, pp. 47–48.
59. Noel-Baker to Nye, 15 March 1949, DO 121/71, UKNA.
60. Lawrence Black, '"The Bitterest Enemies of Communism": Labour Revisionists, Atlanticism and the Cold War', *Contemporary British History* (15, 3) (2001), p. 44.
61. Richard J. Aldrich, *The Hidden Hand: Britain, America and Cold War Secret Intelligence* (London: John Murray, 2001), p. 116.
62. 'Civil Service: Exclusion of Communists and Fascists from Certain Branches', 25 March 1948, CAB 128/12, UKNA.
63. 'Inner Circle', 19 January 1949, DO 142/363, UKNA.
64. Sanjeevi to Iengar, 6 January 1949, DIB D.O.2(i)/49, File No. 2/301, Private Papers of Sardar Patel, (PSP), National Archives of India (NAI).

NOTES TO PAGES 62–66

65. Sanjeevi to Iengar, 4 January 1949, DIB D.O.2/49, File No. 2/301, PSP, NAI.
66. Sanjeevi to Iengar, 6 January 1949, DIB D.O.2(i)/49, File No. 2/301, PSP, NAI.
67. Patel to Nehru, 6 January 1949, File No. 2/301, PSP, NAI.
68. Nehru to Patel, 6 January 1949, File No. 2/301, PSP, NAI; Nehru to Menon, 11 January 1949, cited in Ramesh, *Chequered Brilliance*, pp. 339–41.
69. Menon to Patel, 30 January 1949, File No. 2/301, PSP, NAI.
70. Menon to Nehru, 16–20 January 1949, cited in Ramesh, *Chequered Brilliance*, pp. 342–43.
71. Nehru to Menon, New Deli, 21 March 1949, *Selected Works of Jawaharlal Nehru (SWJN)* 2nd series, vol. 10, ed. S. Gopal, (New Delhi: Oxford University Press, 1990), pp. 23–28.
72. Liddell note, 31 May 1949, KV/2/2512-1, UKNA.
73. 'The India League', 30 May 1949, KV/2/2512-20, UKNA.
74. Liddell note, 31 May 1949, KV/2/2512-1, UKNA.
75. 31 May 1949, Liddell Diaries, pp. 115–16, KV/4/471, UKNA.
76. See Liddell Diaries, entries for 14 June 1949, p. 127; 27 June 1949, p. 135; 29 June 1949, p. 137; 21 and July 1949, p. 155, KV/4/471, UKNA.
77. 'The India League', 30 May 1949, KV/2/2512-20, UKNA.
78. Sillitoe to Chief Constable, County Durham, 24 February 1950, KV/2/2512-18, UKNA.
79. 22 July 1949, Liddell Diaries, p. 157, KV/4/471, UKNA.
80. 'V. K. Krishna Menon', 10 March 1950, KV/2/2512-18, UKNA.
81. Costley-White to Shaw, 14 March 1951, KV/2/2512-16, UKNA.
82. For an insight into MI5's opinion of Dutt, see Thurlow, 'British Communism and State Surveillance', pp. 1–21.
83. A note on a conversation between Sillitoe and Gordon Walker, 17 April 1951, KV/2/2512-15/16, UKNA.
84. Jairam Ramesh, *Intertwined Lives: P. N. Haksar and Indira Gandhi* (New Delhi: Simon & Schuster India, 2018), pp. 38–39.
85. U'ren note, 2 April 1951, KV/2/2512-2/3, UKNA.
86. Conversation between Sillitoe and Gordon Walker, 17 April 1951, KV/2/2512-15/16, UKNA.
87. Ibid.
88. Garner, *Commonwealth Office*, p. 299.
89. Clutterbuck, to Saville Garner, 21 October 1954, KV/2/2514-3, UKNA.
90. 'Statement made by D. G. of MI5 at JIC meeting, 1 August 1947', KV/2/2512-20., UKNA.
91. T. J. S. George, *Krishna Menon: A Biography* (London: Cape, 1964), p. 155.
92. Sir Percy Sillitoe, *Cloak without Dagger* (London: Cassell, 1955), p. 176; Andrew, *Defence of the Realm*, p. 333.
93. Conversation between Sillitoe and Attlee, 7 May 1951, KV/2/2512-13, UKNA.
94. 'The India League', 30 May 1949, KV/2/2512-20, UKNA.
95. Nye to Liesching, 28 December 1950, FO 371/92925, UKNA.
96. Kellar note, 2 July 1951 KV/2/2512-4, UKNA.
97. A. J. Kellar minute, 2 July 1951, KV/2/2512-4, UKNA.
98. Garner, *Commonwealth Office*, p. 310.
99. Shaw to SLO New Delhi, 2 May 1951, KV/2/2512-13; Shaw to Sillitoe, 25 April 1951, KV/2/2512-3, UKNA.
100. U'ren to SLO New Delhi, 28 May 1951, KV/2/2512-10, UKNA.

NOTES TO PAGES 66–69   281

101. U'ren note, 28 June 1951, KV/2/2512-4, UKNA.
102. Gopal, *Nehru, 1947–1956*, p. 142.
103. U'ren note, 2 April 1951, KV/2/2512-2/3; 'Inside Information', *Daily Graphic*, 3 April 1951, KV/2/2512-16; Conversation between Sillitoe and Gordon Walker, 17 April 1951, KV/2/2512-15/16, UKNA.
104. Kellar note, 2 July 1951, KV/2/2512-4, UKNA.
105. Nye to Liesching, 8 November 1951, KV/2/2513-10, UKNA.
106. Liesching to Nye, 1 January 1952, KV/2/2513-10, UKNA.
107. Patrick Gordon Walker, *Political Diaries, 1932–1971* (London: The Historians Press, 1991), p. 241.
108. Spooner note, 24 January 1951, KV/2/2512-16, UKNA; Judith M. Brown, *Nehru: A Political Life* (New Haven, CT: Yale University Press, 2003), p. 248.
109. Nye to Liesching, 8 November 1951, KV/2/2513-10, UKNA.
110. M. O. Mathai, *Reminiscences of the Nehru Age* (New Delhi: Vikas Publishing, 1978), p. 165.
111. U'ren note, 11 December 1951, KV/2/2513-10, UKNA.
112. Nye to Liesching, 8 November 1951, KV/2/2513-10, UKNA.
113. Gopal, *Nehru, 1947–1956*, pp. 141-43.
114. Nye to Liesching, 8 November 1951, KV/2/2513-10, UKNA.
115. Liesching to Nye, 1 January 1952, KV/2/2513-10, UKNA.
116. U'ren note, 2 April 1951, KV/2/2512-2/3, UKNA.
117. Saville Garner monthly letter No. 16, 8 July 1952, DO 133/56, UKNA; Gopal, *Nehru, 1947–1956*, p. 144; Arora, *Menon*, p. 111.
118. 'Mr. Kher in London', 14 July 1952, *Times*, p. 6.
119. Spooner note, 8 July 1952, KV/2/2513-8; 'The Present Position and Views of Krishna Menon', 19 July 1952, KV/2/2513-5, UKNA.
120. U'ren to Costley-White, 29 May 1953, KV/2/2514-8; Saville Garner to Combie, 9 February 1954, DO 35/9014, UKNA.
121. Gopal, *Nehru, 1947–1956*, p. 144.
122. 'Current Intelligence Weekly Summary', 16 June 1955, CIA-RDP79 -0927A000500110001-6, CIA Records Search Tool, USNA.
123. Harold R. Issacs, *Scratches On Our Minds: America Images of China and India* (New York: John Day Company, 1958), pp. 313-4.
124. Garner to Clutterbuck, 11 October 1954, KV 2/2514-5; Roberts to Garner, 11 October 1954, FO 371/112194, UKNA.
125. Roberts to Garner, 11 October 1954, FO 371/112194, UKNA.
126. Kurt Stiegler, 'Communism and "Colonial Evolution": John Foster Dulles' Vision of India and Pakistan', *Journal of South Asian and Middle Eastern Studies*, 12 (Winter 1991), pp. 74–75.
127. US Embassy to Curry, 5 August 1947, KV/2/2511-2; MI5 to US Embassy, 15 August 1947, KV/2/2511-2, UKNA.
128. SLO Washington to DG MI5, 7 December 1954, KV/2/2514-2; DG to SLO Washington, 9 December 1954, KV/2/2514-2, UKNA.
129. 198th Meeting of the National Security Council, Thursday 20 May 1954, *Foreign Relations of the United States (FRUS), 1952–54, Volume XII* (USGPO: Washington, DC, 1984), p. 497; Allen to State Department, 31 March 1954, *FRUS, 1952–1954, Volume XIII* (USGPO: Washington, DC, 1982), pp. 1193–94.
130. Sarvepalli Gopal, *Jawaharlal Nehru: A Biography, vol. 3, 1956–1964* (London, 1984), p. 46.

282 NOTES TO PAGES 69–73

131. Mathai, *Nehru Age*, p. 55.
132. 'Dulles-Menon Talks', 13 July 1955, CIA-RDP79R00904A000200030007-9, CREST, NARA; Extract from *Economist*, 5 July 1955, FO 371/115054, UKNA.
133. *New York Times*, 7 April 1957, p. 216.
134. John Kenneth Galbraith, *A Life in Our Times*, (Boston: Houghton Mifflin, 1981), p. 407.
135. Phillips Talbot Oral History, 27 July 1965, Oral Histories, John F. Kennedy Library (JFKL).
136. *New York Times*, 22 November 1961, p. 35.
137. Gore-Booth to Sandys, 29 December 1961, PREM 11/3837, UKNA.
138. Mountbatten to Gore-Booth, 20 December 1961 MSS.Gorebooth 85, Paul Gore-Booth Papers, Bodleian Library, Oxford.
139. *Time*, 29 December 1961; Gore-Booth to Sandys, 29 December 1961, PREM 11/3837, UKNA.
140. CIA Report, 'Afterthoughts', 16 January 1962, Box 106 A, National Security File, JFKL.
141. Nehru to Menon, 12 January 1957, cited in Ramesh, *Chequered Brilliance*, p. 473.
142. Transcript of Moscow Radio Peace and Progress Broadcast to India, 11 February 1971, Box 10, Folder Miscellaneous Items, RG 84, Ambassador Keating Subject Files, 1968–1972, USNA.
143. Ibid. See also, John D. Smith. *I Was a CIA Agent in India* (New Delhi: New Age Printing Press, 1967); Pauly V. Parakal. *CIA Dagger against India* (New Delhi: New Age Press, 1973).
144. Nehru to Ramakrishna Bajaj, 21 November 1961, *SWJN Volume 72*, ed. Madhavan K. Palat (New Delhi: Oxford University Press, 2017), pp. 202–3; Ramakrishna Bajaj to Nehru, 26 December 1961, *SWJN Volume 73*, ed. Madhavan K. Palat (New Delhi: Oxford University Press, 2017), pp. 657–58.
145. *Time*, 24 August 1962.
146. Christopher Andrew and Vasili Mitrokhin, *The Mitrokhin Archive II: The KGB and the Wider World*, (London: Penguin, 2006), pp. 314–15.
147. Komer to McGeorge Bundy, 16 July 1962, Box 441, National Security File, JFKL.
148. New Delhi to CRO, 3 July 1962, DO 133/151, USNA.
149. Gore-Booth to Saville Garner, 3 February 1962, DO 196/209, UKNA.
150. Belcher to Sandys, 25 August 1962, DO 196/127, UKNA.
151. Gore-Booth to Saville Garner, 26 October 1962, DO 196/75, UKNA
152. CRO to Delhi and Karachi, 15 November 1962, FO 371/164929, UKNA; Roger Hilsman, To Move a *Nation: The Politics of Foreign Policy in the Administration of John F. Kennedy* (New York: Doubleday, 1967), pp. 331–32; Chester Bowles, *Promises to Keep: My Years in Public Life, 1941–1969*, (New York: HarperCollins, 1971), p. 437; Entry for 23 October 1962, John Kenneth Galbraith, *Ambassador's Journal: A Personal Account of the Kennedy Years* (London: Hamish Hamilton, 1969), pp. 428–31.
153. Entry for 23 October 1962, Galbraith, *Ambassador's*, p. 431; Galbraith to Rusk, 21 October 1962, Box 107A, National Security File, JFKL.
154. Galbraith to Kennedy, 25 October 1962, NSF, Countries Series, India, General, 9/27/62-10/5/62, JFKL.
155. B. K. Nehru Meeting, 26 October 1962, Meetings Recordings, Tape No. 40, JFKL.
156. Kaysen to Galbraith, 27 October 1962, NSF, Countries Series, India, Ambassador Galbraith, Special File, JFKL.

NOTES TO PAGES 73–77   283

157. New Delhi to Sandys, 14 November 1962, DO 196/172, UKNA.
158. Ormsby Gore to FO, No. 2717, 29 October 1962, DO 196/166, UKNA.
159. *New York Times*, 1 November 1962, p. 30.
160. Gore-Booth to Saville Garner, 7 November 1962, DO 196/75, UKNA.
161. Sir Paul Gore-Booth, *With Great Truth and Respect* (London: Constable, 1974), p. 295; Gopal, Nehru: 1956–1964, p. 13; Steven Hoffmann, *India and the China Crisis*, (Berkeley: University of California Press, 1990), pp. 203–6.
162. G. Parthasarathi, (ed.), *Jawaharlal Nehru: Letters to Chief Ministers, vol. 5, 1958–1964* (London, 1989), p. 571; 58th meeting of the U.S./Australian/British/ Canadian co-ordinating group, 19 December 1963, DO 164/72, UKNA.
163. Delhi to CRO, 19 August 1963, DO 196/154, UKNA; Rusk to Karachi, Washington, 28 August 1963, *FRUS, 1961–1963*, Volume XIX, Document #326 (Washington, DC: USGPO, 1996).
164. Michael Brecher, *India and World Politics: Krishna Menon's View of the World* (London: Oxford University Press, 1968), p. 289.
165. Saville Garner to Clutterbuck, 11 October 1954, KV/2/2514-5; Roberts to Saville Garner, 11 October 1954, FO 371/112194, UKNA.
166. Costley-White to Kitchin, 19 October 1954, KV/2/2514-5; Kitchin note, 25 October 1954, KV/2/2514-1, UKNA.
167. Snelling to Saville Garner, 25 June 1962, DO 189/371, UKNA.
168. Eric Norris minute, 22 August 1972, FCO 37/1096, UKNA.
169. 'The President's Daily Brief', 8 March 1967, DOC_0005968824, CIA FOIA Electronic Reading Room, www.foia.cia.gov.
170. Andrew and Mitrokhin, *Mitrokhin Archive II*, pp. 314–22; and Arthur Stein, *India and the Soviet Union: The Nehru Era* (Chicago: University of Chicago Press, 1969), p. 237.
171. Washington Embassy Fortnightly Political Report, 1–15 May 1962, MEA Records, WWII/101(S)/61, NAI.

4   Quiet Americans: The CIA and the Onset of the Cold War in South Asia

1. Howard Imbrey, 21 June 2001, Foreign Affairs Oral History Collection, Library of Congress (hereafter FAOHC).
2. Robert Baer, *See No Evil: The True Story of a Ground Soldier in the CIA's War on Terrorism* (London: Penguin Random House, 2002), pp. 67–70.
3. Imbrey, FAOHC.
4. Ibid.
5. One of the first books to document CIA activity was published in India, L. Natarajan's, *American Shadow over India* (Bombay: People's Publishing House, 1952). From the 1960s, communist publishing houses in the subcontinent joined in uncovering alleged Agency misdeeds. See, John D. Smith, *I Was a CIA Agent in India* (New Delhi: New Age Printing Press, 1967); Pauly V. Parakal, *CIA Dagger against India* (New Delhi: New Age Press, 1973); and Kunhanandan Nair, *Devil and His Dart: How the CIA is Plotting in the Third World* (New Delhi: Sterling Publishers, 1986). The CIA's operations in India remain largely absent from intelligence literature. See, for example, Victor Marchetti and John D. Marks, *The CIA and the Cult of Intelligence*

284   NOTES TO PAGES 77–79

(London: Jonathan Cape, 1974); John Ranelagh, *The Agency: The Rise and Decline of the CIA* (London: Weidenfeld & Nicolson, 1986); Rhodri Jeffreys-Jones, *The CIA and American Democracy* (London: Yale University Press, 1998); or, Tim Weiner, *Legacy of Ashes: The History of the CIA*, (London: Allen Lane, 2007). Exceptions include Kenneth Conboy and James Morrison. *The CIA's Secret War in Tibet* (Lawrence: University of Kansas Press, 2002). The memoirs of former CIA Directors mostly omit reference to India. See, Richard Helms, *A Look Over My Shoulder: A Life in the Central Intelligence Agency* (New York: Random House, 2003); and George Tenet, *At the Center of the Storm: My Years at the CIA*, (London: Harper Press, 2007). Some senior CIA officers have reflected on India in print. See, Duane R. Clarridge, *A Spy for All Seasons: My Life in the CIA* (New York: Scribner, 1997); and Baer, *See No Evil*. Accounts of ambassadorial tours in the subcontinent also provide glimpses of CIA activity. See, John Kenneth Galbraith, *Ambassador's Journal: A Personal Account of the Kennedy Years*, (Boston: Houghton Mifflin, 1969), and *A Life in Our Times: Memoirs* (London: Andre Deutsch, 1981); *Chester Bowles, Promises to Keep: My Years in Public Life, 1941–1969* (New York: Harper and Row, 1971); and Daniel Patrick Moynihan, *A Dangerous Place* (Boston: Little Brown, 1978).

6. Richard J. Aldrich, 'American Intelligence and the British Raj: The OSS, the SSU and India, 1942–1947', *Intelligence and National Security*, 13: 1, (Spring 1998), pp. 132–64.

7. 'O.S.S. Organization in India', 8 April 1943, CAB 122/1589, United Kingdom National Archives, Kew, London (UKNA).

8. Elizabeth P. MacDonald, *Undercover Girl* (New York: Macmillan, 1947), p. 18.

9. 'American Penetration in INDIA', 3 May 1943, CAB 122/1589, UKNA; India Office to Wavell, No. 226, 14 May 1943, CAB 122/1589, UKNA.

10. Cawthorn to Wavell, 'American Intelligence and Cognate Activities in India', 17 May 1943, CAB 122/1589, UKNA; Aldrich, '*American Intelligence*', pp. 132–64.

11. Deane to Donovan, 13 September 1943, CIA-RDP13X00001R000100290006-7, CIA FOIA.

12. US Central Intelligence Agency, NIE-23: 'India's Position in East-West Conflict', 4 September 1951, *FRUS*, 6:2174-5, p. 2179.

13. 'Communist Activities in India', 3 January 1950, CIA-RDP82-00457R004000330003-2, CIA FOIA.

14. Sherman Kent to Deputy Director/Intelligence, 'Situation in India', 17 December 1953, CREST, CIA-RDP79R00904A000100040004.

15. John D. Jernegan, Address to American Academy of Political and Social Science, Philadelphia, 3 April 1954, DL/10345/7, FO 371/112212, UKNA.

16. Berry to Matthews, 8 February 1952, *FRUS 1952–54*, vol. 11, part 2, p. 1634.

17. Donovan, 'Biographical document on Sanjeevi', 16 May 1949, RG59, Lot file 57D373, Box 2, Folder Memorandum to the Secretary 1949, USNA.

18. Satterthwaite to Webb, 15 June 1949, RG59, Lot file 57D373, Box 2, Folder Memorandum to the Secretary 1949, USNA.

19. Nehru to Pandit, 20 May 1949, Vijaya Lakshmi Pandit Papers (hereafter VLPP), Subject File 60, Nehru Museum and Memorial Library New Delhi (hereafter NMML); Nehru to Pandit, June 22, 1949, VLPP, Subject File 60, NMML; Iengar to Sanjeevi, 25 June 1949, File No. 40/21/49, Police II, Home Ministry Records, National Archives of India (hereafter NAI).

NOTES TO PAGES 80–83

20. 'Deputation of Mr T. G. Sanjeevi, I. B. Director', 12 May 1949, File No. 40/21/49, Police II, Home Ministry Records, NAI.
21. Bhashyam Kastur, *Intelligence Services: Analysis, Organisation and Functions* (New Delhi: Lancer Publishers, 1995), p. 27.
22. Satterthwaite to Webb, 15 June 1949, RG 59, Lot file 57D373, Box 2, Folder Memorandum to the Secretary 1949, USNA.
23. Parsons to Sparks, 24 May 1949, Box 1, Folder 26, Georgetown University Library Special Collections Research Center, Washington, DC.
24. Henderson to Sparks, 17 April 1950, and Klise to Henderson, 18 April 1950, RG59, Lot file 57D373, Box 2, Folder Official informal Jan–May 1950, USNA.
25. Sparks to Henderson, 8 July 1949, RG59, Lot file 57D373, Box 2, Folder Official Informal July 1949, USNA.
26. Henderson to Sparks, 17 April 1950, and Klise to Henderson, 18 April 1950, RG59, Lot file 57D373, Box 2, Folder Official informal Jan–May 1950, USNA.
27. Satterthwaite to Webb, 15 June 1949, RG59, Lot file 57D373, Box 2, Folder Memorandum to the Secretary 1949, USNA. Periodic attempts were subsequently made by the FBI to establish a liaison presence in India. These fell on fallow ground until 2000. In the autumn of 1971, for example, the US Embassy in New Delhi rejected a proposal from the FBI Director to establish a permanent presence in India. Kenneth Keating noted at the time that, 'All-in -all, I believe we [the US Embassy] presently have the facilities and contacts to respond positively and productively to FBI requests for investigations in India and Nepal.' See, Stone to Secretary of State, 'FBI Proposal to Establish Additional Liaison', No, 16789, 28 October 1971, Box 5, Folder FBI, RG 84, Ambassador Keating Subject Files, 1968–1972, USNA.
28. Satterthwaite to Webb, 15 June 1949, RG59, Lot file 57D373, Box 2, Folder Memorandum to the Secretary 1949, USNA.
29. Klise to Henderson, 18 April 1950, RG59, Lot file 57D373, Box 2, Folder Official informal Jan–May 1950, USNA.
30. Christopher Andrew. *The Defence of the Realm: The Authorized History of MI5* (London: Allen Lane, 2009), pp. 445–46.
31. Nehru to Foreign Secretary, 4 February 1951, File No. 41-6/51-AMS, MEA, INA.
32. Nehru to Cabinet Secretary, 9 October 1956, *Selected Works of Jawaharlal Nehru* (hereafter *SWJN*), vol. 35 (New Delhi: Oxford University Press, 2005), p. 207.
33. Nehru speech to heads of Indian Missions in Europe, Salzburg, Austria, 28–30 June 1955, *SWJN*, vol. 29 (New Delhi: Oxford University Press, 2001), p. 257. See also, Subimal Dutt, *With Nehru in the Foreign Office* (Calcutta: Minerva Associates, 1977) p. 241.
34. Nehru speech to heads of Indian Missions in Europe, Salzburg, Austria, 28–30 June 1955, *SWJN*, vol. 29 (New Delhi: Oxford University Press: 2001), p. 257.
35. Nehru to Shriman Narayan, 24 May 1955, New Delhi, *SWJN*, vol. 28 (New Delhi: Oxford University Press, 2001), pp. 284–86, f. 10.
36. Sahay to Radhakrishnan, 17 February and 31 October 1966, Radhakrishnan Papers, NMML, quoted in Sarvepalli Gopal, *Jawaharlal Nehru: A Biography, Vol. 3, 1956–1964* (London: Jonathan Cape, 1984), p. 122.
37. Gopal, *Nehru, 1956–1964*, p. 122. A biographer of Nehru's, who received privileged access to his private papers, found no evidence linking Mathai to the CIA. See, Judith M. Brown, *Nehru: A Political Life* (London: Yale University Press, 2003), pp. 382–83. While maintaining his innocence, Mathai admitted to circumventing Indian

286   NOTES TO PAGES 83–88

government security protocols by keeping, 'a spare copy of everything Nehru wrote and also copies of important telegrams and documents'. M. O. Mathai, *Reminiscences of the Nehru Age*, (New Delhi: Vikas Publishing House 1978), p. 249.

38. Mary Olmsted, 8 April 1992, FAOHC.

39. Henderson to Field, 7 June 1978, Loy W. Henderson Papers (hereafter LWHP), Library of Congress, Manuscripts Division, Box 8, India Misc folder.

40. Henderson memorandum 'Jawaharlal Nehru', undated, Box 8, India Misc folder, LWHP.

41. Nehru/Henderson talk, New Delhi, 15 September 1951, *SWJN*, vol. 16 (New Delhi: Oxford University Press, 1994), p. 627.

42. Nehru to Birla, 6 February 1956, *SWJN*, vol. 32 (New Delhi: Oxford University Press, 2003), pp. 481–82; Interview with Attwood, *Look* correspondent, New Delhi, 31 August 1954, *SWJN*, vol. 26, (New Delhi: Oxford University Press, 2000), pp. 310–16.

43. Nehru to Mountbatten, New Delhi, 30 July 1951, *SWJN*, vol. 16 (New Delhi: Oxford University Press, 1994), pp. 336–41.

44. Nehru to Pillai and Dutt, 27 May 1960, *SWJN*, vol. 61 (New Delhi: Oxford University Press, 2015), pp. 625–26.

45. Nehru to R. K. Nehru, 27 May 1960, *SWJN*, vol. 61 (New Delhi: Oxford University Press, 2015), pp. 482–83.

46. Nehru to J. K. Bhonsle, 13 May 1961, *SWJN*, vol. 69 (New Delhi: Oxford University Press, 2016), pp. 349–40.

47. Fred J. Cook, 'The CIA', *The Nation*, 192,25 (26 June 1961), pp. 439–572.

48. Cook, 'The CIA', pp. 439–572.

49. Nehru to M. J. Desai, 17 July 1961, *SWJN*, vol. 70 (New Delhi: Oxford University Press, 2017), p. 589.

50. Nehru to Tyabji, 'Intelligence Policy', 26 February 1962, *SWJN* vol. 75, ed. Madhavan K. Palat (New Delhi: Oxford University Press, 2018), pp. 507–8.

51. National Security Council Report 5701, *FRUS* 1955–1957 vol. 8, 10 January 1957, pp. 29–43.

52. 'Indian Financial Problems', 4 June 1957, 891.00/6-457, USNA; Bunker to John Foster Dulles, 19 November 1957, 791.5 MSP/11-1957, USNA.

53. Rosenthal to Salisbury, undated, Box 159, CIA Series 1965–66, Raw Data, Harrison Salisbury Papers, Butler Library, Columbia University (hereafter HSP).

54. Albert Lakeland Jr., 27 July 1992, FAOHC.

55. Eugene Rosenfeld, 28 November 1989, FAOHC.

56. Rosenthal to Salisbury, undated, Box 159 CIA Series 1965–66 Raw Data, HSP.

57. James Strodes, *Allen Dulles: Master of Spies* (Washington DC: Regnery Publishing, 1999), pp. 11–12, pp. 35–38; See also, Stephen Kinzer, *The Brothers: John Foster Dulles, Allen Dulles and Their Secret World War* (New York: St. Martin's Griffin, 2013), p. 8, p. 16.

58. Leonard Mosley, *Dulles: A Biography of Eleanor, Allen, and John Foster Dulles and their Family Network* (London: Hodder and Stoughton, 1978), p. 34.

59. Kinzer, *The Brothers*, pp. 19–20.

60. Strodes, *Master of Spies*, p. 489.

61. 'What's Behind Allen Dulles' Mystery Mission to India? Let Asia Beware of Us Intelligence agency!' *Blitz*, 29 September 1956.

62. 'Delhi Spy Scandal', *Blitz*, 29 September 1956.

NOTES TO PAGES 88–93

63. Radio Moscow, 11 January 1961, Folder Central Intelligence Agency vol. II [1 of 2], Oct 1965–Feb 1966, NSF, LBJL.
64. 'India: CIA planned assassination of Nehru, 10 January 1966, *Komsomolskaya Pravda*', Folder Central Intelligence Agency Vol. II [1 of 2], Oct 1965–Feb 1966, NSF, LBJL.
65. MacDonald to Home, 'India: General Elections, 1957', 30 April 1957, DO 35/3167, UKNA.
66. Indian Embassy, Washington to Foreign Secretary, 'Fortnightly Political Report for the period February 1–15, 1957', File 48-1-AMS-57, Americas Division, MEA, NAI.
67. Ramsey to State Department, no. 347, 1 May 1957, RG59, Lot 57D373, Box 8, Folder Kerala Aug–Dec 1957, USNA.
68. MacDonald to Macmillan, 'Communism in Kerala', 28 September 1957, DO 201/8, UKNA.
69. Simons to Adams, 21 November 1957, RG59, Lot file 57D373, Box 8, Folder Kerala Aug–Dec 1957, USNA.
70. See, Ellsworth Bunker, Oral History, 18 June and 17 July 1979, Butler Library, Columbia University, New York, pp. 67–68. Other US officials, such as David S. Burgess, have corroborated Bunker's revelation. See, David. S. Burgess, 7 April 1991, FAOHC. Daniel Patrick Moynihan, US Ambassador to India in the early 1970s, also confirmed that the CIA was used to fund Congress Party campaigns against the CPI in Kerala and West Bengal. See, Moynihan, *Dangerous Place*, p. 41.
71. Nehru to Home Minister, 19 June 1956, *SWJN*, vol. 33 (New Delhi: Oxford University Press, 2005), pp. 251–52.
72. Ellsworth Bunker, Oral History, 18 June and 17 July 1979, Butler Library, Columbia University, New York, pp. 67–68.
73. Nehru to Secretary General and Foreign Secretary, 28 April 1957, *SWJN*, vol. 37 (New Delhi: Oxford University Press, 2006), p. 339.
74. Fulbright to Allen Dulles, 18 February 1959, CIA-RDP80R01731R000100070040-0, CIA FOIA, www.foia.cia.gov.
75. Allen Dulles to Fulbright, 27 February 1959, CIA-RDP80R01731R000100070040-0, CIA FOIA, www.foia.cia.gov.
76. Allen Dulles, 'Resume of OCB Luncheon Meeting, 3 February 1960', 10 February 1960, CIA-RDP80B01676R002700020051-7, CIA FOIA, www.foia.cia.gov.
77. 'Special Report: Exploitation of Kerala Elections', OCB,17 February 1960, *FRUS*, 1958–1960, vol. XV, document 254, https://history.state.gov/historicaldocuments/frus1958-60v15/d254
78. David S. Burgess, 7 April 1991, FAOHC.
79. Komer to Jessup, 20 March 1964, NSF, Robert W. Komer Files, Box 23, Folder 1 India – December 1963–1964 [1 of 4], LBJL.
80. Clarridge, *Spy for All Seasons*, pp. 91–92.
81. MacDonald to CRO, 'India: Communist Rule in Kerala', 24 October 1959, DO 201/10, UKNA.
82. The 'Panch Sheel' or 'Five Principles of Peaceful Co-existence' were incorporated into the 1954 Sino-Indian Treaty on Trade and Intercourse with Tibet. These encompassed commitments to mutual non-aggression and respect for national sovereignty. The slogan and policy of *Hindee Chinee bhai-bhai*, or Indian-Chinese

288 NOTES TO PAGES 93–98

brotherhood, was popularised in India following the Treaty. See, A. Appadorai (ed.), *Select Documents on India's Foreign Policy and Relations, 1947–1972, vol. 1* (New Delhi: Oxford University Press, 1982), pp. 459–66.

83. William J. Barnds, *India, Pakistan and the Great Powers* (London: Pall Mall Press, 1972), p. 143; Dennis Kux, *India and the United States: Estranged Democracies, 1941–1991* (Washington DC: National Defense University Press, 1993), pp. 161–62.

84. 'Chinese Intentions against India', JIC report, 22 November 1962, CAB 158/47, UKNA. See also, Gopal, *Nehru 1956–1964*, p. 81 and p. 89, and Robert J. McMahon, 'U.S. Policy toward South Asia and Tibet during the Early Cold War', *Journal of Cold War Studies*, 8, 3 (Summer 2006), p. 141. For a Chinese perspective on Sino-Indian relations, see Chen Jian, *Mao's China and the Cold War* (Chapel Hill: University of North Carolina Press, 2001), pp. 78–79.

85. 'Tibet', J. I. C. (49) 131st Meeting, 16 December 1949, CAB 159/6 Part 2, UKNA.

86. Nehru to Pillai, 18 June 1954, 'Prime Minister's Secretariat', Top Secret, Nehru for Pillai, R. K. Nehru, 'Tibet – escape of the Dalai Lama', Subject File No. 6, Subimal Dutt Papers, NMML.

87. See, Conboy and Morrison, *Secret War in Tibet*; and John Kenneth Knaus, *Orphans of the Cold War: America and the Tibetan Struggle for Survival* (New York: Public Affairs, 1999).

88. Nehru to Mountbatten, 18 September 1954, New Delhi, *SWJN*, vol. 26 (New Delhi: Oxford University Press, 2000), pp. 221–23.

89. Nehru to Pillai, 18 June 1954, 'Tibet – escape of the Dalai Lama', Subject File No. 6, Subimal Dutt Papers, NMML.

90. Nehru talks with Chou Enlai, 20 April 1960, New Delhi, P. N. Haksar Papers, III Instalment, Subject File 24; and, Conversation between R. K. Nehru and Chou Enlai, 21 April 1960, P. N. Haksar Papers, III Instalment, Subject File 26, NMML.

91. Nehru talks with Chou Enlai, 25 April 1960, New Delhi, P. N. Haksar Papers, III Instalment, Subject File 24, NMML.

92. John Kenneth Galbraith, *The Affluent Society* (London: Penguin Books, 1958), and *The Liberal Hour* (London: Hamish Hamilton, 1960).

93. Richard Parker, *John Kenneth Galbraith: His Life, His Politics, His Economics* (New York: Farrar, Straus and Giroux, 2005), pp. 324–25.

94. Arthur M. Schlesinger Jr., *A Thousand Days: John F. Kennedy in the White House* (Cambridge, MA: Riverside Press, 1965), p. 523.

95. Hagerty to Schaffer, 26 September 1967, RG 59, Box 4, India 1967, M. C. Chagla, USNA.

96. Galbraith, *Ambassador's Journal*, 29 March 1961, Washington, p. 51.

97. Galbraith, *Life in Our Times*, pp. 394–96.

98. Clarridge, *Spy for All Seasons*, p. 84.

99. 'The Year of the Spy (in a Manner of Speaking)', *New York Times*, 5 January 1986, p. E19.

100. Galbraith, *Life in Our Times*, p. 396.

101. Ibid., p. 396.

102. Jeffreys-Jones, *CIA and American Democracy*, p. 128. See also, Marchetti and Marks, *Cult of Intelligence*, p. 340.

103. Knaus, Orphans of the Cold War, pp. 146–47.

NOTES TO PAGES 98–101 289

104. Galbraith to Harriman, Ball and McGhee, 30 November 1961, Box 463, Folder J. K. Galbraith 1 of 2, Averell Harriman Papers, Manuscript Division, Library of Congress, Washington DC.
105. Parker, *John Kenneth Galbraith*, p. 354. See also, Steven B. Hoffman, 'Rethinking the Linkage between. Tibet and the China-India Border Conflict: A Realist Approach', *Journal of Cold War Studies* 8 (Summer 2006), pp. 179–81; Prem Mahadevan, 'The Failure of Indian Intelligence in the Sino- Indian Conflict', *Journal of Intelligence History*, 8:1 (2008), pp. 11–12.
106. Joseph Greene, JR., 12 March 1993, FAOHC,
107. Mary Olmsted, 8 April 1992, FAOHC.
108. Clarridge, *Spy for All Seasons*, p. 78.
109. *Times*, 23 October 1962, p. 10; and *FRUS, 1961–1963, vol. XIX* (Washington, DC: Government Printing Office, 1996), Galbraith to State Department, 18 October 1962, pp. 346–47.
110. Gore-Booth to Saville Garner, 26 October 1962, DO 196/75, UKNA; Neville Maxwell, *India's China War* (London: Penguin Books, 1972), p. 414; and, CIA Daily Intelligence Bulletin, 28 October 1962, USNA.
111. Gopal, *Nehru, 1956–1964*, p. 223.
112. Gore-Booth to Saville Garner, 26 October 1962, DO 196/75, UKNA.

5 Confronting China: The Sino-Indian War and Collaborative Covert Action

1. D. K. Palit, *War in High Himalaya: The Indian Army in Crisis, 1962* (London: Hurst, 1991), p. 240; Neville Maxwell, *India's China War* (London: Cape, 1970), pp. 388–89
2. S. N. Prasad et al (eds.), *History of the Conflict with China, 1962* (New Delhi: History Division, Ministry of Defence, 1992), p. 372. Available through Parallel History Project on Cooperative Security, Zurich, www.php.isn.ethz.ch/collections/coll_india/SecretHistory.cfm?navinfo=96318
3. *Times*, 22 October 1962, p. 10.
4. *Times*, 23 October 1962, p. 10.
5. Prasad, *Conflict with China*, p. 386; Gore-Booth to Saville Garner, 26 October 1962, DO 196/75, UKNA.
6. Maxwell, *India's China War,* p. 392 and p. 411.
7. Gore-Booth to Saville Garner, 26 October 1962, DO 196/75, UKNA.
8. See Maxwell's, *India's China War;* Yaccov Vertzberger, 'India's Border Conflict with China: A Perceptual Analysis', *Journal of Contemporary History*, 17, 4, (October 1982), pp. 607–31; Michael Brecher, 'Non-Alignment Under Stress: The West and the India-China Border War', *Pacific Affairs*, 52, 4 (Winter 1979–80), pp. 612–30; and John Garver, *Protracted Contest: Sino-Indian Rivalry in the Twentieth Century* (Seattle: University of Washington Press, 2001), pp. 58–62.
9. Yaacov Vertzberger, 'Bureaucratic-Organizational Politics and Information Processing in a Developing State', *International Studies Quarterly* 28, 1 (March 1984), p. 76.
10. Mullik dismissed criticism of the IB's 'alleged failure of intelligence' as ill-informed. B. N. Mullik, *My Years with Nehru: The Chinese Betrayal* (Bombay: Allied Publishers, 1971), p. 497. Other senior IB officers rejected Mullik's defence and

290 NOTES TO PAGES 102–6

argued that the spy chief had 'let down' Nehru by furnishing India's premier with 'erroneous assessment[s] of Chinese military strength, claims and consequent designs on our border territories in 1961 and 1962'. K. Sankaran Nair, *Inside IB and RAW: The Rolling Stone that Gathered Moss* (New Delhi: Manas Publications, 2013), p. 98.

11. Y. D. Gundevia, *Outside the Archives* (New Delhi: Sangam Books, 1984), pp. 211–12; Prem Mahadevan, 'The Failure of Indian Intelligence in the Sino-Indian Conflict', *Journal of Intelligence History*, 8, 1 (2008), p. 23.

12. Manoj Shrivastava, *Re-Energising Indian Intelligence* (New Delhi: Vij Books, 2013), p. 55; K. S. Subramanian, *Political Violence and the Police in India* (New Delhi: Sage, 2007), pp. 84–86.

13. Nehru to Bhonsle, 'Intelligence is Satisfactory', 13 May 1961, SWJN vol. 69, ed. Madhavan K. Palat (New Delhi: Oxford University Press, 2016), pp. 349–40.

14. Whitehead (Calcutta) to Smedly, undated, c. February 1960, DO 133/148, UKNA.

15. Srinath Raghavan, *War and Peace in Modern India: A Strategic History of the Nehru Years* (New Delhi: Permanent Black, 2009), pp. 91–97.

16. Embassy of India, Washington to Foreign Secretary, MEA, 'Fortnightly Political Report for the period April 16–30, 1960', No. FR-8/61, 4 May 1961, File 48-1-AMS-57, Americas Division, Ministry of External Affairs, National Archives of India.

17. Delhi to CRO, 9 January 1960, DO 133/148, UKNA.

18. Pandit to Nehru, 1 October 1959, Vijaya Lakshmi Pandit Papers, Subject File 62, 1st Instalment, Nehru Museum and Memorial Library (NMML).

19. Ibid.

20. Nehru to Pandit, 'Researching Maps at the India Office', 6 October 1959, *SWJN* vol. 53, ed. Madhavan K. Palat (New Delhi: Oxford University Press, 2014), p. 488.

21. 'Whitehall Says Briton Did Not Contact Gopal', *Hindustan Times*, 26 February 1960.

22. Dobbs to Anderson, 26 February 1960, DO 133/48, UKNA.

23. Sydney Wignall, *Spy on the Roof of the World* (Edinburgh: Canongate Books, 1996). See also, Francine R. Frankel, *When Nehru Looked East: Origins of India-US Suspicion and India-China Rivalry* (Oxford: Oxford University Press, 2020), p. 252; and Chandra B. Khandur, *Thimayya: An Amazing Life* (New Delhi: Knowledge World International, 2007), p. 206.

24. Jan Morris, *Coronation Everest* (London: Faber & Faber, 2003), p. 31, p. 44.

25. Wignall, *Roof of the World*, p. viii.

26. Wignall, *Roof of the World*, pp. 256–67.

27. A more detailed account of this episode is provided in Chapter 9, 'Battle of the Books'.

28. Sanjeevi to Iengar, 24 November 1948, DIB D.O. 336/48, File No. 40/21/49, Police II, Home Ministry Records, National Archives of India.

29. Nehru to Lal Bahadur Shastri, 17 May 1961, SWJN vol. 69, ed. Madhavan K. Palat (New Delhi: Oxford University Press, 2016), p. 405.

30. Herbert Passin, 'Sino-Indian Cultural Relations', *The China Quarterly* 7 (July–September 1961), pp. 85–100.

31. CRO to Gautrey, 4 May 1956, FO 371/120992, UKNA.

32. Nehru to Foreign Secretary, 'Intelligence for Foreign countries', 30 October 1957, *SWJN* vol. 39, ed. Mushirul Hasan (New Delhi: Oxford University Press, 2007), pp. 302–3.

NOTES TO PAGES 107–11 291

33. Nehru to Pillai, Dutt and Desai, 2 December 1959, *SWJN* vol. 55, ed. Madhavan K. Palat (New Delhi: Oxford University Press, 2014), pp. 365–66.
34. John Kenneth Galbraith, *A Life in Our Times: Memoirs* (London: Andre Deutsch, 1981), pp. 427–28.
35. John Kenneth Galbraith, *Ambassador's Journal: A Personal Account of the Kennedy Years* (Boston: Houghton Mifflin, 1969), 26 October 1962, pp. 435–36.
36. Noam Kochavi, *A Conflict Perpetuated: China Policy during the Kennedy Years* (London: Praeger, 2002), pp. 148–50.
37. Sarvepalli Gopal, *Jawaharlal Nehru: A Biography, vol. 3: 1956–1964* (London: Jonathan Cape, 1984), p. 223.
38. Gore-Booth to Saville Garner, 26 October 1962, DO 196/75, UKNA.
39. Galbraith, *Ambassador's Journal*, 26 and 29 October 1962, New Delhi, p. 440 and p. 447; Delhi to CRO, No. 1629, 21 October 1962, FO 371/164914, UKNA; Ormsby Gore to FO, No. 2723, 29 October1962, FO 371/164880, UKNA.
40. *New York Times*, 20 November 1962, p. 1.
41. Ormsby Gore to Macmillan, 20 November 1962, DO 196/168, UKNA.
42. Galbraith, *Ambassador's Journal*, 19 November 1962, New Delhi, p. 486; Galbraith to Rusk, 20 November 1962, NSF, Box 108, JFKL.
43. Sino-Indian War', 19 November 1962, Meetings Recordings, Tape No. 62, JFKL; Kennedy to Harriman and Galbraith, 23 November 1962, *FRUS, 1961–1963*, vol. XIX, p. 405, and Galbraith to Washington, 24 November 1962, *FRUS, 1961–1963*, vol. XIX, p. 405.
44. Ormsby Gore to FO, 19 November 1962, FO 371/164929, and Ormsby Gore to FO, 20 November 1962 FC1063/16 (C), UKNA; Sandys to Macmillan, 13 November 1962, DSDN 8/12, Duncan Sandys Papers (DSP), Churchill College, Cambridge.
45. Ledward to McKenzie-Johnston, 24 November 1962, FO 371/164930, UKNA.
46. Sino-Indian Conflict: policy Situation', 22 November 1962, DO 196/172, UKNA.
47. Nitin A. Gokhale. *R. N. Kao: Gentleman Spymaster* (New Delhi: Bloomsbury, 2019), p. 105.
48. See, Komer to McGeorge Bundy, 14 October 1965, LBJL, NSF, Robert W. Komer Papers, Box 13, Folder 6 Bundy, McG – Decisions 1965–66; and Rostow to Johnson, 30 April 1966, LBJL, NSF, Intelligence File, Box 2, Folder India's Unconventional Warfare Force; M. S. Kohli and Kenneth Conboy, *Spies in the Himalayas: Secret Missions and Perilous Climbs* (Lawrence: University Press of Kansas, 2003); and John Kenneth Knaus, *Orphans of the Cold War: America and the Tibetan Struggle for Survival* (New York: Public Affairs, 2000), pp. 265–76.
49. 'Report to the Joint Chiefs of Staff by General Paul D. Adams on Indian Military Situation, 3 December 1962 ['Adams Report']', Folder India: Military Situation, Box 112, NSF, 1961–1963, Asia and the Pacific, First Supplement, JFKL.
50. 'Adams Report', Enclosures I: Appraisal of the Indian Intelligence System and K: Survey of Special Warfare requirements, Folder India: Military Situation, Box 112, NSF, 1961–1963, Asia and the Pacific, First Supplement, JFKL.
51. Galbraith, *Life in Our Times*, p. 436.
52. Knaus, *Orphans of the Cold War*, pp. 264–65.
53. Ibid., pp. 265–66; 271–72.

292 NOTES TO PAGES 111-17

54. 'Adams Report', Folder India: Military Situation: A Report by General Paul Adams, 3 December 1962', Box 112, NSF, 1961–1963, Asia and the Pacific, First Supplement, JFKL.
55. 'Adams Report', Enclosure I: 'Appraisal of the Indian Intelligence System', Box 112, NSF, 1961–1963, Asia and the Pacific, First Supplement, JFKL.
56. 'Adams Report', Enclosure K: 'Survey of Special Warfare requirements', Folder India: Military Situation, Box 112, NSF, 1961–1963, Asia and the Pacific, First Supplement, JFKL.
57. 'Mark Scrase-Dickens', *Times*, 23 March 2003, p. 55.
58. Nehru to Chavan, 25 November 1962, *SWJN* vol. 79, ed. Madhavan K. Palat (New Delhi: Oxford University Press, 2018), pp. 575–76.
59. Gokhale, *Gentleman Spymaster*, p. 106.
60. Komer to McGeorge Bundy, 14 October 1965, NSF, Robert W. Komer Files, Box 13, Folder 6 Bundy, McG – Decisions 1965–66, LBJL.
61. Rostow to Johnson, 30 April 1966, NSF, Intelligence File, Box 2, Folder India's Unconventional Warfare Force, LBJL.
62. Bowles to Rostow, 26 July 1966, NSF, Walt W. Rostow Files, Box 15, Folder 3, [Non-Vietnam July–September 1966] [1 of 2], LBJL.
63. Mountbatten to Chaudhuri, 7 May 1965, Mountbatten Papers, MB1/J507 Visit to India, May 1965, MBP.
64. Mountbatten to Freeman, 7 May 1965, Mountbatten Papers, MB1/J507 Visit to India, May 1965, MBP.
65. 'Adams Report', Enclosure K: 'Survey of Special Warfare requirements', Folder India: Military Situation: A Report by General Paul Adams, 3 December 1962', Box 112, NSF, 1961–1963, Asia and the Pacific, First Supplement, JFKL.
66. Memorandum for the Special Group, Washington, 9 January 1964, 'Review of Tibetan Operations', *FRUS*, 1964–1968, vol. XXX, China, Document 337, https://history.state.gov/historicaldocuments/frus1964-68v30/d337
67. Memorandum for the 303 Committee, Washington, 26 January 1968, 'Status Report on Tibetan Operations', *FRUS*, 1964–1968, vol. XXX, China, document 342 https://history.state.gov/historicaldocuments/frus1964-68v30/d342.
68. Memorandum Prepared for the 40 Committee, Washington, 11 January 1971, 'Status Report on Support to the Dalai Lama and Tibetan Operations', *FRUS*, 1969–1976, vol. xvii, China, 1969–1972, Document 278. https://history.state.gov/historicaldocuments/frus1969-76v17/d278; 'US Suspends spy forays into southern China', *Guardian*, 4 October 1971.
69. 'Chinese Foreign Ministry Protests Against Indian Government's use of Chinese Tibetan Traitors for Anti-China Activity', 29 March 1967, FCO 21/72, UKNA.
70. Hopson to Brown, 'China: Chinese Actions Against the Indian Embassy in Peking', 26 June 1967, FCO 21/72, UKNA.
71. 'Adams Report', Enclosure I: 'Appraisal of the Indian Intelligence System', Folder India: Military Situation: A Report by General Paul Adams, 3 December 1962', Box 112, NSF, 1961–1963, Asia and the Pacific, First Supplement, JFKL.
72. Nehru to Chavan, 'Airfields for American Use', 5 May 1963, *SWJN* vol. 82, ed. Madhavan K. Palat (New Delhi: Oxford University Press, 2019), p. 775. See also, Desai conversation McNamara, May 1963, T. T. Krishnamachari Papers, NMML; Krishnamachari to Nehru, 20 May 1963, T. T. Krishnamachari Papers, NMML.

NOTES TO PAGES 117–22

73. Gokhale, *Gentleman Spymaster*, pp. 101–2.
74. 'State-JCS Meeting on 14 December 1962 at 1130', 14 December 1962, CIA-RDP80R01580R001603320006-3, CIA FOIA Electronic Reading Room, www.foia.cia.gov.
75. Gregory W. Pedlow and Donald E. Welzenbach, 'The Central Intelligence Agency and Overhead Reconnaissance: The U-2 and OXCART Programs, 1954–1974' (History Staff, Central Intelligence Agency, Washington, DC, 1992), pp. 231–32.
76. CIA [Officials name redacted] to Galbraith, 11 January 1963, CIA-RDP78B04558A001800010014-7, CIA FOIA Electronic Reading Room, www.foia.cia.gov.
77. Harriman conversation with Senator William J. Fulbright, 4 December 1962, Box 537, Folder 1, Harriman Papers, Library of Congress, Washington DC.
78. Gregory W. Pedlow and Donald E. Welzenbach, 'The Central Intelligence Agency and Overhead Reconnaissance: The U-2 and OXCART Programs, 1954–1974' (History Staff, Central Intelligence Agency, Washington, DC, 1992), pp. 231–32.
79. Gregory W. Pedlow and Donald E. Welzenbach, 'The Central Intelligence Agency and Overhead Reconnaissance: The U-2 and OXCART Programs, 1954–1974' (History Staff, Central Intelligence Agency, Washington, DC, 1992), pp. 231–32.
80. Ibid., pp. 174–76; Michael Beschloss, *May Day: Eisenhower, Khrushchev, and the U-2 Affair* (New York: Faber & Faber, 1986).
81. Howard Kohn, 'The Nanda Devi Caper: How the CIA used American mountaineers to plant a nuclear-powered spy station in the Himalaya', *Outside Magazine* (May 1978).
82. 'President Kennedy News Conference 59', Washington DC, 1 August 1963, *Public Papers of the President of the United States* (hereafter PPP-US)*, John F. Kennedy, 1963*, American Presidency Project, www.presidency.ucsb.edu/ws/.
83. Entry for 11 December 1964, Crossman, *Minister of Housing 1964–66*, p. 94.
84. Zuckerman to Wilson, 15 March 1965, 'India and the Bomb', PREM 13/973, UKNA.
85. 'On Reported Planting of a Nuclear Device by the CIA in the Nanda Devi', 17 April 1978, Session IV, Lok Sabha Debates (New Delhi: Government of India, 1978).
86. Goheen to State Department, 17 April 1978, *FRUS, 1977–1980*, vol. XIX, South Asia (Washington DC: GPO, 2019), p. 261.
87. 'CIA Put Nuclear Spy Devices in Himalayas', *Washington Post*, 13 April 1978, p. A3.
88. Kohli and Conboy, *Spies in the Himalayas*.
89. Joseph N. Greene interview, 13 March 1993, Foreign Affairs Oral History Collection, Library of Congress, https://tile.loc.gov/storage-services/service/mss/mfdip/2004/2004gre09/2004gre09.pdf
90. Christopher to Carter, 14 April 1978, *FRUS, 1977–1980*, vol. XIX, South Asia (Washington DC: GPO, 2019), 260; 'On Reported Planting of a Nuclear Device by the CIA in the Nanda Devi', 17 April 1978, Session IV. Lok Sabha Debates (New Delhi: Lok Sabha Secretariat, 1978); 'CIA Mischief in Himalayas?' *Times of India*, 14 April 1978, p. 8.
91. Lukas to Wicker, 18 October 1965, Box 159 CIA Series 1965–66 Raw Data, HSP. See also, 'Ducks Reprieved at a U.S. Embassy', *New York Times*, 6 June 1965, p. 8.

294 NOTES TO PAGES 122-29

92. Joseph N. Greene interview 13 March 1993, Foreign Affairs Oral History Collection, Library of Congress, https://tile.loc.gov/storage-services/service/mss/mfdip/2004/2004gre09/2004gre09.pdf
93. Thomas Powers, *The Man Who Kept the Secrets: Richard Helms and the CIA* (New York: Simon & Schuster, 1979), p. 169.

6 Peddling Propaganda: The Information Research Department and India

1. For insights into the British approach to Cold War propaganda, see A. Defty, *Britain, America, and Anti-Communist Propaganda, 1945–53: The Information Research Department* (Abingdon: Routledge, 2003); John Jenks, *British Propaganda and News Media in the Cold War* (Edinburgh: Edinburgh University Press, 2006); and Gary Rawnsley (ed.), *Cold-War Propaganda in the 1950s* (London: Palgrave Macmillan, 1999).
2. SLO Letter, undated and unsigned, c May 1962; Williamson to Welser, 8 May 1962; and Welser to Williamson, 10 May 1962, FCO 168/430, United Kingdom National Archives, Kew, London (UKNA).
3. Ralph Murray, 7 January 1949, FO 1110/22, UKNA.
4. Nye to CRO, 5 May 1951, FO 371/92864, UKNA.
5. Joyce to CRO, 15 January 1952, DO 35/2657, UKNA.
6. Nye to CRO, 15 January 1952, DO 35/2657, UKNA.
7. FO memorandum, 17 November 1951, FO 953/1051, UKNA.
8. John Christopher Edmonds interview, 21 May 2009, British Diplomatic Oral History Project, pp. 7–8, www.chu.cam.ac.uk/media/uploads/files/Edmonds.pdf.
9. King to Joyce, 2 February 1950, FO 1110/293, UKNA.
10. Bennett to Glass, 25 January 1962, FO 1110/1560, UKNA.
11. Hoghton note, 3 November 1954, FO 371/112211, UKNA.
12. 'Vilification of Gandhi: Soviet Blunder in India', *Manchester Guardian*, 20 October 1954; BBC Monitoring report, 4 December 1954, FO 371/112211, UKNA.
13. 'Counter-Subversion Structure: Annex D – Interdepartmental Review Committee', 27 July 1966, DEFE 28/146, UKNA; Paul Lashmar and James Oliver, *Britain's Secret Propaganda War: Foreign Office and the Cold War, 1948–77* (Stroud: Sutton Publishing, 1998), pp. 140–41.
14. Hans Welser, handwritten note, 11 February 1966, FCO 168/2386, UKNA.
15. 'United States-United Kingdom Information Working Group Meetings: United Kingdom Brief', June 1960, FCO 168/19, UKNA.
16. 'Clandestine Subversive Activities by Sino-Soviet Bloc Representatives in Public Information Media', December 1958, CIA-RDP78-00915R001000360002-9, CIA FOIA.
17. Glass, minute, 30 December 1964, FCO 168/1992; Üre to Glass, 19 January 1965, FCO 168/1992, UKNA.
18. 'Chinese Peace Committee Letters', undated, FO 1110/2363, UKNA.
19. Peter Joy, 'I.R.D. Work in India (1964)', FCO 168/1161, UKNA.
20. Selborne to Churchill, 23 October 1944, CAB 301/11, UKNA.
21. Borron minute, 23 April 1952, DO 133/134, UKNA.
22. Minute by Murray, 28 March 1950 CAB143/3, UKNA.

NOTES TO PAGES 129–36

23. 'Meeting of the Chiefs of Staff: Cold War Organisation', 10 March 1948, FO 1093/375, UKNA.
24. 'Information Research Department', c. 1970, FCO 79/182, UKNA.
25. Lawson to Stephens, 23 August 1965, Declassified Documents Reference System-295501-i1-14.
26. Murray to Joyce, 7 January 1948, FO 1110/44, UKNA.
27. King to Joyce, 27 November 1948, FO 1110/44, UKNA.
28. Hughes note, 11 August 1951, DO 133/116, UKNA.
29. Nicholls to MacDonald, 21 November 1951, DO 133/116, UKNA.
30. Hughes to Cockram, 25 March 1955, FO 1110/818, UKNA.
31. Michele L. Louro, *Comrades Against Imperialism: Nehru, India, and Interwar Internationalism* (Cambridge: Cambridge University Press, 2018), p. 12.
32. Nye to CRO, 5 May 1951, FO 371/92864; Hughes to Cockram, 25 March 1955, FO 1110/818, UKNA.
33. Borron, 23 April 1952, DO 133/134, UKNA.
34. 'Minoo Masani speech to Detroit Economic Club', 13 November 1951, DO 133/134, UKNA.
35. V. S. Naipaul, *An Area of Darkness: A Discovery of India* (New York: Vintage Books, 2002), p. 113.
36. Young to Kitchin, 18 March 1952, DO 133/134, UKNA.
37. Symon to Patrick, 14 February 1948, DO 133/128, UKNA.
38. Y. D. Gundevia, *Outside the Archives* (New Delhi: Sangam Books, 1984), pp. 208–9.
39. Mayhew to Gordon Walker, 22 November 1948, FO 1110/22, UKNA.
40. Murray minute, 22 July 1948, FO 1110/22, UKNA.
41. Nye to CRO, 5 May 1951, FO 371/92864, UKNA.
42. Bozman minute, 28 March 1956, FO 1110/929, UKNA.
43. Hughes to Cockram, 25 March 1955, FO 1110/818, UKNA.
44. Cole to Bozman, 22 June 1956, FO 1110/929, UKNA.
45. Jenks, *British Propaganda*, pp. 67–69.
46. Bozman to Cole, 28 June 1956, FO 1110/929, UKNA.
47. Meeting between Bozman, Costley-White, Middleton, 28 March 1956, FO 1110/929, UKNA.
48. Martin to Bozman, 7 October 1953, FO 1110/603; Bozman minute, 15 April 1955, FO 1110/818, UKNA.
49. Cole to Bozman, 23 April 1956, FO 1110/929, UKNA.
50. James to Belcher, 31 August 1960, FO 371/152546, UKNA.
51. Nehru to Tyabji, 'Intelligence Policy', 26 February 1962, SWJN vol. 75, ed. Madhavan K. Palat (New Delhi: Oxford University Press, 2018), pp. 507–8.
52. 'India', 5 December 1967, FCO 95/290, UKNA.
53. Bennett to Glass, 25 January 1962, FO 1110/1560, UKNA.
54. The phrase 'dolphin' families appeared in a Kipling short story, 'The Tombs of His Ancestors', *Pearson's Magazine* (December 1897). See also, David Gilmour, *The British in India: Three Centuries of Ambition and Experience* (London: Allen Lane, 2018), p. 72.
55. Rivett-Carnac Minute, 6 February 1962, FO 1110/1560, UKNA.
56. Bennett to Glass, 25 January 1962, FO 1110/1560, UKNA.
57. COS (62) 9th Meeting, 6 February 1962, DEFE 32/7, UKNA.
58. COS (62) 75th Meeting, 27 November 1962, DEFE 32/7, UKNA.

296   NOTES TO PAGES 136–46

59. Hopson minute 13 May 1961, FCO/168/255; Murray minute, 15 May 1961, FCO/168/255, UKNA.
60. 'India', 5 December 1967, FCO95/290; Bennett to Glass, 25 January 1962, FO 1110/1560, UKNA.
61. Joy minute, 18 November 1963, FO 1110/1698, UKNA.
62. Norton minute, 23 April 1963, FO 371/170671, UKNA.
63. Kerr to Bishop, 30 October 1962, DO 191/99; Drinkall minute, 14 November 1962, DO 191/99, UKNA.
64. Gore-Booth to CRO, 28 December 1962, FO 371/170669, UKNA.
65. Foreign Office Note, 23 November 1962, DO 191/99, UKNA.
66. Sandys talk with Nehru, 26 November 1962, DO 196/199, UKNA.
67. Drinkall minute, 14 November 1962, DO 191/99, UKNA.
68. Joy minute, 18 November 1963, FO 1110/1698, UKNA.
69. Kerr to Bishop, 19 December 1962, DO 191/99, UKNA.
70. 'India', 5 December 1967, FCO95/290, UKNA.
71. 'India', 5 December 1967, FCO 95/290, UKNA.
72. Joy minute, 18 November 1963, FO 1110/1698, UKNA.
73. 'India', December 1967, FCO 95/290, UKNA.
74. Joy minute, 18 November 1963, FO 1110/1698, UKNA.
75. Kristin Roth-Ey, *Moscow Prime Time: How the Soviet Union Built the Media Empire that Lost the Cultural Cold War* (Ithaca, NY: Cornell University Press, 2011), pp. 153–56.
76. Joy minute, 18 November 1963, FO 1110/1698, UKNA.
77. The question of declaring IRD's field officer to the Indian government was raised again in February 1964 and July 1967. Continued opposition from the British high commission quashed the idea. 'India', 5 December 1967, FCO95/290; Allen to Costley-White, 22 May 1963, FO 1110/1685, UKNA.
78. 'India', 5 December 1967, FCO95/290, UKNA.
79. Stephenson minute, 20 April 1964; Joy to Barclay, 9 April 1964, FO 1110/1829, UKNA.
80. 'India', 5 December 1967, FCO 95/290, UKNA.
81. Miles to Brinson, 28 July 1972, FCO 95/1278, UKNA.
82. 'India', 5 December 1967, FCO 95/290, UKNA.
83. Joy to Tucker, 9 September 1963, FO 1110/1698, UKNA
84. Peter Joy, 'I.R.D. Work in India (1964)', FCO 168/1161, UKNA.
85. Joy to Tucker, 9 September 1963, FO 1110/1698, UKNA.
86. 'India', 5 December 1967, FCO 95/290, UKNA.
87. Joy to Barclay, 21 June 1965, FCO 168/1161, UKNA.
88. Scott to Costley-White, 23 July 1965, FCO 168/1161; McMinnies to Drinkall, 24 July 1965, FCO 168/1161, UKNA.
89. Joy to Bowman, 30 July 1965, FCO 168/1161, UKNA.
90. Peter Joy, 'I.R.D. Work in India (1964)', FCO 168/1161, UKNA.
91. Stella Rimington, *Open Secret: The Autobiography of the Former Director-General of MI5* (London: Hutchinson, 2002), p. 75.
92. Joy minute, 18 May 1963, FO 1110/1698, UKNA.
93. Joy to Duke, 6 February 1964, FO 1110/1829, UKNA.
94. Joy to Norris, 10 December 1964, FO 1110/1830, UKNA.
95. Jonathan Davidson interview, Washington DC, June 2013.

NOTES TO PAGES 146–54 297

96. McMinnies to Stephenson, 2 March 1966, FO 1110/2081; Tucker to McMinnies, 18 April 1966, FO 1110/2081, UKNA.
97. 'India', 5 December 1967, FCO95/290, UKNA.
98. McMinnies to Stephenson, 23 March 1966, FO 1110/2081, UKNA.
99. *Times*, 3 January 1966, p. 9.
100. Tony Benn, *Out of the Wilderness: Diaries 1963–67* (London: Hutchinson, 1987), pp. 375–76; Waterfield to Duff, 14 August 1968, FCO 168/3215, UKNA.
101. Barclay minute, 22 June 1966, FCO 168/2246, UKNA.
102. Meeting between James and Freeman, Karachi, 1 and 2 February 1966, FO 371/186952, UKNA.
103. McMinnies to Stephenson, 23 March 1966, FO 1110/2081, UKNA.
104. Chester Bowles, *Promises to Keep: My Years in Public Life, 1941–1969* (New York: Harper, 1971), p. 544.
105. Crook to Joy, 4 July 1967, FCO 95/290, UKNA.
106. 'India', 5 December 1967, FCO 95/290, UKNA.
107. Freeman to Saville Garner, 11 April 1967, FCO 95/290, UKNA.
108. Waterfield to Duff, 31 March 1967, FCO 168/2649, UKNA.
109. Commonwealth Office to New Delhi, 10 February 1967, FCO 37/74, UKNA.
110. Duff to Johnston, 15 February 1967, FCO 37/74, UKNA.
111. Saville Garner to Johnston, 17 February 1967, FCO 37/74, UKNA.
112. Waterfield to Duff, 2 March 1967, FCO 37/74, UKNA.
113. Freeman to Commonwealth Office, 18 February 1967, FCO 37/74.
114. 'Did KGB Man Forge Freeman Telegram?' *Young India*, pp. 11–13, January 1968.
115. Lancashire to Joy, 16 June 1967, FCO 37/36, UKNA.
116. Garvey to Wright, 29 December 1971, FCO 95/1278, UKNA.
117. 'South Asian Heads of Mission Conference – Information Work', 3 May 1973, FCO 37/1213, UKNA.
118. Barker to Sutherland, 5 January 1972, FCO 95/1278, UKNA.
119. Kerr to Cortazzi, 14 July 1976, FCO 84/52, UKNA.
120. Brinson to Hennings, 14 January 1972, FCO 95/1278, UKNA.
121. 'IRD Work', c. February 1975, FCO 95/1768, UKNA.
122. Hum to Seaward, 15 October 1975, FCO 37/1595, UKNA.
123. 'Annual Report of IRD in India, 1967–1968', FCO 37/43, UKNA.
124. Kerr to Cortazzi, 14 July 1976, FCO 84/52, UKNA.
125. Ibid.
126. Susan L. Carruthers, *Winning Hearts and Minds: British Governments, the Media and Colonial Counter-Insurgency, 1944–60*, (Leicester: Leicester University Press, 1995), pp. 266, 269.

7   From Russia with Love: Dissidents and Defectors in Cold War India

1. S. Mulgaokar, 'The Right of Asylum', *Weekend Review*, II, 5 (6 January 1968), pp. 3–4.
2. Cole to Hunt, 5 January 1968, FCO 37/62, United Kingdom National Archives, Kew, London (UKNA).
3. Mulgaokar, 'Right of Asylum', pp. 3–4.
4. *Times of India*, 21 December 1967, p. 1.
5. A. R. Wic, 'The Ulug-Zade affair', *Weekend Review*, II, 5 (6 January 1968), pp. 6–7.

298   NOTES TO PAGES 154–56

6. See, Christopher Andrew, *The Defence of the Realm: The Authorized History of MI5* (London: Allen Lane, 2009); Rhodri Jeffreys-Jones, *Cloak and Dollar: A History of American Secret Intelligence* (New Haven, CT: Yale University Press, 2003. Some works have engaged with the intelligence Cold War from a broader global perspective, notably, Philip Davies and Kristian Gustafson (eds.), *Intelligence Elsewhere: Spies and Espionage Outside the Anglosphere* (Washington, DC: Georgetown University Press, 2013).

7. Scholarship addressing India's Cold War relations invariably elides the issue of political asylum. See, for example, Dennis Kux, *India and the United States: Estranged Democracies, 1941–1991* (Washington, DC: National Defense University Press, 1993). Howard Schaffer provides a brief account of the Alliluyeva episode in *Chester Bowles: New Dealer in the Cold War* (Cambridge MA: Harvard University Press, 1993). Rosemary Sullivan also offers insightful analysis of Alliluyeva's defection in, *Stalin's Daughter: The Extraordinary and Tumultuous Life of Svetlana Stalin* (London: Fourth Estate, 2015). See also, Svetlana Alliluyeva's own account of her defection in, *Only One Year* (New York: HarperCollins, 1969).

8. Scholarship addressing the secret intelligence dimension of South Asia's Cold War has typically excluded consideration of defection and political asylum. See, Eric D. Pullin, 'Money Does Not Make Any Difference to the Opinions That We Hold': India, the CIA, and the Congress for Cultural Freedom, 1951–58, *Intelligence and National Security*, 26 (2–3), (2011), pp. 377–98; P. M. McGarr, '"Quiet Americans in India": The Central Intelligence Agency and the Politics of Intelligence in Cold War South Asia', *Diplomatic History*, 38 (5), (2014).

9. On the centrality of human rights in Indian foreign policymaking, see Manu Bhagavan, *The Peacemakers; India and the Quest for One World* (New Delhi: Harper Collins, 2012).

10. Vladislav Krasnov, *Soviet Defectors: The KGB Wanted List* (Stanford, CA: Hoover Institution Press, 1986), p. 116.

11. 'Working Party on Russian and Satellite Defectors and Refugees', CAB 301/136, UKNA.

12. Donaldson, 4 August 1950, CAB 301/136, UKNA. See, also, Jeffrey Richelson, *The US Intelligence Community* (Boulder, CO: Westview Press, 2008), pp. 328–32.

13. Alistair Horne, *Macmillan, 1957–1986: Vol. 2 of the Official Biography* (London: Macmillan, 1989), p. 457; and, D. R. Thorpe, *Supermac: The Life of Harold Macmillan* (London: Pimlico, 2011), p. 310.

14. Meeting between Churchill, Nutting, Rennie and Kirkpatrick, 1 May 1954, PREM 11/773, UKNA. A fictional rendering of SIS's enthusiasm for extracting propaganda value from Soviet defectors, that bears resemblance to the Khokhlov case, appears in John le Carrè's, *Secret Pilgrim* (London: Hodder & Stoughton, 1991), p. 152.

15. 'Petrov Defection Policy', The Royal Commission on Espionage, 1954–55, Series Number A4940, C926, National Archives of Australia, Canberra. See also, Vladimir and Evdokia Petrov, *Empire of Fear* (London: Andre Deutsch, 1956).

16. Cheney to Rumsfeld, 'Solzhenitsyn', 8 July 1975, Box 10, folder "Solzhenitsyn, Alexander," Richard B. Cheney Files, Gerald R. Ford Presidential Library (GFPL).

17. Hutchinson to Foreign Office, 15 November 1950, FO 371/92207, UKNA; 'Sinkiang Refugees' Leaders in Delhi', *Statesman*, 5 February 1950; 'Chinese Fugitive Governor in Delhi', *Hindustan Times*, 6 February 1950.

NOTES TO PAGES 157–61

18. 'Discussion with Prime Minister on Indian Foreign Policy', February 1950, Box 8, India Misc. folder, Loy W. Henderson Papers, Manuscripts Division, Library of Congress.
19. Allen to Jones, 6 August 1955, RG59, Lot 59 D 75, folder India 1955, US National Archives, College Park, Maryland (USNA).
20. 'Sinkiang Refugees' Leaders in Delhi', *Statesman*, 5 February 1950.
21. Selby to Maclennan, 7 February 1950, FO 371/84261, UKNA.
22. Lamb to Scott, 12 October 1951, FO 317/92897, UKNA. See also, Justin M. Jacobs, 'Exile Island: Xinjiang Refugees and the "One China" Policy in Nationalist Taiwan, 1949–1971', *Journal of Cold War Studies*, 18, 1 (Winter 2016), pp. 188–218.
23. William J. Barnds, *India, Pakistan and the Great Powers* (London: Pall Mall Press, 1972), p. 143.
24. Nehru to Apa B. Pant, 11 July 1958, Subject File 6, 1st Instalment, Apa B. Pant Papers, Nehru Museum and Memorial Library, New Delhi (NMML); 'Chinese Intentions against India', Joint Intelligence Committee report, 22 November 1962, CAB 158/47, UKNA.
25. *Hindustan Times*, 13 January 1960; *Times of India*, 13 January 1960, p. 1.
26. 'Czechs in Bombay', 25 May 1950, CIA-RDP82-00457R004900500003-4, CIA FOIA Electronic Reading Room, www.foia.cia.gov.
27. New Delhi to CRO, 13 March 1948, DO 133/1, UKNA.
28. CRO to New Delhi, 18 March 1948, DO 133/1, UKNA.
29. Shone to Noel-Baker, 27 April 1948, DO 133/1, UKNA; Shone to Noel-Baker, 8 May 1948, DO 133/1, UKNA.
30. Selby to Shattock, 4 August 1948, DO 133/1, UKNA; Cables WN#2305827 and WN#23155, 27 April 1945 and 14 May 1945, RG 226, Entry 211, 250/64/32/1, CIA Accession: 85-0215R, Box 7, USNA.
31. Prague to FO, 7 March 1951, FO 371/94540, UKNA; *Daily Mail*, 5 March 1951, p. 1.
32. *Daily Mail*, 13 March 1951; *Times*, 6 March 1951, p. 4.
33. 'Notes on Communism in India, Pakistan and Ceylon No. 24 for the period January/March 1951', FO 371/92864, UKNA.
34. Ibid.
35. Nehru to Pandit, 12 March 1948, *SWJN* 2nd series, vol. 5, ed. S. Gopal, (New Delhi: Oxford University Press, 1987), p. 546.
36. Pierson to Roberts 24 October 1950, DO 133/2, UKNA.
37. Cumming-Bruce to Roberts, 3 November 1950, DO 133/2, UKNA.
38. Nye to Liesching, 24 November 1950, DO 133/2, UKNA.
39. US House of Representatives, 'Defection of a Russian Seaman: testimony of Vladislaw Stepanovich Tarasov', Eighty-Eight Congress, First Session, 19 September 1963 (Washington DC: GPO, 1963), p. 790.
40. 'Russian Defector Gives Witness to the Effectiveness of the Voice of America', Congressional Record, A5978, 23 September 1963, CIA FOIA CIA-RDP65B00 383R000100050038-7.
41. US House of Representatives, 'Defection of a Russian Seaman', p. 790.
42. C. L. Sareen, *Bid for Freedom: USSR vs. Tarasov* (Englewood Cliffs, NJ: Prentice Hall, 1966), pp. 13–16.
43. *New York Times*, 22 December 1962, p. 2.
44. *New York Times*, 20 December 1962, p. 4.

NOTES TO PAGES 162–67

45. *Jugantar,* 29 November 1962.
46. Eastland to Lodge, 1 May 1956, *Foreign Relations of the United States, 1955–1957,* United Nations and General International Matters, Volume XI, Document 23 https://history.state.gov/historicaldocuments/frus1955-57v11/d23. See also, *Life,* 7 May 1956, pp. 45–46.
47. 'Vladimir Stepanovich Tarasov', 20 December 1962, FCO 168/911, UKNA.
48. Ormerod to Allen, 29 December 1962, FCO 168/911, UKNA.
49. Delhi to IRD, 27 December 1962, FCO 168/911, UKNA.
50. Allen to Norris, 24 December 1962, FCO 168/911, UKNA.
51. Delhi to IRD, 24 December 1962, FCO 168/911, UKNA.
52. Joy to Welser, 18 January 1963, 18 January 1963, FCO 168/912, UKNA.
53. Joy to IRD, 27 December 1962, FCO 168/911; Welser to American Embassy, London, 24 January 1963, FCO 168/912, UKNA.
54. Rayner to Joy, 7 February 1963, FCO 168/913, UKNA.
55. Joy to Rayner, 18 February 1963, FCO 168/913, UKNA.
56. *Times of India,* 7 January 1963, p. 7.
57. *Washington Post,* 5 January 1963, p. A6.
58. See, Soviet Embassy to MEA, 30 November 1962; MEA to Soviet Embassy, 30 November 1962; and MEA to Soviet Embassy, 29 December 1962, National Archives of India, New Delhi (NAI).
59. G. D. Khosla, ex-Chief Justice, Punjab High Court, foreword in Sareen, *Bid for Freedom,* pp. iii–iv.
60. *Times of India,* 11 January 1963, p. 8.
61. *Guardian,* 11 January 1963, p. 9.
62. *New York Times,* 31 January 1963, p. 2.
63. *Times of India,* 4 March 1963, p. 3.
64. Sareen, *Bid for Freedom,* pp. 153–54.
65. *Guardian,* 30 March 1963, p. 7.
66. *Statesman,* 1 April 1963.
67. *Times of India,* 1 April 1963, p. 6.
68. Bowles, 'Defection of Svetlana Alliloueva, [sic]', 15 March 1967, N[ational] S[security] F[ile] Box 3, Folder Svetlana Alliluyeva (Stalin), Lyndon Baines Johnson Library, Austin, Texas (LBJL).
69. *Economist,* 29 April 1967, p. 465.
70. Chester Bowles interview, 11 November 1969, Foreign Affairs Oral History Collection (FAOHP), Library of Congress, https://tile.loc.gov/storage-services/service/mss/mfdip/2004/2004bow05/2004bow05.pdf
71. Bowles to Rostow, 18 March 1967, NSF, Box 3, Folder Svetlana Alliluyeva (Stalin), LBJL.
72. Bowles, 'Defection of Svetlana Alliloueva, [sic]', 15 March 1967, NSF, Box 3, Folder Svetlana Alliluyeva (Stalin), LBJL; Chester Bowles interview 11 November 1969, FAOHP.
73. Bowles to Rostow, 18 March 1967, NSF, Box 3, Folder Svetlana Alliluyeva (Stalin), LBJL.
74. Delhi to Washington, 8 March 1967, NSF, Box 3, Folder Svetlana Alliluyeva (Stalin), LBJL.
75. *Times of India,* 7 June 1967, p. 8.
76. Schaffer, *Chester Bowles,* p. 301.

NOTES TO PAGES 168–74

77. Delhi to Washington, 9 March 1967, NSF, Box 3, Folder Svetlana Alliluyeva (Stalin), LBJL.
78. Bowles to Jha, 10 March 1967, see also 'Defection of Svetlana Alliluyeva', 15 March 1967, Box 326, Bowles Papers, Yale University Library.
79. Sullivan, *Stalin's Daughter*, p. 9.
80. Bendall to Smith, 17 March 1967, FCO 28/397, UKNA; Trench to Duff, 31 March 1967, FCO 37/76, UKNA.
81. Thompson to Rusk, 21 March 1967, NSF, Box 3, Folder Svetlana Alliluyeva (Stalin), LBJL.
82. Maxey to Clift, 17 March 1967, FCO 28/397, UKNA.
83. Thompson to Rusk, 21 March 1967, NSF, Box 3, Folder Svetlana Alliluyeva (Stalin), LBJL.
84. Bowles to Rusk, 20 March 1967, NSF, Box 3, Folder Svetlana Alliluyeva (Stalin), LBJL.
85. Rusk to Bowles, 21 March 1967, NSF, Box 3, Folder Svetlana Alliluyeva (Stalin), LBJL.
86. Gore-Booth to Lord Hood, 27 April 1967, FO 95/14, UKNA.
87. Memorandum, 'Svetlana', undated, FO 95/14, UKNA.
88. Anne Applebaum, *Gulag: A History of the Soviet Camps* (London: Allen Lane, 2003), pp. 476–77; Mark Hopkins, *Russia's Underground Press: The Chronicle of Current Events* (New York: Praeger, 1983), pp. 1–14.
89. Mittal, 'Unending Soviet War on Intellectuals', undated, FCO 168/3402, UKNA.
90. Greenhill to P.U.S., 28 April 1967, FO 95/14, UKNA.
91. *Times of India*, 7 June 1967, p. 8.
92. Giffard to Greenhill, 20 September 1967, FCO 28/397; Day to Stewart, 22 September 1967, FCO 28/397, UKNA.
93. McMinnies minute, 20 October 1969, FCO 37/375, UKNA.
94. 'Svetlana Letter', 18 August 1967, FCO 168/2847, UKNA.
95. Welser to Clive, 28 July 1967, FCO 168/2847, UKNA.
96. Thomas to Bayne, 19 July 1967, FCO 168/2847, UKNA.
97. Welser minute, 20 July 1967, FCO 168/2847, UKNA.
98. Bayne to Welser, 19 July 1967, FCO 168/2847, UKNA.
99. KGB Department ('DEZINFORMATSIYA'), undated. August 1967, FCO 168/2847, UKNA.
100. 'Victor Louis', undated. August 1967, FCO 168/2847, UKNA.
101. 'Svetlana STALIN's Memoirs', 9 August 1967, FCO 168/2847; Memorandum to Crook, 31 August 1967, FCO 168/2847, UKNA.
102. *National Review*, 19 (18), 9 May 1967, p. 1.
103. *Times of India*, 7 June 1967, p. 8.
104. Intriguingly, John le Carré's Swiss publishers attempted sometime later to persuade the British author to co-write a work of 'philosophical non-fiction' with Alliluyeva. Alliluyeva was keen, le Carré was not, and the project proved abortive. le Carré to Sir Alec Guinness, 27 January 1982 in Tim Cornwell (ed.). *A Private Spy: The Letters of John le Carré* (London; Viking, 2022), p. 241.
105. Harrison to FO, 27 May 1967, FCO 28/397, UKNA.
106. *Daily Mail*, 3 November 1984.
107. Alliluyeva Press Conference, 16 November 1984, FCO 168/2847, UKNA.
108. *Times of India*, 21 December 1967, p. 1.
109. Ibid.

302   NOTES TO PAGES 174–82

110. See John D. Smith, *I Was a CIA Agent in India* (New Delhi: New Age Printing Press, 1967).
111. *Times of India*, 21 December 1967, p. 1.
112. *Times*, 22 December 1967, p. 1.
113. *Times of India*, 21 December 1967, p. 1.
114. Stella Rimington, *Open Secret: The Autobiography of the Former Director-General of MI5* (London: Arrow Books, 2002), p. 74.
115. Greene interview, 12 March 1993, FAOHP.
116. *Times of India*, 22 December 1967, p. 1.
117. Ibid.
118. Greene interview, FAOHP.
119. *Times of India*, 27 December 1967, p. 9.
120. Ibid. p. 1.
121. *Times of India*, 28 December 1967, p. 12.
122. *Times of India*, 29 December 1967, p. 5.
123. MEA to Diplomatic Missions in New Delhi, 30 December 1967, FCO 37/62, UKNA.
124. Cole to Hunt, 5 January 1968, FCO 37/62, UKNA.
125. Hunt to Cole, 4 March 1968, FCO 37/62, UKNA.
126. *Lok Sabha*, Unstarred Question No. 360, 14 February 1968.
127. Clive to Jackson, 5 January 1968; Payne to Welser and Clive, 8 January 1968, FCO 168/2850, UKNA.
128. McMinnies to Lancashire, 22 December 1968; Lancashire to McMinnies, 4 January 1968, FCO 168/2850, UKNA.
129. Peck to Greenhill, 12 February 1968, FCO 168/ 2850, UKNA.
130. Tucker to Hamilton, 20 February 1968; O'Connor Howe to Bayne, 29 November 1968, FCO 168/2850, UKNA.
131. *Hindustan Times*, 3 January 1968.
132. *Times of India*, 4 January 1968, p. 8.
133. *Times of India*, 10 February 1970, p. 1.
134. *Times of India*, 21 June 1972, p. 1.
135. Hunting, 'Amnesty International Report 1975/1976: Section on India', 29 November 1976, FCO 37/1933, UKNA.
136. Vance to Embassy Delhi, 4 February 1977, Document no. 1977STATE025389, USNA.

8   The Foreign Hand: Indira Gandhi and the Politics of Intelligence

1. Sol Stern, 'An Expose: The CIA and the National Students Association', *Ramparts*, 5, 7 (March 1967), pp. 29–38.
2. See, Neil Sheehan, 'A Student Group Concedes It Took Funds from the CIA', *New York Times*, 14 February 1967, p. 1; Walter Lippmann, 'The CIA Affair', *Washington Post*, 21 February 1967, p. A21.
3. Frank Church, 25 September 1975, Select Committee to Study Governmental Operations with Respect to Intelligence Activities, Washington D. C.INTERNET, www.aarclibrary.org/publib/church/reports/vol2/pdf/ChurchV2_3_Brennan.pdf
4. Richard J. Aldrich, '"The Value of Residual Empire": Anglo-American Intelligence Co-operation in Asia after 1945' in *Intelligence, Defence and*

NOTES TO PAGES 182–87   303

Diplomacy: British Policy in the Post-War World, eds., Richard J. Aldrich and Michael F. Hopkins (London: Frank Cass, 1994), p. 246.

5. Pauly V. Parakal, *CIA Dagger against India* (New Delhi: New Age Press, 1973), pp. 53–54.
6. Lancashire to Joy, 10 and 21 February 1967, FCO 37/35, UKNA.
7. A. Maslennlkov, *Pravda*, 'The Long Arms of the C.I.A.', 31 January 1967.
8. John Kenneth Galbraith, 'CIA Needs a Tug on Its Purse Strings', *Washington Post*, 12 March 1967, p. B1.
9. Helms to Lyndon Johnson, 28 March 1967, Box 9, Folder CIA vol. 3 [1 of 2], N[ational] S[ecurity] F[ile], Lyndon Baines Johnson Library, Austin, Texas (hereafter LBJL). See also, Hugh Wilford, *The Mighty Wurlitzer: How the CIA Played America* (Cambridge, MA: Harvard University Press, 2008), p. 241.
10. John D. Smith, *I Was a CIA Agent in India* (New Delhi: New Age Printing Press, 1967). See also, Eric D. Pullin, '"Money Does Not Make Any Difference to the Opinions That We Hold": India, the CIA, and the Congress for Cultural Freedom, 1951–58', *Intelligence and National Security*, 26, 2–3 (2011), pp. 377–98.
11. Simons to Purcell, 'The Indian General Election', 13 March 1967, FCO 37/36, UKNA.
12. Lok Sabha Starred Question No. 1, George Fernandes regarding activities of CIA, 20 March 1967, WII/125/11/76 P&I, AMS Division, Ministry of External Affairs (MEA), National Archives of India (hereafter NAI).
13. Ibid.
14. Ibid.
15. 'Half hour discussion in. Lok Sabha on C.I.A.', 23 March 1967, WII/125/11/76 P&I, AMS Division, MEA, NAI.
16. 'India to Conduct Inquiry on C.I.A.', *New York Times*, 24 March 1967, p. 1.
17. 'What has been the extent of K.G.B.'s involvement in India's fourth General Election? Soviet KGB Support 129 Candidates', *Young India*, June 1967, pp. 5–8, p. 45.
18. Lancashire to Joy, 'Allegations of CIA and Communist Financial Involvement in Indian General Elections', 16 June 1967, FCO 37/36, UKNA.
19. Lancashire to McMinnies, 'Alleged KGB Involvement in Indian General Elections', 18 October 1967, FCO 37/36, UKNA.
20. 'New Delhi Report Says C.I.A. Helped Rightists in Elections', *New York Times*, 13 June 1967, p. 6.
21. 'Inquiry ordered into "leakage" of CIB report: Chavan', *Hindustan Times*, 16 June 1967.
22. Christopher Andrew and Vasili Mitrokhin, *The Mitrokhin Archive II: The KGB and the Wider World* (London: Penguin, 2005), pp. 317–18. See also, John Barron, *KGB Today: The Hidden Hand* (London: Hodder and Stoughton, 1984).
23. 'India', 15 November 1967, FCO95/290, UKNA.
24. Leonid Shebarshin, *Ruka Moskvy* (Moscow: Tsentr-100, 1992), cited in Andrew and Mitrokhin, *The Mitrokhin Archive II*, pp. 317–18.
25. 'South Asian Heads of Mission Conference – The Communist Powers and South Asia', 2 May 1973, FCO 37/1213, UKNA.
26. 'Brief Progress Report on IRD work in India, 1 January–30 June 1967', and 'India', 15 November 1967, FCO 95/290, UKNA.
27. 'Where "I spy" is a national industry', *The Observer*, 3 December 1967.
28. McNally to Weston, 20 August 1975, FCO 37/1593, UKNA.

304 NOTES TO PAGES 187–92

29. Biographical Sketch of Indira Gandhi, 23 March 1966, NSF, Country File, India, Box 133, Folder 4 Prime Minister Gandhi Briefing Book 3-27-4-1-66, LBJL.
30. Krishna Bhatia, *Indira: A Biography of Prime Minister Gandhi* (London: Angus & Robertson, 1974), p. 21.
31. Bowles to Johnson, No. 1820, 16 January 1966, NSF Country File, India, Box 130, Folder 1 India Cables [1 of 3] vol. VI 9-65 to 1-66, LBJL.
32. 'National Intelligence Survey: India September 1973', CIA-RDP01 -00707000200070032-3, CREST.
33. 'Mrs. Indira Gandhi', 15 January 1964, RG59, Lot 68D207, Box 5, USNA.
34. Moynihan to Kissinger, No. 3458, 'Mrs Gandhi on the Hustings', 27 March 1973, RG 59, Central Foreign Policy Files, Electronic Telegrams, 1/1/1973-21/31/1973, USNA.
35. Telecon between Rogers and Kissinger, Washington, 24 October 1970, *Foreign Relations of the United*, 1969–1976 Volume E-7, Documents on South Asia, 1969–1972, Document 89, INTERNET, http://history.state.gov/historicaldocu ments/frus1969-76ve07/d89
36. Saxbe to Secretary of State, No. 03530, 'Prime Minister Gandhi Comments on CIA Activity', 13 March 1975, RG59, Central Foreign Policy Files, Electronic Telegrams, 1/1/1975-21/31/1975, USNA.
37. Russell Jack Smith, *The Unknown CIA: CIA: My Three Decades with the Agency* (New York: Berkley Books, 1992), p. 13.
38. Daniel Patrick Moynihan, *A Dangerous Place* (Boston: Little Brown, 1978), p. 41.
39. Saxbe to Secretary of State, No. 03530, 'Prime Minister Gandhi Comments on CIA Activity', 13 March 1975, RG 59, Central Foreign Policy Files, Electronic Telegrams, 1/1/1975-21/31/1975; Saxbe to Secretary of State, No. 03606, 'Indo-US Intelligence Cooperation Reported in Press', 14 March 1975, RG 59, Central Foreign Policy Files, Electronic Telegrams, 1/1/1975-21/31/1975, USNA.
40. 'India Party Chief Leads New Anti-CIA Drive', *Los Angeles Times*, 5 October 1972, p. A21.
41. Roberts to Martin, 'The Poodle Not House-Trained', 19 October 1972, FCO 95/ 1347, UKNA.
42. Garvey to FCO, No. 2595, 23 October 1972, FCO 95/1388, UKNA.
43. 'Hitting Out Wildly', *Statesman*, 12 October 1972.
44. USIS Media Reaction Report, New Delhi, 26 September 1972, FCO 95/1388, UKNA.
45. Christophe Jaffrelot and Pratinav Anil, *India's First Dictatorship: The Emergency, 1975–1977* (London: Hurst, 2020), p. 10.
46. India Issues Paper, 9 July 1975, RG 59, Lot file 77D389, Box 26, Folder General 1973, USNA.
47. Jaffrelot and Anil, *India's First Dictatorship*, p. 61.
48. Schneider to Secretary of State, No. 07903, 16 June 1975, RG 59, CFP, Electronic Telegrams, 1/1/1975-21/31/1975, USNA.
49. Schneider to Secretary of State, No. 08067, 19 June 1975, CFP, Electronic Telegrams, 1/1/1975-21/31/1975, RG 59, USNA; and, Moynihan (1978), p. 150.
50. Kissinger to Moynihan, No. 242175, 10 December 1973, CFP, Electronic Telegrams, 1/1/1973-21/31/1973, RG 59, USNA.
51. India Issues Paper, 9 July 1975, RG 59, Lot file 77D389, Box 26, Folder General 1973, USNA.

NOTES TO PAGES 192–97

52. Maloy Krishna Dhar, *Open Secrets: India's Intelligence Unveiled* (New Delhi: Manas Publications, 2012), p. 245.
53. Nixon to Haldeman, Ehrlichman, and Kissinger, 2 March 1970, *FRUS 1969–1976*, I, 61.
54. 'Indo-American Relations 1970', 2 March 1970, RG59, Lot file 74D17, Box 14, USNA.
55. R. N. Kao to Indira Gandhi, 3 December 1972, P. N. Haksar Papers, III Instalment, Subject File 265, NMML.
56. Richard Nixon, *RN: The Memoirs of Richard Nixon* (New York: Simon & Schuster, 1978), p. 131; Henry Kissinger, *The White House Years* (London: Weidenfeld & Nicolson, 1979), p. 849.
57. Krishna Bhatia, *Indira: A Biography of Prime Minister Gandhi* (London: Angus & Robertson, 1974), p. 250.
58. Bajpai to Banerjee, No, 1382-D(AMS)/67, 27 April 1967, File No. WII/102 (II)/76, Volume 1, American Division, MEA, NAI.
59. Summary of Conclusions, Washington Special Actions Group Meeting, 'India and Pakistan', 17 August 1971, LOC-HAK-559-30–10-7, CIA FOIA Electronic Reading Room, www.foia.cia.gov.
60. Nixon, *RN*, pp. 526–31.
61. 'Discussion between Richard Nixon and Edward Heath', Bermuda, 21 December 1971, FCO 82/21, UKNA.
62. Conversation between President Nixon and Kissinger, 26 May 1971; Conversation between Nixon, Kissinger, and Haldeman, 5 November 1971, *Foreign Relations of the United States, 1969–1976*, vol. E–7, Documents on South Asia, 1969–1972, Documents 135 and 150, INTERNET http://history.state.gov/historicaldocuments/frus1969-76ve07; Memorandum on NSC meeting, 16 July 1971, *FRUS 1971*, pp. 264–67; and, Kissinger, *White House Years*, p. 848.
63. Thomas Powers, *The Man Who Kept the Secrets: Richard Helms and the CIA* (New York: Simon & Schuster, 1979), pp. 255–56.
64. George Carver interview with Harold Ford, Washington DC, 12 February 1987, cited in Ford, *William E. Colby*, p. 16.
65. Nixon to Haldeman, 18 May 1972, cited in Bruce Oudes, ed., *From the President: Richard Nixon's Secret Files* (New York: Andre Deutsch, 1998), p. 448.
66. 'Indo-American Relations 1970', 2 March 1970, RG59, Lot file 74D17, Box 14, USNA.
67. Richard N. Viets, 6 April 1990, FAOHC.
68. 'Indo-American Relations 1970', 2 March 1970, RG59, Lot file 74D17, Box 14, USNA.
69. Viets, FAOHC.
70. Howard B. Schaffer, 10 March 1997, FAOHC.
71. Leonard J. Saccio, 30 September 1990, FAOHC.
72. Ibid.
73. Transcript of Moscow Radio Broadcast to India, 2 February 1971, RG 84, Box 10, Folder Miscellaneous Items, USNA.
74. Keating to Galbraith, 25 February 1971, RG 84, Box 5, Folder Galbraith, USNA.
75. Garvey to Douglas-Home, 'Annual Review 1972', 3 January 1972, FCO 37/1281, UKNA.
76. Garvey to Appleyard, 'Indo/US Relations', 19 July 1972, FCO 37/1097, UKNA.

306 NOTES TO PAGES 198–203

77. Keating to Secretary of State, No. 9257, 25 July 1972, RG 84, Box 28, Folder Gandhi, Prime Minister Indira, Miscellaneous Cables, USNA.
78. Bernard Weinraub, 'Daniel Moynihan's Passage to India', *New York Times Magazine*, 31 (March 1974), p. 256.
79. Tom Wicker, 'Out of the Frying Pan, Into the Fire', *New York Times* News Service, 1972, Box I-352, Folder India Correspondence B7 1973–1975, Daniel Patrick Moynihan Papers, Library of Congress (DPMP).
80. Barreaux to Moynihan, 13 December 1972, Box I-352, Folder India Correspondence Congratulatory 2, DPMP.
81. 'Current Topics', *Times of India*, 12 December 1972.
82. 'A New Ambassador', *Indian Express*, 18 December 1972.
83. 'Tricky Dick's Ayaram!' *Blitz*, 6 January 1973.
84. Draft Manuscript for 'A Dangerous Place', I-350 Speeches and Writings File Folder A, DPMP; Moynihan, *Dangerous Place*, p. 16.
85. Moynihan to Kissinger, 22 November 1973, Box 370, DPMP.
86. Moynihan to Professor Lockwood, 29 July 1974, Box 361, DPMP.
87. Moynihan notes, 20 February 1974, Box 361, DPMP.
88. Moynihan to Davis, 19 June 1974, Box 361, DPMP.
89. G. K. Reddy, 'United States, India and Moynihan', *The Hindu*, 18 April 1973.
90. Moynihan to Kissinger, 10 March 1973, Box I-377 Folder India Subject File White House 1973, DPMP.
91. Moynihan to Galbraith, 10 May 1973, Box I-377 Folder India Subject File Soviet Union 1973–74, DPMP.
92. Steven R. Weisman (ed.), *A Portrait in Letters* (Public Affairs: New York, 2010), Moynihan diary entry 7 January 1974, pp. 323–24.
93. Weisman, *A Portrait in Letters*, Moynihan diary entries 6 August and 5 September 1974, pp. 346 and 351–52.
94. First draft manuscript for 'A Dangerous Place', III-4, I-348 Speeches and Writings File Folder A, DPMP.
95. Bernard Weinraub, 'Daniel Moynihan's Passage to India', *New York Times Magazine*, 31 March 1974, p. 256.
96. Swaran Singh Statement at UN Assembly, MEA Press Relations Section, 3 October 1973, WII/101/20/73, NAI.
97. See P. N. Dhar, *Indira Gandhi, the 'Emergency' and Indian Democracy* (New Delhi: Oxford University Press 2000); Katherine Frank, *Indira: The Life of Indira Nehru Gandhi* (London: Harper Collins, 2002); and Inder Malhotra, *Indira Gandhi: A Personal and Political Biography* (London: Hodder & Stoughton, 1989).
98. S. K. Singh to Indian Delegation in New York, 17 September 1973, MEA, WII/101/20/73, NAI.
99. Fidel Castro, 'Brave Calmness of a Dedicated Leader' in G. Parthasarathi and H. Y. Sharada Prasad (eds.), *Indira Gandhi: Statesmen, Scholars, Scientists, and Friends Remember* (New Delhi: Vikas Publishing, 1985), p. 103.
100. J. K. Gujral, *Matters of Discretion: An Autobiography* (New Delhi: Hay House, 2011), p. 85.
101. *Socialist India*, 13 April 1974, p. 31.
102. Kuldip Nayar, *The Judgement: Inside Story of the Emergency in India* (New Delhi: Vikas, 1977), p. 83.

NOTES TO PAGES 203–8   307

103. Appleyard to Seward, 'Indo/American Relations', 20 September 1973, FCO 37/1287, UKNA.

104. 'Address to the plenary session of the fourth Summit conference of the Non-aligned countries', Algiers, 6 September 1973, in Indira Gandhi, *Selected Speeches and Writings of Indira Gandhi, Volume II, September 1972–March 1977* (New Delhi: Ministry of Information and Broadcasting Government of India, 1984), pp. 668–72.

105. Schneider to Secretary of State, No. 07903, 16 June 1975, RG 59, CFP, Electronic Telegrams, 1/1/1975-12/31/1975, USNA.

106. *Socialist Weekly*, 15 August 1975.

107. Girilal Jain, 'Where India has Faltered: No Parallel with Chile', *Times of India*, 19 September 1973.

108. Moynihan to Secretary of State, No. 12063, 10 September 1974, RG 59, CFP, Electronic Telegrams 1/1/1974-12/31/1974, USNA.

109. See, *Patriot* and *Times of India*, 9 September 1974.

110. Moynihan to Secretary of State, No. 12063, 10 September 1974, CFP, Electronic Telegrams, 1/1/1974-12/31/1974, RG 59, USNA.

111. 'Concern by India on C.I.A. Related', *New York Times*, 13 September 13, 1974, p. 11.

112. Galbraith to Moynihan, 26 September 1974, I-354, Folder India Galbraith, John Kenneth, 1973-74, DPMP.

113. 'United States Relations with Communist Countries', United States Senate, Committee on Foreign Relations, 19 September 1974, 'Foreign Policy of USA', FCO 82/423, UKNA.

114. William E. Colby, 'The View from Langley', address to the Fund for Peace Conference on 'The CIA and Covert Actions', 13 September 1974, Box I: 371, Folder India: Central Intelligence Agency, DPMP.

115. Moynihan to Kissinger, No. 16066, 3 December 1974, Box I-371, Folder India: Central Intelligence Agency, DPMP.

116. Weisman, *Portrait in Letters*, diary entry 27 November 1974, p. 360.

117. Last press conference in India, I-352 Folder India Correspondence B7, 1973–1975, DPMP; Moynihan, *Dangerous Place*, p. 16.

118. Saxbe to Secretary of State, No. 09951, 24 July 1975, RG 59, Central Foreign Policy Files, Electronic Telegrams, 1/1/1975-21/31/1975, USNA.

119. 'Charges of CIA Meddling in India Draw Saxbe's Ire', *Los Angeles Times*, 12 August 1975, p. A1.; Bernard Weintraub, 'Saxbe Follows an Off-Beat, Aloof Course as American Ambassador in India', *New York Times*, 27 May 1975, p. 9.

120. Saxbe to the Department of State, No. 1767 5 February 1976, Presidential Country Files for Middle East and South Asia, Box 12, India, State Telegrams to Secretary of State NODIS (3), Gerald Ford Presidential Library, Ann Arbor, Michigan (hereafter GFPL).

121. Saxbe to the Department of State, No. 787, 15 January 1976, 'Mrs. Gandhi's Attacks on US', Presidential Country Files Middle East and South Asia, Box 12, India, State to Sec State NODIS (3), GPFL.

122. Millington to Hum, 'Indo-US Relations', 23 February 1976, FCO 37/1724 UKNA.

123. Greenhill to Prime Minister, 'Meeting with Mrs Gandhi on 1 September', 1 September 1980, FCO 37/2321 UKNA.

124. Kao to Bush, 30 June 1984, Country File India 1984 [3] [OA-ID 19779], GWBL.

125. Jaffrelot and Anil, *India's First Dictatorship*, p. 54.

308   NOTES TO PAGES 208–15

126. Hum to Christopher, 'Sanjay Gandhi', 11 December 1975, FCO 37/1597, UKNA.
127. 'C.I.A. Study Details Failures; Scouring of System Is Urged', *New York Times*, 3 June 1998, p. A1.; 'CIA Faces Heavy Fallout over India Nuclear *Tests*', *Wall Street Journal*, 13 May 1998.
128. 'Moscow's anger grows: Role of the CIA condemned', *Times*, 2 November 1984, p. 5.
129. 'Superpower clash: Blaming of CIA arouses US fury', *Times*, 3 November 1984, p. 5.

9   Battle of the Books: Daniel Patrick Moynihan, Seymour Hersh, and India's CIA 'Agents'

1. Daniel Patrick Moynihan, *A Dangerous Place* (Boston: Little Brown, 1978).
2. Howard Kohn, 'The Nanda Devi Caper', *Outside Magazine* (May 1978).
3. Thomas Powers, *The Man Who Kept the Secrets: Richard Helms and the CIA* (New York: Simon & Schuster, 1979), p. 262; 'CIA talked of spy in Indira govt', *Times of India*, 15 November 1979, p. 9.
4. Thomson to White, 28 May 1979, FCO 37/2151, United Kingdom National Archives, Kew (UKNA).
5. Seymour Hersh, *The Price of Power: Henry Kissinger in the Nixon White House* (New York: Faber & Faber, 1983).
6. 'Kissinger Takes The Stand', *Washington Post*, 3 October 1989, p. D1.
7. 'On Reported Planting of a Nuclear Device by the CIA in the Nanda Devi', 17 April 1978, Session IV, Lok Sabha Debates (New Delhi: Lok Sabha Secretariat, 1978).
8. Howard Kohn, 'The Nanda Devi Caper', *Outside* (May 1978).
9. Dingell and Ottinger to Carter, 12 April 1978, CIA-RDP81M00980R001200070 033-6, CIA FOIA Electronic Reading Room, www.foia.cia.gov (CIA FOIA).
10. Dingell and Ottinger to Palkhivala 12 April 1978, CIA-RDP81M00980R00 1200070033-6, CIA FOIA.
11. 'CIA planted device may pollute Ganga', *Indian Express*, 13 April 1978.
12. Asrani minute, 13 April 1978, File No. WII/504/7/78, Ministry of External Affairs (MEA), National Archives of India (NAI).
13. Mehta to Mathur, undated. c. 13 April 1978, File No. WII/504/7/78, MEA, NAI.
14. 'CIA Mischief in Himalayas?' *Times of India*, 14 April 1978, p. 8.
15. *Associated Press*, New Delhi, 13 April 1978.
16. Evening Reports, April 1978, Box 20, Subject File Brzezinski Material, National Security Affairs, Jimmy Carter Presidential Library, Atlanta, Georgia.
17. Note for Supplementaries, Rajya Sabha, undated, c. April 1978, File No. WII/504/7/78, MEA, NAI.
18. Goheen to State Department, 17 April 1978, *Foreign Relations of the United States, 1977–1980*, vol. XIX, South Asia (Washington DC: GPO, 2019), p. 261.
19. Balasubramani to Joint Secretary, 20 April 1978, File No. WII/504/7/78, MEA, NAI.
20. Moynihan's time in India is represented as a political and intellectual interregnum in, Godfrey Hodgson, *The Gentleman from New York: Daniel Patrick Moynihan – A Biography* (New York: Houghton Mifflin, 2000); Steven R. Weisman ed., *Daniel Patrick Moynihan: A Portrait in Letters of an American Visionary* (New York: Public

NOTES TO PAGES 215–22

Affairs, 2010); Robert Katzmann (ed.), *Daniel Patrick Moynihan: The Intellectual in Public Life* (Washington DC: Johns Hopkins University Press, 1998); and, Gil Troy, *Moynihan's Moment: America's Fight Against Zionism as Racism* (New York: Oxford University Press US, 2013).

21. 'Moynihan to Quit Senate Panel Post in Dispute on CIA', *New York Times*, 6 April 1984, p. A1.
22. Moynihan, 'Will Russia Blow Up?' *Newsweek*, 19 November 1979, pp. 36–39.
23. Richard Gid Powers, 'Introduction' in Daniel Patrick Moynihan, *Secrecy: The American Experience* (New Haven, CT: Yale University Press, 1998), p. 4.
24. Moynihan, 'Do We still Need the C.I.A.?' *New York Times*, 19 May 1991, p. E17.
25. Moynihan, 'The Central Intelligence Agency Abolition Act of 1995', *Congressional Record*, vol. 141, no. 1, 4 January 1995 (Washington DC: USGPO, 1995).
26. Moynihan, *Secrecy*, p. 3.
27. Bob Woodward, *Veil: The Secret Wars of CIA 1981–1987* (New York: Simon and Schuster, 1987), p. 51.
28. Daniel Patrick Moynihan, 'The United States in Opposition', *Commentary*, March 1975, p. 42.
29. Moynihan, *Dangerous Place*, p. 41; Draft manuscript for 'A Dangerous Place', Box I-348, Folder A, Daniel Patrick Moynihan Papers, Library of Congress (DPMP).
30. Draft manuscript for 'A Dangerous Place', Box I-348, Folder A, DPMP.
31. 'Moynihan's charges baseless: Mrs Gandhi', *Indian Express*, 12 April 1979, p. 1.
32. 'Gandhi Alleges Close Ties between Moynihan, Militant Hindus', 25 April 1979, Box II-2965, Folder 'A Dangerous Place' India's Reaction, DPMP.
33. New Delhi to Secretary of State, 'Further Reaction to "A Dangerous Place"', 20 April 1979, Box II-2965, Folder 'A Dangerous Place' India's Reaction, DPMP.
34. 'Congress (I) Leaders Embarrassed', *The Statesman*, 12 April 1979.
35. 'Deoras wants Mrs Gandhi to prove innocence', *Indian Express*, 16 April 1979.
36. 'Congress (I) Leaders Embarrassed',*The Statesman*, 12 April 1979.
37. 'A Serious Affair', *Statesman*, 14 April 1979.
38. 'Patel urged to disclose CBI report', *Times of India*, 14 April 1979.
39. New Delhi to Secretary of State, 'Further Reaction to "A Dangerous Place"', 20 April 1979, Box II-2965, Folder 'A Dangerous Place' India's Reaction, DPMP.
40. Binns to Pearce, 'Internal Politics: Congress Parties', 19 April 1979, FCO 37/2151, UKNA.
41. 'CIA and CIB worked together: Moynihan', *Indian Express*, 28 April 1979.
42. Fortescue to Binns, 'CIA and Mrs Gandhi', 10 May 1979, FCO 37/2160, UKNA.
43. Jay to FCO, 1 May 1979, FCO 37/2160. UKNA.
44. Fortescue to Binns, 'CIA and Mrs Gandhi', 10 May 1979, FCO 37/2160, UKNA.
45. Goheen to State Department, 'Stormy Debate on Moynihan's Disclosures', 10 May 1979, Box II-2965, Folder 'A Dangerous Place India's Reaction May 1979', DPMP.
46. Weisman, *Portrait in Letters*, diary entry 7 January 1974, pp. 323–24.
47. Powers, *Man Who Kept the Secrets*, pp. 262–63; Tad Szulc, 'Soviet Move to Avert War Is Seen in Pact with India', *New York Times*, 13 August 1971, p. 1; President's Daily Briefs, Dec 1–Dec 16, 1971, Nixon Presidential Materials, NSC Files, Box 37, USNA.
48. Richard Viets interview, 6 April 1990, FAOHP.
49. Simons to Secretary JICS, 21 December 1971, FCO 37/755, UKNA.
50. Cromer to Douglas-Home, 17 December 1971, FCO 37/754, UKNA.

310 NOTES TO PAGES 222–30

51. Conversation between Home and Kissinger, Bermuda, 20 December 1971, FCO 37/754, UKNA.
52. 'CIA talked of spy in Indira govt.', *Times of India*, 15 November 1979, p. 9.
53. 'Raj Narain say J. Ram may have been CIA Agent', *Indian Express*, 19 November 1979, p. 1.
54. 'From Bad to Worse', *Times of India*, 20 November 1979, p. 8.
55. 'C.I.A. Issue Injected into Indian Election', *New York Times*, 20 November 1979, p. A7.
56. 'Indian election campaign gathers momentum', *Times*, 20 November 1979, p. 10.
57. 'Report of High CIA Tipster Stirs Furor in India', *Washington Post*, 22 November 1979, p. A33.
58. Haksar/Jha correspondence quoted in Jairam Ramesh, *Intertwined Lives: P. N. Haksar and Indira Gandhi* (New Delhi: Simon & Schuster India, 2018), pp. 250–51.
59. 'Desai Calls It a "Sheer Mad Story,"' *UP*, New Delhi 2 June 1983; Seymour Hersh, *The Price of Power, Henry Kissinger in the Nixon White House* (New York: Faber & Faber, 1983), pp. 449–50; pp. 459–60.
60. Seymour Hersh, *The Dark Side of Camelot* (Boston: Little Brown & Company, 1997); Lloyd Grove, 'Was the Writing on the Wall?' *Washington Post*, 27 October 1997, p. C1; Edward Jay Epstein, 'Recovered Memories', *Los Angeles Times*, 28 December 1997, p. F6; Ramesh Chandran, 'Letter from America', *Times of India*, 23 November 1997, p. 11.
61. Hersh, *Price of Power*, p. 450; pp. 459–60.
62. 'Blatant holes in charge against Desai', *Times of India*, 4 June 1983, p. 1.
63. Hersh, *Price of Power*, p. 450.
64. 'Blatant holes in charge against Desai', *Times of India*, 4 June 1983, p. 1.
65. 'Hersh sticks to charge', *Times of India*, 5 June 1983, p. 9.
66. 'U.S. may have referred to another Desai', *Times of India*, 5 June 1983, p. 9.
67. 'Morarji may file suit against Hersh', *Times of India*, 18 June 1983, p. 1.
68. Mehta, 'Complaint Law', 17 June 1983, Folder 1, Box 55, Desai v Hersh 1983, Elmer Gertz Papers, Library of Congress, Manuscripts Division (EGP).
69. 'Remarks as to motion concerning interrogatories', Folder 1, Box 55, Desai v Hersh 1983, EGP.
70. 'Around the World', *New York Times*, 14 July 1983, p. A5.
71. 'Morarji's plea for stay rejected', *Times of India*, 4 August 1983, p. 1.
72. Reuters report, New Delhi, 19 June 1983.
73. 'US silence on Hersh charge queried', *Times of India*, 17 July 1983, p. 9.
74. 'Stephen hits out at Vajpayee', *Times of India*, 19 July 1983, p. 9.
75. 'Plea for discussion on Hersh's charge', *Times of India*, 29 July 1983, p. 5.
76. 'Morarji's "CIA link', *Times of India*, 27 August 1983, p. 1.
77. 'Allegations by Mr Seymour Hersh against Shri Morarji Desai', 26 August 1983, *Session XII, Lok Sabha Debates* (New Delhi: Lok Sabha Secretariat, 1983).
78. 'Secrecy ordered in Morarji case', *Times of India*, 26 May 1984, p. 1.
79. 'Morarji Desai rejects Hersh offer', *Times of India*, 13 October 1987, p. 1.
80. 'CIA sticks to usual "no" in Desai case', *Times of India*, 11 May 1985, p. 9.
81. 'Kissinger Takes The Stand', *Washington Post*, 3 October 1989, p. D1; 'Desai an honest man: Kissinger', *Times of India*, 4 October 1989, p. 15.
82. 'Indian's Libel Case Nearing Decision', *New York Times*, 3 October 1989. p. A19.

NOTES TO PAGES 230–38

83. 'U.S. Journalist Cleared of Libel Charge by Indian', *New York Times*, 7 October 1989, p. 24.
84. 'People angry over verdict', *Times of India*, 8 October 1989, p. 11.
85. 'P. V. Narasimha Rao misled Parliament on help to writer Seymour Hersh who called Morarji Desai a CIA mole', *Times of India*, 8 November 2011, p. 1.
86. R. K. Yadav, *Mission R&AW* (New Delhi: Manas Publications, 2014), p. 360.
87. Parthasarathy to Dixit, 16 November 1979, No. WAS/ISI/303/1/79, File WII/103/6/79, AMS, MEA, NAI.
88. Associated Press, New Delhi, 28 February 1977.
89. Yadav, *Mission R&AW*, p. 361; See also Christophe Jaffrelot and Pratinav Anil, *India's First Dictatorship: The Emergency, 1975–1977* (London: Hurst, 2020), p. 11.

10   Indian Intelligence and the End of the Cold War

1. Bahukutumbi Raman, *The Kaoboys of R&AW: Down Memory Lane* (New Delhi: Lancer, 2007), p. 23.
2. Bush to Kao, 19 June 1984, Country File India 1984 [1] [OA-ID 19779], George W. Bush Library, College Station, Texas (GWBL).
3. Kao to Bush, 13 April 1984, Country File India 1984 [3] [OA-ID 19779], GWBL.
4. Gregg and Doran to Bush, 'Comments on Meetings between Indian Foreign Secretary Rasgotra and Pakistani Foreign Secretary Naik', 13 June 1984, Country File India 1984 [1] [OA-ID 19779], GWBL.
5. 'When a kidnap marred George H. W. Bush's only India visit', *Hindu*, 1 December 2018, www.thehindu.com/news/national/when-a-kidnap-marred-george-hw-bushs-only-india-visit/article62020680.ece
6. Bush to Kao, 19 June 1984, Country File India 1984 [1] [OA-ID 19779], GWBL.
7. Ibid.
8. Kennedy to Nehru, 18 January 1962, National Security Files, Countries Series, India, Nehru Correspondence, 1/15/62-3/31/62, John. F. Kennedy Library, Boston, Massachusetts (JFKL).
9. *Times of India*, 28 June 1975, p. 2.
10. Kao to Bush, 30 June 1984, Country File India 1984 [3] [OA-ID 19779], GWBL.
11. 'US Congressional Perspectives of India', Twenty-Sixth Session, 1983–84, United States Department of State, Foreign Service Institute, Country File India 1985 [3] [OA-ID 19797], GWBL.
12. Raman, *Kaoboys of R&AW*, p. 43.
13. Joseph E. Persico, *Casey: From the OSS to the CIA* (New York: Viking, 1990), p. 313.
14. 'South Asian Heads of Mission Conference – The Communist Powers and South Asia', 2 May 1973, FCO 37/1213, United Kingdom National Archives, Kew, London (UKNA).
15. Ibid.
16. 'MOD Paper for Sir Clive Rose's Working Group on Policy Towards India: Defence Relations with India', 2 March 1977, FCO 37/1935, UKNA.
17. Eagleburger, Spiers, Wolfowitz to Haig, 13 April 1981, 'Countering Soviet Covert Action and Propaganda', *Foreign Relations of the United States (FRUS)*, 1981–1988, vol. III, doc. 41, https://history.state.gov/historicaldocuments/frus1981-88v03/d41
18. Haksar to Gandhi, 9 July 1982, Subject File 287, Instalment III, P. N. Haksar Papers, Nehru Museum and Memorial Library (NMML).

312   NOTES TO PAGES 238–46

19. Haksar to Gandhi, 19 November 1974, P. N. Haksar Papers, III Instalment, Subject File 269, NMML.
20. Haksar to Gandhi, 9 July 1982, Subject File 287, Instalment III, P. N. Haksar Papers, NMML.
21. 'P. M's Meeting with Selig Harrison, 22 March 1984, Parliament House', Polish Intelligence Files, IPN BU 0 449/5t. 62, Central Military Archive, Military Historical Office, Warsaw.
22. Bob Woodward, *Veil: The Secret Wars of CIA 1981–1987* (New York: Simon and Schuster, 1987), p. 56.
23. T. V. Rajeswar, *India: The Crucial Years* (Noida, UP: Harper Collins India, 2015), pp. 139–40.
24. Blitz quoted in *New York Times*, 2 September 1981, p. A-10.
25. 'India Bars Senior U.S. Diplomat, Stirring a Dispute', *New York Times*, 2 September 1981, p. A-10.
26. See, Henry Kissinger, *The White House Years* (London: Weidenfeld & Nicolson, 1979); and Lawrence Lifschultz, *Bangladesh: The Unfinished Revolution* (London: Zed Press, 1979).
27. 'Reported Indo-United States difference over posting of diplomats', Cols. 287-300, 8 September 1981, Lok Sabha Debates, *Seventh Series*, no. 17 (New Delhi: Lok Sabha Secretariat, 1981).
28. 'Indians explain rejection of envoy', *Guardian*, 9 September 1981.
29. *Associated Press*, New Delhi, 6 December 1983.
30. 'U.S. diplomat ousted from India', *United Press International*, 8 December 1983.
31. Williams to James, 21 December 1983, FCO 37/3229, UKNA.
32. 'India: 3 Spied for U.S.', *New York Daily News*, 25 July 1985, p. C-8.
33. 'Soviet "Active Measures": Forgery, Disinformation, Political Operations', Special Report No. 88, October 1981, United States Department of State, Bureau of Public Affairs (Washington, DC: USGPO, 1981).
34. Christophe Jaffrelot and Pratinav Anil, *India's First Dictatorship: The Emergency, 1975–1977* (London: Hurst, 2020), p. 414.
35. Melinda Beck and David C. Martin, 'The Soviets' Dirty-Tricks Squad', *Newsweek*, 98,21 (23 November 1981), pp. 52–53.
36. Soviet 'Active Measures': Forgery, Disinformation, Political Operations', Special Report No. 88, October 1981, United States Department of State, Bureau of Public Affairs (Washington, DC: USGPO, 1981).
37. 'Pro-Soviet Press in India Mounts Propaganda Drive Against U.S.', *Washington Post*, 17 February 1983, p. A33.
38. BBC Summary of World Broadcasts, Radio Moscow, 29 March 1983, '"Destructive Acts" of CIA in Indian North-East', GB898 BBC/PUB/SWB, BBC Written Archives Centre, Caversham Park, Reading (BBC). Soviet propaganda had publicised alleged CIA operations in northeast India from the 1950s. See, John D. Smith. *I Was a CIA Agent in India* (New Delhi: New Age Printing Press, 1967), pp. 20–21; Rustem Galiullin, *The CIA in Asia: Covert Operations against India and Afghanistan* (Moscow: Progress Publishers, 1988), pp. 83–85.
39. BBC Summary of World Broadcasts, Radio Moscow, 17 August 1983, '"Komsomolskaya Pravda" on CIA Support for Indian Separatists', GB898 BBC/PUB/SWB, BBC.
40. The Patriot, 'AIDS may invade India: mystery disease caused by U.S. lab experiments', 16 July 1983, p. 1. See also, Thomas Rid, *Active Measures: The*

NOTES TO PAGES 246–53

Secret History of Disinformation and Political Warfare (London: Profile Books, 2020), pp. 302–4.
41. Rid, *Active Measures*, p. 304.
42. Robert to Stephenson, 12 September 1968, FCO 168/3215, UKNA.
43. Rid, *Active Measures*, p. 428.
44. Dean to Secretary of State, 'The Indo-Soviet Relationship', No. 15164, 21 June 1986, Digital National Security Archive (DNSA), https://nsarchive.gwu.edu/dnsa-collections
45. 'CIA Dagger Behind Plot to Oust Rajiv', *Blitz*, 1 August 1987, p. 1.
46. 'Forgery? Here's Final Proof', *Blitz*, 8 August 1987, p. 1.
47. *Soviet Influence Activities: A Report on Active Measures and Propaganda, 1987–1988*, United States Department of State (Washington DC: USGPO, 1989).
48. 'Gandhi Accepts Assurance of CIA Non-Interference', *Associated Press*, 21 October 1987.
49. 'Gandhi Reports Bush Assurance On CIA Activity', *Washington Post*, 22 October 1987, p. A33.
50. 'CBI Could have handled it better', *Times of India*, 17 December 2015, p. 1.
51. '24 arrests in Delhi spy ring case', *Times*, 21 January 1985, p. 1.
52. Harry Anderson and Sudip Mazumdar, 'Cleaning Out a Nest of Spies', *Newsweek*, 105, 4 (28 January 1985), p. 43; 'Envoy quits Delhi after spy scandal', *Times*, 2 February 1985, p. 5.
53. 'India-USSR-US: Placing Blame in Spy Scandal', 31 January 1985, DOC_0000263061, CIA FOIA Electronic Reading Room, www.foia.cia.gov
54. *United Press International*, New Delhi, 30 January 1985.
55. 'Towards an Even-handed Foreign Policy', 4 February 1985, DOC_0000263067, CIA FOIA Electronic Reading Room, www.foia.cia.gov; 'The Indian Spy Scandal: Soviet bloc contacts are ordered out', *Times*, 6 February 1985, p. 7.
56. 'Intelligible Intelligence', *Times of India*, 21 September 2000, p. 10; 'A Spy Ring at the Center', *Newsweek*, 105, 5 (4 February 1985), p. 35.
57. Hall to Dickinson, 'India: Rama Swarup Espionage Case', 31 January 1986, FCO 37/4442, UKNA.
58. Ibid.
59. 'PM warns MPs against shady invitations', *Indian Express*, 21 February 1986.
60. Broomfield to Wilson, 27 February 1986, FCO 37/4442, UKNA.
61. Hall to Dickinson, 'India: Rama Swarup Espionage Case', 7 March 1986, FCO 37/4442, UKNA.
62. 'Govt Must Explain', *Times of India*, 7 March 1986, p. 8.
63. Wade-Gery to Evans, 14 November 1986, FCO 37/4442, UKNA; 'In Secret Trial, India Sentences 6 for Spying for U.S.', *New York Times*, 30 October 1986, p. A 5.
64. 'Foe of Gandhi Stung by Accusations of C.I.A. Role', *New York Times*, 19 November 1989.
65. 'Moynihan Assails India – C.I.A. charge', *New York Times*, 21 November 1989.
66. 'Foe of Gandhi Stung by Accusations of C.I.A. Role', *New York Times*, 19 November 1989.
67. 'Forgeries blamed on Soviets', *Washington Times*, 23 November 1989.
68. 'Rajiv got Soviet funds: daily', *Times of India*, 29 June 1992, p. 1.
69. Yevgenia Albats and Catherine Fitzpatrick, *The State Within a State: The KGB and Its Hold on Russia, Past and Present* (New York: Farrar Straus & Giroux, 1994), p. 223.

314 NOTES TO PAGES 255–62

70. 'India's Search for Villains Finds Old Culprit: The CIA', *Washington Post*, 14 June 1991, p. A19.
71. Sudheendra Kulkarni, 'Days of the Jackal', *Sunday Observer*, 9 July 1991; 'India's Search for Villains Finds Old Culprit: The CIA', *Washington Post*, 14 June 1991, p. A19.
72. 'India's Search for Villains Finds Old Culprit: The CIA', *Washington Post*, 14 June 1991, p. A19.

Conclusion

1. R. N. Kao to Vappala Balachandran, 12 May 1998, cited in Vappala Balachandran, *National Security and Intelligence Management: A New Paradigm* (Mumbai: Indus Source Books, 2014), p. 312.
2. John le Carré, *Silverview* (London: Viking, 2021), pp. 110–11.
3. Alistair Campbell and Bill Hagerty (eds.), *The Alistair Campbell Diaries: Volume 4: The Burden of Power, Countdown to Iraq*, (London: Arrow Books, 2013), 5 October 2001, p. 39.
4. *The Blair Years: Extracts from the Alastair Campbell Diaries*, ed. Alastair Campbell and Richard Stott (London: Hutchinson, 2007), p. 577.
5. Ibid., pp. 577–78.
6. Campbell and Hagerty, *Campbell Diaries: Volume 4*, 5 October 2001, p. 39. For insights into Dearlove's political perspicacity see, Richard J. Aldrich and Rory Cormac, *The Black Door: Spies, Secret Intelligence and British Prime Ministers* (London: William Collins, 2016), p. 418.
7. Campbell and Hagerty, *Campbell Diaries: Volume 4*, 2 & 5 January 2002, pp. 125–26; p. 129.
8. 'Delhi clumsily bugged Blair's room', *Times of India*, 30 July 2007 https://time sofindia.indiatimes.com/world/uk/delhi-clumsily-bugged-blairs-room/article show/2243144.cms See also, Rashmee Roshan Lall, 'Blair's spin doctor spills the beans: View from London', *Times of India*, 30 July 2007, p. 21.
9. 'Vajpayee govt tried to bug Blair's bedroom in Delhi, IBNlive.com, 20 July 2007, https://web.archive.org/web/20120929145020/http://ibnlive.in.com/news/vaj payee-govt-tried-to-bug-blairs-bedroom-in-delhi/45265-2.html
10. Vir Sanghvi, 'The Foreign Hands', *Hindustan Times*, 23 July 2006 www.hindustan times.com/india/the-foreign-hands/story-otQJcwNAIiDGZrdUBc4F9L.html
11. Ibid.
12. For insights into the role of Suez in fuelling Middle Eastern conspiracism, see, M. Zonis, and C. M. Joseph, 'Conspiracy Thinking in the Middle East', *Political Psychology* 15, 3 (1994), pp. 443–59; and, M. Gray, 'Explaining Conspiracy Theories in Modern Arab Middle Eastern Political Discourse: Some Problems and Limitations of the Literature', *Critique: Critical Middle Eastern Studies* 17, 2 (2008), pp. 155–74.
13. 'US Congressional Perspectives of India', Country File India 1985 [3] [OA-ID 19797], George W. Bush Library, College Station Texas.
14. For an illuminating reassessment of the Shah of Iran, Mohammad Reza Pahlavi, in this context, see Roham Alvandi, *Nixon, Kissinger and the Shah: The United States and Iran in the Cold War* (Oxford: Oxford University Press, 2014).

NOTES TO PAGES 262–66

15. O'Brien to Duff, 'Sino-Indian Relations', 3 March 1966, FO 371/186998, United Kingdom National Archives, Kew (UKNA).
16. Calder Walton, *Empire of Secrets: British Intelligence, the Cold War and the Twilight of Empire* (London: Harper Press, 2013), p. 304.
17. Chikara Hashimoto, *Twilight of the British Empire: British Intelligence and Counter-Subversion in the Middle East, 1948–68* (Edinburgh: Edinburgh University Press, 2017), p. 176.
18. Ruchir Sharma, *Democracy on the Road: A 25-Year Journey through India* (London: Allen Lane, 2019), p. 202.
19. Tony Benn. *Office Without Power: Diaries, Papers, 1968–1972* (ed.) Ruth Winstone (London: Hutchinson, 1988), Thursday 7 March 1968, p. 40.
20. Bill Clinton, 'Remarks at the One America Meeting with Religious Leaders', 9 March 2000, www.presidency.ucsb.edu/documents/remarks-the-one-america-meeting-with-religious-leaders; Barak Obama, 'Remarks on United States Military and Diplomatic Strategies for Afghanistan and Pakistan', 27 March 2009, www.presidency.ucsb.edu/documents/remarks-united-states-military-and-diplomatic-strategies-for-afghanistan-and-pakistan-0
21. For an overview of India's nuclear history, encompassing the 1998 tests, see George N. Perkovich, *India's Nuclear Bomb: The Impact of Global Proliferation* (Berkeley: University of California Press, 1999).
22. 'India: BJP Flexing Muscles, But How Far Will It Go?' CIA Intelligence Report, 29 May 1998, https://nsarchive2.gwu.edu/NSAEBB/NSAEBB187/index.htm
23. Manoj Shrivastava, *Re-Energising Indian Intelligence* (New Delhi: Vij Books, 2013), p. 51.
24. 'N-tests baffle CIA officials', *Times of India*, 13 May 1998, p. 9.
25. George Tenet, *At the Centre of the Storm: My Years at the CIA* (New York: Harper Collins, 2007), p. 69.
26. Praveen Swami, 'India's new language of killing', *The Hindu*, 1 May 2014, www.thehindu.com/opinion/lead/indias-new-language-of-killing/article5963505.ece

BIBLIOGRAPHY

Manuscript Collections

United Kingdom

Bodleian Library, University of Oxford
Clement Attlee Papers
Paul Gore-Booth Papers
Harold Macmillan Papers
Harold Wilson Papers

British Library, India Office Select Materials, London
Olaf Caroe Papers
Indian Civil Service (Retired) Association Papers
Sir John Gilbert Laithwaite Papers
Alexander Symon Papers
BBC Written Archives Centre, Caversham Park, Reading
BBC Summary of World Broadcasts

Churchill Archives Centre, Churchill College Cambridge
Leopold Amery Papers
Thomas Elmhirst Papers
Dingle Foot Papers
Baron Gordon Walker Papers
Lord Hailsham Papers
William John Haley Papers
Duncan Sandys Papers
Earl of Swinton Papers

Royal Commonwealth Society Library, University of Cambridge
Cyril Pickard Papers

BIBLIOGRAPHY   317

Hartley Library, University of Southampton
Lord Mountbatten Papers

Houses of Parliament Archives, London
Reginald Sorenson Papers
John Tilney Papers

Palace Green Library, University Of Durham
Malcolm MacDonald Papers

School of Oriental and African Studies, University of London
Frank Moraes Papers

Unpublished UK Government Documents,
National Archives, Kew, London
Records of the Cabinet Office
Records of the Colonial Office
Records of the Commonwealth Relations Office
Records of the Foreign Office
Records of the Ministry of Defence
Records of the Prime Minister
Records of the Security Service
Records of the Treasury

United States

Library of Congress, Washington, DC
William O. Douglas Papers
Elmer Gertz Papers
Averell Harriman Papers
Loy W. Henderson Papers
Daniel Patrick Moynihan Papers

Butler Library, Columbia University, New York
Dorothy Norman Papers
Harrison Salisbury Papers

Sterling Memorial Library, Yale University, Connecticut
Chester Bowles Papers
Walter Lippmann Papers

318 BIBLIOGRAPHY

Harry S. Truman Library, Independence, Missouri
Dean Acheson Papers
Harry S. Truman Papers

Dwight D. Eisenhower Library, Abilene, Kansas
John Foster Dulles Papers
Dwight D. Eisenhower Papers

John F. Kennedy Library, Boston, Massachusetts
George Ball Papers
McGeorge Bundy Papers
John Kenneth Galbraith Papers
Roswell Gilpatric Papers
Roger Hilsman Papers
Carl Kaysen Papers
John F. Kennedy Papers
Robert Komer Papers

Lyndon Baines Johnson Library, Austin, Texas
George Ball Papers
Lyndon B. Johnson Papers
Robert Komer Papers
Drew Pearson Papers
Bromley Smith Papers

Jimmy Carter Presidential Library, Atlanta, Georgia
Brzezinski Material, National Security Affairs

George H.W. Bush Library, Colleges Station, Texas
National Security Affairs, Country File India

Unpublished US Government Documents, USNA, National Archives of the United States II, College Park, Maryland
Record Group 59, General Records of the Department of State
Record Group 218, Records of the Joint Chiefs of Staff
Record Group 306, Records of the United States Information Agency
Record Group 273, Records of the National Security Council
Central Intelligence Agency Records Search Tool (CREST)

BIBLIOGRAPHY 319

India

Nehru Memorial Museum and Library, New Delhi
G. D. Birla Papers
Subimal Dutt Papers
P. N. Haksar Papers
R. N. Kao Papers
T. N. Kaul Papers
K. P. S. Menon Papers
Vijaya Lakshmi Pandit Papers
C. Rajagopalachari Papers
T. T. Krishnamachari Papers

National Archives of India
Records of the Ministry of External Affairs
Records of the Home Ministry

Published Primary Sources

United Kingdom

Benn, Tony. *Office Without Power: Diaries, Papers, 1968–1972*. London: Hutchinson, 1988.

Campbell, Alistair, and Richard Stott. *The Blair Years: Extracts from the Alastair Campbell Diaries*. London: Hutchinson, 2007.

Campbell, Alistair, and Bill Hagerty (eds.). *The Alistair Campbell Diaries: Volume 4: The Burden of Power, Countdown to Iraq*. London: Arrow Books, 2013.

Mansergh, Nicholas. *Transfer of Power 1942–1947 (TOP)*, vol. III. London: HMSO, 1971.

United States

Committee on Foreign Relations, United States Senate, Eighty-Third Congress, Second Session. Washington, DC: Government Printing Office, 1954.

Foreign Relations of the United States, 1952–54, vol. XI, Africa and South Asia, Part I. Washington, DC: Government Printing Office, 1983.

Foreign Relations of the United States, 1952–54, vol. XI, Africa and South Asia, Part II. Washington, DC: Government Printing Office, 1983.

Foreign Relations of the United States, 1952–54, vol. XII, East Asia and the Pacific. Washington, DC: Government Printing Office, 1984.

Foreign Relations of the United States, 1952–1954, vol. XIII, Indochina. Washington, DC: Government Printing Office, 1982.

320   BIBLIOGRAPHY

Foreign Relations of the United States, 1955–57, vol. VIII, South Asia. Washington, DC: Government Printing Office, 1987.
Foreign Relations of the United States, 1958–60, vol. XV, South and Southeast Asia. Washington, DC: Government Printing Office, 1992.
Foreign Relations of the United States, 1961–1963, vol. XIX, South Asia. Washington, DC: Government Printing Office, 1996.
Foreign Relations of the United States, 1964–1968, vol. XXV, South Asia. Washington, DC: Government Printing Office, 2000.
Foreign Relations of the United States, 1964–1968, vol. XI, South Asia Crisis 1971. Washington, DC: Government Printing Office, 2005.
Foreign Relations of the United States, 1977–1980, vol. XIX, South Asia. Washington, DC: Government Printing Office, 2019.
Foreign Relations of the United States, 1981–1988, vol. III, Soviet Union. Washington, DC: Government Printing Office, 2016.
Galbraith, John Kenneth. *Letters to Kennedy.* London: Harvard University Press, 1998.
Kennedy, John F. *A Compilation of Statements and Speeches Made During His Service in the United States Senate and the House of Representatives.* Washington, DC: Government Printing Office, 1964.
Norman, Dorothy. *Indira Gandhi: Letters to an American Friend, 1950–1984.* New York: Harcourt Brace Jovanovich, 1985.

India

Appadorai, A (ed.). *Select Documents on India's Foreign Policy and Relations, 1947–1972*, vol. 1. New Delhi: Oxford University Press, 1982.
Appadorai, A *Select Documents on India's Foreign Policy and Relations, 1947–1972*, vol. 2. New Delhi: Oxford University Press, 1985.
Chakravorty, B. C. *History of the Indo-Pak War, 1965.* Edited by S. N. Prasad. New Delhi: History Division, Ministry of Defence, Government of India, 1992.
Choudhary, Valmiki (ed.). *Dr. Rajendra Prasad: Correspondence and Select Documents*, vol. 21, January 1960 to February 1963. New Delhi: Allied Publishers Limited, 1995.
Gandhi, Indira. *India: The Speeches and Reminiscences of Indira Gandhi, Prime Minister of India.* London: Hodder & Stoughton, 1975.
Gandhi, Indira. *Selected Speeches and Writings of Indira Gandhi, Volume II, September 1972–March 1977.* New Delhi: Ministry of Information and Broadcasting Government of India, 1984.
Gopal, Sarvepalli (ed.). *The Essential Writings of Jawaharlal Nehru*, vol. 2. Oxford University Press, 2003.
Hasan, Mushirul (ed.) *Selected Works of Jawaharlal Nehru*, Second Series, vol. 36, 1 December 1956–21 February 1957. New Delhi: Oxford University Press, 2005.
Hasan, Mushirul, Sharad Prasad, H. Y. and Damodaran, A. K. (eds.). *Selected Works of Jawaharlal Nehru*, Second Series, vol. 33, 1 May 1956–20 June 1956. New Delhi: Oxford University Press, 2004.
Kumar, Ravinder and Sharada Prasad, H. Y. (eds.). *Selected Works of Jawaharlal Nehru*, Second Series, vol. 27, 1 October 1954–31 January 1955. New Delhi, Oxford University Press: 2000.

BIBLIOGRAPHY   321

Kumar, Ravinder and Sharada Prasad, H. Y. *Selected Works of Jawaharlal Nehru*, vol. 28, 1 February–31 May 1955. New Delhi: Oxford University Press, 2001.

Parthasarathi, G. (ed.). *Jawaharlal Nehru: Letters to Chief Ministers, 1947–1964, vol. 3: 1952–1954.* New Delhi: Oxford University Press, 1989.

Parthasarathi, G. (ed.). *Jawaharlal Nehru: Letters to Chief Ministers, 1947–1964, vol. 5: 1958–1964.* New Delhi: Oxford University Press, 1989.

Parthasarathi, G. and Sharada Prasad, H. Y. (eds.). *Indira Gandhi: Statesmen, Scholars, Scientists, and Friends Remember.* New Delhi: Vikas Publishing, 1985.

Prasad, S. N. (ed.). *History of the Conflict With China, 1962.* New Delhi: History Division, Ministry of Defence, 1992.

Prasad, S. N. *Prime Minister on Chinese Aggression.* New Delhi: Publications Division, Ministry of External Affairs, 1963.

Prasad, S. N. *We Accept China's Challenge: Speeches in the Lok Sabha on India's Resolve to Drive out the Aggressor.* New Delhi: Government of India, Ministry of Information and Broadcasting Publications Division, 1962.

Soviet Union

Bulganin, N. A. and Khrushchev, N. S. *Visit of Friendship to India, Burma and Afghanistan: Speeches and Official Documents, November–December 1955.* Moscow: Foreign Languages Publishing House, 1955.

Newspapers and Periodicals

Daily Mail
Daily Telegraph
Economist
Guardian
Times
Sunday Express
New Republic
New York Times
Time
Newsweek
Wall Street Journal
Washington Post
Los Angeles Times
Commentary
Amrita Bazar Patrika (Calcutta)
Business Week
The Hindu (Madras)
The Hindustan Times (New Delhi)
Indiagram

322   BIBLIOGRAPHY

India Today
The Indian Express (Bombay)
National Herald (Lucknow)
Patriot
Sunday Observer
The Statesman (Calcutta)
The Sunday Statesman (Calcutta)

Online Primary Sources

The Cold War International History Project Digital Archive, Woodrow Wilson International Centre for Scholars, Washington, DC, www.wilsoncenter .org/digital-archive

The Foreign Affairs Oral History Collection, Library of Congress, Washington, DC, http://memory.loc.gov/ammem/collections/diplomacy/

Hansard, 1803–2005, London, http://hansard.millbanksystems.com

Miller Centre Presidential Recordings Program, University of Virginia, Virginia, http://millercenter.org/academic/presidentialrecordings

The National Security Archive, The George Washington University, Washington, DC, www.gwu.edu/~nsarchiv/

Public Papers of the Presidents of the United States, The American Presidency Project, www.presidency.ucsb.edu

Secondary Sources and Memoirs

Albats, Yevgenia and Fitzpatrick, Catherine. *The State Within a State: The KGB and Its Hold on Russia, Past and Present*. New York: Farrar Straus & Giroux, 1994.

Aldrich, Richard J. *The Hidden Hand: Britain, America and Cold War Secret Intelligence*. London: John Murray, 2001.

'American Intelligence and the British Raj: The OSS, the SSU and India, 1942–1947'. *Intelligence and National Security* 13: 1, (Spring 1998), 132–64.

'"The Value of Residual Empire": Anglo-American Intelligence Co-operation in Asia after 1945' . In *Intelligence, Defence and Diplomacy: British Policy in the Post-war World*. Edited by Richard J. Aldrich and Michael F. Hopkins. London: Frank Cass, 1994.

Aldrich, Richard J., and Rory Cormac. *The Black Door: Spies, Secret Intelligence and British Prime Ministers*. London: William Collins, 2016.

Allen, Charles. *Plain Tales from the Raj: Images of India in the Twentieth Century*. London: Andre Deutsch, 1975.

Alliluyeva, Svetlana. *Only One Year*. New York: HarperCollins, 1969.

BIBLIOGRAPHY

Alvandi, Rohan. *Nixon, Kissinger and the Shah: The United States and Iran in the Cold War*. Oxford: Oxford University Press, 2014.

Applebaum, Anne. *Gulag: A History of the Soviet Camps*. London: Allen Lane, 2003.

Andrew, Christopher. *The Defence of the Realm: The Authorized History of MI5*. London: Allen Lane, 2009.

Andrew, Christopher and Mitrokhin, Vasili. *The KGB and the World: The Mitrokhin Archive II*. London: Allen Lane, 2005.

Arora, K. C. *Indian Nationalist Movement in Britain,1930–1949*. New Delhi: South Asia Books, 1993.

V. K. Menon: A Biography. New Delhi: Sanchar Publishing House, 1998.

Baer, Robert. *See No Evil: The True Story of a Ground Soldier in the CIA's War on Terrorism*. London: Penguin Random House, 2002.

Barnds, William J. *India, Pakistan and the Great Powers*. London: Pall Mall Press, 1972.

Barron, John. *KGB Today: The Hidden Hand*. London: Hodder and Stoughton, 1984.

Bayley, Viola. *Memoir of Life in India, 1933–46: One Woman's Raj*. Unpublished manuscript, 1975/76.

Bayly, C. A. *Empire and Information: Intelligence Gathering and Social Communication in India, 1780–1870*. Cambridge: Cambridge University Press, 1996.

Benn, Tony. *Out of the Wilderness: Diaries 1963–67*. London: Hutchinson, 1987.

Beschloss. Michael R. *Mayday: The U-2 Affair*. New York: Harper and Row, 1986.

Bhagavan, Manu. *The Peacemakers: India and the Quest for One World*. New Delhi: Harper Collins, 2012.

Bhatia, Krishna. *Indira: A Biography of Prime Minister Gandhi*. London: Angus & Robertson, 1974.

Biney, A. 'The Development of Kwame Nkrumah's Political Thought in Exile, 1966–1972'. *The Journal of African History* 50, 1 (2009), 81–100.

Black, Lawrence. '"The Bitterest Enemies of Communism": Labour revisionists, Atlanticism and the Cold War'. *Contemporary British History* 15, 3, (2001), 26–62.

Blake, George. *No Other Choice: An Autobiography*. London: Jonathan Cape, 1990.

Bowles, Chester. *Ambassador's Report*. New York: Harper, 1954.

Promises to Keep: My Years in Public Life, 1941–1969. New York: Harper, 1971.

'The "China Problem" Reconsidered'. *Foreign Affairs* 38 (April 1960), 476–86.

Brands, H. W. *The Spectre of Neutralism: The United States and the Emergence of the Third World, 1947–1960*. New York: Columbia University Press, 1989.

Inside the Cold War: Loy Henderson and the Rise of the American Empire, 1918–1961. New York: Oxford University Press, 1991.

Brecher, Michael. *Nehru: A Political Biography*. London: Oxford University Press, 1961.

BIBLIOGRAPHY

India and World Politics: Krishna Menon's View of the World. London: Oxford University Press, 1968.

'Non-Alignment Under Stress: The West and the India-China Border War'. *Pacific Affairs* 52, 4, (Winter 1979–80), 612–30.

Brown, Judith M. *Modern India: The Origins of an Asian Democracy.* Oxford University Press, 1985.

Nehru: A Political Life. New Haven, CT: Yale University Press, 2003.

Buchan, John. *Greenmantle.* London: Hodder & Stoughton, 1916.

Butler, Lord. *The Art of the Possible: The Memoirs of Lord Butler.* London: Hamish Hamilton, 1971.

Buzan, Barry and Gowher, Rizvi (eds.). *South Asian Insecurity and the Great Powers.* New York: St. Martin's Press, 1986.

Campbell-Johnson, Alan. *Mission with Mountbatten.* London: Hamish Hamilton, 1985.

le Carré, John. *The Spy Who Came in from the Cold.* London: Gollancz, 1963.

Tinker, Tailor, Soldier, Spy. London: Hodder and Stoughton, 1974.

Smiley's People. London: Hodder and Stoughton, 1979.

Secret Pilgrim. London: Hodder & Stoughton, 1991.

Silverview. London: Viking, 2021.

Carruthers, Susan L. *Winning Hearts and Minds: British Governments, the Media and Colonial Counter-Insurgency, 1944–60.* Leicester: Leicester University Press, 1995.

Cold War Captives: Imprisonment, Escape and Brainwashing. Berkeley: University of California Press, 2009.

Carton de Wiart, Sir Adrian. *Happy Odyssey: The Memoirs of Lieutenant-General Sir Adrian Carton de Wiart.* London: Jonathan Cape, 1950.

Chakravarty, Suhash. *Crusader Extraordinary: Krishna Menon and the India League, 1932–1936.* New Delhi: India Research Press, 2006.

Chamberlain, Paul Thomas. *The Cold War's Killing Fields: Rethinking the Long Peace.* New York: HarperCollins, 2018.

Cherkashin, Victor. *Spy Handler: Memoir of a KGB Officer – The True Story of the Man Who Recruited Robert Hanssen and Aldrich Ames.* London: Basic Books, 2005.

Clarridge, Duane R. *A Spy for All Seasons: My Life in the CIA.* New York: Scribner, 1997.

Coll, Steve. *Directorate S: The C.I.A. and America's Secret Wars in Afghanistan and Pakistan, 2001–2016.* London: Allen Lane, 2018.

Conboy, Kenneth and Morrison, James. *The CIA's Secret War in Tibet.* Lawrence: University of Kansas Press, 2002.

Cormac, Rory. *Disrupt and Deny: Spies, Special Forces, and the Secret Pursuit of British Foreign Policy.* Oxford: Oxford University Press, 2018.

Cornwell, Tim. (ed.). *A Private Spy: The Letters of John le Carré.* London: Viking, 2022.

BIBLIOGRAPHY 325

Crocker, Walter. *Nehru: A Contemporary's Estimate.* New York: Oxford University Press, 1966.

Curry, John. *The Security Service, 1908–1945: The Official History.* London: PRO, 1999.

Danchev, Alex and Todman, Daniel. (eds.). *War Diaries, 1939–1945: Field Marshal Lord Alanbrooke,* London: Weidenfeld and Nicholson, 2001.

Dauer, Richard P. *A North-South Mind in an East-West World: Chester Bowles and the Making of United States Cold War Foreign Policy, 1951–1969.* Westport, CN: Praeger, 2005.

Davies, Philip, and Gustafson, Kristian (eds.). *Intelligence Elsewhere: Spies and Espionage Outside the Anglosphere.* Washington, DC: Georgetown University Press, 2013.

Defty, A. *Britain, America, and Anti-Communist Propaganda, 1945–53: The Information Research* Department. Abingdon: Routledge, 2003.

Desai, Morarji. *The Story of My Life.* New Delhi: S. Chand, 1978.

The Story of My Life, vol. 2. Oxford: Pergamon Press, 1979.

Desai, Tripta. *Indo-U.S. Relations, 1947–1974.* Washington, DC: University Press of America, 1977.

Dhar, Maloy Krishna. *Open Secrets: India's Intelligence Unveiled.* New Delhi: Manas Publications, 2012.

Dhar, P. N. *Indira Gandhi, the 'Emergency' and Indian Democracy.* New Delhi: Oxford University Press, 2000.

Dorril, Stephen. *MI6: Fifty Years of Special Operations.* London: Fourth Estate, 2000.

Douglas, William O. *Strange Lands and Friendly People.* New York: Harper & Brothers, 1951.

Beyond the High Himalayas. New York: Doubleday, 1952.

Exploring the Himalaya. New York: Random House, 1958.

Dulat, A. S. and Sinha, Aditya. *Kashmir: The Vajpayee Years.* Noida: Harper Collins India, 2015.

Dulat, A. S., Sinha, Aditya, and Durrani, Asad. *The Spy Chronicles: RAW, ISI and the Illusion of Peace.* Noida (India): HarperCollins India, 2018.

Dutt, Subimal. *With Nehru in the Foreign Office.* Calcutta: Minerva, 1977.

Eisenhower, Dwight D. *The White House Years: Mandate for Change, 1953–1956.* New York: Doubleday & Co, 1963.

The White House Years: Waging Peace, 1956–1961. New York: Doubleday & Co, 1965.

Engerman, David C. *The Price of Aid: The Economic Cold War in India.* Cambridge, MA: Harvard University Press, 2018.

Faulkner, Simon and Ramamurthy, Anandi (eds.). *Visual Culture and Decolonisation in Britain.* Aldershot: Ashgate Publishing, 2006.

Frank, Katherine. *Indira: The Life of Indira Nehru Gandhi.* London: HarperCollins, 2002.

326 BIBLIOGRAPHY

Frankel, Francine R. *When Nehru Looked East: Origins of India-US Suspicion and India-China Rivalry.* Oxford: Oxford University Press, 2020.

French, Patrick. *Liberty or Death: India's Journey to Independence and Division.* London: HarperCollins, 1997.

Galbraith, John Kenneth. *The Affluent Society.* London: Penguin Books, 1958.

The Liberal Hour. London: Hamish Hamilton, 1960.

Ambassador's Journal: A Personal Account of the Kennedy Years. Boston: Houghton Mifflin, 1969.

A Life in Our Times. London: Andre Deutsch, 1981.

Name-Dropping: From F. D. R. On. New York: Houghton Mifflin, 1999.

Galiullin, Rustem. *The CIA in Asia: Covert Operations against India and Afghanistan.* Moscow: Progress Publishers, 1988.

Garner, Joe. *The Commonwealth Office, 1925–1968.* London: Heinemann, 1978.

Garver, John. *Protracted Contest: Sino-Indian Rivalry in the Twentieth Century.* Seattle: University of Washington Press, 2001.

George, T. J. S. *Krishna Menon: A Biography.* London: Cape, 1964.

Gilmour, David. *The British in India: Three Centuries of Ambition and Experience.* London: Allen Lane, 2018.

Gokhale, Nitin A. *R. N. Kao: Gentleman Spymaster.* New Delhi: Bloomsbury, 2019.

Gopal, Sarvepalli. *Jawaharlal Nehru: A Biography,* vol. 1: *1889–1947.* London: Jonathan Cape, 1975.

Jawaharlal Nehru: A Biography, vol. 2: *1947–1956.* London: Jonathan Cape, 1979.

Jawaharlal Nehru: A Biography, vol. 3: *1956–1964.* London: Jonathan Cape, 1984.

Gordon Walker, Patrick. *Political Diaries, 1932–1971.* London: The Historians Press, 1991.

Gore-Booth, Paul. *With Great Truth and Respect.* London: Constable, 1974.

Gray, M., 'Explaining Conspiracy Theories in Modern Arab Middle Eastern Political Discourse: Some Problems and Limitations of the Literature'. *Critique: Critical Middle Eastern Studies* 17, 2 (2008), 155–74.

Groffman, Nicolas. 'Indian and Chinese espionage'. *Defense & Security Analysis* 32:2 (2016), 144–162.

Guha, Ramachandra. *India After Gandhi: The History of the World's Largest Democracy.* London: Macmillan, 2007.

Gujral, J. K. *Matters of Discretion: An Autobiography.* New Delhi: Hay House, 2011.

Gundevia, Y. D. *Outside the Archives.* New Delhi: Sangam Books, 1984.

Guyet-Réchard, Bérénice. *Shadow States: India, China and the Himalayas, 1910–1962.* Cambridge: Cambridge University Press, 2017.

Harlan, Josiah. *A Memoir of India and Afghanistan.* Philadelphia: J Dobson, 1842.

Hashimoto, Chikara. *Twilight of the British Empire: British Intelligence and Counter-Subversion in the Middle East, 1948–68* (Edinburgh: Edinburgh University Press, 2017).

BIBLIOGRAPHY 327

Helms, Richard. *A Look Over My Shoulder: A Life in the Central Intelligence Agency.* New York: Random House, 2003.

Hersh, Seymour. *The Price of Power, Henry Kissinger in the Nixon White House.* New York: Faber & Faber, 1983.

The Dark Side of Camelot. Boston: Little Brown & Company, 1997.

Hilsman, Roger. *To Move a Nation: The Politics of Foreign Policy in the Administration of John F. Kennedy.* New York: Delta, 1967.

Hoffmann, Steven. *India and the China Crisis.* Berkeley: University of California Press, 1990.

'Rethinking the Linkage between. Tibet and the China-India Border Conflict: A Realist Approach'. *Journal of Cold War Studies* 8 (Summer 2006), 179–81.

Hodgson, Godfrey. *The Gentleman from New York: Daniel Patrick Moynihan – A Biography.* New York: Houghton Mifflin, 2000.

Hopkins, Mark. *Russia's Underground Press: The Chronicle of Current Events.* New York: Praeger, 1983.

Hopkirk, Peter. *The Great Game: On Secret Service in High Asia.* London: John Murray, 1990.

Horn, Robert C. *Soviet-Indian Relations: Issues and Influence.* New York: Praeger, 1982.

Horne, Alistair. *Macmillan, 1894–1956.* London: Macmillan, 1988.

Macmillan, 1957–1986. London: Macmillan, 1989.

Inder Singh, Anita. *The Limits of British Influence: South Asia and the Anglo-American Relationship, 1947–56.* London: Pinter, 1993.

Issacs, Harold. *Scratches on Our Minds: American Views of China and India.* New York: John Day, 1958.

Jaffrelot, Christophe and Anil, Pratinav, *India's First Dictatorship: The Emergency, 1975–1977.* London: Hurst, 2020.

Jeffrey, Keith. *MI6: The History of the Secret Intelligence Service, 1909–1949.* London: Bloomsbury, 2010.

Jeffreys-Jones, Rhodri. *The CIA and American Democracy.* London: Yale University Press, 1998.

Cloak and Dollar: A History of American Secret Intelligence. New Haven, CT: Yale University Press, 2003.

Jenks, John. *British Propaganda and News Media in the Cold War.* Edinburgh: Edinburgh University Press, 2006.

Jervis, Robert. *Why Intelligence Fails: Lessons from the Iranian Revolution and the Iraq War.* Ithaca, NY: Cornell University Press, 2010.

Jian, Chen. *Mao's China and the Cold War.* Chapel Hill: University of North Carolina Press, 2001.

Johnson, Chalmers. *The Sorrows of Empire: Militarism, Secrecy and the End of the Republic.* London: Verso, 2004.

Johnson, Robert. *Spying for Empire: The Great Game in Central and South-East Asia, 1757–1947.* London: Greenhill Books, 2006.

328   BIBLIOGRAPHY

Kalugin, Oleg. *Spymaster: My Thirty-Two Years in Intelligence and Espionage against the West*. London: Smith Gryphon, 1994.

Kasturi, Bhashyam. *Intelligence Services: Analysis, Organisation and Functions*. New Delhi: Lancer Publishers, 1995.

Katzmann, Robert. *Daniel Patrick Moynihan – A Biography*. New York: Houghton Mifflin, 2000.

Kaul, Chandrika. *Communication. Media and the Imperial Experience: Britain and India in the Twentieth Century*. Basingstoke: Palgrave Macmillan, 2014.

'India, the Imperial Press Conferences and the Empire Press Union: The Diplomacy of News in the Politics of Empire, 1909–1946'. In *Media and the British Empire*. Edited by Kaul, Chandrika. London: Palgrave, 2006.

Kaul. T. N. *Diplomacy in Peace and War: Recollections and Reflections*. New Delhi: Vikas, 1979.

Reminiscences: Discreet and Indiscreet. New Delhi: Lancers, 1982.

Khandur, Chandra B. *Thimayya: An Amazing Life*. New Delhi: Knowledge World International, 2007.

Khilnani, Sunil. *Incarnations: A History of India in 50 Lives*. London: Allen Lane, 2016.

Khrushchev, Nikita S. *Khrushchev Remembers: The Last Testament*. Boston: Little Brown, 1974.

Memoirs: Time, People, Power, vol. 3. Moscow: Moskovskie Novosti, 1999.

Kinzer, Stephen. *The Brothers: John Foster Dulles, Allen Dulles and Their Secret World War*. New York: St. Martin's Griffin, 2013.

Kipling, Rudyard. *The Phantom 'Rickshaw and Other Tales*. Allahabad: A. H. Wheeler & Co., 1888.

Kim. London: Macmillan, 1901.

Kissinger, Henry. *The White House Years*. London: Weidenfeld & Nicolson, 1979.

Knaus, John Kenneth. *Orphans of the Cold War: America and the Tibetan Struggle for Survival*. New York: PublicAffairs, 1999.

Knight, Amy. *How the Cold War Began: The Igor Gouzenko Affair and the Hunt for Soviet Spies*. New York: Carroll & Graf, 2005.

Knightley, Philip. *Philby: KGB Masterspy*. London: Andre Deutsch, 2003.

Kochavi, Noam. *A Conflict Perpetuated: China Policy during the Kennedy Years*. London: Praeger, 2002.

Kohli M. S. and Conboy, Kenneth. *Spies in the Himalayas: Secret Missions and Perilous Climbs*. Lawrence:University Press of Kansas, 2003.

Krasnov, Vladislav. *Soviet Defectors: The KGB Wanted List*. Stanford, CA:Hoover Institution Press, 1986.

Kumar, Satish. *CIA and the Third World: A Study in Crypto-Diplomacy*. London: Zed Press, 1981.

Kux, Dennis. *India and the United States: Estranged Democracies, 1941–1991*. Washington, DC: National Defense University Press, 1993.

Lashmar, Paul and Oliver, James. *Britain's Secret Propaganda War: Foreign Office and the Cold War, 1948–77*. Stroud: Sutton Publishing, 1998.

BIBLIOGRAPHY 329

Lifschultz, Lawrence. *Bangladesh: The Unfinished Revolution*. London: Zed Press, 1979.

Louro, Michele L. *Comrades Against Imperialism: Nehru, India, and Interwar Internationalism*. Cambridge: Cambridge University Press, 2018.

Lownie, Andrew. *Stalin's Englishman: The Lives of Guy Burgess*. London: Hodder, 2016.

Lüthi, Lorenz M. *Cold Wars: Asia, the Middle East, Europe*. Cambridge: Cambridge University Press, 2020.

MacDonald, Elizabeth P. *Undercover Girl*. New York: Macmillan, 1947.

Macintyre, Ben. *Josiah the Great: The True Story of the Man Who Would Be King*. London: Harper Press, 2004.

    A Spy Among Friends: Kim Philby and the Great Betrayal. London: Bloomsbury, 2014.

Macmillan, Harold. *Riding the Storm, 1956–1959*. London: Macmillan, 1971.

    Pointing the Way, 1959–1961. London: Macmillan, 1972.

    At the End of the Day, 1961–1963. London: Macmillan, 1973.

Mahadevan, Prem. 'The Failure of Indian Intelligence in the Sino- Indian Conflict'. *Journal of Intelligence History* 8, 1 (2008), 1–27.

Mahmud Ali, S. *Cold War in the High Himalayas: The USA, China and South Asia in the 1950s*. New York: St. Martin's Press, 1999.

Malhotra, Inder. *Indira Gandhi: A Personal Memoir and Political Biography*. London: Hodder & Stoughton, 1989.

Manning, Toby. *John le Carré and the Cold War*. London: Bloomsbury Academic, 2018.

Manor, James. *Politics and State-Society Relations in India*. London: Hurst & Company, 2017.

Marchetti Victor, and Marks, John D. *The CIA and the Cult of Intelligence*. London: Jonathan Cape, 1974.

Mastny, Vojtech. 'The Soviet Union's Partnership with India'. *Journal of Cold War Studies* 12, 3 (2010), 50–90.

Mathai, M. O. *Reminiscences of the Nehru Age*. New Delhi: Vikas, 1978.

Maxwell, Neville. *India's China War*. London: Cape, 1970.

Maugham, Somerset. *Ashenden: Or the Secret Agent*. London: Heinemann, 1928.

Maxwell, Neville. *India's China War*. London: Pelican, 1972.

McGarr, P. M. *The Cold War in South Asia: Britain, the United States and the Indian Subcontinent, 1945–1965*. Cambridge: Cambridge University Press, 2013.

    '"Quiet Americans in India": The Central Intelligence Agency and the Politics of Intelligence in Cold War South Asia'. *Diplomatic History* 38, 5 (November 2014), 1046–82.

    'The Information Research Department, British Covert Propaganda, and the Sino-Indian War of 1962: Combating Communism and Courting Failure?'. *The International History Review* 41, 1 (2019), 130–56.

    'The Neo-Imperialism of Decolonisation: John le Carré and Cold War India'. *Intelligence & National Security* 38, 2 (2023), 271–84.

BIBLIOGRAPHY

McMahon, Robert J. *The Cold War on the Periphery: The United States, India and Pakistan*. New York: Columbia University Press, 1994.

'U.S. Policy toward South Asia and Tibet during the Early Cold War'. *Journal of Cold War Studies* 8, 3 (2006), 133–44.

Menon, K. P. S. *Many Worlds Revisited*. Bombay: Bharatiya Vidya Bhavan, 196.

Merrill, Dennis. *Bread and the Ballot: The United States and India's Economic Development*. Chapel Hill: The University of North Carolina Press, 1990.

Mishra, Pankaj. *From the Ruins of Empire: The Revolt Against the West and the Remaking of Asia*. London: Allen Lane, 2012.

Moon, Pendrel (ed.). *Wavell: The Viceroy's Journal*. London: Oxford University Press, 1973.

Moore, R. J. *Escape from Empire: The Attlee Government and the Indian Problem*. Oxford: Clarendon Press, 1983.

Montgomery, Mary E. *The Eyes of the World Were Watching: Ghana, Great Britain and the United States 1957–1966* (PhD Diss., University of Maryland, 2004).

Morgan, Kenneth O. *Labour in Power, 1945–1951*. Oxford: Clarendon Press, 1984.

Morris, Jan. *Coronation Everest*. London: Faber & Faber, 2003.

Mosley, Leonard. *Dulles: A Biography of Eleanor, Allen, and John Foster Dulles and their Family Network*. London: Hodder and Stoughton, 1978.

Moynihan, Daniel Patrick. *A Dangerous Place*. Boston: Little Brown, 1978.

Secrecy: The American Experience. New Haven, CT: Yale University Press, 1998.

Mullik, B. N. *My Years with Nehru, 1948–1964*. New Delhi: Allied Publishers, 1972.

Murphy Christopher J. '"Constituting a Problem in Themselves": Countering Covert Chinese Activity in India: The Life and Death of the Chinese Intelligence Section, 1944–46'. *The Journal of Imperial and Commonwealth History* 44, 6 (2016), 928–51.

Murphy, Philp. 'Intelligence and Decolonization: The Life and Death of the Federal Intelligence and Security Bureau, 1954–63'. *The Journal of Imperial and Commonwealth History* 29, 2 (2001), 101–30.

'Creating a Commonwealth Intelligence Culture: The View from Central Africa, 1945–1965'. *Intelligence and National Security* 17, 3 (2002), 131–61.

Naipaul, V. S. *An Area of Darkness: A Discovery of India*. New York: Vintage Books, 2002.

Nair, Kunhanandan. *Devil and His Dart: How the CIA is Plotting in the Third World*. New Delhi: Sterling Publishers, 1986.

Nair, K. Shankaran. *Inside IB and RAW: The Rolling Stone that Gathered Moss*. New Delhi: Manas Publications, 2013.

Nanda, B. R. (ed.). *Indian Foreign Policy: The Nehru Years*. New Delhi: Sangham Books, 1990.

'Nehru and the British'. *Modern Asian Studies* 30, 2 (1996), 469–79.

Natarajan, L. *American Shadow over India*. Bombay: People's Publishing House, 1952.

Nayar, Kuldip. *The Judgement: Inside Story of the Emergency in India*. New Delhi: Vikas, 1977.

BIBLIOGRAPHY   331

Nehru, Jawaharlal Nehru. *Discovery of India*. New York: John Day, 1946.
Soviet Russia: Some Random Sketches and Impressions. Allahabad: Law Journal Press, 1928.
Nitze, Paul H. *From Hiroshima to Glasnost: At the Centre of Decision, A Memoir*. New York: Grove Weidenfeld, 1989.
Nixon, R. N. *RN: The Memoirs of Richard Nixon*. New York: Grosset and Dunlap, 1978.
Oudes, Brue (ed.). *From the President: Richard Nixon's Secret Files*. New York: Andre Deutsch, 1998.
Owen, Nicholas. *British Left and India: Metropolitan Anti-Imperialism, 1885–1947*. Oxford: Oxford University Press, 2008.
Palit, D. K. *War in High Himalaya: The Indian Army in Crisis, 1962*. London: Hurst, 1991.
Paliwal, Avinash. 'Colonial Sinews of Postcolonial Espionage – India and the Making of Ghana's External Intelligence Agency, 1958–61'. *The International History Review* (2001), 1–21.
Pandit, Vijaya Lakshmi. *The Scope of Happiness: A Personal Memoir*. London: Weidenfeld & Nicolson, 1979.
Panikkar, K. M. *In Two Chinas: Memoirs of a Diplomat*. London: Allen and Unwin, 1955.
An Autobiography. Madras: Oxford University Press, 1977.
Parakal, Pauly V. *CIA Dagger against India*. New Delhi: D. P. Sinha for Communist Party of India, 1973.
Parker, Richard. *John Kenneth Galbraith: His Life, His Politics, His Economics*. New York: Farrar, Straus and Giroux, 2005.
Passin, Herbert. 'Sino-Indian Cultural Relations'. *The China Quarterly* 7 (September 1961), 85–100.
Perkovich, George N. *India's Nuclear Bomb: The Impact of Global Proliferation*. Berkeley: University of California Press, 1999.
Persico, Joseph E. *Casey: From the OSS to the CIA*. New York: Viking, 1990.
Petrov, Vladimir and Evdokia. *Empire of Fear*. London: Andre Deutsch, 1956.
Popplewell, Richard J. *British Intelligence and the Defence of the Indian Empire, 1904–1924*. London: Routledge, 1995.
Powers, Thomas. *The Man Who Kept the Secrets: Richard Helms and the CIA*. New York: Simon & Schuster, 1979.
Pullin, Eric D. '"Money Does Not Make Any Difference to the Opinions That We Hold": India, the CIA, and the Congress for Cultural Freedom, 1951–58'. *Intelligence and National Security* 26, 2–3 (2011), 377–98.
Raghavan, Srinath. *War and Peace in Modern India*. Basingstoke: Palgrave Macmillan, 2010.
Rajeswar, T. V. *India: The Crucial Years*. Noida, UP: Harper Collins India, 2015.
Raman, B. *The Kaoboys of R&AW: Down Memory Lane*. New Delhi; Lancer, 2007.
Ramesh, Jairam. *Intertwined Lives: P. N. Haksar and Indira Gandhi*. New Delhi: Simon & Schuster India, 2018.

BIBLIOGRAPHY

A Chequered Brilliance: The Many Lives of V. K. Krishna Menon. Gurgaon, India: Penguin Random House India, 2019.

Ranelagh, John. *The Agency: The Rise and Decline of the CIA.* London: Weidenfeld & Nicolson, 1986.

Rawnsley, Gary (ed.). *Cold-War Propaganda in the* 1950s. London: Palgrave Macmillan, 1999.

Reid, Escott. *Envoy to Nehru.* New York: Oxford University Press, 1981.

Richelson, Jeffrey. *Spying on the Bomb: American Nuclear Intelligence from Nazi Germany to Iran and North Korea.* New York: W. W. Norton, 2006.

The US Intelligence Community. Boulder, CO: Westview Press, 2008.

Richterova, Daniela and Telepneva, Natalia (eds.). 'The Secret Struggle for the Global South: Espionage, Military Assistance and State Security in the Cold War'. *The International History Review* 43, 1, (2021), 1–5.

Rid, Thomas. *Active Measures: The Secret History of Disinformation and Political Warfare.* London: Profile Books, 2020.

Rimington, Stella. *Open Secret: The Autobiography of the Former Director-General of MI5.* London: Arrow Books, 2002.

Rohtagi, Manila. *Spy System in Ancient India from Vedic Period to Gupta Period.* Delhi: Kalpaz Publications, 2007.

Roosevelt, Kermit. *A Sentimental Safari.* New York: Knopf, 1963.

Roth-Ey, Kristin. *Moscow Prime Time: How the Soviet Union Built the Media Empire that Lost the Cultural Cold War.* Ithaca, NY: Cornell University Press, 2011.

Sareen, C. L. *Bid for Freedom: USSR vs. Tarasov.* Englewood Cliffs, NJ: Prentice Hall, 1966.

Schaffer, Howard B. *Chester Bowles: New Dealer in the Cold War.* Cambridge, MA: Harvard University Press, 1993.

Ellsworth Bunker: Global Troubleshooter, Vietnam Hawk. Chapel Hill: University of South Carolina Press, 2003.

Schlesinger Jr, Arthur M. *A Thousand Days: John F. Kennedy in the White House.* Boston: Houghton Mifflin, 1965.

Schofield, Camilla. *Enoch Powell and the Making of Postcolonial Britain.* Cambridge: Cambridge University Press, 2013.

Shaffer, Ryan. 'Indian Intelligence Revealed: An Examination of Operations, Failures and Transformations'. *Intelligence and National Security* 33, 4 (2018), 598–610.

Sharma, Ruchir. *Democracy on the Road: A 25-Year Journey through India.* London: Allen Lane, 2019.

Shrivastava, Manoj, *Re-Energising Indian Intelligence.* New Delhi: Vij Books, 2013.

Singh, V. K. *India's External Intelligence: Secrets of Research and Analysis* Wing *(RAW).* New Delhi: Manas Publications, 2007.

Sood, Vikram. *The Unending Game: A former R&AW Chief's Insights into Espionage.* Gurgaon: Penguin Viking, 2018.

Srivastava, C. P. *Lal Bahadur Shastri: A Life of Truth in Politics.* New Delhi: Oxford University Press, 1995.

BIBLIOGRAPHY 333

Stein, Arthur. *India and the Soviet Union: The Nehru Era*. Chicago: University of Chicago Press, 1972.

Stiegler, Kurt. 'Communism and "Colonial Evolution": John Foster Dulles' Vision of India and Pakistan'. *Journal of South Asian and Middle Eastern Studies* 12 (Winter 1991), 68–89.

Strodes, James. *Allen Dulles: Master of Spies*. Washington DC: Regnery Publishing, 1999.

Sillitoe, Sir Percy. *Cloak without Dagger*. London: Cassell, 1955.

Smith, John D. *I Was a CIA Agent in India*. New Delhi: New Age Printing Press, 1967.

Smith, Russell Jack. *The Unknown CIA: My Three Decades with the Agency*. New York: Berkley Books, 1992.

Subramanian, K. S. *Political Violence and the Police in India*. New Delhi: Sage, 2007.

Sullivan, Rosemary. *Stalin's Daughter: The Extraordinary and Tumultuous Life of Svetlana Stalin*. London: Fourth Estate, 2015.

Tenet, George. *At the Center of the Storm: My Years at the CIA*. London: Harper Press, 2007.

Tharoor, Shashi. *Inglorious Empire: What the British Did to India*. London: Hurst and Company, 2017.

Thomas, Martin. *Empires of Intelligence*. Berkeley: University of California Press, 2008.

Thorpe, D. R. *Supermac: The Life of Harold Macmillan*. London: Pimlico, 2011.

Tinker, Hugh. *The Banyan Tree: Overseas Emigrants from India, Pakistan, and Bangladesh*. Oxford: Oxford University Press, 1977.

Tromly, Benjamin. 'Ambivalent Heroes: Russian Defectors and American Power in the Early Cold War'. *Intelligence & National Security* 33, 5 (2018), 642–58.

Tory, Gil. *Moynihan's Moment: America's Fight Against Zionism as Racism*. New York: Oxford University Press, 2013.

Vappala, Balachandran. *National Security and Intelligence Management: A New Paradigm*. Mumbai: Indus Source Books, 2014.

Vaughan, Bruce. 'The Use and Abuse of Intelligence Services in India'. *Intelligence & National Security* 8, 1 (January 1993), 1–22

Vertzberger, Yaccov. 'India's Border Conflict with China: A Perceptual Analysis'. *Journal of Contemporary History* 17, 4 (1982), 607–31.
'Bureaucratic-Organizational Politics and Information Processing in a Developing State'. *International Studies Quarterly* 28, 1 (March 1984), 69–95.

Von Tunzelmann, Alex. *Indian Summer: The Secret History of the End of an Empire*. London: Simon & Schuster, 2007.

Wagner, Kim A. *Amritsar 1919: An Empire of Fear and the Making of a Massacre*. New Haven, CT: Yale University Press, 2019.

Walton, Calder. *Empire of Secrets: British Intelligence, the Cold War and the Twilight of Empire*. London: HarperPress, 2013.

Wavell, Archibald Percival. *Wavell: The Viceroy's Journal*. Edited by Pendrel Moon. London: Oxford University Press, 1973.

Weiner, Tim. *Legacy of Ashes: The History of the CIA*. London: Allen Lane, 2007.

Weisman, Steven R. (ed.). *Daniel Patrick Moynihan: A Portrait in Letters of an American Visionary*. New York: Public Affairs, 2010.

Westad, Odd Arne. *The Global Cold War: Third World Interventions and the Making of Our Times*. Cambridge: Cambridge University Press, 2007.

Wignall, Sydney. *Spy on the Roof of the World*. Edinburgh: Canongate Books, 1996.

Wilford, Hugh. *The Mighty Wurlitzer: How the CIA Played America*. Cambridge, MA: Harvard University Press, 2008.

America's Great Game: The CIA's Secret Arabists and the Shaping of the Modern Middle East. New York: Basic Books, 2013.

Wilson, Jon. *India Conquered: Britain's Raj and the Chaos of Empire*. London: Simon & Schuster, 2016.

Woodward, Bob. *Veil: The Secret Wars of CIA 1981–1987*. New York: Simon and Schuster, 1987.

Yadav, R. K. *Mission R&AW*. New Delhi: Manas Publications, 2014.

Yadav, Yatish. *RAW: A History of India's Covert Operations*. Chennai: Westland Publications, 2020.

Zachariah, Benjamin. *Nehru*. London: Routledge, 2004.

Ziegler, Philip. *Mountbatten: The Official Biography*. London: Collins, 1985.

Zonis, N., and Joseph C. M. 'Conspiracy Thinking in the Middle East'. *Political Psychology* 15, 3 (1994), 443–59.

INDEX

A Dangerous Place, 188, 209, 216, 218, 219
Abel, Jane, 232
Adams, General Paul, 109
Afghanistan, 3, 7, 235, 239, 240, 250, 257, 259, 265
  Soviet invasion 1979, 3
Agee, Philip, 218
Ahluwalia, Sagar, 142, 149, 185
Air India, 240
Aksai Chin, 93, 101, 108
Al Qaeda, 257
Alanbrooke, Lord, 27
Albats, Yevgenia, 253
Alexander, A. V., 15
Alexander, Padinjarethalakal Cherian (P. C.), 249
All India Radio (AIR), 138, 139
All the President's Men, 190
Allahabad, 6
  Allen Dulles, 87–88
  High Court, 151, 190, 203
Allen, Catherine, 145
Allen, John
  MI5 SLO, 36, 37
Allen, Mary, 234
Allen, Stanley Bryson, 234
Allende, Salvador
  CIA denials of complicity in death, 261
  CIA efforts to destabilise government, 204
  Indian reaction to death, 201–4
Alliluyeva, Svetlana Iosigovna, 3, 154, 165
  defection to West through India, 165
All-India Congress Committee (AICC), 253

All-India Trade Union Congress (AITUC), 141
American Shadow over India, 10
Amery, Leo, 58
Amnesty International, 180
Amrita Bazar Patrika, 130
Amritsar, 234, 235
Anderson, Jack, 221, 231
Andhra Pradesh, 146, 245
Andley, K. B., 243
Andropov, Yuri, 8, 171
Arthashastra, 8
Arunachal Pradesh, 93, 101, 121
Asia Foundation, 86, 181
Assam, 100, 102, 117, 146, 207, 245
Attlee, Clement, 22, 31
  Attlee Directive on intelligence, 21
  transfer of power in India, 14
Australia, 21, 134, 184
  foreign intelligence organisation, 29
  intelligence liaison, 37
  MI5 station, 50
  Petrov defection, 155
  training of Indian intelligence officers, 82
Australian Security Intelligence Organisation (ASIO), 134
Aviation Research Centre (ARC), 117
Awami League, 241

Baer, Robert, 260
Bajpai, Katyayani Shankar (K. S.), 193
Bajpai, Sir Girija Shankar, 126
Bakkar, N. L
  Tarasov defection, 164
Baltimore Sun, 214
Banerjee, R. N., 20

335

336 INDEX

Bangalore, 146
Bangladesh, 150, 194, 203, 255
  India-Pakistan war (1971),
    221, 241
  Sheikh Mujibur Rahman
    assassination, 190
Barnes, Harry G., 239
Barreaux, Theodore, 198
Bay of Pigs (1961), 84, 97, 102
Bayley, Vernon Thomas, 24
  SIS officer in India, 23
Bell, Walter
  MI5 SLO, 36
Benediktov, Ivan, 166, 167
Benn, Anthony Wedgwood 'Tony', 147,
  263, 264
Beria, Lavrentiy, 172
Berlin, 7, 136
Berlin Blockade, 61
Berlin Wall, 3, 155, 252
Bernstein, Carl, 190
Besant, Annie, 52
Bevan, Aneurin, 53
Bevin, Ernest, 16
Bezemenov, Youri, 180
Bhagavad Gita, 230
Bharatiya Janata Party (BJP), 228
Bhatia, Prem, 165
Bhutan, 111, 112
Bissell Jr., Richard M., 96
Blair, Tony
  bugged by Indian intelligence
    services, 258
  Kashmir dispute, 259
Blake, George, 7
Blee, David, 118
Blitz, 88, 141, 149, 199, 217, 240, 244,
  247, 253
  anti-CIA propaganda, 88
Blunt, Anthony, 149
Boidevaix, Serge, 249
Boies, Robert, 71
Bolley, Alain, 249
Bombay, 8, 10, 32, 41, 58, 67, 68, 70, 76,
  137, 214
Bourne, Kenneth, 36
  MI5 SLO in India, 23
Bowles, Chester, 196

Central Intelligence Agency (CIA),
  97, 98, 99, 122–23
  communist propaganda, 47
  Indira Gandhi, 188
  Indo-US relations, 17, 196
  Ramparts, 181
  Svetlana Alliluyeva defection, 166
  Ulug-Zade defection, 154, 175
  US support for Indian
    unconventional warfare, 114
Brady, Tom, 162
Brasenose College, Oxford, 260, 263
British Council, 125–26, 150
British Foreign Office Research
  Department (FORD), 134
British Guiana, 2
British India
  destruction of colonial intelligence
    records, 15
  empire of intelligence, 9
  intelligence focus on nationalism, 14
British Information Service (BIS), 125,
  129
British Joint Intelligence Committee
  (JIC), 16, 18, 35, 60, 93
  Ulug-Zade defection, 178
British Ministry of Defence (MOD),
  139
British Secret Intelligence Service (SIS
  or MI6), 1, 7, 10, 19, 31, 263
  authorised history, 11
  bid to secure primacy over MI5 in
    India, 21
  black propaganda, 127, 139
  British India, 9
  closure of SIS station in India, 27
  covert operations in India, 109
  covert propaganda in India, 26
  liaison with IB on China, 106
  operations in post-independent
    India, 17
  reintroduction to India in 1964, 33
  Sino-Indian border, 105
  Special Political Action (SPA), 127
  Whitehall debate over role in India,
    20
British Security Service (MI5), 9, 18
  Attlee Directive, 49

INDEX

authorised history, 11
British India, 9
concern at Soviet penetration in
    India, 45
financial pressure, 49
impact of Attlee Directive, 29
MI5 concern over SIS operations in
    India, 27
MI5 SLO in India, 31
operations in post-independent
    India, 17
plots against Krishna Menon, 63
Security Liaison Officer (SLO)
    system, 34
Ulug-Zade defection, 178
Whitehall debate over role in India, 20
Brook, Norman, 49
Bucher, General Sir Roy, 4
Bulganin, Nikolai, 46
Bundy, McGeorge, 71, 97
Bunker, Ellsworth, 85
    CPI victory in Kerala (1957), 88
Burdick, Eugene, 83, 84
Burgess, David, 91
Burgess, Guy, 3, 64, 149
Burma, 41, 117
    OSS operations, 76
Bush, George H. W., 207, 234
    criticism of India accusations against
        CIA, 234
Bussi, Hortensia, 201

Cabinet Mission (1946), 15
Cairncross, John, 149
Calcutta, 8, 26, 101, 137, 146, 163, 218
Cambodia, 239
Cambridge Five spy ring, 3, 149
Campbell, Alistair, 257
    Research and Analysis Wing, 258
Canada, 21, 239, 246
    foreign intelligence organisation, 29
    intelligence liaison, 37
Cancun, 241
Carter, James Earl 'Jimmy', 212, 221
    Nanda Kot, 213
Casey, William 'Bill', 215, 236, 247
    target of communist forgery in India,
        247
    view of India, 236

Castro, Fidel
    CIA assassination plots, 201
Central Intelligence Agency (CIA), 3, 7,
    11, 12, 31
    Church committee revelations, 181
    concern at Soviet penetration of
        India, 47
    coup in Iran (1953), 10
    covert action in Kerala, 89
    covert action in Tibet, 94
    cultivation of T. G. Sanjeevi, 80
    Dalai Lama, 115
    Indian accusations of interference in
        Punjab, 234
    Indian trades unions, 92
    presence in India, 7
    Project Brahmaputra, 182
    Tibet, 95, 97, 115
    Tibetan Task Force, 108
    Western-centric, 87
Ceylon, 125
    IRD publications, 132
    OSS operations, 76
    Security Liaison Officer (SLO), 50
Chagla, Mohammadali Carim (M. C.),
    183
Chamberlain, Paul Thomas, 2
Chandra, Prakash, 162
Charbatia air base, 113
Chaudhuri, General Jayanto Nath, 114
Chavan, Yashwantrao Balwantrao
    (Y. B.), 113
Chebrikov, Viktor, 253
Chile, 2
    Allende government, 261
    coup (1973), 201, 261
    Indian reaction to 1973 coup, 201–5
Christopher, Warren, 219
Church, Senator Frank, 181
Churchill, Sir Winston, 27, 128, 155
Clarridge, Duane 'Dewey', 92
Clinton, William Jefferson 'Bill', 264
Clive, Robert, 235
Clutterbuck, Sir Alexander, 52, 103
    Attlee Directive, 50
    opinion of Krishna Menon, 52
Colby, William, 200
    Congressional testimony on CIA and
        Chile, 204

338 INDEX

Colonialism, 6
Communist Party of Great Britain
(CPGB), 53
support for Krishna Menon and
India League, 56
Communist Party of India (CPI), 4, 16,
35, 77, 185
Russian funding, 42, 46
Congo, 2, 70, 122, 205, 208
Congress for Cultural Freedom (CCF),
181, 183
Congress Party, 4, 16, 18, 20, 39, 59, 89,
117, 120, 146, 185, 209, 218
Conservative Party, 18
Cook, Fred, 84
Cripps Mission, 57
Cripps, Sir Stafford, 15, 53, 60
Critchfield, James, 108, 110
US support for Indian paramilitary
force, 111
Cuba, 84, 97, 107, 136, 205
Cuban Missile Crisis, 107, 154, 160
Current, 143
Curry, John 'Jack', 9
Curzon, Lord, 147
Czechoslovakia, 159
coup (1948), 61, 159
Kratochvil defection, 159–60

Daily Express, 162
Dalai Lama
CIA and flight to India, 8
exile in India, 158
Dange, S. A., 141
Darjeeling, 102
Davidson, Jonathan
Calcutta Symphony Orchestra, 146
IRD officer in Calcutta, 145
de Gaulle, Charles, 255
Dean, Sir Patrick, 35
Dearlove, Richard
Research and Analysis Wing, 258
Secret Intelligence Service, 257
Defections, 3
Denniston, Alistair, 9
Desai, M. J., 72, 84
accused of receiving CIA funds, 184
Desai, Morarji, 180, 209, 225
accusation of acting as a CIA agent, 225

accusation of acting as CIA agent, 209
Indo-US relations, 209
libel case against Seymour Hersh,
227
libel trial, 209
Operation Hat, 120, 121, 210
Dhar, Maloy Krishna, 192
Dhar, Prithvi Nath (P. N.), 200
Dharamshala, 158
Dick White
V. K. Krishna Menon, 63
Dingell, John, 212
Dixit, Jyotindra Nath (J. N.), 232
Doctor Zhivago, 170
Donovan, Howard, 79
Donovan, William 'Wild Bill', 78
Douglas-Home, Sir Alec, 222
Doval, Ajit
covert action, 12–13
Dulles, Allen, 10
affinity for Kipling, 88
Dulles family connection with India,
87
Ewing Christian College, Allahabad,
87
friendship with Nehru family, 87
trips to India, 87
Dulles, John Foster, 88, 188
Krishna Menon, 69
Dutt, Rajani Palme, 56

Eagleburger, Lawrence, 200, 237
East Germany, 240
East India Company
intelligence operations, 8
East Pakistan, 41, 221
Eccles, Sir David, 72
Economic Times, 144
Economist, 165
Eelam People's Revolutionary
Liberation Front (EPRLF), 234
Eisenhower, Dwight D., 7
Indo-US relations, 7
Elmhirst, Air Marshal Sir Thomas, 4, 20
Enlai, Zhou
Central Intelligence Agency (CIA),
95
Dalai Lama, 95
Sino-Indian border, 93

INDEX

Falshaw, Chief Justice Donald, 164
Federal Bureau of Investigation (FBI), 79, 103
Fedoseev, Anton
  Tarasov defection, 163
Fernandes, George, 183, 264
First war of Indian independence or Indian mutiny (1857), 8, 14, 30
Firyubin, Nikolay, 168
Fitzgerald, Desmond, 110
  Chester Bowles and covert action, 123
Fleming, Ian, 33
Fogg, Lennox, 76
Foot, Michael, 53
Ford, Gerald, 215, 221
Forsyth, Frederick, 255
Freeman, John, 114
  importance of MI5 SLO in India, 50
  IRD in India, 143
  victim of communist disinformation ploy in India, 148
Fulbright, William, 91
Furnival Jones, Martin, 51

Galbraith, John Kenneth
  blowback from CIA operations, 97
  dismissal of Krishna Menon, 72
  nomination as US ambassador to India, 96
  opposition to CIA activity in India, 96
Gandhi, Indira, 147
  assassination attempts against, 203
  bank nationalisation, 189
  British intelligence, 6
  charge that CIA subverting Indian democracy, 190
  CIA agent in cabinet, 209, 221
  criticism of CIA, 236
  death (1984), 208
  fear of US backed coup, 201
  forms Congress (R), 189
  Indo-British relations, 147
  Indo-US relations, 238
  installed as Indian prime minister (1966), 187
  Operation Hat, 210, 211
  purported anti-Americanism, 188

relations with Salvador Allende, 203
  State Department view on, 187
  suspicion of CIA, 190
  Ulug-Zade defection, 176
Gandhi, Mohandas
  assassination (1948), 62
  IRD propaganda, 127
Gandhi, Rajiv, 236, 247
  accusations of CIA involvement in assassination, 254
  impact of Coomer Narain scandal, 250
  receipt of funding from Soviet Union, 253
  view of CIA, 248
Gandhi, Sanjay, 208
Garner, Sir Saville 'Joe', 52
  Freeman forgery, 149
Garvey, Sir Terence
  Indian use of CIA to vilify US, 197
  questions need for IRD in India, 150
  Soviet penetration of India, 237
George, Claire
  Desai libel trial, 229
Ghana
  MI5 SLO, 50
Gibraltar, 50
Goa crisis (1961)
  Krishna Menon, 70
Goheen, Robert
  Operation Hat, 212, 214
Gopal, Sarvepalli
  Sino-Indian border dispute, 103
Gordon Walker, Patrick, 64, 132
Gore-Booth, Sir Paul
  support for Information Research Department, 135
  Svetlana Alliluyeva defection, 170
Government Code and Cypher School (Bletchley Park), 9
Grady, Henry, 47
Great Game, The, 10, 105, 257
Greene, Joseph, 121, 122
  Chester Bowles distaste for covert action, 98
  Ulug-Zade defection, 176
Greenhill, Denis, 207
Griffin, George
  India declares *persona non grata*, 240

340 INDEX

GRU (Soviet foreign military
  intelligence), 7, 11, 47, 163
Guardian, 127, 241
  Tarasov defection, 165
Guatemala, 2, 205
Guha, Ramachandra, 2
Gulag Archipelago, 155
Gundevia, Yezdezard Dinshaw (Y. D.),
  43

Haig, Alexander, 237
Haight, Hugh
  Tarasov defection, 163
Haksar, Parmeshwar Narayan (P. N.),
  64
  view of Ronald Reagan, 238
  formation of Research & Analysis
    Wing (R&AW), 30
  opinion of B. N. Mullik, 45
Haldeman, H. R., 194
Haley, William, 35
Han-Fu, Chang, 157
Harlan, Josiah, 7
Harriman Mission
  limited Indian intelligence exchange
    with US, 110
  US report on Indian intelligence, 109
Harriman, Averell, 108
Harrison, Selig, 238
Harrop, John, 105
Hauptverwaltung Aufklärung (HVA)
  or Stasi, 240
Hayter, William, 21, 24
  support for SIS station in India, 28
Heath, Edward, 222
Helms, Richard, 182, 193, 209
  Watergate, 194
Henderson, Loy, 156
  Nehru as anti-American, 83
  T. G. Sanjeevi, 80
Hersh, Seymour, 204, 209, 225
  allegation Morarji Desai acted as CIA
    agent, 225
Hillary, Edmund, 104
Hillenkoetter, Roscoe, 80
Hindustan Times, 128, 141, 144, 153,
  179, 189, 252, 253, 260
HIV/AIDS
  Stasi disinformation and India, 245

Hollis, Roger, 33, 45, 50
  Krishna Menon, 57
  opposition to SIS activity in India,
    49
Holt-Wilson, Sir Eric, 35
Hong Kong, 107, 116, 130, 138
Hoover, J. Edgar, 80
Hopson, Donald, 136
Hyderabad, 42, 61, 146

I was a CIA Agent in India, 183
Iengar, Haravu Venkatanarasimha
  Varadaraja, 133
Imbrey, Howard, 76
India
  State of Emergency, 151, 180, 190,
    208, 218
India League, 52, 53, 55
India Office Library (IOL), 103
Indian Air Force (IAF), 4, 117
Indian Atomic Research Centre, 214
Indian Committee for Cultural
  Freedom, 142, 181
Indian Congress for Cultural Freedom,
  70
Indian Express, 144, 148, 198, 212
  Tarasov defection, 165
Indian Intelligence Bureau (IB)
  overseas stations, 105
Indian Intelligence Bureau (IB), 9, 12,
  15, 30, 35
  collaboration with US, 219
  knowledge of CIA covert action in
    Tibet, 98
  limited coverage of China, 106
  limited external operational capacity,
    101
  London station, 37
  posting of officer to Beijing, 106
  relations with CIA, 222
  Security Liaison Unit (SLU), 38
  Soviet propaganda in India, 131
  unconventional warfare operations,
    111
  US use of Indian airfields, 117
  working with British intelligence to
    target Soviet Union, 40
Indian Joint Intelligence Committee
  (JIC), 20

INDEX 341

Indian Ministry of External Affairs (MEA), 7, 37, 47, 102, 126, 134, 138, 148, 153, 173, 183, 193, 212, 231
Indian National Congress (INC), 55
Indian Police Service (IPS), 9
Indian Political Intelligence (IPI), 18, 20, 60
  Krishna Menon, 53
  relations with MI5, 9
Indian Press Information Bureau (PIB), 138
Indians for Truth Abroad, 227
India-Pakistan war (1965), 262
India-Pakistan war (1971), 150, 190, 195, 207, 209, 222, 224, 226, 230, 231
India-Soviet Cultural Society (ISCUS), 140
Indochina, 68, 155
Indonesia, 2, 113, 129, 205
Indo-US Joint Unconventional Warfare Operations Base (JUWOB), 112
Information Research Department (IRD), 12, 26, 124
  Asian Analyst, 133
  Basic Papers, 133
  black propaganda, 124
  China Records, 138
  China Topics, 138
  counter propaganda aimed at the Soviet Union, 140
  field officer programme, 136
  financial payments to Indian contacts, 142
  Indian article redistribution scheme, 142
  Indian counter-subversion propaganda training, 140
  Indian field officer linked to SIS, 148
  Interpreter, 133
  material fed to B. N. Mullik, 134
  support for India during Sino-Indian border war, 138
  suspension of IRD activities in India, 148
  Tarasov defection, 162
  use of Indian publishers, 141
Inside the Company: CIA Diary, 218

Iran, 2, 80, 205, 239
  coup (1953), 10, 261
Iran-Contra affair, 92
Izvestia, 16, 253

Jaipur, 31
Jaisalmer, 31
Jaish-e-Muhammad, 13
James, Morrice, 45
Jan Sangh, 185
Janata Party, 218, 225, 227, 242
Japan, 24, 184, 197
Jha, Chandra Shekhar (C. S.), 167
  Svetlana Alliluyeva defection, 168
Jha, Lakshmi Kant (L. K.), 224
Jieshi, Jiang, 156
Jinnah, Muhammad, 59
Johnson, Lyndon B., 122
Joint Unconventional Warfare Task Force (JUWTF), 112
Joy, Peter, 138, 147
  first IRD field officer in India, 136

Kabul, 240
Kalimpong
  base for international espionage, 95
Kalugin, Oleg, 8
Kao, Rameshwar Nath (R. N.), 200
  relations with CIA, 233
  relations with George H. W. Bush, 233
Karaka, D. F., 143
Karamessines, Thomas, 221
Karnataka, 241, 245
Kaul, Triloki Nath (T. N.), 148, 207
Kautilya, 8
Kaysen, Carl, 73
Keating, Kenneth, 195
  attitude to CIA, 196
  Indian misperceptions of CIA, 196
  Indo-US relations, 197
  valedictory interview with Indira Gandhi, 197
Kellar, Alex, 15, 28, 66
Kennan, George, 173
Kennedy, John F., 69, 215, 226
  Bay of Pigs (1961), 97
  competition between India and China, 7, 85

342 INDEX

Kennedy, Robert, 97
Kent, Sherman, 78
Kerala, 35, 52, 146, 148
Kerr, Donald, 139, 142
Kerr, Philip Marquess of Lothian, 6
KGB (Soviet Committee for State
  Security), 7, 8, 11, 47
  active measures in India, 243
  penetration of Indian government, 8,
    47
  smears CIA during 1967 Indian
    elections, 186
  Svetlana Alliluyeva defection, 169,
    171
Khan, Dost Mohamed, 7
Khan, Yahya, 231
Kher, Bal Gangadhar, 67
Kher, Balasaheb Gangadhar (B. G.), 38
Khokhlov, Nikolai, 155
Khrushchev, Nikita Sergeyevich, 46,
  165
  Indo-Soviet relations, 7
  secret speech (1956), 171
Kim, 10
  Allen Dulles, 88
King, W. F., 126
Kipling, Rudyard, 7, 10, 17, 135
  Allen Dulles a devotee of, 10
  impact on post-war US intelligence, 10
  link to Harold 'Kim' Philby, 10
  required reading for British
    diplomats, 10
Kirkpatrick, Jeanne
  subject to communist
    disinformation in India, 244
Kissinger, Henry, 192, 209, 222, 241,
  261
  criticism of India, 193
  Morarji Desai libel trial, 230
Kitchen, Eric
  MI5 SLO, 36, 45, 65
Klise, Dick, 77, 81
Knaus, John, 108
Knight Smith, Ian, 146
Kohler, Foy, 168
Kohn, Howard, 209
Komer, Robert, 71, 92
  US support for Indian
    unconventional warfare, 113

Korea, 68, 100
Korean War, 130, 139
Kratochvil, Dr. Bohuslav
  defection to West through India,
    159
Kulkarni, Sudheendra, 255
Kuomintang, 156

Ladakh, 101, 103
Lal, Diwan Chaman, 164
Lancashire, David, 149, 185
Laos, 84
Larkins, Air Vice Marshal Ken, 242
Larkins, Major General Frank, 242
Laski, Harold, 52, 53
le Carré, John, 1, 3, 103
Lenin, Vladimir Ilyich Ulyanov, 35
Lhasa, 8
Liddell, Guy, 37
  Indian dependence on British
    intelligence, 34
  intelligence transfer of power in
    India, 17
  Krishna Menon as a security threat,
    53
  MI5 employment of British Indian
    intelligence officers, 19
  MI5 SLO in India, 22
  opinion of B. N. Mullik, 43
  opinion of T. G. Sanjeevi, 19, 39
  surprise at B. N. Mullik's assessment
    of British intelligence, 46
Lifschultz, Lawrence, 241
Lincoln's Inn, 57, 263
Link, 141
Linlithgow, Marquess of, 58
London School of Economics (LSE), 52,
  57
Lucknow, 6, 14
Ludhiana, 7
Lukas, Anthony, 122
Lüthi, Lorenz, 2

MacDonald, Malcolm
  CPI victory in Kerala (1957), 89
Maclean, Donald, 3, 64, 149
Macmillan, Harold, 155
  Attlee Directive, 50
  Krishna Menon, 68

INDEX

Madan, K. L.
  subject to Chinese espionage
    operation, 103
Madras, 8, 27, 41, 52, 76, 89, 97, 129,
  137, 146
Maharashtra, 89
Mainstream, 141
Malaya, 24, 44
Malaysia, 184
Marshall, George, 17
Masani, Minocher Rustom 'Minoo', 57,
  176
  Krishna Menon, 70
  Soviet propaganda in India, 131
Masaryk, Jan, 159
Mathai, M. O.
  accusation of being CIA agent, 82
Mathur, Shiv Narain
  Operation Hat, 213
May, John Peter
  SIS officer in India, 24
Mayhew, Christopher, 132
McMinnies, John Gordon, 147
McNamara, Robert
  Indian military aid programme, 118
Meerut Conspiracy, 35
Mehta, Jagat Singh, 212
Mehta, Lieutenant Colonel B. N. 'Baij',
  105
Menon, Kumara Padmanabha
  Sivasankara (K. P. S.)
  view of Krishna Menon, 59
Menon, Shivshankar, 266
Menon, V. K. Krishna, 52
  appointed Indian High
    Commissioner to UK, 52
  departure from Indian cabinet, 73
  first meeting with Nehru, 52
  ill-health, 66
  Labour Party, 56
  relations with Nehru, 55
  Secretary of India League, 53
  Sino-Indian border war (1962), 100
  Soviet attempts to cultivate, 74
  Soviet funding, 71
  touted as sucessor to Nehru, 71
Menshikov, Mikhail, 90
Menzies, Stewart, 19
  closure of SIS station in India, 27, 28

establishment of SIS station in India,
  23
insistence on SIS station in India, 24
Mexico, 241
Mittal, Gopal, 141
Modi, Narendra, 12
Modin, Yuri
  Freeman forgery, 149
Molotov, Vyacheslav, 58, 69
Moraes, Frank, 148
Morgan, Ellis, 29
Morris, James (later, Jan), 104–5
Mosaddegh, Mohammad, 10
Mountbatten, Lord Louis, 15, 59, 83
  Indian unconventional warfare, 114
Moynihan, Daniel Patrick, 209, 215,
  261
  allegation of CIA funding of
    Congress Party, 188, 216
  appointment as US ambassador to
    India, 198
  criticism of CIA, 215, 220
  criticism of Colby public comments
    on covert action, 205
  departure from India, 205
  fractious Indo-US relations, 199
  impact of CIA revelations on Chile
    on Indira Gandhi, 204
  Indian request for intelligence
    cooperation with US, 200
  Indira Gandhi and intelligence
    agencies, 188
  Indira Gandhi receipt of CIA funds,
    216, 219
  low public profile in India, 199
  Peter Burleigh incident, 200
  rebuffs charge Morarji Desai was
    CIA agent, 227
  relations with CIA in India, 200
Mulgaokar, Suman, 153
Mullik, Bhola Nath (B. N.)
  anti-communism, 44
  appointment as DIB, 43
  dissatisfaction with British
    intelligence, 37
  Krishna Menon, 65
  Nehru's view of intelligence, 6
  relations with MI5, 33
  relationship with Nehru, 43, 102

344 INDEX

Murray, Ralph
Information Research Department (IRD), 129
Muslim League, 59
My Lai massacre, 225

Naipaul, Vidiadhar Surajprasad (V. S.)
Soviet propaganda in India, 131
Nair, K. Sankaran
opinion of T. G. Sanjeevi, 19
Nanda Devi, 119, 121, 210
Nanda Kot, 121, 213
Narain, Coomer
espionage scandal, 249
Narain, Raj, 222
Narasimha Rao, Pamulaparthi Venkata (P. V.), 228
Natarajan, L., 10
Nation, 84
Near and Far East News (NAFEN), 162
Nehru, Braj Kumar, 72
Nehru, Jawaharlal, 6, 7, 10, 35, 37
aversion to secret intelligence, 15
British colonial intelligence, 6
Central Intelligence Agency (CIA), 38, 82, 84
CIA operations in Tibet, 95
death (1964), 45, 119
frustration with performance of IB, 42
Hindu nationalism, 15
Indian non-aligned foreign policy, 36
Indian reliance on British intelligence, 4, 15
Indo-Soviet relations, 36
intelligence cooperation with UK and US, 4, 81
Soviet propaganda in India, 131
threat posed by communalism, 42
wary of links between IB and MI5, 39
Nehru, Ratan Kumar (R. K.), 106
Nepal, 104, 105, 115, 150
New Age, 130, 182
New Delhi, 8
New York Times, 69, 86, 87, 122, 161, 162, 181, 185, 190, 194, 198, 204, 211, 215, 221, 223, 225, 230, 253
New Zealand
intelligence liaison, 37

Nixon, Richard, 215, 221
animus for India and Indira Gandhi, 193
criticism of CIA, 194
misogyny directed at Indira Gandhi, 194
tilt to Pakistan, 192
Noel-Baker, Philip, 61
North-Eastern Frontier Agency (NEFA), 100, 117
Novikov, Kirill, 47
Novosti, 141, 176
Nye, Lieutenant-General Sir Archibald, 27, 32, 61
British propaganda, 125
feeding anti-communist propaganda to Indian government, 133
friendship with Jawaharlal Nehru, 27
Indian communism, 35
Kratochvil defection, 160
Krishna Menon, 65
opposition to SIS station in India, 27

O'Connor Howe, Josephine
review of IRD operations in India, 135
Obama, Barack, 264
Observer, 172
Office of Strategic Services (OSS), 76, 77, 159
Oldfield, Maurice, 29, 31
Olmstead, Mary
scale of CIA operation in India, 98
Operation Blue Star, 234
Operation Hat, 119, 120, 121, 209, 210
Operations Coordinating Board (OCB), 78
Ormsby Gore, David, 73
Orwell, George, 173
Ottinger, Richard, 212
Owen, David, 151

Pakistan, 12, 13, 30, 31, 43, 73, 88, 101, 106, 107, 109, 114, 125, 150, 192, 193, 236, 240, 241, 245, 249, 250, 255, 257, 259, 265
India-Pakistan relations, 73, 193
IRD publications, 132
Kashmir dispute, 16, 33, 36, 61, 109, 147, 257

INDEX

MI5 SLO, 23
terrorism, 257
U-2 incident, 119
US-Pakistan relations, 69, 192
Palkhivala, Nani
Operation Hat, 212
Palkhivala, Nani Ardeshir, 219
Panch Sheel, 94, 157
Pandit, Vijaya Lakshmi, 160, 217
British-India relations, 33
Chinese intelligence, 104
V. K. Krishna Menon, 72
Panikkar, Kavalam Madhava (K. M.),
157
Pant, Apa, 264
MI5 target, 263
Parsons, J. Graham, 80
Parthasarathy, Gopalaswami, 231
Pasternak, Boris, 170
Patel, Vallabhbhai, 4, 19, 30, 43
intelligence transfer of power, 18
Patil, S. K., 89
Patriot, 141
Pegov, Nikolai, 175
People's Liberation Army (PLA), 72,
94, 100, 105
People's Republic of China (PRC), 4, 6,
12, 16, 41, 109, 129, 130
Sino-Indian relations, 8
Pethick-Lawrence, Frederick, 15, 58
Petrie, Sir David, 9
Petrov, Vladimir, 134, 155
Philby, Harold 'Kim', 3, 10, 149, 178
Philby, St John, 10
Pillay, Patsy, 64
Pinochet, Augusto, 201
Pollitt, Harry, 56
Powell, Enoch, 18
Powers, Thomas, 209, 221
The Man Who Kept the Secrets, 222
Powles, Viola, 23
Praja Socialist Party, 106, 146, 185
Pravda, 173
Punjab, 7, 164

Quit India (1942), 57, 77

Raborn, William, 88
Radhakrishnan, Sarvepalli, 115, 119

Radio Moscow, 88
Raghunath, K., 116
Rajagopalachari, Rajaji, 66
Rajasthan, 31
Rajeswar, Thangavelu (T. V.)
view of Bill Casey, 239
Ram, Jagjivan
allegation of being CIA agent, 222
Ramparts, 148, 169, 181
Ramsey, Henry, 89
Rashtriya Swayamsevak Sangh (RSS),
41
Rayle, Robert, 166, 170
Reagan, Ronald, 3, 233
meeting with Indira Gandhi in
Cancun, 241
Reddy, P. Thimma, 146
Research and Analysis Wing (R&AW),
12, 30
covert action, 13, 265
India nuclear test (1998), 264
relations with CIA, 222
Sri Lanka, 234
Reuther, Walter, 91
Richard Helms, 221
Rimington, John, 32
Rimington, Stella, 31, 32
expansion of Cold War in India, 32
Soviet penetration of India, 47
target of Soviet intelligence
operation in India, 48
Ulug-Zade defection, 175
work for IRD in India, 145
Rivett-Carnac, Douglas, 135
RMS *Caledonia*, 32
Roberts, P. H., 150
Rogers, William
view of Indira Gandhi, 188
Roosevelt, Kermit 'Kim', 10, 80
Rosenfeld, Eugene, 86
Rosenthal, Abraham Michael 'Abe', 86
Rositzke, Harry
CIA operations in India, 98
CIA operations in Tibet, 98
proactive approach to CIA
operations in India, 99
Rostow, Walt
US support for Indian
unconventional warfare, 114

Roy, Manabendra Nath (M. N.), 35
Royal Indian Navy mutiny, 58
Royal Navy, 4
Rusk, Dean, 97
Russell, Bertrand, 53
Russian revolution (1917), 30

Salisbury, Harrison, 225
Samyukta Socialist Party, 183
Sandys, Duncan, 74, 108, 138
Sanjeevi Pillai, Tirupattur
    Gangadharam (T. G.), 19, 39
  animus for J. Edgar Hoover, 80
  British concern over attitude to
    communist subversion, 41
  clash with Krishna Menon, 62
  dismissal as DIB, 42, 106
  first Indian Director of IB, 19
  inexperience as an intelligence
    officer, 20
  London visit (1948), 39
  visit to Washington (1949), 79
Sargent, Sir Orme, 21, 27
Saxbe, William 'Bill', 206
  Indian attacks on CIA and Indo-US
    relations, 207
Scarse-Dickens, Mark
  British support for Indian
    unconventional warfare, 113
Schaffer, Howard, 195
Schlesinger, Arthur, 131
Sejnoha, Jaroslav
  defection in India, 159
Semichastny, Vladimir, 8
Sethi, Jai Gopal, 164
Sharma, Shankar Dayal, 189, 190
Shastri, Lal Bahadur, 71, 75, 101, 115,
    120, 147, 210
Shelepin, Alexander, 8
Shone, Sir Terence
  concern at SIS profile in India, 25
  debate over MI5 or SIS primacy in
    India, 22
  opposition to SIS station in India, 24
Sikhism, 234
Sikkim, 111
Silkwood, Karen, 211
Sillitoe, Sir Percy, 40
  Attlee Directive, 29

covert action, 21
Indian Intelligence Bureau (IB), 64
MI5 efforts to remove Krishna
    Menon, 64
relations with Clement Attlee, 28, 65
T. G. Sanjeevi, 39
V. K. Krishna Menon, 60, 63, 64
Simon Commission, 65
Singapore, 37, 97, 129
  Japanese occupation (1942), 24
Singh Deo, Brigadier Kamakhya
    Prasad, 250, 251, 252
Singh Gill, Jaspal, 242, 243
Singh Kohli, Manmohan, 120
Singh, Ajeya, 253
Singh, Brajesh, 166
Singh, Dinesh, 168
Singh, Jasbir, 243
Singh, Karan, 223
Singh, Lieutenant Colonel Jasbir, 242
Singh, Manmohan, 265
Singh, Ram, 141, 143
Singh, Swaran, 201
Singh, Vishwanath Pratap, 252, 253
Sinha, Justice Jagmohanlal, 190
Sinha, Yashwant, 259
Sino-Indian border war (1962), 29, 31, 50,
    54, 72, 75, 99, 100, 101, 102, 103,
    105, 107, 108, 113, 115, 117, 118,
    123, 124, 125, 138, 139, 147, 154, 210
  British aid for India, 138
  impact of Chinese propaganda, 138
  Indian intelligence failure, 102
  lack of Indian propaganda, 138
Sinyavsky, Andrei, 170, 172
Sirisena, Maithripala, 13
Smiley, George, 1, 5
Smith, John Discoe, 174, 182
Smith, Norman, 18, 19, 22
Smith, Russell Jack, 227, 229
Sobolev, Arkady, 162
Socialist Weekly, 203
Solzhenitsyn, Alexander, 155–56, 171
Somerville College, Oxford, 55
South Africa, 127
  Commonwealth security
    conferences, 37
  Communist Party, 64
  Indian response to apartheid, 129

INDEX   347

South Vietnam, 108
Soviet Union, 4, 6, 7, 16, 129
  economic aid to India, 7
  Indo-Soviet relations, 16
  Kashmir dispute, 7
  propaganda in India, 131, 140
Special Frontier Force (SFF), 111, 113, 114
Special Operations Executive (SOE), 128
Spiers, Ronald, 237
Sri Lanka, 13, 150, 234, 240, 250
St Kitts and Nevis, 253
Stalin, Joseph, 3, 16, 131, 153, 154, 165, 166, 170, 172, 173
  death, 78, 131, 155
  Indo-Soviet relations, 36, 126
Stasi, 246, *See* Hauptverwaltung Aufklärung (HVA)
Statesman
  Tarasov defection, 165
Stephen, Chembakassery Mathai (C. M.), 217
Stilwell, Colonel Richard, 80
Suez crisis (1956), 37, 68, 88, 261
Sunday Telegraph, 172
Sunday Times, 171, 172
Swarup, Rama
  espionage scandal, 250
Swatantra Party, 176, 185
Symon, Alec, 132

Taiwan, 250
Taiwan straits crises, 68, 69
Tanzania, 50
Tarasov, Vladislav Stepanovich
  defection, 160–65
Tashkent, 35, 147
TASS, 131, 173, 208, 240, 245, 248
Telangana, 26, 35, 77
Tenet, George, 264
  Indian nuclear test (1998), 264
Tenzing, Norgay, 104
Tereshkov, A. V., 180
Tezpur, 100
Thailand, 118, 119, 184, 200, 207
The Affluent Society, 96
The Liberal Hour, 96
The Man Who Kept the Secrets, 209, 223

The Man Who Would Be King, 7
The Price of Power, 209
The Spy Who Came in from the Cold, 1
The Ugly American, 83
The White House Years, 231
Thimayya, General Kodandera Subayya 'Timmy', 105
Thomas, Alunkal Mathai, 120
Thompson, Gordon, 19
Thought, 141, 143
Tibet, 101, 104, 105, 117
  CIA operations, 8
  Indian policy, 93
Tihar jail, 5, 241
Tiltman, John, 9
Times, 35, 68, 104, 147, 223
Times of India, 165, 174, 179, 180, 198, 203, 213, 223, 226, 251, 252, 259
Tinker, Tailor, Soldier, Spy, 1, 3
Today Show (NBC), 212, 248
Trade Unions, 26, 38, 41, 127, 183, 237
Trend, Sir Burke, 50
Tripathi, Kamlapati, 217
Tripura
  communist subversion, 44
Trombay, India atomic research centre, 214
Truman, Harry S., 11
  disinterest in India, 17
  V. K. Krishna Menon, 69
Tunnard, Bridget, 63
Turner, Stansfield, 239
  CIA agents within the Indian government, 239
  Operation Hat, 213
  Senior Indian official operating as CIA agent, 239
Tyabji, Badruddin, 84, 134

U'ren, William (Bill)
  Indian intelligence and MI5, 46
  MI5 SLO, 23, 36, 45, 65
U-2 aerial reconnaissance, 136
  Indian programme, 117
  May 1960 incident, 98
Ukraine, 16
Ulug-Zade, Aziz Saltimovitch
  defection, 153–54, 173–79

348 INDEX

United Kingdom, 7
  intelligence relations with India, 5
  postcolonial relations with India, 4
  transfer of power in India, 14
United Nations, 68, 88, 162, 201, 244
  human rights, 171
  Kashmir dispute, 36
United Nations Security Council
    (UNSC)
  Kashmir dispute, 7
United States, 7, 31
United States Information Agency
    (USIA), 126
United States Information Service
    (USIS), 11, 173
Urban, Major General Sujan Singh, 111
US Agency for International
    Development (USAID), 176, 196,
    234
US Atomic Energy Commission, 213
US State Department, 52, 69, 77, 78, 79,
    80, 83, 89, 96, 97, 98, 162, 163, 168,
    170, 171, 187, 192, 195, 200, 207,
    208, 212, 213, 214, 215, 219, 220,
    228, 237, 238, 240, 243, 244, 248, 252
  view of Krishna Menon, 52
Uttar Pradesh, 14, 117

Vajpayee, Atal Bihari
  India nuclear tests (1998), 264
  Indian intelligence services, 259
  Indira Gandhi and CIA, 219
  Janata links to CIA, 220
  Morarji Desai and CIA, 228
  Operation Hat, 210, 213
  talks with Tony Blair, 257
  terrorism, 257
Vallabhbhai Patel
  Krishna Menon, 62
  MI5 SLO in India, 21
Venkataraman, Ramaswamy, 242
Verma, Anand Kumar (A. K.), 232
Verma, S. P., 34
  MI5 SLO system, 51
Vickery, Philip
  Indian Political Intelligence (IPI), 18
  V. K. Krishna Menon, 60, 61, 63
Vietnam
  My Lai, 225

Vietnam War, 98, 168
Viets, Richard
  CIA in India, 195
Vijai, P., 116
Vijaya Lakshmi Pandit
  Allen Dulles, 87
  T. G. Sanjeevi Pillai, 79
Vishinsky, Andrey, 36
Vladislaw Stepanovich Tarasov, 154

Washington Post, 182, 184, 194
  CIA and Indira Gandhi
    assassination, 254
  Ramparts, 181
Wave, 217
Wavell, Field Marshal Archibald, 16, 59
  transfer of power, 14, 59
Welser, Hans
  Information Research Department,
    127
West Bengal, 35, 112, 115, 161, 164,
    188, 216, 263
West Germany, 3, 155
Wetherbee, Harry, 242
White, Lincoln, 163
White, Sir Dick
  Attlee Directive, 49
Wicker, Tom, 198
Wignall, Sydney
  Indian covert action, 105
  Indian military intelligence, 104
Williams, Shirley, 171
Wilson, Harold
  British-Indian relations, 33
  India-Pakistan war (1965), 147, 175
  nuclear proliferation, 120
Wolfowitz, Paul, 237
Woodward, Bob, 190
World Health Organisation (WHO), 246

Xinjiang, 93, 101, 105, 117, 119, 120,
    156, 157, 158

Yew, Lew Yuan, 97
Young, Sir John Robertson 'Rob', 258

Zedong, Mao, 99, 130, 157
  political dissidents, 157
  Sino-Indian border war (1962), 75